DATE DUE

Demco, Inc. 38-293

Anglo-Saxon England 28

Her mon mæg giet gesion hiora swæð

ANGLO-SAXON ENGLAND
28

Edited by

MICHAEL LAPIDGE
University of Notre Dame

MALCOLM GODDEN SIMON KEYNES
University of Oxford *University of Cambridge*

PETER BAKER CARL BERKHOUT
University of Virginia *University of Arizona*

MARTIN BIDDLE MARK BLACKBURN
University of Oxford *University of Cambridge*

DANIEL DONOGHUE ROBERTA FRANK
Harvard University *University of Toronto*

RICHARD GAMESON HELMUT GNEUSS
University of Kent at Canterbury *Universität München*

PATRIZIA LENDINARA ANDY ORCHARD
Università di Palermo *University of Cambridge*

FRED ROBINSON DONALD SCRAGG
Yale University *University of Manchester*

CAMBRIDGE UNIVERSITY PRESS

Published by the Press Syndicate of the University of Cambridge
The Edinburgh Building, Cambridge CB2 2RU, United Kingdom
40 West 20th Street, New York, NY 10011-4211, USA
10 Stamford Road, Oakleigh, Melbourne 3166, Australia

© Cambridge University Press 1999

First Published 1999

Typeset by
Servis Filmsetting Ltd
Manchester

Printed in the United Kingdom by
Redwood Books Ltd
Trowbridge

ISBN 0 521 65203 0
ISSN 0263-6751

COPYING

This journal is registered with the Copyright Clearance Center, 222 Rosewood Drive, Danvers, MA 01923, USA. Organizations in the USA who are also registered with C.C.C. may therefore copy material (beyond the limits permitted by sections 107 and 108 of US copyright law) subject to payment to C.C.C. of the per-copy fee of $9.50. This consent does not extend to multiple copying for promotional or commercial purposes. Code 0263-6751/99 $9.50. Organizations authorized by the Copyright Licensing Agency may also copy material subject to the usual conditions.

For all other use, permission should be sought from Cambridge or the American Branch of Cambridge University Press.

SUBSCRIPTIONS: Anglo-Saxon England (ISSN 0263-6751) is an annual journal. The subscription price including postage (excluding VAT) of volume 28 is £68 for institutions (US$115 in the USA, Canada and Mexico), £51 (US$78 in the USA, Canada and Mexico) for individuals ordering direct from the Press and certifying that the annual is for their personal use. EU subscribers (outside the UK) who are not registered for VAT should add VAT at their country's rate. VAT registered subscribers should provide their VAT registration number. Japanese prices for institutions are available from Kinokuniya Company Ltd., P.O. Box 55, Chitose, Tokyo 156, Japan. Orders, which must be accompanied by payment, may be sent to a bookseller, subscription agent, or direct to the publishers: Cambridge University Press, The Edinburgh Building, Shaftesbury Road, Cambridge CB2 2RU, UK. Orders from the USA, Canada or Mexico should be sent to Cambridge University Press, 40 West 20th Street, New York, NY 10011-4211, USA. Prices include delivery by air.

Back volumes: £68.00 (US$115.00 in the USA, Canada and Mexico) each available from Cambridge or the American Branch of Cambridge University Press.

A catalogue record of this book is available from the British Library.

Contents

List of illustrations	*page* vii
King Alfred's ships: text and context M. J. SWANTON *University of Exeter*	1
What use are the Thorkelin transcripts of *Beowulf*? JOHAN GERRITSEN *University of Groningen*	23
The iconography of the Utrecht Psalter and the Old English *Descent into Hell* JESSICA BRANTLEY *University of California, Los Angeles*	43
Anti-Judaism in Ælfric's *Lives of Saints* ANDREW P. SCHEIL *University of Hartford*	65
The earliest texts with English and French DAVID W. PORTER *Southern University, Baton Rouge*	87
Unfulfilled promise: the rubrics of the Old English prose Genesis BENJAMIN C. WITHERS *Indiana University, South Bend*	111
The *West Saxon Gospels* and the gospel-lectionary in Anglo-Saxon England: manuscript evidence and liturgical practice URSULA LENKER *University of Munich*	141
The scribe of the Paris Psalter RICHARD EMMS *Diss, Norfolk*	179
The Office of the Trinity in the Crowland Psalter (Oxford, Bodleian Library, Douce 296) BARBARA C. RAW *Oxford*	185

Contents

Hereward and Flanders   201
    ELISABETH VAN HOUTS   *Emmanuel College, Cambridge*

The cult of King Alfred   225
    SIMON KEYNES   *Trinity College, Cambridge*

Bibliography for 1998   357
    DEBBY BANHAM, *Newnham College, Cambridge*
    CARL T. BERKHOUT, *University of Arizona*
    CAROLE P. BIGGAM, *Strathclyde University*
    MARK BLACKBURN, *Fitzwilliam Museum, Cambridge*
    and SIMON KEYNES, *Trinity College, Cambridge*

Abbreviations listed before the bibliography (pages 357–9) are used throughout the volume without other explanation

The editorial assistance of Clare Orchard and Peter Jackson is gratefully acknowledged

Illustrations

PLATES

between pages 54 and 55

I Utrecht, Universiteitsbibliotheek, 32, 8r
II London, British Library, Harley 603, 71r
III Cambridge, University Library, Ii. 2. 11, 31v–32r
IV Cambridge, Trinity College, B. 10. 4, 164v
V Paris, Bibliothèque Nationale de France, lat. 8824, 188r
VI*a* London, British Library, Harley 5431, 15v (detail)
VI*b* Paris, Bibliothèque Nationale de France, lat. 8824, 19r (detail)

between pages 246 and 247

VII*a* Diagram by Matthew Paris (*c.* 1250), in his *Chronica Maiora*, pt I, showing the Heptarchy, King Alfred, and King Alfred's descendants. (Cambridge, Corpus Christi College 26, iv verso, detail.)
VII*b* Drawing by Matthew Paris, in his *Chronica Maiora*, pt I, showing King Alfred as first sole ruler of England. (Cambridge, Corpus Christi College 26, 65r, detail.)
VII*c* Marginal annotation by Matthew Paris, in his 'History of the Abbots of St Albans', with reference to 'Ælfredus Magnus'. (London, British Library, Cotton Nero D. i, 30v, detail.)
VIII*a* Portrait of King Alfred the Great, commissioned by Thomas Walker, Master of University College, Oxford, in 1661–2. (The Master's Lodge, University College, Oxford.)
VIII*b* Portrait of King Alfred the Great made and engraved by George Vertue to accompany the folio edition of Rapin's *History of England* (1732–3). *Private collection.*
IX*a* Nicholas Blakey, 'Alfred in the Isle of Athelney receiving news of a victory over the Danes', from *English History Delineated* (1751). *Private collection.*
IX*b* Mason Chamberlin, RA, 'Alfred the Great in the neatherd's cottage', painted in 1764, from an engraving published in 1794. (British Museum, Department of Prints & Drawings, 1950-11-11-99.)
X*a* Samuel Wale, RA, 'Alfred makes a collection of laws, and divides the kingdom into counties', from Mortimer's *History of England* (1764). *Private collection.*
X*b* Edward Edwards, 'Alfred in the neat-herd's cottage', from an engraving first published in *The Copper-Plate Magazine*, 1 September 1776. *Private collection.*
XI*a* Richard Westall, 'Prince Alfred before Pope Leo III [*recte* IV]', painted for Bowyer's 'Historic Gallery' and published in 1794. (The British Library.)

Illustrations

XI*b* Francis Wheatley, 'Alfred in the house of the neat-herd', painted for Bowyer's 'Historic Gallery' in 1792 and published in 1795. (The British Library.)
XII*a* Richard Westall, 'Queen Judith reciting to Alfred the Great, when a child, the songs of the bards' (1799), watercolour. (British Museum, Department of Prints & Drawings, Oo.3-12.)
XII*b* Thomas Stothard, 'Alfred disguised as a harper in the Danish camp' (*c.* 1793), from an engraving published in 1802. (British Museum, Department of Prints & Drawings, 1849-7-21-1412.)
XIII*a* David Wilkie, 'Alfred reprimanded by the neatherd's wife' (1806), from an engraving published in 1828. (British Museum, Department of Prints & Drawings, 1836-11-24-3.)
XIII*b* C. W. Cope, 'The first trial by jury'. Cartoon for a fresco, exhibited at Westminster Hall in 1843, from a lithograph published in 1847. (British Museum, Department of Prints & Drawings, 1854-12-11-135.)
XIV*a* John Bridges, 'Alfred submitting his code of laws for the approval of the witan'. Cartoon for a fresco, exhibited at Westminster Hall in 1843, from a lithograph published in 1847. (British Museum, Department of Prints & Drawings, 1854-12-11-142.)
XIV*b* Marshall Claxton, 'Alfred in the camp of the Danes, A.D. 880'. Cartoon for a fresco, exhibited at Westminster Hall in 1843, from a lithograph published *c.* 1847. (British Museum, Department of Prints & Drawings, 1852-6-12-421.)

FIGURES

1 Alfred's ships
2 The relationship of manuscripts of the *Excerptiones de Prisciano*.

ACKNOWLEDGEMENTS

By permission of the Trustees of the British Museum the design on the cover is taken from the obverse of a silver penny issued at London in the early 880s, reflecting Alfred's assumption of political control over the city.

Permission to publish photographs has been granted by: the Universiteitsbibliotheek, Utrecht (pl. I); the British Library (pls. II, VI*a*, VII*c*, XI*a* and XI*b*); the University Library, Cambridge (pl. III); the Master and Fellows of Trinity College, Cambridge (pl. IV); the Bibliothèque nationale de France, Paris (pls. V and VI*b*); The Conway Library, Courtauld Institute of Art, and the Master and Fellows of Corpus Christi College, Cambridge (pls. VII*a* and VII*b*); the Master and Fellows of University College, Oxford, and the Photographic Survey, Courtauld Institute of Art (pl. VIII*a*); the Trustees of the British Museum (pls. IX*b*, XII*a*, XII*b*, XIII*a*, XIII*b*, XIV*a* and XIV*b*).

CONTRIBUTIONS FOR FUTURE EDITIONS ARE INVITED

Material should be submitted to the editor most convenient regionally, with these exceptions: an article should be sent to Martin Biddle if concerned with archaeology, to Mark Blackburn if concerned with numismatics, to Daniel Donoghue if concerned with Old English metrics, to Richard Gameson if concerned with art history, to Simon Keynes if concerned with history or onomastics, and to Michael Lapidge if concerned with Anglo-Latin or palaeography. Whenever a contribution is sent from abroad it should be accompanied by international coupons to cover the cost of return postage. A potential contributor is asked to get in touch with the editor concerned as early as possible to obtain a copy of the style sheet and to have any necessary discussion. Articles must be in English.

The editors' addresses are:

Professor P. S. Baker, Department of English, University of Virginia, Charlottesville, Virginia 22903 (USA)

Professor C. T. Berkhout, Department of English, University of Arizona, Tucson, Arizona 85721 (USA)

Mr M. Biddle, Hertford College, Oxford OX1 3BW (England)

Dr M. A. S. Blackburn, Fitzwilliam Museum, Cambridge CB2 1RB (England)

Professor D. Donoghue, Department of English, Harvard University, 8 Prescott Street, Cambridge, Massachusetts 02138 (USA)

Professor R. Frank, Centre for Medieval Studies, University of Toronto, 39 Queen's Park Crescent East, Toronto, Ontario M5S 1A1 (Canada)

Dr R. Gameson, Faculty of Humanities, Rutherford College, University of Kent at Canterbury, Canterbury, Kent CT2 7NX

Professor H. Gneuss, Institut für Englische Philologie, Universität München, Schellingstrasse 3, D-80799 München (Germany)

Professor M. R. Godden, Pembroke College, Oxford OX1 1DW (England)

Professor S. D. Keynes, Trinity College, Cambridge CB2 1TQ (England)

Professor M. Lapidge, Department of English, University of Notre Dame, Notre Dame, Indiana 46556 (USA)

Professor P. Lendinara, Cattedra di Filologia Germanica, Università degli Studi di Palermo, Facoltà di Magistero, Piazza Ignazio Florio 24, 90139 Palermo (Italy)

Dr A. Orchard, Emmanuel College, Cambridge CB2 3AP (England)

Professor F. C. Robinson, Department of English, Yale University, New Haven, Connecticut 06520 (USA)

Professor D. G. Scragg, Centre for Anglo-Saxon Studies, The University of Manchester, Manchester M13 9PL (England)

King Alfred's ships: text and context

M. J. SWANTON

The *Anglo-Saxon Chronicle*'s well-known reference to King Alfred's plan for a new design of war-ships is problematic both in general and in detail. In the account of the year 897 (*recte* 896), we are told how, after the raids made along the coast of Wessex by Danish gangs based in East Anglia and Northumbria, and in particular with raiding-vessels (OE *æscas*, ON *askar*) which they had built 'many years before', Alfred ordered ships of a new type to be constructed to meet the Danish menace. In the near-contemporary Winchester manuscript (A) the critical passage reads:

Þa het Ælfred cyng timbran langscipu ongen ða æscas. Þa wæron fulneah tu swa lange swa þa oðru. Sume hæfdon lx ara, sume ma. Þa wæron ægðer ge swiftran ge unwealtran ge eac hieran þonne þa oðru; næron nawðer ne on fresisc gescæpene ne on denisc, bute swa him selfum ðuhte þæt hie nytwyrðoste beon meahten.[1]

What was it that was going to be 'most useful' in the circumstances? Given the, as yet, dispersed nature of Anglo-Saxon land-forces, it seems that once small, rapidly moving predatory bands had landed, there was little that could be done to bring them to stand. Ideally they should be prevented from landing at all. Indeed, earlier we apparently hear, at least twice, of intending invaders successfully encountered and repelled while still at sea. In 851 the king of Kent and Ealdorman Ealhhere are said to have 'fought in ships',[2] attacking a great raiding-army at Sandwich, the major point of entry in east Kent, capturing nine ships

---

[1] 'Then King Alfred ordered "long-ships" to be built to oppose the *askar*. They were well-nigh twice as long as the others, some had sixty oars, some more; they were both swifter and less "walty", and also *hieran* than the others; they were neither of Frisian design nor of Danish, but as it seemed to himself that they might be most useful': *The Anglo-Saxon Chronicle MS A*, ed. J. M. Bately, The AS Chronicle: a Collaborative Edition, ed. D. Dumville and S. Keynes 3 (Cambridge, 1986), 60; cf. N. R. Ker, *Catalogue of Manuscripts containing Anglo-Saxon*, 2nd ed. (Oxford, 1990), pp. 57–9; *The Parker Chronicle and Laws*, ed. R. Flower and H. Smith, EETS os 208 (London, 1941), 19a.

[2] Thus in all the later versions of the Chronicle, although in the early Winchester version (A), in common with Asser and the Annals of St Neots, they are said merely to have fought 'at Sandwich': *Two of the Saxon Chronicles Parallel*, ed. C. Plummer, 2 vols. (Oxford, 1892–9) I, 64–5; *Asser's Life of King Alfred*, ed. W. H. Stevenson (Oxford, 1904, repr. 1959), p. 6; *The Annals of St Neots with Vita Prima Sancti Neoti*, ed. D. Dumville and M. Lapidge, The AS Chronicle: a Collaborative Edition, ed. D. Dumville and S. Keynes 17 (Cambridge, 1985), 44.

and putting the others to flight. Then in 875, and again in 882, Alfred himself is said to have put out to sea with an English raiding-fleet (*sciphere*), capturing one or two enemy ships.[3] These are unlikely to have been the only instances of such strategy in the intervening years – but it is important in this context to differentiate between records of what are merely ship-borne forces and what are naval tactics *per se*. For example, Professor Smyth is probably going too far in saying that Ecgfrith 'launched a naval attack' on the coast of Ireland in 684,[4] although it is true that any Northumbrian troops must certainly have been conveyed there in ships.

There is a growing body of evidence for contemporary Danish ship-design, and some – though rather less – for Frisian;[5] but the significant thing seems to be that Alfred's new design favoured neither of these. He had obvious different requirements; for example, his ships, if specifically designed for the protection of home waters, rather than long-distance conveyance craft, would need no space for storage of any kind, whether traded goods or loot, which was necessary to the ships of the *wic*-men.

It was natural enough for the chronicler to refer to these two contemporary maritime nations; there were many Frisian seamen – and no doubt Danish mercenaries – in Alfred's employ.[6] But probably there was little to learn. Perhaps because of the relative dearth of physical evidence for Anglo-Saxon ship-design,[7] it is easy to forget that the native Saxons – island-dwellers, and during the Migration Age master seamen and themselves notorious pirates[8] – were even now employing sea-borne raiding armies against their neighbours.[9] They

---

[3] *Two Chronicles*, ed. Plummer I, 74–9. The term *sciphere* was not used of the second occasion, but this is presumably incidental. [4] A. P. Smyth, *King Alfred the Great* (Oxford, 1995), p. 109.

[5] For general contacts of Frisians with England and with Denmark, see D. Jellema, 'Frisian Trade in the Dark Ages', *Speculum* 30 (1955), 15–36; also S. Lebecq, 'On the Use of the Word "Frisian" in the 6th–10th Centuries Written Sources: Some Interpretations', *Maritime Celts, Frisians and Saxons*, ed. S. McGrail, Council for British Archaeol. Research Reports 71 (London, 1990), 85–90; D. Ellmers, 'The Frisian Monopoly of Coastal Transport in the 6th–8th Centuries AD', *ibid.* pp. 91–2, and references there cited; and L. Whitbread, 'The "Frisian Sailor" Passage in the Old English Gnomic Verses', *RES* 22 (1946), 215–19.

[6] See *Two Chronicles*, ed. Plummer I, 91, for the names of, presumably prominent, Frisian seamen who died in Alfred's service; cf. *Asser's Life of King Alfred*, ed. Stevenson, p. 60. Frisians fought together with Old Saxons in a ship-borne onslaught against the Franks, according to Æthelweard, *The Chronicle of Æthelweard*, ed. A. Campbell (London, 1962), p. 45.

[7] For the background, see O. Crumlin-Pedersen, 'The Boats and Ships of the Angles and Jutes', in *Maritime Celts*, ed. McGrail, pp. 98–116; M. O. H. Carver, 'Pre-Viking Traffic in the North Sea', *ibid.* pp. 117–25; A. C. Evans and R. Bruce-Mitford, 'The Ship', *The Sutton Hoo Ship-Burial*, ed. R. Bruce-Mitford, 3 vols. (London, 1975–83) I, 345–435; V. Fenwick, *The Graveney Boat: a Tenth-Century Find from Kent*, BAR Brit. ser. 53 (Oxford, 1978).

[8] For the background generally, see J. Haywood, *Dark Age Naval Power: a Re-Assessment of Frankish and Anglo-Saxon Seafaring Activity* (London, 1991), pp. 59–61.

[9] Against Danish East Anglia *ASC* 885; Scotland 933 A, 934 DEF: *Two Chronicles*, ed. Plummer I, 78–9 and 106–7.

cannot have been lacking ship-designs suitable to home waters. Of course, it is not said that the English boats were unsatisfactory – nor indeed that they could not successfully withstand the Danes; rather that Alfred has found a *better* design – denoted by the long list of comparatives: longer, swifter, less 'walty' etc. than 'the others'. It is not absolutely clear whether the 'other' ships with which the Chronicler was comparing Alfred's ships were the Viking *askar*, or other English ships.

Britain's Atlantic location, lying along 'the greater part of Europe: Germany, France and Spain',[10] meant that immigrants from many parts, as well as temporary visitors, will have introduced vessels of many different designs.[11] Foreign trading vessels will have been closely inspected; occasionally raiding vessels were captured. Consequently native ship-building traditions are likely to have been more varied than elsewhere – some ancient types continuing with little change, others developing as a result of interaction, changing needs or the availability of alternative materials. Any over-taxonomized account of ship design will inevitably fail to take account of differing local conditions, or allow for either precosity or conservatism – the issue of culture-lag with which we are all too familiar in the built environment and other areas of material development. And as the excavator of the Graveney boat rightly says, the accumulation of evidence, far from simplifying the picture of the way ship-building has developed, teaches us to be cautious in drawing evolutionary patterns; each new discovery tends to confound an old theory and to furnish new problems of interpretation.[12]

Let us start with the boats which Alfred's ships were designed to oppose, the Danish *askar*, for which we do have some evidence. We normally suppose the Chronicler's word *æsc* to have been borrowed from Old Norse *askr* – assuming it to have been familiar to ninth-century Englishmen in the way that German words like Dornier or Heinkel were known to UK citizens during World War II. But the word *æsc* may well have been used of certain English ships – just as the term *here* was used of certain English armies. Although not much documented of any kind of boat, native or foreign, it *is* an Old English word referring, by a kind of metonymy, to anything made of ash-wood to which the distinctive characteristics of this long-grained material were especially suited – whether the

---

[10] Thus Bede, *Historia ecclesiastica* II.3: *Bede's Ecclesiastical History of the English People*, ed. B. Colgrave and R. A. B. Mynors (Oxford, 1969), pp. 14–15, following Pliny, *Historia naturalis* IV.16 (30), ed. L. v. Jan (Leipzig, 1865–78) I, 178. The conception is well represented in early medieval maps such as the Isidore T-O diagram map: P. D. A. Harvey, *Mappa Mundi, The Hereford World Map* (London, 1996), p. 25.

[11] Bede describes London as 'an emporium for many nations who come to it by land and sea', *Historia ecclesiastica* II. 3: *Bede's Ecclesiastical History*, ed. Colgrave and Mynors, pp. 142–3.

[12] Fenwick, *The Graveney Boat*, p. 193. See also generally *Sources and Techniques in Boat Archaeology*, ed. S. McGrail (Oxford, 1977), pp. 137–256 *passim*.

watertight property needed for a trough or bowl,[13] the supple strength needed for a hand-spear shaft,[14] or the various requirements of a certain type of boat. Although the word is in Common Germanic distribution, its usage in this latter sense is, understandably perhaps, confined to the littoral tribes.[15]

Æsc was used by Anglo-Saxon scholars to gloss Latin words like *dromo* and *cercilus*, that is to say, small fast rowing-boats for which a later age might have used the term 'gig'.[16] The best latter-day parallel might be the Cornish or Scilly Isles gigs[17] – rapid, ten-oared interceptors, designed to put pilots on board incoming vessels on a competitive basis, or for salvage or rescue work – easily manœuvered across dangerous currents or to avoid rocks or sandbanks. In these a scratch crew can achieve eight or nine knots; and there are records of 250-mile round sea trips, for up to thirty hours at the oars – which no cutter could overtake, the crew simply pulling into the wind if hard pressed.

Early medieval nautical terminology is complicated, and it is still generally impossible to assign a specific vernacular term like *snacc* or *scegð* to any particular vessel;[18] but the practical application of *æsc/askr* seems secure; as with bowls or spears of a particular kind, the name seems to derive from the material of which the majority of the hull – or at least its prominent upper strakes – were made. Unlike ships of the Norwegian Gokstad type, which were made wholly of oak,[19] these boats were probably in origin predominantly, if not entirely, ash wood (*Fraxinus excelsior*). Ash is outstanding among European timbers for its flexibility and lightness; and, especially where grown over chalk and limestone, it achieves an extraordinary hardness and strength. Place-names like Shebbear and possibly Gargrave suggest that sources of timber suitable for use as shafts and handles were recognized and cultivated,[20] and it is not impossible that uncoppiced standards suitable for ship-building may have been in cultivation too.

In early Germanic usage the word **askiz* seems to refer to an attack-vessel of

---

[13] For the occurrence of ash-wood bowls in early 'pagan' Saxon contexts I am grateful for a personal communication from Jacqui Watson; and for later Saxon contexts, see *Aspects of Saxo-Norman London*, ed. A. Vince, 3 vols. (London, 1988–92) II, 242 and 275–6.

[14] M. J. Swanton, 'The Spear in Anglo-Saxon Times' (unpubl. PhD dissertation, Durham Univ., 1966) I, 453–5.

[15] J. Pokorny, *Indogermanisches etymologisches Wörterbuch*, 2 vols. (Bern, 1959–69) I, 782 *passim*; J. de Vries, *Altnordisches etymologisches Wörterbuch* (Leiden, 1962), p. 15.

[16] *Anglo-Saxon and Old English Vocabularies*, ed. T. Wright and R. P. Wülcker, 2 vols. (London, 1884) I, cols. 181.29, 287.31 and 363.34; *The Corpus Glossary*, ed. W. M. Lindsay (Cambridge, 1921), p. 36.281; *Old English Glosses (A Collection)*, ed. H. D. Merritt (London, 1945), p. 60.18; *Old English Glosses in the Épinal–Erfurt Glossary*, ed. J. D. Pheifer (Oxford, 1974), p. 11.180.

[17] E. J. March, *Inshore Craft of Great Britain*, 2 vols. (London, 1970) II, 221–46.

[18] For simple listings, see H. Schnepper, *Die Namen der Schiffe und Schiffsteile im Altenglischen: eine kulturgeschichtlich-etymologische Untersuchung* (Kiel, 1908).

[19] N. Nicolaysen, *The Viking-Ship Discovered at Gokstad in Norway* (Oslo, 1882), p. 54 *et passim*.

[20] A. H. Smith, *English Place-Name Elements*, 2 vols., EPNS 25–6 (Cambridge, 1956) I, 194 and II, 99.

a particular kind: a light personnel-carrier. It is probable that the *auxilia ascarii* mentioned in the *Notitia dignitatum* were so called because they used boats of this kind.[21] In 365 they were used by Jovinus to approach and plunder the tents of Alamanni camped on the Marne.[22] In the Frankish Salic Laws the word *ascus* is used of a boat sufficiently valuable to be kept under lock and key, theft of which incurs a punitive fine.[23] Since this kind of boat is latterly identified with robber bands, perhaps the term fell out of use except to refer to hostile invaders like the Danes – for whom the term *æsc-man* was still current in the Chronicle in 921, and used by Adam of Bremen as late as the 1070s[24] (it is perhaps significant that the Vikings seem not to have used this word of themselves).[25] In any case, with the establishment of secure land-bases more or less wherever needed, the importance of the *askr* or assault-craft *per se* would have been superseded. When Ælfric, writing *c.* 990, refers to the Vikings Ívarr and Ubbi landing in Northumbria *mid æscum*,[26] so sophisticated a writer might well have sought an appropriate word for an invasion which took place well over a century earlier in 866. And the reference to the Viking army in *The Battle of Maldon*, 991, as an *æschere* (line 69) could well be explained as poetic conservatism.

But if the ninth-century Anglo-Saxon had reason to fear the Viking *askr*, his Migration Age predecessor was well accustomed to using this kind of ship himself, when it was said that 'the Saxon would come whatever wind might blow'.[27] A fifth-century Romano-Gallic bishop at the Visigothic court, Sidonius Apollinaris, characterized the 'blue-eyed Saxon' as 'a master of salt water, if timid enough on land here' (i.e. in Bordeaux).[28] Writing to a naval officer stationed at Saintes, who had been patrolling against the Saxons' curved gigs (*pandos myoparones*), he gives a graphic, if rhetorical, account of their descent on the Atlantic coast:

quorum quot remiges uideris, totidem te cernere putes archipiratas: ita simul omnes imperant parent, docent discunt latrocinari. . . . inprouisus aggreditur praeuisus elabitur; spernit obiectos sternit incautos; si sequatur, intercipit, si fugiat, euadit. ad hoc exercent

[21] In parallel with the *numeri barcarii* (heavy barge-men): *Notitia Dignitatum*, ed. O. Seeck (Berlin, 1876), pp. 122, 138, 210 and 215; D. Hoffmann, *Das spätrömische Bewegungsheer und die Notitia Dignitatum*, Epigraphische Studien 7 (Düsseldorf, 1969–70), *passim*. R. Much, 'Ascarii', *ZDA* 41 (1897), 94–5, preferred to associate them with the word *æsc*, 'spear'.
[22] *Ammien Marcellin, Histoire*, ed. E. Galletier *et al.*, 5 vols. (Paris, 1968–96) V, 106.
[23] MGH, Leges Nationum Germanicarum IV, ed. K. A. Eckhardt, 2 vols. (Hanover, 1962–9) I, 86; II, 68–9 and 226.
[24] *Gesta Hammaburgensis ecclesiae pontificum*, ed. G. H. Pertz, MGH SS 7 (Hanover, 1846), 317 and 370.
[25] C. Fell, 'Old English *wicing*: a Question of Semantics', *PBA* 72 (1986), 295–316, at 313.
[26] Cf. G. I. Needham, *Ælfric: Lives of Three English Saints*, 2nd ed. (Exeter, 1976), p. 45.
[27] *Claudii Claudiani Carmina*, ed. J. B. Hall (Leipzig, 1985), p. 215.
[28] Sidonius Apollinaris, *Epistulae at Carmina*, ed. C. Lütjohann, MGH, Auct. antiq. 8 (Berlin, 1887), 136.

illos naufragia, non terrent. est eis quaedam cum discriminibus pelagi non notitia solum, sed familiaritas. . . . in medio fluctuum scopulorumque confragosorum spe superuentus laeti periclitantur.[29]

For a Roman officer, accustomed to heavily built ships designed for deep water and safe anchorage, this mode of making landfall, that is, beaching rather than coming into harbour, must have seemed tantamount to shipwreck. Double-ended, light and, above all, flexible, the *æsc* was designed to come to land through the surf, as North Danish fishing-boats did until recently, even in rough conditions. The distinctive characteristics of this type of ship would be determined by the fact that the principles of hull design were laid down on the beach.[30] As an assault craft, required primarily for swift conveyance, it was exemplary. Slender, low-boarded and light, it was fast enough to overtake, or flee if need be, most other ships by oar or sail. The flexible (walty) construction, shallow draught and flat unkeeled bottom would permit landfall at any point – beaching on broad sandy shores or penetrating far up muddy, as yet undredged, rivers; it was perhaps even light enough to allow portage over short distances.

The *æsc* would suit the beach trader no less than the raider. In fact raiding vessels were not readily distinguished from trading vessels – or indeed, raiders from traders by their appearance or immediate deportment. The king's reeve Beaduheard, who went to three *dromones* landed in Dorset *c.* 787, approached the arrivals thinking they were traders rather than raiders, and died as a result.[31] Similarly, vessels of Northmen sighted off Narbonne could be mistaken for traders from the Levant or from Africa or from Britain – only the wise Charlemagne (*sapientissimus*) recognizing them for marauders as distinct from merchantmen on account of their complement and speed, *ex instructione [implere] uel agilitate*.[32] Just as the Viking *askr* was a multi-purpose craft, so the 'Viking' himself may well have been ambivalent – trader one day, raider the next – happy to flirt with 'trade's dark sister' piracy if opportunity arose.[33] The word *wicing*

---

[29] 'in whose every oarsman you might detect so many pirate-chiefs, inasmuch as they all issue commands at once, instruct in brigandage . . . [he] attacks unforeseen, and when foreseen slips away; he scorns opposition, destroys the careless. If he pursues he overtakes; if he flees he escapes. Moreover, shipwreck, far from terrifying them, is their business; with the perils of the sea they are not merely acquainted, they are familiar; . . . they gladly face any danger of surf and jagged rocks in the hope of achieving a surprise': *ibid.* p. 132. For the background, see I. Wood, 'The Channel from the 4th to the 7th Centuries AD', *Maritime Celts*, ed. McGrail, pp. 93–7.

[30] Cf. O. Crumlin-Pedersen, 'The Ships of the Vikings', *The Vikings: Proceedings of the Symposium of the Faculty of Arts of Uppsala University, June 6–9, 1977*, ed. T. Andersson and K. I. Sandred (Uppsala, 1978), pp. 32–41, at 40.   [31] Æthelweard, *Chronicle*, ed. Campbell, pp. 26–7.

[32] As related by a monk of St Gallen (pseudo-Notker): MGH, SS 2, ed. G. H. Pertz (Hanover, 1829), p. 757; whether or not the circumstances were actual, the emperor's discriminating eye is already part of the romantic cult of the personality.

[33] The expression is from G. Jones, *A History of the Vikings* (Oxford, 1968), p. 199.

itself originally denoted merely 'man of the *wics*, i.e. entrepôts',[34] and the first documented record of the word, glossing *piratici* in the combination *wicing sceaþa, sæsceaða, æscmen* ('hostile men of the *wics*, or of the sea, *askr*-men') in the late-seventh-century Épinal–Erfurt–Corpus group of glossaries, seems to imply that there might have been another, more peaceable, kind;[35] it perhaps marks a moment (understandably abrupt) of semantic shift.

At this stage, the *wic* (*qua* entrepôt site) had a typically shallow approach. Quays seem not to have developed until eventually an increasing volume of low-value bulk trade would require new sites capable of accommodating deeper-draught merchantmen.[36] It was the eleventh and twelfth centuries which saw Quentovic abandoned in favour of Montreuil-sur-mer, *Hamwic* in favour of Southampton. For the time being, however, even in the port of London where the Roman quay may have survived, the normal mode of landfall was beaching.[37] As the *Beowulf*-poet put it, ships were 'moored in the sand', *sælde to sande*, and Hygelac's harbour-guard, *hyðweard*, would supervise little more than a sand-dune parking-space.[38] In the mind of an Anglo-Saxon poet, ships would be imagined as beached even in exotic deep-water Mediterranean locations.[39] For a ship beached in some such conditions, a falling or rising tide will have made it more or less easy to embark; a tender might be needed to go on a vessel which on another occasion might merely require wading.[40]

We tend to assume that all Vikings, and all Viking boats, were much the same; and our historical imagination is fixed on ships of the Norwegian

---

[34] W. Vogel, 'Wik-Orte und Wikinger: eine Studie zu Anfängen des germanischen Städtewesens', *Hansische Geschichtsblätter* 60 (1935), 5–48; R. Boyer, 'Les Vikings, des guerriers ou des commerçants?', *Les Vikings et leur civilisation, problèmes actuels*, ed. R. Boyer (Paris, 1976), pp. 211–40; P. H. Sawyer, 'Wics, Kings and Vikings', *The Vikings*, ed. Andersson and Sandred, pp. 23–31, at 29. For what the word meant to the Anglo-Saxons, see generally Fell, 'Old English *wicing*'.

[35] *Corpus Glossary*, ed. Lindsay, p. 138.391; *Épinal–Erfurt Glossary*, ed. Pheifer, p. 39.736.

[36] R. W. Unger, *The Ship in the Medieval Economy, 600–1600* (London, 1980), pp. 95, 109, 136 *et passim*.

[37] Albeit on an artificially supplemented 'hard', cf. B. Hobley, 'The London Waterfront – the Exception or the Rule?', *Waterfront Archaeology in Britain and Northern Europe*, ed. G. Milne and B. Hobley (London, 1981), pp. 1–9, at 2–4, with fig. 3. For much of the period mooring took place upstream of the City in the Aldwych (*eald wic*) area on a wide, naturally shelving beach: J. Haslam, *Anglo-Saxon Towns in Southern England* (Chichester, 1984), pp. 297–9.

[38] Lines 1914, 1917, cf. 1896, and 212–15: *Beowulf*, ed. and trans. M. Swanton, 2nd ed. (Manchester, 1997), pp. 124–7, and cf. pp. 44–5.

[39] Cf. *Andreas* 253–4, ed. K. R. Brooks, *Andreas and the Fates of the Apostles* (Oxford, 1961), pp. 8 and 70 (note to line 236).

[40] Contrast the modes of embarking from the foreshore at Bosham, Sussex, as described in *ASC* 1046 E (= 1049): *Two Chronicles*, ed. Plummer I, 169, with that depicted in the Bayeux Tapestry: *The Bayeux Tapestry*, ed. D. M. Wilson (London, 1985), pl. 5.

Gokstad type.[41] We now know that there was a variety of types of ship, developed in response to local circumstances, available materials and intended use. Whether or not the Gokstad vessel was a war-ship *per se*, it was almost certainly not the type of ship which Alfred confronted. This Gokstad type was a deep-fjord design – a broad-bosomed, keeled boat built of rigid oak rather than ash. What the Danes who raided Alfred's kingdom were using – as the Saxons before them – was the type developed on and for the sand-dune coast from Jutland *via* Friesland to Flanders, the requirements of which were very different from the drowned valleys of northern Scandinavia. It is perhaps not surprising that it was the Danes who settled in eastern England, attracted to its sandy beaches and broad shallow rivers, while the deeper channels of the rocky north and west coasts were colonized by the Norse. The Anglo-Saxon annalists were notoriously confused as to the precise origins of the Scandinavian invaders,[42] but place-name evidence makes their distinctive distribution quite clear.[43]

Our best opportunity to observe the nature of a ship built for flat, sandy Danish beaches comes with one of a number of old boats sunk at Skuldelev at the end of the tenth century as block-ships to seal a known channel approaching the royal centre of Roskilde (Sjælland).[44] Wreck 5 was a personnel-carrier for twenty-six to thirty men; it closely parallels in design and method of construction the rather larger Sutton Hoo ship built *c.* 600 which survived as a mere imprint with iron rivets.[45] Long and low on the water, with slender 7:1 proportions, it was 18 m long, and 2.6 m wide amidships (only half the beam measurement of the Gokstad ship), with lower sides, 1.1 m high, and a maximum draught of 0.5–0.6 m; it had 12 thwarts (i.e. 24 oars), at intervals of about 90 cm, with square ports cut in the gunwale strake, provided with oak shutters to prevent shipping water in rough seas. The upper strakes were of ash, and the lower, beach-scraping ones and T-shaped keel-plank, of oak. The bow-stem was missing, but was scarfed in a manner suggesting it may have been designed to carry a figure-head. The gunwale shows some evidence for a shield-ledge. And there was stepping for a mast, indicating the availability of a sail when running before the wind – but with no evidence for the kind of stays. Nor is there any evidence for any steering-oar on the starboard (*steor-bord*) stern, since that part of

---

[41] Cf. A. Binns, 'The Ships of the Vikings, were they "Viking Ships"?', *Proceedings of the Eighth Viking Congress*, ed. H. Bekker-Nielsen *et al.* (Odense, 1981), pp. 287–94.

[42] *The Anglo-Saxon Chronicle*, ed. and trans. M. J. Swanton (London, 1996), p. 54, n. 4.

[43] See generally the early survey by E. Ekwall, 'The Scandinavian Settlement', *An Historical Geography of England before 1800*, ed. H. C. Darby, 2nd ed. (Cambridge, 1951), pp. 132–64, and subsequently G. Fellows Jensen, 'The Vikings in England: a Review', *ASE* 4 (1975), 181–206, and references there cited.

[44] O. Olsen and O. Crumlin-Pedersen, 'The Skuldelev Ships (II)', *Acta Archaeologica* 38 (1967), 73–174, at 132–45. [45] Evans and Bruce-Mitford, 'The Ship'.

the boat is missing.[46] In trials, a reconstruction rode the waves buoyantly, and even when fully manned proved highly manœuvrable. When transporting horses, it could be beached broadside, tilting over to allow the beasts to disembark with a step of little more than 60 cms.[47] But this very lack of draught could prove hazardous in rough conditions further out at sea. A Danish fleet no less than a hundred and twenty strong was wrecked in stormy weather off the Dorset coast in 877.[48]

The Skuldelev *askr* was old when sunk, repairs and wear on the underside showing that it had been hauled up the beach innumerable times. Caulking material (animal hair and wood tar) was Carbon-14 dated 960 +/− 100[49] but this is likely to have post-dated the construction of the hull itself by any number of years, especially given its deliberately flexible build. The Chronicler of 897 thinks it worth remarking that the late-ninth-century Danish *askar* in question were now old – but exactly how old we have no way of knowing. One or two clinker-built Scilly gigs are still racing 150 years and more after they were first built; and some of the little boats used to evacuate men from the beaches of Dunkirk in 1940 had been constructed in the previous century – and are still afloat and in use today.[50]

Hitherto, the primary requirement of a 'war-ship' – whether those that brought Germanic war-bands to the shores of Roman Britain or their latter-day Viking descendants – was for transports that might convey men from land-point to land-point, rather than for fighting at, or on, the sea as such. Now what was needed 'to oppose' the Viking *askar* – that is, to prevent their beaching – was an interceptor; as Asser put it:

Tunc rex Alfred iussit cymbas et galeas, id est longas naues, fabricari per regnum, ut nauali prælio hostibus aduentantibus obuiaret; impositisque piratis in illis uias maris custodiendas commisit.[51]

---

[46] Evidence for this part of the boat is rarely found, but for side rudders in general, see S. McGrail, *Ancient Boats in N.W. Europe: the Archaeology of Water Transport to AD 1500* (London, 1987), pp. 244–51, and D. Goodburn, 'A Side Rudder from the London Waterfront', *A Spirit of Enquiry*, ed. J. Coles *et al.* (Exeter, 1993), pp. 56–60 *passim*. The fact that in manuscript illustrations the steering-oar is sometimes seen on the larboard stern is presumably a question of artistic licence, since it is easier to depict what is happening if the oar is seen on the side viewed.
[47] See generally B. Almgren, 'Vikingatågens höjdpunkt och slut', *Tor* 9 (1963), 215–50.
[48] *Two Chronicles*, ed. Plummer I, 74–5; C and D say it was as a result of fog, *mycel myst*, rather than tempest, *micel yst*.   [49] Olsen and Crumlin-Pedersen, 'The Skuldelev Ships', p. 163.
[50] March, *Inshore Craft*; and personal communication from David Knight, archivist of The Association of Dunkirk Little Ships.
[51] 'Then King Alfred commanded *cymbas* and galleys, that is long ships, to be built throughout the kingdom, in order that he might offer naval battle to the enemy *as they were coming*; and on board these he placed adventurers (*piratis*) and appointed them guardians of the seaways': *Asser's Life of King Alfred*, ed. Stevenson, p. 39. Whether the term *cymbas* is used in any specialist sense is unclear; classically it should mean 'small ships', but that sense would be relative. In dealing with

The incoming *askar* were fast and manœuvrable. Alfred's interceptor would need to be at least their equal in speed and manœuvrability; and having once made contact, to be able to offer violence: damaging the hull, breaking the oars, or at the very least interrupting their stroke. Though good at attacking inshore through surf and cross-currents, when further out at sea the *askr* would be easily swamped, and highly vulnerable to being rammed by a more rigid vessel.[52] The sixty-oared galley would certainly have proved an effective ram. This is presumably what is understood by John (*alias* Florence) of Worcester's use of the word *uiolentia* describing how Alfred's ships overcame the Danish, although he was writing from a twelfth-century perspective:

aduersum quos bis longiores, altiores, celeriores minusque nutantes, ex præcepto regis Alfredi fabricantur naues, quarum uiolentia predicte hostium superari possent.[53]

Old English glosses which equate 'keel' with Latin *rostrum*, 'beak', strongly suggest that sea-ramming was understood, whether currently practised or merely read about in ancient texts, though the Alfredian paraphrase of Orosius omits his account of Brutus' confrontation with the Venetii off the Loire, which described the specific virtues of oak-built ships in ramming tactics:

Bruto circumspicienti imparem longe nauium esse conflictum, quia barbarorum naues solido robore intextae cauernisque praeualidis obduratae saxorum modo adactos rostratarum ictus retundebant.[54]

The translator of the Orosius similarly ignores the word *rostrum/rostrata* on the one or two occasions it occurs elsewhere in the text.[55] However, the Épinal–Erfurt-Corpus glossaries offer *rostrum: neb uel scipes cæle*.[56] That this was understood to be more than merely a dragon or bird figure-head of the 'beaked' kind

---

the same incident, later historians prefer to use the word *cylas*: Matthew Paris, *longas naues, quas cyulas siue galeias appellant*, *Chronica Majora*, ed. H. R. Luard, 7 vols., RS 57 (London, 1872–4) I, 433; cf. Roger of Wendover, *Chronica*, ed. H. O. Coxe, 3 vols. (London, 1841–4) I, 363. Both use very much the same words in dealing with the earlier events of 877: *cyulas et galeias, id est longas naues* (*ibid.* pp. 409 and 327 respectively). Possibly the 'adventurers' in question were the Frisian mercenaries we hear of in ASC 897 (= 896): *Two Chronicles*, ed. Plummer I, 91.

[52] Cf. S. McGrail and E. McKee, *The Building and Trials of the Replica of an Ancient Boat: the Gokstad Faering*, 2 vols. (Greenwich, 1974), vol. II.

[53] 'against which, at King Alfred's command, ships were built, twice as long, higher, swifter and less "nodding", by the violence of which the aforementioned enemy (ships) might be overcome' (my translation): *The Chronicle of John of Worcester* II, ed. R. R. Darlington and P. McGurk, with trans. by J. Bray and P. McGurk (Oxford, 1995), p. 350.

[54] 'Brutus was aware that the naval battle would be very unequal because the ships of the barbarians had been joined with beams of solid oak and, enduring like rock, their powerful hulls weakened the force of blows struck by rams': *Orose, Histoires (contre les Païens)*, ed. M-P. Arnaud-Lindet, 3 vols. (Paris, 1990–1) II, 185.

[55] See conveniently the parallel text edited by H. Sweet, *King Alfred's Orosius*, EETS os 79 (London, 1883), 80–1, 246–7.

[56] *Épinal–Erfurt Glossary*, ed. Pheifer, p. 45.862; *Corpus Glossary*, ed. Lindsay, p. 155.204.

dredged from the river Scheldte,[57] and perhaps alluded to by the poets in such phrases as *hea hornscip* or *hyrnde ciolas*,[58] might be confirmed by the further Épinal–Erfurt–Corpus gloss: *rostratum, tindicti*,[59] the curious tenth-century Harley 3376 gloss: *celox, uel cilion, i. species nauis, i. ceol, uel stempingisern*,[60] or the early-eleventh-century Brussels gloss *rostrata nauis, i. barda*,[61] perhaps best explained by reference to Snorri's *Óláfs saga Tryggvasonar*:

Eiríkr jarl hafði barða einn geysimikinn, er hann var vanr at hafa í viking. Þar var skegg á of anverðu barðinu hváru tveggja, en niðr frá járnspǫng þykk ok svá breið sem barðit ok tók allt í sjá ofan.[62]

A strategy of occasional interception would not, of course, keep at bay a large-scale centrally organized invasion fleet, but might certainly check the frequent, and locally very destructive hit-and-run raids.[63] If Alfred could only control the narrow seas he could at least look to protect the West Saxon shoreline against marauders preying on coastal settlements. Perhaps Alfred's ships were already associated with the kind of coastal watch that his successor Edward successfully employed along the southern edge of the Bristol Channel a dozen years later.[64] This may have been visual rather than physical – like the watch, perhaps complete with pass-control, as kept by Hrothgar's coast-guard described in the epic *Beowulf*.[65]

References to sea and ships are frequent enough in Old English literature – which means, for the most part, poetry – but set *topoi* and formulaic phraseology are of questionable value as realistic, transferable evidence.[66] Broadly speaking,

---

[57] R. Bruce-Mitford, 'Ships' Figure-Heads of the Migration Period', *Aspects of Anglo-Saxon Archaeology: Sutton Hoo and other Discoveries* (London, 1974), pp. 175–87.

[58] *Andreas* 274; *The Metres of Boethius* 26.23.

[59] *Épinal–Erfurt Glossary*, ed. Pheifer, p. 46; *Corpus Glossary*, ed. Lindsay, p. 155.208.

[60] *Anglo-Saxon Vocabularies*, ed. Wright and Wülcker, col. 203.30. Cf. *Middle English Dictionary*, ed. H. Kurath *et al.* (Ann Arbor, MI, 1952–; in progress), *s.v. stampne* (a) Naut.

[61] Brussels, Bibliothèque Royale, 1828–30: *Anglo-Saxon Vocabularies*, ed. Wright and Wülcker, col. 289.12.

[62] 'Jarl Eric had a particularly large *barði* which he used to have on his Viking raids; there was a 'beard' uppermost on each of the two stems (fore and aft), and below it a stout iron plate which was as broad as the stem and went right down to the waterline': Snorri Sturluson, *Heimskringla*, ed. B. Aðalbjarnarson, 3 vols., Íslenzk Fornrít 26–8 (Reykjavik, 1941–51) I, 355; cf. *An Icelandic Dictionary*, ed. R. Cleasby and G. Vigfusson, 2 vols. (Oxford, 1874), *s.v. barð*, and de Vries, *Altnordisches Wörterbuch*, *s.v. barð*.

[63] For estimations of the size of invading fleets, small or large, cf. N. P. Brooks, 'England in the Ninth Century: the Crucible of Defeat', *TRHS* 5th ser. 29 (1979), 1–20, at 1–11. H. Marwick convincingly estimated the full strength of the Orkney fleet as sixteen or seventeen vessels: 'Naval Defence in Norse Scotland', *Scottish Hist. Rev.* 28 (1949), 1–11.

[64] We are not told the precise date of its institution, or even that it was more than temporary – but it seems to have been more or less effective during daylight hours in 917 (= 918 A, 915 D), *Two Chronicles*, ed. Plummer I, 98–9. [65] Lines 240–7, ed. Swanton, pp. 44–7.

[66] For a comparative account of what might be found among the skalds, see P. Hallberg, 'The

narrative texts describe the passage of parties of warriors in terms of sailing: wind- rather than oar-propulsion. Perhaps, irrespective of actuality, the handling of an oar is considered less than heroic. Classical heroes are never depicted at the oar themselves,[67] and the same appears to be true of Germanic stories: neither Beowulf nor his companions are represented as rowing, but rather 'driven by the wind'.[68] Though the Wanderer figure is said to 'stir the sea with his hands',[69] his situation is portrayed as one of exceptional hardship. Even prose writers have other things on their minds than accurate representation. So far as a sermon-writer, biblical commentator, or even chronicler is concerned, the transmission of precise nautical information may not be the point of a nautical reference. Furthermore there is no way of judging the nautical competence of the commentator.

Given this general *caveat*, Alfred's new interceptors, if that is what they were, are said to be: (a) *langscipu*; (b) *fulneah tu swa lang (swa þa oðru), sume hæfdon lx ara, sum ma*; (c) *ægðer ge swiftran*; (d) *ge unwealtran*; (e) *ge eac hieran*.

(a) *langscipu*. The question of what exactly is meant by 'long-ship' is itself unclear. The chronicler of 897 expects to be understood, although the word is found nowhere else in vernacular texts. The etymology must be relative, but relative to what? They were presumably built to accommodate a relatively larger number of oarsmen. Speaking of the three ships that brought the Jutish-led Germanic mercenaries employed by Vortigern in 449, Bede says they arrived in three 'long ships', *longis nauibus*.[70] If this is the translation of a Germanic word, the Alfredian translator of Bede is uncertain what to do with it, since he simply renders it *þrim myclum scypum* 'three big ships'. The Peterborough and Worcester Chronicles use the word *ceol (on þrim ceolum)*, whereas the Canterbury Chronicle says *ðrim langon scipan*;[71] and Gildas equates the two: *cyulis, nostra [lingua] longis nauibus*.[72]

Ship – Reality and Image in Old Norse Poetry', *The Vikings*, ed. Andersson and Sandred, pp. 42–56; P. Foote, 'Wrecks and Rhymes', *ibid.* pp. 57–66.

[67] Cf. Homer, *The Odyssey*, ed. A. T. Murray, rev. G. E. Dimock, 2 vols. (Cambridge, MA, 1995) I, 366–9, etc.

[68] Lines 17–23 and 1905–13. It is technically possible that what is normally considered simply a swimming-contest between the two boys Beowulf and Breca (lines 506–81, ed. Swanton, pp. 58–61 and 192) also involved rowing: cf. K. P. Wentersdorf, 'Beowulf's Adventure with Breca', *SP* 72 (1975), 140–66, at 155–62.

[69] *The Wanderer*, 4, ed. I. Gollancz, *The Exeter Book* I, EETS os 104 (London, 1895), 286–7.

[70] *Historia ecclesiastica* I. 15: *Bede's Ecclesiastical History*, ed. Colgrave and Mynors, pp. 50–1.

[71] *Two Chronicles*, ed. Plummer I, 12–13; *An Anglo-Saxon Chronicle*, ed. E. Classen and F. E. Harmer (Manchester, 1926), p. 6.

[72] Gildas, *De excidio et conquestu Britanniae*, ed. M. Winterbottom, *The Ruin of Britain and Other Works* (Chichester, 1978), pp. 26 and 97.

(b) *fulneah tu swa lang (swa þa oðru), sume hæfdon lx ara, sum ma.* Given a thwart-interval similar to Skuldelev 5 (i.e. 90 cm), provision for 60 oars in double alignment must have required a length of at least 27 m even before allowance for bow and stern. That would more than confirm Alfred's design as 'well-nigh twice as long as the others', supposing these others to have been of the Skuldelev type. Even allowing for some exaggeration, it would have meant proportions something in the order of 12:1 and a total length of perhaps 35 m.

A one-piece monoxylous keel was obviously not possible for a ship of this length. From felling-point to point of crown-break, the average clear stem of either *Quercus* or *Fraxinus sp.* found in semi-natural woodland, depending on how tightly they were planted, or whether they were high pruned, both present an upper limit of fifteen metres – although much of later medieval felling was typically of 7·5 to 9 m standards.[73] So Alfred's ships must have had scarfed keels. The technical difficulty of scarfing a keel, an argument formerly raised against the physical construction of such a long ship, we now know would not have been a problem, as a result of the discoveries at Skuldelev and elsewhere.[74]

Anglo-Saxon scholars will have known of the *trireme* from ancient texts like Orosius or Boethius,[75] and it is not impossible that so large a number of oarsmen (sixty or more) might have been accommodated in some manner other than simple alignment – perhaps more like that which Alfred and others in his entourage might have seen on Mediterranean ships during visits to Rome: in particular the various types of double-banked Byzantine *dromones*, or even the lesser *dromia* specifically developed for use against the Viking Rus.[76] Some of the current Mediterranean designs were equipped with a spike, *calcar*, above the waterline (similar to that sported by Jarl Eric's *barði*), rather than the ancient ram, *rostrum*, below the waterline, now intended not to sink the enemy, but to immobilize it with a view to capture.

One way of accommodating a greater number of oarsmen is to row *alla zenzile*, whereby two men sit on the same bench but each with his own oar and his own port or thole-pin – a style demanding great skill, the oars almost

---

[73] For general information I am indebted to Professor Julian Evans of The Forestry Commission Research Division.   [74] McGrail, *Ancient Boats*, p. 117, table 8.2.
[75] *The Old English Orosius*, ed. J. Bately, EETS ss 6 (London, 1980), 54 and 129; *King Alfred's Old English Version of Boethius De Consolatione Philosophiae*, ed. W. J. Sedgefield (Oxford, 1899), pp. 115 and 194.
[76] *Asser's Life of King Alfred*, ed. Stevenson, pp. 7 and 9; and see generally L. Bréhier, 'La Marine de Byzance du VIIIe au XIe siècle', *Byzantion* 19 (1949), 1–16, at 11–12; A. R. Lewis, *Naval Power and Trade in the Mediterranean, A. D. 500–1100* (Princeton, NJ, 1951), chs. 4–5 and references there cited. For a convenient summary, see J. H. Pryor, *Geography, Technology and War: Studies in the Maritime History of the Mediterranean, 649–1571* (Cambridge, 1988), pp. 57–8, and also references there cited.

touching.[77] At Gokstad two shields were lodged between each oar-port,[78] which suggests either plentiful provision, or passengers (unlikely), or possibly the technique of rowing *alla scallocca*, that is, where two or more men pull on one oar, although this is normally thought to have been introduced only in much later medieval times. It is debatable as to whether or not oars came in pairs of variable length in early English galleys, as was certainly the case later.[79] But if so, and this meant that one of the pair stood or sat at a higher level, it might make sense of the assumption that Alfred's ships were built, or looked, 'higher'.[80] We know that three galleys commissioned in Norway in 1206 had two tiers of oar-ports amidships.[81] Certainly Cnut's great galley of sixty thwarts (that is, a hundred and twenty oars), or even Jarl Hákon's with forty thwarts,[82] must have had some such arrangement; the length would be incredible, unless the thwart interval was reduced in some way. If Cnut's oarsmen were simply aligned, sixty oars a side would result in a vessel fifty-four metres long even before bow and stern allowance, which in a shallow wooden hull ought to be quite unviable.

(c) *ægðer ge swiftran*. Swiftness would depend in part at least on size, allowing a higher ratio of oarsmen to length. But much would depend on maintaining a shallow draught. The seventeenth-century commentator Sir John Spelman, who was presumably closer to the actualities of sea-travel, was unable to reconcile the incompatibility of height, draught and speed in the chronicler's account of Alfred's ships; and concludes that if there was no level decking beneath which the rowers sat cramped, the height spoken of referred merely to some sort of partial superstructure like a poop-deck at either end.[83] Hydrodynamic resistance to vessels of different forms is very variable; it increases rapidly with speed, mainly, though not wholly, due to skin-friction or drag, and to wave-making or wash. Turbulence increasing at the edges, it may then require a disproportionate amount of effort to pass through the incoherent waves which act as speed barriers. Only experience, or sophisticated calculations, would tell whether any increase in speed was worth the weight of additional bodies.[84] But then, Alfred's oarsmen may have served an additional function as fighters if occasion arose.

---

[77] R. C. Anderson, *Oared Fighting Ships from Classical Times to the Coming of Steam*, 2nd ed. (Kings Langley, 1976), pp. 42–51. [78] Nicolaysen, *Gokstad*, pp. 62–3.
[79] See generally R. C. Anderson, 'The Oars of Northern Long-Ships', *The Mariner's Mirror* 29 (1943), 190–5; J. T. Tinniswood, 'English Galleys, 1272–1377', *ibid*. 35 (1949), 276–315, at 292–6. For general oar-propulsion data, see McGrail, *Ancient Boats*, pp. 207–16.
[80] But see below, p. 16. [81] Cf. Nicolaysen, *Gokstad*, p. 29.
[82] If we are to credit Snorrri's account: *Heimskringla*, ed. Aðalbjarnarson II, 273.
[83] *Ælfredi magni Anglorum regis invictissimi vita tribus libris comprehensa* (Oxford, 1678), pp. 110–11.
[84] See generally C. A. Marchaj, *Sailing Theory and Practice* (London, 1964), pp. 231–92 *passim*; McGrail, *Ancient Boats*, pp. 195–8.

Bow and stern shape are clearly important to laminar flow, but there is no evidence for developments of the kind at this stage. To preserve laminar flow and minimize friction it is important for the leading edge to be smooth, since the slightest roughness will cause turbulence. The clinker-built method of construction presents a relatively large wetted area, and hence a high a degree of surface drag. The use of wider planks would reduce this. And of course the hulls might have been regularly painted, greased or tarred: quite small factors could prove crucial if pulling boats over some distance.

(d) *ge unwealtran*. The new design is said to be less 'walty'. The expression is otherwise undocumented at this date, although there are Middle English parallels meaning something like 'tossed or thrown about', and it survives as a nautical expression through the seventeenth century to present-day yachting circles.[85] *Nutantes*, the word used in John of Worcester's Latin rendering of this passage,[86] suggests a vertical 'nodding' rather than a sideways yawing.[87] Though *wealt is often thought to mean 'unsteady',[88] there is no reason to suppose that the country's long ship-building history would have resulted in unseaworthy craft. Walt was probably the determining characteristic of the *æsc* hull, the walty or flexible construction a distinct advantage for beaching that type of vessel. Flexibility was not so important to Alfred's ships as it was to the incoming *askr*. Alfred's ships would not necessarily be required to beach – or even go out through surf – since they were leaving friendly territory. And of course greater rigidity would be a positive virtue in physically striking the indubitably walty *askr*. Greater rigidity might be supplied either in build or with sturdier materials. The major feature of later hull development from about 1000 to 1250 was that the original system of frames and cross-beams remained in position at the bottom while the sides of the ship grew upward and consequently had to be braced with a new system of cross-beams, which in turn permitted high-level decking.

In the meantime better-quality timber would certainly be required for such a highly stressed function as Alfred's interceptor would have been expected to perform. It may have been a question of using oak rather than ash now.

---

[85] 'We say a ship is walt when shee is not stiffe', Captain John Smith, *A Sea Grammar, with the plaine exposition of Smiths accidence for young sea-men enlarged* (London, 1627), p. 55; *The Oxford English Dictionary*, 2nd ed., 20 vols. (Oxford, 1989) XIX, *s.v.* walt, walty, and XX, *s.v.* welt v^2; *The English Dialect Dictionary*, ed. J. Wright, 6 vols. (London, 1898–1905) VI, *s.v.* walt, welt v^2; and personal communication from Robin Ward, Esq.

[86] See above, p. 10.

[87] *Thesaurus Linguae Latinae*, ed. F. Vollmer *et al.* (Leipzig, 1900–, in progress) IX, 1, *s.v.*

[88] Thus both G. N. Garmonsway, *The Anglo-Saxon Chronicle* (London, 1953), p. 90, and D. Whitelock, *English Historical Documents, c. 500–1042*, Eng. Hist. Documents 1, 2nd ed. (London, 1979), p. 206, render *unwealt* 'steadier'.

Whatever may have been used earlier – and it seems that a variety of woods were pressed into service[89] – the evidence from waterlogged sites in London from the mid-ninth century onwards is overwhelmingly for oak-built construction.[90] The single sample of ash wood identified is unfortunately undated, but there is no evidence that the material continued to be much, if at all, used for shipbuilding. There is no reason to suppose the word *æsc* was abandoned because of its hostile connotations (this did not stop the Anglo-Saxons using the word *here* of their armies), but perhaps the material itself ceased to be used – or the form of vessel itself became outmoded. Radially split planking,[91] which gives greatest strength for thickness, was generally used at least until the twelfth century. Any movement noticed in the oak-built Gokstad type of hull (resilient rather than *æsc*-flexible)[92] is due to method rather than materials of construction.

(e) *ge eac hieran*. The final adjective used of Alfred's new ships is *hieran*. Later versions of the *Chronicle* render the early Winchester manuscript form *hieran* as *hearran*, presumably understood to be a comparative of *heah*. The 'Abingdon' versions (BC) read *hearran* and the Worcester manuscript (D) *hearra*, which John of Worcester, who is closest to the Abingdon version of the *Chronicle* in general, renders *altiores*.[93]

Anglo-Saxon poets typically apply the adjectives *bront* and *heah*, 'steep, tall', to notable ships, but perhaps metaphorically.[94] Of course, greater height might be a virtue simply on account of being more imposing. This was presumably the function of a figure-head, where used, or when used. Apparently detachable, the gaping and perhaps gilded zoomorphic head was put on after the boat was launched, either to indicate the presence of a man of status[95] or to denote the intention of setting out on a war expedition[96] – perhaps the only distinguishing

---

[89] Unfortunately at Sutton Hoo and Snape little more than sand-stain profiles remained; see generally Evans and Bruce-Mitford, 'The Ship'; Bruce-Mitford, 'The Snape Boat-Grave', *Aspects of Anglo-Saxon Archaeology*, pp. 114–40. But wood grain preserved on oxidized plank-rivets from Sutton Hoo is thought to have a density similar to that of oak (Evans and Bruce-Mitford, 'The Ship', p. 354).

[90] D. M. Goodburn, 'Anglo-Saxon Boat Finds from London, are they English?', *Crossroads in Ancient Shipbuilding, Proceedings of the Sixth International Symposium on Boat and Ship Archaeology, Roskilde 1991*, ed. C. Westerdahl (Oxford, 1994), pp. 97–104 (summary table at p. 98).

[91] The method of preparation is well explained in McGrail and McKee, *Building and Trials* I, 42–4.

[92] In reconstruction trials, the keel was reported to move 2 cm and the sides to writhe by as much as 15 cm: M. Andersen, *Vikingefærden* (Oslo, 1895), p. 190. For a general *caveat* on the scientific value of reconstruction trials, see McGrail, *Ancient Boats*, p. 193.

[93] See above, p. 10.   [94] *Andreas* 266 and 273; *Beowulf* 238; *Elene* 238; *The Whale* 13.

[95] Cf. the capture of Gruffydd's figure-head and its *bone* (*ornatura*) described in *ASC* 1063 D: *Two Chronicles*, ed. Plummer I, 191 and II, 251.

[96] 'þá mælti Sveinn konungr: "Hræddr er Óláfr Tryggvason nú, eigi þorir hann at sigla með

feature of a warlike as distinct from a more peaceable purpose. But even when used, a boat with a figure-head need not necessarily appear markedly higher than one without, to judge by representation in early waterside graffiti from Bergen.[97]

Certainly in this context to have interpreted *hieran* as 'higher' is puzzling, since the speed of a galley would be in inverse proportion to its height, and yet the chronicler specifies that Alfred's boats were in fact faster. Greater height would have pushed the hull lower in the water[98] with some increased drag on the wetted-area as a result. Moreover, greater height would add to the likelihood of the vessel toppling over. Alfred might recall Orosius' account of the 'very famous' sea-battle off Actium, where Mark Antony's ships were said to have made up in size what they lacked in number. It is pertinent to see how the Alfredian translator, or rather paraphraser, treats the original – what he adds, misunderstands, or chooses to change. Orosius reads:

Classis Antonii centum septuaginta nauium fuit, quantum numero cedens tantum magnitudine praecellens, nam decem pedum altitudine a mari aberant[99]

which the Alfredian translator renders:

Antonius hæfde eahtatig scipa, on þæm wæron farende x legian, for þon swa micle swa he læs hæfde, swa micle hie wæron beteran 7 maran, for þon hie wæron swa geworht þæt hie mon ne mehte mid monnum oferhlæstan, þæt hie næren x fota hea bufan wætere.[100]

Where Orosius said that Antony's ships were better because they rose fully ten feet out of the water, the Alfredian translator inserts another clause and adds a negative, emphasizing their lowness in the water – their virtue residing in the fact that they could not be overladen because they did *not* rise ten feet out of the water. Whatever the nautical credentials of the Anglo-Saxon translator, he seems clear that the matter of height is linked with the question of vulnerability, suggesting that the issue might have been a current concern.

hǫfuðin á skipi sinu"' ('Then King Swein said: "Now Olaf Tryggvason is afraid; he has not the courage to sail with a figure-head on his ship"'): Snorri Sturluson, *Heimskringla*, ed. Aðalbjarnarson I, 353. For a survey of references to ships' figure-heads in Old Norse literature, see A. Campbell, *Encomium Emmae Reginae*, Camden 3rd ser. 72 (1949; Camden Classic Reprints 4 (Cambridge, 1998)), 94–5.

[97] A. E. Herteig, 'The Excavation of "Bryggen", the Old Hanseatic Wharf in Bergen', *MA* 3 (1959), 177–86, at 185, fig. 68; cf. A.-E. Christensen, 'Ship Graffiti and Models', *Miscellanea 1: Medieval Dublin Excavations 1962–81*, Series B 2, ed. P. F. Wallace (Dublin, 1988), pp. 13–26.

[98] As Bray and McGurk recognize, translating John of Worcester's *altiores* as 'with a bigger draught', pp. 350–1.

[99] 'Antony's fleet had a hundred and seventy ships, which were fewer in number (than Octavianus' ships) but greater in size, inasmuch as they rose ten feet above the sea.'

[100] 'Antony had eighty ships, in which travelled ten legions; but by so much as he had fewer (than Octavianus) by so much were they better and larger, because they were so built that they could not be overladen with men, in that they were not ten feet high above the water': *The Old English Orosius*, ed. Bately, pp. 129 and 317.

In due course greater overall size (and height) would certainly render the ship more formidable as a fighting-platform; but Alfred's ships are said to be longer, rather than 'bigger' or 'wider'. When in 885 Alfred sent a raiding-fleet from Kent to Danish East Anglia, where there were two engagements in the mouth of the Stour, the first of which the English won, and the second of which they lost,[101] Asser's account tantalizingly speaks of the Viking ships being *paratae ad bellum*, but whether understood as 'cleared for action' (Conybeare) or 'rigged for battle' (Keynes and Lapidge),[102] either suggests the sense of later tactics; and the issue is bedevilled by the disputed chronological status of that text. Æthelweard says, more credibly, *deponunt scarmos*, 'dropped their rowlocks'.[103] It was all too easy for scribes copying out the *Chronicle* in later times more accustomed to sea-engagements, and certainly John of Worcester writing in the twelfth century, to assume that because the war-ship was a fighting-platform, height was a necessary virtue. It is important to remember that John of Worcester was well-nigh as remote from Alfred as Alfred was from Orosius. By the same token, Snorri Sturluson's account of the thirty-four-thwart 'Long Serpent', built for Óláf Tryggvason in 998, which suggests that it towered over its adversaries, with fore- and aft-castles, is looking back from the standpoint of the thirteenth century.[104]

Despite greater carrying potential, any additional height would bring commensurate problems of propulsion and manœuvrability. This in turn would lead to the development of stern-post rudder and bow-sprit sail. But in the ninth century at least, war-ships employed sails merely adventitiously, since they were efficient only when running before the wind. Indeed, the use of sail for primary manœuvring purposes must have resulted in such considerable local stress to the structure that would, of itself, have revolutionized building technology. The introduction of the deep-draught hull, stern-rudder and multiple-rigging that mark the major stages in the evolution of the ship are all normally reckoned developments much later than the age of Alfred.

At this stage higher sides might suit merchantmen like the Scandinavian *byrðingar*, which took their name from the high-boarded bulwarks (*byrði*) which allowed goods to be piled up between them,[105] but would have been impractical in the case of a war vessel, where oars might need to be rapidly unshipped. Garmonsway's less-than-literal translation represents *hieran* as 'with more freeboard',[106] which apparently led Professor Logan to assume this meant 'with more deck space',[107] though in view of their shallow draught there could be no

[101] *Two Chronicles*, ed. Plummer I, 78–9.
[102] *Asser's Life of King Alfred*, ed. Stevenson, p. 51; E. Conybeare, *Alfred in the Chroniclers* (London, 1900), p. 101; S. Keynes and M. Lapidge, *Alfred the Great: Asser's 'Life of King Alfred' and Other Contemporary Sources* (Harmondsworth, 1983), p. 87.   [103] *Chronicle*, ed. Campbell, p. 45.
[104] Snorri Sturluson, *Heimskringla*, ed. Aðalbjarnarson I, 335–6, 344–6, 356 *et passim*.
[105] de Vries, *Altnordisches Wörterbuch*, p. 67, *s.v.*   [106] See above, p. 15, n. 88.
[107] F. D. Logan, *The Vikings in History*, 2nd ed. (London, 1991), p. 149, and cf. p. 178.

decking in any conventional sense. Additional free-board would gain nothing in terms of transfer ship-to-ship unless there was equally high decking – which would put the rowers at too inefficient an angle to the water; on the other hand, it might deter boarding by an enemy. A high free-board would certainly facilitate awkward manœuvres without shipping water – and perhaps worth compromising efficiency in respect both of the weight involved and the additional length of oar necessary to provide maximum purchase. If the oar-ports were cut in too low a strake, then it would prove difficult to unship the oars rapidly. The Gokstad ship adds a further wash-strake to the gunwale as compared with the Oseberg ship, but retains its rowing geometry by leaving the thwart where it was and cutting the oar-port in the sheer-strake. What it gained in comfort as a princely transport it would lose in safety; its crew could not have successfully encountered an enemy at sea. Ships of the Sutton Hoo type had been provided with thole-pins (that is, pins inserted in the top of the gunwale) rather than ports, so that oars need prove no encumbrance in such circumstances.

Finally, if *hieran* does mean 'higher', this word sits rather oddly where it does in the list of attributes. We might have expected that, in a considered account, such an adjective might have been placed with the physical characteristics which begin the list. John of Worcester modifies the text to do just this; having rendered the Abingdon manuscript *hearran* as *altiores*, he naturally transferred it earlier in the list (see fig. 1).

Winchester Chronicle (*ASC* MS A)	Abingdon Chronicle (*ASC* MS B)	John of Worcester
contemporary	*late tenth century*	*twelfth century*
longer and more oars	longer and more oars	longer
swifter	swifter	*altiores*
less flexible	less flexible	swifter
hieran	*hearran*	less flexible

Fig. 1 Alfred's ships

It seems likely that by *hieran*, the earliest scribe intended not the comparative of *heah*, 'high', which as we see is physically improbable, but rather of *hiere*, 'obedient, responsive', which is exactly what we would expect, since manœuvrability is the essential quality of the interceptor. The sense of the *hapax legomenon* is provided easily enough from the negative *[ofer]hyre*, '[dis]obedient'[108] or the substantive compound *hiere[mann]*, 'one obedient to another', or associated words

[108] Cf. *Wulfstan's Canons of Edgar*, ed. R. Fowler, EETS os 266 (London, 1972), 2–3.

such as *hiernes*, 'obedience' or *hieran* 'to obey', all familiar from the Alfredian 'Pastoral Care'.[109]

Manœuvrability, then, consists of what? – not sail, since all the evidence seems to confirm the later chroniclers' conviction that Alfred's ships were in fact *galeias*.[110] In any case, the very winds that drove the attacking ships onto the English coast stood direct in the face of, and evidently impossible for, any intending interceptor to utilize. It was apparently under sail that the Danish fleet came to grief in 877 having taken advantage of favourable winds[111] – but in 897 when pressed (in retreat, that is) enemy ships are said to row.[112] For some time sail was primarily of use to mercantile vessels which did not need to move fast or reliably and where space was needed for cargo rather than men. Unlike a heavy cargo-boat, the interceptor could not afford to wait for a propitious wind; by definition it would be needed instantaneously, irrespective of weather conditions, and then might need to manœuvre tightly. For this purpose oars would remain the primary mode of propulsion for centuries.

Greater draught or greater breadth might increase the ship's stability; a keel especially would give added purchase and thus more efficient sailing, but not necessarily better oar-propulsion. Greater drag impedes manœuvrability under oar. Indeed, greater draught and greater breadth could both prove a decided disadvantage when negotiating the shoals and strong tidal currents of the English estuaries or coastline. Of course if Alfred's ships *were* higher, and thus had greater draught, they would be more likely to go aground in shallow conditions. Shortly after being built, nine of these new ships were sent in after a group of Danish *askar* which had entered an estuary somewhere on the south coast, and were said to have 'grounded' – 'and also very awkwardly, *uneðelice*, grounded'.[113] This is a curiously detailed comment, unless the writer intended to stress that the boats were badly handled or simply not intended to beach.[114] Anglo-Saxon boatmen will surely have had good experience of the dangerous cross-currents and shifting sands of native estuaries, and knowledge even of irregular tides;[115] but exceptional length would not have been easy to handle across inshore shoals. Of course, if *uneðelice* is understood to mean 'inconveniently' rather than 'awkwardly', it could refer to the fact that they had

---

[109] *King Alfred's West Saxon Version of Gregory's Pastoral Care*, ed. H. Sweet, 2 vols., EETS os 45 and 50 (London, 1871–2), 29, 55, 128 *et passim*.   [110] See above, pp. 9–10, n. 51.
[111] See above, p. 9.   [112] *Two Chronicles*, ed. Plummer I, 91.   [113] *Ibid.* I, 90–1.
[114] Alan Binns ingeniously supposes that the deliberately beached *askar* were using rollers (perhaps spare oars), unlike the accidentally grounded English ships: 'The Navigation of Viking Ships round the British Isles in Old English and Old Norse Sources', *The Fifth Viking Congress*, ed. B. Nicolasen (Tórshavn, 1968), pp. 103–17, at 109–10.
[115] See Bede, *De temporum ratione liber*, c. xxix, ed. C. W. Jones, CCSL 123 B (Turnhout, 1977), 366–71, and generally W. M. Stevens, *Bede's Scientific Achievement* (Jarrow, 1985), pp. 13–18.

beached deliberately, albeit in the wrong place, rather than merely inadvertently.[116] Whether or not the whole *Chronicle* account records a failed experiment – as the most recent commentator concludes,[117] assuming the annalist to have been no less an apologist than Asser – there were certainly difficulties associated with the sole report specifically made of their use. And the incident in question immediately follows the writer's description of their design. If the difficulties experienced could be regarded as a consequence of Alfred's design, one might reconsider the thrust of *swa himselfum ðuhte*.[118] Regal war-leaders from Marius to Shaka are conventionally credited with improved weapon-design. But to follow so specific a description of the king's new ships merely with an account of their tactical failure would represent a remarkably objective reservation in the context of a bulletin we might suppose to have derived at one or other remove from Alfred's circle.

Whether or not Alfred's innovatory design outlasted his time we have no way of knowing. It may have been so successful as to be taken for granted; or it may have been such a failure that there was never occasion to mention it again; either way, the record is curiously silent. However, the tactics of interception are implicit thereafter, and in turn provoke a revival of the naval engagement *per se* which may not have been much seen since classical times. The subsequent importance of the English fleet is undeniable. Within a very few years Alfred's son and successor Edward could gather a fleet of a hundred vessels, and by 1008 it seems that there was a navy firmly under royal direction, funded from national taxation.[119] John of Worcester claimed that Edgar was able to summon 3,600 ships for annual manœuvres after Easter, divided into three fleets commanding eastern, western and northern coasts respectively, so that the whole island was circumnavigated.[120] The numbers look like an exaggeration, but the practice seems credible, inasmuch as Æthelred attempted to maintain customary post-Easter naval manœuvres.[121] In 1066 Harold could guard the Channel coast at least during the summer and autumn.[122]

Whatever Alfred's achievement in strategy or design, subsequent generations seemed to have looked back not to Alfred but to Edgar, *rex marium Brittaniæ*, as

---

[116] For a general account of what might have been happening, see F. P. Magoun, 'King Alfred's Naval and Beach Battle with the Danes in 896', *MLR* 37 (1942), 409–14; Binns, 'The Navigation of Viking Ships', pp. 108–10. [117] Smyth, *King Alfred*, pp. 112–13.
[118] 'as it seemed to himself', see above, p. 1, n. 1.
[119] *ASC* 911, 1008, *Two Chronicles*, ed. Plummer I, 96–7 and 138. On the later Anglo-Saxon navy, see C. W. Hollister, *Anglo-Saxon Military Institutions on the Eve of the Norman Conquest* (Oxford, 1962), pp. 103–26, and R. P. Abels, *Lordship and Military Obligation in Anglo-Saxon England* (London, 1988), *passim*.   [120] *Chronicle*, ed. Darlington and McGurk, pp. 424–7.
[121] V Æthelred 27 and VI Æthelred 33: *Die Gesetze der Angelsachsen*, ed. F. Liebermann, 3 vols. (Halle, 1903–16) I, 242–3 and 254–5.   [122] *Two Chronicles*, ed. Plummer I, 194–7.

the origin of English naval aspirations.[123] Alfred's more recent reputation on which so much national myth is based, of the kind identifying him as founder of the Royal Navy,[124] inspiration of Arne's 'Rule Britannia'[125] and presiding spirit of the dreadnought race,[126] is an eighteenth-century perception, presumably based on the need for a more romantic national figure than Edgar.[127]

[123] Cf. *The Libelle of Englyshe Polycye: a poem on the use of sea-power, 1436*, ed. G. Warner (Oxford, 1926), pp. 45–9; *The Diary of Samuel Pepys*, ed. R. Latham and W. Matthews, 11 vols. (London, 1970–83) VI, 81, n. 1.

[124] Thus, for example, J. Abbott, *History of King Alfred of England* (London, 1850), p. 111; J. A. Giles, *Memorials of King Alfred* (London, 1861), pp. 310–11; E. A. Freeman, *The History of the Norman Conquest of England*, 6 vols. (Oxford, 1867–79) I, 57; J. R. Green, *The Conquest of England* (London, 1883), pp. 137–8.

[125] Written for *Alfred: a Masque represented before their royal highnesses the Prince and Princess of Wales, at Cliffden, on the First of August, 1740* [David Mallet and James Thomson] (London, 1740), pp. 42–3; cf. A. Scott, 'Arne's "Alfred"', *Music and Letters* 55 (1974), 385–97. The topic was obviously *en vogue*; shortly afterwards Haydn set to music Alexander Bicknell's drama *The Patriot King: or Alfred and Elvida*; cf. H. C. Robbins Landon, *Haydn: The Years of 'The Creation', 1796–1800* (London, 1977), pp. 107–8.

[126] Cf. A. Bowker, *The King Alfred Millenary* (London, 1902), pp. 146–51.

[127] For further discussion, see S. Keynes, 'The Cult of King Alfred', below, pp. 225–356.

What use are the Thorkelin transcripts of *Beowulf*?

JOHAN GERRITSEN

The Thorkelin transcripts of *Beowulf* (Copenhagen, Royal Library, N.K.S. 512 and 513 4°) are useful for a number of purposes. Two of these involve *Beowulf* itself: they offer a number of readings lost from its unique manuscript (London, British Library, Cotton Vitellius A. xv) and they afford an insight into the genesis of its first printed edition (Thorkelin's) published, after many vicissitudes, in Copenhagen in 1815. For reasons that will become clear, these purposes should be kept well apart. The present study, accordingly, will concern itself with the first of them only, and will investigate the contribution made by the two transcripts to our knowledge of the manuscript as it was at two points of time in 1787 (more than half a century after the fire of 1731) when the two transcripts purport to have been made. With respect to the second transcript, Thorkelin B, for the most part a line-for-line and page-for-page copy written by Thorkelin himself in his English copperplate hand, this date has been queried, but no satisfactory evidence has been produced and it is not evident where any can now be found. As the dates appear, however, to have been recorded at least a quarter-century after the event, they need not necessarily be trusted wholly in either case. It is certain that in adding the date 1787 to another transcript[1] Thorkelin was a year out; it may thus merely represent a memory of an intensive spell of copying. We shall see below that the first transcript, Thorkelin A, made by an amanuensis in an imitation of the manuscript's Insular script, suggests that there may not have been so very much time between it and Thorkelin B.

Before anything useful can be said about the information provided by the two transcripts, it is necessary to examine their genesis in some detail. The physical aspect of this has been dealt with in an earlier study, but there remains the essential matter of how their text was put on paper and came to have its ultimate form.[2] The point has not remained wholly unnoticed, but to date no sufficiently

---

[1] Copenhagen, N.K.S. 513b 4°, Lydgate's Life of St Edmund, apparently copied in the first half of 1788, not 1787 as stated in a late addition to its title.
[2] The principal earlier work is the Introduction to Kemp Malone's facsimile (*The Thorkelin Transcripts of Beowulf in Facsimile*, EEMF 1 (Copenhagen, 1951)), where several of the points now made afresh can already be found. Kevin Kiernan's *The Thorkelin Transcripts of Beowulf*, Anglistica 25 (Copenhagen, 1986) should not be used without expert verification at source.

thorough analysis has appeared that satisfies the requirements of method, expertise and verification (not to mention detachment and charity).[3] Kemp Malone, in the facsimile, tries to distinguish the inks and gives some other useful information, but does not even tell his reader that the opening leaf of the facsimile does not mirror the make-up of the manuscript but presents verso and recto of two different leaves as recto and verso of the same leaf. Kevin Kiernan, in his *Beowulf* book of 1981,[4] had much to say about Thorkelin shifting leaves, and similar matters, in B, but in fact could never have analysed that manuscript's make-up. His book on the transcripts, like the *Beowulf* book, was written by an enthusiastic, persuasive and intelligent writer without adequate training and experience in the arcane skills required, and lacking in the historical perspective needed to understand Thorkelin's mind and purpose. As a result, in these two books, no-one can separate fancy from truth, or indeed from sometimes quite acute observation, who has not thoroughly familiarized himself with the needed skills, and only then with the documents. That the skills involved are not merely technical, but include both an awareness that one must allow the documents to speak for themselves and a readiness to do so is not entirely irrelevant either. And it is perhaps not superfluous, in this technical age, to remind ourselves that

---

Such footnotes as have been added in support of this observation cite the work as *TTB*. For the codicology, see now my 'The Thorkelin Transcripts of *Beowulf*: a Codicological Description, with Notes on their Genesis and History', *The Library*, ns 12 (1990), 1–22 [cited as *TCD*]. The account presented on p. 13 of my 'Beowulf: the Foundations of the Text' (*N[etherlands] S[ociety for] E[nglish] S[tudies] Bulletin* 1.1 (April 1991), 1–22), when the A transcript had not yet been fully analysed, now needs correction, as does, on some points, the paper delivered to the International Society of Anglo-Saxonists at Oxford in 1993. Reference to A is by page and line (the same for transcript and facsimile), to B by present page followed by slash and facsimile page (prefixed M). Reference to the Vitellius manuscript is by folio and line according to the current foliation of 1884 (also used in Kemp Malone's facsimile edition, *The Nowell Codex: British Museum Cotton Vitellius A. XV Second MS*, EEMF 12 (Copenhagen, 1963)) which is correct for *Beowulf* as it originally was, as it is now, and as it was when Thorkelin knew it. The historically interesting but now misleading 'old' foliation was unknown to Thorkelin and is irrelevant to these studies. It should perhaps be added that though the work of others is occasionally mentioned, the whole analysis has, for very good reason, been done entirely afresh.

[3] *TTB* wholly ignores the evidence which the state of the quill can provide; and its one reference (p. 92: 'new ink and pen begin', B66r/M131a:19) is wrong as to the ink and guesswork as to the pen. When the pen has been mended the ink may look different to the naked eye, and any such judgement should therefore rest (and for the present study does rest) on examination under magnification and with proper illumination; and one can tell that a quill has been mended, but hardly if it is the same or a new one. It is not evident from *TTB* that its author was aware that steel nibs did not become common until their perfection and popularization by James Perry in the 1830s, so after Thorkelin's death; no steel nib would have worn so quickly that a new one was needed for virtually every page.

[4] K. S. Kiernan, *Beowulf and the Beowulf Manuscript* (New Brunswick, NJ, 1981). A revised edition, reprinting the original text with a new introductory essay, adding the text of his 'The State of the Beowulf Manuscript 1882–1983' (*ASE* 13 (1984), 23–42), and with a new Foreword by K. O'Brien O'Keeffe, was published at Ann Arbor, MI, in 1996.

we deal with hypothesis and interpretation. Whether, for instance, we enhance an image by photographic or by electronic means, the outcome is never absolute truth. A sign *is* not an *a*, it is not even *interpreted* as one, it is interpreted as having been *intended* for one. Such interpretations have been and will undoubtedly continue to be, occasionally, faulty. Even in modern writing hands, as in some early ones, there is often no way of deciding objectively between, for instance, *cl* and *d* except through context. I well remember a student whom, from the papers she sent in, we registered as *Thecla* but who called herself *Theda* when she arrived. It cannot be said that we *misread* her, but we certainly *misinterpreted*. No enhancement could ever change that.[5]

Though the present study cannot claim to be definitive, what is said here does attempt to meet the requirements stated; and while it may occasionally cite the work of others, the analysis presented has, for good reason, been done entirely afresh. Some of the principles applied are illustrated below;[6] others will appear from the discussion as required.

In studying the two transcripts there is good reason to proceed from B to A. Neither transcript was left untouched after its original scribe had completed his original job: back in Denmark, maybe earlier, Thorkelin interfered with the record, and about Thorkelin, at least, more can be learnt. Of the amanuensis we know nothing for certain so far, except what may be learnt from this one text; so before looking at A in depth it is wise to examine B.

Before doing so, however, an important point should be made about Grímur Jónsson Thorkelin. Those who have so far concerned themselves with this eminent scholar and his two transcripts have been (without exception, it would seem) philologists, and we should not perhaps blame them for having mistaken Grímur Jónsson for one of their own breed. This is particularly evident in the case of Kevin Kiernan, and it is therefore no marvel that that is where it has done most harm. To understand what went on in the transcripts it is essential to realize that Thorkelin was in no way a philologist, even less a literary scholar, but an eighteenth-century historian and antiquary who lived on into the nineteenth. Like historians generally, *then as now*, he saw a text as a source of historical information: what mattered was its content, not its form. What Thorkelin set out to do when he copied *Beowulf* was to record not the manuscript – of which in any case he already owned a quasi-facsimile transcript (regrettably, not linear and paginary) – but the *text* of a *document* that seemed relevant to early Danish *history* (the purpose for which he was in Britain). The spine labels on his two transcripts, both of them produced in Denmark, particularly that on A (*HIST. Da[n] Anglosax*), but also that on B (*Poëma Anglos de rebus Daniciis*), as well as the title of

---

[5] It should be emphasized that no technical enhancement should be accepted that does not, as a check, include an adequate portion of unambiguous surrounding text. If the enhancement alters this text in any significant way, it is suspect.   [6] See, for instance, n. 12.

his edition (*De Danorum Rebus Gestis Secul. III. & IV.*) make this abundantly clear. This *text*, and no more, he set out to transcribe, accurately, according to the historian's normal practice. 'Accurate exscripsit' he says on the title-page of his own transcript (as he could not of A, another man's work – even had he thought so, which we may doubt). It is a claim that, it is here maintained, is reasonably substantiated by a critical but impartial examination of his transcript *as he originally made it,* though (like A) it does contain errors (more errors than we, or he, would have wished) and (in contrast to A) contains the historian's usual, conscious formal departures from the exemplar in such matters as capitalization, punctuation and the expansion of abbreviations. To the historian this is merely part of the modernization process inherent in any transcription of a text from an obsolete to a modern graphic system, and textually they are small matters.

But Thorkelin does not unthinkingly follow this system, however accepted and respectable. It requires capitals for proper names and for the beginnings of sentences, so when he starts copying, the first line, full capitals in the manuscript, is reduced except for one initial one, at once indicating that this is a historian's transcript, not a philologist's. But he only gradually comes to recognize the proper names: of the first two capitalized, both on his first page, the one, *Dena,* is a late alteration pretty certainly made in Denmark, the other is sentence initial; we have to wait several pages before the first name is capitalized as such as part of the original copying.[7] Besides, he does not always identify names correctly, and he quite soon recognizes that a single point is not necessarily a period. On his first page each one of them is followed by a capital, but this practice has already ceased by page two. His expansion of abbreviations shows a similar development, though he never learns the meaning of **g** with a macron on it till after the transcript is finished.

But what is, for us, a serious problem caused by Thorkelin's historical background is that he would have considered himself fully justified to copy, as text readings, his own reconstructions on the basis of what he found before him. In cases where he was clearly wrong, we can tell, but they are the only ones. Where A shows a gap, and B does not, we must always consider the possibility that what we have is Thorkelin's reconstruction, right or wrong, on the basis of what remained plus his knowledge of language and, perhaps, verse. We should treat him with respect, for he may have seen more than we do now or than A dared copy, but we should not rely on him.

---

[7] The record in *TTB* is inaccurate. All four names on 2r/M3a have capital *H* written over original *h*, not *Heorogar* alone. *Scyldinga* 4v/M8a:11 (line 170) is the first name, *Hroðgar* 8v/M16a:1 (line 339) the first actor in the poem to be given a first-time capital where no stop precedes, so presumably because it has been recognized as a name. For the one this was the fourth occurrence in the manuscript text, for the other the seventh.

What use are the Thorkelin transcripts of Beowulf?

THORKELIN B

Thorkelin B, as already stated, is almost throughout a linear and paginary copy of the manuscript as Thorkelin found it, written, in an English copperplate hand, on paper folded for outer margins but not ruled.[8] A suspected lacuna in the manuscript, or one left in the transcript for possible later suppletion, is of fitting size, and is marked by one or more dots (though, *pace* Malone, without guessing at the number of letters wanting). Where a lacuna was filled (whether almost immediately or later), the dots were generally written on, often making them hard to ascertain with the unaided eye. Thorkelin's consistency in this respect appears good enough to make it quite unsafe to hypothesize an original lacuna where not one dot can be observed.[9] An examination of the use of pen and ink shows the copying to have been very rapid and fluent. This should be obvious at a glance, but it is also demonstrated more objectively by the behaviour of the ink, particularly in many linking strokes where the width of the line remains the same but the middle part of the stroke shows a lighter colour because not enough ink was deposited. In the lettered A this phenomenon is absent.

With rare exceptions, the original transcript is entirely consistent as to colour of ink, direction, and thickness of point; this strongly suggests that Thorkelin, while making his transcript, did not allow himself to be distracted by anything except the genuine puzzles, and, apart from plentiful corrections as he wrote, did not as a rule go over the same ground a second time before the transcript was complete. It would seem illogical, moreover (and quite out of character), that with the manuscript before him and justifiably confident in his knowledge of the script and the language, he should have impeded his

---

[8] Exceptions are that Thorkelin, like his amanuensis, generally gives the fitt numbers a line to themselves, irrespective of the manuscript situation, that on the crowded final page he finds it impossible in some lines to get in as much as his copy-text does, and that he occasionally transposes a (part of a) word from one line to the next (or vice versa), presumably because he did not memorize the text in manuscript lines. That this occasional transposition is unintentional is suggested by the general practice of his transcription, and evidenced more particularly by the cases he noticed and corrected. Where an original reading gets onto the wrong page in this way it is always within the same opening; no argument for the use of A can therefore depend on it. It is to be noted that, tailed letters apart, Thorkelin's general faith in A was such that in his edition he repeatedly adopts A's error for his own correct reading, even when the form of that reading is supported elsewhere in his text.

[9] The usual criteria of ink, state of the quill, etc. are of course also available; in fact only a single case has been observed where these betray the filling of an original lacuna and no dot has been identified with certainty. It should be added that examination of such letters as **c** and **o** in places where no dots are suspected shows that it is all too easy to discover imaginary dots in their bottom curve.

progress in the laborious manner which any consultation of A would have implied.[10]

That he did compare the two, and in fact did so on several occasions, is testified by his alterations to both transcripts; but as always in manuscript studies, *what was originally written* constitutes the primary evidence. It is not impossible that while in Britain he may have again compared B with its original here or there (which given the method of his transcript was reasonably easy), but there is nothing to prove consultation of A, nothing to show any sustained rechecking with the manuscript, and nothing to prove or even suggest any substantial collation of the two transcripts before he was back in Denmark and had started work on his edition. It is far more likely that he wrote B because it was faster, and more reliable, than collating and correcting A. That B is, like A, based on the Vitellius manuscript is certain; had it been based even partly on A it would have avoided a number of errors, have copied some others, and have had notably fewer lacunae. Corresponding observations prove (superfluously, to be sure) that the original writer of A at no time depended on B.

The phrase 'what was originally written' is not superfluous, for Thorkelin eventually prepared an edition, and in fact had to do so twice, as the first version was lost through the bombardment of Copenhagen in 1807. The transcripts, but especially his own B, bear witness to this in a number of respects. In A, apart from an interlinear Latin translation on some pages, later erased, we are (exclusively or mainly) concerned with alterations to its literal record, occasionally felicitous,[11] too often not. In B we have not only these but also a great many pencil strokes on some leaves to divide the verse, a spate of added ink commas (and perhaps points, but these are not always easy to identify as to ink) on some pages, a long but mistaken side-note on one leaf, and a variety of other, smaller matters. Among the literal changes, two are pervasive. In the first place many **ds** were later, in Denmark, crossed to turn them into **ð**, not infrequently errone-

---

[10] His notebook in Rigsarkivet (6431.5.E3, notebook *Biblioth. Cotton.*) contains two Old English passages copied out with accustomed rapidity on 2 October 1786, with corrections *currente calamo*: *gl* struck through and followed immediately by *geleornis*; and *neath: t* struck through and continued as *neahterne*. Note that the second one already shows the problem with Old English *h* that *TTB*, p. 142 mistakenly wishes to link with his visit to Scotland of a year later (cf. below, p. 41, n. 35).

[11] Like his suppletion of A's *gio..ntas* to *gigantas* at 134r.20 (A4:16; the facts are misrepresented by *TTB* pp. 48–9 and 124, but correctly stated by Zupitza, who, however, did not recognize the correcting hand as Thorkelin's; the correction from *e* to *a* in *ntas* of the next manuscript page appears to be done in A's ink). The amanuensis apparently only wrote *gio* at first (the pointed *o* is not really that, but apparently imitates what he thought he saw in the manuscript; in view of the spacing, the *ga* of *gantas* must have been lost on the verso), added *..ntes* at the correcting stage, then changed *e* to *a*; the rest is shown by the ink and hand to be late Thorkelin. As to the erased Latin translation, which *TTB*, p. 121, claims was written before B, such traces as remain show Danish script.

What use are the Thorkelin transcripts of Beowulf?

ously.[12] And secondly, most **v**s were later altered to **w**, Thorkelin having realized (p. 3v/M6a, 134v.01) that *Beowulf* is no exception to the rule that in Old English manuscripts there is generally no *v*, so that the character was legitimately (and to someone with his background naturally) available to transcribe *wynn*.[13] The ink of this change, mostly much lighter than the original, and especially the ductus, shows that the change was made at a late date in Denmark when Thorkelin had become unaccustomed to the copperplate hand he had written so well in his younger, English years.[14]

THORKELIN A

The copying

Thorkelin A is a script facsimile of the manuscript beginning in strong dark brown ink, soon changing to a paler colour, and ending in a very light brown. Its text appears to have been copied continuously on lines ruled in pencil; the number of lines on the page ranges from fourteen to twenty-three, but is generally around eighteen; the lines are fully written except for the fitt numbers standing alone. The procedure with respect to lacunae is more or less the opposite of B's. Gaps are left for problems, generally much larger than needed (perhaps for

---

[12] The number of original ð, however, proves on proper examination to be rather larger than suggested by *TTB*. Thus of the eighteen cross-strokes on ð on 181v (50v/M100a), one of which does duty for two adjoining characters, one (in *eðel*, 12) is clearly late. Its ink is lighter, it is written with a quill scraped thinner and so making a thinner line when drawn sideways than the pen which wrote the original page, it is not the firm stroke that all the others are, and it is written at a different angle. These others all have the colour of their surroundings, have the same width and direction, and in ten cases show ink running from the stem into the cross-stroke, either one way or both ways. It is thus evident that all seventeen are original, and that *eðel* provides a guide for judging other alterations on this page. According to *TTB*, however, eight of the seventeen (including six of those with ink running from the stem into the cross-stroke) are, without argument, later changes. The recto page tells a similar story; further checking on this point seems supererogatory.

[13] To call this a mistake, and knowingly changing the manuscript (*TTB*, p. 119), though helping to bolster up claims of Thorkelin's inaccuracy, is merely silly. The whole purpose of transcription is to reproduce the manuscript in a (to us) more legible form. On the graphemic level what is done here is unexceptionable, and no different from transcribing the Old English form of *r* by a modern one (simple one-to-one correspondence). If this sort of argument is to be used, the first candidates for complaint should be the different forms of *s* in the manuscript, which Thorkelin (be it said with full justification) indiscriminately transcribes as long and short *s*, while the amanuensis is obviously at pains to keep them. The matter of the ð, to be sure, is much more disturbing, though (see previous note) less so than *TTB* suggests.

[14] *TTB*'s query (p. 140) – how do we 'confidently date the inks, not to mention the four hands' is perfectly capable of an answer, but it requires the sort of careful palaeographical scrutiny that *TTB* does not give (cf. above, p. 24, n. 3). This does not, of course, mean that no doubt remains, or that calendar dates can be appended. The only real question is what was done while Thorkelin was still in England.

easy finding); on subsequent suppletion the excess space is filled with dots unless, it would seem, the suppletion is known to be partial. Corrections on the first thirty-two pages are mostly in a strong dark brown ink, almost black to the naked eye; further corrections and additions are in various inks, from apparent black to a very light yellowish brown.

It is clear that Thorkelin's amanuensis started from scratch, without any very useful instruction in the Insular hand, and without any knowledge of Old English. He copied the manuscript so far as he could make it out, leaving gaps where it appears he could not. His initial unfamiliarity with the script is evident from the shape of some, and the fairly large size of all his characters on starting, but also from the sorts of mistakes that someone familiar with the script would expect from such a person. As a copyist he must therefore have been essentially more reliable than the sophisticated Thorkelin, and with a good knowledge of Old English it should be possible, where the manuscript fails, to recover the original behind many if not most of his errors.

As, however, his transcript is just over eighty-nine pages long, in the course of his work he must have become to some extent familiar with script and language, will have acquired certain expectations, and may similarly have been influenced by these to make errors. On the other hand, his transcript is not cursive but lettered and thus provides a better safeguard against impressionistic error than does B. All the same one is surprised fairly often by errors that the state of the manuscript could hardly have caused; the section below on, correction, will go further into these matters.

After a while, developments become visible. A growing familiarity not only reduces the size of the script but also brings changes to the execution of some of the characters. Thus **t**, apparently first taken for a form of **c**, becomes more like what it should be, but the most notable development is perhaps in the *yogh*. This starts as a large figure **3**, with the tail a wide, open bow ending in a pronounced bulb; first the bulb disappears, and then the character starts narrowing and the bow begins to turn back and eventually recross, the final result being a graceful narrow character, easily written, that does not perhaps resemble its original too much, but is eminently legible (it is in fact the copperplate **z**).

The amanuensis eventually does learn to distinguish between **c** and **t**, and to give **t** a proper form; and his **d**, starting with a double-curved top, eventually terminates with a simple reverse-leaning stroke. But, as Malone already observed, the most marked change in the whole manuscript occurs at p. 29, four lines before the page-end. Up to this point the script has indeed been gradually improving and reducing in size, but now it takes on a fresh look. It is still the same man, the same hand, and the same character formation, but one detail has suddenly changed: the amanuensis now knows that *thorn* and *wynn* must not have

What use are the Thorkelin transcripts of Beowulf?

round bowls. As it becomes here, the hand, with certain further developments, remains with us to the end of the transcript. Moreover, although the preceding twenty-nine pages are heavily corrected, particularly the mistakes in the tailed letters, and the bowls of *thorn* and *wynn*, this correction now soon comes to an end. Three pages on, and we have the usual erasures and corrections made instantly or nearly so, but that is all; even the lacunae mostly remain unfilled, except where Thorkelin eventually filled them. It looks as if at this point the amanuensis had instruction in reading and writing Insular script, and then went on confidently with the rest, in the knowledge that he would not henceforth be able to do better than he was doing now.

This does not mean that he made no further mistakes, but their number is now comparatively small until he hits scribe B in the manuscript, when his troubles begin afresh. Most of this has been observed before, beginning with Malone in his Introduction to the facsimile, but there is no point in listing the errors in A unless it is first shown as objectively as possible who wrote what to begin with.

There is no evidence, and no reason to think, that anyone else was concerned with the transcript other than the amanuensis and Thorkelin. From early June until late October, Thorkelin was away on a trip to the north, receiving an honorary doctorate at St Andrews on 26 October,[15] but his presence at the British Museum before June is only recorded with any certainty on fourteen days in those five months. This refers, however, to his use of the Reading Room: there is no telling how often he visited the Department; and since there is no Reading Room record for it, unless we assume that Thorkelin was allowed to take the manuscript home (which is absurd), both transcripts must have been prepared in the Department. But whenever it took place, coming as late in the transcription as it did, the intervention that caused the change at p. 29 can hardly be ascribed to anyone but Thorkelin, and the question therefore is what were his grounds for deciding that some instruction was indicated, and what else he might conceivably have done.

What is certain is that, having reached p. 29, the amanuensis continued to the end in a fashion greatly superior to what he had done before, even though collation of his work with the manuscript shows that a renewed confrontation could have been as profitable there as elsewhere. But having got to the end he seems indeed to have gone back to fill in blanks where possible, but not to have got further than p. 15. The hand and ink that fill some lacunae here and add three accidentally omitted lines plainly belong to the final stage of his task, when the

---

[15] The only evidence found for the date of his return is in his manuscript autobiography at Copenhagen (Rigsarkivet, Personal File 6431.5, D: Selvbiografiske optegnelser), written a very long time after the event. He does not appear in the British Museum records again until January 1788.

hand had come to differ in some further points from what it was on pp. 30ff., and the ink was the lightest of those he had employed.

The corrections

As indicated above, the A transcript is very extensively corrected, and it is essential for an appreciation of it as a record of the Vitellius codex that the status, and thereby the authority, of the corrections be properly ascertained. Though different selections of errors and corrections have been published, few criteria for the judgements given have been presented, and no systematic analysis has been made.

A first distinction that must be made is between running corrections made by the amanuensis while he was copying, more or less *currente calamo* (though erasing, of course, makes for something of a break), and those made at some later stage: those of the former type should be virtually indubitable reflexes of the original, for those of the latter type this is a question that must be determined.

Corrections made as part of the copying process are of two kinds: those involving the use of the pen only, and those involving some form of erasure. The first type is not always easy to attribute as, once written, the text is open to the ministrations of whoever gets it into his hands. Where a character has been touched up or altered one must therefore judge whether pen, ink and ductus agree with what we find authentic in its surroundings, and this can be quite hard. Erasure is much easier to deal with, for when it occurs at the point of writing, the final text will agree with its surroundings in all its features, most particularly in its spacing. It is, moreover, a characteristic of the amanuensis that his erasure is not generally so thorough that the original text cannot be made out. Evidently, the eraser which he used was pumice: one or two letters preceding the erasure have generally become much lighter than the preceding text, pumice being rather less precise in its use than the knife. Its advantage, however, is that it will leave a much smoother surface, and that if the space is to be written over again, there is no need to rub out the original text completely.[16] Consequently we can also form an opinion on the types of error he was most prone to, and which may therefore remain in other places of the transcript, where he failed to catch them. Besides eyeskip, so general an error that one must necessarily expect it, two others stand out: the transposition of two successive letters (as his uncorrected

[16] In contrast to the use of the knife, which generally will do so, erasure with pumice need not, in good writing paper (which this is), show any obvious thin spot against the light; though thorough erasure, like that of a premature fitt capital (B[eowulf] 54:08, 172v.14), will of course show one. It is accordingly characteristic that the amanuensis touches up the last character (or more) before the erasure when beginning to write the correct text, making it quite plain what is text and what is imperfect erasure. There are also a very few instances (e.g. *hiora* 85:11) where, for some reason, he appears to have begun erasing a word and then stopped.

What use are the Thorkelin transcripts of Beowulf?

bolde for *blode* at A30:06, 153r.16; *folda* for *floda* at A80:13, 195r.1; *halden* for *hladen* at A88:16, 201r.10), and the skipping of a single character (as *manige*, with *ig* on erased *g*, A13:07, 139r.19; *genehost*, A26:11, 150r.12, with *h* on erased *o*; or uncorrected *hfalan*, A16:18, 142r.02; *maplode*, A22:03, 146v.02).[17] This last feature is textually significant in at least one place (141v.1, A16:6) where the relevant reading of A is *wedra*, that of B *.edera*, while the manuscript now only has *ra*.[18]

The second type of corrections, those made at some later stage, involve not merely the attribution problem alluded to above, but also the question of date. Thorkelin presumably received the transcript in 1787, and did not turn it over to the nation until well after the completion, in 1815, of his edition. At any time between, and in fact even before the transcript was complete, it would have been possible for him to tinker with its record. It is true that, from a textual point of view, the record should be what the amanuensis left as his final text, irrespective of later correction, but this still entails the problem of determining which corrections are his, and later corrections by Thorkelin might conceivably be based on the manuscript.

Some of the later suppletions should definitely be the amanuensis's, namely those which are clearly in the same hand and ink that were active on the final pages of the transcript. These are confined to the first fifteen pages, and they either fill gaps left earlier, or interline omissions. Of the gaps and omissions filled or rectified later, three[19] are in Thorkelin's Danish cursive and date from well after his return to Denmark (one of them, *swa me*, also has a *w*, not the *v* he used for *wynn* in London), and must be based on B, with which they also agree in their one error. There remain some dozen more[20] that are not evidently the amanuensis's and which on balance have a good chance of being Thorkelin's.

If such a balance is to be properly struck, however, it is necessary to analyse the whole matter of the secondary correction in A in some detail. This type of correction starts with the very first line of the transcript, where two big capital *P*'s have been turned into *wynns* through erasure followed by correction with pen and ink. The ink looks exactly like the original, a very dark brown, but traces of the *P* remain in the two bowls, and holding the sheet to the light shows what has happened. The ink of the corrections to single letters that follow similarly shows a fairly dark crystalline deposit under magnification, quite different from

---

[17] For further examples of these and others, see Malone's Introduction to the facsimile, pp. 5–21.
[18] An examination of B's treatment of this word elsewhere in the Transcript suggests that an editor should read *wedera* here.
[19] þæim 140v.05, A15:02; swa me 141v.12, A16:12; full line 142v.05–06, A17:13–14.
[20] 132v.19/2:06 þady; 135v.01/6:10 æglaca ehtende; 162v.01/41:06 swy... scolde; 178v.01/61:02 figende, 181v.02/64:09 don; 182r.15,16/ 65:10 rege þ nat; 182r.18/65:11 & ðær; 182v.09/65:18 leoda; 182v.17/ 66:05 þhu nu hruce... [preceding cwæð has r corrected to *wynn* in A's ink], 183r.01/66:08 f; 183r.02/66:09 dug; 192r.20/77:06 nægling...

Johan Gerritsen

what we meet in the amanuensis's undoubted suppletions and in his capitals. The vast majority of the corrections involve the production of proper *thorns* and *wynns*, at first by thorough erasure of the original by means of the knife, followed by rewriting, but quite soon by simply touching up the character found (especially **p** doing duty for *wynn*, but **p** is also found for **þ** and **r**, and the amanuensis also produced a curious mixture, an Insular **r** with the stem lengthened into a hasta and doing duty for **þ**, very occasionally for another of the tailed letters). Other corrections occur, but are incidental.

This type of correction, in dark ink, and with strong emphasis on the tailed letters but in other respects rather haphazard, continues in some form as far as p. 32, but on some pages is rather cursory, affording a very fair view then of what the transcript looked like in its original state, with its plethora of **p**s (*flet perod pig heap gepanod hie pyrd for speop*, 142v.12, A17:17; *pord pæron pynsume* 146r.04, A21:13; *beopulf maplode* – omitting an **e** as well – 146v.02, A22:03).[21] On p. 12 we begin to see signs that the corrector is tiring of the job: bowls of **þ** are left uncorrected, and gradually the whole becomes more and more negligent until it picks up at p. 26. After p. 32 it stops completely. But there is more to it. The correction of pp. 26–9 is on the whole comparable to that of the early pages, though after 26:09 it suddenly gets to be quite thorough: up to the end of 29 only ten errors remain, and two (*witela* 152r.06, A28:13, and *sciwes* 152v.01, A29:3; both places are entirely clear in the Vitellius manuscript) are added through miscorrection. That of pp. 30–2 is not thorough at all, being wholly confined to the *wynns* and overlooking twenty-six other errors of all kinds.[22]

What is most remarkable about these corrections to pp. 26–32, however, is the fact that they use a form of *wynn* that is straight-topped, not round. It is a form found nowhere else in the transcript, except in the two capitals of line 1 and in four consecutive corrections on p. 41. As a first-written form it never occurs at all.

When we recall the change in the amanuensis's script near the bottom of p. 29, the suggestion seems inescapable that at that point Thorkelin intervened, not merely by giving instruction in Insular script, but by checking over and cor-

---

[21] It is *TTB*'s decision not to note 'corrections of "p" to *thorn* or *wynn* in the first 918 lines of A' (p. 46) that effectively barred Kiernan from finding out the truth. By no means all other corrections have been noted by him, particularly not those of *p* to *r*, but also e.g. on the first page *aldon* (or what may have looked like it to the corrector) corrected to *aldor* (14), or similarly on the verso *ante* corrected to *ahte* (9), both done by means of over-heavy dark downstrokes. Nor has the original reading always been correctly identified. In addition, *TTB* eventually develops a highly idiosyncratic view of how some of A's graphs should be interpreted, a view that has the effect of enhancing A's apparent accuracy. Thus the objective *p*'s of *pæron* and *pado* (A19:14, 144ᵛ.1,2) are silently accepted as *w*'s.

[22] The miscorrection of *scoldon*, 151r.05, A27:7, reported by *TTB*, is in fact (as the letter spacing confirms) the opposite, correction of *scoldan* to *scoldon* in a manner wholly uncharacteristic of the amanuensis – which (and the failure to use magnification?) probably explains *TTB*'s error. Malone (p. 17) seems to have similarly mistaken the correction.

recting the last few pages written, so as to see how things stood. In view of the errors overlooked and the miscorrections made, Thorkelin must then have done so without looking at the Vitellius manuscript. At any rate, up to p. 26:09 the number of errors remaining is quite on a par with what we find in what goes before, and so is the number of those overlooked by the corrector. After the instruction at the end of 29 the amanuensis will have continued his copying, and after three more pages Thorkelin made another check, of the *wynn*s only, and let him carry on to the end. He then apparently allowed him to start recollating, but after fifteen pages of it presumably paid him off. One other point seems significant: the correction of *wynn* did not merely consist in drawing a straight-topped bowl over and past the bowl of *p*. In very many cases it included the erasure of the (too high) top of its stem; and this erasure was done with the knife, a good sharp erasing knife, and not with pumice (which would never have produced the small, often ragged marks that the lens discovers). Not infrequently it took part of the new straight top with it, and in no case was it thought necessary to replace this; the corrector, apparently, thought it distinctive, but not essential. In many cases one need only hold the leaf up to the light to see the difference, but scrutiny of the surface tells the same story.

At this point it becomes significant that it is precisely this same process, erasing with the knife and rewriting in dark ink, that can be seen at work in the first ten lines of the text, after which it is abandoned in favour of simple pen-and-ink correction; and that we have here precisely the same type of correction that we found on pp. 26–9, attending primarily to the tailed letters, correcting other errors as they are noticed and miscorrecting every now and then. The dark ink of these corrections is throughout quite unlike what we see in the amanuensis's undoubted later work on the early pages.[23]

To summarize:

(1) we see the hand and ink of the amanuensis showing a clearly identifiable development from large to small and from dark to light;
(2) the hand and ink of the final stage can also be recognized as a secondary agent in certain suppletions in the first fifteen pages, and nowhere else;
(3) the eraser habitually used by the amanuensis is pumice,[24] while the corrections in dark ink involve the use of the knife;
(4) the corrections in dark ink fall into three groups affecting pp. 1–26:09, pp. 26:10–29 and pp. 30–2 respectively;

---

[23] It should be said that a very dark ink was also used at what appears to have been a later stage, when Thorkelin, again haphazardly, retopped a few characters that had suffered in his erasure of the interlined Latin. But it seems more likely that the only changes still made at that late date consisted in the suppletion, from B and in Insular script, of a few of the remaining gaps, rather than that all the corrections in dark ink would have been made so late. See also below, n. 24.

[24] India-rubber was not yet available; as a soft pencil-eraser it was just coming in at this time.

(5) the corrections on pp. 26:10–32:end, but not the earlier ones, employ a straight-topped *wynn*; those on pp. 30–2 involve *wynn* only;

(6) many readings which the manuscript even today clearly shows to be wrong are left uncorrected; some corrections are made that the manuscript still clearly shows to be wrong.

If these observations are to make coherent sense, it seems inevitable to conclude that apart from the few suppletions clearly in the amanuensis's late hand and ink, all the later corrections are not his, and are the work of one man. And though there is no absolute proof, it is hard to imagine any person other than Thorkelin, the transcript's commissioner, being sufficiently interested first to correct and then to check in the manner shown. After having attended to pp. 26–32, while the copying was still proceeding, the corrector later starts at the beginning doing a thorough job quite fairly, then tires of it after eight or nine lines, carries on in a quicker way, and after some twenty pages gradually abandons it altogether. It is tempting to think that he then decided to do B. Identifying the corrector as Thorkelin seems not merely a matter of Occam's razor: his work is quite in character with that of the transcriber of B. An outsider would hardly have operated in this manner, even less have made the errors we see. But however little we may like it, if this is what happened, also as regards the time-scheme,[25] a whole set of puzzles disappears. We are no longer surprised that the amanuensis should have defaced his own work in the manner we see on so many of the early pages: the letters altered without benefit of any sort of eraser give them a very untidy look (the total absence of pumice is striking), and the often heavy correcting strokes suggest an impatience never seen in what is undoubtedly the amanuensis's work. We understand how so many obvious errors can have been overlooked and correct transcriptions spoilt. We understand how, fifteen or twenty years later, Thorkelin could adopt *Wite, la* into his text twice where we, with hindsight, see two transcripts fully supporting *fitela* (the name occurs twice on the same page, four independent records, and the Vitellius *f* is still very clear; as the inks show, the vertical stroke turning it into two words in A is very much later than the miscorrection of *f* to *w* (not *v*, note); Thorkelin was far too prone anyway, in his edition, to follow A against B, but here he must have thought his correction genuine).[26]

---

[25] There can of course be no certainty, but the initial use of erasure suggests a certain continuity from the earlier correction; its quick abandonment, and the premature abandonment of the whole process suggest a young man in a hurry, rather than the older Thorkelin or the amanuensis. If against this there is the fact that none of the early corrected *wynns* have the straight top, neither does that in *fitela* (cf. next note), which can in no case be due to the amanuensis. Correction in the early pages would no longer be for the latter's benefit.

[26] It should be remarked that the miscorrection of *fitela* (A28:13, 152r.6) has been done with the *wynn* used in correcting the early part of the manuscript, not that with the straight top. Its ink also looks darker than that of the other corrections on this page.

RELATIONS BETWEEN A AND B

As has been indicated above, in spite of claims to the contrary, there is not merely no evidence that when Thorkelin copied B, he had in any real sense studied A (and good evidence that he had not), nor any evidence that he used A in tandem with the Vitellius manuscript; there is in fact no possibility at all of establishing a case for either. So far as its original writing (however hard this is sometimes to determine) goes, it is entirely safe to accept B, with all its faults upon its head, as a reflex of the manuscript and of nothing else. What we must very carefully remember, however, is that before being committed to paper this reflex had passed through the mind of G. J. Thorkelin.

That Thorkelin, though having indeed gone (too) rapidly over its first thirty-two pages, had not studied A beforehand is most evident from his treatment of the names, for which evidence has already been quoted above.[27] The historian's practice demanded their capitalization, yet no original capitals occur, even for names with which he might not have been entirely unfamiliar (such as Scylding) until he has let them pass several times uncapitalized. He could have no help from underlinings in A here (whose existence or non-existence at this time there is in any case nothing to show), for these do not start till the fourth fitt, with Ecgþeow in 263 (all the same B, failing to recognize the inserted *yogh* as a character separate from the *c*, has *egþeov*). After *Dena* and *Beowulf* in lines 1 and 16 which, as we saw, are otherwise explained, there are no capitalized names till the first fitt, and even here the trio in 61, like *Hrod-gare* in 64, were copied small and capitalized later.[28] It is not till the top of B's 8v, line 339b, that Hroþgar gets a first-time capital and that we find Thorkelin familiar with certain other names of the type that interested him, viz those from Scandinavian antiquity. (Adam is an understandable exception, but Cain and Grendel follow the rule; Hygelac long remains troublesome; at 159r.7 (B28r, M55a) he capitalizes the verb *healdan*.) He does learn, but only gradually: we see it happen in the course of B as he gains experience from practice. *Beowulf* is not recognized as a name until the unmistakable 'Beovulf is min nama' on 8v, the third occurrence of the name, and the second of the hero.

That he should have used A in tandem with the manuscript (in fact should have used it at all while copying) is even anteriorly improbable. Thorkelin had an evident (and justified) faith in his ability to read Insular script, and can have seen little reason to trust A in this respect. Moreover A, a non-linear and non-paginary copy, is by no means easy to use in conjunction with the

---

[27] See p. 26 and n. 7.
[28] He might indeed have turned back to capitalize these after reaching line 339 (at the earliest), but this would seem quite out of character.

manuscript,[29] and the pre-eminent feature of B, as we saw, is that it was copied at speed. The present investigation has not revealed one single piece of evidence that suggests such a use (and not for want of looking), and the investigation of earlier claims on this point has merely shown these to be illusory, or worse.[30]

It is quite true that, as originally written, the two transcripts show a fair amount of coincidental error (though not significantly greater than that of difference), but none of this is strong enough to support more than the common notion that identical stimuli may produce identical responses. In a great many cases these stimuli are still easily verifiable, the principal ones being, as might be expected, the condition of the manuscript and the context. The only clear early link between the two could be their agreement in placing the fitt number XXXVIIII at line 2821, but if the number was wanting in the manuscript, it would be Thorkelin, not A, who must have been the stimulus in both cases. However, as Zupitza saw, the number in B is a later addition (it is in a different ink, and two of the X's have flags whose formation belongs to Thorkelin's Danish hand), so that this argument lapses. The fact remains, however, that the number is not now in the manuscript, and more particularly that it is not in the position where Vitellius Scribe B would normally have put it (in the space after the preceding line-end, which could easily have accommodated it). But in contrast to any earlier places where a number may have been wanting (we lack XXVIIII and XXX), Thorkelin here followed his invariable custom of leaving a separate line for the number, whether the manuscript did or not (in fourteen cases it did not). Ink and style show that there can be no doubt that A's number is original, and as A showed a similar preference for numbers in a line by themselves (on pp. 17 and 54 he erased an already perfect capital *H*

---

[29] This is probably also the reason why in his correction of A he ignored the manuscript.

[30] The amount of special pleading in *TTB* (pt 3) is remarkable, and the hares it starts are pursued with such vigour that it rarely finds breath to ask itself questions. P. 129 begins with half a page of speculation based on the notion that Thorkelin wrote *holme* in 230/B6 = T7 = M11a:1, when the naked eye can tell (and a lens confirms) that there is no form of *e* there, but only a small downward hook terminating the offstroke of *m*, while of the claimed erasure there is no trace. The conclusions drawn and explanations offered in the other half of the page thus lack any support. The 'many times' Thorkelin 'began or ended a line with the wrong word' [*ibid*.; in fact fifteen for nearly 2900 lines] are easily explained by his working rapidly and not keeping discrete manuscript lines in his head, and the whole discussion is futile, starting from the mistaken notion that as we have it B was bound in England. The odd coincidences quoted to show B's dependence on A are not balanced by an equal consideration of the numerous cases where A is right and B wrong or absent, and too many of those cited do not survive investigation. Thus the cases on 182v listed on p. 131 can merely show that the page was then as bad as now: that A, though using a slower copying process, got them wrong was to be expected; that Thorkelin, trying to keep up some speed, should have done the same, even more so. On the (much poorer) recto he does not even bother to transcribe some still perfectly legible letters that would never have served him to produce any *text*.

What use are the Thorkelin transcripts of Beowulf?

resp. *B* for the purpose, but there the manuscript also has the numbers on separate lines),[31] the most likely hypothesis would be that Scribe B put the number in the left margin, and that Thorkelin found only traces of it. (At the speed at which he worked it is not remarkable that he should not have bothered to turn back in the manuscript or to rummage among his completed bifolia for what in any case he should have no trouble determining afterwards; whether A found the whole number or looked back is a good question.)

Furthermore, it should be noted that, unlike the amanuensis, Thorkelin did not rule his paper, while numerous irregularities prove that he did not employ a ruled underlay either. Thus his top line is particularly liable to changes of direction, and this repeatedly creates an impression of discontinuity which a closer examination shows to be illusory.[32]

There is plenty of evidence that B was altered in Denmark, but since that is where Thorkelin prepared his edition, this is hardly remarkable. Features of his Danish hand – especially the double bends in tailed letters, but also such a feature as two-stroke *c* and the pointed first limb correcting *v* to *w* – are clearly in evidence in a number of corrections and correlate positively with the use of a much lighter ink than is normal for the original transcript. This allows us to date other alterations made in the same ink to the same time, also when, as in some parts of the manuscript, a darker ink, but still contrasting with that of the original copying, was used for the *w*'s.

Changes made by Thorkelin at the time of original writing, so presumably with the manuscript available, but not while the page involved was still being

---

[31] In the present case, though, there is a single word (three letters) at the beginning of the line in which the number stands.

[32] Such a statement as that *spręc*, beginning 164r.1 (33r/M71a:1, line 1398), is a later addition by Thorkelin on the basis of A *(TTB,* p. 128; the dots printed there are not found in pt 2 or in the transcript; the late correction of *v* in *va* to *þ* should of course be discounted), is disproved by the condition of the quill point as well as the ink and the direction, which show that the whole line must have been written as a single effort. As so often (though not invariably, see e.g. 3r/M5a:13, 8r/M15a:3, 9r/M17a:12, 25r/M49a:5, 36r/M71a:15, 37v/M74a:8), the pen was mended before the new page, and the word was written with the newly mended pen. Other cases cited will similarly not support this claim. The 'three occasions' of p. 126 are all later or indeed very much later than the original copying. Similarly, *selest* (25r/M49a:7) is misreported as being on erasure; its miswritten first *e* was retopped by Thorkelin with a broader pen and in a light ink, both features exactly like the correction of *v* to *w* on this page. (The whole word was indeed first written to begin the previous line and not too thoroughly erased there before the correct line was begun over it.) The claim that, when copying B, Thorkelin sometimes wrote line-initial words first, before writing the rest of a page, to facilitate consultation of A, cannot therefore rest on it, nor do we find any series or sequence, however small, of line-initial words written with the quill-point in similar condition and contrasting progressively with the rest of the page, which such a practice would occasion. On the present page the pen was mended after *gumena* in line 5, but all the words beginning the following lines, including the erased *selest*, are written with the mended pen. No other evidence is adduced.

copied, are extremely rare. So far as can be told, they are restricted to the names he might have gone back to capitalize and merely serve, it would seem, to make the transcript conform further to its rules of transcription, here linked with an interest of Thorkelin's own; authority can only rest with the original reading. Changes without the manuscript have certainly been made at various times (though not, so far as we can tell, to B in England), but the time at which those were made is not in itself important, as none of them can have any authority.[33]

For A, as for B, then, it is in most cases possible to isolate and date the separate layers of alteration, at least relatively, so as to distinguish between London and Copenhagen. Ideally, we should therefore attempt such an analysis on either transcript, and certainly this should be done here if we were investigating Thorkelin's edition of *Beowulf*. There is no reason to suppose that we are dealing with more than two people, and though we know nothing of the amanuensis except what can be learned from his transcript, in Thorkelin's case we possess plentiful material for comparison in the form of letters, transcripts, and other documents spanning his career.

---

[33] One of the prominent weaknesses of the record in *TTB*'s pt 2 is its indiscriminate use of the term 'later' for alterations made at once, as shown by e.g. the (letter or word) spacing taking the alteration into account; alterations made clearly in the same ink and with the quill in the same state and therefore presumably still at the time of original writing; and alterations evidently made at some time (mostly long) after the completion of the whole transcript, such as the correction of *v* to *w*, made in the same light ink throughout most of the manuscript. The claim (p. 136) that certain errors prove that Thorkelin, while copying, was consciously emending the text ignores all evidence for correction *currente calamo*, plentiful though it is, by simply classifying it as 'later'. Thus of the five instances cited there of *for* written for *rof*, one (146r.11) was so corrected, a second was never written (145v.20: *f* written and erased, then *rof*), vitiating the argument; of the list of seventeen then presented as examples, only the first two, and perhaps the last, were corrected afterwards. For word-spacing evidence see such a case as 138v.2 (7v/M14a:2) *to*, which has normal placement and word-spacing without the (later) alteration of *v* to *w* (*TTB*, p. 51: 'to (later, when v changed to w in weder)'). At 191v.14 (60v/M120a:14: 'man dryhten') Thorkelin wrote some dots, and continued with *dryhten* (also with a re-topped *e*). He then mended his pen, added *man,* and continued the transcript with *mægenes* (it is of course not demonstrable that *man* was not inserted a very little later, but it has the same ink and the same state of the newly mended quill as *mægenes*, and the mending implies a pause). *TTB*, p. 87 reads 'man (later, with space left before m)'. Similarly 140v.1 (9r/M18a:1) *tiges* was not written 'in a different ink from the rest of the line,' (*TTB*, p. 126) but the pen was mended *after* it had been written, the ink remains the same, and the state of the pen is that of 9v/M17a:20. But one's judgement of the ink can apparently also differ: of eight cases cited *TTB*, p. 139 as later additions, only the interlined *and* of 153v.1 (22v/M44a:1) appears genuine; the others look like their surroundings. The cross-strokes of *ð* (cf. above, p. 29, n. 12) tell a similar tale. Conversely, the term 'later' is frequently wanting where it would clearly have been in place, e.g. 176r.6 (45r/M89a:7) where *TTB*'s 'him (im x um)' (i.e. *um* replaced by *im*) represents *him*, with *im* written above deleted original *um* in the same light ink that corrected *d* to *ð* in the next word. Roughly, *TTB*'s 'later' appears to extend from twenty years or more after the original inscription to the mere fact that writing is a linear process. A tantalizing instance, apparently with future reference, occurs at 201r.17 (70r/M139a:18), where *TTB* quotes B as '§17 wud[u] (MS? cf.A), rec (r later?)'. When last seen (October 1997), B still read *wud... ec* (*w* corrected from *v*). Cf my *TCD*, n. 8.

What use are the Thorkelin transcripts of Beowulf?

But our interest is in *Beowulf* and, damaged though it is, Vitellius A. xv still exists, and the interest of the two transcripts is, in the literal sense of the word, almost wholly marginal. We know their nature, and we know something of their history. We also have a reasonable knowledge of their language, and we know the problems of the Insular hand. These points are not new; they were fully realized by Zupitza, who, in his facsimile, generally quotes the transcripts only where the Vitellius codex is damaged. This is the area where the two are useful; the only other use, where the text of *Beowulf* is concerned, is in the opportunity they provide for determining the limitations within which they are to be trusted as a record of what we can no longer check. We should also remember that these lost parts of the codex may have been in a condition where even the most conscientious transcript cannot always be trusted as an accurate record of what was originally written. Both transcripts repeatedly make the same errors in places where we can check; we can tell, because we have a better knowledge of the language, and particularly of the poetry, than either of their scribes. Their agreement is not therefore to be trusted absolutely, and there is no point in trying to compile statistics of their common errors or their relative reliability as such, because the area where we can check their work against their exemplar is not representative for the area where that exemplar does not run. All we have to go upon, besides our knowledge of the language and so on, are the general features of their work. The amanuensis is reliable as a facsimilist of what he saw, but cannot be relied upon to have made correct graphetic identifications and separations;[34] Thorkelin is a historian, with the historian's attitude towards his text, and if he will make fewer graphetic errors than his amanuensis, he will compensate (and probably over-compensate) for this by deviations due to a certain linguistic (and occasionally historical) expectation, to speed, and to method (such as the capitalization of proper names). On the other hand, where the exemplar was problematic he *may* be more reliable than usual, and than A, because he had to look more closely, and because his knowledge of script and language was better. But, by way of unwelcome compensation, he will almost certainly have tried to reconstruct from their remnants readings that were no longer wholly there. He was indeed better qualified to do this than A, but for all that he will not always have been right. In addition he has some problems due to his origins, of which perhaps the most striking are his difficulty with the Old English use of *h* to render the sound [χ] and his troubles in copying *d* and *ð*.[35]

---

[34] He evidently tries to keep the characters grouped as they are in the manuscript, but for one reason or another often departs from this aim. Similar observations can be made about his linkages.

[35] *TTB*, p. 142 claims: 'A favorite emendation was changing the Old English spelling *burg* to the Scottish spelling *burgh,* another sign that Thorkelin made his transcript after returning from Scotland in 1788', but this is fanciful. If the Old English form had indeed been *burg* it could have been argued, but the instances quoted are all of *burh,* to which (in five out of its twelve

Johan Gerritsen

In evaluating the transcripts, an editor is thus left with a simple question, and a limited task. The question: what places are there in the text where only one or both transcripts are extant (but not the Vitellius codex) and their original readings differ or, when in agreement, are unsatisfactory from a textual point of view? The task: to identify these places and, given our knowledge of the poem and the language and what we think we know about the characteristics of the two transcribers, to determine what their exemplar probably read.[36] To a very large extent, this will merely mean duplicating Zupitza.

But we can be sure, at last, that the Insular suppletions that stick out in A as not being by the amanuensis are by Thorkelin and rest on B. Therefore Kevin Kiernan, whose praise of the amanuensis I would not detract from, credited him with virtues that, rightly, should belong to his *bête noire* Thorkelin. If indeed they are virtues.

This does not mean that no puzzles remain. The four corrected *wynns* on p. 41 still worry me. It is puzzling that they are so far apart in time from the others as this reconstruction implies. And why would they suddenly appear here, unless they were linked with the immediately preceding suppletion of *swy . . . scolde*? But it is hardly imaginable that this should have come directly from the manuscript, though B shows that it must still have been legible, for B shows no problem and its *swy* has the *v* that belongs to the original copying. And the formation of the suppletion in A seems to belong with the other suppletions indicated, and the ink of several of these also with a restoration of the top of a letter erased with the interlinear Latin.

But these are matters of detail; the general conclusion remains clear: as a supplement to the manuscript, the A transcript can be used so far as its original text is concerned, plus the few suppletions made by the amanuensis himself in the first fifteen pages; the B transcript can be used only so far as its original text is concerned. A is then a record of the graphic, B of the linguistic form as it appeared to their respective scribes. In interpreting these records, the very different backgrounds and interests of these scribes – particularly the fact that Thorkelin was a historian and an antiquary, but not a philologist – should not for a moment be lost sight of.

instances) he adds the (to him) more usual *g*. Cf. such cases as *leohg* for *leoht* 166v.1 (35v/M76:1), the weird and wonderful *beohrhte* originally written in the same line (after which the first *h* was expuncted in the same ink), or the end of n. 10 above.

[36] If in any case a difference should appear between the report in the two transcripts and that in 'The State of the *Beowulf* Manuscript 1882–1983', pp. 23–42, this would also have to be taken into account, but no such difference appears. The procedure suggested here allows the passing over of a vast number of cases where the present writer's judgement differs from that of *TTB*. This should not be taken to mean, however, that there are not a fair number of agreements also.

The iconography of the Utrecht Psalter and the Old English *Descent into Hell*

JESSICA BRANTLEY

The Old English *Descent into Hell* fits uneasily into the poetic corpus remaining to us from Anglo-Saxon England. The poem is an oddity both thematically and generically, and (insofar as it has attracted any attention at all) the history of its criticism has been an unrewarding search for sources. The *Descent* presents a sourcing problem at its most basic, for its parts are so disparate that it is difficult even to construct a horizon of expectations from which to read the work.[1] I hope to suggest here a new analogue, as well as a new way of thinking about sources and analogues in Old English literary studies, that may prove fruitful. The more rewarding context for comparative study of the *Descent into Hell* is not textual, but pictorial;[2] I argue that visual exegesis of the psalms reveals both the source and the nature of the connection between the poem's two primary topics. In particular, iconography derived from the enormously influential Utrecht Psalter (Utrecht, Universiteitsbibliotheek, 32) provides a structural model, if not for the composition of the text in the most direct sense, then certainly for both medieval and modern understanding of it.

Before turning to this visual analogue, it will be useful to outline some of the interpretative questions it can help to answer. Critics have long been puzzled by the basic difficulties of determining the poem's sense,[3] but even when linguistic

---

[1] An idiosyncratic exception to this general rule is S. A. J. Bradley, 'Grundtvig's Palm Sunday 1867 and the Anglo-Saxon *Descent into Hell*', *Grundtvig-Studier* (1993), 198–213, which makes unlikely use of the Old English poem to create a context for Grundtvig's even more perplexing prophecies. Bradley suggests that in the reassuring company of the *Descent into Hell* the nineteenth-century theologian's 'prophetic optimism' 'look[s] less like the rambling of a mind unhinged and more like learning and wisdom' (p. 208). The poem has had its defenders, but by far the greater number of readers has agreed with T. A. Shippey's characterization of it as 'a series of confident trespasses on the reader's good nature' (*Poems of Wisdom and Learning in Old English* (Cambridge, 1976), p. 42).

[2] Links between the visual and the narrative arts in the Anglo-Saxon period remain largely unexplored. See, however, J. Leyerle, 'The Interlace Structure of *Beowulf*', *Univ. of Toronto Quarterly* 37 (1967–8), 1–17; A. Renoir, 'Judith and the Limits of Poetry', *ES* 43 (1962), 145–55; P. R. Schroeder, 'Stylistic Analogies between Old English Art and Poetry', *Viator* 5 (1974), 185–98; and R. D. Stevick, *The Earliest Irish and English Bookarts: Visual and Poetic Forms Before A.D. 1000* (Philadelphia, PA, 1994).

[3] Most recent critical discussion of the *Descent* has centered on the troublesome 'git Iohannis' in line 135. On the model of the elliptical dual in the first person, the phrase is construed most

43

Jessica Brantley

cruces have been resolved, substantial mysteries remain. Lasting uncertainty about the poem's subject is documented tellingly by discomfort over its title: once called a version of the *Harrowing of Hell*, it is more commonly known today simply as the *Descent into Hell*.[4] The text implies Christ's forceful entry into the underworld, and gestures towards his liberation of the damned from their torments, but it does not strictly narrate these episodes. Although it is clear that the narrative of the Harrowing underlies the work in a significant way, the events of the poem are in fact more fairly described as mere 'descent', if indeed as that. The poem is composed of two distinctly different parts: it opens with the arrival of sorrowing women at the sepulchre (1–22), then turns abruptly to John the Baptist's welcome of the triumphant Christ into Hell (23–137). This welcome itself comprises several sections: John's memory of Christ's promise 'þæt he me gesoht' (23–32); a short inset narrative of Christ's arrival in Hell (33–55); formal welcome and praise (56–75); apostrophes to Gabriel (76–83), Mary (84–98), Jerusalem (99–102) and the river Jordan (103–6); and a concluding prayer for baptism (107–37). This enigmatic series of fragments does not much resemble what we know of Anglo-Saxon traditions of the Harrowing. These traditions were wide and varied – impossible to summarize succinctly in a study of this length[5] – but among them all the *Descent into Hell* remains so unusual as to have

---

naturally to mean 'you two (the other being John)'. This reading introduces a complex set of problems, however, since the poetic context would seem to indicate that John the Baptist is himself the figure speaking at this point. Scholars have attempted various solutions to this puzzle, ranging from the suggestion of an alternate speaker (see F. Holthausen, 'Zur altenglischen Literatur. V', *Beiblatt zur Anglia* 19 (1908), 49–53); to emendation of the line (see G. Crotty, 'The Exeter *Harrowing of Hell*: A Re-Interpretation', *PMLA* 54 (1939), 349–58); to liberal construction of the syntax (see R. A. Kaske, 'The Conclusion of the Old English Descent into Hell', *Paradosis: Studies in Memory of Edward A. Quain*, ed. H. G. Fletcher and M. B. Schulte (New York, 1976), pp. 47–59). R. M. Trask, '*The Descent into Hell* of the Exeter Book', *NM* 72 (1971), 419–35 raises the possibility that the final speech is 'a kind of dual peroration of the poet as persona as well as John' (p. 422); see also J. E. Anderson, 'Dual Voices and the Identity of Speakers in the Exeter Book *Descent into Hell*', *Neophilologus* 70 (1986), 636–40; and T. D. Hill, 'Cosmic Stasis and the Birth of Christ: The Old English *Descent into Hell*, Lines 99–106', *JEGP* 71 (1972), 382–9.

[4] Earlier English critics of the poem, following Benjamin Thorpe in his 1842 edition of the *Codex Exoniensis*, refer to the poem as a *Harrowing*. The poem has long been known to German scholarship, however, as 'Der Höllenfahrt Christi' (after C. W. M. Grein, *Bibliothek der angelsächsischen Poesie in kritisch bearbeiten Texten und mit vollständigem Glossar*, 4 vols. (Göttingen, 1857–64)), and Dobbie makes an argument on this model for calling it a *Descent* (see G. P. Krapp and E. V. K. Dobbie, *The Exeter Book*, ASPR 3 (New York, 1936), lxi). Most subsequent critics in English have adopted his suggestion.

[5] See J. J. Campbell, 'To Hell and Back: Latin Tradition and the Literary Use of the "descensus ad inferos" in Old English', *Viator* 13 (1982), 107–58; and R. V. Turner, '*Descendit ad inferos*: Medieval Views on Christ's Descent into Hell and the Salvation of the Ancient Just', *Jnl of the Hist. of Ideas* 27 (1966), 173–94.

seemed to some readers incomplete.[6] But the text surprises both by what it omits and by what it includes; any exploration of its sources must help to account for both kinds of peculiarity.

Most conspicuous of the poem's omissions is any mention of the devil, or of Christ's conquest and overthrow of him; this is a remarkably peaceful vision of divine triumph. Although the Harrowing of Hell is an episode in Christian history that invites (or even insists upon) a Satanic presence,[7] and although widespread and vital demonology was a hallmark of the Anglo-Saxon period,[8] the *Descent* presents the dramatic story without resort to the usual machinery of epic battle or even a characterization of the Adversary. In this, the poem has surprisingly little to do with the most familiar exposition of the Harrowing-story: the *Descensus ad inferos*, a section of the apocryphal *Gospel of Nicodemus*.[9] This work was known in the late Anglo-Saxon period – a mid-eleventh-century translation from the Latin demonstrates that – but despite the efforts of early editors nothing in the *Descent* can be definitively traced to it.[10] To begin with, the

---

[6] J. H. Kirkland calls the poem 'a mere fragment' (*A Study of the Anglo-Saxon Poem 'The Harrowing of Hell'* (Halle, 1888), p. 5). Dobbie grants that the *Descent* is 'somewhat unusual in style and structure', but he finally judges it 'a complete poem' (*The Exeter Book*, p. lxi). Indeed, the text opens with a clearly articulated beginning ('Ongunnon him on uhtan…') and concludes equally clearly with a formulaic prayer ('Sie þæs symle meotude þonc!').

[7] Kirkland's assumption that the poem is fragmentary stems directly from the absence of Satan. He imagined in a hopeful vein that the larger tradition of the Harrowing would have been represented in the *Descent*, were it complete: 'That the overthrow of Satan and these other incidents were fully treated in H. [the *Descent into Hell*] we are bound to believe…' ('The Harrowing', p. 13). Although no modern reader would subscribe with such confidence to this speculation, his certainty does reflect the degree to which the devil has been expected in an Anglo-Saxon Harrowing.

[8] That Anglo-Saxon England was especially captivated by demons is a commonplace of its criticism. To cite just one example, Rosemary Woolf ('The Devil in Old English Poetry', *RES* ns 4 (no. 13) (1953), 1–12) explains the many literary manifestations of Anglo-Saxon demonology as a fortuitous correspondence between the Judeo-Christian Satan, leading his routed angels into exile, and an unfaithful retainer, condemned by a pagan heroic code to leave his lord's mead-hall. Satan could be explained in cultural terms already well established, and Anglo-Saxon Christianity often capitalized on this chance to ease the introduction of the new religion. The *Descent into Hell* provides a notable counter-example to Woolf's thesis, however.

[9] The *Gospel of Nicodemus* exists in three versions, two Latin and one Greek, varying primarily in the order in which they present material and the relative weight given to each episode. For editions of the text in languages pertinent to the *Descent into Hell*, see W. H. Hulme, 'The Old English Gospel of Nicodemus', *MP* 1 (1903–4), 579–614; W. H. Hulme, 'The Old English Version of the Gospel of Nicodemus', *PMLA* 13 (1898), 457–542; 'The Gospel of Nicodemus, or the Acts of Pilate', *The Apocryphal New Testament*, ed. M. R. James (Oxford, 1924), pp. 94–146; and *The Gospel of Nicodemus: Gesta Salvatoris*, ed. H. C. Kim (Toronto, 1973).

[10] Campbell's main interest, in fact, is to show that none of the Old English poetic accounts of the Harrowing is demonstrably indebted to the *Gospel of Nicodemus*. Although the *Gospel of Nicodemus* had an enormous influence on poetry of the later Middle Ages, Anglo-Saxon writers seem to have drawn their ideas of the Harrowing from other sources.

plot is markedly different, for the Old English poem does not dramatize contrasting infernal responses to the coming of Christ in the squabbling confrontation of Satan and Hell. More important, the two versions could hardly be more unlike in their tone or their purpose. The *Gospel of Nicodemus* relies on swift and decisive movement: Christ's descent, the prophets' assumption. The Old English *Descent into Hell* is all the more remarkable, then, as a poem built instead around stasis.[11] The poem makes a surprisingly static tableau of what is traditionally a dynamic story.

The poem accomplishes its extraordinarily peaceful effect by insisting on its fiction, by calling explicit attention to the figurative nature of its narrative. The entry of Christ into hell is described as a battle, but a battle unlike any known on earth. What could be the scene of a dramatic military confrontation of the powers of good with the powers of evil is actually quite different:

>   Fysde hine þa to fore   frea moncynnes;
>   wolde heofona helm   helle weallas
>   forbrecan ond forbygan,   þære burge þrym
>   onginnan reafian,   reþust ealra cyninga.
>   Ne rohte he to þære hilde helmberendra,
>   ne he byrnwigend   to þam burggeatum
>   lædan ne wolde,   ac þa locu feollan,
>   clustor of þam ceastrum;   cyning in oþrad,
>   ealles folces fruma   forð onette,
>   weoruda wuldorgiefa.   (33a–42a)[12]

This triumph is explicitly spiritual and not physical. In anticipation of the event, the poet imagines that Christ 'wolde' break down the walls of hell and carry off its population, but the Saviour does not think in these militaristic terms: 'ne rohte he...' Christ himself rejects the standard battle-imagery associated with the Harrowing; when he actually approaches, there is no need for fighting. Christ defeats Hell in a sort of anti-battle; its fortifications dissolve miraculously

---

[11] The poem can be understood as an exploration of the tradition of universal stasis at liminal moments (Nativity, Resurrection, Harrowing) in Christ's life. See, for example, Hill, 'Cosmic Stasis'; C. B. Hieatt, 'Transition in the Exeter Book *Descent into Hell*: the Poetic Use of a "stille" yet "geondflow[ende]" River', *NM* 91 (1990), 431–8; and B. Raw, 'Why Does the River Jordan Stand Still?' *Leeds Stud. in Eng.* 23 (1992), 29–47.

[12] 'Then the Lord of mankind hastened to his journey; the heavens' Protector would demolish and lay low the walls of hell and, most righteous of all kings, carry off the stronghold's populace. For that battle he gave no thought to helmet-wearing warriors, nor was his will to lead armoured fighting men to the stronghold gates. But the locks and the bars fell from those fortifications and the King entered in; onward he advanced, Lord of all the people, the multitudes' Bestower of glory.' Quotation of the *Descent into Hell* is taken throughout from B. J. Muir, *The Exeter Anthology of Old English Poetry: an Edition of Dean and Chapter MS 3501*, 2 vols. (Exeter, 1994). Translation is taken, except where otherwise indicated, from *Anglo-Saxon Poetry*, trans. S. A. J. Bradley (London, 1982).

The Utrecht Psalter and the Old English Descent into Hell

at his approach, even though he is alone. The poem invokes martial language only to resist it immediately (and on the greatest authority), denying its relevance to this salvific context. The triumph of salvation itself, rather than the warlike means by which it is procured, is this poet's interest.[13]

In a further denial of the combative potential of the Harrowing-story, the *Descent*-poet even removes Satan from the crowd present when Christ enters. The assembly that greets him upon his triumphal entry is surprisingly homogeneous.

>   Wræccan þrungon,
> hwylc hyra þæt sygebearn   geseon moste,
> Adam ond Abraham,   Isac ond Iacob,
> monig modig eorl,   Moyses ond Dauid,
> Esaias   ond Sacharias,
> heahfædra fela,   swylce eac hæleþa gemot,
> witgena weorod,   wifmonna þreat,
> fela fæmmena,   folces unrim. (42b-49b)[14]

Christ needs no 'helmberendras' upon his entry into hell because he encounters no opposition. There are no devils among the 'helwaran' who welcome him in this context. The explicit addition of countless unidentified women and virgins to the named patriarchs, a detail to my knowledge unique in Anglo-Saxon accounts of the Harrowing, emphasizes the pacific nature of the occasion. The king enters as a beloved monarch in a royal progress through his realm, rather than as a conqueror. The Adversary is nowhere to be found.

Not only is Satan as a speaking character omitted from the Old English *Descent*; he is pointedly said not to be in residence in hell at the time that Christ is there. One of the few — cryptic — references to him seems to make a point of his absence. The unnamed 'burgwarena ord' of line 56 gives this tribute:[15]

---

[13] Many critics have noted that the elision of a battle is unusual in this context. C. L. Wrenn is most forthright (even disappointed?): 'The Exeter book poem ends only with the welcoming of Christ by Adam, and has no fighting' (*A Study of Old English Literature* (New York, 1967), p. 156). Although Stanley Greenfield asserts that 'the most interesting aspect of this poem is its heroic-Christian mode of presentation of Christ's conquest of hell', this peculiar reading was silently dropped in Greenfield and Calder: see S. B. Greenfield, *A Critical History of Old English Literature* (New York, 1965), p. 141; and cf. S. B. Greenfield and D. G. Calder, *A New Critical History of Old English Literature* (New York, 1986).

[14] 'The exiles came crowding, trying which of them might see the victorious Son — Adam and Abraham, Isaac and Jacob, many a dauntless man, Moses and David, Isaiah and Zacharias, many patriarchs, likewise too a concourse of men, a host of prophets, a throng of women and many virgins, a numberless tally of people.'

[15] Holthausen ('Zur altenglischen Literatur. V', p. 51) was the first to identify the 'burgwarena ord' as Adam, rather than John. A case can be made for either, but the choice of Adam solves the semantic problem of 'git Iohannis' (line 135). Choosing Adam invariably presents its own

Jessica Brantley

> þe þæs þonc sie, þeoden user,
> þæt þu us[ic sar]ige secan woldest,
> nu we on þissum bendum bidan [sceoldon]
> þonne monige bindeð broþorleasne
> wræccan [.........] – he bið wide fah –
> ne bið he no þæs nearwe under nið loc [can
> oððe] þæs bitre gebunden under bealuclommum,
> þæt he þy yþ ne mæge ellen habban,
> þonne he his hlafordes hyldo gelyfeð,
> þæt hine of þam bendum bicgan wille. (59a–68b)[16]

This passage is, unfortunately, damaged so severely that the explicit mention of the devil can only be inferred. But the chance absence of his name seems fitting, in a playful sense, with the meaning of the passage, insofar as it can be reconstructed: the devil is 'an enemy abroad', in Bradley's phrase.[17] The poet does not imagine the devil as a threat within the walls of hell, but as a constant threat elsewhere. Here the heroic ideal does inform the demonology of the poem: drawing on contiguous meanings of the word 'fah' – both 'guilty, criminal, inimical, hostile', and also 'proscribed, outlawed' – the *Descent*-poet paints the devil as a traitorous retainer outlawed even from the fellowship of hell. The very appropriateness of the devil to heroic ways of thought 'outlaws' him from representation in this poem. The guilty retainer is banished from his lord's presence, so the devil is not in hell for Christ's triumphant visit.

> complications, however, for this speaker claims to have bathed in the Jordan with Christ. He prays:
>
>> ond for Iordane in Iudeum –
>> wit unc in þære burnan baþodan ætgædre. (131–2)
>
> This problem can be solved by an appeal to the apocryphal *Vitae Adae et Evae*, which establishes a tradition in which the first couple bathed in the river for forty days. An alternative hypothesis is given by J. N. Garde, who identifies the 'burgwarena ord' as David and proposes that John and David speak antiphonally throughout the final passage (*Old English Poetry in Medieval Christian Perspective: a Doctrinal Approach* (Cambridge, 1991), pp. 113–30). Many critics (Dobbie and Bradley, among others) accept Holthausen's identification, but John still seems to me the most likely speaker.

[16] 'Thanks be to you, our Prince, because you were willing to seek out us sinful men since we have had to languish in these bonds. Although the traitorous devil – he is an enemy abroad – ensnares many a brotherless exile, that man is not bound so closely beneath oppressive locks nor so cruelly beneath painful fetters that he may not quite easily acquire courage, when he trusts in his Lord's good faith, that he will ransom him from those bonds.'

[17] Different translations of course treat the lacuna differently, but each must acknowledge a hostile presence, an enemy of man, in the missing word. Although the suggestion of an evil presence is less explicit in Shippey's more secular translation, for example, it is still present: 'When *they* tie up the brotherless outcast, the man with no resources (?) – he is proscribed everywhere – he can never be so tightly shut up under hostile bars, or fastened so cruelly in evil chains, that he cannot take heart the easier if he believes in his lord's good grace, and that he will ransom him out of his bondage' (*Poems*, p. 115; emphasis mine).

The Utrecht Psalter and the Old English Descent into Hell

Even the most direct reference to the devil in the *Descent into Hell* is still decidedly oblique and unmilitaristic. Again a battle is obviated, this time by the actions of sinful humanity. The speaker laments:

>   We þurh gifre mod
> beswican us sylfe;   we þa synne forþon
> berað in urum breostum to bonan honda,
> sculon eac to ussum feondum   freoþo wilnian.   (95b–98b)[18]

Insofar as any battle is implied by these lines, it is a battle between the devil and humankind, not a conflict in which Christ plays any role. The devil is invoked here to emphasize human culpability over the miracle of the redemption; rather than Christ triumphant over a bested Satan, the poet gives us a vision of humans defeating themselves. The poem's vocabulary speaks of betrayal ('beswican') and pleading ('freoþo wilnian'), rather than of martial encounters. This heroic struggle is the ongoing metaphorical one between humans and their own sin, not a part of a traditional account of the Harrowing of Hell.

The *Gospel of Nicodemus* was of course not the only source of the Harrowing of Hell available in Anglo-Saxon England, and it is possible to discover more likely analogues to the poem's pacific tone. Although the episode is not strictly biblical, several intimations of it can be found in the canonical New Testament. The *Descent into Hell* little resembles the most spectacular and combative New Testament account, the Apocalyptic binding and imprisonment of the dragon (Rev. XIX–XX), but has perhaps more to do with I Peter III.18–19, which describes Christ engaged in preaching to the souls in hell:

quia et Christus semel pro peccatis mortuus est, iustus pro iniustis, ut nos offerret Deo, mortificatus carne vivificatus autem spiritu; in quo et his qui in carcere erant spiritibus veniens praedicavit.[19]

This is not an account of a military encounter, but of the salvation of the souls in hell,[20] which accords with the joyful tone of the Old English poem. But although Christ's activity in I Peter is more salvific than martial, there is no

---

[18] 'By our greedy mind we have betrayed ourselves; therefore we deliver those sins in our hearts into the destroyer's hands and likewise to our foes we are forced to supplicate for peace.'

[19] 'Because Christ also died once for our sins, the just for the unjust: that he might offer us to God, being put to death indeed in the flesh, but enlivened in the spirit. In which also coming he preached to those spirits that were in prison.' (All translations of the Vulgate Bible are taken from the Douai–Rheims version.)

[20] Early elaborations of the doctrine of the Harrowing seem to have had their origin in this salvific idea. The release of the patriarchs, derived from biblical suggestions such as I Peter, seem to have formed the basis of the account, which only afterwards acquired the trappings of an epic battle. See J. A. MacCulloch, *The Harrowing of Hell: a Comparative Study of an Early Christian Doctrine* (Edinburgh, 1930), p. 227. The early history of the doctrine of the Harrowing does not explain completely the oddity of the *Descent*, however, since in Anglo-Saxon literary usage the Harrowing is nearly always a militaristic episode.

mention in the *Descent* of Christ's preaching to the souls in prison. Instead, the poem (like the *Gospel of Nicodemus*) focuses on the joy of John the Baptist and the other inhabitants of hell – a reception perhaps implied by, but in fact absent from, the apostolic account.

The most convincing source for an Anglo-Saxon Harrowing without a devilish presence, comparable to the *Descent into Hell*, is the liturgy.[21] The polyphonic utterances in the *Descent*'s final verses, for example, could be explained as a reflection of the poem's liturgical sensibility. The attribution of the poem's words to a speaker (the poet) outside the fictional narrative opens the possibility that the sentiment extends mimetically to the work's readers, as well. This slippage of voice can be likened to a liturgical model familiar from settings such as the *Magnificat* and *Nunc Dimittis*, in which the celebrant's narration is primary and Mary's or Simeon's words are heard as reported speech. More particularly, the *Descent into Hell* has obvious thematic affinities with the Eastertide liturgy, especially the Light and Baptismal services for Holy Saturday. The *Vespere autem* antiphon used before and after the *Magnificat* at the end of the Holy Saturday mass gives an account of the visit of the three women to the tomb, and the *Vidi aquam* antiphon used before the Easter mass shows certain correspondences with the poem's four apostrophes.[22] More generally, baptismal imagery pervades the poem and brings the theme of spiritual rebirth into a liturgical realm. Christ's resurrection and his salvation of hell's inhabitants are both 'births', and baptismal echoes link these to the spiritual rebirth of any Christian. The women's sudden shift from grief to joy, emphasized in the poem, mirrors the larger revelation implicit in the salvation of the patriarchs:

>   Huru þæs oþer þing
>   Wiston þa wifmenn,   þa hy on weg cyrdon.   (14b–15)[23]

The poet's knowing aside can be taken as a touchstone for the poem's general mood of comic reversal, a mood that might be called broadly baptismal. Such a mood obviates the need for the devil, for it generates a version of the Harrowing

---

[21] For the most detailed discussion of the liturgy as the 'highest model for artistic imitation' in the *Descent*, see P. W. Conner, 'The Liturgy and the Old English "Descent into Hell"' *JEGP* 79 (1980), 179–91, at 191. Conner claims that the *Descent into Hell* is 'a conflation of materials from the Mass and Divine Office of Holy Saturday' (p. 180).

[22] Conner reports that the *Vidi aquam* replaces the *Asperges me* in the Easter Sunday procession as recorded in the early-tenth-century Hartker Antiphonary (St Gallen, Stiftsbibliothek, 390 + 391), which has been linked to the Exeter Book through the antiphons unquestionably echoed in *Christ I* (*ibid.* pp. 189–90). See *Antiphonaire de Hartker: manuscrits Saint-Gall 390–391*, ed. J. Froger, Paléographie musicale, 2nd ser. [Monumentale] I (Bern, 1970).

[23] 'Something different indeed from this those women would know when they turned on their way.'

The Utrecht Psalter and the Old English Descent into Hell

more concerned with salvation than with epic struggles.[24] There is neither devil nor divine preaching in the liturgical account of the Harrowing of Hell, and in this it is tempting to identify it as a source for the Anglo-Saxon poem.

In its salvific content and polyphonic form, the liturgy is the most persuasive of sources which critics have thus far identified for the *Descent*; yet the liturgical connection, too, remains insufficient to explain the peculiarity of this poet's choice. The liturgy explains the mode (and mood) of the poem at the end, but does not account very well for the particular juxtaposition that distinguishes its beginning: the combination of the Visit to the Sepulchre and the Harrowing of Hell. Conner cannot prove definitively that the women's visit derives from liturgical rather than biblical sources,[25] and even if the visit is liturgical it is not clear how the liturgy suggests that it alone should be joined with the Harrowing. Why are only these two episodes, of the Passion's many evocative moments, included in this poet's meditation on the events of Easter morning? No textual source thus far proposed provides a compelling answer to this question. Although the *Descent into Hell* is undeniably indebted to liturgical modes and themes, to take full account of the poem's aesthetic project another source must be sought.

The absence of the devil may be the most conspicuous of all the oddities presented by the *Descent into Hell*, but the inclusion of the Holy Women at the Sepulchre as a prelude to the story of Christ's descent is perhaps more fundamental. There are Anglo-Saxon examples of a Harrowing without Satan, but no source has been convincingly established for a Harrowing paired exclusively with a Visit to the Sepulchre. The account of the women's visitation is based on the canonical gospels.[26] But nothing in these gospels (or elsewhere in Christian tradition) suggests the direct association of that story with the Harrowing of Hell. The significant void that the *Descent*-poet creates in omitting the fiery confrontation between Christ and Satan, he fills with the account of the women's visitation; sorrowing women replace the bellicose devil in this poetic version of the story. One might seek, then, to understand the devil's strange absence by explaining the stranger presence of the three Marys.

Although the pairing of these episodes is unusual, the poem asserts an association without any explanatory connective material. The scene shifts brusquely from the meeting of the women and the angel(s) at the sepulchre to John's speech in hell:

---

[24] See H. A. Kelly, *The Devil at Baptism: Ritual, Theology, and Drama* (Ithaca, NY, 1985), who notes: 'The liturgy of Good Friday, which commemorates the crucifixion and death of Christ, should, we might expect, lay great stress on the Savior's struggle with his chief adversary, the devil. Instead, however, as in the Gospels, the events are portrayed largely on the level of human guilt and antagonism' (p. 213).

[25] He admits as much in his discussion ('Liturgy', p. 181).

[26] It is not clear which particular gospel forms the basis of this account, but Matthew (XXVIII.1–8) comes the closest.

Jessica Brantley

>   Ac þær cwom on uhtan   an engla þreat,
>   behæfde heapa wyn   hælendes burg.
>   Open wæs þæt eorðærn,   æþelinges lic
>   onfeng feores gæst,   folde beofode,
>   hlogan helwaran.   Hagosteald onwoc
>   modig from moldan,   mægenþrym aras
>   sigefæst ond snottor.   Sægde Iohannis,
>   hæleð helwarum,   hlyhhende spræc
>   modig to þære mengo   ymb his mæges [sið].   (17a–25b)[27]

Linked only by their time of arrival ('on uhtan'), the angels of the Resurrection and the grieving Marys give way to the quaking earth and laughing patriarchs of the Harrowing. The poet engages in a bit of interlace to link the scenes;[28] lines 19–22 describe alternately both events in hell and events at the tomb. But no more informative connection is made.

If the devil's absence from hell is striking in the *Descent*, Christ's bodily presence there is suggested in a way at least as unusual. The poem's movement from the visit at the sepulchre to the scene in hell at Christ's descent, although unexplained, implies a very unorthodox temporal sequence. The surprising sequence of narration in the *Descent into Hell*, what Z. Izydorczyk calls an 'inversion of paschal events',[29] has peculiar implications: if the Resurrection preceded the Harrowing, as the chronology of the poem seems to argue, it would appear that Christ descended into hell bodily, rather than spiritually. Whereas Ælfric, for example, is especially careful to explain that the opposite is true,[30] the *Descent*-poet flouts theological nicety and suggests that Christ's resurrected body was in hell. Izydorczyk accounts for this startling chronology doctrinally. To make his own theological point, the poet may have sacrificed traditional ordering: 'If the

---

[27] 'For in the dawning there came a throng of angels; the rapture of those hosts surrounded the Saviour's tomb. The earthy vault was open; the Prince's corpse received the breath of life; the ground shook and hell's inhabitants rejoiced. The young man awoke dauntless from the earth; the mighty Majesty arose, victorious and wise. The man John explained to hell's inhabitants; dauntless, he spoke rejoicing to the multitude about his kinsman's coming...'

[28] 'Interlace', of course, is in its origins a term describing patterns common in the Anglo-Saxon visual arts, used by analogy to describe a feature of poetic practice in the period. The primary study of the sister arts in the Anglo-Saxon period capitalizes on this parallel: see Leyerle, 'Interlace Structure'.

[29] See Z. Izydorczyk, 'The Inversion of Paschal Events in the Old English *Descent into Hell*', *NM* 91 (1990), 439–47.

[30] The famous Palm Sunday sermon makes this distinction: 'And *his lic* læg on byrgene þa sæterniht and sunnan-niht; and *seo godcyndnys* wæs on ðære hwile on helle...' ('And *his corpse* lay in the sepulchre the Saturday night and Sunday night; and *the Divinity* was during that while in hell...' (Text and translation are taken from *The Homilies of the Anglo-Saxon Church. The First Part, Containing the Sermones Catholici, or Homilies of Ælfric*, ed. B. Thorpe, 2 vols. (London, 1844–6) I, 216–17; my emphasis). In this position Ælfric is following such theologians as Augustine (PL 33, 834) and Jerome (CCSL 78, 381), who assert that Christ's presence in hell is only spiritual.

resurrection was a cause of salvation, it had to be given priority and mentioned first, even if such an order violated the usual chronology of paschal events.'[31]

Although this sequence is unusual in medieval treatments of the Harrowing, it is not entirely unheard of. Izydorczyck cites a homily from Cambridge, Corpus Christi College 41 as a rare correspondence: 'ure Drihten, Hælend Crist ... of deaðe aras to midre nihte, and he astahg niþer to helwarum to þan, þæt he wolde þa helle bereafian, and swa gedyde, and þæt ealdor deoful oferswiðan'.[32] *Blickling Homily VII*, also, a *locus classicus* for Anglo-Saxon ideas of the Harrowing, rather sloppily suggests the strange chronology, even as it later explicitly endorses the more usual one. The homily opens, in part, with the following offhand assertion: '... Drihten of deaþe aras mancynne to bysene æfter his þrowunga, and æfter þæm bendum his deaþes, and æfter þæm clammum helle þeostra; and þæt wite and þæt ece wræc asette on þone aldor deofla, and mancyn freolsode ...'.[33] These homilies demonstrate that passion-chronology was not absolutely fixed at this period, but they bear little relation, finally, to our poem. The homilist of CCCC 41 imagines a resurrected Christ in hell, and the Blickling homilist allows for such a possibility, but both writers also – importantly – conceive of this bodily presence in the context of a Satanic battle.

These homilies offer an analogue for the *Descent*'s unusual sequence, but because they differ in their most significant respect – the devilish presence – from the Anglo-Saxon poem, they cannot explain adequately its peculiarities. I argue that the poem's ostensible sequence should not be read as a 'sequence' at all, and that although it appears to set forth a chronology in the succession of its episodes, the poem does not, in fact, make an argument about the 'sequence of paschal events'. In noting the work's indebtedness both to liturgy and to the lyric mode, some commentators have intimated that sequence is not the issue.[34] But I

---

[31] Izydorczyck, 'Inversion', p. 444. He thinks the *Descent* in this respect an early example of subsequent theological developments in representations of the Harrowing (p. 441).

[32] *Ibid.* p. 440. 'Our Lord, Holy Christ ... rose from death in the middle of the night, and he journeyed below to the hell-dwellers because he wished to seize them from hell, and did so, and overcame the old devil' (my trans.). This homily is printed in its entirety at the end of Hulme's edition of 1904 of the Old English *Gospel of Nicodemus*. Campbell says of this 'poorly written' homily that 'the chronology is skewed in odd ways at several points' ('To Hell and Back', pp. 141–2), and even imagines that the homilist was composing based on his memory of Harrowing-accounts rather than on any written copy-text.

[33] '... for our example the Lord arose from the dead after his passion, after the bonds of his death, and after the bonds of hell's darkness; and he laid upon the prince of devils eternal torment and vengeance, and delivered mankind ...' (text and translation are taken from *The Blickling Homilies*, ed. R. Morris, EETS 58, 63, 73 (repr. as 1 vol., London, 1967), pp. 82–3).

[34] See above for a discussion of the poem's liturgical qualities. Dobbie minimizes the importance of narrative in the course of his argument that the *Descent* is primarily lyrical: 'The poet's interest is not in an orderly and sequential narrative, but in a lyrical development of those aspects of his theme which lend themselves most readily to the lyric form' (*The Exeter Book*, p. lxii). Indeed the liturgy is often more interested in thematic associations than in strict chronology, but the

would like to suggest a new potential source both liturgical and lyric, and even more radically atemporal: visual exegesis of Ps. XV.10 in the iconographical tradition of the Utrecht Psalter. The most apt analogue for the static prospect of the Harrowing presented by the Old English *Descent* is revealed, finally, not by textual associations but by visual ones, for the naturally less temporal structures of visual representation suggest ways of meaning that facilitate interpretation of a hitherto opaque 'narrative'. The psalm-illustration is useful as an analogue to the *Descent into Hell,* for it juxtaposes a pacific Harrowing with the Visit to the Sepulchre, while denying the importance of narrative sequence. When read in the light of Utrecht iconography, the many perplexing features of the *Descent* clarify and reinforce each other, for its aim is to present a pacific tableau, rather than a dynamic, confrontational – and properly sequenced – narrative.

Ps. XV was one of many biblical sites in which medieval commentators discovered material to elucidate the doctrine of the Harrowing of Hell.[35] Verses 9–11, in particular, seem to intimate a divine descent:

Propter hoc laetatum est cor meum, et exultavit lingua mea: insuper et caro mea requiescet in spe.
Quoniam non derelinques animam meam in inferno: nec dabis sanctum tuum videre corruptionem.
Notas mihi fecisti vias vitae, adimplebis me laetitia cum vultu tuo: delectationes in dextera tua usque in finem.[36]

David's hope for his own salvation, both in soul and body, was imagined in explications of these verses as a prophetic figure of Christian resurrection. Verse 10 was seen not only to prefigure the Harrowing ('Quoniam non derelinques animam meam in inferno'), but also to refer specifically to the Resurrection of Christ ('nec dabis sanctum tuum videre corruptionem'). The words *sanctum tuum* can refer to David in particular, or simply to any faithful soul, but in the

> Eastertide liturgy is among the most 'plot-driven' sequences. Critics have also tended to read the opening of the poem narratively, even if they read the end lyrically. Campbell agrees that the poem focuses on the 'meaning of the events, rather than their order', but contends that 'a bit of narrative introduces this mainly thematic poem' ('To Hell and Back', p. 150). Crotty also thinks 'the interest of the poem, as it proceeds, shifts more and more from narrative to lyric and liturgy' ('Exeter *Harrowing of Hell*', p. 356). Understanding even the account of the women's visit in a non-narrative context, as I seek to do here, integrates the composition as a whole along lyrical lines.

[35] See Campbell for a detailed discussion of biblical and patristic support for the doctrine of the Harrowing. He discusses Ps. XV only in passing, however ('To Hell and Back', p. 120). Trask also mentions Ps. XV tangentially in connection to the *Descent into Hell* ('Descent into Hell', p. 423, n. 4).

[36] 'Therefore my heart hath been glad, and my tongue hath rejoiced: moreover my flesh also shall rest in hope. Because thou wilt not leave my soul in hell; nor wilt thou give thy holy one to see corruption. Thou hast made known to me the ways of life, thou shalt fill me with joy with thy countenance: at thy right hand are delights even to the end.'

XIIII
DNEQUISHABITA
BITINTABERNA
CULOTUO·AUTQUIS
REQUIESCITINMONTE
SCOTUO
QUIINCREDITURSINE
MACULA·ETOPERATUR
IUSTITIAM
QUILOQUITURUERITA
TEMINCORDESUO
QUINONECITDOLU
INLINGUASUA

PSALMUS
NECFECITPROXIMOSUO
MALUM·ETOBPROBRIU
NONACCEPITADUER
SUSPROXIMOSSUOS
ADNIHILUMDEDUCTUS
ESTINCONSPECTUEIUS
MALIGNUS·TIMENTES
AUTEMDNMGLORIFICAT
QUIIURATPROXIMO
SUOETNONDECIPIT
QUIPECUNIAMSUA
NONDEDITADUSURA

ETMUNERASUPER
INNOCENTES
NONACCEPIT
QUIFACITHAEC·NON
MOUEBITURINAETER
NUM

I Utrecht, Universiteitsbibliotheek, 32, 8r

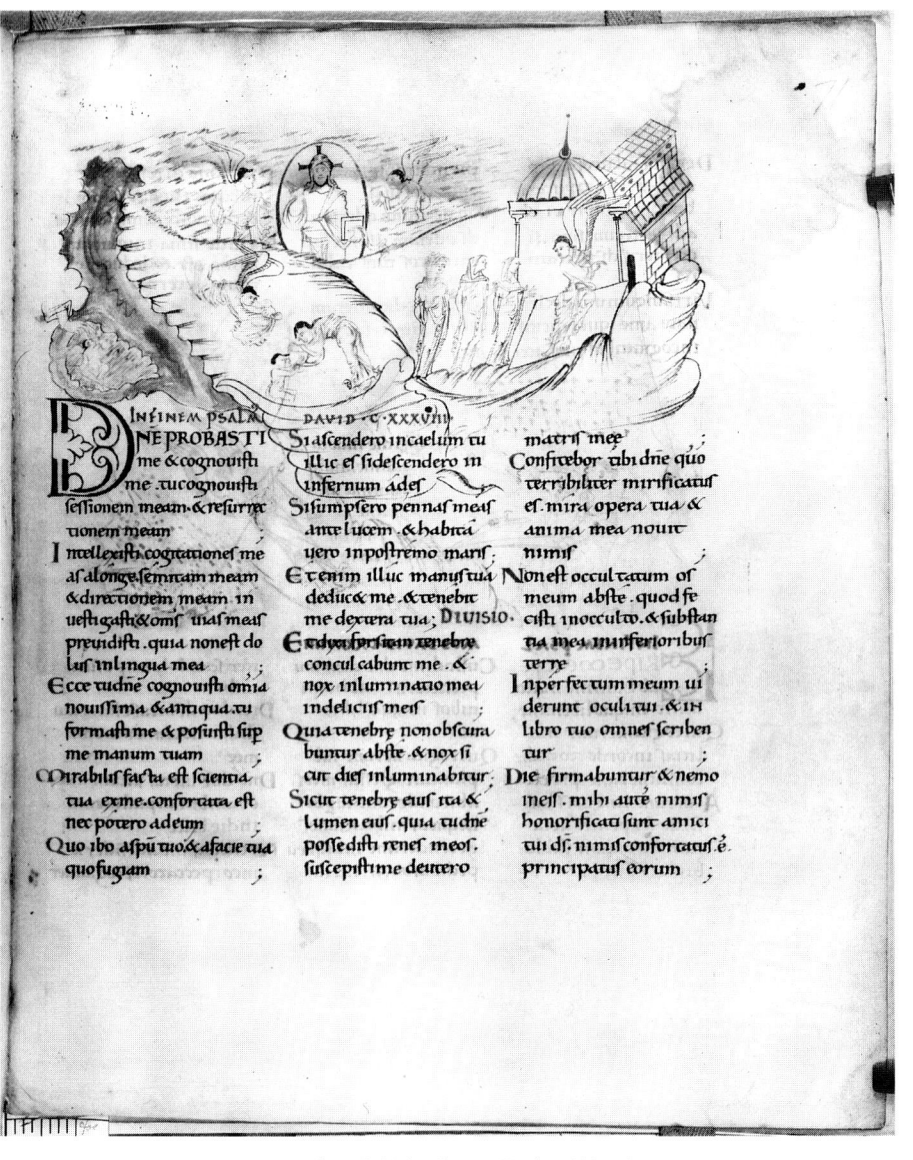

INCIPIT PSALM
DAVID C XXXVIII

DNE PROBASTI
me & cognouisti
me. tu cognouisti
sessionem meam. & resurre
ctionem meam
Intellexisti cogitationes me
as a longe. semitam meam
& directionem meam in
uestigasti. & omnes uias meas
preuidisti. quia non est do
lus in lingua mea
Ecce tu dne cognouisti omnia
nouissima & antiqua. tu
formasti me & posuisti sup
me manum tuam
Mirabilis facta est scientia
tua ex me. confortata est
nec potero ad eum
Quo ibo a spu tuo. & a facie tua
quo fugiam

Si ascendero in caelum tu
illic es. si descendero in
infernum ades
Si sumpsero pennas meas
ante lucem. & habitau
ero in postremo maris
Etenim illuc manus tua
deducet me. & tenebit
me dextera tua; DIUISIO·
Et dixi forsitan tenebre
conculcabunt me. &
nox inluminatio mea
in deliciis meis
Quia tenebre non obscura
buntur abs te. & nox si
cut dies inluminabitur
Sicut tenebre eius ita &
lumen eius. quia tu dne
possedisti renes meos.
suscepisti me de utero

matris meae
Confitebor tibi dne quo
terribiliter mirificatus
es. mira opera tua &
anima mea nouit
nimis
Non est occultatum os
meum abste. quod fe
cisti in occulto. & substan
tia mea in inferioribus
terre
Inperfectum meum ui
derunt oculi tui. & in
libro tuo omnes scriben
tur
Die firmabuntur & nemo
meis. mihi autem nimis
honorificati sunt amici
tui ds. nimis confortatus e
principatus eorum

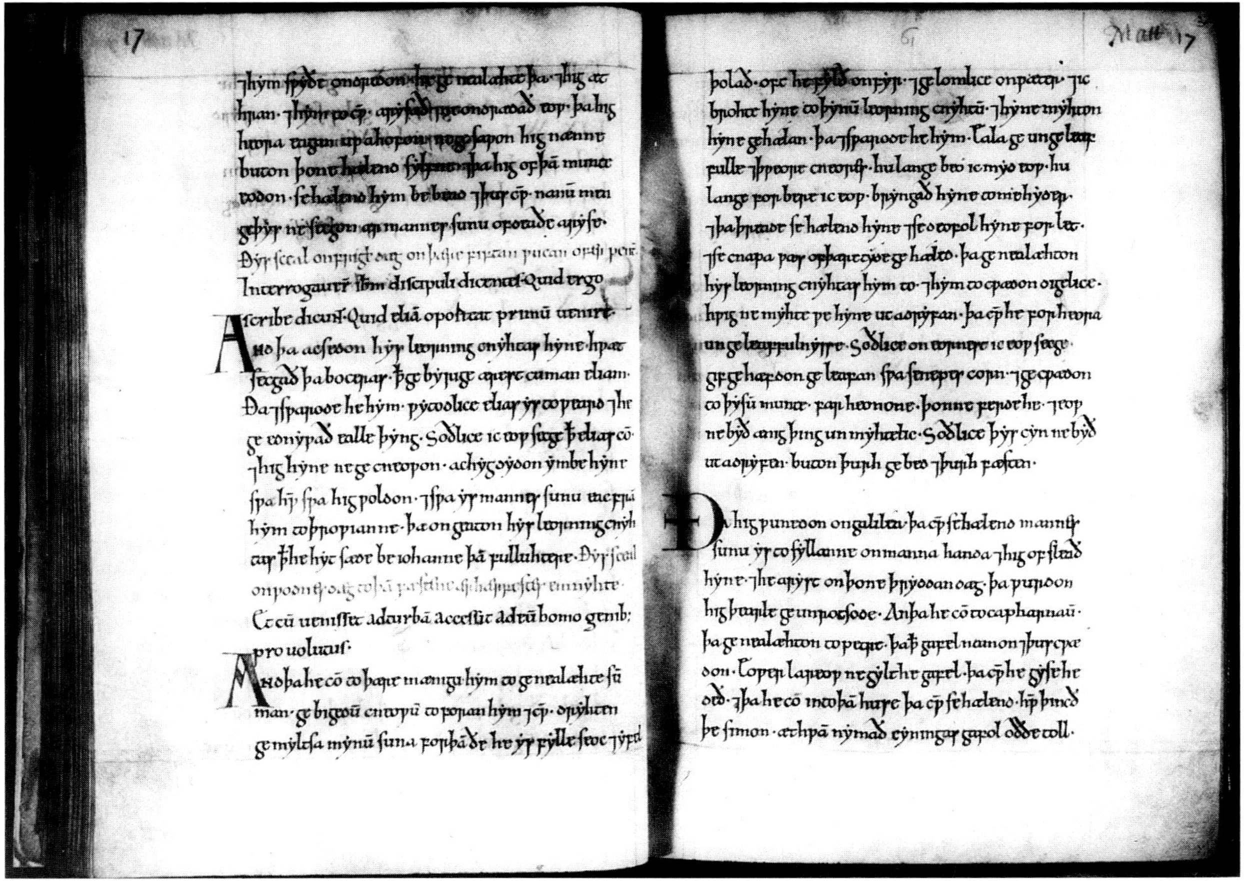

III Cambridge, University Library, Ii. 2. 11, 31v–32r

tem aliud. Eug̃ Sedm marcum. Cap̃ xxvi. Exeuntes autem statim pharisaei cum
herodianis. Usq̃: curandi infirmitates & eiciendi daemonia.

Jnnat' Sc̃i Sebastiani. Eug̃ Sedm lucam. Cap̃ xlv. Inttł. Descendens ihc de monte
Usq̃: merces ũr multa est incaelo.

te quosup̃n. Jnat' Sc̃i fabiani. Eug̃ Sedm marh Cap̃ cclxiii. Inttł. Dix ihc discipuł
suis. Vigilate ergo. Usq̃: construx eum.

osic~v. p̃ theophania. Eug̃ Sedm matheum. Cap̃ lxviiii. Ascendente ihu innauicula.
Usq̃: quia uenti & mare oboediunt ei.

Jnat' Sc̃ae Agnae. Eug̃ Sedm matheum. Cap̃ cclxvii. Inttł. Dix ihc discipulis suis
Simile ẽ. regnum caeloẓ dece̊ uirginib: Usq̃: quia nescitis diem neq̃: horam.

er·iiii. Eug̃ Sedm marh. Cap̃ lxviii. Inttł. Loquente ihu adturbas ecce princeps uñs
Usq̃: inuniuersam terram illam.

tem aliud. Eug̃ Sedm lucam. Cap̃ c·v. Factum est autem ambulantibus illis
inuia. dix quidam aditm. Usq̃: aptus est regno di.

er·vi. Eug̃ Sedm marcum. Cap̃ xli. Inttł. Dixit ihc discipulis suis & turbis. Videte
quid audiatis. Usq̃: discipulis suis disserebat omnia.

tem aliud Eug̃ Sedm marcum. Cap̃ c·vi. Inttł. Offerebant ihu paruulos. Usque
benedicebat eos.

S abb. Eug̃ Sedm lucam. Cap̃ clxxviii. Inttł. Dicebat ihc parabolam hanc. intendens
quomodo primos accubitos eligerent. Usq̃: beat quimanducabit panem inregno di.

tem aliud Eug̃ Sedm Iohem. Cap̃ iii. Inttł. Dix ihc turbis Operamini noncybum
qui periit. Usq̃: nonsitis inaeternum.   meum

osican. p̃ theoph̃. Eug̃ Sedm marh. Cap̃ cxxxvi. Inttł. Dix ihc discipulis suis parabola
hanc Simile ẽ. regnũ caeloẓ homini quiseminauit bonũ semen inagro. Usq̃: inhorreũ.

tem aliud Eug̃ Sedm marcum. Cap̃ xlviiii. Inttł. Cum etranscendisset ihc innauim
omisfretauit. Usq̃: & estu sanus aplaga sua.

tem Eug̃ Sedm matheum. Cap̃ cx. Inttł. Respondens ihc dix. Confiteor tibi dñe pat
caeli & terrae. Usq̃: & onus meum leue est.

Jnat' Sc̃ae Agnae denatiuitate. Eug̃ Sedm marh. Cap̃ cxl. Inttł. Dix ihc discipu
lis suis parabolam hanc Simile ẽ. regnũ caeloẓ thesauro abscondito. Usq̃: noua & uetera.

er·vi. Eug̃ Sedm marcũ. Cap̃ lxviii. Inttł. Uenit ihc transfretum inregione gerasenoẓ

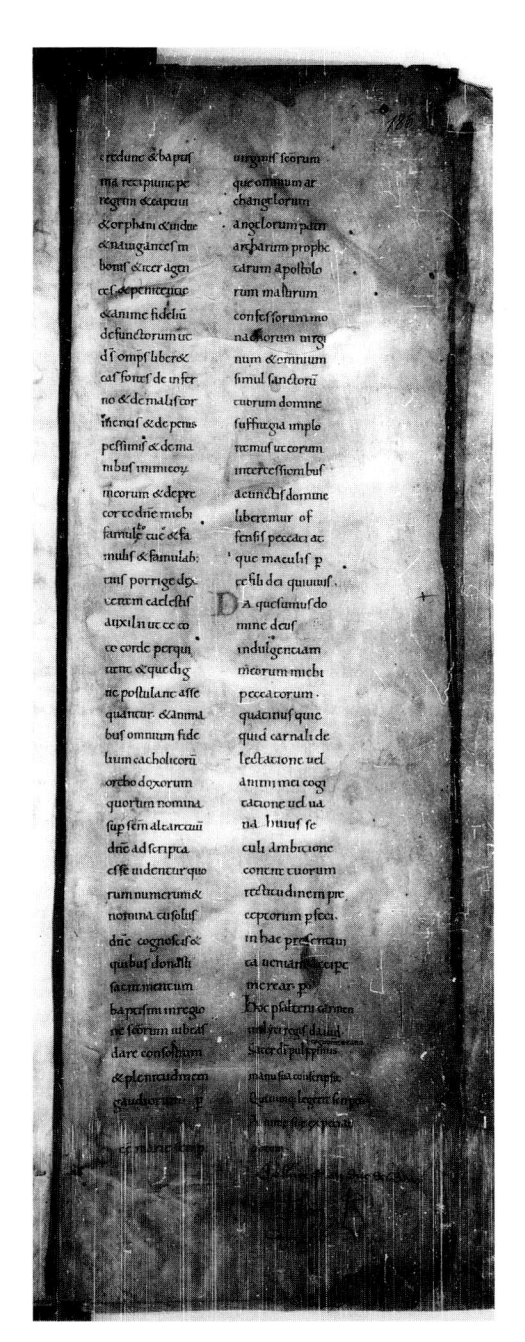

credunt & baptis-
ma recipiunt pe-
regrini & catpaui
& orphani & indue
& tangentes in
bonis & ter agen-
tes & penitentiae
& anime fideliu
defunctorum ut
ds omps liber &
eas fortes de infer-
no & de malis cor-
ripiens & de penis
pessimis & de ma-
nibus inimicoy.
meorum & depre-
cor te dne mihi
famule tue & fa-
mulis & famulabz
tuis porrige dex-
teram celestis
auxilii ut ex to-
to corde per qui-
nne & que dig-
ne postulant asse-
quantur. & animi-
bus omnium fide-
lium catholicorū
ortho doxorum
quorum nomina
sup̄ s̄c̄m altare cuiu
dn̄e ad scripta
esse uidentur quo-
rum numerum &
nomina tu solus
dn̄e cognoscis &
quibus donasti
sacramentum
baptismi in regio-
ne s̄c̄orum ubi as-
dare consolatio-
& plenitudinem
gaudiorum p

uirginis s̄c̄orum
que omnium ar-
changelorum
angelorum patri-
archarum prophe-
tarum apostolo-
rum martirum
confessorum mo-
nachorum uirgi-
num & omnium
simul sanctoru
tuorum domine
suffragia implo-
ramus ut eorum
intercessionibus
actu ĉ h̄ ſ domine
liberemur of-
fensis peccati ac-
que maculis p-
ce filii dei quiuuis
Da quesumus do-
mine deus
indulgentiam
meorum mihi
peccatorum.
quatinus quic-
quid carnali de-
lectatione uel
animi mei cogi-
tatione uel ua-
na huius se-
culi ambicione
contra tuorum
rectitudinem pre-
ceptorum psci.
in hac presenti
ta ueniam recipe-
re mereat po-
Hoc psalteri carmen
uili ur iosep dauid
Sacerdis pulfpinus
manu sua conscripsit
Quicumq; legerit semp
manus for exp̄cat

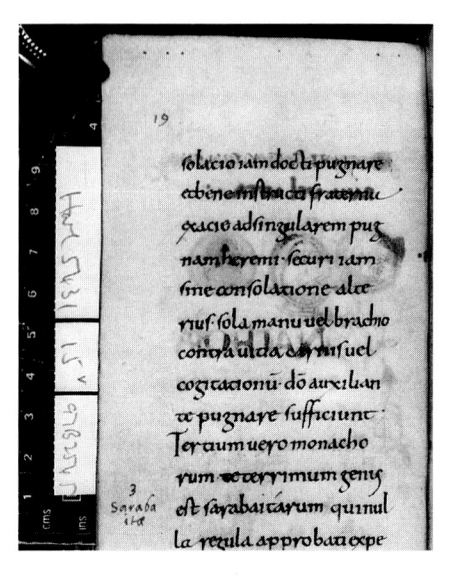

VI*a* London, British Library, Harley 5431, 15v (detail). The open-topped **a** can be seen at the end of line 2.

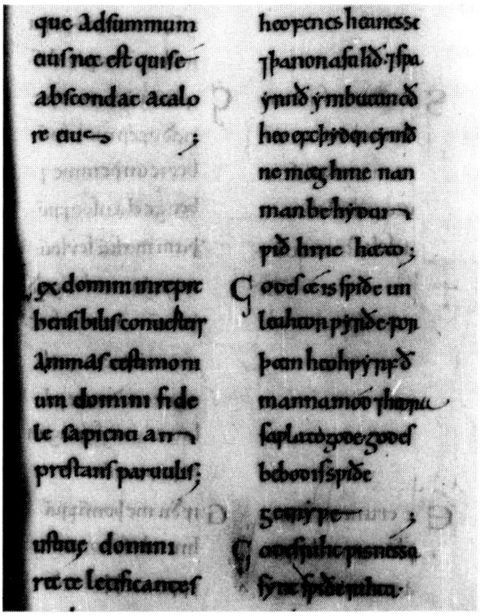

VI*b* Paris, Bibliothèque Nationale de France, lat. 8824, 19r (detail). The open-topped **a** can be seen at the end of line 11 (line 26 in the manuscript).

minds of medieval exegetes the referent became Christ himself whose body was not only uncorrupted but also raised from the dead. Thus the verse was understood to celebrate both the release of the faithful from hell and the resurrection of the body of Christ.

There is abundant evidence for traditions of both patristic and medieval interpretation of Ps. XV.10 along these lines. Both Augustine and Jerome, among others, explicitly understand the ones who are not left in hell to be the patriarchs, the first part of the verse to be an intimation of the Harrowing.[37] The connection was current in Anglo-Saxon literary production, too. The psalm figures, for example, in the early liturgical drama preserved in the *Book of Cerne*: Adam, speaking from hell in snatches of psalms, includes the plea 'Ne derelinques in inferno animam meam' (line 41).[38] *Blickling Homily VII*, which seems to be related textually to the *Book of Cerne* dialogue,[39] includes Ps. XV.10 in a similar speech. Anglo-Saxon audiences, then, could have had little difficulty seeing in this psalm-verse a reference to New Testament events.

Early Christian exegesis of the psalms in Acts II.31 demonstrates that the typological connection in the second half of the verse had been made with equal ease:

Providens locutus est de resurrectione Christi, quia neque derelictus est in inferno, neque caro eius vidit corruptionem.
Hunc Iesum resuscitavit Deus, cuius omnes nos testes sumus.[40]

And the incorrupt Holy One is affirmed as Christ rather than David even more explicitly in Acts XIII.35:

Ideoque et alias dicit: Non dabis sanctum tuum videre corruptionem.
David enim in sua generatione cum administrasset voluntati Dei, dormivit, et appositus est ad patres suos, et vidit corruptionem.
Quem vero Deus suscitavit a mortuis, non vidit corruptionem.[41]

---

[37] See Augustine, *Ep.* clxxxvii (PL 33, 833–4); Jerome, *Tractatum in Psalmos series altera* (CCSL 78, 382). These passages are quoted and discussed in Campbell, 'To Hell and Back', pp. 117 and 120.

[38] For an edition and discussion of the play, see D. N. Dumville, 'Liturgical Drama and Panegyric Responsory from the Eighth Century? A Re-Examination of the Origin and Contents of the Ninth-Century Section of the Book of Cerne', *JTS* 23 (1972), 374–406. Dumville points out the close relationship of the psalter to the development of the Harrowing-doctrine, and he notes that a full study of the subject would be valuable.

[39] Dumville suggests that the two share a common Latin homiletical source (*ibid.* p. 375).

[40] 'Forseeing this, he [the patriarch David] spoke of the resurrection of Christ. For neither was he [Christ] left in hell, neither did his flesh see corruption. This Jesus hath God raised again, whereof we are all witnesses.'

[41] 'And therefore, in another place also, he [God] saith: Thou shalt not suffer thy holy one to see corruption. For David, when he had served in his generation, according to the will of God, slept: and was laid unto his fathers, and saw corruption. But he whom God hath raised from the dead, saw no corruption.'

Jessica Brantley

Here David is explicitly refused as the referent of *sanctum tuum*; because the apostles were certain that the flesh of the patriarchs had indeed seen corruption, they did not doubt that the holy one of the psalm must be Christ.

Given these suggestions from the New Testament and patristic sources, it is not surprising to find that the Utrecht Psalter artist illustrated Ps. XV along these interpretative lines.[42] It is the first of many typological/liturgical illustrations to be found in the Psalter's programme.[43] The image chosen to depict the first phrase of verse 10 is the Harrowing of Hell: the magnificently dynamic Christ in fluttering draperies bending deeply over the pit of hellmouth, raising up the naked souls of Adam and Eve (pl. I). He tramples on a prostrate human figure, most likely a personification of Hades, and certainly not a more particularized demon. Like the *Descent into Hell*, the picture presents the merest suggestion of Christ's metaphorical triumph over hell, rather than a literal battle with Satan as its prince.[44] Juxtaposed with the Harrowing-scene is the spatially unrelated one of the Holy Women at the Sepulchre: they approach the angel seated in front of the tomb, within which a portion of Christ's uncorrupted body is visible. Clearly this juxtaposition serves a thematic rather than a visual purpose; like all the Utrecht drawings, this one responds to a complexity of

---

[42] It is possible to illustrate the psalm without asserting a typological interpretation, and psalters outside the Utrecht tradition, from the early Christian to the late medieval period, sometimes did so. The Ormesby Psalter (*c.* 1320) is a late English example: the initial introducing Ps. XV depicts a Last Judgement (23v). See S. C. Cockerell and M. R. James, *Two East Anglian Psalters at the Bodleian Library, Oxford*, Roxburghe Club (Oxford, 1926), pl. XX (a).

[43] This point is made by E. T. DeWald, *The Illustrations of the Utrecht Psalter* (Princeton, NJ, 1932), p. 10. See also S. Dufrenne, *Les Illustrations du Psautier d'Utrecht: sources et apport carolingien* (Paris, 1978); C. Gibson-Wood, 'The *Utrecht Psalter* and the Art of Memory', *RACAR: Revue d'Art Canadienne/Canadian Art Rev.* 14 (1987), 9–15; *The Utrecht Psalter in Medieval Art: Picturing the Psalms of David*, ed. K. van der Horst, W. Noel, and W. C. M. Wüstefeld ('t Goy-Houten, 1996); and F. Wormald, 'The Utrecht Psalter', *Francis Wormald: Collected Writings*, ed. J. J. Alexander, T. J. Brown and J. Gibbs, 3 vols. (Oxford, 1984–8) I, 36–46. The facsimile edition is *The Utrecht Psalter*, ed. K. van der Horst and J. H. A. Engelbrecht, Codices Selecti 75 (Graz, 1982).

[44] Most artistic representations of the Harrowing of Hell in the Anglo-Saxon period, even some clearly derived in other respects from the Utrecht image, emphasize the battle between Christ and Satan. The Tiberius Psalter, for example, a manuscript roughly contemporary with the Harley Psalter and the *Descent into Hell*, depicts in its prefatory cycle a triumphant Christ trampling a marvellously unrepentant demon. The striking curve of Christ's body argues for its distant relation to the Utrecht image, but the Tiberius artist shows a more characteristic interest in developing the demonic aspect of the episode. For a general treatment of the *Tiberius Psalter*, see F. Wormald, 'An English Eleventh-Century Psalter with Pictures: British Library Cotton MS Tiberius C.VI', *Francis Wormald: Collected Writings*, ed. J. J. Alexander, *et al.* I, 123–37. For a discussion of the psalter in this particular connection, see K. M. Openshaw, 'The Battle Between Christ and Satan in the Tiberius Psalter', *Jnl of the Warburg and Courtauld Inst.* 52 (1989), 14–33, where she argues that the battle between Christ and Satan is the principle of thematic coherence for the psalter's illustrative programme. See also K. M. Openshaw, 'Weapons in the Daily Battle: Images of the Conquest of Evil in the Early Medieval Psalter', *Art Bull.* 75 (1993), 17–38.

verbal suggestion rather than to the visual imperative of a coherent picture-space. The artist uses space casually, expanding on themes explicit or implicit in the text to create a chaotic but richly evocative pictorial interpretation of individual moments in each psalm. The illustration of Ps. XV accordingly reflects both of the emphases in verse 10, as medieval Christians read them: the righteous shall not be left in hell, as the Harrowing demonstrates, and the body of Christ will not be corrupted, as the Holy Women at the Sepulchre discover.

Although the visit of the Holy Women to the Sepulchre is a standard subject, its representation here includes an unusual detail that emphasizes further the textual origins of the image. The scene archetypally implies, if it does not actually depict, the Resurrection of Christ; the women's surprise and joy at the discovery of the empty tomb communicates dramatically the miracle of the Resurrection. The origin of medieval drama in the *Quem quaeritis* dialogues demonstrates the power with which this scene recalls the primary mystery celebrated in Christian history.[45] In the visual arts as well, the image of the Women at the Sepulchre is the earliest and most common way in which Christ's Resurrection is depicted in the Middle Ages.[46] However, the women in this drawing in the Utrecht Psalter do not approach an empty tomb, but one with an uncorrupted and incorruptible body inside. Christ is not risen yet, it seems, but is perhaps about to be resurrected on the spot. The surprise the women have in store for them, the 'oþer þing' they are about to discover, is not that the tomb is empty, but that Christ's body within it is undecayed. The artist's inconsistency with (or innovations from) other depictions of the women at the tomb demonstrates the direct derivation of this scene from the verse of the psalm.[47] And the psalm celebrates only implicitly the resurrection itself. The scene of the Holy Women at the Sepulchre functions rather in this context as pictorial proof of the body's incorruptibility.

The Utrecht Psalter is a Carolingian book, but it was in England as early as the tenth century, and its iconographic legacy survives in three copies made at the scriptorium of Christ Church, Canterbury: the Harley Psalter (London, British Library, Harley 603), the Eadwine Psalter (Cambridge, Trinity College R. 17. 1), and the Canterbury Psalter (Paris, Bibliothèque Nationale, lat. 8846). The

---

[45] See O. B. Hardison, Jr, *Christian Rite and Christian Drama in the Middle Ages* (Baltimore, MD, 1965). Hardison notes that the *Quem quaeritis* trope is 'above all a resurrection play' (p. 162).

[46] G. Schiller locates the earliest instance of the Women at the Sepulchre in a wall-painting from Dura Europos, *c.* 250, now in the Yale Art Gallery, New Haven. For a reproduction, and general discussion of the development of this iconography, see G. Schiller, *Ikonographie der christlichen Kunst*, 5 vols. (Gütersloh, 1971) III, 18–30.

[47] There are apparently no other medieval examples, visual or textual, of the holy women discovering an uncorrupted body inside Christ's tomb. The depiction of an open, empty tomb is a relatively late development in the iconographic tradition of this scene, but the inclusion of an uncorrupted body seems unique to the Utrecht Psalter and its derivatives.

Harley copy, thought to have been made in the early eleventh century,[48] is of primary interest for the *Descent into Hell*, for it testifies to Anglo-Saxon knowledge of and interest in Utrecht iconography. The Harley illustration to Ps. XV follows its predecessor closely: Christ bends low over the pit of hell, lifting out the patriarchs and trampling on an insignificant and indeterminate figure.[49] Nearby, the three Holy Women approach the sepulchre with the uncorrupted body guarded by an angel. The visual apparatus connected to the psalm is an almost exact copy of its Carolingian exemplar. The association of the visit of the Holy Women with a Harrowing of Hell in the context of Ps. XV, then, was available not only textually, but also visually, in Anglo-Saxon England.

In the Utrecht Psalter, the illustration of Ps. XV is the only one to pair a representation of the Harrowing with one of the Holy Women at the Sepulchre. But in the Harley version, that unusual iconography is tellingly repeated.[50] Ps. CXXXVIII is illustrated with a collection of images that includes, in part, a Harrowing and a Visit to the Sepulchre (pl. II). The relationship between text and image is especially close here, for the artist's inclusion of the Harrowing, a clear departure from Utrecht iconography, was clearly prompted by independent textual interpretation. The pertinent verses of Ps. CXXXVIII are 8–10:

Si ascendero in caelum, tu illic es: si descendero in infernum, ades.
Si sumpsero pinnas meas diluculo et habitavero in extremis maris etenim illuc manus tua deducet me et tenebit me dextera tua.[51]

Verse 8 affirms the presence of God in hell, and therefore is easily understood christologically as a reference to the Harrowing. The Carolingian iconography that this artist rejects includes as its response to this verse a personification of Hades about to devour a sinner. DeWald suggests that 'a demon is prodding another victim towards him'.[52] Although it seems impossible to imagine this

---

[48] The most thorough study of the Harley Psalter is W. Noel, *The Harley Psalter* (Cambridge, 1995). See also R. Gameson, 'The Anglo-Saxon Artists of the Harley 603 Psalter', *JBAA* 143 (1990), 29–48.

[49] It is perhaps significant that, of all the images illustrating this psalm, the Anglo-Saxon artist seemed especially interested in the captivating figure of Christ bending over the pit of hell. A dry-point outline of the figure is barely visible in the lower left margin of the Utrecht page – perhaps a trial or a means of transferring the picture from one manuscript to another.

[50] The Harley Psalter is described only advisedly as a 'copy' of the Utrecht. Noel has shown that the production of the Anglo-Saxon book, a very complex interaction of many different scribes and artists over a period of some years, is more accurately conceived as an interpretation of the earlier codex than as an exact copy. Noel's Artist A is the illustrator of Ps. XV, and his Artist F of Ps. CXXXVIII.

[51] 'If I ascend into heaven, thou art there: if I descend into hell, thou art present. If I take my wings early in the morning, and dwell in the uttermost parts of the sea: Even there also shall thy hand lead me: and thy right hand shall hold me.'

[52] DeWald, *Illustrations*, p. 60.

figure as an angelic one, come to liberate rather than to torment the soul, the Harley artist seems to have understood the drawing that way, for he replaces this group with the Harrowing-image from Ps. XV. The deep curve of the demonic figure must have provided a visual stimulus for this substitution, recalling the earlier image of Christ's salvific effort. The Harley drawing makes the joy of God's presence in Hell unambiguous by aligning this psalm visually with the familiar tradition of the salvation of the patriarchs.

The Harrowing of Hell illustrating Harley Ps. CXXXVIII is the logical conclusion of a steady devaluation of the role of the demonic from the Utrecht Psalter to its direct and indirect descendants in Harley 603: there is no devil at all. This Harrowing-image is always a relatively pacific one, for there is no devil, properly speaking, even in the Utrecht exemplar. Instead, the power of Hades has *already* been overthrown; its personification lies inert and unthreatening under the feet of the Saviour. The two Harley interpretations of the image reflect the incidental nature of this figure, minimizing still further the role of the demonic. In the first Harley Harrowing (Ps. XV), Christ tramples a figure, but he is less evidently human, in the end simply less present.[53] The Utrecht Hades and the Harley adversary are similarly insignificant in the design of the iconography of the Harrowing of Hell, for this is not the depiction of an epic battle between good and evil, but of the joyful liberation of prisoners. The second Harley Harrowing (Ps. CXXXVIII) understands the insignificance of the devil in this context, for it omits any adversary at all. The devil which Christ was trampling has metamorphosed, in the way of images copied, into what appears to be a small outcrop of rock.[54] This outcrop serves the same visual purpose of elevating the divinity a little, thereby emphasizing in the curve of his bending figure the depth of his condescension and the extent of his mercy. This visual purpose reflects the most important thematic purpose of the Utrecht and Harley artists: the figure of the devil – indeed, the whole image – exists only to demonstrate the extent of the redemptive sacrifice and the intensity of the joy of the redeemed.

As Noel notes, the hellmouth from which Christ liberates the righteous dead is actually drawn around the words from Ps. CXXXVIII that prompted it; the visual forms conjured up by the word *infernum* encircle and highlight the verse in which it is contained. In this close association of word and image, the Harley artist follows

[53] Harley Artist A used demons for effect when it interested him. Tselos credits him, for example, with the transformation of the Utrecht humanoid into a full-fledged demon in Ps. VI; see D. Tselos, 'English Manuscript Illustration and the Utrecht Psalter', *Art Bull.* 41 (1959), 137–49, at 139. See also Gameson, 'Anglo-Saxon Artists', p. 38.

[54] The Ps. CXXXVIII Harrowing introduces a hellmouth: one might argue that the demonic presence has been transferred from a bested Satan to a permanently gaping orifice. Christ's triumph, in this case, is not so much a defeat of Satan as a deprivation of Hell through the rescue of the patriarchs.

Jessica Brantley

the spirit, if not the visual 'letter', of his Utrecht exemplar, which derives its images independently from internal verbal cues, rather than external pictorial models.[55] But the independent draftsman known as Artist F is not impervious to visual suggestion in his willingness to respond to the psalm-text. Although Noel characterizes Artist F's images as 'moulded' by the psalter's text,[56] in this particular case it seems to me more likely that the artist replaced the Utrecht images with adventurous iconography derived in part from different *visual* prototypes.

Artist F clearly used visual associations to build upon verbal cues when he imported the Harrowing of Hell into Ps. CXXXVIII. And the patterns of thought that impelled him to include the Holy Women at the Sepulchre in conjunction with this psalm are even less obviously textual. The *resurrectionem* of verse 2 prompts in the Utrecht exemplar an open and empty sarcophagus, and perhaps that was enough to remind the Anglo-Saxon artist of the sorrowing women. Verse 9 could also have reinforced such a connection: the Utrecht psalmist takes his wings *diluculo*, recalling vaguely the early morning visit of the women to Christ's empty tomb.[57] Verse 18 implies the resurrection still more strongly in the words of the psalmist: *Exsurrexi et adhuc sum tecum*.[58] But still there is no strong suggestion of the women at the tomb, and the Utrecht artist did not include their image in his illustration of the psalm's text. Most likely, the Harley artist's main inspiration for the inclusion of the sepulchral visit was his previous decision to use the Harrowing. Taking a suggestion from the text of Ps. CXXXVIII, he followed the pictorial exemplar of Ps. XV, importing an earlier artist's imaginative association into a new verbal context.[59] The pairing of the Harrowing of Hell with the visit of the grieving Marys must have remained powerfully in the imagination of Artist F, and it proved useful in his attempt to explicate visually the text of the later psalm.

The reliance of the Harley Artist F on visual memory as well as on word-suggestion shows that the imagistic combination of the Holy Women at the Sepulchre and the Harrowing of Hell had a life in Anglo-Saxon England outside the confines of illustrations of Ps. XV. The conjunction of these two images was powerful enough in one artist's mind to spread from its original context as commentary on Ps. XV into the new exegetical environment of Ps. CXXXVIII.

---

[55] The illustrator of the Harley Psalter's Ps. CXXXVIII was especially likely to depart from his visual models. Noel observes that 'while artists A-D2 followed the *Utrecht Psalter* extremely closely, artist F did not' (*Harley*, p. 85).   [56] *Ibid.*

[57] That the morning was obviously suggestive of the Resurrection is illustrated by the *Descent into Hell*, in which both the angels of the Resurrection and the women start out 'on uhtan'.

[58] R. Gameson, *The Role of Art in the Late Anglo-Saxon Church* (Oxford, 1995), p. 67, traces the lineage of the picture from this verse.

[59] In keeping with his characteristic attention to the text of the psalms, though, Artist F does not include Christ's uncorrupted body in the sepulchre that accompanies Ps. CXXXVIII. In the context of Resurrection proper, rather than incorruptability, it makes little sense.

And given the distance at which the influence of the Utrecht Psalter was felt, it is not difficult to imagine that this particular imagery was similarly influential beyond the confines of the Harley manuscript.[60] The visual logic of the pictorial conjunction in the Utrecht Psalter seems to have been imported not only into new artistic environments, but into literary contexts as well; an association originally discovered by patristic commentary in the text of a psalm was not only codified visually, but also rewritten into the words of an Old English poem. The iconography of the Utrecht Psalter was not the only source upon which the Old English poet drew, nor does his poem follow these pictures slavishly in every particular.[61] But the idea for the structural juxtaposition of these two scenes comes to the poem by way of the psalm; the obscure literary mechanisms of the *Descent into Hell* are thus clarified by analogy with the Harley illustrations.

So little is known with certainty about the origins of the Exeter Book, in which *Descent into Hell* is uniquely preserved, that any physical connection between that manuscript and the iconography of the Utrecht Psalter must necessarily be hypothetical. And of course a great distance is possible even between the artistic intelligence(s) responsible for the *Descent into Hell* and the scribe(s) who wrote the Exeter Book. But if it seems certain that the *Descent*-poet knew Ps. XV and traditions of its commentary, it is by no means impossible that he also knew the Utrecht illustrations themselves. The origins of the Exeter Book remain obscure, but it has been persuasively argued that 'the hypotheses which seem most compatible with the scanty facts at our disposal are production at Glastonbury or Christ Church, Canterbury'.[62] This latter possibility is intri-

---

[60] Broderick's identification of Utrecht Psalter iconography in the illustration of Junius 11 demonstrates that the influence of the continental book in Anglo-Saxon England extends beyond the psalter that is its direct descendant, and even into one of the great poetic codices. See H. R. Broderick, 'Observations on the Method of Illustration in MS Junius 11 and the Relationship of the Drawings to the Text', *Scriptorium* 37 (1984 for 1983), 161–77.

[61] The motif of the Women at the Sepulchre, used in common by picture and poem, manifests itself in slightly different ways in each. Whereas the poet specifies the presence of Mary and one other 'eorles dohtor' (9–11), reflecting the textual tradition in one of its many variations (cf. Matt. XXVIII.1, Mark XVI.1, Luke XXIV.10 and John XX.1–10), the artist includes the three female figures more typical and in fact nearly ubiquitous in visual representations of the scene.

[62] R. Gameson, 'The Origin of the Exeter Book of Old English Poetry', *ASE* 25 (1996), 135–85, at 179. The uncertain history of the Exeter Book continues to spark debate. P. W. Conner, *Anglo-Saxon Exeter: a Tenth-Century Cultural History* (Woodbridge, 1993) has provided very thorough documentation in support of his daring contention that the manuscript was produced in Exeter itself. Gameson's reading of the evidence is more cautious (and to my mind more persuasive), but even at his most conservative, Gameson posits an origin for the Exeter Book that preserves a link with the scriptorium at Christ Church: 'We would seem, therefore, to be looking for a major scriptorium in the south-west which was active in the mid- to third quarter of the tenth century, which included a talented calligrapher who was skilled in the native tradition of script, *which had connections with Canterbury* and whose other products seem largely to have disappeared' ('Origin', p. 179; emphasis mine).

guing, for the Utrecht Psalter was available at the Christ Church scriptorium *c.* 970, and thus the Exeter Book – if it is a contemporary Canterbury production – could reasonably show signs of its influence. If the Exeter Book and the Harley Psalter were produced in the same scriptorium at roughly the same time, they might be expected to exhibit similar iconographic patterns. They might even be conjectured to represent two related responses in different media to the influential illustrations in the Carolingian book. Given the striking nature of the parallels between illustration and poem – and the inscrutability of the poem otherwise – we may be forgiven for imagining, however tentatively, such a mechanism of transmission.

Illustration of Ps. XV.10, then, is especially instructive for readers of the Old English *Descent into Hell*. Visual exegesis of the psalm in the tradition of the Utrecht Psalter helps to explain why this Anglo-Saxon Harrowing omits any mention of Christ's Apocalyptic binding of the devil. More important, the Utrecht pictures suggest why the poet has chosen the unusual iconographic conjunction of the Holy Women at the Sepulchre and the Harrowing of Hell. In Ps. XV.10, typologically understood, a pacific Harrowing and the Visit to the Sepulchre are paired; the poem is derived thematically from the complex of ideas expressed most succinctly in this verse. More important still, illustration of the psalm illuminates some of the structural strangeness of the poem. Neither illustration of Ps. XV in the Utrecht tradition nor the Anglo-Saxon poetic *Descent into Hell* makes chronology its most fundamental concern. The poet's willingness to imply Christ's bodily presence in Hell matches the artist's willingness to include a completely unattested incorruptible body in the sepulchre: in the service of local effect, neither seeks consistency with orthodox narratives, or indeed seeks narrative at all. The point of these Harrowings, both verbal and visual, is not the fight with the devil nor the Resurrection itself, but an impressionistic celebration of the salvation of the just. If the imagery presented in the *Descent* stems originally from Ps. XV and its commentary, the manifestation of that imagery in the Harley picture is the analogue that demonstrates crucially the nature of the source-relationship. The psalter's pictorial mode of representing this complex of associated exegetical ideas parallels most closely the atemporal methods behind the Old English poem.

It is almost impossible to imagine that a picture could serve as the direct source for words – the mere translation of an idea from one medium to another requires more interaction than our common notion of 'source' implies. In making these connections, then, we are forced to operate with a degree of reserve in the murkier area of 'analogue'. And yet the critical conjunction of a literary text with an artistic object is especially fortuitous in this case because visual art implies sequence less powerfully than do written words. Rather than considering temporal relationships, the visual arts more often portray related events on the undifferentiated plane of their common meaning. The word-painting of the Utrecht Psalter tradition, in particular, in spite of its demonstrated verbal interest, defies both spatial and temporal ordering. Manuscript artists and the Old English poet created in the same vein; the poem responds to the psalm and its commentary in the same lyrical way as the pictures, simply associating two episodes in the passion-narrative in order to produce affective response. The analogue cannot reveal precisely the ways in which these ideas or the modes of their expression were transmitted between artist and poet – which will always remain a matter for supposition only – but the comparison is none the less instructive. What is to be gained from a critical enterprise of this sort is not so much insight into how a text was written, but rather into how we are to read it.[63]

[63] For their learned and helpful advice at various stages during the preparation of this article, I would like to thank C. Cannon, R. Gameson, H. A. Kelly, M. Lapidge, N. E. R. Perkins and C. Sanok.

Anti-Judaism in Ælfric's *Lives of Saints*

ANDREW P. SCHEIL

Anti-Judaism existed in Anglo-Saxon England without the presence of actual Jewish communities.[1] The understanding of Jews and Judaism in Anglo-Saxon England is therefore solely a textual phenomenon, a matter of stereotypes embedded in longstanding Christian cultural traditions.[2] For instance, consider the homily *De populo Israhel* (written between 1002 and 1005), a condensation and translation of selections from Exodus and Numbers by the prolific monk Ælfric of Eynsham (*c.* 955–*c.* 1020).[3] The text narrates the tribulations of the Israelites in the desert: Ælfric explains that although God 'worhte feala wundra

---

[1] Scholarly consensus maintains that Jews only settled in England after the Norman Conquest: see the *Encyclopedia Judaica*, ed. C. Roth *et al.*, 16 vols. (Jerusalem, 1971) VI, col. 747; J. Jacobs, *The Jews of Angevin England* (London, 1893), p. ix; A. M. Hyamson, *A History of the Jews in England* (London, 1908), pp. 1–6; E. N. Calisch, *The Jew in English Literature as Author and Subject* (Port Washington, NY, 1909), p. 33; H. Michelson, *The Jew in Early English Literature* (Amsterdam, 1926), pp. 12–21; S. W. Baron, *A Social and Religious History of the Jews*, 2nd ed., 20 vols. (New York, 1952–93) IV, 76; C. Roth, *A History of the Jews in England*, 3rd ed. (Oxford, 1964), p. 2; H. H. Ben-Sasson, *A History of the Jewish People*, trans. G. Weidenfeld (Cambridge, MA, 1976), p. 394; L. Poliakov, *The History of Anti-Semitism: from the Time of Christ to the Court Jews*, trans. R. Howard, 4 vols. (New York, 1965–85) I, 77; L. K. Little, *Religious Poverty and the Profit Economy in Medieval Europe* (Ithaca, NY, 1978), p. 45; H. Pollins, *Economic History of the Jews in England* (Rutherford, NJ, 1982), p. 15; K. R. Stow, *Alienated Minority: the Jews of Medieval Latin Europe* (Cambridge, MA, 1992), p. 41. On Jews in Roman Britain, see S. Applebaum, 'Were there Jews in Roman Britain?', *Trans. of the Jewish Hist. Soc. of England* 17 (1951–2), 189–205. For nearby continental communities, see *Encyclopedia Judaica* VII, cols. 7–14 ('France: Roman and Merovingian Periods', esp. the map cols. 11–12).

[2] Thus, this study deals with an understanding of Jews little influenced by Jewish culture. R. Mellinkoff suggests, in 'The Round, Cap-Shaped Hats Depicted on Jews in BM Cotton Claudius B. iv', *ASE* 2 (1973), 155–65, that the observation of real Jews could be responsible for the iconographic innovation of round hats on Jews (as opposed to pointed ones) in the illustrations of London, British Library, Cotton Claudius B. iv. For knowledge of Hebrew in the period, see S. Larratt Keefer and D. R. Burrows, 'Hebrew and the *Hebraicum* in late Anglo-Saxon England', *ASE* 19 (1990), 67–80. Such bits of evidence do not argue for a substantial impact of Jewish culture on Anglo-Saxon England. Any influence of Hebrew literature on Anglo-Saxon literary culture was probably through an intermediary text; see F. M. Biggs and T. N. Hall, 'Traditions concerning Jamnes and Mambres in Anglo-Saxon England', *ASE* 25 (1996), 69–89, at 85–6.

[3] For the date of *De populo Israhel*, see P. Clemoes, 'The Chronology of Ælfric's Works', *The Anglo-Saxons: Studies in some Aspects of their History and Culture presented to Bruce Dickins*, ed. P. Clemoes (London, 1959), pp. 212–47, at 244.

on ðam westene', the Israelites were 'wiðerræde witodlice to oft' and angered him.[4] The intractable attitude of God's chosen people in the desert demands an explanation; why did the Israelites spurn the heaven-sent manna and long for the repasts of their Egyptian captivity? Ælfric clarifies their behaviour through a string of typological associations. He explains that the manna 'hæfde þa getacnunge ures Hælendes Cristes'.[5] Christ is the bread of life, but '[þ]one acwealdon syððan þæt ylce Iudeisce cynn, and noldon hine habban heora sawlum to bigleofan'.[6] Ælfric explicates the rebelliousness of Israel by equating the defiant Israelites with the 'evil' Jews of the New Testament; the Jews were rebellious then, just as they later betrayed Christ, but, as Ælfric emphasizes, 'we gelyfað on hine'.[7] Following this typological logic, Ælfric continues to interpret the narrative, drawing binary oppositions to firm up the difference between Jew and Christian. The 'spiritual' people of the New Covenant supplant the 'carnal' people of the Old Law: the Israelites 'wæron flæsclice menn, and underfencgon heora wite on ðyssere worulde, æfter Moyses æ'' while 'we [Ælfric's community] syndon gastlice menn under Godes gife nu'.[8] Ælfric safely situates the corporeal Jew in the past tense, under the Old Law, and thus clearly demarcates the inherent difference of the Christian, spiritual community in the here and 'nu'.[9] This traditional opposition is the signature of an early medieval understanding of Jews frequently replicated in Ælfric's writings; it is, in effect, a multifaceted strategy for the construction of social identity, a way to delimit and explore the boundaries of the Christian community.

Drawing mainly on Ælfric's collection of homilies known as the *Lives of Saints*, this study examines his hermeneutic strategies when confronted by Jews in the course of his vernacular translations, and then, having established a template for Ælfric's understanding, investigates in detail the representation of Jews in his homily on the Maccabees in the *Lives of Saints*.[10] This close attention to one

---

[4] Ælfric, *De populo Israhel*, in *Homilies of Ælfric: a Supplementary Collection*, ed. J. C. Pope, 2 vols. EETS os 259–60 (London, 1967–8) II, 638–66, lines 38–40: 'created many miracles in the desert'; 'indeed rebellious too often'. Further references to *De populo Israhel* will be cited by title and line numbers. Although *De populo Israhel* and other texts in this study sometimes push beyond the generic definition of 'homily', I have retained the term throughout for convenience. All translations are my own.

[5] *De populo Israhel*, lines 128–9: 'had the signification of our Saviour Christ'.

[6] *Ibid.* lines 132–3: 'afterwards that same Jewish people killed him and would not take him as a sustenance for their souls'. [7] *Ibid.* line 134: 'we believe in him'.

[8] *Ibid.* lines 297–9: 'were carnal men and suffered their torment in this world, according to the law of Moses'; 'now we are spiritual men under the grace of God'.

[9] For a similar contrast in the homily between the earthly rewards of the Israelites and the greater spiritual rewards of the Christian community, see *ibid.* lines 376–89.

[10] The *Lives of Saints* was written over a number of years, but was probably completed between 992 and 1002: see Clemoes, 'Chronology', p. 244. M. Lapidge argues for a *terminus ante quem* of 998 in 'Ælfric's *Sanctorale*', *Holy Men and Holy Women: Old English Prose Saints' Lives and their*

particular use of anti-Judaism reveals not only the contours of anti-Judaism particular to Ælfric, but also shows the potential ideological role of anti-Judaic discourse in late Anglo-Saxon England.

We have already seen some common characteristics of medieval anti-Judaism in *De populo Israhel*: the Jews are guilty of deicide and they are also deficient in their mental faculties. They are 'spiritually blind' and therefore unable to recognize the spiritual meaning of the manna; their carnal nature entails an insufficient understanding that prevents them from recognizing the divine presence of Christ in the offering from God.[11] As might be expected from a monk so concerned with orthodox interpretation, Ælfric's understanding of Jews resides in the mainstream of early medieval theology. The paradigm for the Christian understanding of Jews in the early Middle Ages was set by Augustine.[12] According to Augustine, the Jews were once God's chosen people, but, due to their spiritual blindness,

---

Contexts, ed. P. E. Szarmach (Albany, 1996), pp. 115–29, at 118. See also J. Hill, 'The Dissemination of Ælfric's *Lives of Saints*: a Preliminary Survey', *ibid.* pp. 235–59.

[11] These stereotypes, in tandem with the notion that the historical dispersion of the Jews is God's punishment for killing Christ, comprise what G. Langmuir calls 'the core of Christian anti-Judaism' (*History, Religion, and Antisemitism* (Berkeley, CA, 1990), p. 285). I follow Langmuir's distinction between the anti-Judaism of the early Middle Ages, characterized by 'logical' (albeit non-rational) conclusions about the Jews that are derived from empirical thinking, and the anti-Semitism of the centuries following 1100, characterized by more fantastical, irrational suppositions. In addition to *History, Religion, and Antisemitism*, see Langmuir's *Toward a Definition of Antisemitism* (Berkeley, CA, 1990) and 'The Faith of Christians and Hostility to Jews', in *Christianity and Judaism*, ed. D. Wood, Stud. in Church Hist. 20 (Oxford, 1992), 77–92. J. Trachtenberg, *The Devil and the Jews: the Medieval Conception of the Jew and its Relation to Modern Antisemitism* (New Haven, CT, 1943) is still a useful survey of medieval anti-semitism. In a recent study, E. Young-Bruehl characterizes anti-Judaism as an ethnocentrism, and anti-semitism as an 'ideology of desire' or an 'orecticism'; see her compelling analysis informed by psychoanalysis and sociology in *The Anatomy of Prejudices* (Cambridge, MA, 1996), pp. 184–99 *passim*.

[12] On the early Christian and patristic background of anti-Judaism, see A. L. Williams, *Adversus Judaeos: a Bird's-Eye View of Christian Apologiae until the Renaissance* (Cambridge, 1935); N. Berdyaev, *Christianity and Anti-Semitism*, trans. A. A. Spears and V. Kanter (New York, 1954); D. D. Runes, *The Jew and the Cross*, 2nd ed. (New York, 1966); G. B. Ladner, 'Aspects of Patristic Anti-Judaism', *Viator* 2 (1971), 355–63; E. Abel, *The Roots of Anti-Semitism* (Rutherford, NJ, 1975), esp. pp. 112–38; R. Radford Ruether, *Faith and Fratricide: the Theological Roots of Anti-Semitism* (New York, 1974) and 'The *Adversus Judaeos* Tradition in the Church Fathers: the Exegesis of Christian Anti-Judaism', *Aspects of Jewish Culture in the Middle Ages*, ed. P. E. Szarmach (Albany, NY, 1979), pp. 27–50; J. Cohen, *The Friars and the Jews: the Evolution of Medieval Anti-Judaism* (Ithaca, NY, 1982), pp. 19–32 and 'The Jews as the Killers of Christ in the Latin Tradition, from Augustine to the Friars', *Traditio* 39 (1983), 1–13; H. Maccoby, *The Sacred Executioner: Human Sacrifice and the Legacy of Guilt* (New York, 1982), pp. 134–62; J. G. Gager, *The Origins of Anti-Semitism: Attitudes toward Judaism in Pagan and Christian Antiquity* (Oxford, 1983), esp. pp. 13–34; *'To See Ourselves as Others See Us': Christians, Jews, "Others" in Late Antiquity*, ed. J. Neusner and E. S. Frerichs (Chico, CA, 1985); Stow, *Alienated*, pp. 6–40. For a collection of important studies, see *Essential Papers on Judaism and Christianity in Conflict: from Late Antiquity to the Reformation*, ed. J. Cohen (New York, 1991).

they killed Christ and were thus forever cast out from God's grace. However, the Jews had an important place within Christian cosmology; they provided proof of God's divine plan as witnesses to the typological potential of the Christian New Testament within the Judaic Old Law, and they were reserved for conversion at the end of time.[13] For Augustine, historical events proved his case; the Jews existed as a scattered and defeated people: 'Iudaei autem, qui eum occiderunt et in eum credere noluerunt, quia oportebat eum mori et resurgere, uastati infelicius a Romanis funditusque a suo regno, ubi iam eis alienigenae dominabantur, eradicati dispersique per terras (quando quidem ubique non desunt) per scripturas suas testimonio nobis sunt prophetias nos non finxisse de Christo . . .'[14] Augustine expressed the connection between Judaism and Christianity as a transition from deficiency to fulfilment: Christianity completed and surpassed the obsolete potential of Judaism.[15] Just as the Old Testament was an incomplete document without the fulfilment of the New, the Jews who were the chosen under the Old Law were to be replaced by the people of the New Covenant. This typological solution requires the ability to hold several contradictory understandings of the Jews in continual suspension: the Old Testament Jews are noble in their own right, but only within the temporal confines of the Old Law; when viewed through the prism of the New Testament, the rebellious Jews of *De populo Israhel* are incomplete, unfinished, 'lack' incarnate. In addition, the Jews of the New Testament are the executioners of Christ, who will nevertheless at the end of time repent and cast off their blindness.

Given these conflicting signals, Ælfric feels that the Jews represent an interpretative conundrum. The Jews of the *Lives of Saints* generally adhere to standard

---

[13] This understanding informed the official policy toward Jews in the kingdoms of Europe in the Middle Ages, and contributed to the relative stability of Jewish life in the period when compared to the later Middle Ages: see B. S. Bachrach, *Early Medieval Jewish Policy in Western Europe* (Minneapolis, MN, 1977) and the legal evidence collected in *The Jews in the Legal Sources of the Early Middle Ages*, ed. A. Linder (Jerusalem, 1997), esp. 'Index of Subjects: Protections of Jews' (p. 714), and 'Violence: against Jews' (p. 717).

[14] Augustine, *De civitate Dei*, CCSL 48, 644, lines 13–18 (XVIII.46): 'However, the Jews who killed him, and would not believe in him, because it pleased him to die and rise again, were more miserably destroyed by the Romans, and cast out from their own kingdom, where aliens had already ruled over them, and they were uprooted and dispersed throughout the lands (so that indeed there is no place where they are not), and thus by their own scriptures they are a testimony to us that we have not made up the prophecies about Christ.' This sentiment is expressed widely in Augustine: see B. Blumenkranz, *Die Judenpredigt Augustins: Ein Beitrag zur Geschichte der jüdisch-christlichen Beziehungen in den ersten Jahrhunderten* (Basel, 1946), pp. 175–81. Cf. Paulus Orosius, *Historiarum adversum paganos libri VII*, ed. K. Zangemeister, CSEL 5, 443 (VII.IV.16): 'Iam hinc post passionem Domini, quem Iudaei quantum in ipsis fuit persecuti sunt, continuae clades Iudaeorum, donec exinaniti dispersique deficiant, incessabiliter strepunt': 'From the passion of the Lord until now, the Jews, who had persecuted him as much as they could, have complained incessantly of continuous disasters for their people, until finally, scattered and desolate, they passed away.'   [15] Cf. Rom. XI.1–31.

early medieval stereotypes. They are guilty of deicide: in *St Apollinaris*, the 'reðan iudeiscan' are condemned for killing Christ[16] and in *Abdon and Sennes*, Abgarus commiserates with Christ: 'Me is eac gesæd þæt ða iudeiscan syrwiað . and runiað him betwynan hu hi þe berædan magon.'[17] *The Forty Soldiers* expands this idea, elaborating the deicide motif: the Jews entrapped Christ with evil intent, but *only* because Christ allowed this to happen. In this homily, Ælfric teaches that Christ turns evil intent to good fortune through his power, and thus the great crime of the Jews, 'þaþa hi syrwdon mid sweartum geþance hu hi crist acwealdon', became the source of Christian salvation.[18] The Jews are 'þurh-scyldige' and have been judged for their treachery 'þeah þe ure drihten þa dæda him geþafode'.[19] Ælfric embellishes this same theme and broadens its application in *The Exaltation of the Holy Cross*. In this text, the Jews hide the true cross so that the Christians cannot find it: 'þa iudeiscan hi behyddon mid hetelicum geðance . noldon þæt se maþm wurde mannum to frofre.'[20] Like a shadow of later fantasies of a 'Jewish conspiracy', the Jews betray and kill Christ, and then actively continue their 'campaign' against the Christian community by hiding the instrument of salvation.[21] Later in the same text, Ælfric discusses the guilt of Judas and the Jews, making clear that although Christ's death meant salvation for humanity, Judas and his people are still guilty and did not simply act according to God's will:

Næron þa iudeiscan ne se dyrna læwe þurh god geneadode . to ðam gramlican geþeahte . ac þa þa crist geseah . se þe ge-sihð ealle þing heora yfelan willan . þa awende þe hit to gode . swa þæt heora yfelnyss us becom to hæle . . . Nu synd þa iudeiscan . and se sceamlease læwa cristes deaðes scyldige . þe syrwdon be him . þeah þe hit us become to ecere alysednysse . and heora nan ne becymð to cristes rice næfre . butan þam þe hit gebettan . and ge-bugan to criste.[22]

---

[16] Ælfric, *St Apollinaris*, *Ælfric's Lives of Saints*, ed. W. W. Skeat, EETS os 76, 82, 94 and 114 (Oxford, 1881–1900; repr. as 2 vols. London, 1966) I, 472, line 6: 'the cruel Jews'. All further references to homilies in the *Lives of Saints* are to this edition by homily title, volume, homily number and line numbers. Cf. the invective of St Stephen against his Jewish executioners in Ælfric's *Passio Beati Stephani Protomartiris*, *Ælfric's Catholic Homilies: the First Series*, ed. P. Clemoes, EETS ss 17 (Oxford, 1997), p. 199, lines 41–6, *passim*.

[17] *Abdon and Sennes*, II, no. 24, lines 99–100: 'It is told to me that the Jews plot and scheme among themselves how they can betray you.'

[18] *The Forty Soldiers*, I, no. 11, lines 318–19: 'when they conspired, with dark thoughts, how they could kill Christ'.

[19] *Ibid.* lines 321 and 323: 'completely guilty'; 'although our Lord allowed them to do the deeds'.

[20] *The Exaltation of the Holy Cross*, II, no. 27, lines 4–5: 'The Jews concealed it with hateful intention; they did not wish the treasure to become a comfort to men.'

[21] Cf. the efforts of the Jews to keep secret the location of the cross in *Elene*.

[22] *Ibid.* lines 165–9 and 176–80: 'Neither the Jews nor the secret traitor was compelled by God to that horrible intent, but when Christ, he who sees all things, saw their evil will, then he turned it to good so that their evil became our salvation . . . Now the Jews and the shameless traitor who plotted against him are guilty of Christ's death, although it became eternal redemption for us; none of them shall ever come to the kingdom of Christ unless they make amends for it and bow to Christ.'

Andrew P. Scheil

Ælfric wants his audience to understand that the Jews did not 'defeat' Christ or ultimately do anything beyond the scope of God's power.[23] Preaching the omnipotence of God on the one hand, and the vulnerability of that same God to Jews on the other, raises the ambiguities of interpretation Ælfric worries about in his Prefaces.[24] The Jews open up a space for *gedwild* ('error' or 'heresy') and Ælfric rushes to fill the gap before Anglo-Saxon minds become confused.

Two homilies exemplify the way anti-Judaic rhetoric can appear with disarming speed in Ælfric's works. Ælfric rails against Jews after extolling the miracles performed at the tombs of two English saints. At the end of *St Swithun*, Ælfric professes his inability to detail all the miracles which Swithun performed and then notes the importance of miracles as signs of Christ's power on earth: 'þyllice tacna cyþað þæt crist is ælmihtig god . þe his halgan geswutelode þurh swylce wel-dæda . þeah ðe ða Iudeiscan þurh deofol beswicene . nellon gelyfan on þone lyfigendan crist . ærðan þe antecrist ofslagen bið þurh god . þonne bugað þa earmingas on ende þysre worulde ðe þær to lafe beoð mid geleafan to criste . and ða ærran losiað þe ær noldon gelyfan.'[25] A very similar invective appears in a discussion of English saints at the end of *St Edmund*:

Synd eac fela oðre on angel-cynne halgan þe fela wundra wyrcað . swa swa hit wide is cuð þam ælmihtigan to lofe . þe hi on gelyfdon . Crist geswutelaþ mannum þurh his mæran halgan þæt he is ælmihtig god þe macað swilce wundra þeah þe þa earman iudei hine eallunge wið-socen . for-þan-þe hi synd awyrgede swa swa hi wiscton him sylfum . Ne beoð nane wundra geworhte æt heora byrgenum . for-ðan-þe hi ne gelyfað on þone lifigendan crist . ac crist geswutelað mannum hwær se soða geleafa is . þonne he swylce wundra wyrcð þurh his halgan wide geond þas eorðan.[26]

---

[23] For the anti-semitism inherent in representations of the passion in the later Middle Ages, see T. H. Bestul, *Texts of the Passion: Latin Devotional Literature and Medieval Society* (Philadelphia, PA, 1996), pp. 69–110.

[24] Ælfric's concern for the possibility of error in the interpretation of scripture is well known: see the Prefaces to the First and Second Series of *Catholic Homilies*, the *Lives of Saints* and the *Preface to Genesis*, collected in *Ælfric's Prefaces*, ed. J. Wilcox (Durham, 1994).

[25] *St Swithun*, I, no. 21, lines 435–42: 'Such signs make known that Christ is almighty God, who revealed his saints through such good deeds, although the Jews, deceived by the devil, will not believe in the living Christ until the Antichrist is slain by God. Then the miserable ones who are left over at the end of the world shall submit to Christ with belief, and the men of old shall be lost who previously would not believe.'

[26] *St Edmund*, II, no. 32, lines 264–75: 'Among the English (as it is widely known) there are also many other saints who work many miracles as praise to the Almighty in whom they believed. Through his glorious saints Christ reveals to men that he is almighty God who makes such miracles, although the miserable Jews completely scorned him because they are accursed, just as they wished for themselves. No miracles are wrought at their tombs because they do not believe in the living Christ, but Christ makes clear to men where the true belief is when he works such miracles through his saints far and wide across this earth.'

Anti-Judaism in Ælfric's Lives of Saints

In both of these cases, Ælfric singles out the Jews for special condemnation even as he presses the validity of these miracles upon his audience.[27] Miracles at the resting places of the saints are continuing expressions of God's power and his ultimate triumph beyond death, but such events might stretch the credulity of the audience, especially if they were performed somewhat recently on English soil. The Jews are the archetypal 'unbelievers' and will pay for their doubts until the end times. Ælfric adds the example of the Jews as a reinforcement to the manifest nature of these divine signs in the earthly realm. He wants to authenticate native English saints, and to establish their claim to the kingdom of heaven beyond any shadow of a doubt. The sterility of Jewish sacred places (whatever those might be in Ælfric's imagination) is a strong contrast to the overflowing divine presence at the tombs of Swithun and Edmund, and thus bolsters the English claims by deflecting any doubts onto the Jews.

In other texts, Ælfric plays the role of 'cultural anthropologist', explaining the strange customs of an unknown people. Old English texts often express a curiosity about other people and places, and Ælfric guides the reader through his understanding of Jewish culture.[28] An episode in the *Chair of St Peter* contains just such a digression. Ælfric comments on the Jewish reluctance, in the Old Testament, to enter a heathen household: 'þa iudeiscan wendon þæt hi ana wæron gode gecorene . and forþy swa cwædon . On ealdum dagum under moyses . æ . noldon þa iudeiscan genealecan þam hæþenum . ne mid him gereordian . and swyþe rihtlice þa . forþan þe hi gelyfdon on þane lifigendan god . and þa hæðenan gelyfdon on þa leasan godas . þaðe næron godas ac gramlice deofle.'[29] Ælfric anticipates questions we can no longer hear: why did the Jews worry about eating with pagans? were the Jews themselves pagans? if they were not pagans, were they beloved of God? We will see similar notes toward a definition of Jewish culture in *Maccabees*. In the *Chair of St Peter* Ælfric carefully situates the Jewish customs in their proper temporal setting 'in the old days, under Moses' Law'. He clearly demarcates Old Testament Jewish culture in order to prevent his people from reaching any uninformed conclusions that might lead them into heresy. As he teaches the English about Jews in this passage, Ælfric notes the righteousness of the Jews in the Old

---

[27] The passage condemning the Jews is not in Ælfric's source for his *vita* of Edmund, the Latin *Passio S. Eadmundi* by Abbo of Fleury: see *Three Lives of English Saints*, ed. M. Winterbottom (Toronto, 1972), pp. 67–87.

[28] Many texts exemplify this ethnographic curiosity, including *Beowulf*, *The Wonders of the East*, *Alexander's Letter to Aristotle*, the voyage of Ohthere and Wulfstan digression in the Old English translation of Orosius, *Widsith*, etc.

[29] *Chair of St Peter*, I, no. 10, lines 176–83: 'The Jews thought that they alone were chosen by God, and therefore spoke thus. In the old days under the law of Moses, the Jews would not come near the heathens or eat with them, and rightly so at that time because they believed in the living God and the heathens believed in false gods, who were not gods but rather fierce devils.'

Testament, especially when compared to their pagan enemies. However, this identification conflicts with Ælfric's lesson that the Jews of the New Testament were the wicked killers of Christ. The paradox is that the 'iudeiscan wæron fram gode. and hi næron fram gode'.[30] Ælfric uses typology to unravel this Gordian knot, but, at a deep level, the tangled representations remain unresolved.

Typological interpretation of the Old Testament allows Jewish narratives to be recast and neutralized for a Christian readership. James Parkes explains that '[f]or the Gentile Church the Old Testament no longer meant a way of life, a conception of the relation of a whole community to God, but a mine from which proof texts could be extracted'.[31] In general, Ælfric follows Augustine's formula: 'Testamentum enim vetus velatio est novi Testamenti, et Testamentum novum revelatio est veteris Testamenti.'[32] Through this process of appropriation, the New Testament encloses or dominates the narratives of the Old Testament and subordinates them to a Christian hermeneutic.[33] In this typological paradigm, the Jews of the Old Testament are God's chosen people, but only within the context of the Old Testament as preparation for the New; the Jews forfeit their chosen status when they murder Christ. The mediating presence of typology renders the Jews and their stories obsolete, a footnote to the overarching story of Christianity; Ecclesia replaces Synagoga.[34] Whether the Jews are right or wrong in their Old Testament struggles with Yahweh does not ulti-

---

[30] *Dominica .V. Quadrigesimae*, *Ælfric's Catholic Homilies: the Second Series*, ed. M. Godden, EETS ss 5 (London, 1979), 128, lines 50–1: 'The Jews were from God and they were not from God.'

[31] *The Conflict of the Church and the Synagogue: a Study in the Origins of Anti-Semitism* (Philadelphia, PA, 1961), p. 374.

[32] Augustine, *Sermones de sanctis (Sermo CCC: In solemnitate martyrum Machabaeorum)*, PL 38, col. 1377: 'Indeed, the Old Testament is the veil of the New Testament, and the New Testament is the revelation of the Old Testament'. P. Clemoes notes the importance of typological interpretation of the Old Testament for Ælfric ('Chronology', p. 240); see also P. E. Szarmach, 'Ælfric as Exegete: Approaches and Examples in the Study of the *Sermones Catholici*', *Hermeneutics and Medieval Culture*, ed. P. J. Gallacher and H. Damico (Albany, NY, 1989), pp. 237–47. E. Auerbach's essay 'Figura', in his *Scenes from the Drama of European Literature* (1944; repr. Minneapolis, MN, 1984), pp. 11–76 contains essential background material.

[33] J. P. Hermann labels this process 'sublation', the 'incorporation of a prior stage or concept by a subsequent one' (*Allegories of War: Language and Violence in Old English Poetry* (Ann Arbor, MI, 1989), p. 55). See also the comments of H. Bloom on the relationship between the Old and New Testament in '"Before Moses Was, I Am": the Original and the Belated Testaments', *Notebooks in Cultural Analysis I*, ed. N. F. Cantor and N. King (Durham, NC, 1984), pp. 3–14.

[34] On the iconography of Ecclesia and Synagoga, see M. Schlauch, 'The Allegory of Church and Synagogue', *Speculum* 14 (1939), 448–64; W. S. Seiferth, *Synagogue and Church in the Middle Ages: Two Symbols in Art and Literature*, trans. L. Chadeayne and P. Gottwald (New York, 1970); M. Camille, *The Gothic Idol: Ideology and Image-Making in Medieval Art* (Cambridge, 1989), pp. 178–80; and R. Mellinkoff, *Outcasts: Signs of Otherness in Northern European Art of the Late Middle Ages*, 2 vols. (Berkeley, CA, 1993) I, 48–51.

mately matter from the Christian perspective; what Ælfric establishes is that, for good or ill, those were the old ways, the old law, the former people, while Ælfric and his audience are the new chosen favourites of God. As Jill Robbins suggests, '[t]he dead letter, the old law, has to be there as something to pass through, to go beyond'.[35] Ælfric's typological understanding of the Old Testament displaces the nation of Israel in order to construct and explore the boundaries of a Christian community.[36] The Jews are emptied of any independent cultural identity of their own and thus resemble a mathematical variable able to be placed into many equations, not valuable in and of itself, but necessary for the final 'answer'; that answer constitutes what Hayden White calls 'ostensive self-definition by negation'.[37]

Honoured yet derided, repudiated yet ever-present, external yet internal, the Jews embody a rhetorical effect of Christian identity. By repudiating Judaism, defining it as lack, Christianity inexorably yokes itself into a tormented relationship with its sibling. This ambivalence gives the Jews a curious ideological mobility, a capacity to be deployed as sheer rhetoric in the flux of everyday life. The anti-Judaism of Ælfric's homily *Maccabees* in the *Lives of Saints* exemplifies this capacity for the Christian understanding of the Jews to function as a mobile, all-purpose political signifier in specific historical circumstances.[38]

Maccabees is a translation and condensation of the Vulgate text (I and II Maccabees), arranged in an original order by Ælfric and interspersed with brief commentary drawn from other parts of the Bible, Ælfric's own reflections and a

---

[35] *Prodigal Son / Elder Brother: Interpretation and Alterity in Augustine, Petrarch, Kafka, Levinas* (Chicago, 1991), p. 40.

[36] M. Godden notes that Anglo-Saxon interpretation of the Old Testament was multifaceted and often moved beyond typology to a use of these narratives as a repository of culturally significant resonances: 'Allegory was used to make the Old Testament safe for Christian readers or to make it consonant with the New Testament by discovering Christian doctrines such as the Trinity hidden within it. But allegorical interpretation soon became a way of using the Old Testament, and the New Testament as well, as a vast store-book of imagery, a source of riddling metaphors and imaginative parallels. The impetus here is not to save the Old Testament for Christianity but to invite the reader to see imaginative parallels between moral truths and physical actuality, or between spiritual experience and historical events' ('Biblical Literature: the Old Testament', *The Cambridge Companion to Old English Literature*, ed. M. Godden and M. Lapidge (Cambridge, 1991), pp. 206–26, at 208).

[37] *Tropics of Discourse: Essays in Cultural Criticism* (Baltimore, MD, 1978), pp. 151–2. P. Stallybrass and A. White call this process the 'law of exclusion' in *The Politics and Poetics of Transgression* (Ithaca, NY, 1986), p. 25, and Mellinkoff describes it as 'who was included in the great feast of life and who was excluded' (*Outcasts* I, p. li).

[38] Cf. the work of S. Gilman, who describes his investigations of nineteenth- and twentieth-century anti-semitism as an attempt to 'understand how stereotypes are generated, how they are embedded in cultural artifacts (texts, in the widest sense of the word), and, most important, how once sanctioned in this arena they form the basis for action' (*Inscribing the Other* (Lincoln, NE, 1991), p. 11).

Andrew P. Scheil

few other sources.[39] At the beginning of the homily, Jewish dietary prohibitions provoke Ælfric into an 'anthropological' digression similar to the one in the *Chair of St Peter*; here Ælfric explains the puzzling customs of Jewish culture to his audience. The first major episode of the homily is the 'martyrdom' of Eleazar from II Maccabees VI. The heathens seize the old scribe Eleazar and 'hi bestungon him on muþ mid mycelre ðreatunge þone fulan mete þe moyses forbead godes folce to þicgenne . for þære gastlican getacnunge'.[40] Before the narrative can move forward, Ælfric interrupts: 'We moton nu secgan swutellicor be ðysum . hwylce mettas wæron mannum forbodene on ðære ealdan . æ . þe mann ett nu swa-ðeah.'[41] Ælfric then attempts to explicate Jewish dietary prescriptions in lines 37–84, relying on Leviticus, Deuteronomy and pseudo-Bede.[42] He first defines the nature of the forbidden meat, condensing material from Leviticus XI.2–47: under the Old Law, unclean beasts do not chew their cud and/or they possess uncloven hooves.[43] Having established what literally defines 'unclean flesh', Ælfric next unfolds the hidden significance behind these distinctions. Clean beasts symbolize men who meditate on God's will and mull over his teachings, like the chewing of cud.[44] Unclean beasts 'getacniað ða þe

---

[39] For the sources of the homily, see G. Loomis, 'Further Sources of Ælfric's Saints' Lives', *Harvard Stud. in Philol. and Lit.* 13 (1931), 1–8, at 2–3, and the more comprehensive discussion by S. Lee, 'Ælfric's Treatment of Source Material in his Homily on the Books of the Maccabees', *Bull. of the John Rylands Univ. Lib. of Manchester* 77 (1995), 165–76. Ælfric's *Maccabees* is extant in several copies. London, BL, Cotton Julius E. vii, s. xi[in.] (Ker no. 162) is the base manuscript for Skeat's edition of the *Lives of Saints*. Other manuscripts include Cambridge, Corpus Christi College 198, s. xi[1] (Ker no. 48); Cambridge, Corpus Christi College 303, s. xii[1] (Ker no. 57); Cambridge, University Library Ii. I. 33, s. xii[2] (Ker no. 18; an acephelous copy, beginning at line 319 according to Skeat's edition). London, BL, Cotton Vitellius D. xvii, s. xi[med.] (Ker no. 222) lacks most of the homily due to fire damage, ending at line 29; Cambridge, Queen's College [Horne] 75, s. xi[in] (Ker no. 81) is only a fragment, containing just the first eight lines of the homily. The 'Ker' numbers refer to N. R. Ker, *Catalogue of Manuscripts containing Anglo-Saxon* (Oxford, 1957). See also Hill, 'Dissemination of Ælfric's *Lives of Saints*', pp. 250–2.

[40] *Maccabees*, II, no. 25, lines 34–6, hereafter cited by line numbers only: 'they stuck in his mouth, with many threats, the foul meat which Moses prohibited God's people to eat because of its spiritual signification'. Note that Ælfric adds the clause 'which Moses forbade God's people to taste because of its spiritual signification' to his source in the Vulgate; he immediately begins to explains *why* this particular meat is anathema to the Jews: 'igitur Eleazarus de primoribus scribarum vir aetate provectus et vultu decorus aperto ore hians conpellebatur carnem porcinam manducare' (II Maccabees VI.18: 'Therefore Eleazar, one of the foremost scribes, a man advanced in age and noble in appearance, was compelled to open his mouth wide and to eat pig's flesh'). All references to the Vulgate are to *Biblia Sacra iuxta vulgatam versionem*, ed. R. Weber, 4th ed. (Stuttgart, 1994).

[41] *Maccabees*, lines 37–9: 'We must now speak more clearly about these things, which meats were forbidden to men in the old law which men eat now nevertheless.'

[42] Lev. XI; Deut. XIV.3–21; pseudo-Bede, *In Pentateuchum commentarii – Leviticus*, PL 91, cols. 345–6. [43] *Maccabees*, lines 40–5.

[44] *Ibid.* lines 46–9. Bede applies the same simile to Caedmon in the *Historia ecclesiastica* IV.24. After displaying his miraculous poetic gifts, Caedmon is taught sacred history, with the result that 'At

tela nellað . ne nellað leornian hwæt gode leof sy . ne on heora mode wealcan þæs hælendes beboda'.[45] Immediately, Ælfric overlays the binary opposition clean/unclean with an opposition between understanding and not-understanding, or proper interpretation and improper interpretation. The Jews are not yet identified with either category in this passage, but Ælfric's binary logic begins to replicate itself analogically, establishing categories he later uses to define the Jews.

Ælfric restates the distinction between clean and unclean in slightly different terms, elaborating the interpretation of these categories. Beasts that cleave their claws and chew cud signify faithful Christians who accept both the Old and New Testament and 'ceowað godes beboda symle mid smeagunge'.[46] Unclean beasts either do not chew their cud, or do not cleave their claws 'for ðære getacnunge þe ða towerd wæs . þæt we to-cleofan ure clawa on þam twam gecyðnyssum . on ðære ealdan . and on ðære niwan þæt is . æ . and godspel'.[47] Ælfric's explanation of the Jewish diet proceeds through three analogical binary oppositions. Why does Eleazar refuse to eat the meat? The meat is unclean because there are clean and unclean beasts. What do clean and unclean beasts signify? They signify those who understand the word of God and those who do not. Who does not understand the word of God? Those who accept the New Testament understand; those who do not accept it do not understand. Having established the parameters of his analysis, Ælfric places the Jews into the paradigm: 'Swa swa ða iudeiscan þe urne drihten forseoð . and his godspel bodunge to bysmre habbað syndon unclæne . and criste andsæte þeah ðe hi moyses . æ . on heora muðe wealcon . and nellað under-standan butan þæt steaflice andgit.'[48] The Jews do not 'cleave their claws' (that is, accept both the Old and New Testament), and are therefore unclean. The irony of Ælfric's interpretation is that he began this analysis in order to elaborate the virtue and heroism of the martyr Eleazar in the face of heathen persecution, but ends the explanation by condemning the Jews. He later clarifies the difference between heroic Old

---

ipse cuncta, quae audiendo discere poterat, rememorando secum et quasi mundum animal ruminando, in carmen dulcissimum conuertebat' ('He learned all he could by listening to them and then, memorizing it and ruminating over it like some clean animal chewing the cud, he turned it into the most melodious verse'): *Bede's Ecclesiastical History of the English People*, ed. B. Colgrave and R. A. B. Mynors (Oxford, 1969), pp. 418–19.

[45] *Maccabees*, lines 51–3: 'signify those who do not desire properly, neither to learn what may be pleasing to God, nor to revolve in their mind the commands of the Saviour'.

[46] *Ibid.* line 60: 'always chew God's commands with reflection'.

[47] *Ibid.* lines 64–6: 'for the signification, which then was still to come, that we cleave our claws in the two testaments, in the Old and in the New, that is the Law and the Gospel'.

[48] *Ibid.* lines 69–73: 'So thus the Jews who reject our Lord and hold his Gospel preaching in contempt are unclean and repugnant to Christ though they revolve the Law of Moses in their mouth and do not wish to understand [anything] except the literal meaning.'

Testament Jews and evil New Testament Jews, but here the rhetoric of binary oppositions, through an inexorable process of analogy, leads him to anti-Judaic invective.

In the remainder of his commentary on the subject, Ælfric retraces the ground he has already covered, driving home the distinction between Old Law and New Testament. Using a citation from Titus I.15, he explains that '[f]ela wæron forbodene godes folce on ðære . æ . þe nu syndon clæne æfter cristes to-cyme . siððan paulus cwæð to þam cristenum ðus *Omnia munda mundis*; Ealle ðincg syndon clæne þam clænum mannum . þam ungeleaffullan and unclænum nis nan þincg clæne'.[49] However, after citing this universal dispensation, Ælfric continues to explicate these confusing categories: 'Hara wæs ða unclæne forðan ðe he nis clifer-fete . and swin wæs ða unclæne forðan þe hit ne ceow his cudu . Sume wæron þa fule þe nu synd eac fule . ac hit biþ to langsum eall her to logigenne be ðam clænum nytenum . oððe be þam unclænum on ðære ealdan . æ . þe mann ett nu swa-ðeah.'[50] Ælfric takes great pains to make these distinctions, yet he refrains from proceeding into further detail: the digression ends abruptly as he closes the argument before it gets too complex for his audience to understand.[51] At this point the forward momentum of the narrative resumes and Eleazar, who refuses to eat the unclean meat, 'mid geleafan his lif ge-endode'.[52]

The text attempts to mediate the 'problem' of Jewish dietary laws, their puzzling nature to a Christian Anglo-Saxon audience, through typology and the rhetoric of binary oppositions. The Jewish dietary prescriptions in the episode of Eleazar call attention to the Jews as a distinct culture, different from Christianity in their customs and ways of life. In addition to spiritual

---

[49] *Ibid.* lines 74–8: 'Many things were forbidden to God's people in the Law, which are now clean after the coming of Christ, since Paul spoke to the Christians in this fashion: "Omnia munda mundis": All things are clean to clean men; there is nothing clean to the unfaithful and unclean.' Cf. Titus I.15: 'omnia munda mundis coinquinatis autem et infidelibus nihil mundum sed inquinatae sunt eorum et mens et conscientia' ('To clean men all things are clean: however, to the corrupt and unbelieving nothing is pure, but both their mind and their conscience are stained').

[50] *Maccabees*, lines 79–84: 'A hare was then unclean, because he is not cloven-footed, and a swine was then unclean because it did not chew its cud. Some were then foul that are still foul; but it will be too tedious to explain here completely concerning the clean beasts or concerning the unclean beasts in the old law, which one nevertheless now eats.'

[51] Cf. the dialogue between master and fisherman in Ælfric's *Colloquy*: 'Quid si immundi fuerint pisces? Ego proiciam immundos foras, et sumo mihi mundos in escam' ('What if the fish are unclean? I throw the unclean ones away, and I take the clean ones for my food') (*Ælfric's Colloquy*, ed. G. A. Garmonsway, 2nd ed. (London, 1947), lines 94–5). Deut. XIV.9–10 prohibits the eating of fish without scales or fins (e.g. eels), but since this is an Old Testament prohibition, and for Ælfric's audience 'omnia munda mundis', why should the fisherman throw back 'unclean' fish? Clearly the matter is one of some confusion for Ælfric.

[52] *Maccabees*, line 107: 'ended his life with faith'.

Anti-Judaism in Ælfric's Lives of Saints

significations, historical and cultural analyses propel Ælfric's explication. In another example of 'cultural lore', when elephants intrude into the narrative of *Maccabees*, Ælfric pauses to identify and describe this strange animal for his Anglo-Saxon audience.[53] Like elephants, Jews are beyond the actual experience of the English, and invite explanation.

In *Maccabees*, Ælfric moves between two opposed representations of the Jewish people: in the Old Testament they are courageous believers in the one true God, but in the New Testament they are the treacherous slayers of Christ. Ælfric depicts the Maccabees as a noble group of God's chosen people, fighting for their land, beliefs and lives against overwhelming heathen opposition. Mattathias leads the first revolt and, with God's help, drives back the enemy: 'þæt werod weox ða swyðe þe wæs mid mathathian . and hi anrædlice fuhton . and afligdon ða hæðenan mid mycelre strængðe . þe modegodon ongean god'.[54] The heroic, martial tone of the homily constitutes a thorough endorsement of the Maccabees and their actions. These are not the archetypal traitors of the New Testament, but rather a noble, idealistic people facing an overwhelming, encircling enemy. Ælfric considerably simplifies his source, emphasizing the nobility of Mattathias and the divine sanction of his enterprise ('and him eac god fylste'), and omitting more problematic behaviour (such as involuntary circumcisions).[55]

After Mattathias dies, the leadership of the revolt passes to his son Judas Maccabeus, a mighty warrior against the heathens: 'Hwæt ða iudas machabeus mihtiglice aras on his fæder stede . and wiðstod his feondum . . . He wearð þa leon gelic on his gewinnum . and dædum . and todræfde þa arleasan . and his

---

[53] *Ibid.* lines 564–73. See J. E. Cross, 'The Elephant to Alfred, Ælfric, Aldhelm and Others', *SN* 37 (1965), 367–73.

[54] *Maccabees*, lines 240–2: 'The army with Mattathias grew a great deal, and they fought in unity, and with great strength they expelled the heathens, who were high-minded against God'.

[55] *Ibid.* line 244: 'and God also helped them'. See I Maccabees II.42–8: 'tunc congregata est ad eos synagoga Asideorum fortis viribus ex Israhel omnis voluntarius in lege et omnes qui fugiebant a malis additi sunt ad eos et facti sunt illis ad firmamentum et collegerunt exercitum et percusserunt peccatores in ira sua et viros iniquos in indignatione sua et ceteri fugerunt ad nationes ut evaderent et circuivit Matthathias et amici eius et destruxerunt aras et circumciderunt pueros incircumcisos quotquot invenerunt in finibus Israhel in fortitudine et persecuti sunt filios superbiae et prosperatum est opus in manu eorum et obtinuerunt legem de manibus gentium et de manibus regum et non dederunt cornu peccatori' ('Then they were joined by a synagogue of Hasidaeans, strong men of Israel, each one a volunteer on the side of the Law: all of those who fled from evils joined them and supported them. They gathered an army and struck down the sinners in their anger, and the evil men in their fury, and the rest who escaped fled to the nations in order to escape. And Mattathias and his companions marched about, and they cast down the altars and circumcised any uncircumcised boys they found within the boundaries of Israel, and they did so bravely. They hunted down the sons of pride and the work prospered in their hands. And they took the Law from the hands of the pagan tribes and the hands of the kings, and did not give the advantage to the sinners').

eðel gerymde.'[56] Judas rallies the Jews against the overwhelming number of their enemies, speaking to his followers in words one can easily imagine Wulfstan using to exhort the English:

Nis nan earfoðnyss ðam ælmihtigan gode on feawum mannum . oððe on micclum werode to helpenne on ge-feohte . and healdan þa ðe he wile . forðan þe se sige bið symle of heofonum . Ðas cumað to us swylce hi cenran syndon and willað us fordon . and awestan ure land . we soðlice feohtað for us sylfe wið hi . and for godes . æ. and god hi eac fordeð ætforan ure gesihðe . ne forhtige ge nates hwon.[57]

These Jews are certainly not afflicted with the adjectives usually employed to describe them in the *Lives of Saints*: treacherous, faithless, blind, unbelieving. The Maccabees are closer to the heroic, martial ethos characteristic of the Jews in *Judith* or *Exodus*; Ælfric encourages his people to appreciate the beleaguered Israelites, a lesson obviously appropriate to an England harassed by Viking raiders. In the *Letter to Sigeweard* Ælfric explains that he has translated Maccabees into English 'for ðan þe hig wunnon mid wæ[p]num þa swiðe wið þone hæðenan here, þe him on wann swiðe, wolde hig adilegian and adyddan of þam earde, þe him God forgeaf, and Godes lof alecgan', and he encourages the reader to 'rædon gif ge wyllað eow sylfum to ræde!'[58] Ælfric clearly thought that the Maccabees, these Old Testament Jews, were a model for the English to emulate.[59]

---

[56] *Maccabees*, lines 274–5 and 282–3: 'Lo, then Judas Maccabeus mightily arose in his father's place, and opposed his enemies . . . He then became like a lion in his struggles and deeds, and destroyed the wicked ones and cleared his country.'

[57] *Ibid.* lines 308–16: 'It is no difficulty for almighty God to help in battle and to support them whom he wishes, in regard to few men or to a large army, because victory is always from heaven. These people come against us as if they are braver, and wish to destroy us and lay waste our land; we truly fight for ourselves against them, and for the law of God, and God shall also destroy them before our sight; fear not at all.'

[58] *The Old English Version of the Heptateuch, Ælfric's Treatise on the Old and New Testament and his Preface to Genesis*, ed. S. J. Crawford, EETS os 160 (London, 1922), 49, lines 785–91 and 51, lines 837–8: 'because they fought mightily with weapons against the heathen army, which fought mightily against them, and wished to destroy them and eliminate them from the land that God had given them, and to suppress the love of God' . . . 'read them (if you wish) for your own instruction'.

[59] Godden observes the 'interest in military and political parallels at the literal level' of *Maccabees* and speculates on the political context of the *Lives*: 'It is probably no coincidence that the collection was commissioned by Æthelweard, the ealdorman responsible for the military defence of the south-west against the Vikings; Æthelweard also commissioned the translation of the book of Joshua, another account of heroic battles against the heathens' ('Biblical Literature', p. 219). See also his 'Apocalypse and Invasion in Late Anglo-Saxon England', *From Anglo-Saxon to Early Middle English*, ed. M. Godden, D. Gray and T. Hoad (Oxford, 1994), pp. 130–62, for more analysis of the Anglo-Saxon 'literary response' to Viking invasion. The tenth century saw a surge of interest in using the Maccabees as exemplars: see J. Dunbabin, 'The Maccabees as Exemplars in the Tenth and Eleventh Centuries', *The Bible in the Medieval World: Essays in Memory of Beryl Smalley*, ed. K. Walsh and D. Wood (Oxford, 1985), pp. 31–41.

Anti-Judaism in Ælfric's Lives of Saints

Although Ælfric overtly praises the virtues of the Maccabees, he eventually needs to include the full arc of Jewish character. Before Ælfric extols their nobility at too great length, he hastens to add more information so that his audience does not think that *all* Jews are worthy of imitation like the Maccabees.[60] After describing the divine intervention of five angels on Judas's behalf, he adds an extended discussion of the Jews:

> þa Iudeiscan wæron ða dyreste gode . on ðære ealdan . æ . forðan þe hi ana wurðodon þone ælmihtigan god mid biggencgum symle . oþ þæt crist godes sunu sylf wearð acenned . of menniscum gecynde of þam Iudeiscum cynne . of marian þam mædene butan menniscum fæder . þa noldon hi sume gelyfan þæt he soð god wære . ac syrwdon embe his lif . swa swa he sylf geðafode; Wæron swa-þeah manega of þam mancynne . gode . ge on ðære ealdan . æ . ge eac on þære niwan . heah-fæderas . and witegan . and halige apostolas . and fela ðusenda þe folgiað criste . þeah þe hi sume wunian wiðerwerde oþ þis . Hi sceolon swa-þeah ealle on ende gelyfan . ac ðær losiað to fela on þam fyrste betwux . for heora heard-heortnysse wið þone heofonlican hælend.[61]

Ælfric vacillates considerably in this comment, moving back and forth between praise and condemnation of the Jews. They were dear to God in the Old Testament because they were monotheists, yet when Christ was born they did not accept him and consequently murdered him. Some of the Jews were good; some even now refuse to believe. All will repent and believe at Judgement Day, but many hard-hearted Jews will die and suffer damnation until then. Ælfric expresses a similar conflict when he relates the death of Antiochus and the tyranny of his son Eupator: 'Se wearð eac ongebroht þæt he ofslean wolde þa geleaffullan iudei . þe gelyfdon ða on god . Hi gelyfdon þa on þa ealdan wisan . on þone ælmihtigan god þeah ðe hi sume wið-socon siðþan þone hælend . and eac swa ofslogon swa swa he sylf wolde.'[62] The whole point of the homily is to praise the fortitude of the Old Testament Jews, and Ælfric applies his considerable aesthetic skills to the task; he intends to write a compelling adaptation of the biblical

---

[60] See J. Wilcox, 'A Reluctant Translator in Late Anglo-Saxon England: Ælfric and Maccabees', *Proc. of the Med. Assoc. of the Midwest II*, ed. M. Storm (Emporia, KS, 1994), pp. 1–18, at 6–7 for a similar conclusion. Wilcox's study complements my analysis of *Maccabees* at several points, although he does not specifically address Ælfric's anti-Judaism.

[61] *Maccabees*, lines 514–29: 'The Jews were the dearest to God in the Old Law, because they alone ever honoured the almighty God with worship, until Christ, the son of God, was himself born of human nature, of the Jewish people, of Mary the maiden, without a human father. Then some of them would not believe that he was the true God, but conspired against his life, just as he himself allowed. However, there were many good men of that race, both in the Old Law, and also in the New, patriarchs and prophets and holy apostles, and many thousands that follow Christ, although some remain rebellious until now. However, they shall all believe in the end, but too many shall perish there, in the period between, for their hard-heartedness against the heavenly Saviour.'

[62] *Ibid.* lines 549–53: 'He [Eupator] also was inclined so that he wished to kill the faithful Jews, who believed then in God. Then they believed in almighty God according to the old ways, although some of them afterwards rejected the Saviour, and also killed him, just as he himself desired.'

Maccabees and inspire the English through the power of his work. However, the logic of typology leads him to the New Testament when narrating the Old, to the Jews who spurned Christ when praising the 'faithful Jews' of *Maccabees*. Concerned as he is with misinterpretation, the task of writing an encomium to Jews that also acknowledges their later crimes was a delicate balancing act.

Ælfric does not stop with drawing these binary distinctions between good and bad Jews, Old and New Testament, as ambivalence over Jews is only part of his anti-Judaism. In *Maccabees*, this anxiety over the correct assessment of Jews and their culture is organized in such a way that it participates in the social conflict of tenth-century England; *Maccabees* fits Fredric Jameson's characterization of narrative as 'a symbolic move in an essentially polemic and strategic ideological confrontation between the classes'.[63] As we shall see, the representation of the Jew serves Ælfric as a strategy to assert a particular vision of society.

The death of Judas Maccabeus occasions another long commentary by Ælfric that sets the stage for his subsequent exposition of Anglo-Saxon society in the text. He begins by praising the might of Judas and his innumerable victories:

Ne synd swa-þeah awritene þæs ðe wyrd-writeras sæcgaþ . ealle iudan gefeoht for his freonda ware . and ealle ða mihte þe he mærlice gefremode his folce to gebeorge . swa swa us bec secgað . Menig-fealde wæron his micclan gefeoht . and he is eall swa halig on ðære ealdan gecyðnysse . swa swa godes gecorenan on ðære godspel-bodunge . forðan þe he æfre wan for willan þæs ælmihtigan.[64]

Ælfric stresses Judas's holiness and right to be considered a 'saint' even though he lived and died before Christ, but in the next lines he places Judas's virtue in a specific context, and shows how the nature of the heroic Old Testament Jew is historically supplanted by the advent of Christ:

On þam dagum wæs alyfed to alecgenne his fynd . and swiþost ða hæðenan þe him hetole wæron . and se wæs godes ðegen þe ða swiðost feaht wið heora onwinnendan to ware heora leoda . ac crist on his tocyme us cydde oðre ðincg . and het us healdan sibbe . and soðfæstnysse æfre . and we sceolon winnan wið þa wælhreowan fynd . þæt synd ða ungesewenlican . and þa swicolan deofla þe willað ofslean ure sawla mid leahtrum.[65]

---

[63] *The Political Unconscious: Narrative as a Socially Symbolic Act* (Ithaca, NY, 1981), p. 85.

[64] *Maccabees*, lines 676–83: 'Nevertheless (as books tell us), according to historians all the battles of Judas for the defence of his friends, and all the mighty deeds which he gloriously performed in defence of his people are not written down. Manifold were his great battles; and he is as holy in the Old Testament, as God's chosen ones in the Gospel-preaching, because he ever struggled for the will of the Almighty.'

[65] *Ibid.* lines 684–92: 'In those days he was allowed to conquer his enemies, and most of all the heathens, who were angry against him; and he was the thane of God who fought most often against their conquerors, in defence of their people. But with his coming Christ taught us another thing, and commanded us ever to hold peace and truthfulness; and we should fight against the blood-thirsty enemies, that is, the invisible ones and the deceitful devils, that wish to slay our souls with sins.'

Ælfric again deploys a binary opposition to understand Judas. By contrasting the 'old days' with the here and now of the Christian era, he shows that to be a servant of God *and* a Jew is inherently deficient; only Christians possess the true knowledge of faithful service. Admirable as Judas's deeds are, according to Ælfric they designate a Jew who cannot move beyond the literal level of interpretation: for Judas Maccabeus, to be a successful servant of God means to fight battles in the physical world because that is the only understanding available to him. Like the blind Jews who cannot recognize the spiritual significance of the manna in *De populo Israhel*, the heroic leader of the Maccabees is deficient in understanding, this time in terms of vocation. The ultimate servant of God, according to Ælfric, is not a worldly warrior, but rather a spiritual one. Yes, it is a good thing to fight for your people, as Judas Maccabeus did, but Christ irrevocably transformed the ideals of service, and now the real, important battle is the one against the invisible, spiritual foe:

> . . . wið ða we sceolon winnan mid gastlicum wæpnum . and biddan us gescyldnysse simle æt criste . þæt we moton ofer-winnan þa wælhreowan leahtras . and þæs deofles tihtinge . þæt he us derian ne mæge . þonne beoð we godes cempan on ðam gastlican gefeohte . gif we ðone deofol forseoþ þurh soðne geleafan . and þa heafod-leahtras þurh gehealtsumnysse . and gif we godes willan mid weorcum gefremmað . þæt ealde godes folc sceolde feohtan þa mid wæpnum . and heora gewinn hæfde haligra manna getacnunge . þe to-dræfað þa leahtras and deofla heom fram on ðære niwan gecyðnysse þe crist sylf astealde.[66]

Ælfric carefully puts together his argument: he lavishly praises the Maccabees and their heroism throughout the homily, but then, in a rhetorical turnabout, he surprises the reader by saying that, admirable as they are, the Maccabees were only Jews and could only do so much. The ultimate service to God is carried on by fighting spiritual battles as opposed to physical ones. Who shall therefore lead the spiritual fight? Who is the best servant of God?

Ælfric gives the answer in his wider discussion of society in the brief exposition entitled *Qui sunt oratores, laboratores, bellatores* appended to the homily.[67] In this epilogue, Ælfric analyses the three orders of society, one of the oldest

---

[66] *Ibid.* lines 693–704: '. . . against them [i.e. the invisible enemies] we should fight with spiritual weapons, and pray continually to Christ for our protection, that we can overcome cruel sins and the temptations of the devil, so that he can not harm us. Then we will be God's champions in the spiritual fight, if we scorn the devil through true belief, and the chief sins through self-control, and if we carry out the will of God with our works. The old people of God had to fight then with weapons, and their struggle had the signification of holy men who drive out sins and devils from them in the New Testament that Christ himself established'.

[67] This item follows the text of *Maccabees* in Julius E. vii, CCCC 198, CCCC 303 and CUL Ii. i. 33 (see above, p. 74, n. 39). In addition, the item is found independently in Cambridge, Corpus Christi College 178, s. xi[1] (Ker no. 41) and Oxford, Bodleian Library, Hatton 115, s. xi[2]–xii[med]. (Ker no. 332). See Hill, 'Dissemination of Ælfric's *Lives of Saints*', pp. 250–2.

examples of the medieval commonplace: 'Is swa-ðeah to witenne þæt on þysre worulde synd þreo endebyrdnysse on annysse gesette . þæt synd *laboratores . oratores . bellatores . laboratores* synd þa þe urne bigleafan beswincað . *oratores* synd þa ðe us to gode geðingiað . *bellatores* synd þa ðe ure burga healdað . and urne eard be-weriað wið onwinnendne here.'[68] After introducing the three orders, Ælfric elaborates their duties: 'Nu swincð se yrðlincg embe urne bigleofan . and se woruld-cempa sceall winnan wið ure fynd and se godes þeowa sceall symle for us gebiddan . and feohtan gastlice . wið þa ungesewenlican fynd.'[69] Here, we see the fruit of Ælfric's earlier commentary in the homily.[70] Having previously

---

[68] *Maccabees*, lines 812–18: 'However, it is apparent that in this world there are three orders, set in unity; these are *laboratores, oratores, bellatores. Laboratores* are they who produce our food; *oratores* are they who intercede with God for us; *bellatores* are they who protect our towns, and defend our land against an invading army.' The recent discussion by T. E. Powell in 'The "Three Orders" of Society in Anglo-Saxon England', *ASE* 23 (1994), 103–32 investigates the use of the tripartite motif by King Alfred, Ælfric, Wulfstan and the author of the *Vita S. Dunstani*, known as 'B'. Powell's discussion of the source of this scheme is exhaustive, but he concludes that Ælfric's direct source (probably Latin and Frankish) remains a mystery (p. 117). See also G. Duby, *The Three Orders: Feudal Society Imagined*, trans. A. Goldhammer (Chicago, IL, 1980), pp. 99–109; M. Godden, 'Money, Power and Morality in Late Anglo-Saxon England', *ASE* 19 (1990), 41–65, at 55–6; and G. Constable, *Three Studies in Medieval Religious and Social Thought: the Interpretation of Mary and Martha, the Ideal of the Imitation of Christ, the Orders of Society* (Cambridge, 1995), pp. 249–341.

[69] *Maccabees*, lines 819–22: 'Now the farmer works for our food, and the worldly warrior must fight against our enemies, and the servant of God must always pray for us, and fight spiritually against unseen enemies.' Cf. Ælfric's repetition of the theme in the Old English *Letter to Sigeweard* (*Old English Heptateuch*, ed. Crawford, pp. 71–2, lines 1204–20) and the Latin *Letter to Wulfstan* (*Councils and Synods, with other Documents relating to the English Church. I. A.D. 871–1204*, ed. D. Whitelock, M. Brett and C. N. L. Brooke, 2 vols. (Oxford, 1981), p. 252). Powell discusses the changing historical circumstances behind these different versions ('Three Orders', pp. 110–15 and 117–24).

[70] At the end of *Maccabees* Ælfric asserts his authority to speak not only about martial conflict in general, but also to demonstrate his knowledge of the peril of Viking attack current in the land: 'Secgað swa-þeah lareowas þæt synd feower cynna gefeoht . *iustum* . þæt is rihtlic . *iniustum* . unrihtlic . *civile* . betwux ceaster-gewarum . *Plusquam civile* . betwux siblingum . *Iustum bellum* . is rihtlic gefeoht wið ða reðan flot-menn . oþþe wið oðre þeoda þe eard willað fordon . Unrihtlic gefeoht is þe of yrre cymð . þæt þridde gefeoht þe of geflite cymð . betwux ceaster-gewarum is swyðe pleolic . and þæt feorðe gefeoht þe betwux freondum bið . is swiðe earmlic and endeleas sorh' (lines 705–14: 'However, teachers say that there are four types of war: *justum*, that is, just; *injustum*, that is, unjust; *civile*, between citizens; *plusquam civile*, between relatives. *Justum bellum* is just war against the cruel seamen, or against other peoples that wish to destroy the land. Unjust war is that which comes from anger. The third war, which comes from strife between citizens, is very dangerous; and the fourth war, that is between friends, is very miserable, and endless sorrow'). Ælfric follows Isidore of Seville's discussion in the *Etymologiae* (*Isidori Hispalensis Episcopi Etymologiarum sive Originum, Libri XX*, ed. W. M. Lindsay, 2 vols. (Oxford, 1911), XVIII.i.1–11). See J. E. Cross, 'The Ethic of War in Old English', *England before the Conquest: Studies in Primary Sources presented to Dorothy Whitelock*, ed. P. Clemoes and K. Hughes (Cambridge, 1971), pp. 269–82, at 272 on Ælfric's use of sources here.

established that worldly war is the province of the 'good Jew' Judas and, in contrast, that spiritual war is the defining element of the Christian, he now proceeds to locate the importance of the monk in this vocation:

Is nu for-þy mare þæra muneca gewinn wið þa ungesewenlican deofla þe syrwiað embe us . þonne sy þæra woruld-manna þe winnað wiþ ða flæsclican . and wið þa gesewenlican gesewenlice feohtað . Nu ne sceolon þa woruld-cempan to þam woruld-licum gefeohte þa godes þeowan neadian fram þam gastlican gewinne . forðan þe him fremað swiðor þæt þa ungesewenlican fynd beon ofer-swyðde þonne ða gesewenlican . and hit bið swyðe derigendlic þæt hi drihtnes þeowdom forlætan . and to woruld-gewinne bugan . þe him naht to ne gebyriað.[71]

Ælfric makes the final link in his extended argument, which began with Judas Maccabeus, by highlighting his own monastic order and accentuating its non-combatant role in English society:

Nu se munuc þe bihð to benedictes regole . and forlæt ealle woruld-ðinge . hwi wile he eft gecyrran to woruldlicum wæpnum . and awurpan his gewinn . wið þa ungesewenlican fynd his scyppende to teonan . Se godes þeowa ne mæg mid woruld-mannum feohtan . gif he on þam gastlican gefeohte . forð-gang habban sceall . Næs nan halig godes þeowa æfter þæs hælendes þrowunga . þe æfre on gefeohte his handa wolde afylan . ac hi for-bæron ehtnysse arleasra cwellera . and heora lif sealdon mid unscæþþignysse . for godes geleafan . and hi mid gode nu lybbað . forðan þe hi furþon noldon . ænne fugel acwellan.[72]

Here Ælfric argues for the social duties and rights of Benedictine monks. Although Timothy Powell has recently asserted that Ælfric is only addressing the infractions of weapon-bearing clergy, the general antagonism or friction *between* classes is unmistakable.[73] Ælfric's elaborate argument answers those who 'wish to compel the spiritual warrior to physical battle'. Malcolm Godden, following a suggestion by Peter Clemoes, notes that this tripartite formulation 'seems indeed to have arisen out of a need to distinguish sharply between

---

[71] *Maccabees* lines 823–32: 'Therefore the struggle of the monks against the invisible devils that plot against us is now greater than that of the worldly men, who struggle against carnal foes and visibly fight against the visible enemies. Now the worldly soldiers should not compel the servants of God away from the spiritual struggle to the worldly fight, because it will benefit them more that the invisible enemies may be overcome than the visible ones; and it will be very harmful that they leave the service of the Lord and submit to the worldly struggle, that in no way concerns them.' Cf. Eph. VI.12 on the struggle against 'invisible enemies'.

[72] *Ibid.* lines 851–62: 'Now the monk who submits to Benedict's rule and leaves behind all worldly things, why will he again turn to worldly weapons and throw aside his struggle against the unseen enemies, to anger his Creator? The servant of God can not fight along with worldly men if he is to have success in the spiritual combat. There was no holy servant of God after the suffering of the Saviour that would ever foul his hands in battle, but they endured the persecution of wicked tormentors, and gave their lives with harmlessness for God's belief, and they now live with God, because they would not even kill a bird.'   [73] Powell, 'Three Orders', p. 122.

military and ecclesiastical duties rather than a wish to give a full account of society'.[74]

Is Ælfric writing this for the English *bellatores* who grumble as they meet the Vikings in battle? Or, if we posit Æthelweard and Æthelmær as potential readers of this text, is he rallying the beleaguered English *bellatores* and aristocracy to maintain their support of the Benedictine reform and its vision of society depicted here? The typological understanding of Jews allows Ælfric to reinforce his social arguments. In this scheme, the insufficient values of the Jews in Maccabees are superimposed on the *bellatores* of Anglo-Saxon England; the thanes defending England from Vikings are incomplete without the spiritual complement of the Benedictine reform. The narrative of the homily functions as an extended exemplum, explicated with reference to Ælfric's society in the *Qui sunt oratores, laboratores, bellatores* appendix. This use of the Old Testament as a way of commenting on current social problems is a common tactic in Ælfric's writings.[75] *Maccabees* and *Qui sunt oratores, laboratores, bellatores* together constitute what Alan Sinfield calls a 'faultline story', an imaginative narrative response to a pressing social conflict.[76] The commentary Ælfric weaves in and around the narrative of *Maccabees* allows us to hear the echo of an ideological conflict between secular and ecclesiastical social groups in late-tenth-century England.[77]

---

[74] Godden, 'Money', pp. 55–6, esp. 56, n. 58; but cf. Powell's dissenting view ('Three Orders', p. 121). For the political use of the Maccabees in the Benedictine reform on the Continent, see Dunbabin, 'Maccabees as Exemplars', pp. 36–8.

[75] E.g. see Ælfric's reason for translating the Book of Judith, that it should be 'eow mannum to bysne, þæt ge eowerne eard mid wæ[p]num bewerian wið onwinnendne here' (*Letter to Sigeweard*, *Old English Heptateuch*, ed. Crawford, p. 48, lines 777–80: 'an example, so that you protect your land with weapons against an invading army'). See also *De populo Israhel*, lines 274–81, 291–3 and 390–6; *Prayer of Moses*, *Lives* I, no. 13, lines 147–77; *Dominica VI Post Pentecosten*, Pope, *Homilies* II, 14, 128–35, 140–6; and others. Godden is particularly sensitive to this aspect of Ælfric's writings: 'For the Anglo-Saxons the Old Testament was a veiled way of talking about their own situation . . . Despite Ælfric's insistence that the old law had been replaced by the new, at least in its literal sense, in many ways the old retained its power for the Anglo-Saxons, and gave them a way of thinking about themselves as nations' ('Biblical Literature', p. 225; in addition, see pp. 207–8 of the same essay, and 'Apocalypse', pp. 131–42, on Ælfric's growing attention to English political matters in his writings, under the increasing threat of Viking invasion at the end of the tenth century).

[76] *Cultural Politics – Queer Reading* (Philadelphia, PA, 1994), pp. 3–4.

[77] For a general historical overview of the connection between the Benedictine reform and the secular politics of England, see, *inter alia*, E. John, 'The King and the Monks in the Tenth-Century Reformation', in his *Orbis Britanniae and other Studies* (Leicester, 1966), pp. 154–80 and 'The World of Abbot Ælfric', *Ideal and Reality in Frankish and Anglo-Saxon Society: Studies presented to J.M. Wallace-Hadrill*, ed. P. Wormald with D. Bullough and R. Collins (Oxford, 1983), pp. 300–16; *Tenth-Century Studies: Essays in Commemoration of the Millennium of the Council of Winchester and Regularis Concordia*, ed. D. Parsons (Chichester, 1975); M. McC. Gatch, *Preaching and Theology in Anglo-Saxon England* (Toronto, 1977), pp. 8–11 and 119–28; B. Yorke, 'Æthelmær: the Foundation of the Abbey at Cerne and the Politics of the Tenth Century', *The Cerne Abbey*

Anti-Judaism in Ælfric's Lives of Saints

Ælfric's anti-Judaism does not exhibit the more sinister attitudes toward Jews that would emerge in the twelfth century.[78] However, his political use of Jewish stereotypes in *Maccabees*, the rhetorical conjunction of ancient scapegoat and current threats to community, bespeaks an understanding of Jews peculiar to the reign of Æthelred. The breakdown of social bonds and obligations is a distinctive concern at the time, reflected in the Old English texts composed and copied in the period, as Hugh Magennis has shown.[79] The centre cannot hold: the ethos of *The Battle of Maldon* cries out to a half-mythical time of noble comitatus values; Wulfstan rages against the dissolution of all natural obligations in the *Sermo Lupi ad Anglos*. In such a climate of change and crisis, with a weak ruler and a growing problem of Danish invasion, the representation of Jews rises to the surface of the 'political unconscious'. In Byrhtferth of Ramsey's *Vita S. Oswaldi* (written between 995 and 1005), Jews are used as political analogues just as they are in *Maccabees*. According to the text, after the death of Edgar (975), anti-monastic sentiment flowered in Mercia; Byrhtferth explains that '[t]anta dementia in Christiano populo ebullivit sicut olim in Judaea cum persecuti fuerant Dominum, in quo scelere languidum Caiphae caput erectum est, et Apostolicus vir vilis apostata factus est, necne facinorosus Pilatus ad te locutus. Discipuli formidolosi extiterant prae timore, sicuti his diebus monachi prae dolore'.[80] Byrhtferth narrates the 'martyrdom' of Edward (978) as a passion narrative, with the English conspirators cast as Jews:

Acceperunt inter se iniquum consilium, qui ita damnatam habebant mentem et nebulosam diabolicam caliginem, ut non timerent manus immittere in christum Domini. . . . Namque cum insidiatores eius ipsum vallarent, et, velut Judaei summum Christum olim circumdarent, ipse intrepidus equo resedit. Dementia quippe una erat in eis, parque insania. Tunc nequitia pessima et dementia truculenta Beelzebutini hostis flagrabat in mentibus venenosorum militum; tum sagittae toxicatae facinoris Pilati exsurrexerunt

---

Millennium Lectures, ed. K. Baker (Cerne Abbey, 1988), pp. 15–26; P. Stafford, 'Church and Society in the Age of Ælfric', *The Old English Homily and its Backgrounds*, ed. P. E. Szarmach and B. F. Huppé (Albany, NY, 1978), pp. 11–42, and also her *Unification and Conquest: a Political and Social History of England in the Tenth and Eleventh Centuries* (London, 1989), pp. 24–68 and 180–200.

[78] See Little, *Religious Poverty and the Profit Economy*, pp. 42–57; R. I. Moore, *The Formation of a Persecuting Society* (Oxford, 1987), pp. 27–45 and 'Anti-Semitism and the Birth of Europe', *Christianity and Judaism*, ed. D. Wood, Stud. in Church Hist. 20 (Oxford, 1992), 33–57; Langmuir, *Toward a Definition of Antisemitism*, pp. 63–133 and *History, Religion and Antisemitism*, pp. 275–305.

[79] *Images of Community in Old English Poetry*, CSASE 18 (Cambridge, 1996).

[80] Byrhtferth of Ramsey, *Vita S. Oswaldi*, *The Historians of the Church of York and its Archbishops*, ed. J. Raine, 3 vols., RS (London, 1879) I, 445: 'Such madness boiled up among the Christian people as once in Judea when they persecuted the Lord, in which crime the feeble head of Caiaphas was raised, and the apostolic man was made a base apostate, not to mention the villainous Pilate. The disciples became timid with fear, just as in these days the monks are with affliction.'

satis crudeliter adversum Dominum, et adversum christum eius, qui erat electus ad tuendum dulcissimae gentis regnum et imperium, derelicto patre.[81]

The anti-Judaism of Ælfric and Byrhtferth mixes indiscriminately with ideological rhetoric. In this context, Jews are both an unsettling variable and a useful rhetorical bludgeon: Ælfric does not want a faulty understanding (and imitation) of Jews to further fray the social fabric, but the Jews provide a useful exemplum (both positive and negative) when the occasion demands.[82] This understanding of Jews and Judaism is sheer ideology; it provides not only for conscious intentional struggles in the socio-political realm, but also constitutes 'the invisible colour of daily life itself'.[83] There can be no Abel without a Cain, no Christianity without Judaism.[84] For Ælfric, Judaism poses an interpretative conundrum, and his 'solution', fraught as it is with contradiction, enables us to trace a thread in the ideological fabric of late-tenth-century England.[85]

---

[81] *Ibid.* pp. 449–50: 'Among them they devised a wicked plan, for they possessed minds so damned and such diabolical blindness that they did not fear to lay hands on the anointed one of the Lord . . . And when his ambushers encircled him, just as the Jews once surrounded Christ, he sat bravely on his horse. Certainly a single madness was in them, and a like insanity. Then the worst wickedness and the savage madness of the devilish enemy flared in the minds of the venomous thegns; then the poisoned arrows of the crime of Pilate rose up most cruelly against the Lord and against his anointed, who had been elected to defend the kingdom and empire of this most sweet race on his father's death.'

[82] B. Cheyette examines similar socio-political uses of Jews in later English history and literature in *Constructions of 'The Jew' in English Literature and Society: Racial Representations, 1875–1945* (Cambridge, 1993); he concludes that 'writers do not passively draw on eternal myths of "the Jew" but actively construct them in relation to their own literary and political concerns' (p. 268). As H. Fisch notes, '[t]he Jew is often (we might even say, most often) a figure of evil [in literature]; but more than he is a figure of evil, he is a nuisance, a problem, a difficulty, something one has to come to terms with before one can come to terms with oneself' (*The Dual Image: the Figure of the Jew in English and American Literature* (London, 1971), p. 13). See also E. L. Panitz, *The Alien in their Midst: Images of Jews in English Literature* (London, 1981).

[83] T. Eagleton, *Ideology: an Introduction* (London, 1991), p. 221.

[84] See Ælfric's typological explication of Cain and Abel in the *Letter to Sigeweard*: 'Abeles slege soðlice getacnode ure Hælendes slege, þe ða Iudeiscan ofslogon, yfele gebroðra swa swa Cain wæs' (*Old English Heptateuch*, ed. Crawford, p. 23, lines 175–8: 'The slaying of Abel truly signified the murder of our Saviour, whom the Jews killed, evil brethren just as Cain was'). On the Cain and Abel tradition, see R. Mellinkoff, *The Mark of Cain* (Berkeley, CA, 1981); R. J. Quinones, *The Changes of Cain: Violence and the Lost Brother in Cain and Abel Literature* (Princeton, NJ, 1991), pp. 23–83. Quinones notes that the Cain and Abel story 'reveals an encounter with the lost brother, the sacrificed other, who must be gone but who can never be gone' and that the story has been used through the ages to 'address a breach in existence, a fracture at the heart of things' (p. 3).

[85] A National Endowment for the Humanities Summer Seminar for College Teachers ('Absence and Presence: the Jew in Early English Literature', SUNY Stony Brook, 1996) provided a helpful forum to test some of the ideas in this argument. I would like to thank the members of the seminar, especially Stephen Spector, Alfred David and Seymour Kleinberg, as well as David Townsend, Scott Westrem, Ian McDougall, Katherine Scheil, Fred Robinson and Malcolm Godden for their help.

The earliest texts with English and French

DAVID W. PORTER

Modern scholars can sometimes reconstruct the methods of medieval glossary-makers by tracking individual glosses along the path from the textual source to the final destination in the glossarial list.[1] Here I wish to pursue a trail of clues through two early-eleventh-century manuscripts of the *Excerptiones de Prisciano* ('Excerpts of Priscian'), a Latin grammatical treatise which has been identified as the source for Ælfric's bilingual *Grammar*.[2] Viewed singly, the manuscripts of this work offer partial views of glossatorial activity; viewed together, these fragmentary glimpses snap into perspective, rendering a dynamic picture of glossary-making as a corporate enterprise undertaken by a group of Anglo-Saxon schoolmen working in several manuscripts simultaneously.

The two manuscripts in question are Antwerp, Plantin-Moretus Museum 16.2 + London, British Library, Add. 32246, and Paris, Bibliothèque Nationale de France, nouv. acq. lat. 586.[3] Antwerp–London is a miscellany. The *Excerptiones de Prisciano* fill the bounding lines of its pages, while an array of texts is copied on flyleaves and margins.[4] Of immediate interest here is the glossarial

---

[1] As P. Lendinara has observed: 'The Abbo Glossary in London, British Library, Cotton Domitian i', *ASE* 19 (1990), 133–47, at 133.

[2] The only general study of the *Excerptiones* is by V. Law, 'Anglo-Saxon England: Ælfric's "Excerptiones de Arte Grammatica Anglice"', *Histoire Épistémologie Langage* 9 (1987), 47–71. The same author's *Insular Latin Grammarians* (Woodbridge, 1982) is the standard point of reference for Anglo-Saxon grammatical studies. For a description of Ælfric's use of the *Excerptiones*, see J. Bender-Davis, 'Ælfric's Techniques of Translation and Adaptation as Seen in the Composition of his Old English Latin Grammar' (unpubl. PhD dissertation, Pennsylvania State Univ., 1985). The *Grammar* is edited in J. Zupitza, *Ælfrics Grammatik und Glossar* (Berlin, 1880) [henceforth cited as *Grammatik*].

[3] See N. R. Ker, *Catalogue of Manuscripts Containing Anglo-Saxon* (Oxford, 1957), pp. 1–3 (no. 2) and 442–3 (no. 371). C. A. Ladd, 'The "Rubens" Manuscript and *Archbishop Ælfric's Vocabulary*', *RES* 44 (1960), 353–64, discusses the modern history and dismemberment of the Antwerp–London manuscript.

[4] Ker, *Catalogue*, no. 2, inventories the contents and the order in which they were written. The additions, beside the glossarial material described below, include Remigius's commentary on Donatus's *Ars minor*, Ælfric's *Colloquy*, several Latin poems, and a letter in Latin prose. M. Förster, 'Die altenglische Glossenhandschrift Plantinus 32 (Antwerpen) und Additional 32246 (London)', *Anglia* 41 (1917), 94–161, describes the manuscript and establishes the original arrangement of the leaves (pp. 97–8). He also edits the additions of the Antwerp segment, with the exception of the Remigius commentary and the poem by the Frenchman Herbert, which is discussed below.

material, five lists in two hands,[5] and particularly the mostly Latin a-order alphabetical list, whose batches are written in the margins, with a new letter beginning at every fourth leaf.[6] The Paris manuscript contains individual components of this list embedded in its text, showing that its scribe was involved somehow in the early stages of glossary compilation. The discovery of this connection will allow us to explore the co-operative working methods of an eleventh-century Anglo-Saxon school and to assign the Paris manuscript to a definite scriptorium. An equally important finding will come from the suggestive evidence for language interaction, of vernacular language with Latin and, surprisingly, the interaction of the two vernaculars Old English and French – an early episode, perhaps the first recorded one, in the long interconnected history of the two languages.

To present the relevant information efficiently, I proceed as follows. First, I examine the general textual relationship of the two manuscripts in order to produce inferences about the overall plan and execution of the Antwerp–London manuscript and particularly of the a-order list that fills its margins. Second, I examine the specific segment of the Paris text where the scribe is constructing an alphabetical glossary with raw material from the *Excerptiones*. Third, I juxtapose the cognate portions of the a-order list with these materials from the Paris Priscian, in order to provide a comparative view that will open an avenue of approach to the compilers' strategies of glossary-making.

---

[5] Ker, *Catalogue*, no. 2, describes the four lists containing English (one on flyleaves, three in margins). The three marginal lists (two alphabetical and one bilingual class list) are in L. Kindschi, 'The Latin-Old English Glossaries in Plantin-Moretus MS 32 and British Museum Add. 32,246' (unpubl. PhD dissertation, Stanford Univ., 1955) [henceforth cited as Kindschi]. All citations below are by page and line from this edition. The glossarial material from the Antwerp segment only is printed in Förster, 'Die altenglische Glossenhandschrift', pp. 101–46. The glossaries are best known from T. Wright and R. Wülcker, *Anglo-Saxon and Old English Vocabularies*, 2nd ed. (London, 1884), cols. 104–91, edited from the Junius transcript (Oxford, Bodleian Library, Junius 71). The relationship of this transcription to the original is elucidated by Ladd, 'The "Rubens" Manuscript'. I discuss the five lists (a Latin–Latin list of architectural terms on Antwerp 43v, in addition to those mentioned by Ker, in 'On the Antwerp–London Glossaries', *JEGP* 98 (1999), 170–92). Other studies touching on this glossarial material include that of R. Gillingham, 'An Edition of Abbot Ælfric's Old English–Latin Glossary with Commentary' (unpubl. PhD dissertation, Ohio State Univ., 1981), which analyses the relationship of the class list to Ælfric's *Glossary*, and that of L. Lazzari, 'Il canto liturgico nel glossario in latino-inglese antico del ms Antwerpen, Plantin Moretus M. 16.2 (47) + London, BL, Add. 32246', *Linguistica e filologia* 2 (1996), 193–221, which examines a discrete batch of the class list. Tania Styles of the University of Nottingham is preparing a thesis on the vocabulary of family relationships in the class list.

[6] Ker, *Catalogue*, no. 2, art. b. It is in the first glossing hand, the same elegant hand that wrote text glosses and marginal scholia but none of the main text aside from two supply sheets. The list is mostly Latin; there are only a half dozen vernacular interpretamenta among the 1000 items.

RELATIONSHIP OF THE MANUSCRIPTS

Paris, BNF, nouv. acq. lat. 586 contains one text, the *Excerptiones de Prisciano*, copied on 131 parchment folios. The eleventh-century segment of the manuscript is written in a single, very legible, Anglo-Caroline hand. A distinctive characteristic of the scribe is the use of the Fleury abbreviation for Latin *est*, a horizontal line followed by a dot: —·[7] Marginal scholia and interlinear glosses are almost entirely by the main scribe. A paper flyleaf has been added at the front during the eighteenth-century rebinding. The first two quires are replacements in an angular twelfth-century continental hand that imitated such Insular features as the Tironian *et*.[8] In these replacement quires, page size measures 19 × 25 cm. Leaves are ruled in pencil, twenty-four lines to the page. Bounding lines, doubled at top and outer margins, demarcate a writing space of 13.5 × 18.5 cm. The catchword *habere* is written in the bottom margin of 15v, the last replacement leaf. The leaves of the original quires are somewhat larger, measuring 19.5 × 26 cm. They have been pricked in the outer margin and ruled across both pages with a dry point, again with twenty-four lines to the page. Double bounding lines mark a writing space measuring 14.5 × 19 cm. The eighteenth-century binding of the manuscript,[9] with a footband as well as a headband, partially obscures the arrangement of the leaves within the quires. There are seventeen gatherings, mostly in eights, as follows: 1^7, 2^8, 3^7 (2 is a half sheet; a stub protrudes in place of 7), 4–16 are quires of eight, 17^5. With the exceptions of quires 15 and 17, all the eleventh-century quires are signed with Roman capitals. Major divisions of the text are indicated with large capitals and/or headings in rustic capitals, both of which are usually rubricated. There are two

---

[7] BNF, nouv. acq. lat. 586 is thus to be added to T. A. M. Bishop's list of nine Anglo-Saxon manuscripts that use this abbreviation ('Lincoln Cathedral MS 182', *Lincolnshire Hist. and Arch.* 32 (1967), 73–6, + 2 plates, at p. 73, n. 3): Lincoln 182 (Bede); Antwerp/London (Priscian); Antwerp, Plantin-Moretus Museum 16.8 (Boethius); Brussels, Bibliothèque Royale, 1650 (Aldhelm); Brussels, Bibliothèque Royale, 1828–30 (glossary); Copenhagen, Kongelige Bibliotek, 1595 (sermons); London, BL, Cotton Cleopatra D.i (Vitruvius); London, BL, Egerton 267, fol. 37 (Boethius); and Vatican City, Biblioteca Apostolica Vaticana, Reg. lat. 123, fol. 114 (misc.). Bishop puts the Lincoln Bede, the Brussels Aldhelm and both the Antwerp and the London Boethius at Abingdon along with the Antwerp–London manuscript. For other evidence linking the Paris manuscript to the same scriptorium, see below.

[8] A stain covers several pages in the first original quire, a probable indication of the mishap that occasioned the twelfth-century repairs. Trimming at the outer top margins of the first four original leaves, fols. 16–20, was probably to remove areas disfigured by the same stain. Small spots of the stain are scattered throughout the manuscript, without impairing legibility.

[9] Beneath the back pastedown, which has separated from the board, is written 'Demigieu 1754, 12ᶜᵗ'. The reference is to the Marquis de Migieu, who acquired the manuscript in 1752 (Ker, *Catalogue*, p. 443). Probably it was during this rebinding that the manuscript was trimmed to its present size.

large display capitals on the first page, one red with green pigment, one in green pigment only, and another red and green capital on 24r. The text is totally without pictorial decoration.[10]

Comparison of the Paris with the Antwerp–London version of the *Excerptiones de Prisciano* shows the two manuscripts to be very close relatives. They share the same layout of headings, large capitals, and text (though consistency is of course not absolute). Sentence divisions in the two manuscripts generally agree, and occasionally *signes de renvoi* are identical. Many glosses are shared, practically all of the text glosses and scholia of the Antwerp–London version being included in the more extensive glossing of the Paris version.

Despite their closeness in time and, as will be demonstrated, place, and though both descend from a common ancestor,[11] neither manuscript is copied directly from the other. The Paris manuscript, in both its original and replacement quires, is an accurate, carefully corrected copy of a good exemplar. It avoids many errors and omissions found in Antwerp–London, and so cannot have been copied from it.[12] On the other hand, despite a good deal of inaccuracy, Antwerp–London sometimes preserves a better reading than Paris, and so must be an independent witness of the common ancestor. One such superior reading is Antwerp–London's correct *Tanton'* in place of Paris's reading *Tantonus*.[13] Another is the paradigm *diripio, -pui, -reptum* which appears in a series of third conjugation verbs in Antwerp–London (Antwerp 28v) but which is

---

[10] The lower left margin of 113v does, however, hold the sketch of a well-dressed man clasping his hands in front of him. Executed in dry-point and only faintly visible, the drawing has no connection with the text.

[11] This ancestor was related to a manuscript used in the composition of Ælfric's *Grammar*. Both Paris and Antwerp–London originally had *deneger* for *degener* (corrected on Paris 34r, uncorrected on Antwerp 6v), a mistake shared with four copies of the *Grammar*, including the oldest, Oxford, St John's College 154 (*Grammatik*, p. 45). And Ælfric's copy of the *Excerptiones* shared the same tradition of scholia with the extant copies, judging from the items of the paratext absorbed by the *Grammar*, e.g., 'quaternio, cine oððe feower manna ealdor' (*Grammatik*, p. 35); 'hic quaternio, qui preest iiii militibus uel quattuor dyplomata' (Paris 31r); 'glabrio, calu oððe hnot' (*Grammatik*, p. 35); 'glabrio, clauus uel sine pilis' (Paris 31r). 'hic lar, ðis fyr/ hi lares, ðas hus. lardum, spic, forðan ðe hit on husum hangað lange' (*Grammatik*, p. 42); 'Lar numero tantum singulari ignem significat. In plurali domus significat. Unde lardum nomen accepit, quod in laribus pendet diu' (Paris 33r).

[12] E.g., the omission of *homuncio* from a list of diminutives on London 9r (cf. Paris 16v and *Grammatik* 17.6); the omission on London 9r of several lines of text (beginning 'ut tignum . . .' and ending '. . . ante um' on Paris 17v); *qui* for *quia* and *sonor* for *soror* on the same page (cf. Paris 18r); and there are many other examples.

[13] The Paris scribe first misinterpreted an apostrophe as the almost identical abbreviation of *-us*. The *-us* ending has been pointed for deletion but no apostrophe has been inserted. This is the context: 'Apostrophus dexter pars est circuli, sed ad summam litteram apponitur. Qua nota deesse ostendimus parti orationis ultimam vocalem, ut Tanton' (*Paris*, Tantonus) pro Tantóne, et similia' (Paris 129rv, Antwerp 46v).

The earliest texts with English and French

lost in Paris (90v). A glance at the same series of verbs in Ælfric's *Grammar* shows the word as part of the original text: 'diripio: ic fram atere, diripui, direptum'.[14]

Mistakes by the scribes of Antwerp–London reveal details of their exemplar. One scribe carelessly copied a page of the exemplar twice, first on Antwerp 11r and again on the verso. An error repeated on both pages (*et* for the neuter third declension ablative ending -*e*) must descend from the exemplar. Another mistake shows the exemplar to have had a form of **m** with a descending right stem and with left and middle stems joining to make a circular shape like the letter **o**. The inexpert scribe interpreted the unfamiliar form as *or*, thus writing on Antwerp 7r *orarcor* for *marcor* and *orarmor* for *marmor*. A third mistake appears on Antwerp 43v, where a scribe wrote *adumbium* for *aduerbium*, evidently misinterpreting the exemplar's *adūbium*. Now the Paris Priscian has a correct reading for ablative -*e*, uses a conventional Caroline **m** for *marcor* and *marmor*, and spells the *aduerbium* of Antwerp 43v without abbreviation. All of this reinforces the earlier inference that Antwerp–London has no direct dependency on the Paris manuscript. Moreover, the mistake on Antwerp fol. 11 probably indicates that the exemplar of Antwerp–London already had a more corrupt text than that of Paris, a hypothesis supported by the manuscript's great number of errors. At any rate, there must have been at least one manuscript intervening between Antwerp–London and the common ancestor, while Paris may have been a direct copy of that ancestor. The following diagram reconstructs this relationship: manuscript α is the common ancestor, which probably had connections to Ælfric's school; β is the lost exemplar of Antwerp–London.

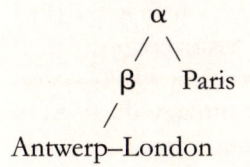

```
         α
        / \
       β   Paris
      /
Antwerp–London
```

1. The relationship of manuscripts of the *Excerptiones de Prisciano*

---

[14] *Grammatik*, p. 168.10. It must be said that there is no evidence in either of the manuscripts for textual contamination from the *Grammar*, copies of which were numerous. Any such editing would become immediately evident, since anomalous words would appear among the lists of illustrations. The *diripio* paradigm, however, is the only example where Antwerp–London and the *Grammar* share material omitted by the Paris manuscript. Some vernacular glosses may have originated with Ælfric's *Grammar*, or perhaps even with Ælfric's own copy of the *Excerptiones* (see Ker, *Catalogue*, p. 442), but there is no reason to suspect that the monolingual Latin text of the *Excerptiones* differs much from its author's autograph copy.

David W. Porter

THE ANTWERP–LONDON **a**-ORDER LIST

Ker describes the marginal **a**-order glossary, whose batches stop at letter **s**, as 'alphabetically arranged . . . and spaced so that a new letter of the alphabet begins at every fourth leaf'.[15] That generalization, however, ignores some anomalies: eight leaves intervene between the **i** and **l** segments, seven between the **q** and **s** segments (there is no **r**-segment). I have compared the readings of both manuscripts to determine if any text is missing at the precise points where an anticipated glossary batch is not found. The **i**-batch begins on the original 35r (now London 16r). Four leaves further, on the original 39r (now London 20r), the scribe of the alphabetical list has made not one stroke on the page but has ruled the top, outer and bottom margins with a dry point. Since comparison with the Paris *Excerptiones de Prisciano* reveals no missing material and hence no missing pages at this point, we may be sure that the compiler originally targeted the margins of this folio for his alphabetical list, probably for a batch of words beginning with the letter **k**. Such words are rare in Latin, and it may be that the compiler found none to hand. Such a plan would be none the less remarkable among Anglo-Saxon glossaries. As a rough gauge, the index to Wright and Wülcker's collection of glossaries contains just one alphabetical batch of three words beginning with **k**, these from the second Cleopatra glossary.[16] Whatever the case, the compiler of the **a**-order list left the margins of London 20r blank, and they were subsequently filled by a scribe who fitted the batches of the class glossary into them with scant regard for the dry-point ruling.

Let us apply the same test to the irregular gap between the **q** and **s** segments. Lemmas beginning with **q** begin on the original 64r (now Antwerp 40r). Four leaves further, between 67v and 68r (now Antwerp 43v and 44r, which begins the ninth quire), Antwerp–London is missing a block of text which in the Paris manuscript has 760 words, an amount comparable to an average folio of Antwerp–London.[17] So at this place Antwerp–London has evidently lost a leaf whose margins held a batch of words beginning with **r**, written in the hand of the **a**-order list. This **r**-batch has not disappeared without a trace, however, because when the compiler dry-ruled the top, bottom and outer margins of the

---

[15] *Catalogue*, p. 1.

[16] *Vocabularies* II, 130. These glossaries have recently been re-edited by P. Rusche, 'The Cleopatra Glossaries: an Edition with Commentary on the Glosses and their Sources' (unpubl. PhD dissertation, Yale Univ., 1996). The Antwerp–London class list has three lemmas beginning with **k**: *Karchesia*, melas; *Kalende* .i. uocationes, gehealddagas uel halige dagas; *Kalo* . g[rece], uoco Latine (Kindschi, pp. 82.14 and 223.8–9). The compiler of the **a**-order list could have found four **k** words in the *Excerptiones*: *karibdis* on London 13r, *kalipso* on Antwerp 5v, *kalende* on Antwerp 15r and *Kartago* on Antwerp 33r.

[17] The block, beginning 'ut si falsum . . .', ending '. . . proderam . proderas . proderat', is on Paris 121v–123v.

lost leaf, he did so with enough force to score the next leaf, Antwerp 44r, lightly.[18]

These observations now allow an articulated description of the **a**-order list. The glossary compiler exploited the physical composition of the manuscript to organize the glossary. His plan was to begin a batch at the beginning and in the central fold, on the recto of fols. 1 and 5, of each of the nine quires, so producing eighteen batches, letters **a–s**. There was a deviation from this plan in that no words beginning with **k** were included, and the **r**-batch, which was perhaps on a singleton at the beginning of the last quire, was subsequently lost. The organization by quire left no room for coherent **t**- and **u**-batches, and these were unsystematically dispersed, often in bottom margins, among the other batches. A lone lemma beginning with the letter **x** is found by itself in the outer margin of Antwerp 28v.[19]

In utilizing the quires of Antwerp–London, the compiler ignored the initial two flyleaves, perhaps originally a bifolium, now separated, one in Antwerp and one in London. Neither did he use the supply leaves, Antwerp 19* and London 24, written in his own hand, that hold text originally omitted by the main scribe. Had he put these pages to use as well, the manuscript would in fact have held all his alphabetical batches **a** through **u** at four-leaf intervals, though without a **k**-batch. For ease of reference, however, he began his glossary batches where the manuscript would tend to open naturally – the easier to enter items as they were collected, the easier to find them again once they were entered.[20] One might consider the manuscript a medieval equivalent of modern dictionaries having thumb-indexed alphabetical divisions. The extreme wear at middle height in outer margins shows that the manuscript did indeed serve for frequent vocabulary reference, in the fashion of a dictionary.

Study of sources gives an important clue about the construction of the **a**-order list. When the compiler was searching out items to copy into his ingeniously organized dictionary, he turned to a text at hand, the *Excerptiones de Prisciano*, whose scholia make up at least 120 of the 1000 items in the glossary. So we can say that in the Antwerp–London manuscript the main text fills the writing area, while many of its original interpretative scholia, now disconnected, are listed alphabetically in the margins. The Antwerp–London version of the *Excerptiones* cannot have been

---

[18] The loss of the first folio of quire nine produced an anomalous quire of seven leaves. It is impossible to say whether this loss occurred during medieval times or during the modern dismemberment of the manuscript. All the **r** words from Wright and Wülcker's edition of the Junius transcript can still be found in the manuscript, but Junius copied only items with English, of which the **r** batch probably had none, because the **a**-order glossary is overwhelmingly Latin–Latin.   [19] 'Xisma. tis .i. nouaculum', omitted by Kindschi.

[20] Each alphabetical batch begins with a capital in the middle of the top margin. Some of these are in red, though now, because of fading, the colour is distinguished only with difficulty. Capitals **l**, **m**, **n** and **o** (Antwerp 20r, 24r, 28r and 32r) are certainly red.

the source for these glosses, however, for the simple fact that for the most part they do not appear there; the large majority are known only from the Paris version.[21]

Let us now turn to the Paris manuscript in order to learn something about the selection of these items for the **a**-order list.

GLOSSARY-MAKING BY THE SCRIBE OF THE PARIS MANUSCRIPT

One remarkable page of the Paris manuscript reveals its scribe involved in more than simply copying a grammar. The page in question, 65v, is heavily glossed in the main scribal hand. When these glossed items, all unglossed in Antwerp–London, are excerpted from the surrounding text, the twenty-two lemmas fall without exception into alphabetical order by the first letter of each word, or in other words, **a**-order:

amminiculor .i. auxilior
auguror augurium exerceo
adorior .i. aggredior . uel incipio loqui
abutor .i. male utor
antestor .i. testimonium fero
adgredior . inuado . incipio
aspernor .i. contemno .
architector .i. aedes construo
assector .i. imitor . uel emulor
argumentor approbo . rei dubie facio fidem
comminiscor .i. commentum facio ɫ excogito
carnificor .i. excrucio
detestor .i. desmentirs .
despicor .i. despicio
demolior .i. uasto
depecul<i>or .i. depredor peculum aufero
ementior .i. ualde mentior
exordior .i. incipio .
experior .i. probo
frustror .i. priuor .i. decipio .
for loquor
metor .i. termino uel designo

This evidence must come from the compilation of an alphabetical glossary with lemmas from the *Excerptiones de Prisciano*. Note, for example, that the glossing skips over items that do not fit the alphabetical scheme, words such as *miror* in line 2 or *machinor* and *polliceor* in line 3 (see p. 96). Since the alphabetical gloss-

---

[21] See the discussion and examples in Porter, 'Glossaries'.

ing begins at line 1 with **a**-words and ends at line nine with **m**-words, one might reasonably assume that it did not descend from the exemplar. And since it seems to have been done for this particular page, the Paris scribe himself is the most likely candidate for its conception and execution. This selective glossing may have been done so that these items could easily be either transcribed onto a working copy such as a vellum scrap or wax tablet, or entered directly into a larger glossary such as the **a**-order list, where all but the last item would fit into the marginal columns of the first three quires. This question will be reopened shortly in the light of internal evidence from the **a**-order list itself.

Hardly less surprising than the alphabetical glossing is the French interpretamentum *desmentirs* above Latin *detestor*. While words of Romance origin (either French or Latin) have long been recognized in Old English texts, they have traditionally been accepted as loans — borrowed words pronounced with English phonological rules, inflected with English endings, and subject to all the evolutionary changes of the native lexicon.[22] *Desmentirs* cannot be counted in this class, however, as there is no recorded instance of its use in either Old or Middle English. Both the form and orthography of the word show it to be simply French, the ancestor of Modern French *dementir*. Dictionaries give the earliest citation from the *Chanson de Roland*, *c.* 1080, where the word means to accuse someone of lying, more particularly to accuse a witness of perjury.[23]

Both the inflectional form and the meaning require comment, as neither is exactly parallel with the Latin lemma. *Desmentirs* is a substantivized infinitive (the *-s* rendering it a nominative). The glossator, one presumes, hit on this as a standard lexicalized form to gloss the lexicalized first-person singular Latin verb *detestor*. Concerning meaning, Classical Latin *detestor* ('to call down a solemn curse' or simply 'to call down')[24] does not have the exact legal associations of *desmentirs*. The pairing of the two words reflects on the one hand the medieval conception of law as religious authority and on the other the grammatical lore of the *Excerptiones*, which frequently interprets derivatives in the light of their roots (*primitiua*).[25] *Detestor* ultimately derives from the Latin root *testis* ('witness'),

---

[22] H. Gneuss, '*Anglicae linguae interpretatio*: Language Contact, Lexical Borrowing and Glossing in Anglo-Saxon England', *PBA* 82 (1992), 107–48, at 134–7.

[23] E.g., *Dictionnaire historique de la langue française* (Paris, 1992), s.v. *mentir*.

[24] *Oxford Latin Dictionary*, ed. P. G. W. Glare (Oxford, 1982), s.v. *detestor*.

[25] London 7r: 'Alia que primitiuorum similem possunt habere significationem'; London 10v: 'Denominatiuum apellatur a uoce primitiui sui non ab aliqua speciali significatione'; London 24v: 'Species uerborum duae sunt, primitiua et diriuatiua, quae inueniuntur fere in omnibus partibus orationis. Est igitur primitiua quae primam positionem ab ipsa natura accepit'; Antwerp 20r: 'Et seruant significationes primitiuorum, quamuis uideantur quedam ex his in alium sensum transire ... Sed si quis attentius inspiciat, non penitus absistunt haec a primitiuorum significatione'; Antwerp 45v: 'Et sciendum quod poete sepe diriuatiuis utuntur pro primitiuis.'

David W. Porter

as do two other verbs from the series on Paris 65v. An etymologically derived legal interpretation of *detestor* is thus reinforced by the semantic influence of the companion words, both of which specifically constitute legal terminology (*antestor* 'to call to witness', *contestor* 'to join legal proceedings').

COMPARISON OF GLOSSES FROM THE TWO MANUSCRIPTS

To recapitulate, so far we have established that both extant versions of the *Excerptiones* contain **a**-order glossarial lists. Let us now compare those lists.

Paris 65v	**a**-order list (cited from Kindschi)
adulor	Amminiculor .i. auxilior . adiuuo [40.14]
amminiculor .i. auxilior	Auguro .i. diuino [40.12]
auguror augurium exerceo	Abhominor .i. detestor uel execror . respuo [39.23]
abhominor	Adorior .i. inuado .i. aggredior . incipio [39.24]
5 consequor	5 Adorior .i. adgredior .i. contra gradior . siue incipio [42.7]
amplector	Abutor .i. male utor [39.25]
adorior .i. aggredior . uel incipio loqui	Antestor .i. presulo . as .i. antistes efficio [40.1]
abutor .i. male utor	Abhominor .i. detestor uel execror . respuo [39.23]
miror	Machinor .i. excogito per fraudem [255.20]
10 antestor .i. testimonium fero	10 Machinor, aris .i. per fraudem excogito [257.9]
execror	Adorior .i. inuado .i. aggredior . incipio [39.24]
machinor	Adorior .i. adgredior .i. contra gradior . siue incipio [42.7]
polliceor	Aspernor .i. fastidio . contempno [40.2]
adgredior . inuado . incipio	Aspernor . aris .i. fastidio [42.14]
15 aspernor .i. contemno .	15 Architrector .i. aedifico . edes construo [40.8]
architector .i. aedes construo	Adsector .i. imitor uel emulor [40.9]
assector .i. imitor . uel emulor	Argumentor .i. approbo uel rei dubie facio fidem [40.11]
argumentor approbo . rei dubie facio fidem	Assentor .i. blandior [42.16]
arbitror	Conspicor .i. intueor [114.15]
20 blandior	20 Comminiscor .i. confingo . excogito [114.16]
consolor	Comminiscor .i. confingo, siue excogito, inde commentus, ta, tum [116.22]
conspicor	Ementior .i. fingo, comminiscor, quasi ualde mentior [190.20]
comminiscor .i. commentum facio uel excogito	Consector .i. emulor [116.23]
consequor	Contestor .i. testimonium do [116.22]
25 consector	25 Calumpnior .i. calumniam sustineo [114.17]
tueor	Calumpnio .i. falso arguor [116.24]
contestor	Carnificor .i. excrucior [117.1]
complector	Carnificor .i. excrucior [114.18]
calumnior	Excarnificio .i. excorio uel excrucio [190.24]
30 carnificor .i. excrucio	30 Abhominor .i. detestor uel execror . respuo [39.23]
dignor	Despicor .i. despicio, deorsum aspicio [149.4]
detestor .i. desmentirs	Despicor .i. despicio [150.1]
despicor .i. despicio	Demolior .i. destruo uel uasto [149.5]
demolior .i. uasto	Dominor .i. presulo, uel presum, rego [149.6]
35 meditor	35 Quirito, .i. clamo uoce romano, et quiritor, dominor [268.3]
dominor	Depeculor .i. deuasto, uel peculium aufero, uel pecore te depredor [149.7]

The earliest texts with English and French

depecul\<i\>or .i. depredor peculum aufero	Delargior .i. distribuo uel prodige dispenso [149.8]
dilargior	Dilargior .i. absque mensura distribuo [150.3]
ementior .i. ualde mentior	Ementior .i. fingo, comminiscor, quasi ualde mentior [190.20]
40 exordior .i. incipio	40 Ementior .i. mendaciter me fingo [191.13]
experior .i. probo	Exordior .i. incipio [190.21]
frustror .i. priuor .i. decipio	Experior .i. probo uel tempto [190.22].
hostor	Opperior, deponens uerbum .i. expecto, sustineo, Et experior. com., .i. probo [259.19]
for loquor, faris, fatur	Frustor .i. priuor, decipio [196.8]
45 obliuiscor	45 Meto .i. mensuram pono, Et metor .i. mensuro, designo uel locum castrorum eligo [256.5]
metor .i. termino uel designo	

This comparison establishes with certainty the interaction of the Paris folio and the **a**-order list. Notice first of all that Paris material is incorporated by the glossary in unbroken segments, for example, a series of five items in the right margin of Antwerp 2r (39.23–40.2), a series of four in the right margin of London 8r (114.115–19), a series of three in the right margin of Antwerp 4r (190.20–2), and so forth. Moreover, in the Paris Priscian, twenty-two words of a forty-six-item verb series are glossed, and nineteen of these twenty-two glossed items then become lemmata of the **a**-order list: nos. 2, 3, 7, 8, 10, 15, 16, 17, 18, 23, 30, 33, 34, 37, 39, 40, 41, 42 and 46. Of these nineteen glosses:

1. six appear verbatim in the **a**-order list (nos. 8, 17, 18, 33, 40 and 42);
2. nine appear verbatim, or nearly so, along with other added material (nos. 2, 7 twice, 15, 16, 34, 37, 39, 41 and 46);
3. one appears twice in the **a**-order list with a minor change of inflection in the interpretamentum (no. 30);
4. and two appear with interpretamenta that paraphrase the Paris folio (no. 3, with a change of ending, and no. 23).

The only glossary headword that receives a Latin interpretation different from that of the Paris page is no. 10, *antestor*, but this is an incorrect definition written on an erasure.[26] And, interestingly, the original Paris interpretation of *antestor* has been transferred to the etymologically related *contestor*, which Paris does not gloss.

Only three glossed items from the *Excerptiones de Prisciano* do not appear as lemmas in the **a**-order list: *adgredior*, *detestor* and *for* (nos. 14, 32 and 44). *Detestor* and *adgredior*, however, become interpretamenta in the glossary (in nos. 11 and 30), so with the exception of the common verb *for* and the French *desmentirs*

---

[26] *Antestor*, 'to call as a witness', probably derives from a contraction of *ante-testor (*Oxford Latin Dictionary*, s.v. *antestor*). The **a**-order list makes a logical but wrong connection with *antistes*, derived from the prefix *ante-* and the verb *sto*, 'to stand'.

all of the glossing on Paris 65v has been absorbed by the **a**-order list of Antwerp–London.

Analysis of the unglossed items on Paris 65v strengthens the inferred connection with the **a**-order list. Of twenty-four unglossed words in the verb series, fourteen make no appearance among the **a**-order batches. But five unglossed words from the Priscian that do appear there (*ab(h)ominor, execror, machinor, consector* and *contestor*) accompany other material from 65v. Only five words (*blandior, conspicor, calumnior, dominor* and *dilargior*) appear in glossary contexts that have no evident connection to the Paris page: cf. above, nos. 18, 19, 29, 35, 38 and 39.

Nor is the evidence cited above the only connection between the glossary and the Paris version of the *Excerptiones de Prisciano*. At this point let us examine the compilers' methods in more detail. In the above list, several of the items from Paris 65v had more than one cognate gloss in the **a**-order list. In fact identical or nearly identical glosses frequently occur in close proximity in the glossary,[27] and sequences of glosses are sometimes repeated, with some variation of content, in exact order.[28] Yet other sequences are repeated with some rearrangement and addition of new items.[29] While the whole process was not very systematic, considering the degree of redundancy that crept into the list, these repeated sequences must in some way represent successive adaptations of the same exemplar: I picture the compiler collecting glosses alphabetically onto a wax tablet or parchment scrap and then using this working copy to transfer glosses into the marginal batches of Antwerp–London.[30]

---

[27] Of the more than 1000 items in the **a**-order list, about 150 contain repeated material. The verb *asciscere*, for instance, appears twice as a headword on London 2r (*asscisco*, Kindschi, p. 42.17; *adscisco, ibid.* p. 43.3). *Aqualiculus* appears on Antwerp 2r and again on 2v (*ibid.* pp. 39.2 and 41.18), as does *aplustra* (*ibid.* pp. 40.13 and 42.4), etc.

[28] Examples include contiguous glosses on *mutuo* and *mentio*, first on Antwerp 24r and again on 24v (Kindschi, pp. 256.7–8 and 257.15–16), on *oria* and *obsonor*, twice on Antwerp 32r (*ibid.* pp. 259.14–15 and 260.11–12), and on *nebulo* and *nequito*, twice on Antwerp 28r (*ibid.* pp. 258.8–9 and 258.13–14).

[29] Cf., for example, Kindschi, pp. 255.16–256.15 and 257.1–257.20, or 259.7–259.15 and 260.1–260.12.

[30] The variations show that the scribe was not copying slavishly but was editing and interpreting as he transferred glosses from the working copy to the margins, as in the following example (Kindschi, pp. 258.8–9 and 258.13–14):

> nebulo .i. mendax
> nequito et nequitor .i. nequiter ago, uel inutilem rem ago
>
> nebulo .i. mendax qui mendaciis quibusdam ueritatem obscurare nititur, uel qui suos fallit auditores
>
> nequito, as .i. nequiter ago. Necatus ferro dicimus. Nectus uero. Alia re peremptus dicitur.

In this instance the compiler expands the original definitions, but in other instances he abbreviates, sometimes severely (e.g., the two glosses on *incubo*, Kindschi, pp. 115.13 and 202.7). At a later date I plan to examine the details of the working methods.

The earliest texts with English and French

An inconsistency of plan lets us view a large batch of *glossae collectae* copied verbatim. The following unalphabetized text glosses from Paris 36v, all again unglossed in Antwerp–London, make up an uninterrupted block in the **s** segment of the **a**-order glossary, on Antwerp 47r.

Paris, 36v	***a**-order list (270.14–19)*
cedes <?> [a word is erased here]	Strages .i. occisio
strages <ubi multa corpora sternuntur>	Cedes .i. interemptio
strues congeries lignorum dicitur (left margin)	Strues .i. congeries i. compositio lignorum
lues <sorditas>	Lues .i. sordiditas l illuvies l interitus
labes <uel interitus>	Labes .i. interitus
clades <.i. morbus>	Clades .i. morbus
labes .i. interitus (left margin)	

Here the relationship between the two texts is a mirror of the case we saw earlier, in that the alphabetical list has again entirely absorbed the Paris text glosses. Note that both ambiguous readings of 'uel interitus' on the Paris page find expression in the glossary, first as a synonym for *sorditas*, glossing *lues*, and again as a sole interpretamentum for *labes*. The erasure above *cedes* was perhaps *interemptio* or another synonym. It may be that a working draft was copied twice, first as the uninterrupted batch on Antwerp 47r, and then again as individual items alphabetized throughout the glossary, for five of the six glossary items appear twice in the **a**-order list.[31]

The Paris manuscript and the **a**-order glossary are connected, that much is clear – yet it is difficult to determine the nature of that connection. The problems spring from the fact that half the evidence has disappeared along with manuscripts α and β. In their absence, I have pursued two hypotheses: that the glossary is directly dependent on the Paris manuscript, or, alternatively, that the selective alphabetical glossing originated with the ancestor α, whence it was transmitted through β to Antwerp–London. In this second hypothesis, the Paris manuscript might have fortuitously inherited the glosses on 65v. Before entering a winding path of details and conjecture, let me point out the unexpected destination: the evidence will not decisively favour either of the hypotheses; or rather it will favour both of them equally, for the clues will suggest that the glossary-makers used manuscript β, and that the Paris scribe was one of the glossary-makers.

Let us state both hypotheses in more explicit terms. So detailed and exact is

---

[31] Kindschi, p. 116.4–5: 'Cedes .i. interemptio . Strages uero est ubi multi occiduntur'; 'Clades .i. morbus'. Kindschi, p. 254.1–2: 'Lues .i. illuuies . sordiditas'; 'Labes .i. interitus'.

the relationship between the glossary and the Paris glosses that it would not be rash to assert the direct dependence of the one upon the other. Yet that judgement would pose a number of problems, since we know the Antwerp–London *Excerptiones* was copied not from the Paris manuscript, but from manuscript β.[32] The glossary makers could, however, have made use of two manuscripts of the *Excerptiones*, copying the main text from β and the paratext from Paris, which was then also ransacked for glossary items. This theory finds support in the script of the text glosses in Antwerp–London, which often contrast strongly with the main text – most are written in the forward-sloping hand of the **a**-order list.

On the other hand, if the sister manuscripts β and Paris shared the same glosses and scholia, the *Excerptiones* glosses for the **a**-order list might have come to Antwerp–London via the lost exemplar β just as we know the main text did. In this case, manuscripts β and Paris are virtually identical, and the batch from Paris 65v, with its French word, could reasonably be assigned to their common ancestor, α. Now three manuscripts of my stemma would seem to have been used in constructing the glossary: α, β and Antwerp–London. The status of the Paris manuscript is here undetermined, but if one assumes the alphabetical glossing to fall neatly on one page by simple chance, there is no necessity of involving the Paris scribe in the compilation of the glossary, or to assume that the presence of *desmentirs* is an indication of his education or native language.

An approach to these questions is difficult, but a close look at the Antwerp–London *Excerptiones* will help us understand the relationship of its scribes and their complex handling of the text glosses.

SCRIBAL DIVISION OF LABOUR IN THE ANTWERP–LONDON MANUSCRIPT

As stated above, in Antwerp–London the text hands usually do not copy accompanying glosses. Yet the treatment is not consistent. In the first twenty-six leaves of the *Excerptiones*, written by a variety of hands, all of the text glossing, marginal and interlinear, is carried out by the forward-sloping hand of the **a**-order list (with the possible exception of a couple of small interlined items). On the twenty-seventh leaf of the text (Antwerp 14r = the original 29r), the copying is taken over by a scribe whose Latin is much better than that of the previous scribes. Writing with a squarish hand, he has the distinctive habit of starting sentences with capitals protruding into the left margin, as many as seven or more per page.[33] Once this scribe's stint begins, the pattern of glossing immediately changes. Now most interlined glosses and short marginal scholia are in the main text hand, while the forward-sloping hand specializes in long notations. On

---

[32] See above, pp. 90–4.
[33] Another distinctive scribal habit is forming the bowl of the **g** as a circle.

The earliest texts with English and French

Antwerp 14v, for example, both interlined and marginal notations are in the main text hand. On the following leaf, Antwerp 15r, the forward-sloping hand copies a long scholion, the text hand a short one. On the following two pages (Antwerp 15v–16r), the text hand copies interlined glosses while the forward-sloping hand copies the marginal annotations. Although the squarish text hand is responsible for one long scholion, in the lower right margin of Antwerp 17r, and the forward-sloping hand still copies a few interlined glosses, as on the first few lines of Antwerp 19v, this section of the manuscript still has a well-established pattern that contrasts sharply with the preceding and following pages. For after the twelve-page stint of the squarish hand, ending on the original 35r (London 16r), there is a reversion to the earlier pattern. This following section, original 35v to 46r (London 16v–24v and Antwerp 20r–22r), has a couple of small items definitely in the hand of the main text, but the burden of glossing is again taken over by the forward-sloping hand. Then begins a second stint by the squarish hand, forty pages long, from the original 46v to 66v (Antwerp 22v–42v), and the same pattern of transition is repeated even more clearly. In this section the forward-sloping hand of the **a**-order glossary makes only two notations (on Antwerp 24v and 29v), while all other glossing, marginal and interlined, some of it quite dense, is in the text hand.

This evidence reveals an important point about the relationship of the Antwerp–London *Excerptiones* to its accompanying set of glosses. The contrast of hands does not result because the main text and glosses were copied from different exemplars. Rather, expertise in Latin is the factor that decides who among the members of the scriptorium was to fit the paratext to the text. It is a job reserved for good Latinists. In the second long stint by the squarish hand, the texts within and without the bounding lines show absolutely no contrast of hand or ink. Clearly in this long section that constitutes more than a fourth of the manuscript the scribe is reproducing the pages of his exemplar, both main text and glosses. This is the clearest picture of the exemplar and though that picture is very similar to the Paris manuscript, it is not the Paris manuscript itself.[34] The important conclusion here is the following: since the scholia and

---

[34] There are, for example, mistakes in Paris that are not repeated in Antwerp–London: incorrect *ma* for *ama* (Paris 80r, Antwerp 23r), incorrect *frigero* for *frigeo* (Paris 87v, Antwerp 27r; cf. *Grammatik*, p. 156.6), and incorrect *indutabilem* for *indubitabilem* (Paris 104v, Antwerp 35r), as well as the omission of the *diripio* paradigm (Paris 90v, Antwerp 28v). Other evidence against direct copying is the relatively large number of text glosses, Latin–Latin or Latin–English, unique to one or other of the manuscripts (especially evident in the section on adverb inflexion, Paris 99v–106r, Antwerp 32v–35v), and the very different pattern of word accents on, for example, Paris 83v and Antwerp 25r. It also seems implausible that an eyeskip error on Antwerp 41r (the omission of the phrase '. . . aduerbia poni debent . Sunt autem pleraque huiuscemodi aduerbia . . .') could have arisen from the Paris manuscript, where the two instances of the word *aduerbia* appear on different pages, 116r and 116v.

glosses of Antwerp–London derived from manuscript β, just as the main text did, β is the most likely source for the *Excerptiones* material that reached the **a**-order list.

Another piece of palaeographical evidence shows that we must not picture the scribe of the forward-sloping hand adding text glosses to an already completed book. On Antwerp 15v, this scribe has copied a scholion just beside a large display capital. Both capital and scholion are written together in identical red ink, showing that they were written at the same time. So the scribe of the forward-sloping hand not only wrote the initial capitals of his alphabetical batches in red, but in the role of rubricator he used red widely for display capitals. Presumably, then, he was involved throughout in the copying of the volume, and throughout he may have simultaneously added text glosses and capitals together, as he demonstrably did in this one instance. His role as primary glossator suggests in fact that he had the principal role in planning and executing the book, a task that would have involved extensive examination and handling of the exemplar, in this case manuscript β. One can only assume, therefore, that he might have used this same exemplar when it came time to collect text glosses to put in the **a**-order list.

Given the incomplete preservation of the manuscript evidence, no precise resolution of these thorny problems is possible. If β was a source for the glossary, it is logical to look also to the ancestor α, as mentioned earlier. Despite this efficient argument, however, further evidence from the Paris manuscript shows that its scribe was no passive recipient of the glossarial information on 65v but was actively involved in its compilation.

DRY-POINT GLOSSING IN THE PARIS MANUSCRIPT

As stated earlier, the presence of a French word like *desmentirs* is highly remarkable in a pre-Conquest manuscript. Yet this is not the only demonstrably French word present in the Paris manuscript. Direct examination, surprisingly, reveals several others accompanying it. Unlike *desmentirs*, these other words are dry-point, that is, scratched with the tip of an uninked stylus into the surface of the parchment, but like *desmentirs* they are all text glosses, either interlined or marginal.

Among the two dozen or more legible scratched glosses, I have identified no fewer than eight French words, all of them accompanying Latin lemmas, and often accompanied by supplementary Latin interpretamenta. These glosses are edited below. Because they are faint, their locations are identified as precisely as possible by numbers indicating the folio and nearest line(s) of script. Glosses above or below the writing block are identified as top or bottom, right or left. Superscripts are put in angle brackets, the ends of lines marked by a slash.

85r17–18, right margin: excellere <.i. surmonter>[35]
88r3, interlined: coniueo <.i. nuo . ceners>
88r2–3, right margin: coniuere <.i. signum facere/.i. ceners>[36]
94v17, interlined: fulcio <fulcire est sufulcirs>[37]
95r21, right margin: suffire <porfumers>[38]
95v10–11, left margin: insignire <.i. merchier>[39]
96r, lower left margin : . . . titillare <.i. catolliers>[40]
96r, lower right margin: . . . tota die .i. soiorners . . .[41]

Since the script of the two replacement quires shows the manuscript to have been on the Continent early in its history, the question is whether the French words were late additions or whether they are linked to the principal scribe who wrote *desmentirs* on 65v, and therefore to the larger glossarial project of which

---

[35] Both lemma and interpretamentum mean 'to surpass' or 'to excel'. The French verb in the form *surmunter* is first attested *c.* 1119, in the form *sormonter c.* 1155 (*Dictionnaire historique de la langue française*, s.v.).

[36] *Coniueo* means 'to wink' or 'to leave uncensured', *ergo* 'to connive at'. Old French *ceners* means 'to give a sign'. Latin *nuo* ('to nod') is a back formation from *adnuo*. *Ceners* is the ancestor of modern *signer* ('to sign', 'to make a sign'). For the environment of all these words in the glossary, see p. 104. The earliest attestation of *ceners* is again the *Chanson de Roland*, with the meaning 'to make the sign of the cross', according to the *Dictionnaire historique de la langue française*. The same source gives the gloss meaning as common from the twelfth and into the seventeenth century.

[37] *Sufulcirs* is a hapax legomenon, cited in neither Godefroy's *Dictionnaire de l'ancien française*, 10 vols. (Paris, 1880–1902) nor in *Altfranzösisches Wörterbuch*, ed. A. Tobler and E. Lommatzsch (Berlin and Wiesbaden, 1925–; in progress). The word is apparently a loan formation from Latin *suffulcio*, 'to prop from below', 'to keep from falling'. The form of the word in the Paris manuscript is certain: the final **s** is tall and quite clear. Old French *foucir* is the well-attested reflex of the Latin lemma, *fulcio* (*Altfranzösisches Wörterbuch*, p. 2178).

[38] Because it is attested only very late (fourteenth century), it is problematic to link *porfumers* with the eleventh-century scribe. Nevertheless, the lemma *suffio* occurs twice in the a-order list (below, p. 104). Ancestor of modern *parfumer* 'to perfume', *porfumers* is of undetermined Romance origin (*Dictionnaire historique de la langue française*, s.v.).

[39] *Merchier*, ancestor of modern *marquer* 'to mark', is attested in this form from *c.* 1120 (*Dictionnaire historique de la langue française*, s.v.). The OE cognate *mearcian* is found in the works of Alfred and Ælfric (*Oxford English Dictionary*, s.v. *mark*). It is interesting that Latin *insignire* is interpreted in Ælfric's *Grammar* by OE *mærsian* (*Grammatik*, p. 192), which is phonetically similar to the French interpretation here.

[40] *Catolliers*, ancestor of modern *chatouiller* 'to tickle' or 'to titillate', is attested *c.* 1220. The primitive spelling *ca-* indicates that the word was in currency at an early date (*Dictionnaire historique de la langue française*, s.v.).

[41] The gloss, damaged by trimming, is illegible at beginning and end. The meaning may be '[?to remain] all day is to sojourn'. Whatever the Latin verb, this is evidently a learned definition arrived at by translating the lemma by a vernacular phrase to which it is linked etymologically. *Soiorners*, ancestor of modern French *séjourner*, has been attested as a late-eleventh-, early-twelfth-century word (*Dictionnaire historique de la langue française*, s.v.); the shift of vowels (/o/ to /e/) is owing to the medieval school-pronunciation of Latin words (A. Ewert, *The French Language* (London, 1933), p. 55).

the **a**-order list is a part. A link between the dry-point glossing and the glossary does in fact exist: some Latin-Latin scratched glosses are incorporated by the **a**-order list, a situation mirroring that of the inked glosses we saw earlier. Given the small number of dry-point glosses, this connection must be considered significant; more than a fourth are replicated with verbatim repetition, as shown in the following list.

Paris scratched glosses	***a**-order list items*
ignaui <stultus> (20r1)	Ambesus i. inscius . seu ignauus . stultus (38.5)
astuti <[c]allidus> (20r2)	Astutus i. callidus . uafer (39.18)
	. . . astutus callere est . . . (115.16)
pellicio <decipio> (24r4)	Pellicio, xi i. blande decipio (201.2)
pellax <deceptor> (24r5)	Pellax .i. deceptor (262.10)
uarix <[l]epr[a]> (41r12)	Varix . cis .i. lepra minuta eo quod uaria cutem (114.24)
officio <noceo> (66r11)	Officio .i. impedio ł noceo (259.7)
	Officio .i. noceo (260.1 and .14)
caluo <decipio> (93r6)	Caluo .i. decipio (114.21)
pernix <[uelo]x> (95r top)	Pernix, citus .i. uelox, a perniciendo .i. a perseruerando (262.15)
	Pernix, nicis i. uelox uel perseuerans (264.13)

Moreover, from the eight glosses with French interpretamenta, no fewer than five lemmas are found among the **a**-order batches of Antwerp–London:

excellere <.i. surmonter>	Excello .i. emineo (191.23)
coniueo <.i. nuo . ceners>	Coniueo, es .i. oculus claudo, ł consentio,
coniuere <.i. signum facere/.i. ceners>	tractum a palpebris qui solent inuicem sibi consentire (115.6)
suffire <porfumers>	Suffio .i. subministro uel suffumigo (269.15)
	Suffio .i. suffumigo (271.5)
insignire <.i. merchier>	Insignio .i. nobilito (202.10)

A form of the word *suffulcio*, of which the hapax legomenon *sufulcirs* is a vernacular adaptation, also appears in the glossary as an interpretamentum: 'Subnixus .i. suffultus' (269.8);[42] and the unusual Latin interpretamentum *nuo* appears as a lemma: 'nuo i. assig[no]' (258.6). In addition to the sharing of text, there is also the connection of style: more than half the French words are infinitives substantivized with -*s*, an exact match with the form of *desmentirs*, a

---

[42] Past participle of *suffulcio* 'to prop below'.

consistency that bespeaks a refined method of scholarship on the part of the glossator.

CONCLUSIONS

The cumulative evidence – the connection to the glossary of the Paris text glossing, whether Latin or French, inked or scratched – argues for the involvement of the Paris scribe in the compilation in the **a**-order glossary of Antwerp–London. And because the scratched glosses can be read only with considerable difficulty one may assume they were written for the glossator's own benefit. They are, in other words, nonce glosses, the scribe's notations to himself. This chain of reasoning leads to some interesting conclusions: that the scribe of the Paris manuscript was a French speaker working in some capacity with the team of Englishmen who wrote the Antwerp–London manuscript, and that the Paris *Excerptiones de Prisciano* is a book he wrote at least in part for his own personal use.

While the exact relationship between this anonymous Frenchman and the compilers of the Antwerp–London **a**-order glossary remains hidden from view, at least on the evidence presented so far, the Paris manuscript holds a tell-tale clue to their co-operative effort. Alone of the 131 Paris folios, 65v has a notation in the extreme top outer margin. Originally at least four lines long, the only legible letters now are

... [?t]io .
... ria .

The notation, apparently in the text hand again, has been partially cut away in trimming, and has been further reduced by a black stain on the corner of the page. Yet the two anomalies of the page, the alphabetical glossing and the notation, must be connected.

Questions such as the exact role of the lost manuscripts α and β in the making of the glossary remain unanswered. What is sure, however, is that the makers of the **a**-order glossary utilized multiple versions of the *Excerptiones de Prisciano* in its compilation. This fact alone – the availability of numerous manuscripts that could have been used interchangeably – may make it impossible to map the exact path whereby the Priscian material found its way into the glossary. At the very least, however, it can be said that the Paris manuscript must have issued from the same scriptorium that produced the Antwerp–London and related manuscripts, and that it was present there at some stage in the compilation of the **a**-order glossary.

Let us now leave a purely textual consideration of the **a**-order list and set our evidence and conclusions into a historical context.

The discovery of a French connection via the Paris *Excerptiones* is particularly intriguing, since the Antwerp–London glossaries have been seen as an important repository of French-derived words in Old English. The French words that occur there are *capun* 'capon' and *custure*, ancestor of modern *couture* 'sewing' or 'seam'. *Capun* appears twice, glossing first the lemma *capo* and then *gallinacius*. *Custure* appears alongside OE *seam* ('seam') in glossing Latin *sutura*.[43] These are rarities among rarities. Among the sparsely attested cross-Channel borrowings, *custure* is a hapax legomenon, and *capun* is found elsewhere only in a late addition to the Brussels glossary.[44] So implausible was the appearance of these words in an early-eleventh-century text that Förster dated the Antwerp–London class list to the twelfth century, while others have denied a French origin altogether.[45] Rather than seeing anomalies to be explained away, however, let us now look to the unnamed French scribe of the Paris manuscript.

There is strong and unmistakable evidence tying the Antwerp–London and related manuscripts to Abingdon. A six-hexameter poem (inc. 'Altaris titulus profusus...') added on Antwerp fol. 1 commemorates SS Eustace and Edward, both of whose relics were venerated at Abingdon.[46] More explicit connections are the hexametrical riddle which describes the Abingdon measure for beer known as 'Æthelwold's bowl',[47] and, on the original fol. 2 (now London 1), an elegy addressed to Wulfgar, abbot of Abingdon 990–1016. The Brussels Aldhelm can also be placed there at about mid-eleventh century, since its glosses were then copied into the Abingdon manuscript Digby 146.[48] This accumulation of evidence for Abingdon provenance – complex and varied, widely distributed – is certainly trustworthy. That same evidence now connects to Abingdon the French scribe who wrote the *Excerptiones de Prisciano* in the Paris manuscript.

The long elegy on London fol. 1 is written in the forward-sloping hand of the a-order list.[49] It is a witty dialogue recording the entreaties of a certain French-born Herbertus who asks for warm winter clothing, and the terse, unsympa-

[43] In Kindschi, pp. 105.10, 105.12 and 272.13. The first two instances are in the Latin–English class list, the third in the mostly Latin a-order list.   [44] Förster, 'Glossenhandschrift', p. 121.
[45] A. Campbell represents the most extreme view in minimizing the French influence: 'No loanwords which can certainly be regarded as French occur in manuscripts older than 1066, except *prūd, prūt* proud, whence are derived *pryte, pryt* pride. There are . . . a few words like *capun, castel*, which might be derived from Latin or French' (*Old English Grammar* (Oxford, 1959), p. 221).
[46] Ker, *Catalogue*, p. 3. The poem (edited by Förster, 'Glossenhandschrift', p. 154) and its Abingdon associations are discussed by M. Lapidge, 'Æthelwold and the *Vita S. Eustachii*', in his *Anglo-Latin Literature 900–1066* (London, 1993), pp. 213–23, at 218.
[47] D. Porter, 'Æthelwold's Bowl and the *Chronicle of Abingdon*', *NM* 97 (1996), 163–7. I omit from discussion here the elegy on the death of Ælfric, archbishop of Canterbury (Ker, *Catalogue*, p. 3), as that reflects as much a Canterbury as an Abingdon connection.
[48] Ker, *Catalogue*, p. 382.
[49] The folio is an originally blank flyleaf. The poem is ed. E. Dümmler, 'Lateinische Gedichte des neunten bis elften Jahrhunderts', *Neues Archiv der Gesellschaft für ältere deutsche Geschichtskunde* 10 (1885), 333–57, at 351–3.

thetic reply of Abbot Wulfgar. The poem is a stylistic *tour de force*, a mock epic describing the ineffectual battles of *Ver* (Spring), girded with white flowers, and *Vulcanus* (Fire), his back armed with wood, against the cruel onslaughts of doughty *Hiems* (Winter). In melodramatic tones the poet laments his own sufferings at the hands of Winter, who sleeps in his bed and traces his every footstep. Wulfgar's deadpan reply parodies the parody – the provisions of Benedict's Rule are sufficient.

Just as the Wulfgar of this agonistic display of wit is a historical personage, so plausibly is the Frenchman named Herbert, though his name occurs in no other Insular manuscript.[50] It is possible that this Herbert was the French scribe of the Paris manuscript. How Herbert might have come to England and made his way to Abingdon is of course not known, but from its inception the Benedictine Reform had much intercourse with France, and in the early eleventh century cross-Channel ties were becoming common.[51]

The details of Herbert's life and career have vanished. The few remaining clues share the common denominator of French, yet in order to guess at a rounded portrait much imagination is necessary. Neither insisting on exactness nor expecting documentary confirmation, we can only aim to construct a plausible account.

Born and reared in France – 'Francia me genuit' – Herbert would have acquired French as his native language, and might have used it for personal

---

[50] Michael Lapidge draws my attention to the tenth-century Horace manuscript of Fleury provenance, Paris, BNF, lat. 7971. On 3r a metrical ex-libris in elegiacs names Herbertus as the donor: 'Hic liber est, Benedicte, tuus, uenerande, per [euum]; / Obtulit Herbertus seruus et ipse tuus'. Another ex-libris on 1v names Constantius, who had close ties with the Ramsey monk Oswald when Oswald was studying at Fleury. See A. Vidier, *L'historiographie à Saint-Benoît-sur-Loire et les miracles de Saint Benoît* (Paris, 1965), p. 53, and M. Mostert, *The Library of Fleury* (Hilversum, 1989), no. BF1140 (p. 222).

[51] Relations between Canterbury and Fleury were particularly strong, for example. V. Ortenberg documents communications over several decades of the late tenth and early eleventh centuries: *The English Church and the Continent in the Tenth and Eleventh Centuries* (Oxford, 1992), p. 10, n. 28. There was likewise considerable communication between Canterbury and Abingdon. Ælfric, archbishop of Canterbury from 995 to 1005, had been an Abingdon monk, and Siward, abbot of Abingdon from 1030 to 1044, travelled to Canterbury in 1044 to become executive assistant to the enfeebled archbishop. He returned to Abingdon in 1048, dying there on 23 October. There must have been many others who travelled between Canterbury and Abingdon, either alone or in the train of great men like Ælfric and Siward. See T. Graham, 'CCCC 57 and its Anglo-Saxon Users', *Anglo-Saxon Manuscripts and their Heritage*, ed. P. Pulsiano and E. Traherne (Aldershot, 1998), pp. 21–69, for an analysis of the historical and codicological links between Canterbury and Abingdon. As for the presence of a Frenchman at Abingdon, it may be relevant that an anonymous redactor of the Abingdon version of the Anglo-Saxon Chronicle exhibited both interest and expertise in French: see *The Anglo-Saxon Chronicle, MS B*, ed. S. Taylor, The AS Chronicle: a Collaborative Edition, ed. D. Dumville and S. Keynes 4 (Cambridge, 1983), p. lxi.

David W. Porter

notations such as the scratched glosses in the Paris manuscript. Scribal training in his native country – 'seu puerum docuit' – would account for the use of the Fleury abbreviation for *est*, an idiosyncratic trait of the script of the Paris *Excerptiones*. The superior education available on the Continent, and at Fleury in particular,[52] would account for the excellent Latin of the Paris *Excerptiones* and for the creativity in Latin verse, as evidenced by the elegiac poem.

That poem, which projects a clear picture of its author as a glib and funny man, recalls neighbouring texts on the same theme of acquisition and consumption. The hexametrical riddle is a ribald description of the size and effect of a gargantuan beer ration. The prose letter at the end of the manuscript, moreover, recalls the relative situation of the elegy's interlocutors in that it is a request to an authority figure ('Ælf' = ?Ælfric) for permission to obtain fish, a food permitted by the Benedictine Rule. Some language in the letter repeats Herbert's elegy practically verbatim, so perhaps this too is his work, or, alternatively, a reflection of his influence in the work of his students.[53] It is also interesting that the poems at the front of the manuscript contain some hermeneutic vocabulary from the glossaries.[54] This textual interaction must arise from the social interaction of teacher and students – the effect of school experience on literary production.

There are indeed indications that the Paris scribe is a teacher and scholar. Every aspect of the glossarial work associated with the **a**-order list evokes the classroom, and the same is true of the short Latin–English list in the top margin of Paris 28v. With interpretations in merographs that conceal the English equivalents, the text is an early form of the teacher's manual. There is also the practical nature of the *Excerptiones* itself, which would most likely have a classroom application, and, as we saw, the likelihood of its personal use by the man who copied it. The dry-point sketch of the Paris manuscript shows its scribe also to have been an expert artist. We may not be too far wrong then to infer this artist's

---

[52] For an example, see *Byrhtferth's Enchiridion*, ed. P. Baker and M. Lapidge, EETS ss 15 (Oxford, 1995) for an assessment of the career and influence of Abbo of Fleury, one of the luminaries of monastic culture near the turn of the millennium.

[53] 'Perlege tamen et, que peto, perfice clemens et mihimet misero miseriis miserere misello...' (Förster, 'Glossenhandschrift', p. 153). Cf. Dümmler, 'Lateinische', p. 351.8: 'Perlege tu pastor perfice quodque precor'; and 353.89: 'Tu mihimet misero miserans miserere misello'.

[54] An entry from the class glossary, for example, holds the solution to the Latin riddle (my 'A Double Solution to the Latin Riddle in MS Antwerp, Plantin-Moretus Museum 16.2', *ANQ* 9.2 (1996), 3–9, at 3). Some lexical rarities from Herbert's elegy, *amphibalis, birrus, cauma*, also appear in the class list (Kindschi, pp. 88.3, 155.13 and 234.10). And it is worth noting the elegy's adjectival forms *lupinus* and *ferinus*, which recall the discussion in the *Excerptiones* of adjectives derived from animal names (London 7v): 'Omnia quae a nominibus mutorum animalium cuiuscumque sint declinationis diriuantur in formam possessiuum i penultimam longam seruant, ut aper aprinus, caper caprinus, ceruus ceruinus, porcinus, taurinus, ferus uel fera ferinus, caninus, leporinus, lupinus. . . .'

classroom influence in the small specimen of pictorial effort from the Antwerp–London manuscript, the sketch of a man's head in the outer top margin of London 24v.

And the French influence, via the loanwords discussed above, demonstrably extends to the first and the last strata of the Antwerp–London glossaries, the **a**-order list and the bilingual class list. This French element is a commonality that links the two glossaries in what appears to be a school tradition. It shows, in other words, that the close proximity of these two very different texts is not a matter of chance but rather of deliberate design.[55] Nor is this the only commonality. Just as the alphabetical list has an indisputable interaction with the text glosses of the Paris manuscript, so does the class list. There, among a list of vocabulary relating to animals (London 6r), the Latin lemma *mutinus* is interpreted by the English words *gadinca* and *hnoc*. Now *mutinus* was thought to be a hapax legomenon, a possible mistake for the relatively common *mutina* 'goat' or 'sheep'. It is therefore intriguing that the word appears as the lemma of a scratched gloss in the bottom right margin of Paris 94v. Although the scratched interpretamentum is, alas, illegible to me, the first and last letters are clearly **m** and **s**, with five or six letters intervening. Whether or not that illegible word is the Old French ancestor of modern *mouton*,[56] the shared lemma by itself directly links the compiler of the class list with the Paris scribe. It is another indication that the varied glossarial lists of Antwerp–London constitute a single corporate enterprise, as asserted at the outset of this paper.

Briefly to recapitulate: the evidence sketches a picture of a group of early-eleventh-century monks compiling a large corpus of glossarial material. They worked, at least some of them, some of the time, at Abingdon, and among their number was a Frenchman, the same one whom we have guessed is Herbert, who was a poet and a wit. This Frenchman was a talented Latin scholar and also had some interest in English, perhaps for its pedagogical use. Conceivably it was exposure to the vernacular educational tradition of English that inspired him to use his native French for textual annotation.[57] The evidence further suggests his

---

[55] Kindschi's comment on this topic is misleading: 'The Latin–Old English class glossary . . . is crowded into such marginal space as remained [after the alphabetical list was written]' (p. 2). Antwerp–London in fact holds much empty marginal space which the scribe of the class glossary chose to ignore. Instead he squeezed his text onto a few leaves, between earlier strata in the forward-sloping hand.

[56] This seems a strong possibility, and if it is so, one with relevance for the word *porfumers*, which as we noted above is unattested before the fourteenth century. The earliest attestation of *mouton* is some 150 years after the date of the glossary, and even then it is considered a dialectal form (*Dictionnaire historique de la langue française*, s.v.). *Mutinus* must be related to *mutina*, which in the Paris Priscian (20v) is glossed '. . . bestia sine cornibus', an animal without horns, i.e. a sheep.

[57] One may speculate whether the hapax *sufulcirs* was a loan formation in imitation of Anglo-Saxon scholastic practice.

influence in school texts, in creative literature, in the scribal and pictorial arts. Several details of scholarly method have been inferred, among them the simultaneous use of several manuscripts. The French scribe's agency may be suspected in the early removal of the Paris manuscript to the Continent, and the later close proximity of an Insular version of the same text (the exemplar of the replacement quires) suggests that the Paris manuscript was only one among several manuscripts he carried with him to his native country.[58]

---

[58] In the course of this work I incurred many debts. I thank the institutions that allowed me to examine manuscripts in their keeping: the British Library, the Bibliothèque Nationale de France and the Plantin-Moretus Museum. Thanks also to the National Endowment for the Humanities, which supported this work with a research fellowship, and to the English Department of Louisiana State University, which welcomed me as a visiting scholar in 1997.

Unfulfilled promise: the rubrics of the Old English prose Genesis

BENJAMIN C. WITHERS

The Old English prose Genesis contains a series of innovative rubrics, unparalleled in the Vulgate tradition, which divide the story of Genesis into a series of holy biographies of the patriarchs Noah, Abraham and Joseph. These rubrics, added to the text in the eleventh century, use formulaic language derived from contemporary documents such as Anglo-Saxon wills and thereby regulate how Genesis was to be read and interpreted by an aristocratic layman or novice monk. The rubrics blend ancient Hebrew narratives, stories of the saints and the legal conventions familiar to the reader in order to portray 'sacred history' as an unbroken, legally sanctioned inheritance. They emphasize the Covenant of God with Abraham and the people of Israel and assure the contemporary reader that he too will inherit an unfulfilled promise manifested in God's covenant with the patriarchs.

These rubrics unexpectedly elevate the story of the patriarch Joseph to a level equal to that of Noah and Abraham. The emphasis given to Joseph by the rubrics leads me to consider how the story is presented in four eleventh-century manuscripts: Oxford, Bodleian Library, Laud Misc. 509, London, British Library, Cotton Otho B. x and Claudius B. iv; and Cambridge, Corpus Christi College 201.[1] In these manuscript contexts, the rubrics announce that the story of Joseph is a significant juncture in sacred history. Because he is the first patriarch to inherit the promise of the covenant without firsthand communication with God, Joseph functions as a prototype for the Anglo-Saxon reader who, like Joseph, must rely on an oral or written transmission of the promised covenant.

Little attention has been devoted to these rubrics or to their specific manuscript contexts, because traditional studies of the Old English prose Genesis are preoccupied with evidence for its authorship and the mechanics of its translation. I re-examine the text in terms of how it was read, instead of how it

---

[1] These manuscripts are described by N. R. Ker, *Catalogue of Manuscripts containing Anglo-Saxon* (Oxford, 1957; repr. with suppl. 1990) and listed by H. Gneuss, 'A Preliminary List of Manuscripts Written or Owned in England up to 1100', *ASE* 9 (1981), 1–60. A facsimile of Claudius B. iv has been published in *The Old English Illustrated Hexateuch: British Museum Cotton Claudius B.IV*, ed. C. R. Dodwell and P. A. M. Clemoes, EEMF 18 (Copenhagen, 1974). The text is ed. S. J. Crawford, *The Old English Version of the Heptateuch, Ælfric's Treatise on the Old and New Testament and his Preface to Genesis*, EETS os 160 (London, 1922; repr. 1969 with the text of two additional manuscripts transcribed by N. R. Ker).

was authored. As previous studies have shown, words on a manuscript page, although written, represent the spoken; the reader's performance involves hearing and speaking, as well as seeing.[2] This interrelationship of oral and literate patterns derived from previously read or heard texts directly informs the experience of reading the Genesis rubrics.[3] The prose Genesis operates in the interstices of oral and literate forms of communication and provides evidence for operation of 'transitional literacy' in late Anglo-Saxon England.[4]

For the medieval audience of the Old English Genesis, the newly added rubrics gloss the text and cue 'sedimented reading habits' which in turn determine the context for the text's interpretation.[5] For the modern reader, the rubrics serve as written records of the reading experience and allow us to filter through the 'sedimented layers' of eleventh-century reading habits and interpretative patterns. These patterns of reading, in turn, provide us with a unique opportunity to reconsider theories of the power of language to unite or divide society and the creation of a cohesive community of texts in Anglo-Saxon England. The vernacular Old Testament translations are based upon and further a distinct outlook on the world, or an ideology; the rubrics promote the close political and social co-operation desired by Anglo-Saxon ecclesiastical and secular hierarchies.[6]

TEXTS AND CONTEXTS OF THE PROSE GENESIS

Origins and provenances of the manuscripts

The prose Genesis is part of a series of compilations that eventually comprised the first seven books of the Old Testament.[7] These paraphrased texts – verses

---

[2] See R. Crosby, 'Oral Delivery in the Middle Ages', *Speculum* 2 (1936), 88–110; M. Camille, 'Seeing and Reading: Some Visual Implications of Literacy', *Art Hist.* 8 (1985), 26–49. Cf. R. Brilliant, 'The Bayeux Tapestry: a Striped Narrative for their Eyes and Ears', *Word and Image* 7 (1991), 113–18.

[3] See K. O'Brien O'Keeffe, *Visible Song: Transitional Literacy in Old English Verse*, CSASE 4 (Cambridge, 1990). I am also expanding the sense of 'community of texts' as it is discussed by B. Stock, *The Implications of Literacy: Written Language and Models of Interpretation in the Eleventh and Twelfth Centuries* (Princeton, NJ, 1983).

[4] I am here concerned with the relationship of oral and literate patterns in the Old English vernacular similar to those explored by O'Brien O'Keeffe, *Visible Song*, pp. 6–14.

[5] 'We never really confront a text immediately, in all its freshness as a thing-in-itself. Rather, texts come before us as the always-already read; we apprehend them through sedimented layers of previous interpretations, or – if the text is brand new – through the sedimented reading habits and categories developed by those interpretive traditions': F. Jameson, *The Political Unconscious: Narrative as a Socially Symbolic Act* (Ithaca, NY, 1981), p. 9.

[6] Ideology refers to 'the means through which man gives meaning to his social world and thereby makes it available to his practical activity': L. Patterson, *Negotiating the Past: the Historical Understanding of Medieval Literature* (Madison, WI, 1987), p. 54.

[7] A paraphrase of all seven books is found in only one manuscript, Bodleian Library, Laud Misc. 509. For this reason, to refer to the texts as they are found in other manuscript contexts as

are shortened, some chapters reduced or left out, and entire books condensed – are derived from the Vulgate.[8] The origin of the text has been traditionally traced to Ælfric of Eynsham, whose *Preface to Genesis*, addressed to the ealdorman Æthelweard, introduces the translation in two of the manuscripts under consideration.[9] Ælfric, it has been conjectured on stylistic grounds, composed his portions of the paraphrase between the years 992 and 1002.[10] A subsequent 'anonymous' compiler gathered material from Ælfric's translations and homilies and joined them with other translations.[11]

These translations seem to have been very appealing to an Anglo-Saxon audience; eight surviving fragments, portions, or 'complete' versions of the text are extant today. Of these eight known versions, three are stray folios from manuscripts now lost and one dates from the twelfth century.[12] The four remaining

---

being part of the 'Old English Heptateuch' is a misnomer. Only the Laud manuscript can accurately be called a 'Heptateuch'; the other paraphrased texts must be seen in the contexts of their own unique compilations to be more accurately understood, as I argue below.

[8] R. Marsden, 'Old Latin Intervention in the Old English Heptateuch', *ASE* 23 (1994), 229–64.

[9] Claudius B. iv and Laud Misc. 509. The initial folio of Claudius B. iv has been lost but was transcribed by Robert Talbot in his notebook, Cambridge, Corpus Christi College 379. See T. Graham, 'Early Modern Uses of Claudius B.IV: Robert Talbot and William L'Isle', *The Old English Hexateuch: Aspects and Approaches*, ed. R. Barnhouse and B. Withers (Kalamazoo, MI, forthcoming).

[10] P. Clemoes, 'The Chronology of Ælfric's Works', *The Anglo-Saxons: Studies in Some Aspects of Their History and Culture Presented to Bruce Dickins*, ed. P. Clemoes (London, 1959), pp. 212–47; repr. as *The Chronology of Ælfric's Work* (Binghamton, NY, 1980); P. Clemoes, 'The Composition of the Old English Text', *The Old English Illustrated Hexateuch*, pp. 42–53, concludes that Ælfric was responsible for Genesis I–III, V.32, VI–IX, XIII–XXII; Numbers XII–end (except XIII.5–17) and Joshua (except I.1–10 and XII).

[11] In his Preface to Genesis, Ælfric states that he has translated the story of Creation up to Isaac (Genesis XXIV) and that 'some other man' had translated the rest. P. Clemoes, in *The Old English Illustrated Hexateuch*, credits 'Anonymous' with filling the gaps in Genesis IV–V.31, X–XI, XXIV.15– XL.25, Exodus, Leviticus, Numbers I–XII and Deuteronomy. Clemoes proposed that the paraphrase was gathered together and compiled by one man, the Ramsey monk and scholar Byrhtferth. P. Baker, 'The Old English Canon of Byrhtferth of Ramsey', *Speculum* 55 (1980), 22–37, rejects Clemoes's attribution, concluding that the non-Ælfrician portions of the paraphrase were translated and compiled by some other anonymous author, probably from the monastery at Ramsey. At present we are left with an agreed division of the text into distinct sections translated by different authors; one is definitely Ælfric of Eynsham, the other an unknown 'anonymous' scholar, possibly Byrhtferth or someone else at Ramsey. See now R. Marsden, 'Translation by Committee?: the "Anonymous" Text of the Old English Hexateuch', *The Old English Hexateuch*, ed. Barnhouse and Withers (forthcoming).

[12] One (Lincoln, Cathedral Library, 298 no. 2) consists of two leaves containing the text of Numbers IX.1–XVI.2. S. J. Crawford, 'The Lincoln Fragment of the Old English Version of the Heptateuch', *MLR* 15 (1920), 1–6, dates the leaves to 'not later than the third quarter of the eleventh century' and states that its text corresponds to that found in Laud Misc. 509 'with phonological variations'. Two other fragments, these preserving portions of the text of Exodus, are the sole remains of another manuscript of the translation. One fragment, now in the Pierpont Morgan Library, contains portions of Exodus XVI.16, XVI.17–XVII.13,

manuscripts all date from the eleventh century and contain the rubrics which are discussed here (the rubrics are not found in the twelfth-century text). One, Cotton Claudius B. iv, contains the Hexateuch illustrated by a cycle of over 400 narrative images. This manuscript is dated to the second quarter of the eleventh century.[13] A second manuscript, Bodleian Library, Laud Misc. 509, dated palaeographically to the third quarter of the eleventh century, contains the Hexateuch as well as a paraphrase of the Book of Judges, ascribed to Ælfric.[14] Two other manuscripts, Cambridge, Corpus Christi College 201 and BL, Cotton Otho B. x, contain the story of Joseph beginning with XXXVII.2. Both are dated by Ker to the first half of the eleventh century, and in both the story of Joseph is associated with a series of homilies and Lives of the Saints.[15]

The surviving manuscripts of the Old Testament paraphrase indicate that its texts were disseminated widely. As discussed above, some portions originated with Ælfric, who lived in south-west England, while, as Clemoes and Baker have shown, other portions appear to have been created by someone with some connection to Byrhtferth at the monastery at Ramsey.[16] Efforts to transmit the text, or at least parts of it, can be attributed provisionally to prestigious English monasteries, including Christ Church and St Augustine's in Canterbury and to the New Minster at Winchester.[17] While the precise origins of the paraphrase, in terms of author or provenance, cannot be traced, the number of extant texts as well as the places and personages associated with their transmission indicate

---

XXIX.46–XXXII.24. Crawford reports that the other fragment, formerly at Norwich but now lost, contained Exodus IX.20–X.9; XIII.19–XIV.23. The translation continued to be influential into the twelfth century. Several exegetical annotations, in Latin and English, were added to the text of Claudius B. iv. One twelfth-century manuscript, Cambridge, University Library, Ii. 1. 33, contains a portion of the beginning of Genesis (to XXIV.22), which belongs to a different recension of the paraphrase text: see F. H. Chase, 'A New Text of the Old English Genesis', *ASNSL* 100 (1898), 241–66. See also Crawford, *Heptateuch*, pp. 424–39, and J. Raith, 'Ælfric's Share in the Old English Pentateuch', *RES* ns 3 (1952), 305–14.

[13] Ker dates the 'two heavy, uncalligraphic, round hands' to the 'middle part of the first half of the eleventh century' ('xi¹' in his shorthand notation): *Catalogue*, p. 179. Ker's date is accepted by Gneuss, 'Preliminary List', p. 22 (no. 315). Art historians, following the lead of Francis Wormald, prefer to date the pictures on stylistic criteria to the 'second quarter of the eleventh century': F. Wormald, *English Drawings of the Tenth and Eleventh Centuries* (London, 1953), p. 67 (no. 26). For an assessment of Wormald's dating, see B. Withers, 'A Sense of Englishness: Claudius B. iv and Colonialism in the Mid-Twentieth Century', *The Old English Hexateuch*, ed. Barnhouse and Withers.

[14] Ker, *Catalogue*, pp. 422–4 (no. 344). Readings variant to Claudius B. iv are given by Crawford, *Heptateuch*. [15] Ker, *Catalogue*, pp. 82–90 and 224–9, and Raith, 'Ælfric's Share'.

[16] See above, n. 11.

[17] Laud Misc. 509 is attributed to Christ Church by Crawford, *Heptateuch*, p. 440. Claudius B. iv was first attributed to St Augustine's by M. R. James, *The Ancient Libraries of Canterbury and Dover* (Cambridge, 1903), no. 95. Corpus 201 has been attributed to the New Minster by T. A. M. Bishop, *English Caroline Minuscule* (Oxford, 1971), p. xv, n. 2.

Unfulfilled promise: the rubrics of the Old English prose Genesis

that it was considered to be a significant and valuable project. Setting aside questions concerning the origins of the text and the rubrics for now, I will concentrate on these manuscripts' present form, as the texts exist now to be read.[18]

The rubrics and the structure of Genesis

Nothing similar to the rubrics in the Old English prose Genesis, to my knowledge, can be found in any Latin version of Genesis.[19] As eleventh-century productions, they communicate a method of reading the text that several different scribes considered to be worth recording in the several different manuscript contexts discussed above. The rubrics therefore reveal attitudes about the text that may have wide-ranging implications for understanding how and by whom it was meant to be read. As I will show below, their presence restructures the text of Genesis in ways that recall patterns of reading generated by other eleventh-century vernacular texts.

Significantly, however, the rubrics divide the Old English text in ways that differ from the standard treatment of the Vulgate. Latin texts of the Bible are usually marked by a consecutive series of small roman numerals, *capitula*, set in the margins of the manuscript.[20] The *capitula* index the brief, narrative summaries of the principal scriptural events or actions found at the beginning of each book. They enable the reader to locate a desired section or story, in particular those lections required in the various monastic services.[21] The paraphrased texts have no numerical divisions. Only in Claudius B. iv, where illustrations punctuate the text at regular intervals, do we find a structure analogous to the *capitula* of

---

[18] See A. J. Frantzen, *Desire for Origins: New Language, Old English, and Teaching the Tradition* (New Brunswick, NJ, 1990), pp. 1–27.

[19] See D. de Bruyne, *Sommaires et rubriques de la Bible latine* (Namur, 1914); M. T. Gibson, *The Bible in the Latin West* (Notre Dame, IN, 1993), pp. 10–11. For the Vulgate in Anglo-Saxon England, see R. Marsden, 'The Old Testament in Late Anglo-Saxon England: Preliminary Observations on the Textual Evidence', *The Early Medieval Bible: its Production, Decoration and Use*, ed. R. Gameson, Cambridge Stud. in Palaeography and Codicology 2 (Cambridge, 1994), 101–24; and Marsden, 'Old Latin Intervention', pp. 229–30.

[20] Only one complete Latin Bible from late Anglo-Saxon England is extant today, London, BL, Royal 1. E. VII + VIII. The manuscript dates from the tenth century with eleventh-century replacements for leaves lost at the beginning of Genesis. In this manuscript the capitula are marked in the text with an ink capital. E. Temple, *Anglo-Saxon Manuscripts 900–1066* (London, 1976), no. 102, pl. 319; A. Heimann, 'Three Illustrations from the Bury St. Edmunds Psalter and their Prototypes', *Jnl of the Courtauld and Warburg Inst.* 29 (1966), 39–59; Marsden, 'The Old Testament in Late Anglo-Saxon England', pp. 109–19; and *idem*, 'Old Latin Intervention', pp. 236–7.

[21] Genesis, as well as other books of the Hexateuch, was read starting at Quadragesima, to provide a historical context for the events of the Passion recounted in the Gospels. Readings from these books were a prominent part of Matins: see A. Hughes, *Medieval Manuscripts for Mass and Office: a Guide to their Terminology* (Toronto, 1982), p. 22.

Latin texts, in that they divide the text into discrete episodes.[22] Yet, unlike *capitula*, the images follow the text they illustrate; in other words they are not markers of textual beginnings but rather visual recapitulations of the narrative. They do not help the reader find a passage within the manuscript as much as help the viewer to recall it.

These illustrations, in turn, fit into a larger structure signalled in Claudius B. iv by larger than normal initials in conjunction with short passages written in red ink capitals.[23] Claudius B. iv has two such rubricated passages in the text of Genesis. One marks the story of Joseph which begins at Genesis XXXVII.2 with the introduction 'Her cydde God ælmihtig hys mildheortnysse þe he Abrahame behet on Iosepe, Abrahames ofsprincge.' As seen in the list below, this introduction to the Joseph story is also found in Laud Misc. 509 and, in a slightly different form, in the Otho B. x and Corpus manuscripts.[24] In the Claudius text, another rubric is found on 21r, at the beginning of our ch. XII, the start of the story of Abraham. A similar rubric is found at the same location in the text of the Laud manuscript. On 12v of the Claudius manuscript a space was left at the top of the page for another rubric.[25] Now only an extra-large initial, similar to those found with the two previous rubrics, marks the beginning of the story of Noah in ch. VI. Fortunately, the Laud manuscript preserves this rubric as well as two others not found in Claudius B. iv. The Laud manuscript introduces Ælfric's 'Preface to Genesis' with the rubricated Latin phrase 'Incipit prefatio Genesis Anglice.' The text of the Preface runs continuously into the rubricated 'Incipit Liber Genesis.' Once again, space has been left in Claudius B. iv but the rubric was never added.[26]

For the convenience of the reader I compare the Old English texts of the rubrics in question, noting their translation.[27]

---

[22] As I explain elsewhere ('Present Patterns, Past Tense: Text and Illustration in London, British Library Cotton Ms. Claudius B.iv', unpubl. PhD dissertation, Univ. of Chicago, 1994), Claudius B. iv contains a variety of visual and textual devices that signal an underlying structure for the narrative and motivate the reader/viewer to understand the biblical text in terms of his or her knowledge of other textual or visual experiences.

[23] For a general history of the use of decoration and initial to mark textual divisions in the Middle Ages, see C. Nordenfalk, 'The Beginnings of Book Decoration', *Essays in Honor of George Swarzenski*, ed. O. Goetz (Chicago, IL, 1951), pp. 9–20.

[24] I will examine these differences below. Some textual variants are noted by Crawford, *Heptateuch*, pp. 424–39. Raith examines the differences in more detail in 'Ælfric's Share'.

[25] Dodwell and Clemoes' facsimile, *Old English Illustrated Hexateuch*, illustrates the arrangement of this page, although the black and white photographs of the facsimile disguise the addition of the writing at the top of the page, belonging to a twelfth-century annotator, which now fills the space originally left for the rubric.

[26] Dodwell and Clemoes, *Old English Illustrated Hexateuch*, 1r.

[27] Untranslated texts to all the quotations from Claudius B. iv, Laud Misc. 509 and Otho B. x can be found in Crawford, *Heptateuch*. The translations, where no other authority is cited, are my own.

Unfulfilled promise: the rubrics of the Old English prose Genesis

Genesis I
    Laud Misc. 509, 3r: 'Incipit Liber Genesis Anglice.'[28]
    Cotton Claudius B. iv, 1v: blank space left in text.

Genesis V.31
    Laud Misc. 509, 6r: 'Her swutelað þas ælmihtigan Godes mildheortnisse 7 his wundru, hu he Noe bearh 7 his wife 7 his teame æt þam miclan flode.'[29]
    Cotton Claudius B. iv, 12v: blank space left in text.

Genesis XII.1
    Laud Misc. 509, 9r: 'Her swutelað þas ælmihtigan Godes mildheortnysse 7 his wundru, hu he Abraham geceas 7 his bletsunga him sealde and his ofspringe.'
    Cotton Claudius B. iv, 20r: 'Her swutelað þæs ælmihtigan Godes mildheortnyss 7 hys wundra, hu he Abraham geceas 7 hys bletsunga him sealde 7 hys ofspringe.'[30]

Genesis XXXVII.2
    Laud Misc. 509, 24v: 'Her cydde God ælmihtig his mildheortnysse þe he Abrahame behet on Iosepe, Abrahames ofspringe.'[31]
    Cotton Claudius B. iv, 53r: 'Her cydde God ælmihtig hys mildheortnysse þe he Abrahame behet on Iosepe, Abrahames ofspringe.'[32]
    Corpus Christi College 201, p. 151: 'Her cydde god ælmihtig his mildheortnisse þe he Abrahame behet and Iosepe and Abrahames ofspringe.'[33]
    Cotton Otho B. x, (now destroyed): 'Her cydde god ælmihtig his mildheortnysse þe he Abrahame behet and Iosepe Abrahames ofspringe.'[34]

Structurally, these rubrics divide the book of Genesis into four distinct parts: creation to Noah, Noah to Abraham, Abraham to Joseph, Joseph to the end of

---

[28] The Laud manuscript begins with a now faded four-line red initial to Ælfric's *Preface to Genesis*. The text of the Preface runs continuously into the rubricated Genesis Incipit. A large two-line green initial 'O' marks the start of the Old English text. Throughout the Laud manuscript, the text is punctuated by black ink, one line initials. Occasionally a larger one-and-one-half-line initial marks sections of the text, though without breaks in the text lines.

[29] 'Here is made known (or manifested) the mercy of Almighty God and his miracles, how he saved Noah and his wife and his offspring at that great flood.' Crawford, *Heptateuch*, p. 99, note to V. 32.

[30] 'Here is made known (or manifested) the mercy of Almighty God and his miracles, how he chose Abraham and gave his blessing to him and his offspring.' *Ibid.* p.114.

[31] *Ibid.* p. 170.

[32] 'Here Almighty God testified his mercy which he promised Abraham, in Joseph, Abraham's offspring.'   [33] Not recorded by Crawford; see Raith, 'Ælfric's Share', p. 305.

[34] Text recorded by H. Wanley, *Antiquæ literaturæ septentrionalis liber alter... catalogus* (Oxford, 1705), p. 192. See Crawford, *Heptateuch*, pp. 5–6, and Raith, 'Ælfric's Share', p. 305.

Genesis.[35] The first three divisions mark the beginnings of the first three divisions of the Six Ages of the World, a medieval historical construct which is based upon a typological relationship to the First Six Days of Creation.[36] Ælfric, in his 'Treatise on the Old and New Testaments', lists the Six Ages as (1) The creation to Noah; (2) Noah to Abraham; (3) Abraham to David; (4) David to the Babylonian Captivity; (5) Restoration to Christ; and (6) Christ to the present.[37] It is surprising, then, that Joseph's life is highlighted by the rubrics since, unlike Abraham's and Noah's, his story does not demarcate the beginning of a new age; instead, in exegetical tradition, Joseph partakes of the same age as Abraham.[38]

A COMMUNITY OF TEXTS: PATRIARCHS, RUBRICS AND WILLS

The rubrics in Genesis accentuate the biographical aspect of Genesis and enshrine the story of Joseph alongside those of Noah and Abraham. The Otho and Corpus manuscripts strikingly remove the story of Joseph from its Old Testament context and present his life as an independent story. This raises the question, why single out Joseph? In the context of Genesis, why rubricate his story and not those of other important figures such as Isaac or Jacob? The rubrics are the key for understanding how the vernacular text of Genesis might be read and why portions of it were included in the Otho and Corpus manuscripts.

Noah, Abraham and wills: receiving a promise

Joseph, I argue, had special importance for the Anglo-Saxons because his life marks an important juncture in sacred history: he was the first patriarch to receive the promise of the covenant without directly speaking to God. Joseph's life, in this way, foreshadows that of the Anglo-Saxon reader who, as a Christian, would receive the same promise handed down in the same way.[39] The rubrics

---

[35] See Withers, 'Present Patterns, Past Tense', where I argue that Ælfric's *Preface* may be seen as an integral component of both the Laud and Claudius manuscripts, in which case the text would be divided by the rubrics into five parts. Structurally the *Preface* serves as a textual intermediary between the Old Testament history and the contemporary Anglo-Saxon reader and in this sense is analogous to the shorter rubricated passages that I discuss in this paper.

[36] Medieval authors recount several methods for structuring history. For a brief survey of the possible formulations, see C. W. Jones, *Saints' Lives and Chronicles in Early England* (Ithaca, NY, 1947), p. 24, and R. S. Farrar, 'Structure and Function in Representative Old English Saints' Lives', *Neophilologus* 57 (1973), 83–93.

[37] Ælfric, *Treatise on the Old and New Testaments*. The Old English text and William Lisle's translation of the treatise are printed in Crawford, *Heptateuch*, pp. 15–75; see esp. pp. 24, 26, 35 and 39.

[38] Ælfric, *Treatise on the Old and New Testaments*, p. 28.

[39] In arguing for a meaningful interplay between the past as recorded in scripture and lived experience for the Anglo-Saxon audience, I follow a line of study formulated by D. Bernstein, *The Mystery of the Bayeux Tapestry* (Chicago, IL, 1986), p. 178, and N. Howe, *Migration and Mythmaking in Anglo-Saxon England* (New Haven, CT, 1989). A continentally based study of similar reuse of the past can be found in S. Nichols, *Romanesque Signs: Early Medieval Narrative and Iconography* (New Haven, CT, 1983), pp. 1–14.

stress the connection between the reader and the Genesis stories by directly addressing the physical performance of reading the text and/or the experience of hearing it read. For example, the rubrics preceding the stories of Noah and Abraham underscore the physical presence of the narrative through the adverb *her*, the dependent adverbial clause beginning with *hu* and the present tense in the verb *swutelað*. *Her* serves in a demonstrative sense, as the equivalent of the Latin *hic*.[40] Literally, it denotes activity *here*, 'in this world, at this time'.[41] The combination of *her* plus a preterite verb is common to both the *Anglo-Saxon Chronicle* and the Bayeux Tapestry. To Peter Clemoes this construction 'with its meaning beamed to the present and its grammar to the past ... welded the two together in a regular formulaic way'.[42] In the same manner, the *hu* clause characterizes the action indicated by the verb *swutelað* which in turn strongly implies a physical immediacy and active presence in its meanings of 'to make manifest, to show, declare, or relate'.[43]

The words and phrases in the rubrics also connect the reader to the vernacular text by evoking the authority of vernacular legal documents such as wills. The verb *swutelað* when combined with *her* forms a phrase which resonates with legal overtones.[44] The *Microfiche Concordance to Old English* records fifty-six

---

[40] As found in Ælfric's *Grammar* as quoted in J. Bosworth and T. N. Toller, *An Anglo-Saxon Dictionary* (Oxford, 1898), p. 531. My findings on this matter are reinforced by Brilliant, 'The Bayeux Tapestry', pp. 113–18.

[41] Bosworth and Toller, *Anglo-Saxon Dictionary*, p. 531; Brilliant, 'The Bayeux Tapestry', p. 118. This is the sense of *her* in the context of the *Anglo-Saxon Chronicle* where it marks the start of the annual entries: see P. Clemoes, 'Language in Context: *Her* in the 890 *Anglo-Saxon Chronicle*', *Leeds Stud. in Engl.* ns 16 (1985), 27–36; E. R. Waterhouse, 'Stylistic Features as a Factor in Detecting Change in the Ninth Century *Anglo-Saxon Chronicle*', *Parergon* 27 (1980), 3–8; A. L. Meaney, 'St. Neot's, Æthelweard, and the *Anglo-Saxon Chronicle*: a Survey', *Studies in Earlier Old English Prose*, ed. P. E. Szarmach (Albany, NY, 1986), pp. 193–243, at 205.

[42] Clemoes, 'Language in Context', p. 28. I owe this reference to Allen Frantzen.

[43] It is the third person singular present tense form of the infinitive *sweotolian*. See Bosworth and Toller, *Anglo-Saxon Dictionary*, p. 951; see also R. Venezky and A. diPaolo Healey, *A Microfiche Concordance to Old English* (Newark, DE, 1980), fiche S0033, 195–9.

[44] The existence of Old English words and word-groupings that functioned as 'Old English legal jargon' is postulated by A. Campbell, 'An Old English Will', *JEGP* 37 (1938), 133–52. F. E. Harmer (*Anglo-Saxon Writs* (Manchester, 1952), pp. 85–92) notes other examples of word-groupings which retain specific legal overtones across textual genres. In particular, she discusses the use of alliteration, rhyme and parallelism in formulas that serve as mnemonic devices for the audience of the text. In this she sees ties between the construction of legal documents and church sermons. K. A. Lowe, '*Swutelung/swutelian* and the Dating of an Old English Charter (Sawyer 1524)', *N & Q* ns 38 (1991), 450–2, argues that the phrase 'Her is geswutelod on þissum gewrite hu' can be localized to Winchester, Old Minster and the years 963–75. N. Brooks sees a similar dependence on formulas in other Anglo-Saxon legal documents, noting that the formulaic character of the Anglo-Saxon writ derives from 'generations of oral messages to the folk courts': 'Anglo-Saxon Charters: the Work of the Last Twenty Years', *ASE* 3 (1974), 211–31, at 219.

instances of the verb form *swutelað*; in forty-two (seventy-five per cent) of these examples the verb combines with *her* to form the phrase *her swutelað*.⁴⁵ Almost all of the recorded examples of the phrase come from legal documents, and it is most commonly found at the beginning of Anglo-Saxon wills.⁴⁶ Two examples, both drawn from the wills of churchmen, illustrate the essential qualities of the formula.⁴⁷ First, the will of Ælfric archbishop of Canterbury, dated to the years 1003–4, begins with the same elements we have encountered in the rubrics: '*Her sutelað hu* Alfric arcebisceop his cwyde gedihte þ[æt] is ærest him to saulsceate he becwæð into cristes cyrcan þæt land æt Wyllan & æt Burnan. & Risenbeorgas. and he becwað his laford his beste scip & þa segelgeræda ðarto & LX. healma. & LX. beornena . . .'⁴⁸ Another example closer in date to the compilation of the Hexateuch/Heptateuch comes from the will of another Ælfric, bishop of East Anglia, written *c.* 1038. It, too, begins with the same formula: '*her swytelað* on þissu[m] gewrite *hu* Ælfric b[iscop] wille his are beteon þe he under gode geernode & under Cnut kyncge his leofue laforde . . .'⁴⁹

In wills, the formulaic expression *her swutelað* introduces a legally binding obligation or promise. This legal connotation carries over into contexts other

---

⁴⁵ Venezky and Healey, *A Microfiche Concordance to Old English*, fiche S0033, 195–9. The *Concordance* also records one instance of the phrase with a variant spelling of the verb, *her swuteleð*. The phrase is recorded with the verb in the past tense four times, *Her is geswutelod*; for the importance of these four instances, see Lowe, '*Swutelung/swutelian*'.

⁴⁶ Sixteen examples of this formulaic beginning can be found in D. Whitelock, *Anglo-Saxon Wills* (Cambridge, 1930): nos. V, VII, IX, XII, XV, XVI(2), XVII, XVIII, XXII, XXIV, XXVI, XXVII, XXXII, XXXVII and XXXVIII. Another example is furnished by D. Whitelock and N. Ker, *The Will of Æthelgifu: a Tenth Century Anglo-Saxon Manuscript* (Oxford, 1968); and *The Charters of Burton Abbey*, ed. P. H. Sawyer (Oxford, 1979), pp. 53–6 (no. 29). The same phrases frequently appear in charters. A few examples suffice: see Harmer, *Anglo-Saxon Writs*, no. XX, and Lowe, '*Swutelung/swutelian*', p. 451, n. 10. Some examples differ in spelling and word order; the nature and importance of these differences are still to be considered. Campbell ('An Old English Will', p. 138, n. 1) considers the phrase 'her is geswutelod an þis gewrit' and its variants to be a later form of the formula 'cyðo & writan hato' and its variants. In his opinion, 'such a formula shows the writing was highly important'.

⁴⁷ Although my examples are from Ecclesiastics, the same phrase also occurs in the wills of secular figures (both men and women): see Whitelock, *Anglo-Saxon Wills*, nos. XVII, XXII, XXVII and XXXII.

⁴⁸ Translated by Whitelock, *Anglo-Saxon Wills*, pp. 52–3: 'Here it is made known how Archbishop Ælfric drew up his will. First as his burial fee, he bequeathed to Christ Church the estates at Westwell and Bourne and Risborough. And he bequeathed to his lord his best ship and the sailing tackle with it, and sixty helmets and sixty coats of mail.' Whitelock in her commentary to her translation points out that the war equipment is not the archbishop's heriot, as he later on in the document makes provisions for its payment. The archbishop's concern with what we consider the attributes of the warrior may provide further evidence of the permeable boundary between the realms of the layman and the ecclesiastic that I discuss below.

⁴⁹ 'It is made known here in this document how Bishop Ælfric wishes to assign his property which he acquired under God and under King Cnut his dear lord . . .' (trans. Whitelock, *Anglo-Saxon Wills*, pp. 70–1).

than wills. For example, the phrase 'Her swutelað, seo gecwydrædnes ðe [...?]' was inscribed in the late tenth or early eleventh century on the south chancel arch of the Anglo-Saxon church at Breamore in Hampshire.[50] Two principal translations have been offered for this somewhat troubling inscription.[51] One translation assumes the inscription to be complete: 'Here is made manifest the covenant (or the word) to thee.'[52] The other assumes the inscription to be incomplete, and that it was continued on one or both of the now altered north chancel or apse arches: 'Here is manifest the covenant which...'[53]

The Breamore inscription implies a binding promise of some sort, although interpreters differ as to exactly what is promised. Du Boulay-Hill suggests that the phrase refers to the completion of a promise made by someone, perhaps to commemorate a vow of construction.[54] R. and F. Gameson argue that the inscription refers to 'God's covenant with mankind as described in Genesis IX.8–17'.[55] This passage establishes the rainbow as a sign of God's promise to Noah and his family not to destroy the earth by water again. The Gamesons claim that 'the fact that these words are written

---

[50] A. du Boulay-Hill, 'A Saxon Church at Breamore, Hants.', *ArchJ* 55 (1898), 84–7, and J. T. Micklethwaite, 'Some Further Notes on Saxon Churches', *ibid.* (1898), 340–9. See also G. B. Brown, *The Arts in Early England*, 5 vols. (London, 1903) II, 234–5; *V.C.H. Hampshire and the Isle of Wight* 5 vols. + Index (London, 1900–14) IV, 598–601; A. R. and P. M. Green, *Saxon Architecture and Sculpture in Hampshire* (Winchester, 1951), pp. 5–8 and 36–8; C. A. Fisher, *The Greater Anglo-Saxon Churches* (London, 1962), p. 392; H. M. and J. Taylor, *Anglo-Saxon Architecture*, 2 vols. (Cambridge, 1965) I, 94–6; E. Fernie, *The Architecture of the Anglo-Saxons* (London, 1982), pp. 112–14; Lowe, '*Swutelung/swutelian*', p. 451, n. 10; E. Okasha, 'The English Language in the Eleventh Century: the Evidence from Inscriptions', *England in the Eleventh Century*, ed. C. Hicks, Harlaxton Med. Stud. 2 (Stamford, 1992), 333–45; and R. and F. Gameson, 'The Anglo-Saxon Inscription at St. Mary's Church, Breamore, Hampshire', *ASSAH* 6 (1993), 1–10.

[51] A third translation has been published by Okasha, 'The English Language in the Eleventh Century', p. 337. This translation, which reads 'Here the agreement which... reveals...', has been rejected by R. and F. Gameson, 'Anglo-Saxon Inscription', p. 9, n. 29.

[52] Green and Green attribute this translation to W. J. Andrews (p. 6–7). Du Boulay-Hill offers the same translation without reference to previous authority ('A Saxon Church', p. 86). Most recently, this interpretation has been affirmed by R. and F. Gameson, 'The Anglo-Saxon Inscription', p. 2.

[53] A. S. Napier, 'Contributions to Old English Lexicography', *TPS* 32 (1903–6), 265–358, at 292. For the alteration in the church fabric, see Green and Green, *Saxon Architecture*, pp. 5–8, and Taylor and Taylor, *Anglo-Saxon Architecture* I, 94–6.

[54] Du Boulay-Hill ('A Saxon Church', p. 86) suggests that the inscription carries 'legal rather than scriptural language, perhaps the fulfilment of a church-building vow.' A third interpretation of the inscription is offered by M. Deanesly, *The Pre-Conquest Church in England* (London, 1961), pp. 349–51; she suggests that the inscription dates to the twelfth century and records the gift of the church to canons regular. A similar claim is attributed to Rev. E. P. Dew by du Boulay-Hill ('A Saxon Church', p. 86). Du Boulay-Hill, and Taylor and Taylor, *Anglo-Saxon Architecture* I, 94–6, dismiss these claims. See also A. R. Green who suggests a textual parallel with Titus I.2–3 (*Saxon Architecture*, pp. 6–7). [55] R. and F. Gameson, 'The Anglo-Saxon Inscription', p. 1.

around an arch gives them added resonance. The external form of the inscription reproduces and alludes to the *arcus* that is the key element in the covenant that the text celebrates.'[56]

The Gamesons link this inscription to an Old Testament covenant through the visual similarity of the curving form of the arch and the rainbow. Their argument may be bolstered by observing how the Breamore inscription combines the legal terminology relayed by the formulaic phrase *her swutelað* with the legal implications of the word *gecwydrædnes*. Although it appears only at Breamore, nearly all translators agree to render *gecwydrædnes* as 'covenant'.[57] Bosworth and Toller describe the word as a feminine abstract form of *gecwidræden* which carries the meaning of an agreement, contract, statute, or conspiration.[58] Hazeltine would place the term in the context of Anglo-Saxon wills. He notes that the term *cwid-ræden* can mean 'an oral decree or ordinance' in Anglo-Saxon sources.[59] If we extend Hazeltine's argument, *gecwidræden* combines two nouns *cwyd* (or *gecwid*) meaning a 'saying or expression' and *ræden* with the senses of 'a decree, ordinance, counsel', all with legal and perhaps scriptural overtones.[60] *Cwid* often generically identifies the will document; the term accentuates the original oral nature of the legal action of will-making.[61] By extension, the word *gecwydrædnes*[62] at Breamore implies a legally binding oral contract, a promise and its fulfilment.[63]

Significantly, the Gamesons point out that the inscription of Breamore was

---

[56] *Ibid.* p. 6.

[57] An exception is Okasha, 'English Language in the Eleventh Century', p. 337. According to Toller's supplement to the *Anglo-Saxon Dictionary*, the word is found only in the context of the Breamore arch inscription. The authority cited for its meaning is Napier, 'Contributions', p. 292, who simply defines the term as 'agreement, covenant'. Du Boulay-Hill ('A Saxon Church', p. 86) explains the term as the 'late form of the word "*gecwidræden*" – "compact", "covenant"'.

[58] Bosworth and Toller, *Anglo-Saxon Dictionary*, p. 382. They note that Ælfric uses the term as a gloss for Latin *conspiratio*. The *Dictionary of Old English* also notes the gloss 'conspiratio' which derives from the Latin–Old English glossary in Antwerp, Plantin-Moretus Museum 47 + British Library, Add. 32246. I am grateful to Peter Baker, Patrizia Lendinara and Greg Rose for their help with this matter.   [59] H. D. Hazeltine, 'Preface', in Whitelock, *Anglo-Saxon Wills*, p. xv, n. 5.

[60] Bosworth and Toller, *Anglo-Saxon Dictionary*, s.v. 'ræd' (pp. 781–3), 'ræden' (p. 783), and '(ge)cwid' (p. 180).   [61] Hazeltine, 'Preface', in Whitelock, *Anglo-Saxon Wills*, p. xiii.

[62] I am not sure if the unusual aspect of 'gecwidrædness' as an abstract feminine noun derived from another abstract feminine noun 'gecwidræden' would affect its interpretation.

[63] The Breamore inscription refers the reader or the audience to the continued relevance of a legal obligation. God's covenant with Noah not to destroy the earth certainly qualifies as this kind of promise. The inscription may also refer to another Old Testament promise, God's covenant with Abraham. The ritual actions – probably baptism, or perhaps, but not very likely, the mass – that would take place below the arch or within the space of the chancel that the arch effectively frames would have been perceived as a partial fulfilment of the covenant given to Abraham. Green and Green (*Saxon Architecture*, p. 8) postulate that the porticus was used as a side chapel, although they note that no signs of an altar have been found. See also R. and F. Gameson, 'The Anglo-Saxon Inscription', p. 6.

probably coloured red in the eleventh century. The colouring of the words at Breamore highlights not only their own letter forms but also their visual connection to rubrics in manuscripts such as those containing the Old English prose Genesis. The rubrication traces these verbal formulas across several textual boundaries. A few revealing discrepancies, however, are found in the formulas shared by the wills, by the Breamore inscription and by the Genesis rubrics. First, unlike the will formula, the Breamore inscription does not seem to mention an authenticating agent.[64] In the will of Bishop Ælfric quoted above, the name of the person whose wishes the will represents is imbedded inextricably within the written text by the adverbial *hu* clause. The verb of this dependent *hu* clause, in the cases of the two examples given above the verbs *gediht* and *beteon*, articulates a process of selection and transferral similar to that announced by the verbs *sealde* and *geceas* in the rubrics. In the wills, the subject of the clause is the donor who 'assigns' his property or 'directs' how it is to be distributed. The donor/subject informs the audience of the will that certain promises have been performed and relies on the legal force of the pronouncement, made before witnesses and enshrined in the written text, to ensure that they are carried out in the future. The will document records a contract, a bilateral, irrevocable and public agreement between the donor and the donee in which goods and/or services are promised for future delivery.[65] The will itself, as a physical thing, was made as a token or symbol of the prior oral promise, as evidence for the legally binding oral ceremony.[66] The audience of the will verifies that the written document is a 'true witness' to the original oral statements of the donor.[67] The absence of this clause at

[64] I have yet to find any specific discussion of the diplomatics of 'authenticating agent' in terms of an originator of a document in Anglo-Saxon wills. The usefulness of a document which makes no mention of any person to give, witness (or possibly receive) the 'covenant' seems limited.

[65] Hazeltine, 'Preface', in Whitelock, *Anglo-Saxon Wills*, pp. xiii-xxx. Campbell, 'An Old English Will', disputes this claim; citing the presence of many different donees in the typical Anglo-Saxon will. Campbell declares that the will 'establishes its possessor in the right to future ownership, and makes known the claim of all donees . . . the contractual settlement has been set aside . . .' (p. 134, n. 5). See also B. Danet and B. Bogoch, 'From Oral Ceremony to Written Document: the Transitional Language of Anglo-Saxon Wills', *Language and Communication* 12 (1992), 95–122, at 97.

[66] Wills are 'after-the-fact records of the binding event': Danet and Bogoch, 'From Oral Ceremony', p. 97.

[67] M. Sheehan, *The Will in Medieval England* (Rome, 1963), p. 53. Hazeltine, 'Preface', suggests that the will could be read to the witnesses who were present at the original oral act in order to strengthen its legal standing (p. xvii). In the terminology of modern 'Speech Act' analysis, wills are 'public constitutive acts' which seek to 'represent, in writing, acts of declaration': see Danet and Bogoch, 'From Oral Ceremony', pp. 95–122; B. Danet and B. Bogoch, '"Whoever Alters This, May God Turn His Face from Him on the Day of Judgement"': Curses in Anglo-Saxon Wills', *Jnl of American Folklore* 105 (1992), 132–65, at 139 and 143. Their arguments are based, in part, on the theories of J. Searle, *Speech Acts: an Essay in the Philosophy of Language* (Cambridge, 1969).

Breamore is in my view the best argument that the inscription as we now have it is incomplete.[68]

The rubrics, on the other hand, follow the will formula. Both the rubrics and the will formulas carefully and elaborately name the specific agent responsible for the actions described. In the wills the agent is a human donor. In the rubrics, however, God himself is portrayed as the one who makes the promise or bequest. In these formulaic expressions the actions of God and man are intermingled. The Deity is held to the same contractual obligations as a mere human testator. At the same time, the actions of men are elevated by comparison to God. The formulas construct a mutually reinforcing system in which God is envisioned as a participant in contemporary eleventh-century legal authority. At the same time, the actions of worldly powers are portrayed as God-like; like the Eternal Father, they promise future blessings.

While in both the wills and the rubrics, the agent is expressed through the dependent clause beginning with *hu*, the rubrics to *Genesis* incorporate a syntactical twist. The subject expressed by the *hu* clause is the pronominal *he*. The reader must look back to or remember the preceding genitive *Godes* to find the necessary antecedent for the pronoun. This direct link of subject to the genitive (of possession) firmly and irrevocably links the agent of the action to those things that are made manifest: the *mildheortnyss* and *wundru*, the 'mercy' and 'wonders' (the latter word the same term used for the miracles of the saints) of God.

Joseph: witness to the promise

The formulaic construction shared by the rubrics of Abraham, Noah and by Old English wills is not found in the rubric preceding the Joseph story. There are three principal differences. First, in the Joseph rubric the word *cydde*, the third person preterite of *cyðan* which carries the senses of 'to make known, tell' and 'to declare, reveal, manifest, testify, and narrate', replaces *swutelað* as the principal verb.[69] Secondly, the *hu* clause has been omitted in favour of a construction that makes *God* the subject of the verb. Finally, the word *wundru* or 'miracles' is not present in the Joseph rubric: only the quality of mercy, of *mildheortnyss*, remains.

---

[68] A stone fragment with the letters 'ðes' is reported by du Boulay-Hill, Green and Taylor and Taylor (see above, p. 121, n. 50). The letters on the fragment are 'of similar size and form' to the surviving inscription on the south arch. The fragment may have come from either of the two altered arches, north porticus and central arches: see Taylor and Taylor, *Anglo-Saxon Architecture* I, 95; W. Rodwell and E. Rouse, 'The Anglo-Saxon Rood and other Features in the South Church of St. Mary's Church, Breamore, Hampshire', *AntJ* 64 (1984), 298–325, at 317; R. and F. Gameson, 'The Anglo-Saxon Inscription', p. 2.

[69] Bosworth and Toller, *Anglo-Saxon Dictionary*, p. 191.

Unfulfilled promise: the rubrics of the Old English prose Genesis

These alterations accentuate the historical validity of the contractual agreement reached by God and Abraham. The switch from the verb *swutelað* to *cydde* alters the emphasis in the rubrics. For the stories of Noah and Abraham, the rubrics characterize the texts they introduce as primary documents that manifest or record the oral promise of the individuals involved, God, Noah and Abraham. In the Joseph rubric, the stress shifts to how God 'makes known' what he *behet*, or promised, previously. God himself literally testifies through the events of Joseph's life that the blessings he promised to Abraham will be passed on to subsequent generations, to Joseph and his offspring.[70]

The Joseph rubric differs from the will by replacing the phrase *on þissum gewrite*, found in the will of the second Ælfric, with the phrase *on Iosepe*.[71] On one level, the omission of the phrase *on þissum gewrite*, whether conscious or unconscious, may signal the compiler's appreciation for the vernacular Genesis as a translated text. He may be unwilling to call attention to the paraphrase as a direct witness to the covenant since it is not in Latin and was not meant to stand as a replacement for the complete and authoritative Latin text. More likely, the compiler may be implying that it is not the text of the translated scripture which stands as the physical manifestation of the spoken covenant but the literal actions of the characters in the Old English narrative. The phrase *on Iosepe* implies that Joseph's life functions as a kind of *writ*, as proof of the validity of Abraham's promised inheritance.

EXTENDING THE TEXTUAL COMMUNITY: THE RUBRICS AND SAINTS' LIVES

Taken together, the legal resonances of these formulaic phrases in the Genesis rubrics validate the authority of the promise that these translated texts transmit. Like the written text of the will, the scriptural stories of Noah and Abraham, when read aloud or experienced in their narrative illustration, are representations of past events. The written word not only preserves these past deeds for posterity; the experience of reading or hearing these written narrations bridges the gap between past and present and future.[72] A will was public performance

---

[70] J. P. Fokkelman, *Narrative Art in Genesis* (Amsterdam, 1975), pp. 238–41. Fokkelman points out that the major narrative theme that unites the stories found in the *Genesis* collection is the history of God's Blessing on the Israelites. In his terms, the Blessing literally 'generates' the story of the 'generations' of Abraham's children.

[71] Hazeltine, 'Preface', notes the descriptive import of the word *gewrit* (Whitelock, *Anglo-Saxon Wills*, p. xiii), while Campbell, 'An Old English Will', lists the varying formulas that call attention to the importance of the written document (p. 138, n. 1). I am grateful to Toby Baldwin for calling this replacement to my attention.

[72] 'The spoken word is always an event, a moment in time, completely lacking the thing-like repose of the written word': W. J. Ong, *Orality and Literacy: the Technologizing of the Word* (London and New York, 1982), p. 75. See also H. R. Jauss, 'Literary History as a Challenge to Literary

which used words to establish the testator's desires in the world.[73] Those who heard the will pronounced or read became witnesses to these desires. The Genesis rubrics convey the experience of the will to the performance of reading the Old Testament so that the reader/hearer becomes a participant, a witness and, finally, a recipient of God's promise to the patriarchs.[74]

What is 'promised' in the texts of Genesis is not tangible property but a legacy of belonging and a bequest of a relationship with God. God, in his repeated miraculous actions revealed in the lives of his chosen ones, literally narrates his unswerving historical plan. As Ælfric reveals in his homily on St Bartholomew,

Sume menn beoð geuntrumode for Godes tacnum, swa swa Crist cwæð be suman blindan men, ðaða his leoringcnihtas hine axodon, for hwæs synnum se mann wurde swa blind acenned. Þa cwæð se Hœlend, þæt he nære for his agenum synnum, ne for his maga, blind geboren, ac forði þæt Godes wundor þurh hine geswutelod wære. And he þærrihte mildheortlice hine gehælde, and geswutelode þæt he is soð Scyppend, ðe ða ungesceapenan eahhringas mid his halwendan spatle geopenode.[75]

In a similar way the lives of the patriarchs and the Christian saints are told in order to 'manifest' God's *mildheortness* and *wundru*. The miracles in these narrations, in turn, 'manifest that he is the true Creator' and stand as a 'true witness' to the continuing validity of the promise of the Christians' divine inheritance in the Last Judgement.

God, the divine narrator

In terms of this promise it is significant that the rubrics to the Joseph story emphasize God's role as witness and narrator. As God speaks through the life of Joseph, he essentially rereads the original covenant which he made to Abraham. He himself witnesses the validity of its contractual terms in the same manner as an Anglo-Saxon witness to a will would reread and stand witness to the terms of

---

Theory', *Towards an Aesthetic of Reception*, trans. T. Bahti (Sussex, 1982), pp. 3–45; and, most recently, C. A. Lees, 'Working with Patristic Sources: Language and Context in Old English Homilies', *Speaking Two Languages: Traditional Disciplines and Contemporary Theory in Medieval Studies*, ed. A. J. Frantzen (Albany, NY, 1991), pp. 157–80, at 165–7.

[73] Danet and Bogoch, '"Whoever Alters This"', p. 153.
[74] Ong discusses the 'unifying sense' of the spoken word: *Orality and Literacy*, p. 73.
[75] 'Some men are afflicted for the miracles of God, as Christ said of some blind man, when his disciples asked him, for whose sins the man was thus born blind. Then said Jesus, that he was born blind not for his own nor his parents' sins, but because that God's miracles might be manifested through him. And he forthwith mercifully healed him, and manifested that he is the true Creator, who opened the unshapen eye-rings with his salutary spittle': *The Homilies of the Anglo-Saxon Church: the First Part, Containing the Sermones Catholici, or Homilies of Ælfric*, ed. and trans. B. Thorpe, 2 vols. (London, 1844–6) I, 474–5 (no. xxxi).

a will before the *witan* or in a public assembly.[76] In the specific wording of the rubrics to Joseph, the Old English grammatical structure foregrounds God's testimonial role by making God himself the subject of the sentence. In the rubric, the subject of the sentence governs the verb *cydde*, which carries a formal sense of a public declaration or proof of evidence. In other texts *cyðan* is used to translate the Latin terms *nuntiare* and *annuntiare* as well as in Old English phrases such as *mid aþe cyþan* (to prove with an oath) or *cyðdon Cristes gebyrd* (they announced Christ's birth).[77]

Cyðan also corresponds to the Latin *narrare*, meaning 'to narrate', 'to tell a story'.[78] In the narratives of Adam, Noah and Abraham, God is the protagonist, the subject of the Old English verbs: he walks, talks, acts. In the illustrated version of the text found in Claudius B. iv, God appears physically as he interacts with the patriarchs.[79] In the story of Joseph, God's presence is felt behind the scenes, not in direct action with the characters. The illustrations to the Joseph story in Claudius B. iv do not show God as physically present. Instead, God acts indirectly, as an invisible guiding hand and protector. The word *cyðan* underscores the point that God's testimony is this narrative, the story of the events which constitute Joseph's life.

In the Joseph story, then, God is made 'to step forward' as a witness and as a narrator at the very time he disappears as an active participant in the narrative. As if to indicate that God is no longer personally present to perform miracles, and to signal the importance of the record rather than of action, the term *wundru* drops from the Joseph rubric. These strategies stress the idea that Joseph is the first of Abraham's children not to see God face to face. This is the key to his importance.

Ironically, when the Vulgate text of Genesis is read literally, the covenant seems to have failed with Joseph.[80] In the covenant, God promises Abraham that his progeny will form a great nation 'as numerous as the stars in the

---

[76] Sheehan, *Wills*, pp. 49–50; Hazeltine, 'Preface', in Whitelock, *Anglo-Saxon Wills*, p. xvii.
[77] Bosworth and Toller, *Anglo-Saxon Dictionary*, p. 191. See also Venezky and Healey, *Microfiche Concordance*, fiche C0015. [78] Bosworth and Toller, *Anglo-Saxon Dictionary*, p. 191.
[79] Weitzmann and Kessler consider the depiction of the active figure of the Creator as one of the hallmarks of the Cotton Genesis iconographical tradition. I would suggest that the inclusion of the figure of God as an active figure in the story can have more to do with the desire of the artist to stress God's role as a protagonist, as a principal subject and main focus of the action than with a proposed line of iconographical descent: see K. Weitzmann and H. Kessler, *The Cotton Genesis, British Library Codex Cotton Otho B. VI* (Princeton, NJ, 1986). A recent assessment of Weitzmann and Kessler's study may be found in J. Lowden, 'Concerning the Cotton Genesis and Other Illustrated Manuscripts of Genesis', *Gesta* 31 (1992), 40–53.
[80] Much of the following discussion is indebted to L. A. Turner, *Announcements of Plot in Genesis*, Jnl for the Study of the Old Testament, Supp. Ser. 96 (Sheffield, 1990), 170. For the sense of fulfilment perceived in the Hexateuch as a whole, see G. von Rad, *The Problem of the Hexateuch and other Essays*, trans. E. W. T. Dicken (New York, 1966).

heavens' and that they will inherit the promised land of Canaan.[81] This grand promise is simply not fulfilled by the end of Joseph's life.[82] The text of Genesis records that the promised 'great nation' consists of the seventy-two members of Jacob's household who migrate from famine-ravaged Canaan to Egypt. The promised land is barren, unfruitful, abandoned. The family is in exile, the blessing of Joseph serves the interests of the Pharaoh who now owns all the land, cattle and services of the people of Egypt.[83]

The rubrics and other additions to the texts of the Old English Genesis restructure Joseph's story in order to stress its future fulfilment and thereby to make clear the validity of the patriarch's testimony to the covenant. This restructuring can clearly be seen in the way that the text of the Joseph story differs in Otho B. x and Corpus 201 from Laud Misc. 509 and Claudius B. iv.[84] In the former two, the text mitigates the lack of fulfilment of the story by prompting the reader to consider biblical events that occur after the death of Joseph. First, the rubric in Corpus 201 differs slightly but significantly from the wording found in the Claudius B. iv and Laud texts. Corpus 201 reads 'Her cydde god ælmihtig his milheortnisse þe he Abrahame behet and Iosepe and Abrahames ofsprincge' whereas both Claudius and Laud (with minor variations between the two texts) have 'Her cydde God ælmihtig hys mildheortnysse þe he Abrahame behet on Iosepe, Abrahames ofspringe.'[85] The principal difference in these two passages is the presence of the preposition *on* in Laud and Claudius. In the Corpus manuscript, the repeated conjunction *and* strings the nouns at the end of the rubric together. This grammatical structure syntactically ties Abraham, Joseph and their offspring together as the recipients of the promise.[86] It effectively reminds the reader that God's promise extends beyond Joseph, and includes all of Abraham's subsequent descendants. The Laud and Claudius rubric identify only Joseph, as Abraham's descendant, as the recipient of the promise.

In the same way, references to future scriptural events added at the end of the Old English texts further temper the pessimistic conclusion to the Joseph story.

---

[81] Genesis XXII.17–18.'

[82] See D. J. A. Clines, *What does Eve Do to Help and Other Readerly Questions to the Old Testament*, Jnl for the Study of the Old Testament, Supp. Ser. 94 (Sheffield, 1990), 49–66.

[83] Genesis XLI.46–56.

[84] The differences found in the rubrics of the various manuscripts were first discussed in depth by Raith, 'Ælfric's Share'.

[85] 'Here almighty God testifies his mercy which he promised to Abraham and to Joseph and to Abraham's offspring.' Otho B. x once had a rubric similar to that in CCCC 201. Unfortunately most of the text was lost in the Cotton fire of 1731, but Humphrey Wanley recorded the rubric before the manuscript's destruction: 'Her cydde god ælmitig his mildheortnysse þe he *Abrahame behet and Iosepe Abrahames ofspringe*' (my emphasis).

[86] This similarity, I suggest, reopens the question of the priority of the texts as shown in Clemoes' *stemma*, especially in regards to the introductory rubrics.

Unfulfilled promise: the rubrics of the Old English prose Genesis

In the Vulgate, we find a straightforward account of Joseph's death and burial: 'Cumque adiurasset eos atque dixisset Deus visitabit vos: apportate ossa mea vobiscum de loco isto: Mortuus est expletis centum decem vitae suæ annis. Et conditus aromatibus, repositus est in loculo in Aegypto.'[87] This ending of the basic story is recast in Otho B. x through references to the story of Joshua:[88]

Iosep forðferde þa þa he wæs an hund wintra and ten wintra, and hine man bebyrigde mid wyrtgemange. He wæs gelæd to his earde of Egypta lande to his agenum gecynde & wearþ bebirged on middon his agenum cynne þær his lichama hine gerestað oð þisne andweardan dæg. Sy lof & wuldor þam well willendan hælande aa on ecnysse. Amen.[89]

With this revised ending the English author looks forward in time in order to tell how Joseph's wishes are to be fulfilled by the Israelites upon their return to Canaan. The definitive statement of the Israelites' return to the promised land cancels the negative connotation of the chosen people's exile. Moreover, the author's concrete reference to Joseph's burial by 'his own kin' underscores the continuing ties of family that we previously observed in the rubricated introduction to the story.[90]

This modified ending turns Joseph's life into a story of Christian hope, one that looks to its fulfilment in future generations. The statement that Joseph's

---

[87] 'And he (Joseph) made them swear to him, saying: God will visit you, carry my bones with you out of this place: And he died being a hundred and ten years old. And being embalmed he was laid in a coffin in Egypt' (Genesis L.24–5).

[88] An abbreviated version of the book of Joshua is found in both the Claudius B. iv and Laud manuscripts.

[89] 'Joseph died when he was one hundred and ten years old, and they buried him with spices. He was taken to his homeland from the land of Egypt into his own kind, and he was buried in the midst of his own kin, where his body rests until the present day. Praise and glory be to the benevolent Saviour forever and ever.' The ending to Otho B. x is now lost due to the destruction of much of the manuscript in the fire of 1731; the same ending may have been found in the text of Corpus 201, since the two manuscripts are closely related textually (see Raith, 'Ælfric's Share', p. 306). The relation of the ending of Otho B. x as recorded by Wanley and the 'standard' text is unclear. Otho may well be a variation from the ending of Genesis in an exemplar of the Laud and Claudius text, therefore suggesting a possible reduction of the ending in the later Laud and Claudius versions.

[90] The theme of Joseph's bones seems to have had some circulation in pre-Conquest England. For the poetical troping of the finding of Joseph's bones, see the prayer of Judas in the Old English poem 'Elene' as discussed by O. F. Emerson, 'The Legend of Joseph's Bones in Old and Middle English', *MLN* 14 (1899), 331–4; R. Schwartz, 'Joseph's Bones and the Resurrection of the Text: Remembering in the Bible', *PMLA* 103 (1988), 114–24. For the attentive reader, as I suspect the author of the passage above was, the mention of the fate of Joseph's bones echoes the final verse of Joshua from Claudius B. iv. There, in a passage which elaborates the text of the Vulgate, we find: 'Iosepes ban witodlice, ðe Israhela bearn broht(on) of Egypta lande, hi bebyrigdon on Sichem, on ðæs landes dæle ðe Iacob bohte æt Emores sunum, Sichemes fæder; hit wæs gehloten to Iosepes bearna lande (for ðam de Iacob hit sealde Iosepe is sune at is forsyðe)' (Claudius B. iv, 155r).

bones rest in Sichem 'to this present day', added as verifiable proof of the historical veracity of the story, effectively bridges the gap between the Old Testament events and the life of the present reader.[91] Similarly, the formulaic phrase 'Sy lof and wuldor þam well willendan hæland aa on ecnysse', which repeats the endings found in several of Ælfric's homilies, appropriates the patriarch's life for the eternal glory of the 'Saviour', the Christianized God.[92] This last phrase allows the Christian Anglo-Saxon reader to associate himself with the spiritual heirs of Abraham. In these ways, the Old Testament Father is joined to the Anglo-Saxon reader, through Christ, in what can be visualized as the infinite spiral of Christian history.[93]

Saints by association: holy biographies

The rubrics discussed above frame the Genesis narrative between verbal resonances of will formulas at the beginning of each section and homiletic echoes in its concluding sentences. These pointed references to other genres make Genesis more understandable and relevant for the contemporary reader because they organize the text into a series of biographies of the patriarchs. The presence of introductory rubrics in the *Genesis* text could have inspired the reader to perceive the biographical structure in the rest of the Hexateuch or Heptateuch. Although they do not have rubricated introductions, the other sections of the biblical texts do conform to this biographical principle. The book of Joshua, for example, is essentially the story of the career of one man. Similarly, Exodus and the significantly reduced and paraphrased books of Leviticus and Deuteronomy in the Claudius and Laud manuscripts narrate the life of Moses.[94]

The various endings to the Joseph story were constructed, I argue, with this biographical principle in mind – and a sensitive awareness of their specific manuscript contexts.[95] In Claudius B. iv and Laud, the Joseph story appears in the

---

[91] '... oð þisne andweardan dæg'.
[92] 'Praise and glory be to the benevolent Saviour always forever and ever'. Raith ('Ælfric's Share', pp. 306 and 313) points out the links between this phrase and homiletic endings.
[93] For the spiralling effect in the Christian notion of time and history, see C. Hahn, 'Picturing the Text: Narrative in the Life of the Saints', *Art Hist.* 13 (1990), 1–33, at 2–5; see also A. Higgins, 'Medieval Notions of the Structure of Time', *Jnl of Med. and Renaissance Stud.* 19 (1989), 227–50.
[94] Raith ('Ælfric's Share', p. 307), associates 'Numbers xiii-xxvi(xxxi) of the Old English Pentateuch' with Ælfric's reference in his homily 'De falsis diis' to his translated account of the Israelites' forty-year sojourn in the desert. Clemoes agrees that Numbers was translated by Ælfric in a way that duplicates and 'goes beyond' his treatment of the theme in *De populo Israhel*: Clemoes, *Chronology*, p. 30.
[95] I suggest that the rubrics of the Old English paraphrase were added in imitation of the practice of rubricating saints' lives; possibly the rubrics became connected to the Joseph text, and hence to the rest of Genesis, through the former's association with the various lives and homilies in Otho B. x and Corpus 201.

Unfulfilled promise: the rubrics of the Old English prose Genesis

context which includes the book of Joshua. In these manuscripts, Joseph's request to have his body transported back to Canaan is fulfilled as the Old English text progresses. The simple reference to future events would lead the reader to continue to follow the story in these manuscripts, where the appropriate details concerning the fate of Joseph's body would be found.

Conversely, in the Otho and Corpus Christi manuscripts, the story of Joseph is isolated, cut out from the immediate context of the rest of the Bible. In these two manuscripts the patriarch's narrative is inserted into a series of other independent narratives: homilies and saints' lives. In this context the story of Joseph has a greater need than it does in the context of the 'complete' Hexateuch or Heptateuch for a textual reminder of the ultimate triumph of the children of Israel, that they carry Joseph's bones back to the Promised Land. In Corpus 201, the Joseph story appears near the end of the manuscript's legal codes and homilies, immediately preceded by three English texts: an English translation of Apollonius of Tyre, then a narrative account of English royal saints, and a list of saints and their resting-places in England.[96] Similarly, Otho B. x surrounded Joseph with Ælfric's biographies of illustrious saints such as Peter and Paul, Æthelthryth, Edmund, and Swithun, written by Ælfric.[97]

In the Otho manuscript, the story of Joseph immediately preceded Ælfric's account of St Swithun.[98] The stories of saint and patriarch are connected by more than mere proximity; they are tied together by the use of the same vocabulary. Ælfric composed the introduction to Swithun to read: 'On Eadgares dagum ðæs æðelan cynincges þaða se cristendom wæs wel ðeonde þurh god on angelcynne under ðam ylcan cynincge þa *geswutelode* god þone sanct swyðun mid manegum *wundrum* þæt he mære is his dæda næron cuðe ærðan þe hi god sylfe *cydde*,' (my emphasis).[99] As with Joseph, God himself *cydde* or testified to the worthiness of the saint. As in the case of Abraham and Noah, God makes known

---

[96] Ker, *Catalogue*, pp. 90–1, and D. Whitelock, 'Wulfstan and the Laws of Cnut', *EHR* 63 (1948), 433–52. The homilies are ed. A. S. Napier, *Wulfstan: Sammlung der ihm zugeschriebenen Homilien* (Berlin, 1883). The lists of saints' resting-places are ed. F. Liebermann, *Die Heiligen Englands* (Hanover, 1889) nos. 1 and 9; see also D. W. Rollason, *The Mildrith Legend: a Study in Early Medieval Hagiography in England* (Leicester, 1982), esp. pp. 28, 57–8, and *idem*, 'Lists of Saints' Resting-Places in Anglo-Saxon England', *ASE* 7 (1978), 61–93, esp. 79–82. For the possible role the text known as the 'Secgan' played in the unification of England, see D. W. Rollason, *Saints and Relics in Anglo-Saxon England* (Oxford, 1989), pp. 133–63, esp. 158.
[97] Ker, *Catalogue*, pp. 229–30; *Ælfric's Lives of Saints*, ed. W. W. Skeat, 4 vols., EETS OS 76, 82, 94 and 114 (London, 1881–1900; repr. in 2 vols., London, 1996).
[98] As reconstructed by Ker, *Catalogue*, p. 226.
[99] 'In the days of the noble King Eadgar when, by God's Grace, Christianity was thriving well in the English nation under that same king, God by many miracles revealed Saint Swithun, (showing) that he is illustrious. His deeds were not known before God Himself manifested them' (trans. Skeat, *Lives of Saints*, p. 440, lines 1–6).

(*geswutelode*) his favour for Swithun through specific actions: miracles (*manegum wundrum*).[100] In fact, the main difference between the rubrics and the introduction to the life of Swithun (besides the relative length of the texts) is that Ælfric tells the reader that the miracles that revealed the saint's holiness occurred 'in Edgar's day', that is within the living memory, perhaps, of at least some of his audience.

The sequence of stories found in the Otho manuscript is tied together by two other homiletic works of a more general introductory nature. The first, the *De initio creaturae*, outlines God's complete plan of Salvation from the story of Creation through the second coming.[101] The second, the *Exameron Anglice*, provides a detailed account of the first six days of the world.[102] These two homilies, written for oral delivery as popular sermons, supply a comprehensive historical background for the corpus of saints' lives and biblical stories found in the manuscript. Both homilies, with their theoretical basis in what James Hurt characterizes as 'the Augustinian view of history: that history has been guided by the hand of God', stress the continuous line of sacred history that unites the patriarchs, the saints and the Christian individual.[103] R. W. Hanning points out the ramification of Augustine's conception of the 'constant principle of God's providence' as the guiding force of history for the Christian individual. Hanning argues that to Augustine, Christian typology explicated 'the continuing life of Christ in Christians, not as the explanation of social and political events'; therefore Augustine's history hinges on the individual, the personal, in the case of the Old English paraphrase, the reader.[104] The *De initio* text in particular, located at the very beginning of the Otho manuscript and addressed 'to the people, whenever you will', introduces its audience to the basic themes developed by the homilies and stories which follow it in the manuscript. Whether read, or heard read in a devotional setting, the *De initio* text initiates its audience into the community of Christian history by providing a condensed version of 'the essential narrative and message of the scriptures interpreted for the ignorant'.[105]

---

[100] A few lines later Ælfric characterizes these actions more completely as 'swutelu[m] wundrum and syllicum tacnum' (Skeat, *Lives of Saints* p. 442, line 13).

[101] The text is ed. Thorpe, *Homilies* I, 8–28. See also V. Day, 'The Influence of the Catechetical "narratio" on Old English and Some Other Medieval Literature', *ASE* 3 (1974), 51–61, at 56–8; J. R. Hurt, 'A Note on Ælfric's *Lives of Saints*, no. XVI', *ES* 51 (1970), 231–4.

[102] Ed. and trans. S. J. Crawford, *Exameron Anglice or the Old English Hexameron, Edited with an Introduction, a Collation of all the Manuscripts, a Modern Translation, Parallel Passages from Other Works of Ælfric and Notes on the Sources*, Bibliothek der angelsächsischen Prosa 10 (Hamburg, 1921).

[103] Hurt, 'A Note', p. 233, adds 'the Old Testament Saints, Christ and his apostles, and the martyrs and confessors of the period since the crucifixion epitomize in their lives the travails of the pious in these three ages' (the Fall, the Incarnation, and the coming Last Judgement).

[104] R. W. Hanning, *The Vision of History in Early Britain from Gildas to Gregory of Monmouth* (New York, 1966), p. 33.

[105] 'Sermo de initio creaturæ, ad populum, quando volueris', in Thorpe, *Homilies* I, 8–9. This characterization of the text is quoted from Day, 'Catechetical "*narratio*"', p. 58. Hurt, 'A Note', p. 231, suggests that Ælfric's homily *De memoria sanctorum* may have played a similar role as introduction and initiation.

Unfulfilled promise: the rubrics of the Old English prose Genesis

The Joseph story has a similar context in the Corpus manuscript. Mary Richards argues that this collection of texts was at least partially organized by Wulfstan, and that 'the organization of texts implies that the laws included among them were part of a group of materials intended for instructional purposes, possibly including delivery from the pulpit'.[106] She then argues that the material towards the end of the manuscript, including the *Apollonius of Tyre*, and the lists of saints' resting-places, was added to the manuscript in order to return to 'a traditional association of laws with historical materials'.[107] While she does not mention the Joseph text as an example, I would argue that it functions like the list of saints' resting-places as an historical text.

The homiletic resonances found in the ending to the Joseph story in Corpus 201 and Otho B. x refashion the Old Testament narrative into an image of the other homilies and saints' lives collected in these two manuscripts.[108] As types of narrative, the lives of saints and patriarchs correspond to one another like threads in a textile. In Raymond Farrar's apt analogy, the stories and lives of the holy individuals form the 'warp and weave' in the fabric of 'salvation history'. 'Salvation history' determines and is determined by the position of the individual in respect to God within the temporal flow of past, present and future events. In this approach, the stories of patriarchs and saints are ultimately similar, for both genres witness the role of God in shaping their lives and the world; both types are 'holy men' perfect in the sight of God. Their stories are a repetitive, mutually reflective genre precisely because they combine to form, spiritually and ideologically, one story which is guided by the hand of God.[109]

The stories of patriarchs and saints share an ultimate referent: the life of Christ. Yet, their relationship to him differs. The saints recreate Christ; they signify their holiness to the world through 'the constant repetition of conventional motifs . . . (that stresses) the collective identity of the saints in fulfilling a divinely ordained pattern originally established by Christ'.[110] The patriarchs take

---

[106] M. P. Richards, 'The Manuscript Context of the Old English Laws: Tradition and Innovation', *Studies in Earlier Old English Prose*, ed. P. E. Szarmach (Albany, NY, 1986), pp. 171–92, at 178.

[107] *Ibid.* p. 180.

[108] K. Jost has suggested that the Joseph story which is found in these two manuscripts bears traces of an earlier homily based on the patriarch's life: 'Unechte Ælfric-Texte', *Anglia* 51 (1927), 177–219, at 217–18. Crawford (*Heptateuch*, p. 427) discounts this theory based on a perceived derivation of the Otho text from the Claudius B. iv and Laud 'standard' version of the paraphrase. [109] Farrar, 'Structure and Function'.

[110] M. Carrasco, 'Sanctity and Experience in Pictorial Hagiography: Two Illustrated Lives of Saints from Romanesque France', *Images of Sainthood in Medieval Europe*, ed. R. Blumenfeld-Kosinski and T. Szell (Ithaca, NY, 1991), pp. 33–66, at 34. See also G. H. Gerould, *Saints' Legends* (Boston, 1916), p. 24; Hahn, 'Picturing the Text', p. 3; Farrar, 'Structure and Function'; and D. Bethurum, 'The Form of Ælfric's *Lives of Saints*', *SP* 29 (1932), 515–33. Bethurum suggests that the metrical alliteration that marks Ælfric's homilies creates a direct link or comparison between the Saints and early Germanic heroes 'with the idea of replacing the latter with the former' (p. 533).

part in the same process; Ælfric, for example, begins his homily called 'On the Memory of the Saints' with an account of the lives of the Old Testament Fathers.[111]

Rosemary Woolf notes that Old Testament stories and saints' lives intertwine in Ælfric's *Life of Eugenia*, a story that features the same type of accusation found in the Joseph story, and in his account of the Old Testament heroine, Judith, which is modelled after a saint's narrative.[112] But instead of recreating Christ, as the saints do, the patriarchs are his authenticating history. As Ælfric writes in his *Preface to Genesis*: 'Eft Iosep, ðe wæs geseald to Egypta lande & he ahredde ðæt folc wið ðone miclan hunger hæfde Cristes getacnunge, ðe wæs geseald for us to cwale & us ahredde fram ðam ecan hungre helle susle.'[113] Ælfric explains Joseph's life as a 'betokening' of Christ. Joseph lived prior to Christ, yet their lives are intimately connected. For Ælfric, the past is not dead, forever separate from the present.[114] An event in the life of a holy man or in history occupies a particular point in the flow of time, but its significance is not limited to that point.[115] God's promise of salvation was present in the past, in the stories of the Old Testament, if only one could interpret those stories properly, as Joseph himself could interpret dreams.[116]

Stories from the Old Testament exist on two levels at once: on what Ælfric calls 'the naked meaning' or literal truth and the 'spiritual meaning' or proper interpretation of the text.[117] Farrar describes this medieval mind set as a view in

---

[111] Skeat, *Lives of Saints*, pp. 337–63; Hurt, 'A Note', pp. 231–4; Farrar, 'Structure and Function', p. 88.

[112] R. Woolf, 'Lives of Saints', *Continuations and Beginnings: Studies in Old English Literature*, ed. E. G. Stanley (London, 1966), pp. 37–67.

[113] Crawford, *Heptateuch*, p. 79, lines 74–7. 'Joseph, who was sold into Egypt and rescued that people from the great famine, betokens Christ who was sold to death for us and rescued us from the eternal hunger of torments of hell' (my translation). For Ælfric's references to Joseph in his other works, see M. P. Richards, 'Fragmentary Versions of Genesis in Old English Prose: Context and Function', *The Old English Hexateuch*, ed. Barnhouse and Withers.

[114] M. Hunter, 'Germanic and Roman Antiquity and the Sense of the Past in Anglo-Saxon England', *ASE* 3 (1974), 29–50, at 46, argues that the Anglo-Saxons saw the past as a 'heroic, idealized present', with different periods and cultures mingled and confused with one another; 'an imperfect awareness of the difference between the past, however alien, and the present'.

[115] In Erich Auerbach's terms, a 'figura' is an event or story that has 'a dual valence as both real in itself and incomplete' (quoted by Farrar, 'Structure and Function', p. 88).

[116] I owe this last point to discussion with Toby Baldwin.

[117] *Preface to Genesis*, ed. Crawford, *Heptateuch*, p. 79. For commentary on Ælfric's concern for interpretation, see D. C. Fowler, *The Bible in Early English Literature* (London 1976), pp. 99–103; S. Greenfield and D. Calder, *A New Critical History of Old English Literature* (New York, 1986), pp. 83–5. Hurt, 'A Note', p. 234, observes that 'the best saints' lives, including Ælfric's, had a double concern with both historical fact and spiritual truth, and their often sensational or garish actions were designed to reveal an "inner truth" usually masked by the confused surface of ordinary life.'

Unfulfilled promise: the rubrics of the Old English prose Genesis

which all events within time are tied together in the life of Christ – and in the experience of the reader.[118] History consists of 'a constant spinning out of its events stretching backward not only to Christ but to the creation of Adam... and from there to the present moment whatever the calendar year.'[119] The past informs the present, because the past has a kind of 'predictive power', 'full of lessons and exempla for the present reader'.[120] For medieval readers the past's 'predictive power' calls for their attention not only as literary lessons, that is as fables of good and bad deeds, but as behavioural guides that demand 'mimetic attention to their actions'.[121] Both Old Testament narrative and the Christian saint's life are didactic texts which the Christian audience is to read (or hear) and emulate.

A 'SEDIMENTAL' VIEW: WHAT FILTERS THROUGH

By recalling the structures of contemporary texts, the vernacular versions of the Old Testament function as history textbooks and primers of social behaviour. Their rubrics, narrative guides created especially for the Old English text, reveal a fundamental strategy for reading the Old Testament. By echoing the verbal formulas found in wills, they stress the text's accurate and valid presentation of past events. Structurally, the rubrics recast Genesis into a series of saints' lives and thereby appropriate the ancient Hebrew stories for the contemporary Christian reader. The readers of the Old English prose Genesis rely on these structures borrowed from other texts (whether oral or written) that they have previously encountered in order to interpret those 'newly read'. These readers themselves may or may not be totally fluent in the 'literate' use of texts; they may have developed a 'pragmatic literacy', a social need for literacy and someone close to them to perform the actual deed.[122]

One last point concerning the readership of the Old English prose Genesis needs to be addressed: just who was this 'contemporary Christian reader'? The paraphrased nature of the text, its lack of capitula, and the presence of portions of the text in homiliaries point to the use of the texts in contexts where complete versions of the Bible were not wanted or needed. This suggests that the vernacular versions of the text, especially in its illustrated form in Claudius

---

[118] This same concern for continuity is found in the *Anglo-Saxon Chronicle*. Clemoes, 'Language in Context', p. 31, writes, 'the series of year numbers starting from Christ's birth must have been significant in its own right and its significance must have lain in its very continuity... This was not the history of cause and effect; it was a declaration of continuity.'
[119] Farrar, 'Structure and Function', p. 88.   [120] *Ibid.*   [121] *Ibid.*
[122] M. Clanchy, *From Memory to Written Record: England 1066–1307* (London, 1979); S. Keynes, 'Royal Government and the Written Word in Late Anglo-Saxon England', *The Uses of Literacy in Early Medieval Europe*, ed. R. McKitterick (Cambridge, 1990), pp. 226–57.

B. iv, was meant to be used by a layman or a novice monk.[123] Since members of both groups could be literate, at least in theory, we can once again seriously consider that the compiler retained Ælfric's preface – which records the dedication of his translation to the Ealdorman Æthelweard – for more than antiquarian or authorial name-dropping. It indicates that men of a certain class and profession were in the conceived audience for this non-Ælfrician composition, at least in part.[124]

The suggestion of a lay readership for Anglo-Saxon texts has been rejected by previous scholars, mainly because modern scholarship tends, I think, to distort the differences between these two closely allied groups.[125] It is becoming more recognized that members of both groups at times show attributes belonging, stereotypically, to the other 'order'.[126] On one side, the activities of reading and composing texts, seen to be attributes of the monastic life, were practised by Ealdorman Æthelweard, who wrote his own Latin chronicle.[127] His son Æthelmær read, in Ælfric's translation, the stories of the *Lives of the Saints* that, to quote from that preface, 'monks honour by special services'.[128] On the ecclesiastical side of the coin, Earl Harold's personal chaplain, who scandalized the more proper monks by refusing to shave off his martial moustache, was killed while leading a battle party against the Welsh – after he became the bishop of Hereford.[129]

Although these are isolated examples, they indicate a widespread phenomenon characteristic of eleventh-century England: that the interests of ecclesiastical and secular society were closely intertwined. It has been argued previously that the hierarchy of the Anglo-Saxon church promoted social cohesiveness and a rough form of national unity through their close economic and political ties to

---

[123] Of course, the texts found in the Otho and Corpus manuscripts were read by a monk or a member of the clergy. The ultimate audience, however, may still have included a substantial lay population: see M. McC. Gatch, *Preaching and Theology in Anglo-Saxon England: Ælfric and Wulfstan* (Toronto, 1977), pp. 37–59, and M. Clayton, 'Homiliaries and Preaching in Anglo-Saxon England', *Peritia* 4 (1985), 207–42.

[124] For a more pessimistic view of lay literacy in regard to the poetic text of Genesis found in Junius 11, see P. J. Lucas, 'Ms. Junius 11 and Malmesbury, Part 1', *Scriptorium* 34 (1980), 197–220, at 211–12.

[125] But now see P. Wormald, 'Anglo-Saxon Society and its Literature', *The Cambridge Companion to Old English Literature*, ed. M. Godden and M. Lapidge (Cambridge, 1991), pp. 1–22, at 18: 'clerics could be as hard to distinguish from laity as in earlier times...'

[126] There is also an increasing appreciation for the 'pragmatic literacy' or 'text-dependency' of the Anglo-Saxon laity; see Keynes, 'Royal Government and the Written Word'.

[127] *The Chronicle of Æthelweard*, ed. A. Campbell (London, 1962).

[128] This is recorded in Ælfric's preface printed in *Lives of Saints*, ed. Skeat, pp. 4–7.

[129] Leofgar, bishop of Hereford, died on 16 June 1056. See the entry in the *Anglo-Saxon Chronicle* for the year 1056 in J. Earle and C. Plummer, *Two of the Saxon Chronicles Parallel*, 2 vols. (Oxford, 1892–9) I, 186–7.

Unfulfilled promise: the rubrics of the Old English prose Genesis

central secular authorities.[130] As Patrick Wormald has recently noted, 'the kingdom of England did not fuse spontaneously: it had to be welded by the mixture of force, cajolery and propaganda that is the stuff of statecraft in any age'.[131] What remains to be established is how the ideological underpinnings of this co-operation were made possible.[132]

The political and spiritual economies of eleventh-century England intersect in the Old English rubrics to the prose Genesis, especially those to the story of Joseph. The textual similarities that I have shown between the rubrics and homiliaries and wills parallel their similar concern with educating the audience and reassuring them that they will receive their proper inheritance. The stories of Joseph, the patriarchs and the saints form a series of promises and fulfilments which themselves are subsets of that larger promise of salvation, which for the Christian reader remains unfulfilled.[133] For a Christian audience, the proper inheritance is determined in the Last Judgement, where one is chosen or not chosen, either inside or outside Christian society.[134]

To be among the chosen depended, in a large measure, on what Ælfric describes as 'bookly lore': 'Gehwa mæg þe eaðelicor ða toweardan costnunge acuman, ðurh Godes fultum, gif he bið þurh boclice lare getrymmed; forðan ðe þa beoð gehealdene þe oð ende on geleafan þurhwuniað.'[135] For Ælfric, 'boclice lare' represents a worldly means to a spiritual end. Reading is a continuous

---

[130] D. J. V. Fisher, 'The Anti-Monastic Reaction in the Reign of Edward the Martyr', *Cambridge Historical Jnl* 12 (1950–2), 254–70. See also P. Stafford, *Unification and Conquest* (London, 1989), 45–69, esp. 58; and the contributions in E. John, *Orbis Britanniae and Other Studies* (Leicester, 1966). Part of the reason for this association seems to be the intellectual debt that English churchmen owed to continental reform movements. On the Continent, reform centres such as Cluny protected their spiritual independence by forming mutually advantageous ties to powerful secular figures.

[131] Wormald, 'Anglo-Saxon Society and its Literature', pp. 14–15.

[132] Howe, *Migration and Mythmaking*, points to the power of myth, especially a myth of communal migration, as one means by which the Anglo-Saxon sense of community and cohesiveness developed. Howe perceives this myth-making as a dynamic, multi-dimensional process which informs the Old English poem *Exodus*. In this work, the poetic, historical tradition of the migrated Germanic tribes fuses with the biblical story of *Exodus*, tribal history merges with Christian allegory, and the identity of the Anglo-Saxon *folc* blends into that of God's chosen people, the Israelites. For an analysis of another influential textual construct of Anglo-Saxon unity, see T. E. Powell, 'The "Three Orders" of Society in Anglo-Saxon England', *ASE* 23 (1994), 103–32.

[133] W. J. Dumbrell, *Covenant and Creation: an Old Testament Covenantal Theology* (Exeter, 1984), p. 43.

[134] In Ælfric's words, 'of þam woruldmannum witodlice beoð on twa wisan gemodode and mislice gelogode, sume beoð gecorene, sume wiðercorene': *Homilies of Ælfric: A Supplementary Collection*, ed. J. C. Pope, 2 vols., EETS os 259–60 (Oxford, 1967–8), 596 (no. xviii).

[135] 'Every one may the more easily withstand the future temptation, through God's support, if he is strengthened by book learning, for they shall be preserved who continue in faith to the end': Ælfric, 'English Preface', ed. and trans. Thorpe, *Homilies* I, 4–5. Quoted and discussed by L. Grundy, *Books and Grace: Ælfric's Theology* (London, 1991), pp. 1–10.

process by which the believer learns the knowledge stored in books with God's help. The texts of the Old Testament which were translated into Old English introduce or represent to the reader those common beliefs, traditions and myths of the past which define Anglo-Saxon and Christian society. The paraphrase's simple, idiomatic prose, especially in its illustrated form in Claudius B. iv, made these beliefs, traditions and myths accessible to a broader audience than that of the Latin scriptures. The knowledge gained by reading this text could strengthen the reader and allow his integration into the community of believers after the coming Judgement.

It is important to note that 'bookly lore', as Ælfric seems to be using the phrase, does not necessarily require the ability to read. As Wormald reminds us, 'one person with the ability to read from parchment could . . . read aloud to many'.[136] In this performative context, the book provides its users with the means for identifying their own role within their societal milieu. Using the same vocabulary as we have seen in the Genesis rubrics, Ælfric describes a hierarchical vision of society:

þa hyrdas ðe wacodon ofer heora eowode on Cristes acennysse, getacnodon ða halgan lareowas on Godes gelaðunge, þe sind gastlice hyrdas geleaffulra sawla; and se engel cydde Cristes acennednysse hyrdemannum, forðam ðe ðan gastlicum hyrdum, þæt sind lareowas, is swiðost geopenod embe Cristes menniscnysse, þurh boclice lare; and hi sceolon gecneordlice heora underþeoddum bodian, þæt þæt him geswutolod is, swa swa ða hyrdas þa heofenlican gesihðe gewidmærsodan.[137]

Book-learning symbolizes the Christian community. 'Boclice lare' stands as a type of what the angels *cydde* (testified or announced) to the shepherds. As 'spiritual shepherds', the 'holy teacher' must reveal what this testimony has made manifest (*geswutelode*). As leaders of the people, Ælfric and his compatriots controlled the 'boclice lare' that determined participation in the ultimate Christian textual community: the community of saints formed on the Day of Judgement. Until the Day of Judgement, however, God's promise remains unfulfilled.

CONCLUSIONS

For the modern reader, the 'book-learning' provided by the prose Genesis can be seen as a means of integrating the eleventh-century reader not only into the

---

[136] See Wormald, 'Anglo-Saxon Society and its Literature', p. 18.
[137] 'The shepherds that watched over their flock at Christ's birth betokened the holy teachers in God's church, who are the spiritual shepherds of faithful souls: and the angels announced Christ's birth to the herdsmen, because to the spiritual shepherds, that is to the teachers, is chiefly revealed concerning Christ's humanity, through book learning: and they shall sedulously preach to those placed under them, that which is manifested to them, as the shepherds proclaimed the heavenly vision': Ælfric, 'Sermon on the Nativity of our Lord', ed. and trans. Thorpe, *Homilies* I, 36–7.

Unfulfilled promise: the rubrics of the Old English prose Genesis

community of the saved but also into the hierarchical textual and political community of Anglo-Saxon England. In theoretical terms, the book, both as symbol and in the knowledge it contains, 'offers cognitive maps that orient present actors in contemporary situations'.[138] The Anglo-Saxon promotion and spread of the vernacular, especially in its written form, can be an effective means of affecting unity, tracing political dominance, and for the user, maintaining contact with the social centre.[139] The rubrics of the Old English prose Genesis structure, define and thereby determine how the Old Testament text will be interpreted by the Anglo-Saxon audience.

For the eleventh-century reader, the impact of these vernacular versions of the Old Testament stories lies in their connections to other contemporary texts. Through its rubrics, the Old English Genesis brings archetypal stories forward in time. The rubrics overtly remind the reader of the promise God gives to Abraham, while they implicitly recall the legally binding formulas of Anglo-Saxon wills. In its biographical focus, the Genesis text asserts the essential similarity of the patriarchs and Christian saints. The stories from the Old Testament present the foundations of Christian history, and as *boclice lare* provide hope for future salvation. Patriarch, saint and the contemporary life of the Anglo-Saxon reader intertwine in the process and performance of reading. Read together, these elements merge into a continuous, unbroken succession: the sacred history of God's 'unfulfilled promise'.[140]

---

[138] A. P. Cohen, *The Symbolic Construction of Community* (London and New York, 1989), p. 100.

[139] R. I. Moore, *The Formation of a Persecuting Society: Power and Deviance in Western Society, 950–1250* (Oxford, 1987). For an analysis of the political ramifications of language and dialect in early Anglo-Saxon England, see T. E. Toon, 'The Socio-Politics of Literacy in Early England: What I Learned at our *hlaford's Knee*', *Folia Linguistica Historica* 6 (1985), 87–106.

[140] I would like to thank Toby Baldwin, Christina von Nolcken, Michael Camille, Robert Nelson, Jonathan Alexander, Peter Baker and Malcolm Godden for reading and commenting on various aspects of this paper. Most importantly, my deepest gratitude goes to Allen Frantzen for his careful attention to the arguments presented here.

The *West Saxon Gospels* and the gospel-lectionary in Anglo-Saxon England: manuscript evidence and liturgical practice

URSULA LENKER

Farað witodlice and lærað ealle þeoda and fulligeaþ hig on naman fæder and suna and þæs halgan gastes. and lærað þæt hig healdon ealle þa ðing þe ic eow bebead (Matt. XXVIII.19–20).

With these words at the end of the gospel according to Matthew, Jesus sends out his disciples to spread the words and deeds of the Lord to all peoples. With respect to the Anglo-Saxons, this order was impressively executed by the earliest translation of the Vulgate gospels into a vernacular, the *West Saxon Gospels* (*WSG*).[1] This text, from the late tenth or early eleventh century, survives in four complete manuscripts (A, B, C, Cp) and two fragments (F, L)[2] from the Old English period and two complete manuscripts from the late twelfth century (R and its copy H).

In Cambridge, University Library, Ii. 2. 11 (A; s. xi[med], from Bishop Leofric's scriptorium at Exeter)[3] and the fragments in New Haven, Beinecke Library, Beinecke 578 (F; s. xi[in], from south-eastern England)[4] rubrics are inserted which show on which day of the liturgical year a certain part of the gospels was read in the liturgy of the mass. Thus in A, the following rubric is found before Matt. XXVIII.16:

> Ðis sceal on frigedæg innan þære easterwucan.
> Undecim discipuli habierunt in galileam.

---

[1] The major editions of the *WSG* are *The Holy Gospels in Anglo-Saxon, Northumbrian and Old Mercian Versions, Synoptically Arranged, with Collations Exhibiting all the Readings of all MSS.*, ed. W. Skeat, 4 vols. (Cambridge, 1871–1900) and now *The Old English Version of the Gospels*, ed. R. M. Liuzza, EETS os 304 (Oxford, 1994).

[2] For the sigla, see the Appendix, below, pp. 175–8. The sigla for the manuscripts of the *WSG* correspond to those chosen by Skeat and Liuzza, with the exception of F for the 'Yale Fragments' ('Y' in Liuzza's edition).

[3] For detailed descriptions, see N. R. Ker, *Catalogue of Manuscripts containing Anglo-Saxon* (Oxford, 1957; reissued with addenda 1991), no. 20, Liuzza, *The Old English Version*, pp. xvii–xx, and *The West-Saxon Gospels. A Study of the Gospel of Saint Matthew with Text of the Four Gospels*, ed. M. Grünberg (Amsterdam, 1967), pp. 19–28. For the rubrics, see also pl. III.

[4] For detailed descriptions of the fragments, see Ker, *Catalogue*, no. 1, Liuzza, *The Old English Version*, pp. xli–xlii and in particular R. M. Liuzza, 'The Yale Fragments of the West Saxon Gospels', *ASE* 17 (1988), 67–82.

Accordingly, the pericope,[5] whose beginning is quoted in Latin, is to be read on the Friday of Easter Week. Altogether, 199 such rubrics are found throughout the text of the four gospels in A. In F, a single rubric which corresponds to that in A marks the text beginning with Mark I.40 to be read in the fifteenth week after Pentecost.

These rubrics connect the Old English gospel text to the eucharistic liturgy and have therefore raised the question whether the gospel of the day was read in the vernacular in Anglo-Saxon times. Madeleine Grünberg, the only editor of the *WSG* who chose A as the basis for her edition, is convinced that the *WSG* were employed in the liturgy of the mass:[6] 'The A-text of the four West-Saxon gospels served the purpose of liturgical reading . . . for this reading special texts, the so-called lectionaries, were in use. The A-text of the West-Saxon gospels, then, served as such a lectionary, but with the unique distinction of being in the vernacular.' Such liturgical use of the Old English gospel text in the Middle Ages would, however, have been revolutionary in the context of the western churches – it was exactly the employment of the vernacular in the liturgy which became one of the main objectives of future church reformers.[7]

Therefore, apart from the origin and organization of the rubrics in A and F,[8] their purpose must first be studied more closely in the light of other Anglo-Saxon witnesses. Such an investigation must be grounded on an inventory of different kinds of documents which inform us about the biblical lections employed in Anglo-Saxon times and, secondly, the evaluation of their functions. Thirdly, the liturgical readings selected in these sources have to be investigated, so that correspondences to and deviations from the tradition recorded in the rubrics may become evident and provide evidence for their purpose.

---

[5] Pericope (from Greek περικόπτειν 'to cut around') is the technical term for a liturgical reading of set length. It was only introduced by Protestant theologians of the sixteenth century. In the Middle Ages, the Latin terms were *capitula euangelii* or *sequentia euangelii* and metonymical *euangelium* (cf. ModE *Gospel (of the day)* and German *Evangelium*). See U. Lenker, *Die westsächsische Evangelienversion und die Perikopenordnungen im angelsächsischen England*, Texte und Untersuchungen zur Englischen Philologie 20 (Munich, 1997), 85–93.

[6] Grünberg, *The West-Saxon Gospels*, p. 369.

[7] In his Preface to the edition of 1571, which was prepared under the supervision of Archbishop Parker (by John Joscelyn?), John Foxe explicitly links the Old English translation with the aims of the Reformation; see also Liuzza, *The Old English Version*, pp. xiii–xv.

[8] The rubrics to the *WSG* have attracted very little scholarly attention; the most important investigations are F. Tupper, 'Anglo-Saxon Dæg-mæl', *PMLA* 10 (1895), 111–241, the notes to J. Bright's edition of the Gospel according to John (*Euangelium Secundum Iohannem. The Gospel of Saint John in West–Saxon* (Boston, 1904), pp. 115–82) and W. H. Frere, *Studies in Early Roman Liturgy: 2. The Roman Gospel-Lectionary*, Alcuin Club Collection 30 (Oxford, 1934), 221.

THE LITURGICAL RUBRICS IN A AND F

The insertion of the liturgical rubrics in manuscripts A and F of the *WSG* was definitely not part of the original translation project.[9] The extant manuscripts can be divided into three broad groups – CpBC, AF and the post-Anglo-Saxon group RH. Compared to the older manuscripts CpBC, A contains a number of apparently deliberate variants in text and layout,[10] such as alteration of prefixes and word order, expansion and shortening of the text, fuller paragraphing and – for that matter – the insertion of liturgical rubrics. Liuzza even refers to A as 'virtually a second edition of the OE version of the gospels'.[11] Unfortunately F defies easy classification, as its text is only preserved in small fragments (Matt. XXVIII.17–19 and Mark I.24–31, 35–42) which do not contain major variants. There are only a few textual agreements which align the fragments with A rather than Cp, suggesting that F represents an earlier version of the text found in A.[12] Apparently the common exemplar of F and A had a slightly altered design in that it also contained the Latin headings, which are found in the margins in other manuscripts, on separate lines (for F, cf. the headings at Mark I.29 and 40).

The Old English rubric in F at Mark I.40 is a later addition, which was squeezed in between the lines by a scribe of unknown date and origin. While palaeographical and dialectal analysis[13] places the origin of F in the Kentish area at the beginning of the eleventh century, the next certain evidence – its provenance at Tewkesbury in the fourteenth century – allows no conclusion as to when it wandered from the eastern to the western part of the country. Hence we do not know where and when the Old English part of the rubric was added.

In A, on the other hand, the insertion of the rubrics is integral to the general design of the whole manuscript. The incipits in the Latin text were written together with the main text in the same ink. This method can be discerned from the fact that the Latin fills two lines where the space was needed, as in the case of the rubrics before Matt. XVII.10 and XVII.14:[14]

---

[9] For the relationship of the manuscripts, see Liuzza, 'The Yale Fragments', pp. 75–80, Liuzza, *The Old English Version*, pp. xliii–lxxiii, and Lenker, *Perikopenordnungen*, pp. 23–7.

[10] Liuzza, *The Old English Version*, pp. lvi–lvii.

[11] The relationship of R and H to the other copies is fairly clear – R is a copy of H, H itself a copy of B. [12] Liuzza, *The Old English Version*, p. lviii.

[13] The Kentish origin is obvious, for example from the spellings <yo> instead of West Saxon <eo> for /e:o/ (e.g. *dyofel, syocnessa* (Mark I.39)) and forms in *-an, -ade* and *-ad* (*geclænsad* Mark I.42) instead of West Saxon *-on, -ode* and *-od* (see A. Campbell, *Old English Grammar* (Oxford, 1959), §§ 297 and 757). *Anwald* without breaking is attested in Mark I.27. See also Liuzza, 'The Yale Fragments', p. 75. [14] Cf. pl. III.

geþys ne secgon ær mannes sunu of deaðe aryse
Ðys sceal on frigedæg on þære fiftan wucan pent*ecosten*.
Interrogauit [*sic*] i*esu*m discipuli dicentes . Quid ergo
scribe dicunt. Quid elia*m* oporteat primu*m* uenire.
And þa acsedon hys leorning cnyhtas hyne hwat

tas þæt he hyt sæde be Iohannes þa*m* fulluhtere. Ðys sceal
on wodnesdæg to *þam* fæstene ær hærfestes emnyhte.
Et cu*m* uenisset ad turba*s* accessit ad eu*m* homo genib*us*
prouolutus.
And þa he co*m* to þære mænigu hym to genealæhte su*m*

Before the Latin incipit a line was left blank for the insertion of the Old English part of the rubric, which was added later by the same scribe in red ink.[15] When this blank line did not provide enough space, the Old English text was squeezed into the blank spaces after the preceding or following Old English gospel text (Matt. XVII.14 above) or the Latin incipit. Rubrics such as the one before Luke XVI.19 prove that the Old English part was added after the completion of both the Old English gospel text and the Latin incipit:

[... unrihthæmð] Ðis godspel
gebyrað on þone oðerne sunnandæg ofer pen
Homo quidam erat diues. tecosten.
[Sum welig man wæs ...]

In all instances, the first word of the Old English pericope is highlighted by an initial.

This procedure of the scribe is important because it informs us that the book(s) he used as (an) exemplar(s) must have contained not only the Old English translation but also the Latin incipits. Textually, these incipits belong to the tradition of lectionaries.[16] Hence the scribe must have used a Latin lectionary in addition to a manuscript of the *WSG* or an exemplar in which these two elements had already been joined.[17] This means that he also had the information about the liturgical day at hand, though probably not in the form of rubrics, but perhaps as marginal notes. This would account for the unsystematic layout by an otherwise extremely careful and competent scribe. The fact that two lines were

---

[15] The later addition of liturgical rubrics in lines left blank for this purpose is not unique to A but is also found in a manuscript of Ælfric's *Catholic Homilies*: 'At the beginning of each homily the scribes left a space for a large initial capital and also one or two blank lines into which the heading and pericope incipit were later inserted' (P. Clemoes, 'Description of the Manuscript', *Ælfric's First Series of Catholic Homilies. British Museum, Royal 7. C. XII, Fols. 4–218*, ed. N. E. Eliason and P. Clemoes, EEMF 13 (Copenhagen, 1966), 22).

[16] See below, pp. 147–9.

[17] Without any obvious reason the scribe changed his method for the last four rubrics (John XX.19, XXI.1, XXI.15 and XXI.19), where the Latin follows the Old English.

The West Saxon Gospels *and the gospel-lectionary in Anglo-Saxon England*

left blank for a pericope which is read on two liturgical days further supports this argument (Luke IV.38):[18]

Ðis sceal on þone ðryddan ðunresdæg innan lenctene
7 to pentecosten on sæternesdæg.
Surgens iesus de sinagoga introiuit in domum simonis.

The Old English text of the rubrics

The Old English part of the rubric is extremely formulaic: only four different phrases are used randomly in the four gospels. The choice is restricted to constructions with *gebyrian* 'it pertains to, it is lawful' and *sceal* 'shall, ought to [be read]', both of which indicate a certain degree of obligation:[19]

+ 'Ðis godspel sceal' (Matt. II.13; Mark VI.17; Luke VII.36; John II.1 etc.)
+ 'Ðis sceal' (Matt. II.1; Mark I.40; Luke I.26; John I.35 etc.)
+ 'Ðis godspel gebyrað' (Matt. I.18; Mark VIII.1; Luke I.1; John II.13 etc.)
+ 'Ðis gebyrað' (Matt. VIII.14; Mark X.46; Luke I.39; John I.19 etc.)

These fixed phrases are not unique to the rubrics of the *WSG* but are also found as rubrics and headings in homiliaries. Consider, for example, two instances from a manuscript of Ælfric's *Catholic Homilies* (London, BL, Cotton Vitellius C. v: s. x/xi), which are identical to the rubrics not only in phrasing but also in contents and design:[20]

FERIA VI IN PRIMA EBDOMADA QUADRAGESIMÆ.
ðis spel gebyrað on Frige-dæg on þære forman Lenctenwucan.
EVVANGELIUM. Erat dies festus Iudæorum, et reliqua.

FERIA VI IN EBDOMADA III:
Ðis spel sceal on frige-dæg on þære þriddan lencten-wucan.
EVVANGELIUM: Venit IHs in ciuitatem samariæ quæ dicitur sichar.

The analysis of the Old English text of the rubrics according to Old English dialect features shows them to be typically late West Saxon.[21] Some of the late features, moreover, attest to a date at the end of the Old English

---

[18] Similarly, two lines are left blank before Matt. XX.29, where the Saturday in the summer Embertide is described in a long phrase: 'þys sceal on sæternesdæg on þære pentecostenes/ wucan to þam ymbrene'.

[19] Only the first instances in each gospel are cited. The Old English term for the pericope is *godspell*, except for the four cases when *passio* refers to the Passion (Matt. XXVI.2, Mark XIV.1, Luke XXII.1 and John XVIII.1).

[20] *Homilies of Ælfric. A Supplementary Collection*, ed. J. C. Pope, 2 vols., EETS os 259–60 (London, 1967) I, 230 and 288.

[21] For a detailed analysis of the different characteristics such as breaking, palatal diphthongization etc., see Lenker, *Perikopenordnungen*, pp. 216–19.

period,[22] in particular syncope in *þuresdæg* (John VII.40) and the already Middle English form *þursdæg* (John V.30) instead of regular *þunresdæg* 'Thursday'.[23]

In addition, two forms (*ucan* and *þæge*) which are not found in the gospel text of A and are thus exclusive to the rubrics, suggest that they originated in the south-western region of England. The form *ucan* with loss of initial /w/ (cf. *wicu/wucu*),[24] also occurs in a manuscript of the *Theodulfi Capitula* (Oxford, Bodleian Library, Bodley 865: s. xi¹)[25] which was presumably written at Exeter. In Old English times, *ucan* is only recorded in manuscripts from the south-western area.[26]

Similarly, the attestations of the pronoun *þæge*[27] (used instead of *þa* in Luke XI.15) are concentrated in the south-west of England, in particular Bath and Exeter.[28] The four instances of *þæge* found in the gospel text of the three south-western manuscripts of the *WSG* (Cp, B and C) are in all cases replaced by *þa* in A (John IV.40, X.16, XIV.12; incorrect *þe* at John XII.20), so that *þæge*-forms in A are only found in the rubrics.

Ucan and *þæge* thus serve as evidence for the origin of the rubrics, which were

---

[22] Other late features are dative plural forms in *-on* instead of *-um*, e.g. *wucon* (Mark XI.1, Luke XIX.29 and John I.15) and *dagon* (Luke XI.5, John XV.12 and XV.17). Cf. also the spelling <mænies> (Matt. XXIV.42) instead of <mæniges> (Luke XII.35) which points towards a vocalization of /j/.

[23] Other instances of syncope of the genitive ending are *sæterndæg* in Mark IX.2 and Luke III.1.

[24] The form *ucan* is attested five times (Luke XVI.10, XXI.20, John XVI.5, XX.11 and XXI.1). For a similar phenomenon of loss of initial *w* before *u*, see the forms *uton* for *wuton* (Campbell, *Old English Grammar*, § 471). The change is probably triggered by *w* being a half-vowel, i.e. an unsyllabic *u*, which was lost before the vowel /u/.

[25] Cf. *Theodulfi Capitula in England. Die altenglischen Übersetzungen zusammen mit dem lateinischen Text*, ed. H. Sauer, Texte und Untersuchungen zur Englischen Philologie 8 (Munich, 1978), 190–1, 377 and 393.

[26] The form *ucan* is found in Luke XVIII.12 ('Ic fæste tuwa on ucan') in the three south-western manuscripts of the *WSG*, Cp (Bath), C (Malmesbury?) and B (unknown origin); in A, however, the form appears as *wucan*. Another instance of *ucan* is recorded in the poem *Seasons of Fasting* (c. 1000). Sisam attributes this form to the 'South Midlands' and comments on its use in Old English: 'The sound-change is concealed by the conventional spelling which spread with the Late West Saxon Literary dialect. It appears commonly in the Domesday record of 1086 where the traditional spelling is no longer followed' (K. Sisam, *Studies in the History of Old English Literature* (Oxford, 1953), p. 52).

[27] For a detailed summary of the attestations of *þæge* and their critical assessment, see M. Förster, 'Die spätae. deiktische Pronominalform *þæge* und ne. *they*', *Anglia Beiblatt* 52 (1941), 274–80 and 'Nochmals: ae. *þæge*', ibid. 53 (1942), 86–7, and in particular W. Hofstetter, *Winchester und der spätaltenglische Sprachgebrauch. Untersuchungen zur geographischen und zeitlichen Verbreitung altenglischer Synonyme*, Texte und Untersuchungen zur Englischen Philologie 14 (München, 1987), 563–7.

[28] See instances 5, 6, 7 and 8 in Förster, 'Die spätae. deiktische Pronominalform *þæge*' and examples 2, 3 and 4 in Hofstetter, *Winchester und der spätaltenglische Sprachgebrauch*, p. 563.

The West Saxon Gospels *and the gospel-lectionary in Anglo-Saxon England*

probably compiled at the end of the Old English period in the south-west of England. Since A itself was certainly written at Exeter in the time of Bishop Leofric,[29] Exeter in the middle of the eleventh century seems a very likely place for the origin of the rubrics themselves, a conclusion which the linguistic evidence would seem to support.

The Latin text of the rubrics

There are two different Latin textual elements in A which have to be separated from one another: first, the Latin incipits of the pericopes and, secondly, the Latin headings which are similarly found in other manuscripts of the *WSG* (Cp, B, R, H).[30] These two elements follow a completely different textual tradition and have furthermore to be distinguished from the Latin exemplar of the translation text itself, as the following examples show:[31]

Luke I.26
Vul: **In mense** *autem* **sexto**   missus est angelus gabriel
WSG: *Soþ*lice **on þam syxtan monðe**   wæs asend gabriel se engel
A: Missus est angelus gabrihel
Qe, Sa: Missus est gabrihel angelus

Luke XXIV.36
Vul: *ipse* stetit   in medio **eorum**
WSG: *se hælend* stod   on **hyra** midlene
A: Stetit *iesus*   in medio **discipulorum suorum**
Qe, Sa: Stetit *iesus*   in medio **discipulorum suorum**

---

[29] The origin and provenance of the manuscript in Exeter is apparent from both palaeographical evidence and the inventory of books procured by Bishop Leofric for the church of Exeter. One copy of this inventory was originally part of A and is now found in a quire prefixed to the Exeter Book (Exeter, Cathedral Library, 3501, fols. 0, 1–7). The manuscript itself can be identified as 'þeos englisce cristes boc' in this list; in another copy (Oxford, Bodleian Library, Auct. D. 2. 16, fols. iv, 1–6) it is called 'englisc Cristes boc'. See M. Lapidge, 'Surviving Booklists from Anglo-Saxon England', *Learning and Literature in Anglo-Saxon England. Studies presented to Peter Clemoes*, ed. M. Lapidge and H. Gneuss (Cambridge, 1985), pp. 33–89, at 64–9. Leofric's donation is also documented in an entry on 1r: 'Hunc textum euangeliorum dedit leofricus episcopus ecclesiae sancti petre apostoli in exonia ad utilitatem successorum suorum. Ðas boc leofric biscop gef sancto petro and eallum his æftergengum into exancestre gode mid to ðenienne.'
[30] For detailed descriptions of the manuscripts, see Liuzza, *The Old English Version*, pp. xvii–xlii.
[31] Abbreviations: 'Vul' refers to the text of the Vulgate (*Nestle-Aland. Novum Testamentum Latine*, ed. K. and B. Aland (Stuttgart, 1982)), '*WSG*' to the Old English translation (ed. Liuzza) and 'A' to the text of the rubrics in the manuscript A. For the text of Latin lectionaries, the incipits cited in the gospel-lists Qe and Sa were chosen (see the Appendix, below, pp. 175–8).

While the first example merely shows a shortening in the text of the lectionary incipits by the deletion of adverbials, the second example documents one of the specific characteristics of lectionary texts, namely the substitution of proper names or nouns for pronouns.[32] In general, all anaphoric items have to be replaced, since the extracts chosen as lessons lack the context of the gospel text, but still have to be fully understandable, coherent stories. In the following example (John XXI.19), the pericope would not be comprehensible without these changes:

Vul:	Et hoc cum dixis**set**,	dic**it** *ei*:	sequere me
WSG:	And þa **he** þæt sæde	þa cwæð **he** *to him*:	fylig me
A:		Dixit **iesus** *petro*:	sequere me
Qe, Sa:		Dixit **iesus** *petro*:	sequere me

The text of the Latin incipits in A clearly derives from the textual tradition of Latin lectionaries.[33]

The second Latin element in the text of A are twenty-five chapter-headings.[34] A mistake of the scribe who could have forgotten to add the Old English part of the rubric is unlikely: apart from four instances there is no line left blank for its insertion. Furthermore, the textual tradition of these chapter-headings does not belong to that of lectionaries but corresponds to the Vulgate text proper. Thus in the chapter-heading for Mark I.29, the Latin text in A and F represents the Vulgate version and is not altered according to the lectionary tradition: 'Et protinus egredientes de sinagoga uenerunt in domum symonis et andree.'[35] The fact that the chapter-headings are mainly found in the beginning chapters of the gospels according to Matthew and Mark suggests that a recension had been started in which all the gospels were to be augmented with chapter-headings.[36] This plan was, however, abandoned after the first chapters of each gospel.

---

[32] The relevant phrases are marked by italics or bold letters.
[33] The exemplar of the Latin incipits in A, however, is as yet unknown. Their comparison with both the incipits attested in extant Anglo-Saxon witnesses and the textual varieties documented in the critical edition of Latin gospelbooks by Fischer (which includes the texts of Roman and Milanese lectionaries) showed too many discrepancies. Their closest textual relative is Paris, Bibliothèque de l'Arsenal, 612 (Rheims, *c.* 850). See B. Fischer, *Die lateinischen Evangelien bis zum 10. Jahrhundert*, 4 vols. (Freiburg, 1988–91).
[34] Cf. the chapter-headings before Matt. V.13, V.27, VI.1, VI.7, VI.22, VII.6, VII.13, VII.22, VIII.5, VIII.28, IX.23, IX.35, X.7, X.11, X.22, Mark I.9, I.14, I.16, I.22, I.29, XII.41 and John III.22, V.24, VI.5 (for VI.1) and VI.37. For chapter-headings in general, see P. Meyvaert, 'Bede's *Capitula Lectionum* for the Old and New Testament', *RB* 105 (1995), 348–80, at 349–52.
[35] Cf. the lack of a proper name or noun as the subject of the sentence ('egredientes, uenerunt'); the adverb 'protinus' is not deleted.
[36] These chapter-headings were a very useful tool in a time when there was no chapter and verse division of the gospels. In the gospels according to Luke and John, major parts of the beginning chapters are used as liturgical readings so that the original chapter-headings were replaced by the rubrics.

The West Saxon Gospels *and the gospel-lectionary in Anglo-Saxon England*

This or a similar project also accounts for the lines which were left blank in A.[37] For these, both Grünberg and Liuzza have suggested[38] a liturgical function, such as the later insertion of rubrics. Yet the verses following the blank lines were not selected for liturgical use in the Roman rite, as a comparison with the incipits of Roman pericopes[39] shows. They agree, however, with the paragraphing and chapter-headings in other manuscripts. The blank lines are therefore due to the altered layout of A and its ancestor, in particular the introduction of new paragraphs for the easier use of the manuscript.

The rubrics in A and F are undoubtedly an addition in one branch of manuscript transmission of the *WSG*. Their common ancestor was a version, revised in text and design, to which the liturgical information was added, presumably in the margins. The combination of the Old English text with the Roman pericope system most probably originated in a centre in the south-western area in the late Old English period, presumably Exeter at the time of Bishop Leofric, according to linguistic and manuscript evidence.

BIBLICAL LECTIONS IN THE LITURGY OF THE EUCHARIST

The reading of the gospel of the day is one of the oldest elements of Christian worship. With regard to the eucharistic liturgy,[40] we have firm evidence for two or three biblical lections from the second century onwards. In the Roman rite,[41] a two-lesson system had gained acceptance by the seventh or eighth century when Roman books entered Gaul. The first text, read by the subdeacon, was taken from the New Testament epistles (hence the term 'epistle'), the Acts of the Apostles, the Apocalypse (Revelation) or the Old Testament.[42] The source

---

[37] For the blank lines, see pl. III (before Matt. XVII.22 'Ða hig wunedon . . .'). There are twenty blank lines in Mark, twenty-one in Luke, eight in Matthew and only two in John. Only four of them are found in the neighbourhood of chapter-headings.

[38] See Grünberg, *The West-Saxon Gospels*, p. 21 and Liuzza, *The Old English Version*, p. xx.

[39] See the index of biblical lessons in Lenker, *Perikopenordnungen*, pp. 529–35.

[40] For general surveys of the subject, see J. Jungmann, *Missarum Sollemnia. Eine genetische Erklärung der römischen Messe*, 5th ed., 2 vols. (Freiburg, 1962) I, 501–83; C. Vogel, *Medieval Liturgy. An Introduction to the Sources*, trans. and rev. W. Storey and N. Rasmussen; and A.-G. Martimort, *Les Lectures liturgiques et leurs livres*, Typologie des sources du moyen âge occidental 64 (Turnhout, 1992), 15–20.

[41] For the development of the elements which surround the readings of the gospel of the day, i.e. the chants, collects, the homily and the *Credo*, see Jungmann, *Missarum Sollemnia*, I; K. Young, *The Drama of the Medieval Church*, 2 vols. (London, 1933; corr. repr. 1962) I, 21–9; and J. Harper, *The Forms and Orders of Western Liturgy from the Tenth to the Eighteenth Century. A Historical Introduction and Guide for Students and Musicians* (Oxford, 1991), pp. 109–26.

[42] Evidence for the first reading in the Anglo-Saxon eucharistic service is provided by the Old English gloss *pistelrædere* for Latin *subdiaconus* in the *Regularis Concordia* (see *Die Regularis Concordia und ihre altenglische Interlinearversion*, ed. L. Kornexl, Texte und Untersuchungen zur Englischen Philologie 17 (Munich, 1993), lines 798, 801, 1011 etc., cf. p. ccxxxix). For the documents for the first reading, see W. H. Frere, *Studies in Early Roman Liturgy: 3. The Roman Epistle Lectionary*,

for the second lection, read by the deacon,[43] has always been one of the four gospels.

The reading of the gospel of the day was, and still is, the central and most important part of the liturgy of the Word. For Christian believers, God is present in the word that is announced and proclaimed, so that Word and Sacrament are inseparable. Accordingly, Latin and vernacular witnesses for the various traditions of biblical lections in the mass[44] have survived in comparatively great numbers from Anglo-Saxon times,[45] in altogether more than sixty different Latin and Old English sources. Before the emergence of the *missale plenum* in the late tenth or eleventh century, the elements that made up the eucharistic liturgy were contained in three separate books: the prayers to be said by the celebrant were found in the 'sacramentary',[46] the chants in the 'gradual'[47] and the readings in various kinds of books, in particular gospelbooks and, later, books written exclusively for liturgical use. Basically, five major groups of witnesses can be distinguished:

Alcuin Club Collection 32 (Oxford, 1935) and for the lack of witnesses from Anglo-Saxon England, see H. Gneuss, 'Liturgical Books in Anglo-Saxon England and their Old English Terminology', *Learning and Literature in Anglo-Saxon England*, ed. Lapidge and Gneuss, pp. 91–141, at 110.

[43] See Jungmann, *Missarum Sollemnia* I, 566–7. For Anglo-Saxon England, the reading of the gospel by the deacon is attested in a number of sources, e.g. the *Regularis Concordia*: 'Diaconus uero, antequam ad euuangelium legendum accedat' glossed by 'se diacon ær þam to godspelle to rædenne toga' (*Regularis Concordia*, ed. Kornexl, line 803) and Ælfric's pastoral letters:'Diaconus is gecweden <þegn> se þenað þæm mæssepreoste oþþe þam bisceope æt þære mæssan and godspel ræt' (*Die Hirtenbriefe Ælfrics in altenglischer und lateinischer Fassung*, ed. B. Fehr, Bibliothek der angelsächsischen Prosa 9 (Hamburg, 1914; repr. with a Supplement to the Introduction by P. Clemoes, Darmstadt, 1966), 108). Cf. also the sign for the deacon in the *Monasterialia Indicia* 'Ðonne þu diacon abban wille þonne stric þu ealgelice mid þinum scyte fingre and wyrc cristes mæl on þin heafod foran on þæs halgan godspelles getacnunge' (*Monasteriales [sic] Indicia. The Anglo-Saxon Monastic Sign Language*, ed. D. Banham (Pinner, 1991), p. 48 (no. 124)).

[44] The present study is restricted to the reading of the gospel of the day as it appears in the context of the eucharistic liturgy. The epistle readings and the lessons included in the daily Office and the occasional offices demand special treatment as they developed independently; for the books for the daily Office, see Gneuss, 'Liturgical Books', pp. 110–35; for their readings, see Martimort, *Les Lectures liturgiques*, pp. 71–103.

[45] See the inventory of manuscripts in the Appendix, which is based on H. Gneuss, 'A Preliminary List of Manuscripts Written or Owned in England up to 1100', *ASE* 9 (1981), 1–60 and in particular Gneuss, 'Liturgical Books', pp. 91–141. See now also R. W. Pfaff, 'Massbooks: Sacramentaries and Missals', *The Liturgical Books of Anglo-Saxon England*, *OEN* Subsidia 23 (1995), 7–34.

[46] Unfortunately, sacramentaries and missals are neither distinguished in Latin, nor in OE or ModE: the terms *missale*, *mæsseboc* and *missal* can denote both books. Cf., for example, the codex known as the 'Missal of Robert of Jumièges' (Rouen, BM, 274 (Y.6)) which is actually a sacramentary. Cf. Gneuss, 'Liturgical Books', pp. 99–100 and Pfaff, 'Massbooks', pp. 7–8.

[47] See Gneuss, 'Liturgical Books', pp. 104–6 and K. D. Hartzell, 'Graduals' in *The Liturgical Books of Anglo-Saxon England*, ed. Pfaff, pp. 35–8.

The West Saxon Gospels *and the gospel-lectionary in Anglo-Saxon England*

(i) marginal notes in gospelbooks[48] (siglum 'M'[49] for the non-Roman tradition, 'N' for the Roman tradition),
(ii) capitularies[50] or gospel-lists, included in gospelbooks ('O', 'P', 'Q', 'S'),
(iii) full lectionaries ('T') and gospel-lectionaries ('V'),
(iv) missals ('W'), and
(v) Latin ('X', 'Y') and vernacular ('Z') homilies and homiliaries.

Bible manuscripts have no importance in this investigation, since evidence from them is restricted to the 'Codex Amiatinus' (Mc) which contains only a single marginal note for a gospel lection.[51]

Systems

In the course of the Middle Ages, several different systems were developed to help the lectors find the proper readings for the recurring feasts. The first documents with information on the nature and arrangement of the readings in the eucharistic liturgy to survive are from the sixth century.[52] With regard to the Roman rite, Anglo-Saxon witnesses employing highly innovative and idiosyncratic methods such as notes to *capitula*-tables (Ma, Mb, Mc)[53] and the so-called

---

[48] See Gneuss, 'Liturgical Books', p. 108 and, in addition, eight notes in Cambridge, University Library, Kk. 1. 24 (Nc) and four in the *Stonyhurst Gospel* (Nk).
[49] The sigla are chosen according to a system in which the first letter of each siglum shows what kind of source the document is.
[50] See Gneuss, 'Liturgical Books', p. 109 and, in addition, the capitularies in Cambridge, Fitzwilliam Museum, 45–1980 (Pc), Hanover, Kestner-Museum, WM XXIa. 36 (Sx), London, BL, Loan 11 (Sc), New York, Public Library, 115 (Qc) and the fragment of a capitulary in Oxford, Bodleian Library, Bodley 381, fols. i–ii (Px). Another extremely important old witness, the epistle- and gospel-list in Würzburg, Universitätsbibliothek, M. p. th. f. 62 (Oa), is included, although its Anglo-Saxon origin is not certain (see below, n. 79). Two lists in Anglo-Saxon manuscripts mentioned by Gneuss (Besançon, BM, 14; no. D. 21) and Klauser (Antwerp, Plantin-Moretus Museum, lat. 194) are post-Anglo-Saxon and were added to these gospelbooks in the twelfth or thirteenth century (for the latter, see T. Klauser, *Das römische Capitulare Evangeliorum. Texte und Untersuchungen zu seiner ältesten Geschichte. 1. Typen*, Liturgiegeschichtliche Quellen und Forschungen 28 (Münster, 1935), p. xxxviii (no. 11)).
[51] For the transmission of the Old Testament in general and for liturgical notes in Old Testament manuscripts, see R. Marsden, *The Text of the Old Testament in Anglo-Saxon England*, CSASE 15 (Cambridge, 1995), 40–1.
[52] For the general development, see Frere, *The Roman Gospel-Lectionary*, pp. iii–iv and 59–61; Klauser, *Capitulare Evangeliorum*, pp. x–xxii; Martimort, *Les Lectures liturgiques*, pp. 15–58; Vogel, *Medieval Liturgy*, pp. 293–304 and 315–20, and Lenker, *Perikopenordnungen*, pp. 94–132.
[53] The notes to the *capitula*-tables in the 'Lindisfarne Gospels' are ed. Skeat, *The Holy Gospels*, pp. 16–22 (Matt.), 2–5 (Mark), 3–11 (Luke) and 3–8 (John). They are described and analysed by T. J. Brown, 'The Latin Text', *Euangeliorum quattuor codex Lindisfarnensis Musei Britannici codex Cottonianus Nero D.IV permissione Musei Britannici totius codicis similitudo expressa. Book I. Part II: The Latin Text*, ed. T. D. Kendrick, T. J. Brown *et al.* (Olten, 1960), pp. 35–6 and his edition of *The Stonyhurst Gospel of Saint John*, Roxburghe Club (Oxford, 1969), pp. 25–7.

Ursula Lenker

'quasi-capitularies' in the 'Lindisfarne Gospels' (Mx) and London, BL, Royal 1. B. VII (My)[54] are among the oldest extant sources.

Marginal Notes

In the oldest manuscripts, marginal notes to gospelbooks appear as the most basic method of marking a gospel text as a liturgical reading (as in M and N),[55] since only the name of the feast is placed in the margin of a codex at the beginning of the pericope.[56] In several of the Northumbrian manuscripts (Md, Me, Mf, Mv/Nd, Nk), crosses mark the beginning of the lection in the gospel text itself. Its conclusion is not similarly indicated: among the Anglo-Saxon manuscripts, London, BL, Add. 40000 (Na) is unique in marking the end of the pericope with *F:n:t*. Since the gospel and the relevant chapter have to be known beforehand, marginal notes represent a somewhat unsystematic and highly provisional means, made for liturgical experts at a time when relatively few readings were fixed. Hence the number of notes scattered over the gospel text is normally small – in seven of the fourteen extant manuscripts[57] from Anglo-Saxon times there are fewer than twenty such notes. Only the notes in the 'Burchard Gospels' (Würzburg, Universitätsbibliothek, M. p. th. f. 68; Mv/Nd) and London, BL, Add. 40000 (Na) cover the major parts of the liturgical year.

Furthermore, both the exact date and place of origin of the notes are often hard to determine. The notes may have been copied together with the gospel text, but they may also have been added to the margins of the texts centuries later. Thus in the 'Burchard Gospels' two sets of notes appear, a non-Roman (Mv) and a Roman system (Nd). In Oxford, Bodleian Library, Auct. D. 2. 14, three different sets of Roman systems are recorded, two from seventh-century Italy (Ng; Nh) and one added in England in the tenth century (Ni). More important than the dating of the manuscripts is therefore that of the notes, which can be summarized as follows:

---

[54] These 'quasi-capitularies' are merely tables of names of church festivals. They are not arranged in the liturgical order and do not indicate which pericopes they refer to. They are thus useless as a means of finding the gospel of the day. Only comparison with the marginal notes to 'Burchard Gospels' allows their allocation to certain liturgical texts. For more detailed descriptions, see Brown, 'The Latin Text', pp. 35–8, J. Chapman, *Notes on the Early History of the Vulgate Gospels* (Oxford, 1908), pp. 52–63 and Lenker, *Perikopenordnungen*, pp. 136–40 and 387–96.

[55] For details, see Klauser, *Capitulare Evangeliorum*, pp. xiii–xiv and xxx–xxxvi, Martimort, *Les Lectures liturgiques*, pp. 22–6, Vogel, *Medieval Liturgy*, pp. 315–16 and Lenker, *Perikopenordnungen*, pp. 102–6 and 387–412.

[56] An exception to this rule are the notes in the 'Burchard Gospels', which are found at the upper margin of the page. The beginning of the pericope in the text is indicated by a cross.

[57] In some manuscripts this is due to later bookbinders who, when rebinding the books and trimming the margins, cut off some of the marginal notes; cf. the seventh-century notes in Oxford, Bodleian Library, Auct. D. 2. 14 (Ng/Nh) and those in Cambridge, University Library, Kk. 1. 24 (Nc) or London, BL, Add. 40000 (Na).

The West Saxon Gospels *and the gospel-lectionary in Anglo-Saxon England*

s. vii   Ng, Nh
s. viii Ma, Mb, Mc, Md, Me, Mf, Mg, Mv, Nd, Nk
s. x   Na, Nc, Ni

Capitularies

The use of marginal notes predominated as long as readings were relatively few. When their number increased, other means became necessary. Thus the most important documents for gospel lections in the early medieval period are gospel-lists (also called 'lists of pericopes' or 'capitularies'). From Anglo-Saxon England, seventeen capitularies have survived (sigla O, P, Q, S).[58] These lists may be placed at the beginning (Pa, Pc, Ph), but are more often found as an appendix at the end of a manuscript. Capitularies provide very precise and detailed information about the date of a feast and in particular the exact beginning and end of the pericope by referring to its Eusebian section and by quoting its opening and closing words. Compare the following examples from the eleventh-century capitulary in Sa (Cambridge, Trinity College B. 10. 4, 164v):[59]

Dom*inica* v p*ost* theophania. Eu*angelium* Sec*undu*m matheum. Cap*itulum* lxviiii. Ascendente Ie*s*u in nauicula Us*que* quia uenti et mare oboediunt ei.
In nat*ale sanct*ae agnae. Eu*angelium* Sec*undu*m matheum. Cap*itulum* cclxvii. In illo *tempore*. Dix*it iesu*s discipulis suis. Simile e*st* regnum caelo*rum* decem uirginibu*s* Us*que* quia nescitis diem neq*ue* horam.

Since the entries are arranged in liturgical order, the lists can be grouped on purely formal grounds, such as the beginning of the list with the first mass of Christmas (Pa, Pb, Pc, Pg) or the vigil mass at None of Christmas Eve (Pc, Ph, Qa, Qb, Qc, Qe, Sa, Sb, Sc, Sd, Se, Sx).[60] Other basically formal criteria provided the basis for the allocation of different sigla: 'Q' indicates that the days of the Sanctorale and Temporale are not combined in one list, but are grouped together (Qa, Qb, Qc) or completely separated (Qe) from one another. While

---

[58] For details, see Frere, *The Roman Gospel-Lectionary*, pp. 59–214, Klauser, *Capitulare Evangeliorum*, pp. xiv–xviii and xxxvii–lxx, Vogel, *Medieval Liturgy*, pp. 316–18 and Lenker, *Perikopenordnungen*, pp. 107–14 and 413–56.   [59] Cf. pl. IV.
[60] The beginning of a list with the first mass of Christmas or the vigil mass at None of Christmas Eve is one of the characteristics which distinguishes the Roman types 2 and 3 (see below, pp. 160–3). In all strictly Anglo-Saxon witnesses investigated here, one of the Christmas masses is chosen as the beginning of the liturgical year, although the shift to the first Sunday in Advent is commonly dated between the eighth and tenth century (see e.g. Vogel, *Medieval Liturgy*, p. 312 and Ælfric's statement in his homily on the Circumcision: 'Sume ure þeningbec onginnað on aduentum domini' (*Ælfric's Catholic Homilies. The First Series. Text*, ed. P. Clemoes, EETS ss 17 (London, 1997), 228)).

'P'-lists count the Sundays after Pentecost according to the Gregorian sections,[61] 'S'-lists name them continuously as 'post pentecosten'.
Most of the surviving capitularies are from the ninth and eleventh centuries:

s. ix   Pa, Pb, Pc, Px, Qc, Qe
s. x   Ph, Qa
s. xi   Pg, Qb, Sa, Sb, Sc, Sd, Se, Sx

For an evaluation of their actual use in the Anglo-Saxon liturgy it has to be remembered, however, that several of these manuscripts were written on the Continent (Pa, Pc, Px, Qa, Qc, Qe; Oa?, Pb?) and only came to England with monks taking refuge from Viking raids or in the wake of the Benedictine reform.

Lectionaries

Unlike gospelbooks with marginal notes and capitularies, lectionaries commonly served liturgical purposes only, because they contain only a selection of biblical texts, namely the readings for the liturgical services. A so-called full lectionary gives the texts for both the first and the second reading. However, the three extant fragments, which consist only of one or two folios, do not provide much evidence for the lection system in Anglo-Saxon England (Ta, Tb, Tc).[62]

Gospel-lectionaries (V)[63] are arranged in the same way as capitularies but give the full texts of all the pericopes in the order of the church year – prefaced by the liturgical formula *In illo tempore*. Within the limits of this narrow definition, Anglo-Saxon evidence is restricted to merely three fragments (Va, Vc, Vf)[64] and one complete gospel lectionary (Florence, Biblioteca Medicea Laurenziana, Plut. xvii. 20 (Vb)).

Another group of manuscripts, which are generally referred to as lectionaries,[65] has to be dealt with separately: Cambridge, Pembroke College 302 (Ub),

---

[61] In the old Roman plan ('Gregorian sections') certain saints' days are chosen as fixed points for counting of the Sundays after Pentecost, namely the feasts of Peter and Paul (29 June), Laurence (10 August), Cyprian (14 September) or Michael (29 September). Accordingly, the Sundays are called 'dominica post natale S(s) Apostolorum (Petri et Pauli) Laurentii, Cypriani, Angeli'). For details, see Lenker, *Perikopenordnungen*, pp. 72–3, 164–6 and 506.

[62] Thus Tb (Oslo, Riksarkivet, Lat. fragm. 201 + Universitetsbiblioteket, Lat. frag. 9) contains only parts of the Passion according to Matthew without reference to the liturgical day.

[63] For details, see Frere, *The Roman Gospel-Lectionary*, pp. 214–20, Gneuss, 'Liturgical Books', p. 107 and Lenker, *Perikopenordnungen*, pp. 115–17 and 457–76.

[64] London, BL, Stowe 944 (Va), Warsaw, Biblioteka Narodowa, i. 3311 (Vc) and London, College of Arms, Arundel 22, fols. 84 and 85 (Vf).

[65] See the descriptions in the manuscript catalogues and hence the classification in Gneuss, 'Liturgical Books', p. 107.

The West Saxon Gospels *and the gospel-lectionary in Anglo-Saxon England*

Oxford, Bodleian Library, lat. liturg. f. 5 (Uc) and a part of Warsaw, Biblioteka Narodowa i. 3311 (Ue) give only a selection of gospel texts.[66] These texts are, however, not given in the liturgical order but in the order of the gospels (Matthew, Mark, Luke, John) and do not name the liturgical day at the beginning of the passage. These witnesses are therefore not lectionaries in the strict sense, as they could not be employed in the mass in this form. They might instead have been intended for private devotion.[67] For present purposes, only the fragments Va, Vc and Vf and the full lectionary Vb, the principal witness, are suitable for analysis.

Missals

Missals, which contain all the prayers, chants and readings for mass, finally replaced three separate volumes, namely sacramentaries, graduals and lectionaries.[68] As a late development, they emerge in the tenth and eleventh centuries. Hence the only extant Anglo-Saxon missal which covers the major parts of the church year is the 'New Minster Missal' (Le Havre, BM, 330; s. xi^2; Wa).

Other manuscripts reflect transitional stages. In the oldest part of the 'Leofric Missal' (Oxford, Bodleian Library, Bodley 579; Wb), marginal notes for the chants and the readings are added to the mass formulas and thus transform the original sacramentary into a provisional missal (s. xi^{med}).[69] Similarly, the sacramentary London, Society of Antiquaries 154* (Wf) is supplemented by an appendix which contains the first and second readings for a number of liturgical days.[70]

More than twenty fragments of Anglo-Saxon missals from the tenth and eleventh centuries, most of which have only recently been identified or discovered

---

[66] The fragments Malibu, John Paul Getty Museum 9 (Ud), in spite of the liturgical formulas *in illo tempore*, do not belong to this group, as their text can be shown to follow the pure Vulgate tradition. See Lenker, *Perikopenordnungen*, pp. 463–4 and for a manuscript similar in textual character, London, BL, Royal 1. A. XVIII (Ua). E. C. Teviotdale has pointed out to me that more Vulgate manuscripts of this kind have survived.

[67] Private devotion seems most likely in the case of Oxford, Bodleian Library, Lat. liturg. f. 5 (S. C. 29744), the 'St Margaret's Gospels', which belonged to Margaret of Scotland, wife of Malcolm III (1057–93).

[68] For details, see Gneuss, 'Liturgical Books', pp. 99–102, Pfaff, 'Massbooks', pp. 7–34 and Lenker, *Perikopenordnungen*, pp. 118 and 477–92.

[69] For the suggestion that Bishop Leofric himself was the executing scribe of the marginal notes, see E. M. Drage, 'Bishop Leofric and the Exeter Cathedral Chapter 1050–1072: a Reassessment of the Manuscript Evidence' (unpubl. DPhil dissertation, Univ. of Oxford, 1978), pp. 139–41.

[70] See F. Wormald, 'Fragments of a Tenth-Century Sacramentary from the Bindings of the Winton Domesday', *Winchester and the Early Middle Ages. An Edition and Discussion of the Winton Domesday*, ed. M. Biddle (Oxford, 1976), pp. 541–9 and Lenker, *Perikopenordnungen*, pp. 487–8.

as flyleaves or binding strips in later manuscripts, indicate that missals were quite common in the last century of the Anglo-Saxon period.

Witnesses for the gospel readings

For an evaluation of the Anglo-Saxon sources, comparison with the witnesses from the Continent, as provided by Klauser for medieval liturgical manuscripts (s. vi–xv), proves to be illuminating. Klauser finds the following distribution[71] for manuscripts from the sixth to the eleventh century:

Century	Notes non-Roman	Notes Roman	Lists Roman	Full lectionaries Roman	Gospel-lectionaries Roman
s. vi	2	–	(2)[72]	–	–
s. vii	11	2	(3)	–	1
s. viii	12	–	9+(2)	–	1
s. ix	–	3	140	6	14
s. x	–	2	96	10	30
s. xi	–	–	101	18	72

Table 1: Continental witnesses

This inventory, according to Klauser,[73] shows that the different forms appear in a chronological order in three consecutive phases. Marginal notes are the original form and are the predominant method for non-Roman and Roman traditions in manuscripts from the sixth century to the eighth. Capitularies in the form described above emerge in the eighth century and are the principal means for marking pericopes before lectionaries and later missals gain full acceptance.

This line of development can now be compared to the data in the following table listing all extant Anglo-Saxon manuscripts which record liturgical gospel readings:

---

[71] This inventory was compiled from Klauser, *Capitulare Evangeliorum*, pp. xxx, xxxv, xxxvi, xxxvii, lxxi, lxxxi, xc and cxiv. The Anglo-Saxon witnesses are included in this list. Altogether, Klauser lists and briefly describes about 1300 medieval manuscripts from the seventh century to the fifteenth (pp. xxx–cxx).

[72] The items in parentheses are witnesses which are not capitularies in the strict sense and thus appear under the rubric 'notes' in my diagram of Anglo-Saxon sources, such as the 'quasi-capitularies' in London, BL, Cotton Nero D. iv (Mx) and London, BL, Royal 1. B. VII (My).

[73] Klauser, *Capitulare Evangeliorum*, pp. xiii–xiv.

The West Saxon Gospels *and the gospel-lectionary in Anglo-Saxon England*

Century	Notes Mss.	Notes non-Roman	Notes Roman	Lists Roman	Full lectionaries Roman	Gospel-lectionaries Roman	Missals Roman
s. vi	1	[–]	[–]	–	–	–	–
s. vii	1	[–]	[2]	–	–	–	–
s. viii	8	[10]	[2]	1	1(f)	–	–
s. ix	–	–	–	6	–	–	–
s. x	1	–	[3]	2	1(f)	2(f)	4(f)
s. xi	3	–	–[74]	8	1(f)	1+2(f)	20(f)

Table 2: Anglo-Saxon witnesses

The findings for Anglo-Saxon England thus basically agree with the data for the Continent, as there is also an obvious development from marginal (non-Roman and Roman) notes to capitularies, lectionaries and finally missals.

For an evaluation of the actual liturgical practice of the Anglo-Saxons, it is necessary to bear in mind that it is documents from gospelbooks – marginal notes and capitularies – which are the most numerous among our surviving sources. The transmission of these mostly sumptuous codices, however, follows very specific paths which lead to their overrepresentation – about a quarter of all illuminated books from the Anglo-Saxon period are gospelbooks.[75] The fact that full lectionaries[76] survive from the eighth, tenth and eleventh centuries, indicates that full lectionaries were much more important for Anglo-Saxon liturgical practice than today's evidence suggests.

The indisputable evidence for two readings in the eucharistic service[77] raises the question from which book the first lesson was sung. No book designed especially for this purpose – such as an epistolary – is extant. The use of bibles in the

---

[74] The rubrics in A and F might be added to this column, as they share more similarities with notes than any other method. See below, p. 170.

[75] Cf. the ratio of gospelbooks in two volumes of the 'Survey of Manuscripts Illuminated in the British Isles' (E. Temple, *Anglo-Saxon Manuscripts 900–1066* (London, 1976) and M. Kauffmann, *Romanesque Manuscripts 1066–1190* (London, 1972)): 'Twenty-nine out of the 106 catalogue entries [in Temple], over a quarter, are gospelbooks or Gospel lectionaries, whereas in the post-Conquest volume in the same series the 106 entries include only seven gospelbooks' (T. A. Heslop, 'The Production of *de luxe* Manuscripts and the Patronage of King Cnut and Queen Emma', *ASE* 19 (1990), 151–95, at 152).

[76] Moreover, lectionaries recording non-Roman traditions are quite numerous from the sixth, seventh and eighth centuries; for an inventory, see Vogel, *Medieval Liturgy*, pp. 320–3 and Martimort, *Les Lectures liturgiques*, pp. 37–9. Strikingly, most of them are palimpsests.

[77] See above, pp. 149–50.

Ursula Lenker

form of a *lectio continua*[78] or with the help of an epistle-list[79] is unlikely because evidence for the production of full and part-bibles[80] is restricted to the beginning and the end of the Anglo-Saxon period. Moreover, apart from the 'Codex Amiatinus' none of the extant bibles contains liturgical notes.

The case for the existence of more full lectionaries is supported by the striking evidence of booklists, which indicate what kind of books were owned by Anglo-Saxons. In six of the thirteen booklists edited by Michael Lapidge, that is almost 50 per cent, a (service-)book[81] called *pistelboc* or *epistolarium* is mentioned.[82] These terms seem to denote an epistolary, that is a lectionary with the full texts for the first reading, a kind of book of which there is not a single trace from Anglo-Saxon England. Yet, the evidence from the *Monasterialia Indicia* helps us to identify what kind of book this *pistolboc* actually is. It is first of all again instructive to note that the *pistolboc* – of which no Anglo-Saxon copy seems to survive – is nevertheless worth a separate sign:[83] 'Ðære pistol boce tacn ys þæt mon wecge his hand and wyrce crystelmæl on his heafde foran mid his þuman forþon þe mon ræt god spel þær on and eal swa on þære cristes bec.' The phrase 'because one reads the gospel in there and likewise in the gospel-books'[84] indicates that the *pistolbec* mentioned in the booklists are most probably not 'epistolaries' but full lectionaries which give the text for the first and the second (gospel) reading.[85] This assumption is also supported by semiotic criteria: the sign for the *pistolboc* 'one moves one's hand and makes the sign of the cross on the front of one's head with one's thumb' resembles the liturgical prep-

---

[78] See below, p. 160.
[79] From Anglo-Saxon England, the only trace of such a document is the epistle-list in Oa (Würzburg, Universitätsbibliothek, M. p. th. f. 62). The Anglo-Saxon origin of this manuscript is, however, highly disputed, so that Gneuss, 'Preliminary List', does not include it. See Lowe, *CLA* IX, no. 1417 and Bischoff's summary: 'Es besteht also durchaus die Möglichkeit einer Abschrift durch einen Boten oder Begleiter Burghards in Rom neben der Herkunft aus England' (B. Bischoff and J. Hofmann, *Libri Sancti Kyliani. Die Würzburger Schreibschule im VIII. und IX. Jahrhundert* (Würzburg, 1952), p. 96 (no. 10)).
[80] For an inventory of Anglo-Saxon bible manuscripts, see Marsden, *The Text of the Old Testament*, pp. 40–1.
[81] The context in the will of Ælfwold, bishop of Crediton (997–1016), is particularly instructive: '. . . and in to Crydian tune þreo þeningbec: mæsseboc, and bletsungboc and pistelboc'. *Mæsseboc* here refers to the sacramentary (see Lapidge, 'Surviving Booklists', p. 56 and Gneuss, 'Liturgical Books', pp. 99–101).
[82] Lapidge, 'Surviving Booklists', pp. 33–89. That the booklists provide helpful evidence can be shown by the fact that the numbers and ratios tally with the extant codices in the case of sumptuous books such as psalters, gospelbooks and bibles: while psalters are listed in eleven, and one or more gospelbook(s) are recorded in nine of them, we find only one instance of a bible.
[83] *Monasteriales [sic] Indicia*, ed. Banham, p. 24 (no. 10).
[84] Banham's translation '(because one reads) the word of God . . .' (*ibid.*) is misleading. It would translate a genitive construction (*Godes spel*) but not the compound *godspel* found here.
[85] For a first suggestion in this direction, see Gneuss, 'Liturgical Books', p. 110.

aration of the deacon who, before reading the gospel of the day, crosses himself and makes the sign of a cross in the gospelbook at the verse where the lesson begins.[86]

The identification of the *pistolboc/epistolarium* as a full lectionary is further strengthened by Ælfric's use of the terms *pistolboc* and *lectionarium* in his *Pastoral Letters*.[87] Ælfric alters the term 'epistolarium' of his source into 'lectionarium, quod quidam uocant epistolarium',[88] thus making *epistolarium* at least partially synonymous with *lectionarium*.

This is, in my opinion, enough positive evidence to suggest that full lectionaries were much more common in Anglo-Saxon times and much more important for Anglo-Saxon liturgical practice than is testified by the evidence of extant manuscripts. These lectionaries were utilitarian, non-durable manuscripts made for everyday use, were worn down, and were discarded when the liturgical tradition changed.[89] Only scraps of them have made their way to the twentieth century.[90] The evidence of gospelbooks must not be overestimated, as they were primarily regarded as objects of worship and not books or documents for the liturgy. They were preserved in their magnificence, almost like relics, on the altar and later passed into the treasury of a monastery or church. They are, however, the principal extant witnesses for the gospel-lectionary in Anglo-Saxon England, since they are most numerous and – in their capitularies – record the most detailed information.

LITURGICAL TRADITIONS

Although the reading of the gospel of the day was one of the central elements of the eucharistic service from early Christian times, there are no traces of a fixed set of readings for the major part of the liturgical year before the sixth

---

[86] For the similar phrases in the sign for the deacon who reads the gospel of the day, see above, n. 43.

[87] *Hirtenbriefe*, ed. Fehr, 13, § 52 (MS O): 'He sceal habban eac þa wæpna to þam gastlicum weorce, ær-þan-þe he beo gehadod, þæt synd þa halgan bec: saltere and pistolboc, godspellboc and mæsseboc, sangboc and handboc, gerim and pastoralem, penitentialem and rædingboc.' For minor variations in other copies and the difficulties with the identification of the manuscripts, see *ibid.* pp. lxxxvi–lxxxvii and 126–7, § 157 and Gneuss, 'Liturgical Books', p. 121.

[88] *Hirtenbriefe*, ed. Fehr, p. 51, § 137: 'Presbyter debet habere etiam spiritalia arma, id sunt diuinos libros, scilicet missalem, lectionarium, quod quidam uocant epistolarium ...'

[89] Most of the extant lectionaries have therefore only survived as palimpsests (see above, n. 76) or as fragments used as binding-strips or flyleaves in later manuscripts. See Lenker, *Perikopenordnungen*, pp. 457–8.

[90] Hartzell similarly argues for the transmission of missals: 'That few missals survive must not convince us they were not written. The missal is, par excellence, the missile of the expanding church, the missionary church, the crusading church, the church in motion ...' (K. D. Hartzell, 'An Eleventh-Century English Missal Fragment in the British Library', *ASE* 18 (1989), 45–97, at 46).

century, that is to say, only shortly before our first Anglo-Saxon witnesses. Until the era of fixed readings, bibles or gospelbooks were probably used in a series of continuous or consecutive readings (*lectio continua*).[91] The special character of annually recurring feasts such as Easter and Christmas, however, suggested early on the selection of readings in harmony with the meaning of the feasts and their seasons. Thus the Roman rite from the late eighth century shows almost no variation in the readings for the masses in Lent, Easter, the 'Great Fifty Days' from Easter to Pentecost, Advent and Christmas. As the progressive organization of the liturgical year rendered a *lectio continua* also for the liturgically more indistinct periods less and less probable, the set of readings becomes increasingly fixed.[92] Yet, nowhere is there to be found a systematic attempt at organizing or reforming a system of readings. For a number of days in the liturgically rather indistinct periods after Epiphany and Pentecost, the choice of readings for the ferial days was only fixed in post-Anglo-Saxon times, so that Anglo-Saxon sources still show a considerable amount of variation. However, it is these varying elements which allow a classification of the witnesses and their rites.

As a basic method of investigation of the different traditions, I compiled two comparative inventories – one for the feasts of the *Proprium de tempore* or Temporale, the other for the *Proprium sanctorum* or Sanctorale.[93] Each liturgical day has been given a separate entry under which all the sources which mention the day are listed, together with their reading(s).[94] Compare the entry for the second Sunday (#74) and the fifth Thursday (#99) in Lent:

○ no reading	Oa, Pa, Pb
■ Matt. XV.21–8	Ni, Ph, Qa, Qb, Qc, Qe, Va, Vb, Vc, Wb, Ya, Yb, Yc, ZÆ (*Ch*II.8)
Matt. XVII.10–23	Pg
Mark I.40–4	Vb

---

[91] See Klauser, *Capitulare Evangeliorum*, pp. x-xiii, Martimort, *Les lectures liturgiques*, pp. 15–20, Vogel, *Medieval Liturgy*, pp. 293–304 and, for the early development, S. van Dijk, 'The Bible in Liturgical Use', *The Cambridge History of the Bible. 2: The West from the Fathers to the Reformation*, ed. G. Lampe (Cambridge, 1969), pp. 220–51, esp. 225, and G. Willis, *St Augustine's Lectionary*, Alcuin Club Collections 44 (London, 1962).

[92] For the development of the liturgical year, see Vogel, *Medieval Liturgy*, pp. 304–14, Harper, *The Forms and Orders of Western Liturgy*, pp. 45–57 and Lenker, *Perikopenordnungen*, pp. 60–80.

[93] The term 'Temporale' refers to the Sundays and ferial days as they run throughout the liturgical year without any regard for their date or interruption by saints' days. The Sanctorale entries contain information about the lessons for days of individual saints or for the *Commune Sanctorum*.

[94] Examples are taken from the inventories for the items for the days of the Temporale (#) and the Sanctorale (‡) in Lenker, *Perikopenordnungen*, pp. 298–351 and 352–83. The affiliation of a reading to different Roman traditions is recorded by the symbols ○ (type 2) and ■ (type 3). See below, pp. 161–3.

The West Saxon Gospels *and the gospel-lectionary in Anglo-Saxon England*

Mark II.13–17	Sa, Sb, Sc, Sd, Se
Mark IX.30–41	Sx
John III.1–[95]	Mv, Mx, My

For this Sunday – the Sunday after the Ember Days in Lent – the sources document a variety of different readings. While the lesson begins with John III.1 in the non-Roman sources (Mv, Mx, My), three Roman capitularies (Oa, Pa, Pb) name only the day but provide no reading. The passage Matt. XV.21–8 is chosen in the majority of Roman sources.

# 99	Fifth Thursday in Lent
○ Luke VII.36–47	Pa, Pb, Pc, Pg, Ph, Qa, Qb, Qc, Sa, Sb, Sc, Sd, Se, Sx, Wb, Ya
Luke XX.1–8	Vb
■ John VII.40–53	Na, Ph, Qe, Sa, Sb, Sd, Se, Yc, A

This entry shows that the fifth Thursday in Lent[96] is not recorded in any of the sources documenting non-Roman traditions (hence no manuscripts with the siglum M). It is only found in the Roman rite, in one witness with marginal notes (Na), in all the capitularies and most of the lectionaries. With regard to the readings chosen, it is possible to distinguish two main groups, one reading Luke VII.36–47, the other John VII.40–53. Five capitularies (Ph, Sa, Sb, Sd and Se) give both texts.[97] The 'Florence Lectionary' (Vb) differs from these two basic groups with the idiosyncratic lesson Luke XX.1–8.

The two main groups recorded in my second example are not only found there but appear in a number of entries. More importantly, the respective sources also show major differences in their plan of the church year, in particular in the number of the Sundays after Epiphany and Pentecost.[98] These discrepancies are not only found in lectionaries but also in sacramentaries and graduals. The variations in the number of Sundays after Pentecost are indeed so distinctive that they allow a distinction of three different phases in the

---

[95] The end of the lesson cannot be determined here as the closing words of the pericope are recorded neither in the *capitula*-tables (Mx, My) nor in the marginal notes to the 'Burchard Gospels' (Mv). See above, pp. 152–3 and n. 95.

[96] For the late introduction of the Thursdays in Lent, see below, pp. 167–8.

[97] The second reading is usually introduced by *Item aliud*. This method is chosen by the common ancestor of Sa, Sb, Sc, Sd and Se for liturgical days whose readings show variation in the tenth and eleventh centuries. See Lenker, *Perikopenordnungen*, pp. 445–6.

[98] The number of these Sundays changes according to the date of Easter, which can fall between 22 March and 25 April. Hence their number varies between one to six after Epiphany and twenty-three to twenty-eight after Pentecost. See the tables in Vogel, *Medieval Liturgy*, pp. 404–10 and Lenker, *Perikopenordnungen*, p. 505.

development of liturgical books. Following Antoine Chavasse,[99] these consecutive phases are called type 1, 2 and 3. For the sacramentaries, Chavasse's type 2 (20 Sundays after Pentecost) is represented by the Gregorian books, type 3 (25–6 Sundays after Pentecost) by the *Gelasiana mixta* or Eighth-Century Gelasian Sacramentaries.[100] Gospel-lectionaries have only survived in the form of type 2 and its augmented version, type 3. The prototype of type 3, which set the model for later developments up to the *Missale Romanum*, is the 'Comes of Murbach' (Besançon, BM, 184, fols. 58–74), an epistle- and gospel-list of the mid-eighth century.[101]

Chavasse's types supersede the distinctions drawn by Frere and Klauser[102] as he was able to show that the different types established by Klauser are merely versions of his type 2.[103] See the comparative diagram of Klauser's, Frere's and Chavasse's classifications:

Frere (1934)	Earlier	Martina	Standard	(Vitus-4 and 15)
Klauser (1935)	Π	Λ	Σ	(Δ)
Chavasse (1952)	type 2	type 2	type 2	type 3

Klauser's extremely fine classification,[104] which is based on alterations in the Sanctorale, allows a very precise local and temporal allocation of the manuscripts. It is so restrictive, however, that only four (six?) Anglo-Saxon manuscripts agree with one of his groups:

---

[99] A. Chavasse, 'Les plus anciens types du lectionnaire et de l'antiphonaire romains de la messe. Rapports et date', *RB* 62 (1952), 1–91. The classification is based on R. Hesbert, 'Les évangiles des dimanches après la pentecôte', *Le Codex 10673 de la Bibliothèque Vaticane. Fonds Latins. Graduel bénéventaine (XIe siècle)*, Paléographie musicale 14 (Tournai, 1931), 129–44.

[100] For the complicated history of different types of sacramentaries and their designations, see K. Gamber, *Sakramentartypen. Versuch einer Gruppierung der Handschriften und Fragmente bis zur Jahrtausendwende*, Texte und Untersuchungen 49–50 (Beuron, 1958), and Pfaff, 'Massbooks', pp. 8–9.

[101] The 'Comes' is ed. A. Wilmart, 'Le Comes de Murbach', *RB* 30 (1913), 25–69; for a description, see also Vogel, *Medieval Liturgy*, p. 347.

[102] Frere, *The Roman Gospel-Lectionary* and Klauser, *Capitulare Evangeliorum*. Investigation into the origin and organization of the liturgical readings has been pursued from the mid-nineteenth century; see the now dated studies by E. Ranke, *Das kirchliche Pericopensystem aus den ältesten Urkunden der Römischen Liturgie dargelegt und erläutert* (Berlin, 1847) and S. Beissel, *Entstehung der Perikopen des Römischen Meßbuches*, Ergänzungshefte zu den Stimmen aus Maria Laach 96 (Freiburg, 1907; repr. Rome, 1967).

[103] See Chavasse, 'Les plus anciens types', p. 6: 'Ces trois variétés [Klauser's Π, Λ, Σ] se distinguent l'une de l'autre par leur sanctoral plus ou moins riche, mais leur temporal demeure identique, à peu de choses près, et c'est pourquoi nous disons qu'elles constituent, en réalité, trois variétés d'un même type fondamental.'

[104] Frere's analyses are comparable to Klauser's in their concentration on changes in the Sanctorale, but his closer investigations anticipate Chavasse's work. For the 'Alternative Ferias', see below, p. 166.

The West Saxon Gospels *and the gospel-lectionary in Anglo-Saxon England*

Π (= 'Earlier'):   (Oa)[105]; Nd
Λ (= 'Martina'):   Pc
Σ (= 'Standard'):   Pa; Pb; Nc(?)[106]

More importantly, the broader lines of development are more easily discerned by changes in the lessons for days of the Temporale. For the analysis of Anglo-Saxon manuscripts, Chavasse's classification is preferable because of its broader approach, its inclusion of other types of liturgical manuscripts and therefore its comparative value.

The gospel-lectionary in Anglo-Saxon England

The investigation of the lessons amounted to the analysis of readings for altogether about 500 days, 270 days of the Temporale and 220 days of the Sanctorale and yielded the general classification and grouping of the Anglo-Saxon sources set out in Table 3 overleaf.

None of the surviving witnesses belongs to a specifically Anglo-Saxon tradition. Even the lessons for the Sanctorale bear no mark of their Anglo-Saxon background: specific pericopes for Anglo-Saxon saints are only recorded in three books from the very beginning and end of the period.[107]

Non-Roman traditions

The main borderline can be drawn in the eighth century, as by the ninth century Roman traditions had ousted various other traditions which are recorded in Northumbrian sources of the seventh and eighth centuries. In the early period, improvisation was still the rule, as is documented by a number of different non-Roman and Roman, but also mixed traditions. Among the non-Roman witnesses, the predominant tradition[108] roots itself in a basically Neapolitan system[109] which was adapted for the needs of the Northumbrian

---

[105] See above, n. 79.
[106] The eight notes in this gospelbook cannot be attributed with certainty. Their only distinctive feature is the provision of two lessons for the second Sunday after Epiphany (#21)) which also occurs in capitularies of the mixed types (e.g. Pg).
[107] See the pericopes for Benedict Biscop (‡1) in Bede's homiliary (Xa), for Cuthbert (‡24, ‡109) in the 'New Minster Missal' (Wa) and for Swithun (‡67) in the 'Red Book of Darley' (Wh).
[108] The only real exception are the seventeen marginal notes (s. viii) in Durham, Cathedral Library, A. II. 16 (Me) which follow an Old Gallican tradition. The notes are ptd C. H. Turner, *The Oldest Manuscripts of the Vulgate Gospels. Deciphered and Edited with an Introduction and Appendix* (Oxford, 1931), p. 217.
[109] Naples is suggested by the lessons for the feasts of St Januarius (‡118, ‡119) and a feast for the main church of Naples ('dedicatio basilicae Stephani'; ‡301). Lapidge also presumes a Naples origin for 'In dedicatione sanctae Mariae' (‡301) and 'Et in dedicatione fontis' (‡302); see B. Bischoff and M. Lapidge, *Biblical Commentaries from the Canterbury School of Theodore and Hadrian*, CSASE 10 (Cambridge, 1994), 157.

Date	Tradition	Witnesses	Origin
s. vii	early Roman	Ng, Nh	Continent
s. vii/viii	Northumbrian-Neapolitan	Ma, Mb, Mc, Mg, Mv, Mx, My	Northumbria
s. vii/viii	Old Gallican	Me	Northumbria
s. viii	Northumbrian-Neapolitan-Roman	Md, Mf, Xa	Northumbria
s. viii	Roman	Nk	Northumbria
	type 2: 'Earlier' (Π)	Nd, Oa	Northumbria
	mixed type	–	
	type 3	–	
s. ix	Roman		
	type 2: 'Standard' (Σ)	Pa, Pb	Continent
	type 2: 'Martina' (Λ)	Pc	Continent
	mixed type 2/3	Px, Qc	Continent
	type 3	Qe	Continent
s. x	Roman		
	type 2	Nc?	England
	mixed type 2/3	Nc?, Ph	England
		Qa	Continent
	type 3	Na, Ni	England
s. xi	Roman	Wz	England
	type 2	–	
	mixed type 2/3	Qb, Pg, Sx	England
	type 3	Sa, Sb, Sc, Sd, Se, Tc, Va, Vb, Vc, Vx, Wa, Wb, Wd, Wj, Wl, Wm, Wn, ZÆ, A, F	England

Table 3: Classification of the Anglo-Saxon witnesses

church.[110] An ancestor of this tradition may have come to England in a volume which Benedict Biscop brought back from one of his journeys to Rome, or, as Michael Lapidge has recently suggested, may have come with Abbot Hadrian to Canterbury and then to Northumbria.[111]

Lessons rooted in this Neapolitan tradition are recorded in the highly innovative and idiosyncratic forms of marginal notes to the *capitula*-tables in the 'Lindisfarne Gospels' (Ma), Royal 1. B. VII (Mb) and the 'Codex Amiatinus' (Mc), in the 'quasi-capitularies' of the 'Lindisfarne Gospels' (Mx) and Royal 1. B. VII (My), and also in the single marginal note to a bible, the 'Codex Amiatinus' (Mg). Supplemented by Roman lessons it serves as the basis for the lessons in Bede's homiliary (Xa) and the notes to Royal 1. B. VII (Md) and Durham, Cathedral Library, A. II. 17 (Mf). Its principal and most precise witness are the marginal notes to the 'Burchard Gospels' (Mv).

This system is only recorded in these Anglo-Saxon witnesses and is in the surviving form certainly not purely Neapolitan. Moreover, none of the extant sources is identical with another:[112] in each manuscript the basic tradition is augmented by new lessons from other, mainly Roman, sources.[113]

Roman traditions

Only representatives of the Roman traditions survive from the ninth century onwards. In the ninth and tenth centuries, we find sources following types 2 and 3, but also mixed types. Therefore the fixing of the readings can be shown to have been a gradual process, which did not exclude the coexistence of different types for a rather lengthy period.

Type 3 emerges in a source of the ninth century (Qe) and has gained acceptance by the eleventh century, when all the important witnesses represent type 3. This is especially true for genuinely liturgical witnesses, such as lectionaries and missals, and for vernacular sources, such as Ælfric's homilies and the rubrics to the *WSG*. But liturgical uniformity was unheard of in the early Middle Ages, so

---

[110] For its readings, see G. Morin, 'Les notes liturgiques de l'Évangéliaire de Burchard', *RB* 10 (1893), 113–26, Brown, 'The Latin Text', 34–43 and Chapman, *Notes on the Early History*, pp. 52–63. For further details, see Lenker, *Perikopenordnungen*, pp. 133–46 and 387–99.

[111] For details, see Chapman, *Notes on the Early History*, pp. 159–61 and Bischoff and Lapidge, *Biblical Commentaries*, pp. 166–7.

[112] The actual use of this system has sometimes been doubted because of the difficult and unsystematic recording of the lessons in the *capitula*-tables and 'quasi-capitularies' or, more generally, because of the attested Northumbrian loyalty to Rome, which would not allow the use of a Neapolitan system. These arguments are, however, somewhat anachronistic, as the sources only testify to liturgical improvisation, by their search for the best method of marking pericopes and by the incompleteness of the lessons. For details, see Lenker, *Perikopenordnungen*, pp. 141–6.

[113] Even its basis should probably rather be described with Chavasse as 'la vieille organisation romaine' (Chavasse, 'Les plus anciens types', p. 74, n. 1).

that even within a given family or type the documents do not always agree at all times and in all places.[114]

While the augmented system of 25 or 26 Sundays after Pentecost, the salient characteristic of type 3, had already gained acceptance in the tenth and eleventh centuries,[115] variations are still found in the lessons for the Sundays after Epiphany[116] and the ferial days after Epiphany and Pentecost. For the ferial days, type 3 was not adjusted from the readings of type 2, but a completely new system was introduced, named 'Alternative Ferias' by Frere.[117] Capitularies of the mixed types (Pg, Ph, Qa, Qb, Qc) use the new series for the Sundays, but retain the old type 2 or an otherwise altered series of the ferial days.

Since a number of witnesses do not give readings for the ferial days but only for Sundays, they can only very generally be classified as 'type 3' and have to be analysed with the help of distinctive readings on other liturgical days.[118] This method can be illustrated by the characteristics which establish the group comprising the rubrics to the *WSG*. Their liturgical tradition follows the new series for the Sundays after Pentecost and after Epiphany, and also employs the 'Alternative Series' for the ferial days:

175 Friday, seventh week after Pentecost
■ Mark V.1–20   Qe, Vb, A
○ Mark VIII.11–26   Pg, Ph, Qb, Sa, Sb, Sc, Sd, Se

205 Wednesday, fifteenth week after Pentecost
■ Mark I.40–45   Qe, Vb, A, F
○ Mark XI.11–18   Pg, Ph, Qb, Sa, Sx

---

[114] The only cases with more or less full agreement are two groups of capitularies (Qa, Qb, Qc and Sa, Sb, Sc, Sd, Se), each of which derives from a common ancestor.

[115] For this new series, six readings for the Sundays were added to the original twenty readings of type 2 (Klauser's Σ and Frere's 'Standard'), to adjust the tradition to the actual number of Sundays after Pentecost. See Chavasse, 'Les plus anciens types', pp. 11–16 and Lenker, *Perikopenordnungen*, pp. 163–6.

[116] The ten readings provided for the Sundays after Epiphany in type 2 are always too many, as the largest possible number of Sundays is six. This means that the need to modify the system was not as urgent as in the case of the too few Sundays after Pentecost – the spare readings were just not used. Thus the capitularies of the mixed types (Ph, Qa, Qb, Qc) give ten Sundays, the group Sa, Sb, Sc, Sd and Se six, and Qe, in accordance with the 'Comes of Murbach', five. For details, see Lenker, *Perikopenordnungen*, pp.167–8.

[117] Frere, *The Roman Gospel-Lectionary*, pp. 119–23. Since Chavasse only describes modifications in the Sundays after Pentecost (and partly Epiphany), the description of the other features is based on the analyses of Frere and the readings in the 'Comes of Murbach' (ed. Wilmart).

[118] For other days with distinctive readings, see Lenker, *Perikopenordnungen*, pp. 168–72.

The West Saxon Gospels *and the gospel-lectionary in Anglo-Saxon England*

The second example is especially instructive, as it shows not only the rubrics in A but also the single rubric in F to belong to a tradition which is only scarcely attested. The group consists of the capitulary 'Qe', the 'Florence Lectionary' (Vb) and the rubrics to the *WSG* (A and F). In some cases, the readings in the 'New Minster' (Wa) and the 'Leofric Missal' (Wb) agree with those of the group:

104 Tuesday in Holy Week
  Mark XIV.1–XV.46   Pg, Ph, Sa, [Sb], Sd, Se, Tc, Vb, Wb, Yc, A
■ **John XII.24–43** **Qe, Vb, Wb, A**
○ John XIII.1–32   Nd, Oa, Pa, Pb, Pc, Ph, Sa, Sb, Sc, Sd, Se
  John XIII.16–32   Pg, Qa, Qb, Qc, Sx

216 Ember Friday in autumn
○ Luke V.17–26   Pg, Qa, Qb, Qc, Sa, Sb, Sd, Se, Sx
■ **Luke VII.36–50** **Ph, Qe, Vb, Wa, Wb, Wn, Ya, A**

For an example from the Sanctorale, see the readings for the feast of St Sylvester:

○ Matt. XXIV.42–7   Oa, Pa, Pb, Pc, Pg, Ph, Qa, Qb, Qc, Sa, Sb, Sc, Sd, Se, Sx, Vx
■ **Matt. XXV.14–23** **Qe, Vb, Wa, Wb, A**

Yet, these agreements do not mean that the manuscripts are direct copies from a common exemplar or from one another. There are too many discrepancies on other days,[119] for example, on the Thursdays in Lent. The stational masses for these Thursdays were established comparatively late under Pope Gregory II (715–31). Thus two distinctive series occur which, according to Frere, afford 'a very valuable criterion for distinguishing and classifying different groups of MSS'.[120] The older series introduced in Frere's subgroup 'Standard' (Klauser's Σ) of type 2 chooses lessons from the synoptic gospels according to Matthew and Luke; in other manuscripts, mainly those representing type 3, only passages from John are selected.[121] However, there are also mixed systems, as the witnesses belonging to the established subgroup show:

---

[119] Cf. the readings for the second Sunday in Lent, above p. 160–1.
[120] Frere, *The Roman Gospel-Lectionary*, p. 65.
[121] The selected passages in the older series are Matt. XV.21–8, Luke XVI.19–31, Luke IV.38–44, Luke VII.11–16 and Luke VII.36–50, in the new series John VIII.31–47, V.30–47, VI.27–35, V.17–29 and VII.40–53; cf. the full entry of the fifth Thursday, above p. 161. Maundy Thursday follows a different tradition.

Ursula Lenker

Thursday in Lent	Qe	Vb	Wb	A
First (#71)	new	old	new	both
Second (#78)	both	old	old	new
Third (#85)	old	new	old	old
Fourth (#92)	both	new	old	new
Fifth (#99)	new	Luke XX.1–8	old	new

Apart from the incongruities of their readings, the manuscripts which form the nucleus of the subgroup (Qe, Vb, A) show considerable variance in their dates and places of origin:

Qe: s. ix^{ex} or x^{in} – Continent, Liège (provenance from s. x^{med}: Canterbury)
Vb: s. xi^1 – Canterbury (provenance from s. xi: Continent)
A: s. xi^{med} – Exeter

The origin of the subgroup is thus definitely not specifically Anglo-Saxon, but can be traced in continental sources of the prototypical type 3. This system was brought to England in different versions and was also modified in England itself. It is the tradition which later served as the basis for the readings in the Sarum and York Missals and also in the *Missale Romanum*.

In summary, the surviving Anglo-Saxon sources of type 3 may be classified tentatively into the following subgroups, which, however, reflect different degrees of conformity and distinctiveness:

mixed type 2 / type 3:	Pg, Ph[122] – Qa, Qb, Qc[123]
unspecific type 3:[124]	Na, Ni, Va, Vc, Wj, Wl, Wm, Wn, ZÆ
Anglo-Saxon group:	Sa, Sb, Sc, Sd, Se[125] – (Sx)
continental–late-Anglo-Saxon group:	Qe, Vb, (Wa), (Wb), A, F

Problems

Some problems emerge when we consider the difficult evidence of gospelbooks. For the ninth century, an era of constant debate in Anglo-Saxon studies, our information is restricted to the – albeit precise – information of six capitularies in gospelbooks. All of these sources were, however, written on the Continent and only came to England in the tenth or eleventh century, so that there is not a single witness of genuine Anglo-Saxon origin from the ninth

---

[122] Pg shares some features with Frere's type 'Vitus-4' (Klauser's Δ), Ph with Frere's type 'Vitus-15'. An overall similarity is therefore notable; for details, see Lenker, *Perikopenordnungen*, pp. 420–8. [123] For details, see *ibid.* pp. 430–7.
[124] These manuscripts only record the augmented series for the Sundays after Pentecost (type 3) or readings for other indistinct days. [125] See below, p. 169.

century. This might serve as another piece of evidence that even the basic liturgical rites were on the decline in this century, especially when compared with the situation on the Continent. More continental capitularies are extant from the ninth century (140) than from the tenth (96) or eleventh (101) centuries.[126] For Anglo-Saxon England, one would expect at least the evidence of fragments of lectionaries or marginal notes in older gospelbooks.[127]

Another example which points towards the specific problems of gospelbooks is the comparison of the liturgical traditions in three manuscripts written by a single scribe, Eadwig (Eadui) Basan:[128]

Pg: mixed type 2/3 (predominantly type 2)
Sx: mixed type 2/3 (predominantly type 3)
Vb: type 3 (subgroup Qe, A, F, [Wa], [Wb])

While two sources record different sorts of mixed types, the lectionary Vb follows a very pure form of type 3. It might be argued that Eadui did not stay at one monastery or that the different monasteries he worked at adhered to different traditions. A much more likely conclusion, however, is that gospelbooks are a dubious source for the investigation of Anglo-Saxon liturgical practice.

The great reverence for gospelbooks also accounts for the overwhelming evidence of four (five) capitularies (that is, almost a third of all extant capitularies) written at the beginning of the eleventh century at Christ Church, Canterbury, or Peterborough – Sa, Sb, Sc, Sd, (Se).[129] This great number of copies is certainly not due to their liturgical material and its intentional distribution, since the tradition recorded is not specifically Anglo-Saxon and was presumably already outdated at the beginning of the eleventh century. The additional material was copied painstakingly because of the sumptuousness of the books. This sumptuousness has made them precious and thus durable.[130]

Hence the evidence of the different sources has to be considered in a certain hierarchy: it is only utilitarian documents such as lectionaries and missals which very possibly record the traditions actually in use, as these are functional books

---

[126] See above, p. 156.
[127] From the tenth century, such notes are found, for example, in Oxford, Bodleian Library, Auct. D. 2. 14 (Ni; s. vi–vii) and Cambridge, University Library, Kk. 1. 24 (Nc; s. viii).
[128] On this scribe, see D. Dumville, *English Caroline Script and Monastic History: Studies in Benedictinism, A.D. 950–1030*, Studies in Anglo-Saxon History 6 (Woodbridge, 1993), 111–40 (in particular 120–2) and R. Pfaff, 'Eadui Basan: Scriptorum Princeps?', *England in the Eleventh Century. Proceedings of the 1990 Harlaxton Symposium*, ed. C. Hicks, Harlaxton Medieval Stud. 2 (Stamford, 1992), 267–83.
[129] For details, see Lenker, *Perikopenordnungen*, pp. 193–5 and 442–56. Se (Cambridge, St John's College 73) is a later copy (after 1081?) of Sd.
[130] Heslop, 'The Production of *de luxe* Manuscripts'.

made exclusively for the liturgy. Capitularies, by contrast, require a more careful investigation, as they may reflect an old tradition which was only copied because it was recorded in a magnificent exemplar.

The rubrics to the West Saxon Gospels

In A, some 170 passages are marked as lessons for the Temporale, twenty-five for the Saints' Days and twelve for the *Commune Sanctorum*.[131] The liturgical system added to the text of the *WSG* in A and also the fragmentary F in its main form – type 3 – agrees with other contemporary manuscripts, not only with capitularies, but also with functional books such as lectionaries (Vb), missals (Wa, Wb) and – seen in a wider perspective – the homilies of Ælfric. As the tradition thus agrees with a system most likely in use in the eleventh century, this could provide evidence for A's use as a gospel-lectionary.

The rubrics show, however, a puzzling idiosyncrasy which not only defeats the theory of the manuscript's employment in the liturgy of the mass but also helps to establish the function of the rubrics. Certain rubrics do not record the commonly chosen Roman text, but mark parallel passage(s) from another of the synoptic gospels,[132] a method which is technically called *concordia*. On Sexagesima Sunday Luke VIII.4–15 ('The Parable of the Sower' and 'The Purpose of Parables') is read in all the Roman sources of type 2 and 3. The rubric in A, by contrast, indicates the beginning of the gospel of the day before Mark IV.3. Mark IV.1–12, however, also relates 'The Parable of the Sower' and is thus a parallel text in the synopsis:

#56 Sexagesima
    Mark IV.3–(20)[133]   **A**
O■ Luke VIII.4–15   Na, Nd, Oa, Pa, Pb, Pc, Pg, Ph, Qa, Qb, Qc, Qe, Sa, Sb, Sc, Sd, Se, Sx, Vb, Vc, Wb, Ya, Yb, Yc, ZÆ (*CH*II.6)

This item is not the only instance of *concordia* readings. Instead of the regular pericope the parallel passages are recorded for the Wednesday in the fourth week after Epiphany (Matt. VIII.19–22) instead of Luke IX.57–62), Sexagesima

---

[131] For a detailed analysis of the readings and an explanation of the unequal numbers of Temporale and Sanctorale items, see Lenker, *Perikopenordnungen*, pp. 263–70.
[132] The so-called 'Synoptic Gospels' (Matthew, Mark and Luke) are very similar in contents and structure. Matthew and Luke knew and used the Gospel according to Mark and only added additional material from other sources into its general framework. John is different in both structure and contents, so that there are only a few parallel passages.
[133] As A does not mark the end of the readings, it can here only be surmised from the parallel passages.

The West Saxon Gospels *and the gospel-lectionary in Anglo-Saxon England*

(Mark IV.3–(20) instead of Luke VIII.4–15), Quinquagesima (Mark X.46–(52) instead of Luke XVIII.31–43),[134] Palm Sunday (Luke XIX.29–(38) instead of Matt. XXI.1–9) and the twenty-third Sunday after Pentecost (Mark XII.13–(17) instead of Matt. XXII.15–21).

Both the regular pericope and a parallel text are recorded for the Ember Saturday in Lent (Matt. XVII.1–9; Mark IX.2–(8)), the third Sunday in Lent (Luke XI.14–28; Matt. XII.22–(30)), the Wednesday in the third week of Lent (Matt. XV.1–20; Mark VII.1–(23)), the Rogation Days (Luke XI.5–13; Matt. VII.7–(11)), the eighth Sunday after Pentecost (Mark VIII.1–9; Matt. XV.32–(9)), the Ember Wednesday in autumn (Mark IX.17–29; Matt. XVII.14–(21)) and the feast of St Peter (Matt. XVI.13–19; Mark VIII.27–(33)). Two parallel passages are given, in addition to the regular pericope, for the fourth Sunday before Christmas (Matt. XXI.1–9; Mark XI.1–10; Luke XIX.29–38).

Most of the alternative passages are taken from the gospel according to Mark, a very good source for *concordia* readings, as it is a synoptic gospel and one only rarely used in the Roman tradition.[135] The majority of these cases of *concordia* occur for important liturgical days, for example, Sundays and days of fasting, such as the Ember Days or the Rogation Days, liturgical days for which homilies are also generally provided.

These parallel passages are evidently not mistakes by a careless scribe who mixed up the beginning words of the gospels. The correct Latin incipits recorded respectively show that the parallel passages are a deliberate choice. Compare the incipits for the Ember Wednesday in autumn:

Ðys sceal on wodnesdæg to þam fæstene ær hærfestes emnyhte. Et cum uenisset ad turbam accessit ad eum homo genibus prouolutus (Matt. XVII.14).
Ðis sceal to þam ymbrene innan hærefeste on wodnesdæg. Respondens unus de turba dixit. magister attuli filium meum ad te (Mark IX.17).

Among our Anglo-Saxon sources, this provision of parallel passages is unique. There are, however, a number of continental witnesses which share this characteristic,[136] in particular the capitulary in Paris, BN, lat. 325 (Northern Italy/ Piedmont, s. xi).[137] The striking similarities of this gospel-list with the rubrics in A (concern-

---

[134] There is no full agreement in this case: the parallel passages are Mark X.46–52 and Luke XVIII.35–43 ('Jesus heals a blind beggar'). A lacks Luke XVIII.31–4 ('Jesus speaks a third time about his death').

[135] In Mark there are only twenty-three rubrics compared to seventy-three in Matthew, forty-six in Luke and fifty-seven in John. Seven of those in Mark are parallel passages, so that only sixteen of the rubrics in A are used in the pure Roman tradition.

[136] For a group of capitularies which were copied in the German–French area (s. x/xi), see Frere, *The Roman Gospel-Lectionary*, pp. 137–9.

[137] For a description of the capitulary, see Frere, *The Roman Gospel-Lectionary*, pp. 200–1, Klauser, *Capitulare Evangeliorum*, p. lx (no. 292) and Lenker, *Perikopenordnungen*, pp. 277–9.

171

Ursula Lenker

ing the plan of the church year, etc.) furthermore suggest a capitulary from the Continent as the exemplar for the liturgical system copied into the rubrics of A.

The function of the rubrics to the West Saxon Gospels

To sum up, the rubrics to manuscripts A and F of the *WSG* are a later addition in one branch of manuscript transmission and are thus not connected with or triggered by the original translation project. Linguistic evidence suggests that the rubrics originated in the south-western area of England at the end of the Old English period. They were copied from a no longer extant exemplar, which probably provided the liturgical information in marginal notes. The liturgical tradition recorded in the rubrics is a very prototypical form of the Roman type 3 and agrees with the type commonly used in the Anglo-Saxon liturgy in the eleventh century.

The manuscripts were, however, most probably not used in the Anglo-Saxon liturgy as gospel-lectionaries. Among our Anglo-Saxon material, there is no (other) indication of an employment of the vernacular for the reading of the gospel of the day. Apart from the lack of signs in the Passion pericopes,[138] and the lack of notes which would indicate the end of the reading in A, the parallel passages in particular contradict this suggestion. Why then was the vernacular translation combined with the contemporaneous liturgical system?

Formally, the similarities of the rubrics to the headings of other manuscripts with homiletic material are striking, in particular the reference to the liturgical day in Old English (or Latin), the provision of the Latin incipit of the text and the formulaic phrases in the Old English part of the rubric. Still more important is the fact that only exegetical homilies show a characteristic which allows for an assumption concerning the function of the parallel passages. Thus in his homily for the third Sunday in Lent, Ælfric exploits both the commonly read pericope Luke XI.14–28 'Jesus and Beelzebul' and its parallel passage in Matt. XII.22–9.[139] In the rubrics of A, both these texts are marked:

81 Third Sunday in Lent
    Matt. XII.22–9   [Ni], **ZÆ (Pope, iv), A**
○■   Luke XI.14–28   Nd, Oa, Pa, Pb, Pg, Ph, Qa, Qb, Qc, Qe,
                     Sa, Sb, Sc, Sd, Se, Sx, Va, Vb, Vc, Wb, Ya, Yb, Yc,
                     ZÆ (Pope, iv), A

---

[138] In lectionaries and a number of gospelbooks, liturgical signs are recorded in the Passion pericopes which are read on Palm Sunday (Matt.), Tuesday (Mark), Wednesday (Luke) and Friday (John) of Holy Week. These signs – *c* ('celeriter') for the commentator, *s* ('sursum') for the Jews and *t* (later †; 'tenere, trahere') for Jesus – tell the deacon in which voice and rhythm the part has to be proclaimed. See Young, *The Drama of the Medieval Church*, pp. 101 and 550 and in particular, B. Stäblein, 'Passion', *Die Musik in Geschichte und Gegenwart* 10 (1962), 886–97.

[139] *Homilies of Ælfric*, ed. Pope I, 259–85.

The West Saxon Gospels *and the gospel-lectionary in Anglo-Saxon England*

On the third Sunday before Christmas (#259), the passage 'The Coming of the Son of Man' is read in the version according to Luke (XXI.25–33). Accordingly, Ælfric's homily starts with the translation of this pericope. In the exegesis, however, its content is then clarified (cf. 'swutelicor') with the help of the parallel verse Matt. XXIV.29:[140] 'Matheus se godspellere awrat swutelicor þas tacna þus cweþende: þærrihte æfter þære miclan gedrefednysse bið seo sunne aþystrod. and se mona ne sylð nan leoht and steorran feallað of heofonum. and heofenan miht beoð astyrede. and ðonne bið ætywed cristes rodetacn on heofenum. and ealle eorðlice mæigða.' In his homily for Sexagesima Sunday, Ælfric illustrates his exegesis of Luke's version of the 'Parable of the Sower' (see above, p. 170) by a deliberate reference to 'se oðer godspellere'. Luke does not tell how manifold the fruit was, information which Ælfric needs in order to continue with his exegesis on the basis of a homily of St Augustine. The exact numbers are, however, given in the parallel passages Matt. XIII.8 and Mark IV.8:[141] 'Se oðer godspellere awrat þæt sum dæl þæs sædes þe on ðan godan lande asprang. ageaf ðritigfealdne wæstm. sum sixtigfealdne. sum hundfealdne.' These similarities suggest that the function of the combination of the vernacular gospels with the liturgical system is related to the homiletic tradition. A homilist could thus have used the text of the *WSG* for the translation of the gospel of the day into Old English, a feature with which almost all exegetical homilies in the vernacular begin.[142] For the exegesis of the text, a preacher trying to elucidate the deeper meaning of the gospel text might have found help in the vernacular gospel text and other versions of the relevant passage.

Both the linguistic evidence and the continental origin of the exemplar suggest that the rubrics originated in Exeter, the scriptorium of A, in the middle of the eleventh century. Accordingly, the 'Leofric Missal' definitely belongs to the same subgroup as the rubrics in A and F. Furthermore, the agreements with the lessons in the capitulary Qe from Liège become even more intriguing when compared to Drage's analysis of book production at Exeter at Leofric's times:[143]

The study of the manuscripts copied at Exeter or owned by Leofric or his Chapter during his episcopate has enabled us to observe that Leofric brought a mixture of English and continental influences to bear upon his and the Chapter's activities. I believe that the continental influences were especially important. William of Malmesbury

---

[140] *Ælfric's Catholic Homilies*, ed. Clemoes, p. 525.
[141] *Ælfric's Catholic Homilies. The Second Series. Text*, ed. M. Godden, EETS ss 5 (London, 1979), 56.
[142] 'For the contemporary congregations these translations must have had the advantage of novelty to add to their normal interest, for the corresponding lessons were read in Latin. Their presence alters the proportions and the emphasis of the homilies, not only making it desirable to shorten the exegesis but giving some encouragement to simplified interpretations of which the chief function is to emphasize the direct meaning of the gospel itself' (*Homilies of Ælfric*, ed. Pope I, 150).   [143] Drage, 'Bishop Leofric', p. 282.

asserted that Leofric was 'apud Lotharingos altus et doctus'. His adoption of the Rule of Chrodegang . . ., his introduction of a Collectar modelled on that of Stephen of Liège, his importing of continental manuscripts (one of which included miniatures added in the Liège area around 1040) combine to suggest strongly that it was in the Liège area, if not in Liège itself, where there was a community living according to the Rule of Chrodegang, that Leofric was educated.

The evidence for Leofric's connections to Liège and the homiletic function of the parallel passages agrees, since Exeter Cathedral was a secular institution and the canons put much emphasis on preaching. Consider, for example, the instructions in the *Rule of Chrodegang*:[144] 'For þi þonne we gesettað þæt tuwa on monþe, þæt is ymbe feowertine niht, man æfre þam folce bodige mid larspelle, hu hi þurh Godes fultum magon to þam ecean life becuman. And þeah hit man ælce Sunnandæge singallice and freolsdæge dyde, þæt wære betere. And do ma þa larbodunge be þam þe þæt folc understandan mage.' Hence Exeter at the time of Leofric might well have been the place where the vernacular translation of the gospels was combined with the gospel-lectionary then in use. The rubrics to the *WSG* do not give evidence for the reading of the gospel in the vernacular at the liturgically proper time for the gospel during the performance of the mass. However, the text of the *West Saxon Gospels* may indeed have been read to the congregation during the mass – instead of or as part of a homily.

---

[144] *The Old English Version of the Enlarged Rule of Chrodegang together with the Latin Original. An Old English Version of the Capitula of Theodulf together with the Latin Original. An Interlinear Old English Rendering of the Epitome of Benedict of Aniane*, ed. A. S. Napier, EETS os 150 (London, 1916), 50 (ch. xlii).

APPENDIX

MANUSCRIPTS AND SIGLA[145]

West Saxon Gospels (WSG)

■ A	Cambridge, University Library, Ii. 2. 11	xi^{med}, Exeter
B	Oxford, Bodleian Library, Bodley 441	xi^1
C	London, BL, Cotton Otho C. i, vol. i	xi^1, Malmesbury?
Cp	Cambridge, Corpus Christi College 140	xi^1, Bath
■ F	New Haven, Beinecke Library, Beinecke 578	xi^1, South-East
H	Oxford, Bodleian Library, Hatton 38	xii/xiii, Canterbury?
L	Oxford, Bodleian Library, Eng. Bib. c. 2	xi^1
R	London, BL, Royal 1. A. XIV	xii^2, Canterbury

Non-Roman Traditions

M Notes (non-Roman traditions)
Notes in *Capitula*-tables

Ma	London, BL, Cotton Nero D. iv	vii/viii, Lindisfarne
Mb	London, BL, Royal 1. B. VII	viii, Northumbria
Mc	Florence, Biblioteca Medicea Laurenziana, Amiatino 1	viii^{in}, Northumbria

Marginal notes to gospel text

Md	London, BL, Royal, 1. B. VII	[viii, Northumbria]
Me	Durham, Cathedral Library, A. II. 16	viii, Northumbria
Mf	Durham, Cathedral Library, A. II. 17	viii^{in}, Northumbria
Mg	Florence, Biblioteca Medicea Laurenziana, Amiatino 1	viii, Northumbria
Mv	Würzburg, Universitätsbibliothek, M. p. th. f. 68	vi, Italy [vii/viii, Northumbria]

'Quasi-capitularies'

Mx	London, BL, Cotton Nero D. iv	vii/viii, Northumbria
My	London, BL, Royal 1. B. VII	viii, Northumbria

---

[145] The dates and places of origin given in square brackets refer to later added (marginal) notes. ○ refers to type 2, ■ to type 3 of the Roman traditions. See above, pp. 160–3.

Ursula Lenker

ROMAN TRADITIONS

N   Marginal notes (Roman traditions)

■	Na	London, BL, Add. 40000	xⁱⁿ, Continent [x/xi]
O■	Nc	Cambridge, University Library, Kk. 1. 24	viii, Northumbria [x, Ely?]
O	Nd	Würzburg, Universitätsbibliothek, M. p. th. f. 68	vi, Italy [viii, Northumbria]
	Ng	Oxford, Bodleian Library, Auct. D. 2. 14	vi/vii, Italy [*ibid.*]
	Nh	Oxford, Bodleian Library, Auct. D. 2. 14	vi/vii, Italy [*ibid.*]
■	Ni	Oxford, Bodleian Library, Auct. D. 2. 14	[ix/x, England]
	Nk	Stonyhurst College, Lancashire, *s.n.* (= London, BL, Loan 74)	vii/viii, Northumbria

O   Gospel-list

O	Oa	Würzburg, Universitätsbibliothek, M. p. th. f. 62	viii, England?, Continent?

P-S Gospel-lists in gospelbooks

P Gospel-lists (Sundays after Pentecost: Gregorian sections)

O	Pa	Coburg, Landesbibliothek, 1	ix^{med}, Metz?
O	Pb	London, BL, Add. 9381	ix/x, Brittany?
O	Pc	Cambridge, Fitzwilliam Museum 45–1980	ix/x, Brittany?
O■	Pg	London, BL, Add. 34890	xi^1, Canterbury?
O■	Ph	Paris, BNF, lat. 272	x, Winchester
O■	Px	Oxford, Bodleian Library, Bodley 381, fols. i and ii	ix/x, Continent

Q Gospel-lists (Separation of Temporale and Sanctorale items)

O■	Qa	Oxford, Bodleian Library, Auct. D. 2. 16	x^1, Landévennec
O■	Qb	Oxford, Bodleian Library, Bodley 155	xi^{in}, Barking?
O■	Qc	New York, Public Library, 115	ix^2, Landévennec
■	Qe	London, BL, Cotton Tiberius A. ii	ix/x, Lobbes (Liège)

S Gospel-lists (Sundays after Pentecost: continuous numbering 1st to 25th/26th Sunday)

■	Sa	Cambridge, Trinity College B. 10. 4	xi^1, Canterbury?
■	Sb	London, BL, Royal 1. D. IX	xi^1, Canterbury?
■	Sc	London, BL, Loan 11	xi^1, Canterbury?

176

The West Saxon Gospels *and the gospel-lectionary in Anglo-Saxon England*

- Sd   London, BL, Harley 76   xi¹, Canterbury?
- Se   Cambridge, St. John's College 73   xi^ex, Bury St Edmunds
- ○■ Sx   Hanover, Kestner-Museum WM XXIa. 36   xi¹, Canterbury

T–V Lectionaries
T Full lectionaries with readings for the first and second reading

Ta   Durham, Cathedral Library, A. IV. 19, fol. 89   viii, Northumbria
Tb   Oslo, Riksarkivet, Lat. fragm. 201 +   x
      Oslo, Universitetsbiblioteket, Lat. fragm. 9   x
- Tc   Oslo, Riksarkivet, Lat. fragm. 211   x/xi

U Gospel-lectionaries without reference to the liturgical days

Ua   London, BL, Royal 1. A. XVIII   ix/x, Brittany
Ub   Cambridge, Pembroke College 302   xi^med, Canterbury
Uc   Oxford, Bodleian Library, Lat. liturg. f. 5   xi^med, Scotland?
Ud   Malibu, John Paul Getty Museum 9   xi^in, Canterbury
Ue   Warsaw, Biblioteka Narodowa, i. 3311   x/xi

V Gospel-lectionaries

- Va   London, BL, Stowe 944, fols. 41–9   xi¹, Winchester
- Vb   Florence, Biblioteca Medicea Laurenziana, Plut. xvii. 20   xi¹, Canterbury?
- Vc   Warsaw, Biblioteka Narodowa, i. 3311   x²
   Vf   London, College of Arms, Arundel 22, fols. 84 and 85   x², Winchester?
- Vx   Cambridge, Fitzwilliam Museum 88–1972, fols. 2–43   xi/xii, Canterbury?

W Missals

- Wa   Le Havre, BM, 330   xi², Winchester
- Wb   Oxford, Bodleian Library, Bodley 579 (Leofric Missal 'A')   [xi^med, Exeter]
   Wc   Oxford, Bodleian Library, Bodley 579 (Leofric Missal 'C')   x/xi
- Wd   London, BL, Royal 5. A. XII, fols. iii-vi   xi^med, Worcester
   Wf   London, Society of Antiquaries 154*   x^ex, Winchester?
   Wh   Cambridge, Corpus Christi College 422   xi, Sherborne
   Wi   Bergen, Universitetsbibioteket, 1549.5   xi/xii
- Wj   Oslo, Riksarkivet, Lat. fragm. 204, fols. 1–4 and 9–10   xi^med
- Wl   Oslo, Riksarkivet, Lat. fragm. 207, 208, 210   x/xi, Winchester

- Wm Oslo, Riksarkivet, Lat. fragm. 228   xi^2
- Wn London, BL, Harley 271, fols. 1* and 45*   xi^{ex}
- Wz Cambridge, Corpus Christi College 391   xi^2, Worcester

X   Homilies (non-Roman tradition)

Xa   Beda (ed. Hurst 1955)

Y   Homilies (Roman traditions)

- Ya   Paul the Deacon (ed. PL 95, 1159–66)
- Yb   Smaragdus (ed. PL 102, 13–552)
- Yc   Haymo (ed. PL 118, 11–804)

Z   Vernacular Homilies

- ZÆ   Ælfric (*CH*1: ed. Clemoes 1997; *CH*2: ed. Godden 1979, ed. Assmann 1889, Irvine 1993 or Pope 1967–8)

ZBl   Blickling Homilies (ed. Morris 1874–80)
ZDiv   various Old English homilies (see Cameron 1973)
ZVer   Vercelli Homilies (ed. Scragg 1992)

The scribe of the Paris Psalter

RICHARD EMMS

The Paris Psalter (Bibliothèque Nationale de France, lat. 8824) has attracted much interest because of its long, thin format, its illustrations in the Utrecht Psalter tradition and its Old English prose translation of the first fifty psalms, which has been convincingly attributed to King Alfred himself.[1] It is a bilingual psalter, with Latin (Roman version) on the left and Old English on the right. The first fifty psalms are in the prose translation connected with King Alfred, the remainder in a metrical version made by an author whose work has not been identified elsewhere. The leaves are approximately 526 × 186 mm, with a writing space of about 420 × 95 mm. It has been estimated that there were originally 200 leaves in twenty-five quires, but fourteen leaves, including those carrying all the major decoration, have been removed. There remain thirteen outline drawings integrated into the text on the first six folios. Some drawings may have functioned as 'fillers' where the Latin text was shorter than the Old English. Further on in the manuscript, in order to solve this problem, the scribe either left gaps or made the columns of Latin thinner than the corresponding Old English ones. The Old English introductions were set out across both columns, suggesting that the book was made for someone who read English more easily than Latin. The manuscript was written around the middle of the eleventh century, and it is clearly the work of a single skilled scribe who used a neat Anglo-Caroline minuscule for the Latin texts, and matching English vernacular minuscule with many Caroline letter forms for the Old English. Unfortunately, his hand has not been identified in any other books or charters; however, he did record in a colophon (186r; see pl.V) that he was called *Wulfwinus cognomento Cada*.

The Old English texts – the metrical and prose psalms – may have had a connection with a centre in Wessex, perhaps Malmesbury; there is Wessex influence

---

[1] *The Paris Psalter*, ed. B. Colgrave, EEMF 8 (Copenhagen, 1958). The most recent discussion is M. J. Toswell, 'Studies in the Paris Psalter, Metrical Version' (unpubl. DPhil dissertation, Univ. of Oxford, 1991). See also her 'The Format of the Bibliothèque Nationale MS lat. 8824: the Paris Psalter', *N&Q* 241 (1996), 130–3. For the authorship of the OE prose psalms, see J. M. Bately, 'Lexical Evidence for the Authorship of the Prose Psalms in the Paris Psalter', *ASE* 10 (1982), 69–95. See also P. Pulsiano, 'Psalters', *The Liturgical Books of Anglo-Saxon England*, ed. R. W. Pfaff, *OEN* Subsidia 23 (Kalamazoo, MI, 1995), 61–85.

in the litany of saints,[2] and it is possible that the relevant exemplar came from that area; however, the production of the Paris Psalter has often been connected with Canterbury on art-historical grounds. Most of the surviving illustrations are related to the Utrecht Psalter tradition and there can be no doubt that the Utrecht Psalter was at Canterbury in the eleventh and twelfth centuries during which time three copies of its illustrations were made there.[3] Of course the influence of the Utrecht Psalter spread to other centres, but the logical inference is that the artwork of the Paris Psalter was done at Canterbury, and hence that the book as a whole was produced there.[4]

Also suggestive of a Canterbury connection is the fact that the two of the books whose proportions come nearest to those of the Paris Psalter were written at St Augustine's Abbey in the late tenth century and are very likely to have remained there in the library of the abbey during the eleventh century. They are the *Regula S. Benedicti* and related documents, now London, British Library, Harley 5431 (230 × 85 mm), and the *Cosmographia* of Aethicus Ister, now Leiden, Bibliotheek der Rijksuniversiteit, Scaliger 69 (140 × 60 mm).[5] The proportions of these books may have given Wulfwinus the idea of producing a bilingual psalter with similarly unusual proportions. An additional clue is provided by the open-topped letter **a**, looking rather like a **u** which is found occasionally at the ends of lines both in the Paris Psalter and in Harley 5431 (see pl.VI (a) and (b)). The Paris Psalter is the only eleventh-century manuscript in which this archaic letter form, which was ultimately derived from New Roman Cursive[6] and which was sometimes used in later scripts, has been noticed.[7] This fact strengthens the hypothesis that Wulfwinus had seen Harley 5431 in the library of St Augustine's Abbey and that he followed not only its unusual shape but also an unusual letter form. He could of course have been a visitor to Canterbury, but to say that he worked there offers a more convincing explanation of these connections.

---

[2] For the (tenuous) Malmesbury connections, see G. T. Dempsey, 'Aldhelm of Malmesbury and the Paris Psalter: a Note on the Survival of Antiochene Exegesis', *JTS* ns 38 (1987), 368–86; for the litany, see *Anglo-Saxon Litanies of the Saints*, ed. M. Lapidge, HBS 106 (London, 1991), 80 and 250–3.

[3] Utrecht, Rijksuniversiteit Bibliotheek, 32 (Hautvillers Abbey, s. ix^{med}). For the most recent study with further bibliography, see *The Utrecht Psalter in Medieval Art*, ed. K. Van der Horst, W. Noel and W. Wüstefeld (London, 1996).

[4] W. Noel, *The Harley Psalter* (Cambridge, 1995), pp. 169–74.

[5] *Aethici Istrici Cosmographia Vergilio Salisburgensi rectius adscripta*, ed. T. A. M. Bishop, Umbrae Codicum Occidentalium 10 (Amsterdam, 1966), pp. xix–xx. For illustration and description of Harley 5431, see *The Golden Age of Anglo-Saxon Art 966–1066*, ed. J. Backhouse, D. Turner and L. Webster (London, 1984), pp. 47–8.

[6] I am indebted to Dr Michelle Brown for this information.

[7] *Paris Psalter*, ed. Colgrave, pp. 13–14 (N. R. Ker's contribution on the handwriting of the manuscript).

The scribe of the Paris Psalter

Whatever the truth of this matter, there is a further piece of evidence which does not appear to have been discussed in connection with the Paris Psalter and which strengthens the claim of Canterbury to be its place of origin, namely an entry in the martyrology and obit book of St Augustine's Abbey, Canterbury (London, BL, Cotton Vitellius C. xii).[8] On 143v, under 30 September, we read an entry *Obit Wulfwinus scriptor frater noster,* written in the original hand of the late eleventh or early twelfth century. *Wulfwinus* (OE *Wulfwine*) was of course a common name and we cannot immediately assume that this obit refers to the scribe of the Paris Psalter.[9] On the other hand the number of men called Wulfwinus who were also scribes must have been limited, so it may be profitable to explore the possible connections between these two references, in the colophon and in the obit, to a scribe named Wulfwinus.

On general grounds it would be surprising if there were two men of this name in the middle of the eleventh century who were both known for their work as scribes. It is just possible that the byname Cada was added to the colophon of the Paris Psalter to distinguish him from another Wulfwinus *scriptor,* but on balance this seems unlikely. Tengvik explained the meaning of the byname Cada as 'likely to denote a stout, lumpish person'.[10] Like other nicknames of the eleventh century, such as those of Eadui Basan and Ælfric Bata,[11] it was hardly complimentary but may offer us a glimpse of a squat figure writing on very tall, thin sheets of parchment.

Wulfwinus *scriptor* was clearly not a monk of St Augustine's Abbey. The scribes of the Cotton Martyrology were consistent in their use of terminology. They described monks of St Augustine's as *monachus et sacerdos* (or *levita*) *huius loci,* while members of other monastic communities were identified as such; for example, a monk of Christ Church would be identified as *monachus ecclesie Christi.* The designation *frater noster* applied, as did *soror nostra,* to a person in a relationship of confraternity to St Augustine's Abbey.[12] It is therefore very likely that the

---

[8] London, BL, Cotton Vitellius C. xii (St Augustine's, Canterbury, s.xi²–xii²); see C. M. Kauffmann, *Romanesque Manuscripts 1066–1190* (London, 1975), pp. 61–2, with colour pl. on p. 23.

[9] W. G. Searle, *Onomasticon Anglo-Saxonicum* (Cambridge, 1897), p. 523, lists seventeen instances of the use of the name *Wulfwinus*. I am grateful to Professor M. Lapidge for pointing out that *Wulfwinus* is probably a latinization of OE *Wulfwine*, but could equally possibly represent OE *Wulfwig*, since the final -g was palatalized by the eleventh century.

[10] G. Tengvik, *Old English Bynames,* Nomina Germanica 4 (Uppsala, 1938), 297.

[11] 'Basan' allegedly means 'the Fat': see D. N. Dumville, *English Caroline Script and Monastic History. Studies in Benedictinism, A.D. 950–1030* (Woodbridge, 1993), pp. 120–4. According to Tengvik, *Old English Bynames,* pp. 287–8, 'Bata is likely to mean a person of stout, heavy appearance'. For a different explanation of 'Bata', see D. W. Porter, 'The Hypocorism Bata – Old English or Latin?', *NM* 96 (1995), 345–9.

[12] Confraternity in English monasteries has received little attention from historians. For a recent discussion, see *The Liber Vitae of the New Minster and Hyde Abbey Winchester,* ed. S. Keynes, EEMF 26 (Copenhagen, 1996), 49–65.

Wulfwinus recorded in the St Augustine's martyrology was a secular cleric, who was well known at the abbey and whose ability as a scribe was recognized.[13]

Where did Wulfwinus *scriptor* do his work as a scribe? Was it in the scriptorium of St Augustine's Abbey, or at Christ Church, or elsewhere in Canterbury? There is little evidence to help us in answering this important question. It is clear that the scriptorium where the Paris Psalter was written must have been well equipped, but evidently this book was not produced for monastic use. It has no surviving lection marks and there is no evidence that it was ever in a monastic library. It was presumably produced for a pious layperson – perhaps, as Wormald suggested, for a lady.[14] The first indication of its medieval provenance is the signature of Jean, duc de Berry, showing that it was still in lay hands *c*. 1400.[15]

If the Paris Psalter was produced in the scriptorium of St Augustine's Abbey, it might be compared with the Old English Illustrated Hexateuch which, although it remained in the library of St Augustine's Abbey, was probably designed for lay use.[16] If, as has been suggested, St Augustine's produced more than one copy of this latter work, the Paris Psalter could be seen as fitting into a pattern of producing illustrated vernacular manuscripts for lay patrons – possibly as commercial ventures.[17]

Recent scholarship has challenged the idea that monastic scriptoria in the eleventh century wrote only for themselves and has shown that they also produced books for each other and for non-monastic clients. It has also demonstrated the potential flexibility of monastic scriptoria in that scribes might be hired, or might move between centres. Non-monastic scribes could and did work in monastic scriptoria; few, if any, would have had their own workshops at this time. The problems of localizing the Paris Psalter appear to reflect this situation and provide evidence for this view.[18] The hypothesis that Wulfwinus *scrip-*

---

[13] In the colophon of the Paris Psalter, Wulfwinus described himself as '*Sacer Dei*'. I am grateful to Mr Tim Graham for pointing out that this term is likely to have been used instead of *sacerdos* for metrical reasons.

[14] F. Wormald, *English Drawings in the Tenth and Eleventh Centuries* (London, 1952), p. 78.

[15] *Paris Psalter*, ed. Colgrave, pp. 11–12. In the fifteenth century the psalter was in the library of the Sainte Chapelle de Bourges.

[16] London, BL, Cotton Claudius B. iv; see *The Old English Illustrated Hexateuch*, ed. C. R. Dodwell and P. Clemoes, EEMF 18 (Copenhagen, 1974).

[17] For an illustration of a layperson commissioning a manuscript from a monastery (if the colloquy in question reflects actual practice), see M. Lapidge, 'Artistic and Literary Patronage in Anglo-Saxon England', in his *Anglo-Latin Literature 600–899* (London, 1996) pp. 37–91, esp. 43–5.

[18] See, for example, T. A. Heslop, 'The Production of *de luxe* Manuscripts and the Patronage of King Cnut and Queen Emma', *ASE* 19 (1990), 151–95. I am grateful to Dr Richard Gameson for the ideas behind this paragraph. For the wider background, see his *The Role of Art in the Late Anglo-Saxon Church* (Oxford, 1995), pp. 248–60.

tor and Wulfwinus Cada are one and the same person fits in with the evidence of the artwork, strengthening the claim of Canterbury to have been the place where the Paris Psalter was produced. It would also imply that the manuscript was the work not of a monk, but of a professional scribe, who both worked for the abbey and produced books for lay patrons. The evidence pointing towards Canterbury as the place of production is admittedly less than conclusive, but it is stronger than the evidence for any other scriptorium.

The named scribes of the eleventh century are a small, distinguished group. If the suggestions made here should be correct, Wulfwinus Cada, creator of one of the most fascinating books surviving from the eleventh century, emerges from the shadows into a documented historical situation, shedding valuable light on the types of scribal careers and on patterns of manuscript patronage that were possible in mid-eleventh-century England.[19]

---

[19] I am grateful to the authorities at the Bibliothèque Nationale de France and the British Library for allowing me to see the manuscripts mentioned here. My thanks go to Dr Michelle Brown, Dr Mildred Budny, Dr Richard Gameson, Mr Tim Graham and Dr Helen McKee for their perceptive and helpful comments on earlier drafts of this article.

The Office of the Trinity in the Crowland Psalter (Oxford, Bodleian Library, Douce 296)

BARBARA C. RAW

The main part of Oxford, Bodleian Library, Douce 296, consists of a psalter (9r–105v), together with the usual accompaniments of calendar (1r–6v), tables (7r–8r), canticles (105v–116v), litany (117r–119v) and prayers (119v –127v). The main part of the manuscript, written by a single scribe, ends halfway down 127v, in the centre of a gathering of six folios. The lower part of 127v and the remaining three folios are taken up by an Office of the Trinity, written by a different scribe. The manuscript is attributed to Crowland on the basis of entries in the calendar and litany.[1] Guthlac's name is entered in capitals in the litany, as are those of SS Mary and Peter; more importantly, Guthlac, like Peter, is invoked twice, a distinction accorded to no other saint in the Douce manuscript. The entries in the calendar include the translation of St Guthlac on 30 August, and a feast of his sister, St Pega, on 8 January, in addition to the usual feast of St Guthlac on 11 April; Pega also occurs, uniquely, in the litany of the Douce manuscript. The Psalter had probably left Crowland by 1091 when most of the monastery, including its library and service books, was destroyed by fire.[2] By the early twelfth century it was in the possession of the Cluniac priory of St Pancras, Lewes, when the *obits* of Lanzo, prior of St Pancras (*ob.* 1 April 1107), Anselm, archbishop of Canterbury (*ob.* 21 April 1109) and Hugh, abbot of Cluny (*ob.* 29 April 1109) were entered on 2v. It is possible that the book was in female hands between leaving Crowland and arriving at Lewes, since the prayers at Lauds in the Office of the Trinity contain feminine forms.[3]

The main part of the manuscript must date from after 1012 since the calen-

---

[1] E. Temple, *Anglo-Saxon Manuscripts 900–1066*, A Survey of Manuscripts Illuminated in the British Isles 1 (London, 1976), 96–7 (no. 79); A. G. Watson, *Catalogue of Dated and Datable Manuscripts c.450–1600 in Oxford Libraries*, 2 vols. (Oxford, 1984), I, 76 (no. 471); calendar ptd F. Wormald, *English Kalendars before 1100*, HBS 72 (1934), 253–65 (no. 20); litany ptd M. Lapidge, *Anglo-Saxon Litanies of the Saints*, HBS 106 (1991), 235–9 (no. xxxii). See also S. Keynes, 'The Crowland Psalter and the Sons of King Edmund Ironside', *Bodleian Lib. Record* 11 (1982–5), 359–70. I am grateful to Dr B. C. Barker-Benfield for discussing the collation of Douce 296 with me.

[2] *Historia Croylandensis*, cited in O. Lehmann-Brockhaus, *Lateinische Schriftquellen zur Kunst in England, Wales und Schottland vom Jahre 901 bis zum Jahre 1307*, 5 vols. (Munich, 1955–60) I, items 1172–6. The manuscript shows no signs of smoke damage.

[3] 'pro me famula tua' and 'ancillam tuam', 129v.

dar includes an entry for Ælfheah, archbishop of Canterbury, who was martyred in 1012. In the past, the manuscript has been dated to before 1057, or even before 1036, on the basis of four *obits* in gold lettering added to the calendar.[4] The *obits* at 10 January (1r) and 19 April (2v), 'ob. Eadmundus clitus' and 'ob. Eadwardus clitus anglorum', refer to the sons of Edmund Ironside, of whom Edward is known to have died in 1057. The *obits* at 18 March (2r) and 24 September (5r), parts of which have been lost when the manuscript was trimmed, cannot be linked to any known person. The suggestion that the entry 'ob. . . . . cl.' on 5r refers to the ætheling Alfred, who died in 1036, and that the manuscript therefore pre-dates 1036, has been shown to be untenable by Simon Keynes, who pointed out that Alfred is known to have died on 5 February, not 24 September.[5] The position of these entries on the page shows that they must have been made after the main text of the calendar was complete. On the other hand, the fact that they were written by the same scribe as the main part of the manuscript suggests that they were added soon afterwards, possibly at the same time as the gold lettering in the rest of the manuscript. This suggests a date for the manuscript as a whole of shortly before or soon after 1057, the year of the ætheling Edward's death. A date around 1057 would suit well with the style of the painting of Christ above the beasts on 40r.[6] This painting is highly unusual in that the drapery spirals round Christ's body instead of being tucked into a fold round the waist. The only other examples of such an arrangement known to me are the paintings of the evangelists Luke and Mark in one of the gospelbooks owned by Judith of Flanders and dated to the period of her stay in England, namely 1051–64.[7] Other details which link the decoration of Douce 296 to the Judith manuscript are the treatment of the acanthus foliage in the borders of the miniatures and the large initial Q with a mask-head and dragon tail.[8]

A Feast of the Trinity on the Sunday after Pentecost was introduced at Liège during the episcopate of Stephen of Liège (902–20) and Ælfric's *Letter to the Monks of Eynsham* shows that by the early eleventh century the feast was being celebrated

---

[4] Keynes, 'Crowland Psalter', p. 359; Temple, *Anglo-Saxon Manuscripts*, p. 97.
[5] Keynes, 'Crowland Psalter', p. 362.   [6] Reprod. Temple, *Anglo-Saxon Manuscripts*, pl. 259.
[7] New York, Pierpont Morgan Library, M 709, 48v and 77v, reprod. T. H. Ohlgren, *Anglo-Saxon Textual Illustration* (Kalamazoo, MI, 1992), pls. 11.5 and 11.7. For a recent discussion of Judith's books, see P. McGurk and J. Rosenthal, 'The Anglo-Saxon Gospelbooks of Judith, Countess of Flanders: their Text, Make-Up and Function', *ASE* 24 (1995), 251–308. The suggestion that the Office of the Trinity was written by the main scribe of Judith's manuscripts must probably be rejected: Dr McGurk tells me that he thinks the hands are not the same and that this was also the view of T. A. M. Bishop (private communication).
[8] Douce 296, 40r (Christ above the beasts) and 40v ('Quid gloriaris'); Morgan 709, 48v, 49r, 77v and 78r (acanthus borders) and 78r ('Quoniam quidem'); reprod. Temple, *Anglo-Saxon Manuscripts*, pls. 259–60, and Ohlgren, *Anglo-Saxon Textual Illustration*, pls. 11.5–11.8.

by the Anglo-Saxon church.[9] The office of the Trinity composed by Stephen has not survived, but several late Anglo-Saxon manuscripts include such offices. The *Leofric Collectar* contains texts for the day hours, headed 'Dominica de Sancta Trinitate'.[10] The *Portiforium Wulstani* includes an office in honour of the Trinity for the Octave of Pentecost, an incomplete set of antiphons and psalms headed 'Antiphonae super nocturnos in festo sanctae Trinitatis' and a second office headed 'Dominica de sancta Trinitate'.[11] Shorter private devotions in honour of the Trinity occur in the Ælfwine and Galba Prayerbooks.[12] The material in these manuscripts can be supplemented by the very full list of chants for the Feast of the Trinity in the tenth- to eleventh-century Hartker Antiphoner,[13] and the texts from the later medieval Hyde and Sarum Breviaries.[14]

Comparison of the available texts shows that there was no agreed form of the office for the Feast of the Trinity in the eleventh century, though there are groups of antiphons and chapters which are found in several manuscripts. The five antiphons to the psalms at First Vespers are the same in most of the antiphoners, in the later Hyde and Sarum Breviaries and in the *Leofric Collectar*.[15] The invitatory to the Night Office, together with the antiphons, psalms and responds to the first nocturn are also common to most of the antiphoners and

---

[9] *Epistula ad monachos Egneshamnenses directa*, ed. H. Nocent, Corpus consuetudinum monasticarum 7.3 (Siegburg, 1984), 149–85, at p. 176. For discussion, see B. C. Raw, *Trinity and Incarnation in Anglo-Saxon Art and Thought*, CSASE 21 (Cambridge, 1997), 10–12, and *The Leofric Collectar (Harl. MS. 2961)*, ed. E. S. Dewick and W. H. Frere, 2 vols., HBS 45 and 56 (London, 1914–21) II, xlix–li.   [10] *Leofric Collectar* I, 187–91.
[11] *The Portiforium of Saint Wulstan (Corpus Christi College, Cambridge, MS 391)*, ed. A. Hughes, 2 vols., HBS 89–90 (London, 1958–60) I, 68–9 (Octave of Pentecost) and II, 48–52 ('Antiphonae' and 'Dominica de sancta Trinitate').
[12] *Ælfwine's Prayerbook (London, British Library, Cotton Titus D. xxvi + xxvii)*, ed. B. Günzel, HBS 108 (London, 1993), 128–31 (no. 49); *A Pre-Conquest English Prayer-Book (BL MSS Cotton Galba A. xiv and Nero A. ii (ff. 3–13))*, ed. B. J. Muir, HBS 103 (London, 1988), 147–9 (no. 69).
[13] *Corpus antiphonalium officii*, ed. R.-J. Hesbert, 6 vols., Rerum ecclesiasticarum documenta, Series maior, Fontes 7–12 (Rome, 1963–79) II, 168–70. Other manuscripts included in Hesbert, vols. I-II, which contain texts for the Feast of the Trinity are: Durham, Cathedral Library, B.III.11 (G); Bamberg, Staatliche Bibliothek, lit. 23 (B); Ivrea, Biblioteca capitolare, 106 (E); Monza, Biblioteca capitolare, c. 12.75 (M); Verona, Biblioteca capitolare, xcviii (V); Zurich, Zentralbibliothek, 28 (R); Paris, Bibliothèque Nationale de France, lat. 17296 (D); Paris, Bibliothèque Nationale de France, lat. 12584 (F); London, British Library, Add. 30850 (S); Benevento, Biblioteca capitolare, V. 21 (L). The Hartker Antiphoner is Sankt Gallen, Stiftsbibliothek, 390 + 391 (H).
[14] *The Monastic Breviary of Hyde Abbey, Winchester, MSS Rawlinson Liturg. e.1 and Gough Liturg. 8 in the Bodleian Library, Oxford*, ed. J. B. L. Tolhurst, 6 vols., HBS 69–71, 76, 78 and 80 (London, 1932–42) II, 129v–132r; *Breviarium ad usum insignis ecclesiae Sarum*, ed. F. Procter and C. Wordsworth, 3 vols. (Cambridge, 1882–6) I, mxlvi–mlx.
[15] The antiphons are: *Gloria tibi Trinitas, Laus et perennis gloria, Gloria laudis resonet, Laus Deo Patri* and *Ex quo omnia*. See Hesbert, *Corpus antiphonalium* I, 232 (no. 97a) and 393 (no. 139a), MSS G, E and M, and II, 168 (no. 43.2a), 454–5 (no. 97a) and 723 (no. 127.3a), MSS H, R, D, F and S; *Hyde Breviary* II, 129v; *Sarum Breviary* I, mxlv; *Leofric Collectar* I, 187.

to the Hyde and Sarum Breviaries;[16] the same antiphons occur in the list of antiphons for the Night Office of the Feast of the Trinity in the *Portiforium Wulstani*.[17] The five antiphons for Lauds also seem to be generally accepted.[18] The chapters and collects are the same in the office for the Octave of Pentecost in the *Portiforium Wulstani* and that for Trinity Sunday in the *Leofric Collectar*, as are the antiphon to the *Magnificat* at First Vespers and the antiphons at Prime, Terce and Sext. Several of these chapters occur also in the Hyde and Sarum Breviaries, though not in the same order.[19]

Whereas the *Leofric Collectar* and *Portiforium Wulstani* contain more or less complete offices for the Feast of the Trinity, the texts in the Galba and Ælfwine Prayerbooks are more restricted. The Office of the Trinity in the Ælfwine Prayerbook combines texts from Prime and Vespers.[20] The Psalms *Deus in nomine tuo* (Ps. LIII), *Confitemini Domino* (Ps. CXVII) and *Beati immaculati* (Ps. CXVIII), together with *Quicumque vult*, are taken from the office of Prime on Sundays,[21] whereas the *Magnificat* belongs to Vespers. Many of the texts correspond to ones found in the Office for Trinity Sunday or the Octave of Pentecost in the *Leofric Collectar* and *Portiforium Wulstani*. The antiphon to the psalms, *O beata et benedicta*, is that for Prime in both manuscripts and the antiphon at the *Magnificat*, *Te Deum Patrem ingenitum*, is that to the *Magnificat* at First Vespers.[22] The chapter, on the other hand, *Tres sunt qui testimonium*, is that for Terce,[23] and the respond after the chapter, *Benedicat nos Deus*, is that to the first reading at the Night Office in the *Portiforium Wulstani*.[24] Three of the six collects in the Ælfwine manuscript occur in the *Leofric Collectar*: *Omnipotens sempiterne Deus coaeterna maiestas* at Lauds, *Omnipotens sempiterne Deus qui dedisti* at First Vespers and *Proflue miserationis ineffabile* at Sext.[25] Five of the collects occur in the *Portiforium Wulstani*: *Omnipotens sempiterne Deus qui dedisti* at First Vespers and Prime, *Domine Deus Pater omnipotens* at Lauds, *Concede nobis quesumus* at Terce, *Proflue miserationis ineffabile* at Sext and *Auge in nobis* among the morning prayers.[26] The four longer prayers, however, have no parallels in these manuscripts.

---

[16] Hesbert, *Corpus antiphonalium* I, 232 (no. 97a) and 393 (no. 139a), MSS G, B, E, M and V, and II, 168 (no. 43.2a), 454–5 (no. 97a), 643 (no. 120.3a) and 723 (no. 127.3a), MSS H, R, D, F, S and L; *Hyde Breviary* II, 130r; *Sarum Breviary* I, mxlvii–mxlix.   [17] *Portiforium Wulstani* II, 48.
[18] See Hesbert, *Corpus antiphonalium* I, 395 (no. 139b), MSS E and M, and II, 170 (no. 43.2b), 456–7 (no. 97b), 645 (no. 120.3b) and 725 (no. 127.3b), MSS H, R, D, F, S and L; *Hyde Breviary* II, 131v; *Sarum Breviary* I, mliii–mliv.
[19] *O altitudo* at Lauds in *Portiforium Wulstani* I, 68, *Leofric Collectar* I, 188, and *Sarum Breviary* I, mliv; *Tres sunt qui testimonium* at Terce in *Portiforium* I, 68, and *Leofric Collectar* I, 189, but at Sext in *Hyde Breviary* II, 132r, and *Sarum Breviary* I, mlvi; *Unus Dominus una fides* at Sext in *Portiforium* I, 69, and *Leofric Collectar* I, 189, but at None in *Hyde Breviary* II, 132r, and *Sarum Breviary* I, mlvi.
[20] *Ælfwine's Prayerbook*, pp. 128–31.
[21] J. Harper, *The Forms and Orders of Western Liturgy from the Tenth to the Eighteenth Century* (Oxford, 1991), p. 258.   [22] *Leofric Collectar* I, 189 and 187; *Portiforium Wulstani* I, 68.
[23] *Leofric Collectar* I, 189; *Portiforium Wulstani* I, 68.   [24] *Portiforium Wulstani* II, 49.
[25] *Leofric Collectar* I, 188 and 190.   [26] *Portiforium Wulstani* I, 68, 69 and 90.

The Office of the Trinity in the Crowland Psalter

The text in the Galba Prayerbook,[27] which begins with *Quicumque vult*, *Pater noster* and *Credo*, seems to be a version of the *preces* which normally end the office of Prime, though with the addition of an unnamed gospel canticle. The antiphon to the canticle—*Te Deum Patrem ingenitum*—is that sung at the *Magnificat* in the Ælfwine Prayerbook office and at First Vespers in the *Leofric Collectar* and *Portiforium Wulstani*,[28] and two of the three collects which end the entry, and which are taken from the liturgy for Trinity Sunday, are also found in the Ælfwine text.[29]

The Office of the Trinity in Douce 296 draws on this common stock of texts, and is similar in many respects to the offices in the *Leofric Collectar* and *Portiforium Wulstani*, though it does not correspond exactly to either. It also contains prayers and readings not found in either of these manuscripts. The Office starts with First Vespers (127v–128r) and ends with Sext at the bottom of 130v. The word 'AMEN' in capitals at this point suggests that this was the end of the entry. Not all texts are written out in full, and it is clear that the Office was intended for use by someone who knew the psalter by heart and who could supply many other texts from memory. Where monastic and secular use differ, it follows secular use. The five psalms for Vespers (CXLIII–CXLVII) are those for secular use on Saturdays; monastic Vespers includes only four psalms.[30] The Office of Compline includes four psalms (IV, XXX, XC and CXXXIII) whereas monastic use includes only three (IV, XC and CXXXIII); the position of the chapter, immediately after the psalms, also corresponds to secular rather than monastic use.[31] The texts at the beginning of the Night Office do not include Ps. III as was usual in monastic use.[32]

All the texts in the Office of Vespers in the Douce manuscript occur in one or both of the *Leofric Collectar* and *Portiforium Wulstani*, and the hour as a whole is based on a combination of texts from First and Second Vespers for Trinity Sunday or the Octave of Pentecost. The psalms and hymn are the usual ones for Saturday Vespers.[33] The antiphons to the five psalms are those for Second Vespers of the feast in the *Leofric Collectar*;[34] the collect is that listed for Second Vespers of the Feast of the Trinity in the *Leofric Collectar* and Second Vespers of the Octave of Pentecost in the *Portiforium Wulstani*.[35] The versicle, antiphon to the *Magnificat* and chapter, on the other hand, are taken from First Vespers of Trinity Sunday (*Leofric Collectar*) or the Octave of Pentecost (*Portiforium*

---

[27] *Pre-Conquest Prayer-Book*, pp. 147–9.
[28] *Leofric Collectar* I, 187; *Portiforium Wulstani* I, 68 and II, 48.
[29] *O. s. Deus, qui dedisti* and *O. s. Deus, trina maiestas* (but with *coaeterna* instead of *trina*), *Ælfwine's Prayerbook*, pp. 129–30.
[30] Those for Saturdays are CXLIV.10–CXLVII; see Harper, *Western Liturgy*, pp. 101 and App. 2.
[31] *Ibid.* pp. 102–3. [32] *Ibid.* p. 93. [33] *Ibid.* p. 258. [34] *Leofric Collectar* I, 190–1.
[35] *Leofric Collectar* I, 191; *Portiforium Wulstani* I, 69.

Wulstani).[36] The responsory after the chapter corresponds to that for Lectio 5 of the Night Office in the *Portiforium*, though the Hyde and Sarum Breviaries list it as the responsory to the chapter at First Vespers.[37]

The texts for Compline (128r–v) normally remain the same each day and are therefore not listed in either the *Leofric Collectar* or the *Portiforium Wulstani*. The four psalms in Douce are the normal ones for Compline in non-monastic churches.[38] The rest of the Office, however, does not follow the usual pattern. The text immediately before the group of psalms, *Te decet laus*, may be the hymn sung after the gospel at the Night Office in monastic churches,[39] though used here as an antiphon. Alternatively, the text *Benedictio et claritas* which follows the group of psalms, and which is used earlier as the fifth antiphon of Vespers, may be intended as the antiphon. However, this would leave the Office without a chapter, and it seems more likely that the text beginning *Benedictio et claritas* is taken from the *Capitula in omnem diem* as found in the Ælfwine Prayerbook.[40] The antiphon to the *Nunc dimittis*, which is written out in full, is not found in either the *Leofric Collectar* or the *Portiforium Wulstani*, but occurs in some antiphoners as the antiphon to the *Magnificat* at Second Vespers of Trinity Sunday.[41] The most problematic text, however, is the prayer at the end of the Office, which does not appear elsewhere.

The Night Office (128v–129r), headed 'Ad Matutinas', shares a number of texts with those for Trinity Sunday in the *Portiforium Wulstani*. There is one major difference, however. The office in the *Portiforium* has three nocturns, as would be expected on Sundays; the office in Douce has only a single nocturn, raising the possibility that it was intended for private recitation. The Invitatory and the responsories to the lections, apart from that to Lection 3, correspond to those for the first nocturn of the office headed 'Dominica de sancta Trinitate' in the *Portiforium Wulstani*; the three psalms with their accompanying antiphons, however, correspond to those listed under the heading 'Antiphonae super nocturnos in festo sanctae Trinitatis'.[42] The lections, too, differ from those in the *Portiforium*, though the same texts are found in the later Sarum Breviary.[43]

Whereas the Night Office is close to that in the *Portiforium*, the office of Lauds draws together texts which are spread over several different hours in other Anglo-Saxon manuscripts. The psalms and hymn are not listed, so they were presumably the normal ones for Lauds on Sundays.[44] The chapter is that for Lauds of Trinity Sunday or the Octave of Pentecost in both the *Leofric Collectar* and the *Portiforium*, and the closing collect is that for Trinity Sunday in the

---

[36] *Leofric Collectar* I, 187; *Portiforium Wulstani* I, 68.   [37] *Portiforium Wulstani* II, 49.
[38] See above, p. 189.   [39] See Harper, *Western Liturgy*, p. 95.
[40] *Ælfwine's Prayerbook*, p. 165, no. 73 [80].   [41] See below, p. 194, n. 65.
[42] *Portiforium Wulstani* II, 48–9.   [43] *Sarum Breviary* I, mxlviii–ml.
[44] See Harper, *Western Liturgy*, p. 258.

Collectar.⁴⁵ In the *Leofric Collectar* and *Portiforium Wulstani* the five antiphons are spread over the day hours from Prime to Vespers, but there is evidence for the use of all five at Lauds in the Hartker Antiphoner.⁴⁶ The antiphon at the *Benedictus* does not occur in the *Portiforium* but corresponds to that sung at the *Magnificat* at Second Vespers of Trinity Sunday in the *Leofric Collectar*.⁴⁷ The long series of *preces* between the *Benedictus* and collect does not occur in either the *Leofric Collectar* or *Portiforium Wulstani*. Prayers of this kind are traditional at this point in the office, but, although there are faint echoes of the prayers in other liturgical books such as the Benedictine Office or the Galba Prayerbook,⁴⁸ an exact parallel to the texts has not been found. The use of feminine forms in these texts, in particular the singular forms *pro me famula tua* and *me . . . ancillam tuam*, suggests that the office may have been put together for private use by a woman.

From this point on, the texts diverge increasingly from those in the *Leofric Collectar* and *Portiforium Wulstani*. The chapter at Prime corresponds to that for Lauds of Trinity Sunday in the *Portiforium Wulstani*⁴⁹ and the antiphon to the psalms at Sext corresponds to the antiphon at the *Benedictus* in the *Leofric Collectar* and that to the *Magnificat* at Second Vespers in the *Portiforium Wulstani*.⁵⁰ The remaining texts, however, several of which are not recorded elsewhere, are completely different and the office as a whole shows the fluidity of liturgical texts in the late eleventh century and the wide range of prayers in honour of the Trinity available at this time.

---

⁴⁵ *Leofric Collectar* I, 188; *Portiforium Wulstani* I, 68.
⁴⁶ *Leofric Collectar* I, 189–90; *Portiforium Wulstani* I, 68–9; Hesbert, *Corpus antiphonalium* II, 170 (no. 43.2b).   ⁴⁷ *Leofric Collectar* I, 191.
⁴⁸ *The Benedictine Office: an Old English Text*, ed. J. M. Ure (Edinburgh, 1957), pp. 89–94; *Pre-Conquest Prayer-Book*, pp. 147–8.   ⁴⁹ *Portiforium Wulstani* II, 51.
⁵⁰ *Leofric Collectar* I, 188; *Portiforium Wulstani* I, 69.

APPENDIX

CURSUS DE SANCTA TRINITATE

(127v) [AD VESPERAS]

DEUS in adiutorium meum intende, Domine ad adiuvandum me festina. Gloria Patri et Filio [et Spiritui Sancto, sicut erat in principio et nunc et semper, et in secula seculorum, Amen].[51]
A. Gloria et honor Deo in unitate Trinitatis, Patri et Filio cum Sancto Spiritu in sempiterna secula.[52]
    Benedictus Dominus Deus meus (Ps. CXLIII).[53]
A. In Patre manet eternitas, in Filio equalitas, in Spiritu Sancto eternitatis equalitatisque connexio.
    Exaltabo te Deus meus (Ps. CXLIV).
A. Sanctus, sanctus, sanctus, Dominus Deus omnipotens, qui erat et qui est, et qui venturus est.
    Lauda anima mea Dominum (Ps. CXLV).
A. Gloria et honor et benedictio sedenti super thronum, viventi in secula seculorum.
    Laudate Dominum quoniam bonus est (Ps. CXLVI).
[*A.*] Benedictio et claritas et sapientia et gratiarum actio, honor, virtus et fortitudo Deo nostro in secula seculorum, Amen.
    Lauda Hierusalem [Dominum] (Ps. CXLVII)

CAPITULUM.

> Pater et Filius et Spiritus Sanctus, unus omnipotens Deus, unus in Trinitate, unus in potestate, unitas Trinitas, sempiterna maiestas, qui nos fecit, nos /(128r) liberavit, et pro merito quemque salvabit.[54]

R. Honor, virtus, et potestas, et imperium sit Trinitati in unitate, unitati in Trinitate, in perhenni seculorum tempore.
V. Trinitati lux perhennis, unitati sit decus perpetim. In perhenni [seculorum tempore].[55]

---

[51] Manuscript abbreviations and cues for well-known texts have been expanded throughout.
[52] The five antiphons are those for 2nd Vespers of Trinity Sunday, *Leofric Collectar* I, 190–1. See also Hesbert, *Corpus antiphonalium* II, 170 (no. 43.2b), 645–7 (no. 120.3b-c) and 727 (no. 127.3c), III, 236 (no. 2943), 276 (no. 3268), 464 (no. 4796), 236 (no. 2944) and 86 (no. 1710).
[53] The five psalms are the normal ones for Saturday Vespers; see Harper, *Western Liturgy*, p. 258.
[54] Chapter at 1st Vespers of Trinity Sunday: *Leofric Collectar* I, 187; *Portiforium Wulstani* I, 68.
[55] Respond 5 at Night Office, *Portiforium Wulstani* II, 49; respond at 1st Vespers, *Hyde Breviary* II, 129v, and *Sarum Breviary* I, mxlvi. See also Hesbert, *Corpus antiphonalium* I, 232 (no. 97a) and 395 (no. 139b), II, 168 (no. 43.2a), 456–7 (no. 97b), 645 (no. 120.3b) and 725 (no. 127.3b), IV, 219 (no. 6870).

The Office of the Trinity in the Crowland Psalter

YMNUS.

> O lux beata Trinitas
> et principalis unitas,
> iam sol recedit igneus,
> infunde lumen cordibus.
> [T]e mane laudum carmine,
> te deprecemur vesperi,
> te nostra supplex gloria,
> per cuncta laudet secula.
> [D]eo Patri sit gloria,
> eiusque soli Filio,
> cum Spiritu paraclito,
> et nunc et in perpetuum. Amen.[56]

V. Benedicamus Patrem [et Filium cum Sancto Spiritu, laudemus et superexaltemus eum in secula].[57]

A. Te Deum Patrem ingenitum, te Filium unigenitum, te Spiritum Sanctum paraclytum, sanctam et individuam Trinitatem, toto corde et ore confitemur, laudamus atque benedicimus, tibi gloria in secula.[58]

[Magnificat].

COLLECTA. Omnipotens sempiterne Deus, qui propter mortalium omnium redemptionem Filium tuum haurire fecisti calicem passionis, te supplices invocamus ut nos per columnas sapientie stabilitos septiformis Spiritus sanctificatione confirmes. Per.[59]

AD COMPLETORIUM.

Converte nos Deus salutaris noster [Et averte iram tuam a nobis] (Ps. LXXXIV.5).

[*A.*] Te decet laus, [te decet hymnus, tibi gloria Deo Patri et Filio cum Sancto Spiritu in secula seculorum].[60]

---

[56] Normal hymn for Saturday Vespers: *Leofric Collectar* I, 357; *Portiforium Wulstani* I, 14, and II, 38 and 40. This is the only hymn noted in the Office; presumably it was repeated at the other hours. See also Hesbert, *Corpus antiphonalium* II, 455 (no. 97a), IV, 516 (no. 8358).

[57] Versicle at 1st Vespers of Trinity Sunday: *Leofric Collectar* I, 187; *Sarum Breviary* I, mxlvi. See also Hesbert, *Corpus antiphonalium* I, 232 (no. 97a) and 393 (no. 139a), II, 168 (no. 43.2a), 454 (no. 97a), 645 (no. 120.3b) and 725 (no. 127.3b), IV, 61 (no. 6238).

[58] Antiphon to *Magnificat* at 1st Vespers of Trinity Sunday: *Leofric Collectar* I, 187; *Portiforium Wulstani* I, 68 and II, 48; *Hyde Breviary* II, 130v. Antiphon at the *Magnificat*, 2nd Vespers of Trinity, *Sarum Breviary* I, mlvii. Also in *Pre-Conquest Prayer-Book*, p. 148, and *Ælfwine's Prayerbook*, p. 129. See also Hesbert, *Corpus antiphonalium* I, 232 (no. 97a) and 393 (no. 139a), II, 168 (no. 43.2a), 456–7 (no. 97b), 645 (no. 120.3b) and 725 (no. 127.3b), III, 502 (no. 5117).

[59] Collect for 2nd Vespers of Trinity Sunday: *Leofric Collectar* I, 191; *Portiforium Wulstani* I, 69.

[60] This is probably the hymn, *Te decet laus*, sung after the gospel at the Night Office in monastic use. It is mentioned in *Benedicti regula*, xi.10, ed. R. Hanslik, CSEL 75 (Vienna, 1960), 58, and included in *Portiforium Wulstani* II, 51, and the offices in BL, Royal 2. B. V and Cotton Tiberius A. iii, ptd *Facsimiles of Horae de Beata Maria Virgine*, ed. E. S. Dewick, HBS 21 (London, 1902), cols. 6 and 22. It seems to be used in Douce as the antiphon to the four psalms of Compline. For the text, see Harper, *Western Liturgy*, p. 270; see also Hesbert, *Corpus antiphonalium* II, 457 (no. 97b).

Ps. Cum invocarem (Ps. IV).[61]
Ps. In te Domine (Ps. XXX).
Ps. Qui habitat (Ps. XC).
Ps. Ecce nunc (Ps. CXXXIII).
[CAPITULUM]
    Benedictio et claritas [et sapientia et gratiarum actio, honor, virtus et fortitudo Deo nostro in secula seculorum, Amen]. (Apoc. VII.12)[62]
Deo Patri sit gloria,
[Eiusque soli Filio;
Cum Spiritu Paraclito,
Et nunc et in perpetuum].[63]
V. Custodi nos, Domine, [ut pupillam oculi; sub umbra alarum tuarum protege nos, Domine.][64]
A. Te gloriosus apostolorum chorus, te prophetarum laudabilis numerus, te martyrum candidatus laudat exercitus, tibi omnes electi voce confitentur unanimes, beata Trinitas unus Deus.[65]
Ps. Nunc dimittis.
ORATIO. Domine sancte Pater, eterne Deus omnipotens, exaudi propitius preces nostras et presta, ut te et unigenitum tuum Dominum nostrum Ihesum Christum, Sanctumque Paraclytum, unum /(128v) Deum in Trinitate, et trinum in unitate credere et confiteri valeamus, quatenus in fide recta et bonis operibus adimplendis eterne beatitudinis mereamur sine fine fieri consortes. Per.[66]
AD MAT[UTINAS].
Domine labia mea aperies [Et os meum annuntiabit laudem tuam].
Deus in adiutorium [meum intende, Domine ad adiuvandum me festina. Gloria Patri et Filio et Spiritui Sancto, sicut erat in principio, et nunc et semper, et in secula seculorum, Amen].
V. Deum verum unum in Trinitate et Trinitatem in unitate. Venite adoremus.[67]
    Venite exultemus Domino (Ps. XCIV).
ANTIPH. Adesto Deus unus omnipotens, Pater et Filius et Spiritus Sanctus.[68]

---

[61] The psalms are the normal ones for Compline in non-monastic churches; monastic use does not include Ps. XXX. See Harper, *Western Liturgy*, p. 258.
[62] *Ælfwine's Prayerbook*, p. 165, no. 73 [80]; also used as antiphon 5 at Vespers, above, p. 192; *Sarum Breviary* II, 33, chapter at Sunday Lauds. See also Hesbert, *Corpus antiphonalium* I, 395 (no. 139b), II, 170 (no. 43.2b) and 645 (no. 120.3b), III, 86 (no. 1710).
[63] This is the final verse of several of the office hymns, including *O lux beata Trinitas*, above, p. 193. See *Sarum Breviary* II, 221.
[64] *Ibid.* II, 225. See also Hesbert, *Corpus antiphonalium* IV, 98 (no. 6385).
[65] Hesbert, *Corpus antiphonalium* II, 458 (no. 97c), III, 503 (no. 5118), antiphon to the *Magnificat* at 2nd Vespers of Trinity Sunday.   [66] Not identified.
[67] Invitatory at Night Office of Trinity Sunday: *Portiforium Wulstani* II, 48; *Hyde Breviary* II, 130r; *Sarum Breviary* I, mxlvii. See also Hesbert, *Corpus antiphonalium* I, 232 (no. 97a) and 393 (no. 139a), II, 168 (no. 43.2a), 454–5 (no. 97a), 643 (no. 120.3a) and 723 (no. 127.3a), III, 7 (no. 1061).
[68] The three psalms and antiphons are those listed as 'Antiphonae super nocturnos in festo sanctae Trinitatis', *Portiforium Wulstani* II, 48; *Hyde Breviary* II, 130r; *Sarum Breviary* I,

The Office of the Trinity in the Crowland Psalter

Ps. Domine Dominus noster (Ps. VIII).
A. Te unum in substantia, Trinitatem in personis confitemur.
Ps. Celi enarrant (Ps. XVIII).
A. Te semper idem esse, vivere, et intelligere profitemur.
Ps. Domini est terra (Ps. XXIII).
V. Sit nomen Domini benedictum [Ex hoc nunc et usque in seculum].[69]
L[ectio] 1.
> Credimus sanctam Trinitatem, id est Patrem et Filium et Spiritum Sanctum, unum Deum omnipotentem, unius substantie, unius essentie, unius potestatis, creatorem omnium creaturarum, a quo omnia, per quem omnia, in quo omnia. Patrem a seipso non ab alio, Filium a Patre genitum, Deum verum de Deo vero, lumen verum de lumine vero: Non tamen duo lumina, sed unum lumen. Spiritum Sanctum a Patre et Filio equaliter procedentem, consubstantialem et coeternum Patri et Filio.[70]

R. Benedicat nos Deus, Deus noster; benedicat nos Deus. Et metuant eum omnes fines terre.
V. Deus misereatur nostri et benedicat nos Deus, Deus noster.[71]
B[enedictio]. Sancta Trinitas et inseparabilis unitas nobis suffragari dignetur.[72]
L[ectio] 2.
> Pater plenus Deus in se, Filius plenus Deus a Patre genitus, Spiritus Sanctus plenus Deus a Patre et Filio procedens, Non tamen tres deos dicimus, sed unum Deum omnipotentem, eternum, invisibilem, incommutabilem, Qui totus ubique est, totus ubique presens, non per partes divisus, sed totus in omnibus, non localiter, /(129r) sed potentialiter, qui sine commutatione sui mutabilia creavit, et creata gubernat.

R. Benedictus Dominus Deus Israhel, qui facis mirabilia solus; et benedictum nomen maiestatis eius in eternum.
V. Replebitur maiestate eius omnis terra, fiat, fiat. Et benedictum [nomen maiestatis eius in eternum].[73]

---

    mxlvii–mxlviii. See also Hesbert, *Corpus antiphonalium* I, 232 (no. 97a) and 393 (no. 139a), II, 168 (no. 43.2a), 454–5 (no. 97a), 643 (no. 120.3a) and 723 (no. 127.3a), III, 31 (no. 1268), 504 (no. 5126) and 503 (no. 5124).

[69] Not in *Portiforium Wulstani*, but in *Hyde Breviary* II, 130r and *Sarum Breviary* I, mlv. See also Hesbert, *Corpus antiphonalium* I, 232 (no. 97a) and 395 (no. 139b), II, 643 (no. 120.3a), III, 485 (no. 4971), IV, 500 (no. 8199).

[70] The lections are from Alcuin, *De fide Sanctae Trinitatis, Invocatio*, PL 101, 56–7. The lections in *Portiforium Wulstani* and *Hyde Breviary* are different, but the Douce lections appear in *Sarum Breviary* I, mxlviii-ml, lections 1–4 for Trinity Sunday, though divided differently.

[71] Respond 1 at Night Office of Trinity Sunday: *Portiforium Wulstani* II, 49; *Hyde Breviary* II, 130r; *Sarum Breviary* I, mxlviii. Also in *Ælfwine's Prayerbook*, p. 129. See also Hesbert, *Corpus antiphonalium* I, 232 (no. 97a) and 395 (no. 139b), II, 168 (no. 43.2a), 454–5 (no. 97a), 645 (no. 120.3b) and 725 (no. 127.3b), IV, 61 (no. 6240).

[72] No Anglo-Saxon parallel, but found in a list of blessings for the readings of the Night Office in a twelfth-century manuscript in the Vatican Library (Palat. lat. 235): P. Salmon, 'Bénédictions de l'office des matines', *Studi e testi* 273 (1974), 47–66, at 53 (no. 6). See also below, p. 198.

[73] Respond to Lectio 2 at Night Office of Trinity Sunday: *Portiforium Wulstani* II, 49; *Hyde Breviary* II, 130r; *Sarum Breviary* I, mxlix. Also in *Pre-Conquest Prayer-Book*, pp. 148–9. See also Hesbert, *Corpus antiphonalium* I, 232 (no. 97a) and 395 (no. 139b), II, 168 (no. 43.2a), 454–5 (no. 97a), 645 (no. 120.3b) and 725 (no. 127.3b), IV, 63 (no. 6249).

L[ectio] 3.

Semper igitur manens Deus quod est, cui nichil accidens esse poterit, quia simplici natura divinitatis, nil addi vel minui potest, quia semper est quod est, cui proprium est, cui sempiternum est, cui idem est, esse, vivere et intelligere. Et hec tria unus Deus et Dominus, hec tria idem Deus et Dominus, vera et sempiterna Trinitas in personis, vera et sempiterna unitas in substantia, quia una est substantia, Pater et Filius et Spiritus Sanctus.

Hec vero sancta Trinitas nil maius est in tribus personis simul nominatis, quam in una quelibet persona semel dicta, quia una queque persona plena est substantia in se. Non tamen tres substantie sed unus Deus, una substantia, una potentia, una essentia, una eternitas, una magnitudo, una bonitas, Pater et Filius et Spiritus Sanctus.

R. Summe Trinitati simplici Deo, una divinitas, equalis gloria, coeterna maiestas, Patri, Prolique, Sanctoque Flamini, qui totum subdit suis orbem legibus.

V. Prestet nobis gratiam Deitas beata, Patris et Nati pariterque Spiritus almi, qui totum [subdit suis orbem legibus].[74]

LAUDIBUS.

A. O beata et benedicta et gloriosa Trinitas, Pater et Filius et Spiritus Sanctus.

[V.] Tibi laus, tibi gloria, tibi gratiarum actio.[75]

[Dominus regnavit] (Ps. XCII)[76]

A. O beata et benedicta et gloriosa Unitas, Pater et Filius et Spiritus Sanctus.

[V.] [M]iserere, miserere, miserere nobis.

[Jubilate] (Ps. XCIX)

A. O vera, summa, sempiterna Trinitas, Pater, et Filius et Spiritus Sanctus.

[V.] Tibi laus, tibi gloria, tibi gratiarum actio.

[Deus, Deus meus] (Ps. LXII)

A. O vera, summa, sempiterna Unitas, /(129v) Pater, et Filius et Spiritus Sanctus.

V. Miserere, miserere, miserere nobis.

[Benedicite]

A. Te iure laudant, te adorant, te glorificant omnes creature tue, O beata Trinitas.

V. Tibi laus, tibi gloria, tibi gratiarum actio.

[Laudate] (Ps. CXLVIII)

---

[74] Respond to Lectio 6 of Night Office for Trinity Sunday: *Portiforium Wulstani* II, 50; *Hyde Breviary* II, 130v, respond to Lectio 8; *Sarum Breviary* I, mliii, respond to Lectio 9. See also Hesbert, *Corpus antiphonalium* I, 232 (no. 97a) and 395 (no. 139b), II, 168 (no. 43.2a), 456–7 (no. 97b), 645 (no. 120.3b) and 725 (no. 127.3b), IV, 422 (no. 7718).

[75] In *Leofric Collectar* I, 189–90, and *Portiforium Wulstani* I, 68–9, the five antiphons are spread over several different hours. In *Hyde Breviary* II, 131v, *Sarum Breviary* I, mliii-mliv, and the Hartker Antiphoner, Hesbert, *Corpus antiphonalium* II, 170 (no. 43.2b), all five are used at Lauds of Trinity Sunday. See also Hesbert, I, 395 (no. 139b), II, 456–7 (no. 97b), 645 (no. 120.3b) and 725 (no. 127.3b), III, 363 (nos. 3992 and 3990), 377 (nos. 4086 and 4087) and 503 (no. 5120). Also in *Ælfwine's Prayerbook*, pp. 128 and 129, A. Wilmart, *Precum libelli quattuor aevi Karolini* (Rome, 1940), p. 165, and Alcuin, *De fide sanctae Trinitatis, Invocatio*, PL 101, 56.

[76] The psalms are not listed in Douce, but are supplied from Harper, *Western Liturgy*, p. 258, Sunday Lauds.

The Office of the Trinity in the Crowland Psalter

CAPITULUM.
O altitudo divitiarum sapientie et scientie Dei, quam incomprehensibilia sunt iudicia eius et investigabiles vie eius. Quoniam ex ipso, et per ipsum, et in ipso sunt omnia. Ipsi honor, et gloria in secula seculorum, Amen (Rom. XI.33 and 36).[77]
V. Magnus Dominus et laudabilis nimis, terribilis est super omnes deos.[78]
IN EVANGELIUM.[79]
A. Gratias tibi Deus, gratias tibi, vera una Trinitas, una et summa veritas, trina et una Unitas.[80]
Ps. Benedictus.
Kyrie eleison.
ORATIO. Deprecor te sancta Trinitas, pro me famula tua et pro omnibus peccatis et angustiis, et necessitatibus meis, et pro omnibus tribulationibus atque infirmitatibus meis.[81]
[Preces] Salvam me fac ancillam tuam sancta Trinitas, Domine Deus meus sperantem in te.
    Salvas fac nos, Domine Deus noster, et congrega nos de nationibus.
    Ut confiteamur nomini sancto tuo, et gloriemur in laude tua.
    Mitte nobis Deus sancta Trinitas auxilium de sancto, et de Sion tuere nos.
    Esto nobis Deus sancta Trinitas turris fortitudinis a facie inimici.[82]
ORATIO. Mitte nobis Deus sancta Trinitas verbum tuum de celo per adnuntiationem tuam et per descensionem tuam, et per conceptionem et incarnationem tuam, et per nativitatem et circumcisionem tuam, et per baptismum tuum, et per passionem et crucem tuam, et sepulchrum tuum, et per resurrectionem et ascensionem tuam, et per adventum Spiritus Sancti paracliti, et per magnitudinem adventus tui, et per ineffabilem maiestatem tuam, et per magnam misericordiam tuam, et per benedictam genitricem tuam, et per suffragia angelica, et per istorum et omnium sanctorum tuorum merita, sana nos ab omnibus infirmitatibus nostris, et dimitte nobis/(130r) omnia peccata nostra preterita, presentia et futura, et erue nos a morte eterna, et de omnibus nostris angustiis quas pro peccatis nostris patimur, et fac tuam clementiam magnam domine

---

[77] Capitulum at Lauds of Trinity Sunday: *Leofric Collectar* I, 188; *Portiforium Wulstani* I, 68. See also *Sarum Breviary* I, mliv.
[78] Ps. XCV.4, Versicle of Trinity Sunday, Hesbert, *Corpus antiphonalium* I, 395 (no. 139b), II, 643 (no. 120.3a), IV, 494 (no. 8131).   [79] i.e. the antiphon to the Gospel Canticle, *Benedictus*.
[80] Antiphon to *Magnificat* at 2nd Vespers of Trinity Sunday, *Leofric Collectar* I, 191. Antiphon to *Magnificat* at 1st Vespers, *Sarum Breviary* I, mxlvi. See also Hesbert, *Corpus antiphonalium* I, 232 (no. 97a) and 393 (no. 139a), II, 168 (no. 43.2a), 454–5 (no. 97a), 643 (no. 120.3a) and 723 (no. 127.3a), III, 241 (no. 2977).
[81] Not identified. Note feminine forms in this and the following prayers.
[82] These five invocations are adapted from the following psalm verses: 'Salvum fac servum tuum Deus meus sperantem in te' (Ps. LXXXV.2); 'Salva fac nos Domine Deus noster: et congrega nos de nationibus. Ut confiteamur nomini sancto tuo: et gloriemur in laude tua' (Ps. CV.47); 'Mitte tibi auxilium de sancto: et de Syon tueatur te' (Ps. XIX.2); 'Deduxisti me quia factus es spes mea: turris fortitudinis a facie inimici' (Ps. LX.3–4). Compare the *preces* in *Pre-Conquest Prayer-Book*, pp. 147–8, *Sarum Breviary* II, 56, and *Hyde Breviary* VI, 20–41 and 99. *Esto nobis ... inimici* also in *Horae of BVM*, col. 40.

sancta Trinitas super nos, et concede nobis spatium vite vivendi, et voluntatem penitendi, ut ante diem exitus nostri per puram confessionem et veram penitentiam, et per rectam fidem operaque bona, tibi sancte Trinitati domino Deo omnipotenti placere mereamur, per.[83]

COLLECTA. Omnipotens, sempiterne Deus, summa maiestas et una Deitas, qui in Trinitate permanes et in Unitate semper consistis, presta quesumus, ut qui peccatorum nostrorum pondere premimur, celerem indulgentiam consequi mereamur, per.[84]

AD PRIMAM.

[A.] Credimus et confitemur Patrem, et Filium et Spiritum Sanctum paraclytum, ipsi gloria per eterna seculorum secula.[85]

> [Deus in nomine] (Ps. LIII)[86]
> [Beati immaculati and Retribue] (Ps. CXVIII.1–16 and 17–32)
> [Quicumque]

CAPITULUM.

> Gratia Domini nostri Ihesu Christi, et caritas Dei, et communicatio Sancti Spiritus sit semper cum omnibus nobis (2 Cor. XIII.13).[87]

R. Laus tibi sancta Trinitas, vera et una Deitas.

V. Pater, et Filius et Spiritus Sanctus.[88]

Gloria Patri.

V. Deus genitor, Deus genitus, in utroque sacer Spiritus coequalis gloria.[89]

[Preces]

Kyrie eleison.[90]

Pater noster.

O beata Trinitas et una Deitas, Pater, et Filius et Spiritus Sanctus.

Credo in Deum.

Sancta Trinitas et inseparabilis [unitas nobis suffragari dignetur].[91]

Domine labia mea aperies [Et os meum annuntiabit laudem tuam] (Ps. L.17).

Verba mea auribus [percipe Domine: intellige clamorem meum] (Ps. V.2).

Intende voci [orationis meae: Rex meus et Deus meus] (Ps. V.3).

Cum ad te orabo [Domine: mane exaudies vocem meam] (Ps. V.4).

Laudemus sanctam Trinitatem et unam Deitatem quam laudant angeli, cui seraphim et seraphim, sanctus, sanctus, proclamant.[92]

---

[83] Not identified.
[84] Collect for Trinity Sunday, *Leofric Collectar* I, 188, *Hyde Breviary* II, 132r (at None). Also in *Pre-Conquest Prayer-Book*, p. 149, and CCCC 422 (ptd *The Leofric Missal as Used in the Cathedral of Exeter during the Episcopate of its First Bishop AD 1050–1072*, ed. F. E. Warren (Oxford, 1883), p. 273).   [85] Not identified.
[86] Psalms for secular use on weekdays, supplied from Harper, *Western Liturgy*, p. 258.
[87] Capitulum for Lauds of Trinity Sunday, *Portiforium Wulstani* II, 51; Capitulum for 1st Vespers, Lauds and Terce, *Hyde Breviary* II, 129v, 131v and 132r; Capitulum at 1st Vespers of Trinity Sunday, *Sarum Breviary* I, mxlvi.   [88] Not identified.   [89] Not identified.
[90] Cf. *preces* in Wilmart, *Precum libelli*, pp. 69–71.
[91] This is identical with the blessing at the Night Office, above, p. 195 and n. 72.
[92] This is adapted from an antiphon for the Feasts of St Michael and of All Saints, Hesbert, *Corpus antiphonalium* III, 314 (no. 3592): 'Laudemus Dominum quem laudant angeli, cui seraphim et cherubim sanctus, sanctus, proclamant.'

The Office of the Trinity in the Crowland Psalter

Exaltare Domine, sancta Trinitas, in virtute tua [cantabimus et psallemus virtutes tuas] (Ps. XX.14).[93]

Benedicamus Dominum in omni tempore, semper laus [eius in ore meo] (Ps. XXXIII.2).[94]

ORATIO. Domine Deus, rex celi et terre, dirige actus nostros in beneplacito tuo, ut in nomine dilecti Filii tui mereamur in bonis operibus habundare, per.[95]

ALIA. O primum et summum omnium recte credentium bonum, sancta Trinitas, Deus omnipotens, exaudi nos in hac hora/(130v) te invocantes, et fac nos hodiernum diem tibi placabiliter et constanter peragere, et adsequentes, te adiuvante, incolomes pervenire, die hac nocte, tua protecti misericordia ab omnibus mereamur adversitatibus liberari, et in tuo sancto famulatu firmiter confortari, et in tuis laudibus iugiter manere valeamus, et in numero tibi placentium secundum tuam voluntatem sine intermissione gaudere mereamur, hic et ubique, et nunc et semper, per omnia secula seculorum, Amen.[96]

AD TERTIAM.

A. Sancta Trinitas, Deus omnipotens, exaudi clemens supplices tuos et relaxa peccatorum nostrorum vincula ut tibi sincera fide in sempiternum servire valeamus.[97]

Ps. Legem pone (Ps. CXVIII.33–80).[98]

CAPITULUM.

Quamvis enim personaliter alius sit Pater, alius sit Filius, alius sit Spiritus Sanctus, ipsa tamen sancta Trinitas unus est Deus.[99]

R. Nulla lingua valet dignas refferre laudes sancte Trinitati quoque unus Deus.

V. Nos tamen prout ipsa concesserit trina maiestas mente devota, assiduas semper agamus, laudes sancte Trinitati.[100]

V. Benedicamus Patrem [et Filium cum Sancto Spiritu. Laudemus et superexaltemus eum in secula].[101]

COLLECTA. Domine sancte Pater, benigne indignas exaudire dignare et per unicum Filium tuum, Sancti Spiritus gratiam cordibus nostris clementer infunde, que nos omnia mala vitare doceat, et in tuis laudibus manere concedat, per.[102]

ORATIO. Trinitas sancta, tuam deprecamur clementiam ut nobis in hac hora perpetuam tribuas gratiam, per.[103]

AD VI.

A. Benedicta sit creatrix et gubernatrix omnium, sancta et individua Trinitas, nunc, semper, per infinita seculorum secula.[104]

---

[93] Cf. *ibid.* III, 214 (nos. 2758–9) and IV, 173 (no. 6682).
[94] Cf. *ibid.* IV, 61 (no. 6236).   [95] Not identified.   [96] Not identified.
[97] Not identified.   [98] Psalm for Terce, Harper, *Western Liturgy*, p. 258.
[99] No exact parallel has been found but cf. Alcuin, *De fide sanctae Trinitatis* I.ii, 'Quamvis personaliter sit alius Pater, alius Filius, alius Spiritus Sanctus', and I.v, 'Et haec Trinitas unus est Deus', PL 101, 15 and 17.   [100] Not identified.
[101] Versicle at 1st Vespers of Trinity Sunday, *Leofric Collectar* I, 187; responsory at Terce, *Sarum Breviary* I, mlv; and at Sext, *Hyde Breviary* II, 132r. See also Hesbert, *Corpus antiphonalium* I, 232 (no. 97a) and 393 (no. 139a), II, 454 (no. 97a), 645 (no. 120.3b) and 725 (no. 127.3b), IV, 61 (no. 6238). See above, n. 57. Cf. *Ælfwine's Prayerbook*, p. 129.   [102] Not identified.   [103] Not identified.
[104] Antiphon at Lauds of Trinity Sunday, *Leofric Collectar* I, 188, and *Sarum Breviary* I, mlv; antiphon to *Magnificat* at 2nd Vespers, *Portiforium Wulstani* I, 69, and *Hyde Breviary* II, 132r. See also Hesbert, *Corpus antiphonalium* I, 234 (no. 97b) and 395 (no. 139b), II, 170 (no. 43.2b), 456–7 (no. 97b), 645 (no. 120.3b) and 725 (no. 127.3b), III, 86 (no. 1707).

[Defecit] (Ps. CXVIII.81–128)[105]
CAPITULUM.
    In Patre manet eternitas, in Filio equalitas, in Spiritu Sancto eternitatis equalitatisque conexio.[106]
R. Domino Deo nostro, Patri omnipotenti, Filioque eius Ihesu Christo, Sanctoque Spiritui, laus et gloria, nunc et in evum per eterna seculorum secula.
V. Laudamus omnes iugiter sanctam Trinitatem, que regnat equaliter in una Deitate, nunc et in evum.[107]
V. Benedictus sit Deus [Pater], unigenitusque [Dei Filius, Sanctus quoque Spiritus qui facit nobiscum misericordiam suam].[108]
Domine Pater, eterne Deus, qui cum Filio tuo et Spiritu Sancto, in una. AMEN.[109]

---

[105] Psalm for Sext in secular use, supplied from Harper, *Western Liturgy*, p. 258.
[106] Alcuin, *De fide sanctae Trinitatis, Invocatio*, PL 101, 57. Identical with second antiphon at Vespers, above, p. 192.   [107] Not identified.
[108] Offertory from mass of Trinity Sunday: R.-J. Hesbert, *Antiphonale missarum sextuplex* (Brussels, 1935), p. 173, no. 172 *bis*.   [109] Not identified.

Hereward and Flanders

ELISABETH VAN HOUTS

Hereward 'the Wake' is renowned as one of the leaders of the English resistance to the Normans in the late 1060s and early 1070s. His involvement in the resistance is noted by all main sources, even though the extent to which he was responsible for actions in Ely and Peterborough remains to be elucidated.[1] He is listed as a pre-Conquest Lincolnshire landholder and tenant in Domesday Book, which is the only contemporary source to mention, but not date, his outlawry.[2] Hereward's career as an outlaw is shrouded in mystery, due to the lack of detail in contemporary sources and also to the rise of stories incorporated in the *Gesta Herewardi* (*The Deeds of Hereward*), written in the twelfth century, which claim that

---

[1] The *Gesta Herewardi* as a narrative representing English ethnic awareness and pride of the English warfare is the topic of an important forthcoming study by Hugh Thomas, who most kindly allowed me to read his article in advance of publication (H. M. Thomas, 'The *Gesta Herewardi*, the English and their Conquerors', *ANS* 21 (1998), pp. 213–32). The relevant sources are: *Two of the Saxon Chronicles Parallel*, ed. J. Earle and C. Plummer, 2 vols. (Oxford, 1892–9) I, 204–5, 208 = *Anglo-Saxon Chronicle*, 'DE', s.a. 1070 [Hereward at Peterborough] and 1071 [Hereward at Ely and his escape]; *The Chronicle of John of Worcester*, ed. R. R. Darlington and P. McGurk, trans. J. Bray and P. McGurk, 2 vols. [II–III] (Oxford, 1995–8) III, 20–1 [Hereward at Ely and escape]; *Willelmi Malmesbiriensis de gestis pontificum Anglorum*, ed. N. E. S. A. Hamilton, RS (London, 1870), p. 420 [Hereward at Peterborough]; *Henry Archdeacon of Huntingdon, Historia Anglorum, The History of the English People*, ed. D. E. Greenway (Oxford, 1996), pp. 396–8 [Hereward at Ely and escape]; *L'Estoire des Engleis by Geffrei Gaimar*, ed. A. Bell, Anglo-Norman Texts 14–16 (Oxford, 1960), lines 5460–5506, pp. 173–81 [Hereward at Peterborough and Ely]; *The Chronicle of Hugh Candidus*, ed. W. T. Mellows (Oxford, 1949), pp. 77–9 and 81 [Hereward at Peterborough and Ely].

[2] *Domesday Book seu Liber Censualis Wilhelmi primi regis Angliae*, ed. A. Farley, 2 vols. (London, 1783) [hereafter DB], fols. 346r, 364v, 376v, 377r and 377v, where he occurs as pre-Conquest landholder of Laughton, Rippingale and Witham (Lincs.) which he held respectively with one Toli, from Crowland Abbey and from Peterborough. Two of the entries (376v and 377v) explicitly mention his outlawry, which is not dated. The Pseudo-Ingulf's history of Crowland Abbey dates the outlawry to 1062 (*Historia Ingulphi* in *Rerum Anglicarum scriptorum veterum Tom. I*, ed. W. Fulman (Oxford, 1684), pp. 1–107, at 67). For discussions of Hereward's origin and status, see J. Hayward, 'Hereward the Outlaw', *JMH* 14 (1988), 293–304; C. Hart, 'Hereward the Wake and his Companions', in his *The Danelaw* (London, 1992), pp. 625–48; E. King, 'The Origins of the Wake Family', *Northamptonshire Past and Present* 5 (1975), 167–77; D. Roffe, 'Hereward the Wake and the Barony of Bourne: a Reassessment of a Fenland Legend', *Lincolnshire Hist. and Archaeol.* 29 (1994), 7–10; and A. Williams, *The English and the Norman Conquest* (Woodbridge, 1995), pp. 49–50 and n. 24.

he went as a mercenary to Cornwall, Ireland and Flanders. Two sections of the *Gesta Herewardi* are devoted to his exploits in the county of Flanders, and there is a curious third passage describing his relationship to Gilbert of Gent, the richest post-Conquest Flemish settler in England, who is said to have been Hereward's godfather.[3] The purpose of this article is to take a fresh look at these passages and to assess them in the light of sources written on the Continent which seemingly confirm the *Gesta* sections on Flanders.

'GESTA HEREWARDI'

The *Gesta Herewardi* survives in one mid-thirteenth-century manuscript known as the *Register of Robert of Swaffham*, which belongs to the Dean and Chapter of Peterborough Cathedral, but is kept at the University Library in Cambridge.[4] It is commonly assumed, correctly I think, that the *Gesta Herewardi* as preserved in the *Register of Robert of Swaffham* is 'the book about Hereward . . . compiled . . . by the venerable man and learned brother, the late Richard', which is mentioned by the compiler of the *Liber Eliensis*.[5] The Ely compiler refers twice to such a biography of Hereward in contexts which strongly suggest that Richard, a monk or clerk, was writing during the episcopacy of Hervey of Ely, that is between 1109 and 1131.[6] If we accept this identification it follows that the anonymous author

---

[3] *Gesta Herwardi incliti exulis et militis*, in *Lestoire des Engles solum la translacion maistre Geffrei Gaimar*, ed. T. D. Hardy and C. T. Martin, 2 vols., RS (London, 1888) II, 339–404; the Flemish passages can be found on 343–4, 353–64 and 370–1. A new edition and translation is in preparation by P. G. Schmidt and J. Mann for OMT. The English translation by M. Swanton (*Three Lives of the Last Englishmen* (New York, 1984), pp. 45–88) needs to be used with caution.

[4] Cambridge University Library, Peterborough, Chapter Library 1, 320r-339r (339v is blank); the whole text is contained in two quires (nos. xxviii–xxix), written in one hand with red chapter headings, and red/blue initials. The *Register* also contains a collection of royal charters for Peterborough, the Chronicle of Hugh Candidus, and the Laws of William the Conqueror. For a description, see J. D. Martin, *The Cartularies and Registers of Peterborough Abbey*, Northamptonshire Record Soc. 28 (Peterborough, 1978), 7–12 and N. R. Ker *et al.*, *Medieval Manuscripts in British Libraries* (Oxford, 1969–; in progress) IV, 162–4. A brief reference to the cartulary can be found in A. Gransden, *Historical Writing in England c. 550 to c. 1307* (London, 1974), p. 520.

[5] *Liber Eliensis*, ed. E. O. Blake, Camden 3rd ser. 92 (London, 1962), 188: 'In libro autem de ipsius gestis Herewardi, dudum a venerabili viro ac doctissimo fratre nostro beate memorie Ricardo edito, plenius descripta inveniuntur.' See also *ibid.* p. xxxiv and n. 10. However, note the doubts expressed by S. Keynes in his unpublished paper 'Hereward the Wake' (1990). I am most grateful to Simon Keynes for allowing me to read his work in advance of publication.

[6] This date (*Liber Eliensis*, ed. Blake, p. xxxiv) is consistent with the references in the Flemish sections of the *Gesta* to the counts of Guînes and Warenne. Count Manasses is called 'Manasses the Old of Guînes' to distinguish him from his grandson Manasses II or Robert (1091–c. 1137) (see below, pp. 211–12, n. 51), while William I of Warenne (d. after 1088) is called 'the old count William of Warenne', contrasting him with his son of the same name who was count from c. 1088 to 1138 (*Early Yorkshire Charters*, ed. W. Farrer and C. T. Clay, 12 vols. (Edinburgh, 1914–65) VIII, 7–12 and C. P. Lewis, 'The Earldom of Surrey and the Date of Domesday Book', *Hist. Research* 63 (1990), 329–36).

of the *Gesta Herewardi* is Richard of Ely. In his prologue to the *Gesta* the author, whom from now onwards I shall call Richard of Ely, explains that he wrote the work in two stages. Firstly he consulted a damaged manuscript which contained an Old English Life of Hereward by Hereward's priest Leofric and he made oral enquiries.[7] For unexplained reasons he then abandoned his project. The second stage took place at an unspecified later time when he stylistically revised his original text. He also incorporated extra oral information from two of Hereward's wounded companions. They are named as brother Siward of Bury St Edmunds and Leofric the Black, who later appear as participants in the struggle against the Normans around Ely.[8] According to the prologue they were also known to the anonymous dedicatee of the *Gesta Herewardi*, who may be identified with some confidence as Bishop Hervey of Ely (1109–31).[9]

Clearly, Richard was working at a time when some of Hereward's companions were still alive. They, like other Conquest veterans, repeated their memories of the battle and subsequent expeditions orally to a generation that had not been present.[10] For example, Abbot Ralph of Battle Abbey, who was born in 1040 and aged 84 when he died in 1124, was the main informant of the author of the *Brevis relatio*, written between 1114 and 1120 at Battle Abbey, while Count Robert of Beaumont, the fifteen-year-old hero of the Battle of Hastings, who died in 1118 at the age of 69, was another likely source of information about the events of 1066 well into the twelfth century.[11] Richard, therefore, had at his disposal a contemporary biography in Old English, oral eyewitness accounts from named companions as well as rumours he had collected at an early stage.[12] His acknowledgement of his sources is impeccable and accords with normal medieval practice by distinguishing between oral and written sources, and by naming informants, where possible.[13] By translating or adapting Old English narratives into Latin he was not unique. Other contemporaries were doing the same: William of Malmesbury translated the now lost vernacular Life of Wulfstan of Worcester by Coleman, Wulfstan's chaplain, and Bishop Hervey of Ely himself

---

[7] The Old English Life of Hereward by Leofric is now lost.
[8] *Gesta Herewardi*, ed. Hardy and Martin, p. 383.   [9] *Ibid.* pp. 339–41.
[10] E. M. C. van Houts, 'The Memory of 1066 in Written and Oral Traditions', *ANS* 19 (1996), 167–80.
[11] E. M. C. van Houts, 'The Brevis relatio de Guillelmo nobilissimo comite Normannorum, written by a Monk of Battle Abbey', *Chronology, Conquest and Conflict in Medieval England*, Camden Miscellany 35, Camden 5th ser. 10 (London, 1997), 1–48, at 14–15; *The Chronicle of Battle Abbey*, ed. E. Searle (Oxford, 1980), pp. 130–2; and D. Crouch, *The Beaumont Twins; the Roots and Branches of Power in the Twelfth Century* (Cambridge, 1986), pp. 3–4; and *The Gesta Guillelmi of William of Poitiers*, ed. R. H. C. Davis and M. Chibnall (Oxford, 1998), pp. 130–1 and 178–9.
[12] For lost Old English texts, see R. M. Wilson, *The Lost Literature of Medieval England* (London, 1970), pp. 72 and 113–15.
[13] E. van Houts, *Memory and Gender in Medieval Europe, 900–1200* (London, 1999), pp. 19–39 (chronicles and annals) and 41–62 (saints' lives and miracles).

commissioned the translation of the Old English records which formed the basis of the *Libellus Æthelwoldi*.[14]

However, the transmission of the text is not as straightforward as this account might suggest. The problem arises from the use made of Richard's work by the compiler of the *Liber Eliensis*. It has been suggested that the compiler used not the *Gesta Herewardi* as preserved in the Swaffham Register but an earlier version which is probably the first version written by Richard and the one he later revised.[15] It is true that there are literary and historical differences between the *Liber Eliensis* and the *Gesta Herewardi*, but it need not follow that an earlier version of the *Gesta Herewardi* must lie behind the *Liber Eliensis*. The compiler of the *Liber* was an accomplished Latinist and would have been quite capable of adapting his sources. His command of Latin would have enabled him to revise the *Gesta Herewardi* stylistically and to make it fit with other material he used, such as the Worcester Chronicle and William of Poitiers' *Gesta Guillelmi*. The differences in content could be attributed to the compiler's readiness to use other Ely traditions, including an otherwise unknown text on Hereward based on an adaptation of the biblical history of Maccabees I and II.[16]

If the text of the *Gesta Herewardi* as we have it was written between 1109 and 1131, then it is contemporary with the chronicles of John of Worcester, Henry of Huntingdon and William of Malmesbury, earlier by perhaps a decade than Gaimar's *L'Estoire des Engleis* (written in 1136–7) and considerably earlier than the late-twelfth-century Peterborough tradition as preserved by Hugh Candidus. On that basis, we should approach the text with the same mixture of trust and professional scepticism that we employ in our approach to those narrative sources.

THE STORY

The most important Flemish material in the *Gesta Herewardi* follows the alleged mercenary career of Hereward in Cornwall and Ireland. From there he travelled, so the story goes, to Flanders via the Orkneys and was shipwrecked on the coast near Saint-Bertin. He was received by the count of that land (*terrae illius*) Manasses the Old and his magnates, who established his identity and the reason for his arrival. Hereward's subsequent adventures in Flanders, which form the centrepiece of the first half of the *Gesta Herewardi*, culminate in his participation in a Flemish expedition against the people of 'Scaldemariland',[17] and about this

---

[14] *The Vita Wulfstani of William of Malmesbury*, ed. R. R. Darlington (London, 1928), pp. viii–ix and 2; *Liber Eliensis*, ed. Blake, pp. xxxiv and li–lii.
[15] *Liber Eliensis*, ed. Blake, pp. xxxvi–xxxvii, 173–6 and 177–88.
[16] *Ibid.* II.102, ed. Blake, pp. 173–6.
[17] P. Grierson, 'The Relations between England and Flanders before the Norman Conquest', *TRHS*, 4th ser. 23 (1941), 71–112, at 102.

Hereward and Flanders

expedition we are told the following facts.[18] Hereward becomes a soldier fighting on the side of the count of Flanders in his struggle against his neighbour, the count of Guînes, and comes up against the latter's nephew or grandson (*nepos*) in particular, a man called Hoibrict. At Saint-Omer Hereward meets Turfrida, a clever girl of wealthy background and skilled in needlework, whose hand is being sought in marriage by the nephew or grandson (*nepos*) of the lord of Saint-Valéry. He spends time travelling around with other soldiers, participates in military contests (probably tournaments) at Bruges and Poitiers, and excels as a fighter and instructor of younger recruits. On one such occasion Hereward defeats Hoibrict and thereby makes a deep impression upon Turfrida, who falls in love with him and shows him her family's heirlooms. He is joined by his paternal cousins Siward the Blond and Siward the Red, who are mentioned earlier in the narrative as having been with him in Cornwall and Ireland, and kills several enemies. He joins the military expedition to *Scaldemariland*, described at some length, under the command of the count's son, Robert, his role as 'leader of the soldiers' (*magister militum*) being to force the people of *Scaldemariland* to pay tribute to the Flemish. Just before peace negotiations are concluded, Hereward manages to buy two beautiful horses named Swallow and Lightfoot. He returns with Robert and the other soldiers to Flanders to find that the count has died and that his successor is absent. Finally, Hereward and his servant Martin Lightfoot revisit England briefly, while both Siwards remain behind to protect Turfrida, who is here called Hereward's wife.

In between the stays in Flanders, Hereward is said to have returned to England, where '... he wished to visit his father's house and his homeland, now subject to the rule of foreigners and almost ruined by the exactions of many men'.[19] This is an unambiguous reference to the conquest of England by the Normans. Hereward throws out the French occupant of his home and revenges the death of his younger brother. He is then knighted at Peterborough by Abbot Brand (1066–9), while his companions are made knights by the monk Wulfwine of Ely, and in this context Richard of Ely provides an interesting digression on the difference of opinion on knighthood between the English and French. Herward's next move involves the murder of Frederick, brother-in-law of William of Warenne, after which he returns to Flanders.

A second, much shorter, Flemish interlude follows when Hereward comes back from England. Rejoining his wife and cousins, he is asked to fight for Baldwin (*quodam praeclarissimo milite provinciae ipsius Baldewyno*, 'a most famous soldier of that province') in a struggle against the lord of Picquigny at which the lord of Brabant was present. Having done so Hereward returns to England for good, accompanied by his wife and by his two cousins.

[18] *Gesta Herewardi,* pp. 353–71.   [19] *Ibid.* p. 364.

'SCALDEMARILAND'

What are we to make of the Flemish incidents mentioned in the *Gesta Herewardi*? In respect of the expedition to *Scaldemariland* the answer is relatively easy, because we possess a hagiographical account, the *Vita S. Willibrordi*, written by Abbot Thiofrid of Echternach (*c.* 1081–after 1105) in 1104–5, which describes what is surely the same expedition from a different point of view.[20] The monastery of Echternach held land and a church dedicated to St Willibrord on Walcheren, one of the islands in the wide estuary of the river Scheldt,[21] and the last miracle appended to the *Vita S. Willibrordi* concerns an attempt by a younger son of Count Baldwin of Flanders to extract unpaid taxes from the inhabitants and those of neighbouring islands. He is said to have led an army of French- and German-speaking troops by land and sea across the *Scaldemermur*. A struggle between his army and local forces ensued and the invaders were driven back with much loss of life, though only three islanders were killed. Feeling victorious, the islanders sent two banners of the Flemish army to Echternach, the home of the saint to whom they credited their victory. However, the victory over the Flemish had left them divided and internal strife broke out. Some time later, therefore, Abbot Thiofrid travelled to Walcheren, where he visited the church of St Willibrord and negotiated a settlement. He took with him as an interpreter and guide a former soldier called Ekehard, whom he acknowledges as his principal informant concerning the earlier fighting. Since the abbot describes him as a monk of Echternach, Ekehard may well have been one of the islanders who took the banners there but stayed behind while the others returned.[22]

One must bear in mind when comparing the stories contained in the *Vita S. Willibrordi* and *Gesta Herewardi* that the two texts were written for different purposes and represent opposite sides of the war described:[23] the *Gesta Herewardi* is centered on the deeds of its hero Hereward, a mercenary in Flemish service, whereas the Echternach text is concerned with the defence of its property against Flemish encroachment. Naturally, the accounts differ. Both, however, identify the leader of the expedition as Robert, and as the count of Flanders's

---

[20] *Vita S. Willibrordi auctore Thiofrido abbate Epternacensi*, ed. A. Poncelet, *Acta SS*, Nov. III (Brussels, 1910), 459–83, at 480–3. For Thiofrid as hagiographer, see *Thiofridi abbatis Epternacensis Flores epytaphii sanctorum*, ed. M. C. Ferrari, CCCM 133 (Turnhout, 1996), pp. viii–ix, where the *Vita S. Willibrordi* is dated to 1104–5.

[21] The *Vita S. Willibrordi* is the earliest written testimony to Echternach's possessions on Walcheren. For later charters referring to Walcheren, see C. Wampach, *Geschichte der Grundherrschaft Echternach im Frühmittelalter*, 2 vols. (Luxembourg, 1930), nos. 204–7 (pp. 335–45). [22] *Vita S. Willibrordi*, pp. 481 and 482.

[23] J. Huizinga, 'Scaldemariland', in his *Verzamelde Werken, I: Oud-Indie, Nederland* (Haarlem, 1948), pp. 554–69 (originally published in: *Mededelingen der Koninklijke Akademie van Wetenschappen, afd. Letterkunde* 84, ser. B, no. 2 (1937), 2–11) at 556.

younger son. He must surely have been Robert 'the Frisian', second son of count Baldwin V (1035–67), who was count of Flanders himself from 1071 to 1093.[24] In 1063 he married Gertrude, widow of Count Floris I of Holland, and as her husband he acted from time to time as regent for her young son Thierry V. During the years 1063 and 1071 he spent time in Flanders and Holland while attempting to extend his authority over the border area between Flanders and Holland, alternately representing Flemish and Dutch interests.[25]

Both accounts also use the same topographical name to describe the target of the expedition, which is the main reason for believing that they refer to the same events. The names *Scaldemermur* and *Scaldemarienses* occur in late medieval records, but they are found in no eleventh- or early-twelfth-century records apart from the *Gesta Herewardi* and the *Vita S. Willibrordi*. J. Huizinga has identified these toponyms with the collection of islands in the estuary of Scheldt which now form part of the province of Zeeland in the Netherlands.[26] In late medieval documents the northern and southern borders of the island area are named respectively *Scoudemarediep* and *Scaldemermur*. The latter name is clearly a composite of *Scalde* (Scheldt) and *mere* (extended sea water) or *mare* (lake or, unusually, sea), these two words being often interchangeable in Old Dutch. Together with its related form *Scaldemare[land]* it applied to the group of islands on the southern fringe of the area; in other words, to the area just north-west of the place where the Scheldt estuary begins. The Echternach text states that across *Scaldemermur* was Walcheren, where Echternach's property was situated; the town of Middelburg is mentioned several times. No specific geographical details are given in the *Gesta Herewardi*, apart from the sand dunes (*montana*), possibly of Walcheren, and unspecified *castra Scaldemariensium*, which may be identified with the fortifications of Middelburg, Domburg and Souburg, originally built by its inhabitants against the Vikings.[27] The references in both texts to the use of ships by the expedition leader illustrates the fact that from Flanders one had to cross water in order to reach the islands.

The *Gesta Herewardi* is unique in saying that the *Scaldemarienses* agreed to pay double the tribute they originally paid to the Flemish as part of a new settlement, rather than reaffirm what they used to pay in the times of their fathers.[28] Nothing is known about tribute or tax being paid by the islands of Zeeland to the count of Flanders. However, the area consisting of the island of Walcheren and some others in the estuary of the Scheldt as well as the land of Waes and the Four Offices had been given to the Flemish count in 1012 by King Henry II

---

[24] *Gesta Herewardi*, p. 360; *Vita S. Willibrordi*, p. 480.
[25] C. Verlinden, *Robert I le Frison, comte de Flandre; étude d'histoire politique* (Antwerp, 1935), pp. 27–39.
[26] Huizinga, 'Scaldemariland', pp. 561–9.
[27] P. H. Sawyer, *Kings and Vikings. Scandinavia and Europe AD 700–1200* (London, 1982), pp. 82–3.
[28] *Gesta Herewardi*, pp. 363–4.

(1002–24) and that grant had been confirmed in 1056 by Agnes, widow of King Henry III (1039–56), on behalf of her son Henry IV (1056–1106).[29] Some renegotiation of the islanders' taxation payable to the count presumably took place and it is likely, but at present unverifiable, that Robert the Frisian's expedition, which according to the *Gesta Herewardi* took place on the orders of Robert's father, was the result of the islanders' refusal to pay their due.[30] The expedition may also have been intended as a warning to Bishop William of Utrecht, who since 1064 had held the former territory of Thierry IV around the delta of the river Rhine: the *comitatus in Westflinge* (the country of *Westflinge*) and the land *circa horas Reni* (around the mouth of the Rhine), due to extensive grants by King Henry IV.[31] The bishop had prepared the way for those royal grants by making sure that the abbey of Echternach, which held many churches in the area, would not object. To this effect Bishop William and Abbot Reginbert, Thiofrid's predecessor, concluded a treaty, confirmed by Henry IV in December 1063.[32] In short, therefore, the historical context of rivalry between the territorial princes, neighbouring the estuaries of the Scheldt and the Rhine, provides a satisfactory explanation for the *Scaldemariland* expedition by Robert the Frisian, who with his father's authorization attempted to force the islanders to pay tribute. The authenticity of such an expedition is strengthened rather than weakened by the account in the *Gesta Herewardi*.

As far as the date of the expedition is concerned, the contemporary sources are very unhelpful.[33] The *Annals of Saint-Bertin* mention that in 1063 'Robert, the younger son of the most powerful count Baldwin, surreptitiously entered Frisia', which is commonly interpreted as a reference to Robert the Frisian's contested acceptance of the regency for Gertrude's son Thierry V.[34] According to Lambert of Hersfeld, who wrote in the late 1070s and early 1080s, Robert was

---

[29] F. Ganshof, *La Flandre sous les premiers comtes* (Brussels, 1944), pp. 33 and 36.

[30] It is significant that Rober 'the Frisian' celebrated Whitsun 1067 with his parents and his brother Baldwin (Verlinden, *Robert I le Frison*, p. 43); on this occasion the planning of the expedition may have begun. For the independence felt by the freemen of the coastal areas of what is now the Netherlands, including the islands of Zeeland, since the Viking attacks, and their reluctance to accept the imposition of taxes, see D. Blok, 'Holland und Westfriesland', *FS* 3 (1969), 347–61, at 356–7.

[31] MGH Dipl. reg. et imp., 6: Diplomata Heinrici IV, ed. D. v. Gladiss and A. Gawlik, 3 vols. (Weimar and Hanover, 1952–78) I, no. 128 (pp. 167–8); Verlinden, *Robert I le Frison*, pp. 38–9; Blok, 'Holland und Westfriesland', pp. 356–7; and R. Nip, *Arnulfus van Oudenburg, Bisschop van Soissons (d. 1087), Mens en Model; een Bronnenstudie* (Groningen, 1995), pp. 116–17.

[32] MGH Dipl. reg. et imp., 6 I, no. 116 (pp. 152–5) and Wampach I, 2, no. 192 (pp. 308–11).

[33] Unaware of the existence of the *Gesta Herewardi*, Verlinden (*Robert I le Frison*, p. 34) suggested a date *c.* 1083, rejecting earlier suggestions for a date between 1061 and 1063.

[34] *Les Annales de Saint-Piere de Gand et de Saint-Amand*, ed. P. Grierson (Brussels, 1937), p. 27: 'Rodbertus, Baldwini potentissimi iunior filius, Fresiam subintrat.' For the most recent discussion of the matter, see Nip, *Arnulfus van Oudenburg*, pp. 115–17.

twice beaten back during expeditions to Frisia, 'the neighbour of Flanders', before he became count of Flanders.[35] The context suggests a period before Florence I's death in 1061, but Lampert's chronology is notoriously weak and would certainly allow the possibility that one of the two Flemish expeditions into neighbouring Frisia was the one to *Scaldemariland*. The account in the *Gesta Herewardi*, however, supplies a date which is extremely plausible. According to this account, the Flemish army returned to Flanders at a time when the old count – Baldwin V – had died and the new count and successor – Baldwin VI, eldest brother of Robert 'the Frisian' – was absent. Since Baldwin V is known to have died on 1 September 1067, and since the future Baldwin VI (1067–70) was very probably occupied at that time with affairs elsewhere, either in Hainault, which he ruled as Baldwin I (1051–70), or in Ponthieu, we may infer that the expedition took place in the (late) summer of 1067.[36]

Before finishing with the *Scaldemariland* expedition it is important to point out that at least one other detail of the *Gesta Herewardi* story can be confirmed from other contemporary material. The availability of horses from the islands, particularly from Walcheren, is also mentioned in the *Translation of St Lewinna* written by Drogo of St Winnocsbergen between 1058 and 1068,[37] and thus supports the likelihood that in reality any mercenary might have taken the opportunity to acquire horses while he was in the vicinity.[38]

CAMBRAI

Having established the authenticity of the expedition by Robert 'the Frisian' to *Scaldemariland* as described in the *Gesta Herewardi* we are still left with the question of whether Hereward was really present, or whether Richard of Ely, or his informants, made up the story of his Flemish mercenary career, inspired perhaps by the historical reality of many English aristocratic exiles and mercenaries who in the mid-eleventh century had flocked to Flanders. Queen Emma was welcomed by Count Baldwin V in 1037; he provided her with a house in

---

[35] Lampert von Hersfeld, *Annalen,* ed. A. Schmidt and W. D. Fritz, Ausgewählte Quellen zur deutschen Geschichte des Mittelalters, Freiherr vom Stein Gedächtnisausgabe 13 (Berlin, 1960), 138: '... in Fresiam, quae confinis est Flandriae, cui Thidericus quondam comes et post hunc Florentius frater eius imperaverat, irruptionem fecit. Bis ibi commisso prelio victus et fugatus est' ('... he [Robert] attacked Frisia, the neighbour of Flanders, which was ruled first by Thierry [IV 1039–49] and later by Florence [I 1049–61]. Twice he launched a war there but was beaten and put to flight'). See Nip, *Arnulfus van Oudenburg*, pp. 116–17.

[36] Huizinga, 'Scaldemariland', p. 561. This date is also accepted by Blok, 'Holland und Westfriesland', p. 357. For Count Baldwin VI's presence in Ponthieu in the (early) autumn, see below, p. 218, n. 80.

[37] N. Huyghebaert, 'Un moine hagiographe: Drogon de Bergues', *Sacris Erudiri* 20 (1971), 191–256, at 211.

[38] *Ex Drogonis translatione S. Lewinnae*, ed. O. Holder-Egger, MGH, SS 15.2 (Hanover, 1888), 782–9, at 789. Cf. Huizinga, 'Scaldemariland', p. 558, n. 1.

Bruges and she stayed till 1040.[39] Osgod Clapa was likewise welcomed by Baldwin in 1049,[40] as were the Godwine family in 1051. Count Baldwin V had married off his half-sister Judith to Godwine's son Tostig,[41] and he offered the couple shelter in the autumn of 1065. In 1068 the count's son and successor, Count Baldwin VI (1067–70), welcomed King Harold's mother Gytha with at least one daughter.[42] Four years later, the then count Robert 'the Frisian' allowed both Edgar the Ætheling and the Northumbrian nobleman Gospatric, later earl of Dunbar, to stay for two years before they left for Scotland.[43] Gospatric, son of Aldgitha, a granddaughter of King Æthelred II, and of Maldred son of Crinan, had the earldom of Northumbria taken away from him by William the Conqueror; with the Ætheling he sought refuge first in Scotland and thereafter in Flanders, a county he knew well because of his earlier connection with Earl Tostig and Judith, whom he had escorted to Rome in 1061.[44] There is no shortage of evidence for the presence of English aristocratic exiles and active soldiers in Flanders in the middle of the eleventh century.

It has been universally accepted that no continental source explicitly mentions Hereward's presence in Flanders. There is diplomatic evidence, however, that may throw light on his mercenary career in Flanders. One of the witnesses to an original charter of Bishop Lietbert of Cambrai (1051–76), datable to early 1065, is listed as *miles Herivvardi*.[45] This Hereward is one of nine *milites*, soldiers or knights, whose names follow those of six archdeacons attesting the bishop's foundation charter of the monastery of Saint-Sepulchre. The charter itself was written and witnessed at Cambrai before it was sent to King Henry IV at Mainz or Worms for confirmation at the end of March or the beginning of April of that year.[46] The building of the monastery was part of an ambitious programme by Bishop Lietbert of Cambrai to enlarge the city and, more importantly, to use

---

[39] *Encomium Emmae reginae*, ed. A. Campbell with a supplementary introduction by S. Keynes, Camden Classic Reprints 4 (Cambridge, 1998), 46–8.

[40] *Anglo-Saxon Chronicle*, 'C', s.a. 1049, ed. Plummer I, 168 and 'D', s.a. 1050 [for 1049], *ibid.* I, 169; John of Worcester, s. a. 1049 (ed. Darlington, McGurk and Bray) II, 550–1.

[41] *The Life of King Edward Who Rests at Westminster*, ed. F. Barlow, 2nd ed. (Oxford, 1992), pp. 38–40.

[42] *Anglo-Saxon Chronicle*, 'D', s.a. 1067 [for 1068], ed. Plummer I, 202.

[43] *Anglo-Saxon Chronicle*, 'D', s.a. 1075 [for 1074], ed. Plummer I, 209; N. Hooper, 'Edgar the Aetheling, Anglo-Saxon Prince, Rebel and Crusader', *ASE* 14 (1985), 197–214, at 204.

[44] *The Life of King Edward*, ed. Barlow, pp. 54–7 and 56, n. 136; *De obsessione Dunelmi* in *Symeonis monachi opera omnia*, ed. T. Arnold, 2 vols., RS (London, 1882–5) I, 215–20.

[45] MGH Dipl. reg. et imp., 6 III, no. 147a (pp. 720–2, at 722). This is the first occasion that the charter has been printed in full with a witness list. It had been known to historians since the eighteenth century but only in an abbreviated form without witnesses; see, e.g., *Gallia Christiana*, ed. D. de Sainte-Marthe, 13 vols. (Paris 1715–85) III, cols. 118–19.

[46] It is one of a few royal confirmation charters not drawn up royal scribes, but instead by the beneficiary (for a discussion, see the introduction to Bishop Lietbert's charter of 1066, MGH Dipl. reg. et imp., 6 I, no. 178 (pp. 231–3, at 232)).

Hereward and Flanders

the new building as part of a new fortification lay-out on the southern fringe of the town.[47] In order to protect the monastery it was brought within its battlements and ditch. The need for new defence work had became imperative due to the endemic strife caused by two political movements. Within the city there was internal warfare between the bishop, who was also count of Cambrai, and the castellans, John of Arras and Hugh, while the city of Cambrai as a whole was in a vulnerable position because of the predatory advances from the counts of Flanders. In 1076 castellan Hugh was defeated and he left for England.[48] Thus internal and external threats encouraged Bishop Lietbert to surround himself with troops of footsoldiers, mounted soldiers and any other military help he could get.[49] Fortification work and fighting required manpower, and one of the bishop's priorities, therefore, would have been to recruit mercenaries to support him. Could not the English Hereward have been one of them? Was he not *Herivvardus*? The name is a Germanic one but known in France, albeit on a very modest scale and mostly in eastern France, it seems.[50] But no other person with that name is known from any Flemish or northern French record. The time, early 1065, and the place, Cambrai in the south-eastern corner of Flanders, could be right and would have offered Hereward an opportunity to show off his mercenary skills. With regard to the time, it is important to return to the *Gesta Herewardi* and look closely at the date given there for Hereward's arrival in Flanders.

According to the *Gesta*, Hereward's host after he was shipwrecked was Manasses the Old, that is, Count Manasses I of Guînes who was active in the mid-eleventh century: he witnessed a charter in 1056 and his son Baldwin, who ruled until 1091, is known to have succeeded him by 1065.[51] The county of

---

[47] *Gesta episcoporum Cameracensium*, ed. L. Bethmann, MGH SS 7 (Hanover, 1846), 489–97; *Chronicon s. Andreae castri Cameracesii, ibid.* 526–50, at 536–7 and the *Vita Lietberti, ibid.* 537, n. 25 (excerpts from the otherwise unpublished *Vita Lietberti* are printed in footnotes to the *Chronicon s. Andreae*). For a commentary on Bishop Lietbert's career and his fortification work, see M. Rouche, 'Cambrai, du comte mérovingien à l'évêque impérial', *Histoire de Cambrai*, ed. L. Trenard (Lille, 1982), pp. 11–42, at 33–5 and 37–8; see also the reconstructed drawing of Cambrai in Bishop Lietbert's time, *ibid.* p. 25.

[48] *Gesta episcoporum Cameracensium*, p. 499: . . . *fugatum Hugonem recepit Anglia* ('. . .England welcomed the fugitive Hugh').

[49] For the bishop's troops of *equites* and *pedites* as well as *milites*, see *ibid.* p. 495. In 1077, shortly after Bishop Lietbert's death under his successor Bishop Gerard II (1076–92), Cambrai established a 'commune' (H. Platelle, 'Les luttes communales et l'organisation municipale (1075–1313)', *Histoire de Cambrai*, ed. Trenard, pp. 43–61, at 45–8).

[50] M. T. Morlet, *Les Noms de personne sur le territoire de l'ancienne Gaule du VIe au XIIe siècle. I: Les noms issus du germanique continental et les créations gallo-germaniques* (Paris, 1968), pp. 124 and 127.

[51] For the counts of Guînes, see L. Vanderkindere, *Histoire de la formation territoriale des principautés belges au Moyen Age*, 2nd ed., 2 vols. (Brussels, 1899–1902) I, 186–7; Manasses I witnessed the 1056 charter of Count Baldwin V of Flanders for St Peter at Gent which was also witnessed by Guy, later bishop of Amiens, Count Guy of Ponthieu, Count Roger of Saint-Pol and Earl

Guînes was situated on the coast of Flanders just south of Bourbourg and adjacent to the estuary of the river Aa that led to the town of Saint-Omer. Any shipwreck off the coast of Guînes was the responsibility of the count of Guînes, rather than of the count of Flanders, and that may explain why Hereward was led to Count Manasses. The *Gesta* states that Hereward arrived while Manasses was still count, which dates his arrival to the early 1060s, possibly to 1064, but certainly not later than 1065. The author of the *Gesta* places Hereward's actions in western Flanders and mentions specifically Saint-Omer, Bruges and (much further south) Poitiers, cities that are singled out for what must have been military competitions, shows or tournaments. Little is known about these shows, but they are usually dated to the late eleventh century, with the first narrative reference, other than in the *Gesta Herewardi*, being to Poitiers in 1067 and the first documentary evidence coming from Valenciennes in 1114.[52] Considering the well-attested military activity in the Cambrai-Valenciennes area in the 1060s and 1070s, tournaments or their early equivalents would surely have attracted mercenary soldiers. And if Hereward was attracted to the neighbourhood he could well have decided to stay at Cambrai and work for Bishop Lietbert before moving on to another master.

A short stay in the Cambrai area may also offer a possible explanation of the *Gesta Herewardi*'s story of Hereward's second stay in Flanders, where he is supposed to have helped the very famous Baldwin, perhaps the later Baldwin II of Hainault,[53] in a battle against the *vidame* of Picquigny,[54] at which the lord

---

Harold of Wessex (see Grierson, 'The Relations between England and Flanders', pp. 100–1; H. J. Tanner, 'The Expansion of the Power and Influence of the Counts of Boulogne under Eustace II', *ANS* 14 (1991), 251–86, at 269, n. 40). Count Baldwin of Guînes' earliest attestation comes in a charter of King Philip I of France issued at Corbie, which can be dated to a time after 4 August 1065 (*Recueil des actes de Philippe I roi de France (1059–1108)*, ed. M. Prou (Paris, 1908), no. xxiii, p. 66). For Count Manasses II, see *Actes des comtes de Flandre 1071–1128*, ed. F. Vercauteren (Brussels, 1938), nos. 13, 17, 21, 41, 90 and 122; his earliest appearance as count seems to have been in 1091 (*Les Chartes de Saint Bertin*, ed. D. Haigneré, 4 vols. (Saint-Omer, 1886–99) I, no. 87, p. 34). In Vercauteren, no. 122, dated to 1122x1127, he is mentioned as Count Baldwin's successor. Lambert of Ardres in his *Historia comitum Ghisnensium* (ed. I. Heller, MGH SS 24 (Hanover, 1879), 550–642) does not mention Manasses I.

[52] *Gesta Herewardi*, p. 356: 'certamina sollempniarum quae apud Pontes iam et Pictavem fiunt' [this text is quoted from the manuscript] ('festive competitions, which then took place at Bruges and Poitiers'). M. Parisse, 'Le tournoi en France des origines à la fin du XIIIe siècle', *Das ritterliche Turnier im Mittelalter. Beiträge zu einer vergleichenden Formen- und Verhaltensgeschichte des Rittertums*, ed. J. Fleckenstein (Göttingen, 1985), pp. 175–211, at 180–2; H. Platelle, 'L' essor des principautés', *Histoire des provinces françaises du nord*, ed. A. Lottin, 2 vols. (Dunkirk, 1989) II, 1–115 at 36–7.

[53] Perhaps Count Baldwin VI of Flanders (1067–70), who was also Baldwin I of Hainault (1051–70) or, more likely, his son Baldwin, who became Baldwin II of Hainault (1076/81–98).

[54] The lord, *vidame*, of Picquigny at this time was Arnulf, father of Wermund of Picquigny who acted alongside Count Charles the Good of Flanders as judge in 1122 (*Actes des comtes de Flandre*,

(*dominus*) of Brabant was also present. The lord of Brabant and Louvain at the time of the conquest was Henry II (1063–79), whose granddaughter Adeliza in 1121 became the second wife of King Henry I of England (1100–35).[55] Due to the geographical position of Picquigny, the likely arena of fighting would have been in the frontier area of Flanders, Amiens and Vermandois, south-west of Cambrai, a country that would have been well known to anyone who had fought for the bishop of Cambrai.[56]

There is no cast-iron proof that the *Herivvardus* of the 1065 Cambrai charter is the same as our Hereward. However, considering the bishop's need for expert military advice and workmanship combined with the story in the *Gesta Herewardi* that Hereward went to Flanders the chances of the two men being the same are surely great. If the identification can be accepted, the omission of any explicit reference to Hereward's possible stay in Cambrai from the *Gesta Herewardi* may be due to the author's prime interest in western Flanders and in particular to Saint-Omer, the home town of Turfrida. It is to that place that we must now turn.

SAINT-OMER

The only place in Flanders that features prominently in the *Gesta Herewardi* is Saint-Omer. Its ties with England have always been strong and they were particularly so in the middle of the eleventh century.[57] Ecclesiastical and secular contacts are prominently recorded in reliable sources, Flemish and English. Most information centres on the monastery of Saint-Bertin at Saint-Omer from which two Flemish monks migrated to England. In 1041–2, a monk of Saint-Bertin wrote the *Encomium Emmae reginae* for the dowager queen Emma of England.[58] The hagiographer Goscelin of Saint-Bertin probably left Flanders *c.* 1058 in the company of Bishop Herman of Wiltshire and spent the next fifty

---

ed. Vercauteren, no. 108). In 1113 Arnulf's daughter, wife of Judhael of Totnes, was delighted to welcome at her house in Barnstaple the monks of Laon on their relic trip and to entertain them for three days on account of the fact that they were compatriots (*Hermanni monachi de miraculis S. Mariae Laudunensis*, PL 156, cols. 961–1018, at 983–4). For Judhael, see J. B. Williams, 'Judhael of Totnes: the Life and Times of a Post-Conquest Baron', *ANS* 16 (1993), 271–89, at 284–5. Another of Arnulf's daughters, Millesende, was married to William II, castellan of Saint-Omer. After the conquest in 1066 Ansculf of Picquigny became sheriff (DB i, fols. 36r and 148v: Ansculf of Picquigny and his son William).

[55] Henry II of Louvain had two sons: Henry III (1079–95) and Godfrey the Bearded (1096–1139; from 1106 duke of Lower Lotharingia). Adeliza was a daughter of the latter (*The Ecclesiastical History of Orderic Vitalis*, ed. M. Chibnall, 6 vols. (Oxford, 1969–80) VI, 308).

[56] For a discussion of the rivalries there, see Ganshof, *La Flandre*, pp. 36–7.

[57] The classic study of relations between Flanders and England remains Grierson, 'The Relations between England and Flanders'; see also V. Ortenberg, *The English Church and the Continent in the Tenth and Eleventh Centuries. Cultural, Spiritual and Artistic Exchanges* (Oxford, 1992), pp. 21–40.

[58] *Encomium Emmae reginae*, ed. Campbell, pp. 46–8.

Elisabeth van Houts

years as a wandering scholar in England. He, or Folcard (see below), is the likely author of the *Vita regis Edwardi*, the biography of King Edward the Confessor.[59] Folcard's arrival in England from Saint-Bertin cannot be dated more precisely than between 1050 and 1069. He knew Archbishop Ealdred of York to whom he dedicated one of his works. He became abbot of Thorney Abbey, but in 1085 was deposed, together with Wulfketel of Crowland, by Archbishop Lanfranc of Canterbury.[60] Despite the fact that Folcard's career is much more obscure than Goscelin's, for our purpose it is intriguing that both men formed living links between Saint-Omer and the Fenland monasteries of Thorney (Folcard) and Peterborough, Ramsey and Ely, where Goscelin spent some time in the 1080s.[61]

The secular ties concern the town of Saint-Omer, rather than its monasteries. When in the autumn of 1065 Count Baldwin V of Flanders offered shelter to his half-sister Judith, he invested her husband Tostig with quite exceptional military power. He appointed Tostig as his deputy commander of Saint-Omer, put his forces there at his disposal, gave him the revenues of the town and provided him with a house and an estate.[62] The military responsibility bestowed upon Tostig is particularly interesting, because it raises the question whether he worked alongside or under the command of Saint-Omer's castellan, who at that time until the battle of Cassel in February 1071 was Wulfric Rabel, son of the previous castellan Lambert.[63] It also raises the question whether those who otherwise received the town's revenues may have felt any resentment against Tostig. Whatever the local sentiments may have been, for us the more important question is when and why would Hereward have gone to Saint-Omer?

We might speculate that he had come to Saint-Omer on account of Earl Tostig's new appointment which he held from the late autumn of 1065 to the spring of 1066.[64] An Englishman in Tostig's position would undoubtedly have attracted mercenaries, and not only English soldiers, looking for a job. If the identification of the *miles Herivvardi* in the Cambrai charter with the Englishman Hereward can be accepted, Hereward would have been in Cambrai when the news of Earl Tostig's arrival spread through Flanders. For Hereward the attrac-

---

[59] *The Life of King Edward*, ed. Barlow, pp. xlvii–xlix.
[60] *Ibid.* pp. lii–lvii; *The Heads of Religious Houses, England and Wales, 940–1216*, ed. D. Knowles, C. N. L. Brooke and V. C. M. London (Cambridge, 1972), pp. 42 and 74.
[61] *The Life of King Edward*, ed. Barlow, p. 140. [62] *Ibid.* pp. 80–3, at 82.
[63] E. Warlop, *The Flemish Nobility before 1300*, trans. J. B. Ross and H. Vandermoere, 4 vols. (Kortrijk, 1975) IV, 1106–16, at 1111 and Verlinden, *Robert I le Frison*, pp. 68–70. At Cassel, Wulfric was involved in the capture of Robert the Frisian. Two weeks later he betrayed Saint-Omer to King Philip I, enabling the latter to launch a vengeful attack on the town. As the castellan of Saint-Omer he disappears from the Flemish sources after March 1071 and his subsequent history is unknown. It is, however, possible that he, like Hugh of Cambrai five years later, may have gone to England. [64] See above, n. 62.

tion of having an English, rather than a Flemish, master would have been great. Although in the autumn of 1065 Tostig's rivalry with his brother Harold would have been known, his aspirations to the throne of England would have peaked after King Edward's death in early January 1066.[65] This might have fuelled Hereward's hope of a legitimate return to England under the aegis of a new king who would abolish his status as an exile.[66] Hereward's stay at Saint-Omer lasted presumably until his employment with Robert 'the Frisian' which, as we have seen, dates from the (early) summer of 1067. While at Saint-Omer he also probably became acquainted with two other individuals mentioned in the *Gesta Herewardi*, Gilbert of Gent, later the the wealthiest Flemish post-Conquest landholder in England, and Frederick of Oosterzele-Scheldewindeke, better known as brother-in-law of William of Warenne, whom he would later kill in England. Before we discuss Turfrida's origin at Saint-Omer we will look at Hereward's connections with Gilbert of Gent and Frederick of Oosterzele.

GILBERT OF GENT

Hereward is linked with Gilbert of Gent in a perplexing story belonging to the Flemish sections of the *Gesta Herewardi*. The most baffling aspect of it is that it is related before the stories of his adventures in Cornwall, Ireland and Flanders and therefore presumably refers to a pre-Conquest period. We have no other reason to suppose that Gilbert, who was clearly the wealthiest Flemish landholder after 1066, was in England at that time.[67] The story in the *Gesta* goes as follows. Allegedly an exile at the time, Hereward comes under the protection of Gilbert of Gent, who is said to be his godfather. Gilbert invites him and his servant Martin Lightfoot to join him in Northumbria, where Hereward engages in a famous fight with a bear brought to England from Norway. So memorable is this encounter that 'women and girls sing about him in their dances'. Hereward

---

[65] For Tostig's claim, see *The Life of King Edward*, ed. Barlow, p. lxv; E. M. C. van Houts, 'The Norman Conquest through European Eyes', *EHR* 110 (1995), 832–53, at 838–9.

[66] J. H. Round, *Feudal England; Historical Studies on the Eleventh and Twelfth Centuries* (London, 1895), p. 162 argues that the exile was caused by Hereward's involvement in the siege of Ely, and post-dates it to a time after the Norman Conquest. The Pseudo-Ingulf (see above, p. 201, n. 2) dates Hereward's exile to 1062, but gives no reasons for this date.

[67] The best modern study of the Gent family in England is M. Abbott, 'The Gand Family in England 1066–1191' (unpubl. Ph.D. dissertation, Cambridge Univ., 1973). Otherwise the following are useful: R. M. Sherman, 'The Continental Origins of the Ghent Family of Lincolnshire', *Nottingham Med. Stud.* 22 (1978), 23–35; R. H. George, 'The Contribution of Flanders to the Conquest of England, 1065–86', *Revue belge d'histoire et de philologie* 5 (1926), 81–99; J. Verberckmoes, 'Flemish Tenants-in-Chief in Domesday England', *ibid.* 66 (1988), 725–99; *Early Yorkshire Charters*, ed. Farrer II (Edinburgh, 1915), pp. 431–6. For the Flemish origins of the Aalst family and its later branches, see Warlop, *The Flemish Nobility* III, 587–3. Dr Warlop, unfortunately, did not use any English source material on the family. None of the authors cited used the *Gesta Herewardi*.

gains the rank and status of a knight, but he choses not take up this honour at once. Overwhelmed by jealousy, his companions attempt to murder him. When this attack founders Hereward decides to part with Gilbert's company despite the pleas of Gilbert's (unnamed) wife that he should stay and perhaps be adopted in place of their sickly son should he die. Hereward ignores this request and leaves.

As far as we can tell, Gilbert I of Gent owed his fortune in England primarily to his participation in the Conquest. Though he is not mentioned in the context of the events of 1066, he was a member of the occupying forces at York in September 1069.[68] It is conceivable that he first arrived in England after the Conquest not having taken part in the battle of Hastings or the early campaigns, but considering the huge grants of land he later received his participation right from the start of the Conquest seems more likely. Flemish charter material shows that he was a younger son of Ralph of Aalst or Alost, hereditary advocate of St Peter's at Gent, and Gisela, daughter of Frederick of Luxembourg. Through his mother, Gilbert was a first cousin once removed of Matilda of Flanders, wife of William the Conqueror, whose paternal grandmother was Gisela's sister Ogiva. Gilbert's eldest brother was Baldwin I of Gent (d. 1082), his second older brother was Ralph, comital chamberlain of Flanders, and his youngest brother was Ragenfridus.[69] Kinship with the counts of Flanders and their officers clearly was not a disadvantage for Gilbert at the time of the Norman Conquest of England. Gilbert married Alice, the daughter of Hugh II of Montfort-sur-Risle, one of the Conqueror's Norman magnates.[70] While based in England and before his death in *c.* 1095,[71] he remained in touch with his Flemish siblings, occasionally travelling to the Continent: in 1075 we find him in the company of his brother Baldwin I of Gent.[72] His eldest son and heir was Gilbert, who died between *c.* 1095 and 1115, and probably very near to the first of these two dates;[73] the second son was Walter (d. 1139), who took Gilbert's place as heir and became his father's successor; the third, Robert (d. 1154), was a priest and became chancellor of King Stephen and dean of York; the fourth, Hugh, in due course inherited his mother's lands in Normandy as Hugh IV of Montfort; and a fifth son Ralph disappears from the

---

[68] Simeon of Durham, *Historia regum*, s.a. 1069, in: *Symeonis monachi opera omnia*, ed. Arnold II, 188.

[69] Abbott, 'The Gand Family', pp. 19–20; Sherman, 'The Continental Origins', pp. 25–6; Warlop, *The Flemish Nobility* III, 590.

[70] *The Gesta Normannorum Ducum of William of Jumièges, Orderic Vitalis and Robert of Torigni*, ed. E. M. C. van Houts, 2 vols. (Oxford, 1992–5) II, 176–7.   [71] Abbott, 'The Gand Family', p. 23.

[72] *Chronicon monasterii Watinensis*, ed. O. Holder-Egger, MGH SS 24 (Hanover, 1883), 169: '. . . Giselbertus, frater Balduini Gandensis, qui ab Anglia tunc venerat . . .' ('Gilbert, brother of Baldwin of Gent, who then came from England').

[73] Abbott, 'The Gand Family', pp. 24, 83 and 252.

sources after 1115.[74] One of his daughters married Hugh of Grandmesnil.[75] Most of his lands were situated in Lincolnshire and Northamptonshire, though little pockets can be identified in the Midlands and further north in Yorkshire.[76] Gilbert (re)founded Bardney Abbey in Lincolnshire, dedicated to St Peter and St Paul and St Oswald, as a cell of Charroux in 1086–7.[77]

Why Richard of Ely should link Gilbert of Gent and Hereward, together with Martin Lightfoot, in a personal relationship against a pre-Conquest Northumbrian background, must remain a mystery, unless new evidence can be found. The easiest solution to this problem is to dismiss it on the grounds that Richard of Ely, or his informers, or indeed Leofric as author of the Old English Life, was confused about the chronology. If Hereward had met Gilbert of Gent before the Norman Conquest of England the most likely place would have been Flanders, and not England.

Other parts of the *Gesta*'s account of Hereward and Gilbert are also suspicious. The reference to a bearfight reads like pure fiction, and the mention of a half-human bear certainly does not inspire confidence. On the other hand, there is evidence for trading in bears for the purpose of fighting and entertainment, for the late-twelfth-century chronicle of the counts of Ardres and Guînes mentions how a bear from England was imported to Guînes for the specific purpose of bear-fighting.[78] The phrase referring to women's songs celebrating Hereward's triumph over this bear comes so close to the Old Testament reference to women rejoicing after David's victory over Saul, that P. G. Schmidt is justified in his caution about using this particular phrase as evidence for pre-Conquest ballads sung about Hereward.[79]

---

[74] *Ibid*. pp. 24–8 based on charter material and *Early Yorkshire Charters*, ed. Farrer II, 426–33; *The Domesday Monachorum of Christ Church Canterbury*, ed. D. Douglas (London, 1944), pp. 67 and 70. Hugh IV was still alive *c*. 1147 (*Calendar of Documents Preserved in France I: AD 916–1206*, ed. J. H. Round (London, 1899), no. 358).

[75] *The Ecclesiastical History of Orderic Vitalis*, ed. Chibnall IV, 230–1.

[76] Abbott, 'The Gand Family', pp. 65–82; Verberckmoes, 'Flemish Tenants-in-Chief', p. 731.

[77] For the early history of Bardney, see *Bede's Ecclesiastical History of the English People*, ed. B. Colgrave and R. A. B. Mynors (Oxford, 1969), pp. 246–51; the charter for the refoundation, which quotes Bede's history, is edited from Bardney's cartulary (London, BL, Cotton Vespasian E. xx, 278v) by Abbott, 'The Gand Family', no. 1, pp. 248–50 and is discussed *ibid*. pp. 190–1. There is no reference to Bardney church or abbey in Domesday Book. For the refoundation, see G. Beech, 'Aquitanians and Flemings in the Refoundation of Bardney Abbey (Lincolnshire) in the Later Eleventh Century', *Haskins Soc. Jnl* 1 (1989), 73–90.

[78] *Lamberti Ardensis, Historia comitum Ghisnensium*, ed. I. Heller, MGH SS 24 (Hanover, 1879), 550–642, at 624–5, and the historical commentary by Warlop, *The Flemish Nobility* I, 71 and II, 391.

[79] P. G. Schmidt, 'Biblisches und hagiographisches Kolorit in den Gesta Herewardi', *The Bible in the Medieval World. Essays in Memory of Beryl Smalley*, ed. K. Walsh and D. Wood, Studies in Church History, Subsidia 4 (Oxford, 1985), 85–95, at 91–2.

FREDERICK, BROTHER-IN-LAW OF WILLIAM OF WARENNE

The *Gesta Herewardi* is one of only two sources to say that Hereward killed Frederick, brother-in-law of William of Warenne, one of William the Conqueror's close advisers. According to the *Gesta*, the murder took place in England during Hereward's brief visit there between his two stays in Flanders. Frederick was a member of the important aristocratic family of Oosterzele-Scheldewindeke, who were the hereditary advocates of Saint-Bertin at Saint-Omer. He was from a sufficiently distinguished background to have acted next after Count Baldwin VI as a witness to Count Guy of Amiens's gift to the abbey of Saint-Riquier in Ponthieu in the autumn of 1067.[80] His sister Gundrada married William of Warenne, one of William the Conqueror's Norman companions and the later earl of Surrey. Most of Frederick's considerable estates in East Anglia passed after his death to Gundreda's husband William and so into the Warenne family.[81] The so-called 'Hyde Chronicle', an early-twelfth-century source emanating from the Warenne circle, confirms the *Gesta Herewardi*'s story that Hereward killed Frederick, who is described as the brother (instead of the brother-in-law) of William of Warenne, in England.[82] The author of the 'Hyde Chronicle' seems to have been unaware of Hereward's career in Flanders, which he does not mention. He was well informed about the Warenne family, knew of the Flemish origins of William of Warenne's wife Gundreda and refers to the Warennes' continuing links with Flanders, explaining that while their eldest son William succeeded his father in England and Normandy, their second son Reginald succeeded to the Flemish family estates.[83] Charter evidence shows that the advocacy of Saint-Bertin stayed with both Warenne sons at least until the late 1090s and it links the Warenne family to land at Roquetoire near Saint-Omer until the late twelfth century.[84] The 'Hyde' Chronicle and the *Gesta Herewardi* reinforce each other's material on this family and the story of Frederick's murder by Hereward.[85] Not only Frederick and Gundreda, but also their brother Gerbod established ties with England as a result of the Conquest.

---

[80] *Ibid.* p. 45 and *Recueil des actes des comtes de Ponthieu (1026–1279)*, ed. C. Brunel (Paris, 1930), no. iv. The date raises the possiblity that Frederick had come back from England to Flanders with his brother Gerbod; see below, p. 219, n. 91.   [81] DB i, 196v and ii, 167v.

[82] *Chronica monasterii de Hida juxta Wintoniam*, in *Liber monasterii de Hyda*, ed. E. Edwards, RS (London, 1866), pp. 183–321, at 295.   [83] *Ibid.* p. 299.

[84] *Early Yorkshire Charters*, ed. Farrer and Clay VIII [Appendix A], pp. 45–6. *Les Chartes de Saint-Bertin*, ed. Haigneré I, nos. 87, 94, 325 and 365. By the beginning of the thirteenth century Lambert of Ardres knew of land in the county of Ardres-Guînes as belonging to the count of Warenne, but thought, erroneously, that the holdings dated back to the late tenth century (*Historia comitum Ghisnensium*, ed. Heller, p. 566: 'predia in manus Warennensis comitis' ('lands in the hand of the count of Warenne')).

[85] *Early Yorkshire Charters*, ed. Farrer and Clay VIII, 1–13 and Appendix A (pp. 40–6).

Hereward and Flanders

For a brief period between 1067 and early 1071 Gerbod was earl of Chester.[86] According to Orderic Vitalis, Gerbod was called back from England to Flanders because he had received a message from the men he had left behind in Flanders to administer his hereditary honour; however, upon his return Gerbod fell into the hands of his enemies and died.[87] But Orderic drew the wrong conclusion. Gerbod no doubt went home in connection with the war of succession following the death of Count Baldwin VI, but he did not die. Two continental chronicles explain that he took part in the battle of Cassel on 22 February 1071, where he killed Count Arnulf III (1070–1).[88] By way of penance he went to Rome where Pope Gregory VII prevented his self-imposed mutilation. Instead the pope recommended him to Abbot Hugh of Cluny, who absolved him from his crime and allowed him to become a monk. Thus Gerbod's 'disappearance' was due to his penitential pilgrimage and subsequent monastic vow, not because he died.[89]

The three 'English' siblings can be connected with an older brother, Arnulf or Arnold II of Oosterzele-Scheldewindeke, who was their father's successor to the extensive estates in northern Flanders.[90] He died in 1067, probably without leaving any children, for his lands near Gent went to two brothers known as Arnulf/Arnold III (d. 1124 x1138) and Gerbod III (d. 1096), whom Warlop has identified as the sons of Gerbod II, known to us as the earl of Chester and monk of Cluny.[91] These two brothers knew Baldwin I of Gent, Gilbert of Gent's eldest brother, who as advocate of St Peter's at Gent was involved in the return of the allodium at Oosterzele by the two brothers to the abbey of St Bavo at Gent, which their uncle Arnulf/Arnold I had alienated.[92] A similar restitution of land there was made to Saint-Bertin.[93] They also presented Saint-Bertin with land at Roquetoire, the very place where, as we have seen, the Warenne family

---

[86] C. P. Lewis, 'The Formation of the Honor of Chester 1066–1100', *The Earldom of Chester and its Charters. A Tribute to Geoffrey Barraclough*, ed. A. T. Thacker, *Jnl of the Chester Archaeol. Soc.* 71 (Chester, 1991), 37–68, esp. 38–40.

[87] *The Ecclesiastical History of Orderic Vitalis*, ed. Chibnall II, 260.

[88] *La Chronique de Saint-Hubert dite Cantatorium*, ed. K. Hanquet (Brussels, 1906), pp. 65–9; *La Chronique de Gislebert de Mons*, ed. L. Vanderkindere (Brussels, 1904), pp. 8–10. The identification of this Gerbod with Gerbod of Saint-Omer can be found in Warlop, *The Flemish Nobility* IV, 1024 and Lewis, 'The Formation', p. 39, n. 16.

[89] Gerbod's presence at Cluny may well explain, as C. Lewis ('The Formation', p. 40) has pointed out, why Gundreda, now the only sibling left, and her husband William of Warenne, were so generous to Cluny.

[90] Warlop, *The Flemish Nobility* IV, 1021–4 and Lewis, 'The Formation', pp. 38–40.

[91] Warlop, *The Flemish Nobility* I, 51–2. We should note that Arnulf/Arnold II's death in 1067 may have necessitated Gerbod II's brief return to Flanders, for in that year he witnessed a charter as advocate of Saint-Bertin (Warlop, *The Flemish Nobility* II, 382, n. 249).

[92] *Liber miraculorum sancti Bavonis*, ed. O. Holder-Egger, MGH SS 15.1 (Hanover, 1887), 598–9.

[93] *Les chartes de Saint Bertin*, ed. Haigneré I, no. 85.

also held land.[94] Thus our knowledge of Frederick of Oosterzele's background and family is at least as extensive as our knowledge of Gilbert I of Gent, even though the precise circumstances of their acquaintance with Hereward in Flanders cannot at present be further illuminated. As younger sons of important noble families in Flanders they turn up in charters and other documents and thus reveal their existence. Through her connection with William of Warenne some knowledge of Gundrada can also be gleaned. Unfortunately, the same cannot be said of Turfrida of Saint-Omer.

TURFRIDA

It is frustrating that we cannot establish where precisely Turfrida fits into the Flemish puzzle. Her name is Gallo-Germanic, distinctly un-English, and as such places her firmly on the Continent. According to the *Gesta Herewardi*, she came from a wealthy family and was learned and skilled in needlework. Her family was rich enough at Saint-Omer to attract as her potential suitor the *nepos* (grandson or nephew) of the neighbouring aristocratic family of Saint-Valéry. This must be a reference to Saint-Valéry-sur-Somme, from which Duke William set out for England in 1066. Identification of the lords of this Ponthieu harbour is rendered difficult by the existence of another Saint-Valéry family who took their name from Saint-Valéry-en-Caux in Normandy. On that account, it is not yet possible to name the lord of Saint-Valéry-sur-Somme in the 1060s, let alone his *nepos*.[95] It is unlikely that Turfrida was connected to the Oosterzele-Scheldewindeke-Warenne family, because if she had been the authors of the *Gesta Herewardi* and the 'Hyde Chronicle' would surely have made a point of the relationship. A plausible conjecture is that she was a daughter or sister of the castellan of Saint-Omer, Wulfric Rabel, but that is no more than an intelligent guess.[96] That she married Hereward, who after all had played an important military role, would fit a common medieval pattern

---

[94] *Ibid.* no. 96; Warlop, *The Flemish Nobility* I, 51.

[95] L. C. Loyd, *The Origins of some Anglo-Norman Families*, ed. C. T. Clay and D. C. Douglas (Leeds, 1951), p. 92 discusses the Norman Saint-Valéry evidence and suggests that the Ranulf of Saint-Valéry mentioned in Domesday Book as an under-tenant of the bishop of Lincoln came from the Pays-de-Caux. This leaves open the possibility that to the Ponthieu family belong the men carrying the names Bernard (Gallia Christiana 11, Instrumenta, cols. 19–20, dated 1096; *Regesta Regum Anglo-Normannorum 1066–1154*, ed. H. W. C. Davis *et al.*, 4 vols. (Oxford, 1913–69) II, no. 1379, dated between 1107 and 1122; J. Green, *The Government of England under Henry I* (Cambridge, 1986), p. 234) and Reginald (spurious charter dated 1106, *Regesta* II, no. 797). From 1144 onwards there is a series of regular charters proving that Reginald (*c.* 1144–*c.* 1164) was the father of Bernard (still alive in 1190), see *Calendar of Documents*, nos. 12, 23, 44, 57, 790, 1057, 1077, 1084–5, 1360 and 1364.

[96] Although it would give added weight to my suggestion (see above, p. 214, n. 63) that in spring 1071 the disgraced Wulfric might have fled from Flanders to England to join, in this hypothesis, his daughter and son-in-law or his sister and brother-in-law.

Hereward and Flanders

whereby mercenary soldiers married women connected with families of their military superiors.

Her later life in England does not reveal anything about her Flemish background either. According to the *Gesta Herewardi*, Hereward repudiated Turfrida in favour of the *uxor* (wife or widow) of 'Earl' Dolfin, named Ælfthryth by Gaimar, whereupon she retired to the monastery of Crowland.[97] The Pseudo-Ingulf adds that she died there after four years.[98] Such information would, if true, have been known in the Fenlands and in particular at Crowland, which at the time of King Edward and before Hereward's outlawry, counted Hereward as their tenant, and one of sufficient status to negotiate an annual rent with the abbot.[99] But how do we explain the 'Earl' Dolfin and his wife or widow who might have been called Ælfthryth? Perhaps there is a connection with Gospatric I, earl of Dunbar, whom we encountered earlier as one of the post-Conquest exiles in Flanders. Gospatric had three sons.[100] The youngest, Gospatric II, eventually succeeded him in Dunbar and Lothian and died at the battle of the Standard in 1138.[101] The middle son was Waltheof, who later (perhaps after a secular career) became a monk at Crowland and was abbot there from 1126 to 1138.[102] Little more than the name of the eldest son, Dolfin, is known. In 1092 he was expelled from Cumbria by William Rufus and after that nothing more is known of him, except indirectly through his brother Gospatric.[103] For Gospatric II as his father's successor was never styled earl or count, but instead was consistently referred to as 'Gospatric, brother of Dolfin'.[104] The conspicuous omission of a title for Gospatric II is intriguing, considering that the whereabouts of his older brother Dolfin are unknown. Could that older brother be the 'Earl' Dolfin of the *Gesta Herewardi*? We do not know whether he was married, but eldest sons usually were for dynastic reasons. If he was still alive but in some way incapacitated and unable to fulfil his comital office, his wife may have left him for someone else. Such information would have been known by members of his family, including Waltheof, who was already at Crowland in the 1080s. All this is pure speculation, of course, but the link with Crowland, where Hereward, Turfrida, 'Earl' Dolfin

---

[97] *Gesta Herewardi*, pp. 397–8; *L'Estoire des Engleis*, ed. Bell, line 5592, p. 177.
[98] *Historia Ingulphi*, ed. Fulman, pp. 67–8.
[99] DB, i, 377v; S. Raban, *The Estates of Thorney and Crowland* (Cambridge, 1977), p. 19.
[100] *Symeonis monachi opera omnia*, ed. Arnold I, 215–20 and II, 199; see also W. G. Searle, *Ingulf and the Historia Croylandensis* (Cambridge, 1894), p. 94.
[101] *The Scots Peerage*, ed. Sir J. Balfour Paul, 9 vols. (Edinburgh, 1904–14) III, 241–6.
[102] *The Ecclesiastical History of Orderic Vitalis*, ed. Chibnall II, 350; Orderic was exceptionally well informed about Crowland, which he visited at least once, probably in 1114–15 (*ibid.* pp. xxiv–xxix), and therefore I see no reason to share the doubt cast on Waltheof of Crowland's identification by the editor of *The Scots Peerage* III, 243.
[103] *Anglo-Saxon Chronicle*, 'E', s.a. 1092, ed. Plummer I, 227. [104] *The Scots Peerage* III, 246.

and, if he was married, the 'earl's' wife were all known, makes the *Gesta*'s unique details worthy of careful scrutiny.

All other information about Turfrida and her descendants derives exclusively from the Pseudo-Ingulf's history of Crowland, which gives Turfrida a daughter, also named Turfrida, who is said to have married Hugh of Envermeu.[105] From this union came another daughter and heiress, unnamed, who is said to have married Richard of Rullos. The existence of Hugh, who was the brother of Bishop Turold of Bayeux (c. 1098–c. 1105), and of Richard can be proven from extant documentation.[106] Unfortunately, in none of this evidence is there any reference to land in Flanders which might help us to elucidate Turfrida's background.

CONCLUSIONS

We have seen how the existence of the *Vita S. Willibrordi* confirms the reliability of the *Gesta Herewardi*'s account of a military expedition to 'Scaldemariland' in 1067. The Echternach account increases dramatically the value of this part of the *Gesta* as an important historical source. The information about Flanders and its neighbouring provinces is, as far as can be established, accurate, even though references to rulers are vague. None of the material presented in the Flemish chapters can be shown to be wrong, from which of course it does not necessarily follow that they are historically correct. But a good case for the *Gesta*'s verifiable contents concerning Flanders can be made. Against this background the presence of a *miles Herivvardus* in a charter of the bishop of Cambrai, who is known to have recruited mercenaries for his defensive strategies at Cambrai, deserves serious consideration as a reference to Hereward 'the Wake'. If this identification can be accepted then Hereward went to Flanders in the mid-1060s. Like other English exiles he put his military expertise at the disposal of Bishop Lietbert of Cambrai early in 1065, in all probability of Earl Tostig at Saint-Omer during the winter of 1065–6, and of Robert 'the Frisian' in 1067. It may have been at Saint-Omer that he became acquainted with Gilbert of Gent and Frederick of

---

[105] *Historia Ingulphi*, ed. Fulman, pp. 67–8. For a discussion of Turfrida's descendants, see Round, *Feudal England*, pp. 132–6, who ultimately rejects the veracity of the Crowland tradition. It should be pointed out, however, that despite the late date of the Crowland chronicle its fifteenth-century compiler had access to genuine eleventh- and twelfth-century documents now lost; see D. Roffe, 'The Historia Croylandensis: a Plea for a Re-Assessment', *EHR* 110 (1995), 93–108.

[106] For Hugh of Envermeu, see *The Ecclesiastical History of Orderic Vitalis*, ed. Chibnall V, 210–11 and *Regesta* II, nos. 601, 727, 794–5, 818, 973 and 1577; for Richard of Rullos, see *ibid.* no. 1592, Loyd, *Origins*, p. 86 and Round, *Feudal England*, p. 165. Richard's brother William, lord of Bourne at the time of Henry I who died without offspring, appears in *Regesta* II, nos. 1031, 1098 and 1187. Richard of Rullos's daughter Adelina married Baldwin FitzGilbert of Clare, who became lord of Bourne 'iure uxoris'. For daughters as the likely missing link in the descent of Bourne from Hereward to Baldwin FitzGilbert, see Roffe, 'Hereward "the Wake"', pp. 7–10.

Oosterzele-Scheldewindeke, and it was surely at Saint-Omer that he met Turfrida, a member of the local nobility (perhaps related to the castellans Lambert and his son Wulfric Rabel) who became his wife. The enhanced status of this part of the *Gesta* as more historically reliable than hitherto thought, ought to invite scholars to renew their acquaintance with this intriguing text.

Perhaps we should see the *Gesta Herewardi* neither as a fictional 'historical adventure novel' as P. G. Schmidt sees it,[107] nor as a chronicle, but as the sort of historical narrative which Gaimar wrote himself and, perhaps jokingly, offered to write about King Henry I to rectify the shortcomings of the now lost work of David:

'But as for the festivities that the king held, as for the drinking and boasting bouts, the courting and the love affairs over which he presided, David's book has hardly anything to say ... Gaimar ... could compose a verse account of the finest exploits [of Henry's court], namely the love affairs and the courting, the hunting and the drinking, the festivities and the pomp and ceremony, the acts of generosity and the displays of wealth, the entourage of noble and valiant knights that the king maintained, and the generous presents that he distributed.'[108]

That Gaimar wrote his *L'Estoire des Engleis* in this vein for a female patron, Constance wife of Ralph FitzGilbert, and that he was prepared to compose something similar for Queen Adeliza of Louvain, King Henry I's widow, inspires me to suggest that the commission of the now lost Old English Life by Leofric, Hereward's chaplain, on which presumably much of the *Gesta*'s narrative is based, came from a female member of his family.[109] Hereward's wife or daughter spring to mind as the likely patrons who successfully rescued the stories of Hereward's adventures in Flanders for posterity.[110]

[107] Schmidt, 'Biblisches und hagiographisches Kolorit', pp. 94–5.
[108] *L'Estoire des Engleis*, lines 6495–6501 and 6504–6511, ed. Bell, pp. 205–6. I am most grateful to Ian Short for allowing me to use his unpublished translation of Gaimar's text. The *Gesta Herewardi*'s likely early-twelfth-century date turns it into a significant source of medieval attitudes to knighthood. The striking story of Hereward's knighting as well as the author's comments on differences between English (Anglo-Norman) and French customs has never been taken into account in scholarly discussions of knighthood (J. Flori, *L'idéologie du glaive; préhistoire de la chevalerie* (Geneva, 1983) and *L'essor de la chevalerie XIe–XIIe siècles* (Geneva, 1986)); J. Gillingham, 'Thegns and Knights in Eleventh-Century England: Who Was Then the Gentleman', *TRHS*, 6th ser. 5 (1995), 129–54; J. Gillingham, 'Kingship, Chivalry and Love, Political and Cultural Values in the Earliest History Written in French: Gaimar's Estoire des Engleis', *Anglo-Norman Political Culture and the Twelfth-Century Renaissance*, ed. C. Warren Hollister (Woodbridge, 1997), pp. 33–58, where Gaimar's work is rehabilitated, but not the very similar *Gesta Herewardi*.
[109] For the exceptional concentration of female patronage of vernacular (Anglo-Norman) patronage in the Lincolnshire area, see I. Short, 'Patrons and Polyglots: French Literature in Twelfth-Century England', *ANS* 14 (1991), 229–50, at 243–4.
[110] In the course of the preparation of this article I have benefited from comments and advice from Judith Everard, Susan Kelly, Renée Nip, Oliver Padel, David Roffe and Ian Short. I am particularly grateful to Simon Keynes for his editorial support and guidance.

The cult of King Alfred the Great

SIMON KEYNES

King Alfred the Great has long been regarded as the archetypal symbol of the nation's perception of itself. Beset throughout his reign with the reality or threat of Viking invasions, Alfred battled fiercely and suffered heroically in leading his people to their eventual victory; at the same time he promoted the causes of religion and learning, and by the example of his government upheld truth, justice and the Anglo-Saxon way. Moreover, although himself fundamentally English (with West Saxon parents and a Mercian wife), he stood for a combination of political interests which made it easier to pass him off as prototypically British. Certainly he has done well, over the years, from the processes which turn history into legend. It may have taken a while for the cult to get going; but once up and running, the bandwagon could not be stopped. My purpose in reviewing the development of the cult of King Alfred is to explore the variety of factors which in their different ways contributed to the process from the ninth century to the present day, and to show how Alfredophilia, and latterly Alfredomania, found expression not only in religious, legal, political and historical writing, but also in much else besides. The overtly 'literary' manifestations of the cult of King Alfred, in poetry, drama, music, and prose, are not unfamiliar; yet they must be taken in connection with manifestations of the cult of King Alfred in sculpture, painting, engraving, and book-illustration, and all placed in whatever contexts may be appropriate, if we are to understand how the image of the king was formed and then transmitted to the next generation. The various manifestations of creative Alfrediana from the late sixteenth to the mid-nineteenth century provided a foundation for the public acts of commemoration which helped in 1849, 1878, and 1901 to transform Alfred from an obsession into an industry. The conventions of historical commemoration are now so well entrenched that in the present century we have already marked the eleventh centenaries of Alfred's birth in 849,[1] of his accession in 871,[2] of his victory at the battle of Edington in

---

[1] An unpublished lecture by Sir Frank Stenton, entitled 'King Alfred and his Place in History', was delivered at Wantage in 1949, and is preserved in the Library, Univ. of Reading, Stenton Papers 16/7. I am grateful to Michael Bott for supplying me with a photocopy of the typescript.
[2] R. H. C. Davis, 'Alfred the Great: Propaganda and Truth', *History* 56 (1971), 169–82, repr. in his *From Alfred the Great to Stephen* (London, 1991), pp. 33–46.

878,[3] of his capture of London in 886,[4] and of his foundation of Shaftesbury abbey in 888.[5] Of course the best is yet to come. King Alfred died eleven hundred years ago, not in 901 (as used to be supposed) but on 26 October 899.[6] And although, as we shall see, the tenth centenary of King Alfred's death was marked by an elaborate 'National Commemoration' in 1901, we are all set to mark the eleventh centenary of his death on 26 October 1999 – prompting the thought that only King Alfred could get two centenaries of his death in one and the same century.[7] Alfred knew well, of course, that glory is transitory; and certainly his own will be short-lived, eclipsed by the big one which follows a few weeks later.

An extended examination of the cult of King Alfred is to some extent an indulgence, from which one would not expect to learn anything whatsoever about Alfred himself, and which may or may not be excused by the special circumstances of an impending centenary.[8] It has to be admitted, moreover, that at every turn the process involves picking on one theme to the exclusion of or in isolation from others; and since at no time was Alfred the only national hero, or the only focus of attention, it is in certain respects misleading to put the emphasis on him. Yet if required to justify the expenditure of time and effort in the

---

[3] D. Whitelock, 'The Importance of the Battle of Edington', repr. in her *From Bede to Alfred: Studies in Early Anglo-Saxon Literature and History* (London, 1980), no. XIII. The lecture was originally delivered in 1978, in the priory church of Edington.

[4] The occasion was marked by a symposium on King Alfred held under the gaze of a portrait of Sir Frank Stenton at the University of Reading. See J. Bately, *The Anglo-Saxon Chronicle: Texts and their Textual Relationships*, Reading Med. Stud. Monograph 3 (Reading, 1991); and S. Keynes, 'King Alfred and the Mercians', *Kings, Currency and Alliances: History and Coinage in Southern England in the Ninth Century*, ed. M. A. S. Blackburn and D. N. Dumville (Woodbridge, 1998), pp. 1–45.

[5] S. Keynes, 'King Alfred the Great and Shaftesbury Abbey', *Studies in the Early History of Shaftesbury Abbey*, ed. L. Keen (Dorchester, 1999), pp. 17–72, being one of a series of lectures first delivered in 1988, and repeated in 1997.

[6] W. H. Stevenson, 'The Date of King Alfred's Death', *EHR* 13 (1898), 71–7.

[7] I have to thank my colleague, Professor David Dumville, for reminding me that the same distinction applies (under the wilder conditions of Irish history) to St Patrick. The 1500th anniversary of Patrick's death in 461 was celebrated, or rather contested, in 1961; the 1500th anniversary of his death in 493 was celebrated in 1993. For further explanation, see D. N. Dumville, *et al.*, *Saint Patrick, A.D. 493–1993* (Woodbridge, 1993).

[8] I should like to record my particular gratitude to the late Jeremy Maule (Trinity College, Cambridge) for discussion of the early modern period (and much else besides) in the early stages of this work, and to Dr Boyd Hilton, Dr David McKitterick, Mr William St Clair, and Dr Tessa Webber (also of Trinity College) for references and suggestions as I strayed further afield. I am also grateful to Dr Nigel Ramsay for reading this paper in typescript, and for making a number of valuable suggestions. Many other debts are mentioned where appropriate below. Papers based on aspects of this material were delivered at the University of Oxford in November 1998, at the University of Notre Dame and at the Newberry Library, Chicago, in March 1999, and at the meeting of the International Society of Anglo-Saxonists, Notre Dame, in August 1999. I am grateful to Professors Rees Davies, Patrick Geary, Paul Szarmach, and Katherine O'Brien O'Keeffe for their good offices in these connections.

The cult of King Alfred the Great

relentless pursuit of Alfrediana through the ages, I would respond in three ways. In the first place, the cult of King Alfred is central to our understanding of the various perceptions of the Anglo-Saxon past which have developed from the sixteenth century onwards, and of the uses which have been made of that past over the same period, whether for religious, political, or more generally nationalistic purposes. Secondly, the cult of Alfred is central to our understanding of the development of Anglo-Saxon studies during the same period, whether pursued in Oxford, Cambridge, or elsewhere. But thirdly, and perhaps most importantly, a necessary stage in the assessment of any historical figure (or period, or event) is the identification of the legendary aspects of that figure's reputation, for only when we understand the circumstances in which received tradition developed can we begin to strip off and clear away the accumulation of preconceptions, assumptions and expectations which might otherwise affect how we formulate the questions that we ask of the available evidence. This applies, for example, to Æthelred the Unready, as the personification of national humiliation at the hands of a foreign power, and to his son, Edward the Confessor, as the embodiment of all that was good in medieval kingship. It applies most particularly, however, to King Alfred the Great, as the symbol or icon of the kind of constitutional monarchy formed when England first became a nation, and as the originator of institutions which were to take their place as the cornerstone of the new polity of Britain. It would be possible to enlarge upon almost any aspect of the developing cult of King Alfred, as set out below, whether in its own right or in a wider context of the appropriate kind; but it is necessary in the first instance to bring the whole range of material under some form of control, in order to establish the parameters and organizing principles of a subject which of its nature extends for well over a thousand years.

FROM THE 'ANGLO-SAXON CHRONICLE' TO POLYDORE VERGIL

The development of the Alfredian myth was set in motion during the king's own lifetime, and it should come as no surprise that there is already some detectable movement away from what we might judge to have been the truth.[9] The concept of Alfred as saviour of his people, and some of the most familiar stories about

---

[9] On aspects of the development of the Alfredian legend, see, e.g., L. W. Miles, *King Alfred in Literature* (Baltimore, MD, 1902); B. A. Lees, *Alfred the Great / The Truth Teller / Maker of England 848–899* (New York and London, 1915), pp. 433–67; C. Hill, 'The Norman Yoke' [1954], repr. in his *Puritanism and Revolution: Studies in Interpretation of the English Revolution of the 17th Century* (London, 1958), pp. 50–122, esp. 96–9; E. Stanley, 'The Glorification of Alfred King of Wessex [1678–1851]' (1981), repr. in his *A Collection of Papers with Emphasis on Old English Literature* (Toronto, 1987), 410–41; S. Keynes and M. Lapidge, *Alfred the Great: Asser's 'Life of King Alfred' and other Contemporary Sources* (Harmondsworth, 1983), pp. 44–8; C. A. Simmons, *Reversing the Conquest: History and Myth in Nineteenth-Century British Literature* (New Brunswick, NJ, 1990), esp. pp. 25–41 and 175–202; and D. Sturdy, *Alfred the Great* (London, 1995), pp. 228–41.

him, originated in the *Anglo-Saxon Chronicle*: notably, his expedition to Rome in 853, and the narrative of his warfare against the Danes. Most of the other stories about him originated in Asser's 'Life of King Alfred', written in 893: Alfred winning a book of 'Saxon' poetry from his mother, learning with divine inspiration how to read in 887, inventing the candle-clock, pursuing wisdom, dispensing justice, and so on. The transmitted corpus of Alfredian prose would have made a strong impression on educated laymen, as well as ecclesiastics, in the tenth century, and would have kept his memory alive in high places. Writing probably in the late 970s or early 980s, Ealdorman Æthelweard recorded Alfred's death in terms which represent the perspective of the West Saxon élite: 'Then in the same year, there passed from the world the magnanimous Alfred, king of the Saxons, unshakeable pillar of the western people, a man replete with justice, vigorous in warfare, learned in speech, above all instructed in divine learning.'[10] For Ælfric, writing in the midst of renewed Viking invasions a decade or so later, Alfred was the first in a line of kings who had been victorious through God: 'just as King Alfred was, who often fought against the Danes, until he won the victory and protected his people';[11] Ælfric also knew Alfred as one who had translated books wisely from Latin into English, including Bede's *Historia ecclesiastica*.[12] When Byrhtferth of Ramsey used Asser in his 'Historical Miscellany', he added words and phrases which afford some indication of an early-eleventh-century view of the king;[13] and to judge from a purported writ of King Æthelred, probably representing a view current at the Old Minster, Winchester, in the eleventh century, Alfred was remembered there as 'the wise King Alfred'.[14] Two of the most familiar stories about Alfred probably arose during the course of the eleventh century: the story of Alfred, at Athelney, sharing his last loaf of bread with a passing pilgrim, who turned out to be St Cuthbert, was first told in the *Historia de Sancto Cuthberto*;[15]

---

[10] Æthelweard, *Chronicon* iv.3 (*The Chronicle of Æthelweard*, ed. A. Campbell (London, 1962), p. 50).

[11] *The Old English Version of the Heptateuch / Ælfric's Treatise on the Old and New Testament and his Preface to Genesis*, ed. S. J. Crawford, EETS os 160 (Oxford, 1922), 416–17; *English Historical Documents c. 500–1042*, ed. D. Whitelock, 2nd ed., Eng. Hist. Documents 1 (London, 1979), 928 (no. 239 (i)).

[12] *Ælfric's Catholic Homilies. The First Series. Text*, ed. P. Clemoes, EETS ss 17 (Oxford, 1997), 174; *Ælfric's Catholic Homilies. The Second Series. Text*, ed. M. Godden, EETS ss 5 (Oxford, 1979), 72.

[13] S. Keynes, 'On the Authenticity of Asser's *Life of King Alfred*', *JEH* 47 (1996), 529–51, at 537–8.

[14] P. H. Sawyer, *Anglo-Saxon Charters: an Annotated List and Bibliography*, R. Hist. Soc. Guides and Handbooks 8 (London, 1968), no. 946: F. E. Harmer, *Anglo-Saxon Writs* (Manchester, 1952), pp. 395–6 (no. 107).

[15] *Historia de Sancto Cuthberto*, chs. 14–19 (an eleventh-century interpolation in a tenth-century source, or, more probably, an integral part of an eleventh-century source). See Keynes and Lapidge, *Alfred the Great*, pp. 21–2 and 211–12; L. Simpson, 'The King Alfred/St Cuthbert Episode in the *Historia de sancto Cuthberto*: its Significance for Mid-Tenth-Century English History', *St Cuthbert, His Cult and His Community to AD 1200*, ed. G. Bonner, *et al.* (Woodbridge, 1989), pp. 397–411; and *The Historia de Sancto Cuthberto*, ed. T. Johnson-South (forthcoming).

The cult of King Alfred the Great

and the story of Alfred and the cakes was first told in the *Vita prima S. Neoti*.[16]

King Alfred's manifold virtues and achievements were fully articulated by those in the late eleventh and early twelfth centuries who did so much to determine the flow in the mainstream of English historical tradition.[17] There was, however, some serious competition. King Arthur fared well from the twelfth century onwards, and was still running in the seventeenth century;[18] but the stronger competition for Alfred came in the form of King Edward the Confessor.[19] It was axiomatic that the Norman regime was founded upon an elaborate if somewhat specious notion of continuity from the Anglo-Saxon past: o'erleaping Harold, but making a great display of William's position as Edward's heir and so on the formal re-establishment of the so-called 'Laws of King Edward'.[20] Of course the conquest had to be justified by assertions of prevailing degeneracy among the English, and of course there was much that was new; but equally there was much to be gained in certain quarters from cultivating a studied respect for the Anglo-Saxon past, whether represented by its saints, by its churches, or by its kings. So, far from scorning the profusion of 'English' local saints as worthless impostors, churchmen were ready to preserve and to promote their cults.[21] In the same way, the historians active in Anglo-Norman England were themselves concerned to advertise the appearance of continuity and to conceal the extent of change. But who would come to be regarded as the king in whose reign the English people had been brought under the rule of a single king, and who would come to be identified in retrospect as the one who had done most to promote their political welfare?

William of Malmesbury based his account on the *Chronicle*, Asser, and the prose preface to the *Pastoral Care*, but famously resisted the temptation 'to follow [Alfred] in [his] narrative, making the circuit of the island (if I may so put

---

[16] Keynes and Lapidge, *Alfred the Great*, pp. 21–2 and 197–202.

[17] For a valuable survey of all this material, see A. Gransden, *Historical Writing in England c. 550 to c. 1307* (London, 1974), and A. Gransden, *Historical Writing in England* II: *c. 1307 to the Early Sixteenth Century* (London, 1982). See also A. Galloway, 'Writing History in England', *The Cambridge History of Medieval English Literature*, ed. D. Wallace (Cambridge, 1999), pp. 255–83.

[18] For the 'historical' Arthur, see O. J. Padel, 'The Nature of Arthur', *CMCS* 27 (1994), 1–31; for the use of the legend in the Middle Ages, see A. MacColl, 'King Arthur and the Making of an English Britain', *Hist. Today* 49.3 (1999), 7–13.

[19] On the cult of St Edward, see further below, pp. 237–8.

[20] The point is made, for example, in King William's famous writ for the citizens of London: *Regesta regum Anglo-Normannorum: the Acta of William I (1066–1087)*, ed. D. Bates (Oxford, 1998), p. 593 (no. 180). See also B. R. O'Brien, *God's Peace and King's Peace: the Laws of Edward the Confessor* (Philadelphia, PA, 1999), esp. pp. 25–8.

[21] S. J. Ridyard, '*Condigna Veneratio*: Post-Conquest Attitudes to the Saints of the Anglo-Saxons', *ANS* 9 (1987), 179–206; but cf. T. A. Heslop, 'The Canterbury Calendars and the Norman Conquest', *Canterbury and the Norman Conquest: Churches, Saints and Scholars 1066–1109*, ed. R. Eales and R. Sharpe (London, 1995), pp. 53–85.

it) in his company'.[22] He was, however, the first to tell the story of Alfred entering the Danish camp disguised as a minstrel, in order to learn the enemy's plans,[23] though we hear nothing from him of shared loaves or burnt cakes. William also supplied some interesting information on the king's literary pursuits,[24] and refined Asser's story of Alfred's time-keeping into a division of the day into three periods of eight hours (one for writing, reading and prayer; one for work; and one for rest).[25] Most importantly, it was William who cast Alfred as the one who had divided the country into hundreds and tithings, as part of an arrangement for the enforcement of the law which required that every man should belong to a tithing, thereby projecting back into the late ninth century measures which had probably evolved in the tenth and eleventh centuries and which could be recognized in retrospect as the origin of the twelfth-century frankpledge system.[26] The Worcester chronicle, whether for this period the work of Florence or of John, retained the annalistic framework of its immediate source, but otherwise introduced material derived verbatim from Asser's 'Life of King Alfred', and thus injected Asser's portrayal of Alfred into the historical mainstream; so, when the Worcester chronicler was inspired to compose a short panegyric on the king, he did so in terms derived from Asser's account.[27] Henry of Huntingdon was more inclined than the others to impose an organizing principle on his narrative, though it happened not to be one which gave special credit to King Alfred. In his view, Ecgberht of Wessex rose to become 'king and monarch of Britain'; and although Alfred was mentioned in passing as one whose authority extended (by implication) beyond the Humber, over all parts of the kingdom, the structure of the work as a whole accorded him a worthy but in political terms relatively unimportant place in the middle of the tale of the Danish wars.[28]

---

[22] William of Malmesbury, *Gesta regum* ii.121.1 (*William of Malmesbury: Gesta regum Anglorum / The History of the English Kings* I, ed. R. A. B. Mynors, R. M. Thomson and M. Winterbottom (Oxford, 1998), 180–2).   [23] William of Malmesbury, *Gesta regum* ii.121.5 (*ibid.* pp. 182–4).

[24] William of Malmesbury, *Gesta regum* ii.123.1–3 (*ibid.* pp. 192–4); see also D. Whitelock, 'William of Malmesbury on the Works of King Alfred' (1969), repr. in *From Bede to Alfred*, no. VII.

[25] Asser, chs. 103–4; William of Malmesbury, *Gesta regum* ii.124.4 (ed. Mynors, Thomson and Winterbottom, p. 194). On the later development of this theme, especially with regard to labour legislation in the nineteenth century, see G. Langenfelt, *The Historic Origin of the Eight Hours Day: Studies in English Traditionalism* (Stockholm, 1954), pp. 122–39.

[26] William of Malmesbury, *Gesta regum* ii.122.1–2 (*ibid.* pp. 188–90). For further discussion, see R. M. Thomson with M. Winterbottom, *William of Malmesbury: Gesta Regum Anglorum / The History of the English Kings*, II: *General Introduction and Commentary* (Oxford, 1999), 98.

[27] *The Chronicle of John of Worcester*, II: *the Annals from 450 to 1066*, ed. R. R. Darlington and P. McGurk (Oxford, 1995), 352–4.

[28] *Historia Anglorum* ii.23, iv.30 and v.7–13 (*Henry, Archdeacon of Huntingdon: 'Historia Anglorum' / The History of the English People*, ed. D. Greenway (Oxford, 1996), pp. 106, 264 and 284–98), ending with a poem praising Alfred's resilience in the face of sustained Danish attack.

The cult of King Alfred the Great

What one misses, therefore, in the first half of the twelfth century, is any clear estimation of Alfred's contribution to the unfolding process of state-formation; which is all the more surprising, given the modern tendency to regard him as the architect of the English state. It was a Norman monk, Orderic Vitalis, writing in the mid-twelfth century, who hailed Alfred as 'the first king to hold sway over the whole of England';[29] and it is Orderic, therefore, who deserves some of the credit or blame for setting off a hare which, in combination with others, would have a long way to run. Sooner or later the hare fetched up at St Albans, where it was nourished by the school of historians who worked there in the thirteenth century, and then sent forth on its way. The school included Roger of Wendover, John of Wallingford, and Matthew Paris; and it also included 'Matthew of Westminster', in the sense that the greater part of this fourteenth-century work was based on Matthew Paris.[30] Roger of Wendover would appear to have been one of the first to create a composite Alfred from various sources, bringing material derived ultimately from the *Chronicle*, and Asser, into proximity with stories (including Alfred and the cakes) derived from less reputable sources. Yet the essential point for present purposes is that, unlike Henry of Huntingdon, Roger fastened on the events which took place at London, in 886, as the moment when the residual political arrangements of the 'Heptarchy' gave way to Alfred's assumption of rule throughout England.[31] The truth may not have been quite so simple, as the self-styled rulers of the English people still had to contend with obstinate Scandinavians and unruly Northumbrians; but there can be no doubt that in fastening on the events at London in 886 Roger had fastened on a political development of the utmost significance.[32] He was followed in this respect by Matthew Paris, who went further in representing Alfred's singular distinction in various graphic forms: in the preliminary matter in the *Chronica Majora*, part I, Alfred is shown at the centre of a diagram symbolizing his rulership as 'prothomonarcha' over the seven kingdoms of the Heptarchy, with links onwards to Edward the Elder and his sons (pl. VII*a*); in the main text of the *Chronica Majora*, part I, at 871, Alfred appears with a banner proclaiming himself to be the first sole ruler or monarch of England (pl. VII*b*); and in the preliminary matter in the *Chronica Majora*, part II, Alfred appears at the head of a genealogical table, showing a book, presumably of his laws, to four appreciative

---

[29] *The Ecclesiastical History of Orderic Vitalis*, ed. M. Chibnall, 6 vols. (Oxford, 1968–80) II, 240 and 340.
[30] For 'Matthew of Westminster', see *A Bibliography of English History to 1485*, ed. E. B. Graves (Oxford, 1975), p. 421 (no. 2871); and Gransden, *Historical Writing* II, 436 and 479.
[31] For Roger of Wendover's account of Alfred, see *Matthæi Parisiensis, Monachi Sancti Albani, Chronica Majora*, ed. H. R. Luard, RS 57, 7 vols. (London, 1872–83) I, 403–35 [passages in small type representing the text of RW].
[32] For the significance of the events of 886, see Keynes, 'King Alfred and the Mercians', pp. 21–9.

231

men.[33] For whatever reason Matthew was otherwise moved to remark, in the context of his own 'History of the Abbots of St Albans', that 'in view of his merits he [Alfred] was called "the Great" ' (pl. VII*c*),[34] representing what would appear to be the earliest occurrence of the title by which the king is set apart in English tradition from all other kings of the English.

The accounts of King Alfred given by the twelfth- and thirteenth-century historians were all capable of further refinement, amplification, and extension, once they came to be absorbed into the mainstream. In many cases, later accounts of Alfred are essentially exercises in the synthesis of earlier writers,[35] though there were some important developments. For example, William of Malmesbury's notion that Alfred instituted hundreds and tithings, once merged with Henry of Huntingdon's remark that it was the kings of Wessex who divided England into shires,[36] and with Roger of Wendover's emphasis on Alfred as first monarch of England, gave rise in time to the notion that it was Alfred who instituted *shires*, hundreds, and tithings, and was thus responsible for determining the shape of the judicial and administrative systems, and much else besides. The development (always open to contradiction, given incidental references in the *Anglo-Saxon Chronicle*, and Roger of Wendover's listing of the shires subject to the rule of King Offa) is found in the *Historia Croylandensis*, a work written by a monk of Crowland, in Lincolnshire, in the fourteenth or early fifteenth century; and it was affirmed further in the same connection that Alfred divided the local rulers into judges (*iudices*), now called justiciaries (*iustitiarii*), and sheriffs (*vice-comites*).[37] It is also instructive to see what happened when the St Albans view of Alfred was adapted at Westminster in the late fourteenth century, and how, in particular, it gave rise there to the notion that the English

---

[33] Cambridge, Corpus Christi College 26, fols. iv verso and 65r, and Cambridge, Corpus Christi College 16, fol. iii recto: see S. Lewis, *The Art of Matthew Paris in the Chronica Majora*, California Stud. in the Hist. of Art 21 (Aldershot, 1987), 165–74, with figs. 95, 96 and 77; and N. Morgan, *Early Gothic Manuscripts [I] 1190–1250*, Survey of Manuscripts Illuminated in the Brit. Isles 4.i (Oxford, 1982), 136–9 (no. 88).

[34] 'Rex Alfredus magnus. Iste regnauit xxix annis, & mensibus vi. Hic meritis exigentibus magnus dicebatur' (BL Cotton Nero D. i, fol. 30v); see S. Keynes, 'A Tale of Two Kings: Alfred the Great and Æthelred the Unready', *TRHS* 5th ser. 36 (1986), 195–217, at 195, n. 2, and Stanley, 'The Glorification of Alfred', p. 441.

[35] The account of Alfred in the vernacular chronicle attributed to Robert of Gloucester, written *c.* 1300, draws on William of Malmesbury and Henry of Huntingdon, but makes more than they do of the significance of the (supposed) fact that Alfred was anointed king by Pope Leo in Rome. See *The Metrical Chronicle of Robert of Gloucester*, ed. W. A. Wright, 2 vols., RS 86 (London, 1887) I, xix and 387–94, at lines 5326–32; see also Gransden, *Historical Writing* I, 405–6 and 432–8. [36] *Historia Anglorum* i.5 (ed. Greenway, pp. 16–18).

[37] H. Savile, *Rerum Anglicarum scriptores post Bedam praecipui* (London, 1596), fols. 484–520, at 495rv; [W. Fulman], *Rerum Anglicarum scriptores* I (Oxford, 1684), 1–132, at 28. For a translation of the operative passage, see H. T. Riley, *Ingulph's Chronicle of the Abbey of Croyland* (London, 1854), p. 56.

coronation regalia had been brought by Alfred from Rome and transmitted onwards to Edward the Confessor.[38] It should be noted, on the other hand, that Alfred was not invoked as a matter of course by those desirous of recovering rights which had been infringed or privileges which had been lost. Monks, nuns, and secular clergy forged charters more often in the names of kings other than Alfred, perhaps because they lacked genuine charters of Alfred for use as models, or perhaps because in most cases there happened to be a more appropriate king on whom to foist their work. In a similar way, those involved in the peasant uprisings of the fourteenth century, who claimed to be tenants in 'ancient demesne' of the king, and whose aspirations represented an early manifestation of the notion that the liberties they coveted had been enjoyed by their forebears in the distant past, tended to have good reasons for invoking the name of some other king, such as Offa, or Athelstan, or Edgar.[39] There was scope in Alfred for further development, but much of it would not be realized until the seventeenth and eighteenth centuries.

Another important theme in the medieval development of the Alfredian legend is the emphasis placed on Alfred's reputation as a sage and scholar, coupled in one way or another with his distinction as a law-maker. The fact that Alfred was described as 'the wise King Alfred' in an eleventh-century writ from Winchester, and that he was regarded in the twelfth century, also at Winchester, as the author of 'proverbs' of some kind,[40] encourages the supposition, or rather the wishful thought, that some of the wise sayings attributed to Alfred in the later twelfth and thirteenth centuries might have been genuinely Alfredian in origin. The tradition, for whatever it might be worth, is represented principally by the several 'Alfredian' sayings incorporated in *The Owl and the Nightingale* (*c.* 1250),[41] and by the more extensive body of material preserved in different

---

[38] For William of Sudbury's tract on the regalia, incorporated in Richard of Cirencester's *Speculum Historiale*, see *Ricardi de Cirencestria Speculum historiale de gestis regum Angliæ*, ed. J. E. B. Mayor, 2 vols., RS 30 (London, 1863–9) II, 26–39. In the early 1640s the box in which St Edward's Crown was kept, at Westminster, bore a label to the effect that it contained the crown with which Alfred, Edward, and others had been crowned; see Spelman, *Life of Alfred*, ed. Hearne [below, n. 127], pp. 200–1. 'St Edward's Crown' seems thus to have been misidentified as 'King Alfreds Crowne' when an inventory was taken of the regalia under the Commonwealth in 1649, shortly before its destruction; see O. Millar, 'The Inventories and Valuations of the King's Goods 1649–1651', *Walpole Soc.* 43 (1972), at 49. See also R. Lightbown, 'The King's Regalia, Insignia and Jewellery', *The Late King's Goods: Collections, Possessions and Patronage of Charles I in the Light of the Commonwealth Sale Inventories*, ed. A. MacGregor (London, 1989), pp. 257–75, at 257–8, and below, n. 64.

[39] See R. J. Faith, 'The "Great Rumour" of 1377 and Peasant Ideology', *The English Rising of 1381*, ed. T. H. Aston and R. H. Hilton (London, 1984), pp. 43–73, at 56–7, and R. Faith, *The English Peasantry and the Growth of Lordship*, Stud. in the Early Hist. of Britain (London, 1997), pp. 266–7.

[40] *Annales Monastici*, ed. H. R. Luard, 5 vols., RS 36 (London, 1864–9) II [Annals of Winchester], 10.   [41] *The Owl and the Nightingale*, ed. E. G. Stanley (London, 1960).

versions of the so-called *Proverbs of Alfred*.[42] Some of this Alfredian wisdom, including the king's last words of advice to his son, was cited by Sir John Spelman in the seventeenth century, and was thus absorbed into the legend.[43] Various other works were attributed to Alfred, including a translation of Æsop's *Fables*, and the authorship of (Adelard of Bath's) *Quaestiones naturales*.[44] The significance of King Alfred's contribution to the making of English law can be appreciated by perusal of his law-code, complemented by Asser, later legislation, and other records;[45] but with help from William of Malmesbury, and some others, the legend of Alfred the law-maker developed dimensions and degrees of elaboration which would lead eventually to his emergence as founder of the Common Law.[46] It is striking that the early-twelfth-century collection of laws known as *Quadripartitus* gave pride of place to the law-code of Cnut, in a way which suggests that Alfred had not yet come to the fore; and that when the material was rearranged and augmented in the early thirteenth century, by the compiler of the so-called 'London Collection', Alfred was again accorded scarcely more than was his due.[47] Similarly, the 'professional' treatises on English law, notably those associated with the names of Glanville, Bracton, and Fortescue, do not display any marked emphasis on King Alfred in particular.[48] It is in the tract known as the *Mirror of Justices*, compiled towards the end of the

---

[42] J. M. Kemble, *The Dialogue of Solomon and Saturn* (London, 1848), pp. 225–57, at 226–48, with translation; H. P. South, *The Proverbs of Alfred* (1931), repr. (New York, 1970); O. Arngart, *The Proverbs of Alfred*, 2 vols., Skrifter utgivna av Kungl. Humanistiska Vetenskapssamfundet i Lund 32 (Lund, 1942–55).

[43] For Spelman's 'Life' of Alfred, see below, pp. 254–6. He cites the *Proverbs of Alfred* from a transcript of a lost Cottonian manuscript (BL, Cotton Galba A. xix), on which see Arngart, *Proverbs of Alfred* II, 11–17.

[44] For Alfred's supposed translation of Æsop, see *Marie de France: Fables*, ed. H. Spiegel (Toronto, 1987), pp. 256–8. In a forthcoming study, Michael Lapidge and Jill Mann suggest that Marie de France may have worked from a lost Latin poem to which Alfred's name had become attached, itself related to the (tenth-century) 'Hexametrical Romulus'. For Alfred's supposed authorship of *Quaestiones naturales*, see B. Smalley, *English Friars and Antiquity in the Early Fourteenth Century* (Oxford, 1960), pp. 207–8.

[45] For an authoritative assessment of Alfred's legislation, see P. Wormald, *The Making of English Law: King Alfred to the Twelfth Century* (Oxford, 1999), and its sequel (forthcoming).

[46] On the glorification of Alfred as a law-maker, in a wider context, see E. G. Stanley, *Die angelsächsische Rechtspflege* (forthcoming), esp. sect. 2.

[47] P. Wormald, '"*Quadripartitus*"', with R. Sharpe, 'The Prefaces of "*Quadripartitus*"', in *Law and Government in Medieval England and Normandy: Essays in Honour of Sir James Holt*, ed. G. Garnett and J. Hudson (Oxford, 1994), pp. 111–72; see also F. Liebermann, 'A Contemporary Manuscript of the "Leges Anglorum Londoniis collectae"', *EHR* 28 (1913), 732–45.

[48] *The Treatise on the Laws and Customs of the Realm of England, Commonly Called Glanvill*, ed. G. D. G. Hall (London, 1965); *Bracton, De legibus et consuetudinibus Angliae*, ed. G. E. Woodbine, rev. S. E. Thorne, 4 vols. (New Haven, CT, 1915–42); *Sir John Fortescue, De laudibus legum Anglie*, ed. S. B. Chrimes (Cambridge, 1942), and *The Governance of England: otherwise called The Difference between an Absolute and a Limited Monarchy, by Sir John Fortescue, Kt*, ed. C. Plummer (Oxford, 1885).

The cult of King Alfred the Great

thirteenth century, that Alfred makes his first appearance in his capacity as the originator of a constitution. Alfred convened parliaments twice a year at London, on which occasions ordinances were made though not set down in written form; the form of appeal for treason could be found 'in old rolls of the time of King Alfred'; and in one year Alfred had forty-four judges hanged for giving false judgements.[49] It is not obvious what might have prompted the compiler of the tract to cast Alfred in this role. Maitland supposed, not unreasonably, that he was making it up; yet we need not doubt that the compiler was committed to the Englishness of our institutions, and it may be that Roger of Wendover's view of Alfred as the First Monarch, established at London in 886, appealed to him as a Londoner. The *Mirror of Justices* was not as well known in the Middle Ages as the early-fourteenth-century tract *Modus tenendi Parliamentum*, which says nothing of Alfred and gives prominence to Edward the Confessor;[50] but it is none the less of special importance for present purposes, for the simple reason that it was regarded in the seventeenth century as a thoroughly reputable source.[51]

One theme which proved to be of crucial importance in the later development of the cult of King Alfred remained to make its first appearance: Alfred's alleged role or complicity in the foundation of the University of Oxford.[52] Towards the middle of the fourteenth century, Ranulph Higden, monk of St Werburgh's, Chester, claimed in his *Polychronicon* that King Alfred had been prompted by St Neot to establish 'public schools for the various arts at Oxford'.[53] The one eighth of the king's annual revenue which (according to Asser, ch. 102) was earmarked for the support of a school for the kingdom's youth was (according to Higden) earmarked for the scholars of Oxford;[54] so it was perhaps no more than the fame of the university in the fourteenth century,

---

[49] *The Mirror of Justices*, ed. W. J. Whittaker, with an Introduction by F. W. Maitland, Selden Soc. 7 (London, 1895), xxiv (date), 8 (parliaments), 54 (treason) and 166–71 (judges). Maitland attributed the work to Andrew Horn, fishmonger of Bridge Street, London; but see J. Catto, 'Andrew Horn: Law and History in Fourteenth-Century England', *The Writing of History in the Middle Ages: Essays presented to Richard William Southern*, ed. R. H. C. Davis and J. M. Wallace-Hadrill (Oxford, 1981), pp. 367–91, at 373–4 and 386–7.

[50] For the *Modus tenendi parliamentum*, see N. Pronay and J. Taylor, *Parliamentary Texts of the Later Middle Ages* (Oxford, 1980), pp. 67–79 (text) and 80–91 (translation), with full commentary.

[51] On the use of the *Mirror of Justices* in the seventeenth century, see further below, p. 249.

[52] The material bearing on the mythical history of the University of Oxford is most conveniently assembled in J. Parker, *The Early History of Oxford 727–1100*, Oxford Hist. Soc. 3 (Oxford, 1885), 24–62 (discussion, with translation of texts) and 305–17 (appendix of texts).

[53] *Polychronicon Ranulphi Higden Monachi Cestrensis*, ed. C. Babington and J. R. Lumby, 9 vols., RS 41 (London, 1865–86) VI, 354. See also J. Taylor, *The 'Universal Chronicle' of Ranulf Higden* (Oxford, 1966), p. 45, and Gransden, *Historical Writing* II, 43–57, at 52. The *Polychronicon* had been translated into English by the end of the fourteenth century, and was printed by Caxton in 1480.

[54] *Polychronicon*, ed. Babington and Lumby VI, 362.

coupled with evidence of Alfred's interest in promoting education, and his developing reputation as an originator of all that was good in England, that led Higden to make the obvious connections. In about 1380, the fellows of University College (established in 1280, with funds bequeathed to the university by William of Durham, who had died in 1249) needed to secure their title to some property in Oxford; so they petitioned the Crown claiming that the college had been founded by King Alfred, and that accordingly King Richard II was now their patron.[55] The petition seems to have had the desired effect, and the claim to Alfredian origin became an integral part of the college's sense of its corporate identity. There were various manifestations of Alfrediana at University College in the late medieval and early modern periods, though much would appear to have been lost during the seventeenth century;[56] but, as we shall see, the cult was revived in the 1660s, and maintained throughout the eighteenth century, in ways which did much to promote the Alfredian and indeed the Anglo-Saxon cause.[57] It should be noted, in this connection, that there is evidence for the production in the late fourteenth century of a manuscript of Asser's 'Life of King Alfred', now lost, which contained a passage about Alfred and Oxford, perhaps produced at that time in an attempt to give the story a greater degree of authority.[58] A more elaborate version of Higden's Oxford story is found in the 'Liber abbatiae' of Hyde Abbey, Winchester, compiled probably by Thomas Rudbourne, of Winchester, in the first half of the fifteenth century.[59] We are told that the University of Oxford was founded in 886, and provided with a distinguished academic staff: St Neot (doctor of theology); Grimbald (professor of divinity); Asser (regent in grammar and rhetoric); John of St David's (reader in logic, music, and arithmetic); and another John (teacher in geometry and astronomy). All this was done in the presence of the most glorious and invincible King Alfred, 'whose remembrance is sweet as honey in the mouths of all'. The Oxford tradition was developed further in the late fifteenth century. According to the antiquary John Rous (1411–91), born in Warwickshire and educated in Oxford, the university was founded by King Alfred in 873, at the instigation of St Neot. There were three 'halls' (*Parva Aula*

---

[55] For further details, see Parker, *Early History of Oxford*, pp. 52–7; *The Victoria History of the County of Oxford* III: *The University of Oxford*, ed. H. E. Salter and M. D. Lobel (London, 1954) [hereafter *VCH Oxon* III], 61–81 (University College); and esp. R. Darwall-Smith, *University College: the First 750 Years* (Oxford, 1999), being the catalogue of an exhibition at the Bodleian Library to mark the 750th anniversary of the founding of University College (in 1249).

[56] For the 'memorials' of Alfred in the windows of the fifteenth-century chapel, and in some of the old chamber windows, see W. Carr, *University College* (London, 1902), pp. 6 and 66–7.

[57] See further below, pp. 260–9 and 322–4.   [58] See further below, n. 95.

[59] *Liber Monasterii de Hyda*, ed. E. Edwards, RS 45 (London, 1866), pp. 41–2, and Parker, *Early History of Oxford*, pp. 45–6. For Thomas Rudbourne, see *The 'Liber Vitae' of the New Minster and Hyde Abbey, Winchester*, ed. S. Keynes, EEMF 26 (Copenhagen, 1996), 45.

(in the High St), *Aula Minor* (near the northern walls of the city), and *Aula Magna* (also in the High St, near the east gate)), for Grammar, the Arts, and Theology; Alfred's youngest son Æthelweard, known from Asser (ch. 75) to have been especially well educated, was sent there; and Grimbald was made the first chancellor.[60] The 'Small Hall' was Brasenose College and the 'Great Hall' was University College, both of which (as we shall see) were pleased to cherish their putatively Alfredian credentials.

All the main elements of the Alfredian myth were now in place. In 1441 King Henry VI, who had been trying for some time to secure the canonization of Osmund of Salisbury, tried hard again through his emissaries also to secure the canonization of King Alfred, 'who was the first monarch of the famous kingdom of England'.[61] Osmund was duly raised to sainthood in 1456, but (for whatever reason) the case for Alfred seems to have made no impression at Rome. Alfred could still not compete, therefore, with King Edward the Confessor; and, indeed, it is important to stress that it was the Confessor who, throughout the Middle Ages, symbolized the identity and continuity of English monarchy, whether represented by his activities as a law-maker,[62] by his cult-centre at Westminster abbey,[63] by the regalia known to have been used by kings from Henry III to Charles I,[64] or by the invention of his coat of arms at

---

[60] For the operative passage from Rous's *Historia regum Angliae*, see Parker, *Early History of Oxford*, pp. 49–51 (with translation) and 315 (text). For Rous himself, and his views on the antiquity of Oxford and Cambridge, see also T. Kendrick, *British Antiquity* (London, 1950), pp. 19–29, and Gransden, *Historical Writing* II, 309–27.

[61] Letters from Henry VI to Pope Eugenius IV, dated 20 March 1441, one concerning Osmund and the other concerning Alfred, in *Memorials of the Reign of King Henry VI: Official Correspondence of Thomas Bekynton, Secretary to King Henry VI, and Bishop of Bath and Wells*, ed. G. Williams, 2 vols., RS 56 (London, 1872) I, 117–19. On the canonization of Osmund, see C. Richmond, 'Religion', *Fifteenth-Century Attitudes: Perceptions of Society in Late Medieval England*, ed. R. Horrox (Cambridge, 1994), pp. 183–201, at 190–1.

[62] For the significance of the so-called 'Laws of Edward the Confessor', see above, n. 20. The author of the *Modus tenendi parliamentum* projected parliament back into Edward's reign (Pronay and Taylor, *Parliamentary Texts*, pp. 67 and 80).

[63] On the cult of St Edward at Westminster, see P. Binski, *Westminster Abbey and the Plantagenets: Kingship and the Representation of Power 1200–1400* (New Haven, CT, 1995), esp. pp. 52–89. Edward was canonized in 1161. His relics were placed in a new shrine at Westminster on 13 Oct. 1163, in the presence of King Henry II and Thomas Becket, and were moved again on 13 Oct. 1269, in the presence of King Henry III. For Richard II at the shrine of Edward in 1381, see *The Westminster Chronicle 1381–1394*, ed. L. C. Hector and B. F. Harvey (Oxford, 1982), pp. 8–10. The shrine was despoiled in the 1540s, restored by Mary I, and restored again by James II.

[64] On the cult of St Edward in relation to the regalia, see Binski, *Westminster Abbey and the Plantagenets*, pp. 134–5, and R. Lightbown, 'The English Coronations before the Commonwealth', *The Crown Jewels: the History of the Coronation Regalia in the Jewel House of the Tower of London*, ed. C. Blair, 2 vols. (London, 1998) I, 53–256, and 'The English Coronation Regalia before the Commonwealth', *ibid*. I, 257–353.

Simon Keynes

Westminster and its subsequent adoption by Richard II.[65] Alfred also continued to face strong competition from King Arthur. The accession of the Welshman, Henry Tudor, as King Henry VII, in 1485, guaranteed the legendary Arthur and his 'British' history an ascendancy which found expression initially in the naming of Henry's first-born son, Arthur, Duke of Cornwall (soon afterwards created Prince of Wales), and which would dominate conceptions of the past current during the reigns of Henry VII (1485–1509), Henry VIII (1509–47), and their Tudor progeny.[66] Unsurprisingly, a scholarly and sceptical note from Italy had little effect. In 1502 the Italian scholar, Polydore Vergil (*c*.1470–1555), came from Urbino to England, and gained the king's patronage. Henry VII asked him to produce a 'History of England', which was completed by 1513, and which, when eventually published in 1534, was dedicated to Henry VIII.[67] What Henry would have made of it is another matter. He was committed to the familiar tales of King Arthur, and might have been deeply disappointed to find that these tales were not to be taken seriously.[68] He might also have had reasons of his own to be dismayed by Vergil's pervasive Romanism. King Ine 'made his realme tributarie to the Busshop of Rome, fininge everie howse at a certaine

---

[65] The coat of arms which would appear to have been devised for Edward the Confessor in the thirteenth century was a cross patonce (or cross flory) between five birds (? eagles, or doves), itself probably derived from his seal and from his coinage (R. H. M. Dolley and F. Elmore Jones, 'A New Suggestion Concerning the So-Called "Martlets" in the Arms of St Edward', *Anglo-Saxon Coins*, ed. R. H. M. Dolley (London, 1961), pp. 215–26). It is seen, for example, in Westminster Abbey: Binski, *Westminster Abbey and the Plantagenets*, p. 79 (fig. 115). For its adoption by Richard II, in the form of a cross patonce (or flory) between five legless birds (presumably martlets), see J. H. Harvey, 'The Wilton Diptych – A Re-examination', *Archaeologia* 98 (1961), 1–28, at 5–6, and Binski, *Westminster Abbey and the Plantagenets*, pp. 87 and 200. The Wilton Diptych (National Gallery), made for Richard II in the late 1390s, shows Richard with his patrons St Edmund (king of East Anglia), Edward the Confessor, and John the Baptist, with Richard's 'Edwardian' arms on the back. For the later adaptation of Edward's coat of arms into one for the kings of all England, including Alfred, see below, n. 114.

[66] For 'The Tudor Cult of British History', see Kendrick, *British Antiquity*, pp. 34–44, and H. A. MacDougall, *Racial Myth in English History: Trojans, Teutons, and Anglo-Saxons* (Montreal and Hanover, NH, 1982), pp. 15–17.

[67] *Polydori Vergilii Urbinatis Anglicæ Historiæ Libri XXVI* (Basel, 1534). Vergil's manuscript, in the Vatican Library, was written in 1512–13. A Tudor translation of his account of the period before the Norman Conquest was edited from BL Royal 18. C. VIII–IX in *Polydore Vergil's English History, I: Containing the First Eight Books, Comprising the Period Prior to the Norman Conquest*, ed. H. Ellis, Camden Soc. 36 (London, 1846), 203–8 and 213–21. See also D. Hay, *Polydore Vergil: Renaissance Historian and Man of Letters* (Oxford, 1952), esp. pp. 79–168; F. J. Levy, *Tudor Historical Thought* (San Marino, CA, 1967), pp. 53–68; and MacDougall, *Racial Myth in English History*, pp. 17–20.

[68] For Vergil on Arthur, see Hay, *Polydore Vergil*, pp. 109–10, 157–8, and 199. Henry VIII was more conscious of King Arthur than of any other king before Edward the Confessor; see *The Inventory of King Henry VIII, I: The Transcript*, ed. D. Starkey, Report of the Research Committee of the Soc. of Antiq. 56 (London, 1998), 174, 326, 384 (nos. 8906 [vestment], 13337 [tapestry], 15377 [picture]).

The cult of King Alfred the Great

peece of monie called a pennie' (a topic of particular interest to Vergil, since he had come to England on his appointment as sub-collector of Peter's Pence);[69] and when King Æthelwulf went to Rome, during the pontificate of Leo IV, 'hee made all that parte of the reallme tributarie to the see of Rome which his father Egbertus had annexed to his native inheritance'.[70] For his part, Alfred, on becoming king, went to Rome and was crowned there by Pope Hadrian II (867–72).[71] Vergil's portrayal of Alfred is otherwise the usual confection from medieval chronicles (notably Matthew Paris), and the king emerges predictably enough as 'a mann shininge in all kinde of vertewse'. This was all very well; but from King Henry's point of view Arthur was simply too potent a force to give way, and as yet there was no good reason why he should be asked to do so.

ALFRED THE GREAT AND THE ELIZABETHAN ANTIQUARIES

In all accounts of Alfred in the fourteenth, fifteenth, and early sixteenth centuries, up to and including Polydore Vergil, it is striking that he is not called 'the Great'; yet it was now only a matter of time before he would take his place as the symbol of a distinctively *English* political order. The antiquary John Leland (1503–52) included a detailed account of Alfred in his register of British authors (compiled in the early 1540s), drawing his information from a variety of manuscript sources (including a copy of Alfred's laws which he had seen at Christchurch (Twynham), Asser's 'Life', and the 'Annals of St Neots').[72] John Bale (1495–1563), drawing on Leland's material for his own very similar purposes, was moved to describe the king as 'Alphredus Magnus',[73] and seems in this way to have reintroduced into scholarly parlance the epithet first registered by Matthew Paris in the mid-thirteenth century. Neither Leland nor Bale had much occasion to reflect on matters of larger historical import, and their estimation of the king is not easy to discern; but both may have been too steeped in the British

---

[69] *Polydore Vergil's English History*, ed. Ellis, pp. 182–3. For Vergil and Peter's Pence, see also Hay, *Polydore Vergil*, pp. 6–7 and 199–200. [70] *Polydore Vergil's English History*, ed. Ellis, pp. 197–8.
[71] *Ibid.* p. 203. For Samuel Wale's illustration of this 'event', made for an edition of Lockman's *History* (1747), see below, p. 305.
[72] *Commentarii de scriptoribus Britannicis, auctore Joanne Lelando Londinate*, ed. A. Hall (Oxford, 1709) I, 144–53, from Oxford, Bodleian Library, Top. gen. c. 4 (S.C. 3120). The heading 'De Alfredo Magno' was supplied by the editors and is not found in Leland's manuscript (as noted by Stanley, 'The Glorification of Alfred', p. 411).
[73] J. Bale, *Illustrium maioris Britanniae scriptorum, hoc est, Angliae, Cambriae, ac Scotiæ, summarium* (Ipswich, 1548), 65r–66r, at 65r; and J. Bale, *Scriptorum illustrium maioris Brytanniae . . . catalogus*, 2 vols. (Basel, 1557–9) I, 125–6. For Alfredian annotations in Bale's copy of the *Catalogus* (BL, Dept of Ptd Books, C.28.m.6), see *Johannis de Trokelowe Annales Edvardi II*, ed. T. Hearne (Oxford, 1729), pp. 276–92, at 279–80. See also *Index Britanniae Scriptorum: John Bale's Index of British and Other Writers*, ed. R. L. Poole and M. Bateson (Oxford, 1902), reptd with an introduction by C. Brett and J. P. Carley (Cambridge, 1990), pp. 28 (writings) and 473–4 (laws). For Leland and Bale, see also M. McKisack, *Medieval History in the Tudor Age* (Oxford, 1971), pp. 1–25.

myth to give him any degree of prominence beyond intellectual distinction. It is not clear what if anything Alfred might have gained or lost by the rampant protestantism of the reign of Edward VI (1547–53), or by the catholic reaction associated with Mary I (1553–8). However, the establishment of more stable foundations during the long reign of Elizabeth I (1558–1603) provided both pretext and opportunity for the development of a view of the past calculated to serve the needs of the new order; and now King Alfred began to come into his own. On one level, the revival of the parochial dispute about the relative antiquity of the universities of Oxford and Cambridge, in the mid-1560s, would have strengthened the feelings of those who cared about such matters, and helped in its own way to focus attention on Alfred.[74] The more significant advance, however, flowed from the provision of new editions of primary texts. William Lambarde's *Archaionomia*, published in 1568 and dedicated to the queen, established the pre-eminence of Alfred's law-code in the corpus of Anglo-Saxon legislation, and (because it did not include Kentish material from the *Textus Roffensis*) gave prominence, perhaps, to the West Saxon tradition.[75] With (or without) the help of a useful warrant from the queen, Matthew Parker (1504–75), formerly Master of Corpus Christi College, Cambridge (1544–53), but latterly archbishop of Canterbury (1559–75), assembled a collection of manuscripts for the express purpose of preserving 'the antient Monuments of the learned Men of our Nation'.[76] Among them was the 'Parker Chronicle and Laws', and an early-eleventh-century manuscript of Asser's 'Life of King Alfred'; others included the Alfredian translations of Gregory's 'Pastoral Care', and 'Dialogues', and an Old English Bede which incorporated a text of the West Saxon regnal table to Alfred and which was furnished by Parker with an even more explicitly 'Alfredian' identity.[77] As architect of the Elizabethan settlement, Parker soon began to publish a range of texts which he thought might help to encourage the study of the early English language and to deepen understanding of early English history, and which might help thereby to provide a firm basis for the newly established 'Ecclesia Anglicana'.[78] The 'St Albans' view of Anglo-Saxon history (featuring

---

[74] Parker, *Early History of Oxford*, pp. 20–40; McKisack, *Medieval History in the Tudor Age*, pp. 70–1.

[75] For Lambarde, see Levy, *Tudor Historical Thought*, pp. 136–41; R. M. Warnicke, *William Lambarde: Elizabethan Antiquary 1536–1601* (Chichester, 1973), esp. pp. 23–6.

[76] R. I. Page, *Matthew Parker and his Books* (Kalamazoo, MI, 1993), pp. 43–4, with plate 24.

[77] Cambridge, University Library, Kk. 3. 18 (N. R. Ker, *Catalogue of Manuscripts Containing Anglo-Saxon* (Oxford, 1957), no. 23), with Parkerian notes on the verso of the flyleaf (to which Tim Graham kindly drew my attention). The manuscript was used by Whelock as the basis of his edition of Bede published in 1643 (below, p. 253).

[78] Levy, *Tudor Historical Thought*, pp. 114–22 and 133–6; F. S. Fussner, *The Historical Revolution: English Historical Writing and Thought, 1580–1640* (London, 1962); pp. 22–4; C. E. Wright, 'The Dispersal of the Monastic Libraries and the Beginnings of Anglo-Saxon Studies', *Trans. of the Cambridge Bibliographical Soc.* 3 (1951), 208–37, at 226–7; McKisack, *Medieval History in the Tudor*

Alfred as First Monarch) was promoted by Parker's publication of 'Matthew of Westminster' in 1567, followed by Matthew Paris in 1571; and in 1574 Parker published his edition of Asser's 'Life of King Alfred'.[79] The publication of Asser facilitated direct access to the text which lies at the heart of the proper appreciation of Alfred's qualities as a ruler of men; and since the book also included a Latin version of King Alfred's will (from a transcript of the *Liber abbatiae* of Hyde abbey), and, most importantly, the prose and verse prefaces to Alfred's translation of Gregory's 'Pastoral Care', with an interlinear translation into modern English followed by a translation into Latin, it did much at the same time to consolidate and substantiate the king's reputation as a statesman and scholar. Not surprisingly, the edition contained nothing which might be construed as being to the advantage of Oxford, though Parker did insert for good measure the story of Alfred and the cakes, taken from the so-called 'Annals of St Neots'.[80]

The effect of Parker's activity is apparent in the earliest works which articulate a view of English history based on printed as opposed to manuscript sources. The particular interest of John Foxe (1516–87), and his 'Acts and Monuments' (or 'Book of Martyrs'), lies elsewhere than in the extended account of English history which appeared for the first time in the edition published in 1570; yet Foxe set a good standard in assembling his picture of Alfred from a wide range of sources, and gave some emphasis to Alfred's virtues as a ruler.[81] In his 'Historie of England', first published in 1577, Raphael Holinshed made effective use of narrative sources, including William of Malmesbury, 'Matthew of Westminster', and even Polydore Vergil;[82] he also used the material published

---

Age, pp. 26–49, esp. 39; P. Williams, *The Later Tudors: England 1547–1603* (Oxford, 1995), pp. 233–7 and 417–18. E. Jones, *The English Nation: the Great Myth* (Stroud, 1998), esp. pp. 31–60, is instructively partisan in its treatment of the same subject.

[79] S. C. Hagedorn, 'Matthew Parker and Asser's *Ælfredi Regis Res Gestæ*', *Princeton Univ. Lib. Chronicle* 51.1 (1989), 74–90; S. C. Hagedorn, 'Received Wisdom: the Reception History of Alfred's Preface to the *Pastoral Care*', *Anglo-Saxonism and the Construction of Social Identity*, ed. A. J. Frantzen and J. D. Niles (Gainesville, FL, 1997), pp. 86–107.

[80] Keynes and Lapidge, *Alfred the Great*, pp. 197–202; see also S. Keynes, *Anglo-Saxon Manuscripts . . . in the Library of Trinity College, Cambridge*, OEN Subsidia 18 (Binghamton, NY, 1992), no. 25 ('Annals of St Neots'), with pl. XXV. For the possibility that Parker's edition gave currency to the tale of Alfred and the cakes, see below, n. 96.

[81] J. Foxe, *Acts and Monuments of these Latter and Perillous Dayes* (London, 1563), as expanded with further historical material in J. Foxe, *The First Volume of the Ecclesiastical History Contaynyng the Actes and Monumentes of Thynges Passed in Every Kynges Tyme in this Realme* (London, 1570). For Foxe's treatment of earlier English history, see W. Haller, *Foxe's Book of Martyrs and the Elect Nation* (London, 1963), esp. pp. 128–30, 141–2 and 152–3 (Alfred).

[82] R. Holinshed, *The Firste Volume of the Chronicles of England, Scotlande, and Irelande* (London, 1577), pp. 211–19. Holinshed's account is illustrated with woodcuts of shipwreck, land-battle, sea-battle, and building activity under royal direction; but the artist would not necessarily have had the specifically 'Alfredian' context in mind. For further discussion, see V. Scholderer, 'The Illustrations of the First Edition of Holinshed', *Edinburgh Bib. Soc. Trans.* 2 (1938–45), 398–403.

in Lambarde's edition of the laws, and in Parker's edition of Asser, though there remained plenty of scope for improvement. In his *Britannia*, first published in 1586, William Camden expressed his reservations about the historicity of the 'British' myth, and introduced new rigour into the investigation of the past.[83] Access to the major narrative sources for early English history was taken a stage further in the 1590s, with the publication in 1592 of Lord William Howard's edition of 'Florence of Worcester',[84] and with the publication in 1596 of Sir Henry Savile's edition of the historical works of William of Malmesbury, Henry of Huntingdon, Roger of Howeden, Ealdorman Æthelweard, and Ingulf of Crowland.[85] Of these sources, the most important would prove to be the one that is now regarded as the most disreputable. The 'History of Crowland' purports to be the work of Ingulf, abbot of Crowland (*c.* 1085–1109); so when it was first published, in Savile's edition, it was accorded all the authority due to an 'early' (late-eleventh-century) source, and thus came to exert a most important influence on the development of the Alfredian myth in the seventeenth and eighteenth centuries. It contained the texts of several Anglo-Saxon charters, which lent it nothing if not an appearance of respectability; and it provided a basis for the development of Alfred's reputation as one who established law and order among the English, and founded what amounted to a new constitution. The fact that 'Ingulf's "History of Crowland"' is a late medieval monastic hoax, albeit one of great literary and historiographical interest, was not fully appreciated until the nineteenth century,[86] by which time, of course, there was no turning back.

Many of the primary texts had been circulating for some time among learned men, whether through the loan or exchange of manuscripts, or through the production and distribution of hand-written transcripts; but the appearance of so much, in print, gave new impetus and direction to the study of early English history. The remarkable circle of learned men who contributed their short

[83] W. Camden, *Britannia, sive florentissimorum regnorum, Angliæ, Scotiæ, Hiberniæ* . . . (London, 1586), rev. ed. (London, 1600); W. Camden, *Britain, or a Chorographicall Description of the Most Flourishing Kingdomes, England, Scotland, and Ireland, and the Islands adjoyning, out of the depth of Antiquitie*, trans. Ph. Holland (London, 1610). For Camden, see P. Collinson, 'One of Us? William Camden and the Making of History', *TRHS* 6th ser. 8 (1998), 139–63. See also Kendrick, *British Antiquity*, pp. 108–9; Levy, *Tudor Historical Thought*, pp. 148–59; and MacDougall, *Racial Myth in English History*, pp. 20–1.
[84] *Chronicon ex chronicis ab initio mundi usque ad annum Domini 1118 deductum, auctore Florentio Wigorniensi monacho* (London, 1592), repr. at Frankfurt in 1601; see *Chronicle of John of Worcester*, ed. Darlington and McGurk, pp. lxxxi–lxxxii.
[85] *Rerum Anglicarum scriptores post Bedam praecipui* (London, 1596), dedicated to Queen Elizabeth, and repr. at Frankfurt in 1601. Sir Henry Savile (1549–1622) was Warden of Merton College, Oxford, from 1585, and provost of Eton College.
[86] See *A Bibliography of English History to 1485*, ed. E. B. Graves (Oxford, 1975), p. 294, with references.

papers to meetings of the Elizabethan 'Society of Antiquaries', in the 1590s, were among the first to capitalize on the access which they enjoyed to published texts, and began at the same time to develop new methods and to set new standards in their various investigations.[87] The members of the group included some of the best of the older hands, such as John Stow (1525–1605), William Lambarde (1536–1601), Arthur Agarde (1540–1615), Francis Thynne (?1545–1608), and William Camden (1551–1623), as well as others who belonged to a younger generation, notably Francis Tate (1560–1616), Henry Spelman (1562–1641), and Robert Cotton (1571–1631). It is possible not only to reconstruct in some detail the range of subjects discussed in successive meetings of the Elizabethan antiquaries, held on a regular basis from 1590 to 1604, but also to peruse the autograph manuscripts of the papers delivered on each occasion;[88] and while much work remains to be done in the elucidation of their activities (on their role, for example, in developing notions of the 'ancient constitution', or in exploding the Arthurian myth),[89] one forms the impression that a notable aspect of their contribution to the development of English historical scholarship was the way in which the evidence of charters and law-codes was integrated by them into the normal processes of academic discourse. It would be interesting to know what Lambarde may have contributed to the proceedings, whether directly or indirectly; for he was the author of a tract on the High Courts of Justice, completed in 1591, which was to have an important impact on political debate in the seventeenth century.[90] Alfred himself featured in one of the two matters discussed in the meeting on 3 November 1591, on the antiquity

---

[87] J. Evans, *A History of the Society of Antiquaries* (Oxford, 1956), pp. 8–13, citing Henry Spelman's account of the gatherings in E. Gibson, *Reliquiæ Spelmannianæ: the Posthumous Works of Sir Henry Spelman Kt* (Oxford, 1698), pp. 69–70. See also Levy, *Tudor Historical Thought*, pp. 164–6; Fussner, *The Historical Revolution*, pp. 92–106; and G. Parry, *The Trophies of Time: English Antiquarians of the Seventeenth Century* (Oxford, 1995), p. 5.

[88] The principal collection of papers is BL, Cotton Faustina E. v. The majority are printed in T. Hearne, *A Collection of Curious Discourses written by Eminent Antiquaries upon Several Heads in our English Antiquities* (Oxford, 1720), supplemented by [Sir J. Ayloffe], *A Collection of Curious Discourses Written by Eminent Antiquaries upon Several Heads in our English Antiquities*, 2 vols. (London, 1771). See also S. Keynes, 'Queen Emma and the *Encomium Emmae Reginae*', *Encomium Emmae Reginae*, ed. A. Campbell, Camden Classic Reprints 4 (Cambridge, 1998), xiii–lxxx, at xlv, n. 7, with references.

[89] Cf. R. F. Brinkley, *Arthurian Legend in the Seventeenth Century*, Johns Hopkins Monographs in Lit. Hist. 3 (Baltimore, MD, 1932), 61–4, and Hill, 'The Norman Yoke', pp. 60–1.

[90] W. Lambarde, *Archeion: or, A Discourse Upon the High Courts of Justice in England*, ed. C. H. McIlwain and P. L. Ward (Cambridge, MA, 1957). For exposition of this work, see also R. J. Terrill, 'William Lambarde: Elizabethan Humanist and Legal Historian', *Jnl of Legal Hist.* 6 (1985), 157–78, at 168–75; J. D. Alsop and W. M. Stevens, 'William Lambarde and the Elizabethan Polity', *Stud. in Med. and Renaissance Hist.* 8 (1987), 233–66; and C. C. Weston, 'England: Ancient Constitution and Common Law', *The Cambridge History of Political Thought 1450–1700*, ed. J. H. Burns with M. Goldie (Cambridge, 1991), pp. 374–411, at 393–4.

of shires in England. Francis Thynne cited Ingulf and William of Malmesbury, giving the credit to King Alfred, but was evidently puzzled to find nothing germane to his purpose in Asser; Thomas Talbot was commendably sceptical, commenting that Alfred was in no position to divide the whole of England into shires; James Ley opined that shires were in fact established before Alfred, and explained that Alfred had instituted the subdivisions into tithings (with view of frankpledge); and Joseph Holland suggested brightly that Alfred had divided the country into shires 'the better to withstand the incursions of the Danes'.[91] Beyond that the antiquaries displayed a certain restraint with regard to Alfred which may suggest that the king still had some distance to run, or perhaps that antiquaries, in the 1590s, were not quite the political animals which they would shortly become.

One member of the fraternity did, however, have something else on his agenda. Some time in the late 1590s, a certain Henry Savile the Elder sent William Camden a passage about Alfred and Oxford which he claimed to have copied from a manuscript of Asser's 'Life of King Alfred' in his own possession.[92] The passage told how a dispute about teaching methods had arisen at Oxford between Grimbald (who had come from Francia to help Alfred with the revival of learning) and the 'old scholars' already established there, how Alfred came to Oxford in order to sort matters out, and how Grimbald retired hurt to Winchester. The story would have appealed to Camden as an Oxford man, and he duly printed the passage in an edition of his *Britannia* published in 1600;[93] and when he republished Parker's edition of Asser's 'Life of King Alfred', in 1602, he simply inserted the passage at the appropriate place in the text.[94] Needless to say, the passage was important to Camden because it implied that the University of Oxford could trace its origins way back *beyond* Alfred, into the dim and distant

---

[91] Hearne, *Curious Discourses*, pp. 29–51, and Ayloffe, *Curious Discourses* I, 19–32, and II, 323; see also Hearne, *Curious Discourses*, pp. lxxix–lxxxvi.

[92] A. G. Watson, 'Henry Savile and the Asser Interpolation', in his *The Manuscripts of Henry Savile of Banke* (London, 1969), pp. 83–5. Henry Savile the Elder was the father of Henry Savile of Banke, and neither is to be confused with Sir Henry Savile, Warden of Merton College (above, n. 85). For his manuscript of Asser, see n. 95.

[93] Camden, *Britannia* [1600], pp. 331–2; Camden, *Britain*, trans. Holland [1610], pp. 378–9. It must have appeared to some that Parker had suppressed the passage in his own edition of Asser. So, when first he heard of the passage about Oxford, the antiquary Thomas Allen asked Thomas James to investigate the matter further. James reported back to Allen by letter, dated 1 April 1600, giving an account of his inspection of the manuscript of Asser which had been used by Parker (and which he had located in Lord Lumley's library), noting that the passage in question was not there. The letter is Oxford, Bodleian Library, Twyne 3, pp. 225–8; and see *Asser's Life of King Alfred*, ed. W. H. Stevenson (Oxford, 1904), pp. xxxvii–xxxix.

[94] W. Camden, *Anglica, Normannica, Hibernica, Cambrica, a veteribus scripta* (Frankfurt, 1602), pp. 1–22, at 16; *Asser's Life of King Alfred*, ed. Stevenson, p. 70 (ch. 83b). For further discussion, see *ibid.* pp. xxiii–xxviii, and Parker, *Early History of Oxford*, pp. 40–52.

past, and because it helped put firmly in their place those who maintained so perversely that the University of Cambridge had been founded by Sigeberht of East Anglia in the seventh century; but while Camden's editorial practices would seem sharp by modern standards, it would perhaps be unfair to accuse him of much more than a wish to provide his readers with the fullest text. There is little that is edifying about the dispute between Oxford and Cambridge, and it is better that the rivalry is now conducted on the rugby field at Twickenham or along a stretch of the river Thames. It was, however, an important episode in the developing self-consciousness of the two universities, and one which had far-reaching consequences for the cult of King Alfred. Matthew Parker had given respectability (in good faith) to the story of Alfred and the cakes, by inserting it into his printed text of Asser, from the 'Annals of St Neots'; and in much the same way Camden gave respectability (in good faith) to the story of Alfred and Oxford, by inserting it into his reprint of Parker's text. The matter remained highly controversial,[95] and those of a more uncritical disposition were always able to believe whatever was convenient for their purposes or compatible with their prejudices. Indeed, as we shall see, the passage in Camden's edition of Asser helped to generate a special enthusiasm for Alfred, in Oxford, which did much to promote his cult there in the later seventeenth century (and beyond); and, one might add, by no means was this the only instance of Alfred's remarkable ability to benefit from a text which on closer inspection would prove not to be what it seemed.

A popular ballad featuring King Alfred and a shepherd, which incorporates the story of Alfred's encounter with a woman and her cakes, would appear to have been published in the late 1570s.[96] The occurrence of the story in such a

---

[95] The implications of the passage in Camden's edition of Asser were pursued, enthusiastically, by B. Twyne, *Antiquitatis academiæ Oxoniensis apologia* (Oxford, 1608), pp. 143–8 and 182–204. On 18 February 1622, Twyne had occasion to raise the matter with Camden himself, and wrote an account of the meeting (Oxford, Bodleian Library, Twyne 22, 235v–236v). It emerges from this account that the manuscript of Asser which had belonged to Savile, and which had been used by Camden, was thought by Camden to have been written at about the time of Richard II, i.e. in the last quarter of the fourteenth century. Such a manuscript might well have contained the offending passage (above, p. 236); and there is no reason to believe that it had been invented by Savile or by Camden.

[96] 'A merry songe of a kinge and a shepherd' was entered on the Stationers' Register for 25 Sept. 1578, and 'King and shepperd' was entered on 14 Dec. 1624; see H. E. Rollins, 'An Analytical Index to the Ballad-Entries in the Register of the Company of Stationers of London', *Stud. in Phil.* 21 (1924), 1–324, at 117–18 (nos. 1354 and 1358). The ballad in question (a seventeenth-century copy of which survives among the Roxburghe Ballads in the British Library [Rox. I. 504–5]) was incorporated in *Wit and Mirth, or Pills to Purge Melancholy*, ed. T. D'Urfey, 6 vols. (London, 1719–20), repr. with an Introduction by C. L. Day, 6 vols. in 3 (New York, 1959) V, 289–97, and in T. Evans, *Old Ballads, Historical and Narrative*, new ed., rev. R. H. Evans, 4 vols. (London, 1810) II, 11–21. For an edition, see W. Chappell, *The Roxburghe Ballads* III.i (Hertford, 1880), 211–19, with a woodcut of Alfred burning the cakes. See also Miles, *King Alfred in Literature*, pp. 48–52, and Lees, *Alfred the Great*, pp. 456–7.

context raises interesting questions about its transmission; for it is not clear whether it represents the survival of a mythology transmitted orally from the Middle Ages (which may or may not have had its origin in a written source), or whether it reflects one or other of the appearances which the story had recently made in print, in the 1560s and 1570s. The ballad itself is essentially a folktale of conventional form, improved for comic effect by the insertion of the story of Alfred and the cakes, and clearly the matter would have to be judged in relation to other material of the same kind.[97] It must suffice for present purposes to infer that the story has long occupied the place in popular mythology which it retains to the present day. No less interesting in the same connection is Thomas Blenerhasset's treatment of Alfred in the 'second part' of the *Mirror for Magistrates*, published in 1578.[98] There is nothing on the cakes, although good use is made of the story of Alfred in the Danish camp; the poet's point, however, is that the king ruined his good name by over-indulgence in carnal activity, and thereby contracted the illness which led to his untimely death.

ALFRED THE GREAT IN STUART ENGLAND

As a creature of national mythology, King Alfred the Great is in all his essentials a product of the first half of the seventeenth century. The advance of scholarship in the sixteenth century had brought the alternative 'Arthurian' mythology under closer scrutiny, and threatened to undermine it altogether. The establishment of the *Ecclesia Anglicana* had given new meaning to the Anglo-Saxon past, and lent it a certain respectability in high circles. There was a developing awareness among antiquaries of the distinctively 'English' origins and identity of the English people. And while it remained the case that the Stuarts were no less keen than their Tudor predecessors to capitalize on their 'British' or Arthurian lineage, it was their pretensions as rulers which helped none the less to create the conditions in which Alfred would eventually prevail over King Arthur, and put Edward the Confessor into the shade. The Anglo-Saxon past, in a relatively impersonal sense, was effectively politicized by lawyers and antiquaries working in response to the rampant or latent absolutism of James I (1603–25) and Charles I (1625–49), and there were other lawyers, of more overtly royalist persuasion, who for their part reinvented Alfred as the very incarnation of constitutional kingship. For a while, in the middle of the century, kings were not

---

[97] For material of this kind in its wider cultural context, see M. Spufford, *Small Books and Pleasant Histories: Popular Fiction and its Readership in Seventeenth-Century England* (London, 1981); N. Würzbach, *The Rise of the English Street Ballad, 1550–1650* (Cambridge, 1990); and T. Watt, *Cheap Print and Popular Piety 1550–1640* (Cambridge, 1991).

[98] *Parts Added to The Mirror for Magistrates by John Higgins & Thomas Blenerhasset*, ed. L. B. Campbell (Cambridge, 1946), pp. 361–496, at 469–76. For successive editions of the original compilation (1559–87), see *The Mirror for Magistrates*, ed. L. B. Campbell (Cambridge, 1938).

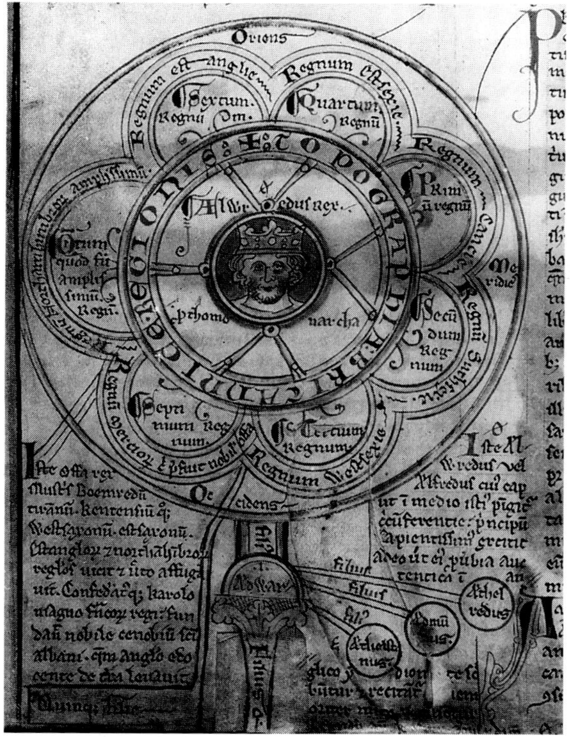

VIIb Drawing by Matthew Paris, in his *Chronica Maiora*, pt I, showing King Alfred as first sole ruler of England. (Cambridge, Corpus Christi College 26, 65r, detail.)

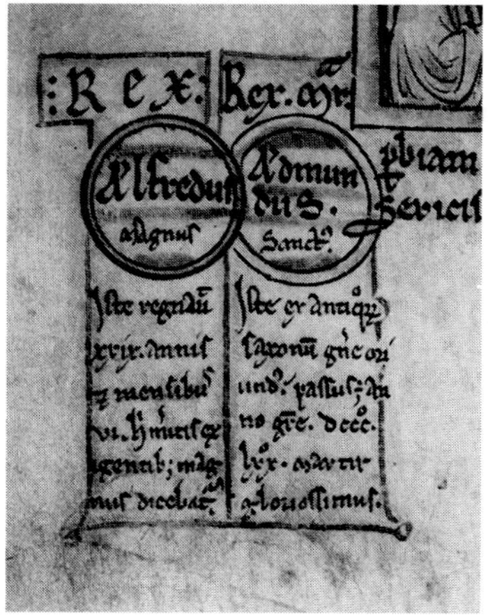

VIIc Marginal annotation by Matthew Paris, in his 'History of the Abbots of St Albans', with reference to 'Ælfredus Magnus'. (London, British Library, Cotton Nero D. i, 30v, detail.)

VIIa Diagram by Matthew Paris (*c.* 1250), in his *Chronica Maiora*, pt I, showing the Heptarchy, King Alfred, and King Alfred's descendants. (Cambridge, Corpus Christi College 26, iv verso, detail.)

VIII*a* Portrait of King Alfred the Great, commissioned by Thomas Walker, Master of University College, Oxford, in 1661–2.

VIII*b* Portrait of King Alfred the Great made and engraved by George Vertue to accompany the folio edition of Rapin's *History of England* (1732–3). *Private collection.*

IX*a* Nicholas Blakey, 'Alfred in the Isle of Athelney receiving news of a victory over the Danes', from *English History Delineated* (1751). *Private collection.*

IX*b* Mason Chamberlin, RA, 'Alfred the Great in the neatherd's cottage', painted in 1764, from an engraving published in 1794. (British Museum, Department of Prints & Drawings, 1950-11-11-99.)

X*a* Samuel Wale, RA, 'Alfred makes a collection of laws, and divides the kingdom into counties', from Mortimer's *History of England* (1764). *Private collection*.

X*b* Edward Edwards, 'Alfred in the neat-herd's cottage', from an engraving first published in *The Copper-Plate Magazine*, 1 September 1776. *Private collection*.

XIa Richard Westall, 'Prince Alfred before Pope Leo III [*recte* IV]', painted for Bowyer's 'Historic Gallery', and published in 1794.

XIb Francis Wheatley, 'Alfred in the house of the neat-herd', painted for Bowyer's 'Historic Gallery' in 1792 and published in 1795.

XII*b* Thomas Stothard, 'Alfred disguised as a harper in the Danish camp', (*c.* 1793), from an engraving published in 1802. (British Museum, Department of Prints & Drawings, 1849-7-21-1412.)

XII*a* Richard Westall, 'Queen Judith reciting to Alfred the Great, when a child, the songs of the bards' (1799), watercolour. (British Museum, Department of Prints & Drawings, Oo.3-12.)

XIII*a* David Wilkie, 'Alfred reprimanded by the neatherd's wife' (1806), from an engraving published in 1828. (British Museum, Department of Prints & Drawings, 1836-11-24-3.)

XIII*b* C. W. Cope, 'The first trial by jury'. Cartoon for a fresco, exhibited at Westminster Hall in 1843, from a lithograph published in 1847. (British Museum, Department of Prints & Drawings, 1854-12-11-135.)

XIV*a* John Bridges, 'Alfred submitting his code of laws for the approval of the witan'. Cartoon for a fresco, exhibited at Westminster Hall in 1843, from a lithograph published in 1847. (British Museum, Department of Prints & Drawings, 1854-12-11-142.)

XIV*b* Marshall Claxton, 'Alfred in the camp of the Danes, A.D. 880'. Cartoon for a fresco, exhibited at Westminster Hall in 1843, from a lithograph published *c.* 1847. (British Museum, Department of Prints & Drawings, 1852-6-12-421.)

fashionable in any form, but after the Restoration, during the reigns of Charles II (1660–85) and James II (1685–8), Alfred was able to make his first appearance in public as a constitutional monarch, albeit with some help from his friends in Oxford.

Seen in the most general terms, the process was inseparable from the early stages in the development of what has come to be known as the 'Whig interpretation of history', or the 'Whig theory of the Ancient Constitution'.[99] There were always those of a royalist persuasion for whom a conquest was a conquest, and who might therefore be inclined to derive a king's exercise of absolute power from the events of 1066, and from his position as the Lord's anointed. There were, on the other hand, others who felt that the liberties of the English people, and the institutions which guaranteed their peace and prosperity, had long been threatened by their kings, and were now threatened in particular by the pretensions of the Stuart monarchs. Magna Carta naturally assumed great importance for the recovery of some liberties and the establishment of others; but those who sought to establish a new political order wished to represent themselves as seeking to restore an order of a kind which they imagined had once existed, and which they supposed had since been lost. So they turned back to Anglo-Saxon England, and found that the liberties and institutions which they coveted had existed before the Norman Conquest, and so before the imposition of a new and self-evidently extraneous regime. Special importance was attached by some commentators to the so-called 'Laws of Edward the Confessor', as a symbol or product of the legal regime which the Normans had claimed to respect, and it could be argued, therefore, that the Norman Conquest had been conducted or effected under circumstances which allowed continuity from whatever was identified as the ancient 'Saxon' constitution. There were, however, others of a more radical persuasion, for whom it was convenient (or, for their purposes, necessary) to regard the Norman Conquest as the enforced imposition of a new political order, and for whom the ancient

---

[99] For accounts with emphasis on historiography, see: H. Butterfield, *The Whig Interpretation of History* (London, 1931); H. Butterfield, *The Englishman and his History* (Cambridge, 1944); and J. Kenyon, *The History Men: the Historical Profession in England since the Renaissance* (London, 1983). For accounts with emphasis on political thought, see: Hill, 'The Norman Yoke' [1954]; J. G. A. Pocock, *The Ancient Constitution and the Feudal Law: a Study of English Historical Thought in the Seventeenth Century* (Cambridge, 1957), reissued with a Retrospect (Cambridge, 1987); and Q. Skinner, 'History and Ideology in the English Revolution', *Hist. Jnl* 8 (1965), 151–78, with particular attention to differing views of the Norman Conquest. See also R. B. Seaberg, 'The Norman Conquest and the Common Law: the Levellers and the Argument from Continuity', *Hist. Jnl* 24 (1981), 791–806; J. P. Sommerville, 'History and Theory: the Norman Conquest in Early Stuart Political Thought', *Political Stud.* 34 (1986), 249–61; Weston, 'England: Ancient Constitution and Common Law'; and M. Chibnall, *The Debate on the Norman Conquest* (Manchester, 1999). For the 'Norman Yoke' in the eighteenth century, see below, p. 270.

'Saxon' constitution was something which might usefully be disassociated from Edward the Confessor and traced back to an earlier stage in the development of English monarchy. Alfred had long been regarded as the First Monarch of all England, and had been credited by reputable authorities with the origin of shires, hundreds, and tithings, and much else besides. By definition, therefore, it was in Alfredian arrangements that lawyers might reasonably expect to uncover the origins of the Common Law (unwritten as opposed to statute law, administered in the king's courts and common to the kingdom as a whole), and of many other familiar aspects of English polity, notably regular parliaments, trial by jury, and the frankpledge system – which came as part of the same package. Other aspects of the medieval regime, notably feudal tenure and all it entailed, might more appropriately be traced back to the Normans, as alien customs imposed on the English by foreign conquerors. Alfred was always there for the royalists; but at the same time he was all set to become a Whig hero.

Richard Rowlands, *alias* Richard Verstegan (*c.* 1545–1620), an Englishman supposedly of Dutch extraction who had been educated at Christ Church, Oxford, in the 1560s, was among those who reacted against the tenets of 'British' history. In his *Restitution of Decayed Intelligence in Antiquities*, first published in 1605 and dedicated to James I, Verstegan put the British in their place and sought to affirm the 'Englishness' of the English people.[100] He took the view that the concept of a single 'English' people had been picked up from Pope Gregory, that it was King Egbert who gave his united realm the name of 'England', and that it was 'the good, and rightly renowned King Alfred' who divided it into shires.[101] In a survey of Roman, sub-Roman and early Anglo-Saxon history published in the following year, John Clapham (1566–1618) set Arthur firmly though sympathetically in his appropriate place, and reaffirmed

---

[100] R. V[erstegan], *Restitution of Decayed Intelligence in Antiquities, Concerning the Most Noble and Renowned English Nation* (Antwerp, 1605), repr. (London, 1673). See Parry, *Trophies of Time*, pp. 49–69; and R. W. Clement, 'Richard Verstegan's Reinvention of Anglo-Saxon England: a Contribution from the Continent', *Reinventing the Middle Ages & the Renaissance*, ed. W. F. Gentrup (Brepols, 1998), pp. 19–36. The thrust of the argument is represented symbolically by the inclusion of a number of engraved illustrations, depicting the pagan gods and two particularly significant historical events ('The arrival of the first ancestors of English-men out of Germany in Britain', and 'The manner of the first bringing and preaching of the Christian faith unto Ethelbert, King of Kent'). The reprint of Verstegan was made necessary, perhaps, by the tenacity of the 'British' point of view, represented latterly (for example) by R. Sheringham, *De Anglorum gentis origine disceptatio* (Cambridge, 1670).

[101] Verstegan, *Restitution of Decayed Intelligence in Antiquities*, esp. pp. 161–4. In the late tenth century, Æthelweard (*Chronicon* i.3) stated that Britain was now called England, 'taking the name of the victors' (ed. Campbell, p. 9); in the twelfth century, Henry of Huntingdon stated that the monarchy of England had originated under Egbert, and had then been divided into shires (ed. Greenway, pp. 12, 16 and 264); and according to Camden, Egbert had issued an edict proclaiming the Heptarchy as 'England'.

Egbert's importance as the one who had named his kingdom 'England'.[102] It is significant that Alfred remained for the time being in a secondary role; but if the ground was changing, so too were the rules. The origins of the more radical view of the Anglo-Saxon past lie hidden (one suspects) in some of the unrecorded deliberations of the Elizabethan antiquaries, in the 1590s, and it was no coincidence that (in Spelman's words) King James I 'took a little Mislike of our Society, not being inform'd, that we had resolv'd to decline all matters of State',[103] and effectively shut them down. Not that the king's 'mislike' made much difference. Three lawyers, in particular, appear to have determined the basic course of the discussion in the early seventeenth century. First, in order of seniority, was Sir Edward Coke (1552–1634), Lord Chief Justice of the Common Pleas from 1606 to 1613, who expounded his views on English law in his several 'Reports' (1600–15) and also in his 'Institutes of the Laws of England' (1628). For example, in the preface to the Eighth Part of his Reports Coke reviewed the early history of English law, with emphasis on the repeated confirmations by Norman and later kings of the Laws of Edward the Confessor, and asserted in passing that Trial by Jury 'was not instituted by the powerful Will of a Conqueror'; and in the preface to the Ninth Part of his Reports Coke summarized some of the provisions contained in the *Mirror of Justices* (noting references to Alfred), extending his survey of early English law with extracts from charters and law-codes, and drawing attention to Alfred's division of England into shires or counties.[104] The second was Sir Henry Spelman (1562–1641), whose work included tracts on 'the Ancient Government of England' and 'Of Parliaments', and also on 'The Original, Growth, Propagation and Condition of Feuds and Tenures by Knight-Service in England' (1639), which, although not published until 1698, reflect his concerns as one of the original 'antiquaries'.[105] The third,

---

[102] [J. Clapham], *The Historie of Great Britannie* (London, 1606), repr. Eng. Experience 719 (Amsterdam, 1975), esp. 296–7. For Clapham, see also Kendrick, *British Antiquity*, p. 109. The title continues: 'declaring the successe of times and affaires in that iland, from the Romans first entrance, untill the raigne of Egbert, the West-Saxon prince; who reduced the severall principalities of the Saxons and English, into a monarchie, and changed the name of Britannie into England'. [103] Gibson, *Reliquiæ Spelmannianæ*, p. 70.

[104] *The Reports of Sir Edward Coke Kt. in English, Compleat in Thirteen Parts*, 7 vols. (London, 1727) IV and V. For Coke's use of the *Mirror of Justices* (above, pp. 234–5), see *Mirror of Justices*, ed. Whittaker, pp. ix–x. See also Hill, 'The Norman Yoke', pp. 58–9 and 65–6; *Complete Prose Works of John Milton*, III: *1648–1649*, ed. M. Y. Hughes (New Haven, CT, 1962), 398–9; Pronay and Taylor, *Parliamentary Texts*, pp. 56–9; and Weston, 'England: Ancient Constitution and Common Law', pp. 392–3. For a valuable exposition of Coke's views in a wider context, see A. Cromartie, *Sir Matthew Hale 1609–1676: Law, Religion and Natural Philosophy*, Cambridge Stud. in Early Modern Brit. Hist. (Cambridge, 1995), pp. 11–29.

[105] Gibson, *Reliquiæ Spelmannianæ*, pp. 1–46 (Feuds and Tenures), 49–55 (Ancient Government) and 57–65 (Parliaments). On the dispersal of Spelman's collections, see S. Keynes, 'The Lost Cartulary of Abbotsbury', *ASE* 18 (1989), 207–43, at 223–4 and 234.

and perhaps the most influential because of the sheer volume of his output, was the young John Selden (1584–1654).[106] Selden's early work on the ancient constitution is represented by his *Analecton Anglobritannicon*, written in 1607 although not published until 1615.[107] His tract on *England's Epinomis* was also written in 1607, and not published until much later.[108] Selden displayed his best command of the material in his *Jani Anglorum Facies Altera* (1610),[109] and, as he worked thereafter on his *Titles of Honour* (1614) and *The Historie of Tithes* (1618), gained renown in the field that was second to none. The vital aspect of the work of these men, for present purposes, is the extent to which their work was seen to depend on close analysis of the texts (including charters and law-codes), matched by the direct and inevitable consequences of the fact that they believed the *Mirror of Justices* to be a pre-Conquest text, and Ingulf's 'History of Crowland' to be an authoritative eleventh-century source. For it was in this way that they were able to deduce, as it were, not only the Alfredian origin of parliament, shires, hundreds, and tithings, but also, in effect, of the whole apparatus of 'subordinate government' and the development of the Common Law. It should be noted, however, that the proper business of these men was to establish the antiquity of English law, as something which had originated before the Norman Conquest, not to project what they found in the image of a particular king; and for this reason there is no pervasive adulation of King Alfred in their writings. One might add that both Coke and Selden are known to have acquired some original Anglo-Saxon charters, leaving only the unfortunate Spelman to complain that charters were so rare in his day 'as though I have seen diverse, yet could I never obtein one originall'.[110] One might also add that all three left copious collections of papers, including transcripts of charters and law-codes, which might yet repay further investigation.[111] Between them, Coke, Spelman, and Selden produced a view of the Anglo-Saxon polity which complemented the narrative histories of an earlier age, and laid the foundations for much of that which would follow.

---

[106] For recent accounts of Selden and his works, see Cromartie, *Sir Matthew Hale*, pp. 30–41; Parry, *Trophies of Time*, pp. 95–129; and P. Christianson, *Discourse on History, Law, and Governance in the Public Career of John Selden, 1610–1635* (Toronto, 1996). On the dispersal of Selden's collections, see S. Keynes, 'A Charter of Edward the Elder for Islington', *Hist. Research* 66 (1993), 303–16, at 304–6.   [107] J. Selden, *Analecton Anglobritannicon* (Frankfurt, 1615).

[108] J. Selden, *England's Epinomis*, in R. Westcot, *Tracts Written by John Selden* (London, 1683) [*England's Epinomis*], esp. pp. 8–11.

[109] J. Selden, *Jani Anglorum Facies Altera* (London, 1610), trans. in Westcot, *Tracts Written by John Selden* [*Jani Anglorum Facies Altera*], esp. pp. 37–42.

[110] H. Spelman, 'Of Antient Deeds and Charters', *The English Works of Sir Henry Spelman Kt* (London, 1723), pt 2, pp. 233–56, at 236.

[111] For Coke's library, see *A Catalogue of the Library of Sir Edward Coke*, ed. W. O. Hassall, Yale Law Lib. Pub. 12 (New Haven, CT, 1950), and the material still preserved at Holkham Hall, Norfolk. For the libraries of Spelman and Selden, see above, nn. 105 and 106.

The cult of King Alfred the Great

While Coke, Spelman and Selden were developing and expounding their views on the nature of the ancient constitution, others continued to indulge in relatively straightforward historical writing about King Alfred. For example, John Speed (1552–1629) produced his magnificent *Theatre of the Empire of Great Britain* and *History of Great Britain* in 1611,[112] which introduced King James to his united realm, and which, in addition to its county maps and decorated title-pages, made good (if essentially decorative) use of Anglo-Saxon coins, courtesy of Sir Robert Cotton,[113] and provided elaborate coats of arms for each successive king.[114] Egbert of Wessex is hailed as the 'First Sole and Absolute Monarch of the Englishmen', taking precedence in this respect over King Alfred, of whom Speed remarks that 'of some Historians he is famoused by the stile of the first absolute Monarch', without much further ado.[115] The poet Samuel Daniel (1562–1619), in the service of the queen, himself produced an interesting (prose) 'Historie of England' in 1612, in which Alfred is accorded an honourable place as a 'mirrour of Princes', but in which the Anglo-Saxons are put firmly in their place by the strikingly positive account of William the Conqueror.[116] For some, perhaps for many, the Norman Conquest remained the natural beginning of English history, as of English royal portraiture.[117] Alfred, did, however, make some impression outside historiographical contexts. The

---

[112] J. Speed, *The Theatre of the Empire of Great Britaine* + *The History of Great Britaine Under the Conquests of the Romans, Saxons, Danes and Normans* (London, 1611). The work was dedicated to King James; the copy which belonged to his queen, Anne of Denmark, is now in the library of Trinity College, Cambridge.

[113] For Cotton's coins, see R. H. M. Dolley, 'The Cotton Collection of Anglo-Saxon Coins', *Brit. Museum Quarterly* 19 (1954), 75–81; G. van der Meer, 'An Early Seventeenth-Century Inventory of Cotton's Anglo-Saxon Coins', *Sir Robert Cotton as Collector: Essays on an Early Stuart Courtier and his Legacy*, ed. C. J. Wright (London, 1997), pp. 168–82; and below, n. 173. For Cotton and Speed, see D. Howarth, 'Sir Robert Cotton and the Commemoration of Famous Men', *Sir Robert Cotton as Collector*, ed. Wright, pp. 40–67, at 65–6, n. 38.

[114] It would appear that separate badges for each of the kingdoms of the Heptarchy were invented in the Middle Ages, to which was added a badge for the kingdom of all England (a cross flory), itself derived from the thirteenth-century arms of Edward the Confessor (above, n. 65). In Speed's system (which may be a refinement of an older system), the cross flory served on its own for kings from Egbert to Eadwig, including Alfred; the badge becomes a cross flory between four martlets, for kings from Edgar to Edmund Ironside; a fifth martlet was then added at the base of the cross, for Edward the Confessor. University College, Oxford, seems to have adopted its own coat of arms (a cross flory between four martlets) from this system, presumably in the fond belief that these arms were Alfred's.

[115] *Ibid.* pp. 348–9 [Egbert] and 356–9 [Alfred].

[116] S. Daniel, *The First Part of the Historie of England* (London, 1612), extending to the reign of King Stephen, later continued as *The Collection of the Historie of England* (London, [1618]), extending to the reign of Edward III.

[117] *Baziliologia, a Booke of Kings, being the True and Lively Effigies of all our English Kings from the Conquest untill this Present* (London, 1618) began with William I: see A. Griffiths, *The Print in Stuart Britain 1603–1689*, Exhibition Catalogue (London, 1998), pp. 49–52 (no. 9).

Catholic divine Dr John Pits (1560–1616), following Bale, included 'Alfredus Magnus' in his catalogue of writers, published in 1619.[118] Another Catholic, William Drury, wrote a Latin play about King Alfred which was first performed in the college of the English Benedictine community at Douay in 1619, and published in 1620.[119] The image of Alfred as a scholarly king also began at this stage to exercise an important influence on the promotion of Anglo-Saxon studies in their own right. William of Malmesbury had harped upon the king's activities as a translator of selected Latin classics, and the publication of the prose and verse prefaces to Gregory's *Regula Pastoralis*, in 1574, had put the king's manifesto for the revival of learning into the public domain. So when, in 1623, William L'Isle ended his extended plea for the study of Old English with 'The complaint of a Saxon King', addressed to the readers of his own day, it was not unnaturally King Alfred who looked down from his vantage-point in Heaven and reflected on the neglect of what he had done when in the lower world:[120]

If any thing here (I say) might offend or greiue me; this it is, that I perceiue there the nation which once I gouerned, which hath also many Kings, both before and after a Norman interruption, descended of my bloud, to make so small account of our writings and language... Haue I translated with my owne hand the godly Pastorall of Saint Gregory, with many his learned Homilies; yea the whole Bible it selfe; haue I sent copies of them all to my Churches, with many Mancusses of gold, for the helpe and incouragement of my Pastors, and instruction of my people; that all should be lost, all forgot, all grow out of knowledge and remembrance? that my English in England, neede to be Englished; and my translation translated; while few now, and shortly perhaps none, shall be able to do it?

The impassioned plea may have helped to encourage Old English studies in general, but it cannot be said that scholars flocked to the cause. In 1638 Sir Henry Spelman established a position at Cambridge for a 'lecturer and reader of the Saxon language and the history of our ancient British churches', which was held first by Abraham Whelock (1593–1653) and then briefly by William Somner (1598–1669).[121] The chief monument of this exercise in the patronage

---

[118] J. Pits, *Relationum historicarum de rebus Anglicis tomus primus* (Paris, 1619), pp. 169–71.
[119] W. Drury, *Alvredus sive Alfredus: Tragi-comoedia ter exhibita in seminario Anglorum Duaceno ab ejusdem collegii juventute, anno Domini M.DC.XIX* (Douay, 1620). For Drury, see the *Dictionary of National Biography* (hereafter *DNB*), and Miles, *King Alfred in Literature*, pp. 52 and 128–30. For another Jacobean drama with an Alfredian theme, in which Alfred defends his kingdom against King Canute, and grants a charter to Newcastle, see R. Howell, 'King Alfred and the Proletariat: a Case of the Saxon Yoke', *AAe* 4th ser. 47 (1969), 97–100.
[120] W. L'Isle, *A Saxon Treatise concerning the Old and New Testament* (London, 1623), Preface. For L'Isle and his projected edition of the OE Psalter, see D. McKitterick, *A History of the Cambridge University Press*, I: *Printing and the Book Trade in Cambridge 1534–1698* (Cambridge, 1992), 187.
[121] For Whelock, see J. C. T. Oates, *Cambridge University Library: a History. From the Beginnings to the Copyright Act of Queen Anne* (Cambridge, 1986), pp. 173–211. For the Saxon lectureship, see the Spelman–Whelock correspondence in Cambridge, University Library, Dd. III. 12.

of Anglo-Saxon studies was the publication in 1643 of Whelock's edition of Bede's *Historia ecclesiastica*, accompanied by what was regarded explicitly as its 'Alfredian' translation, and by a text and Latin translation of the *Anglo-Saxon Chronicle* (based on MS G).[122] Whelock also produced a new edition of Lambarde's *Archaionomia* in 1644, and in the same year reissued both works together, making a useful compendium of Alfredian works (the OE Bede, the *Chronicle* and the laws). It was not, however, for another fifty years that other works by (or attributed to) King Alfred would begin to find their way into print, and then not in Cambridge but in Oxford.

The foundations laid by Coke, Spelman and Selden, during the reign of James I (1603–25), were put to good use by two men working during the reign of his successor, Charles I (1625–49). One was a Gloucestershire solicitor called Robert Powell, who flourished in the 1630s.[123] In his 'Treatise of the Antiquity, Authority, Uses and Jurisdiction of the Ancient Courts of Leet, or View of Franck-Pledge', Powell traced the history of the particular legal institutions in which he was interested back to their Alfredian origins, and beyond that to their Mosaic roots; so we read of the 'first division of this kingdome by Alfred into Counties, Hundreds and Tythings', and of Alfred's 'appointment of officers and making Lawes for the better ordering of the Kingdome'. The tract was written apparently in the early 1630s (during the period of Charles's 'Personal Rule'), for it was approved by none other than Sir Edward Coke, who died in 1634. It might not, however, have appealed to those of a different political persuasion, and its publication was delayed for some years by decree of the Star Chamber. When published in 1642, it was dedicated to the knights, citizens and burgesses assembled in Parliament, and to their speaker, John Selden.[124] Powell's 'Life of Alfred', published in 1634, conveyed much the same message in a rather more palatable form, and must be accorded pride of place (after Asser) in the long line of Alfredian biography.[125] Powell represents Alfred as a model of Christian kingship, and as the first 'that reduced this confused Kingdome into an orderly rule of subordinate government' (shires, hundreds, and tithings); all of which is set

---

[122] [A. Whelock], *Historiæ ecclesiasticæ gentis Anglorum libri V* (Cambridge, 1643); see also McKitterick, *A History of the Cambridge University Press*, pp. 187–91.

[123] For Powell, see the entry on him in the *DNB*.

[124] R. Powell, *A Treatise of the Antiquity, Authority, Uses and Jurisdiction of the Ancient Courts of Leet, or View of Franck-Pledge, and of Subordination of Government Derived from the Institution of Moses, the First Legislator; and the First Imitation of him in this Island of Great Britaine, by King Alfred and Continued Ever Since* (London, 1642), published again in 1668.

[125] R. Powell, *The Life of Alfred, or, Alured. The First Institutor of Subordinate Government in this Kingdome, and Refounder of the University of Oxford. Together with a Parallel of our Soveraigne Lord K. Charles untill this year, 1634* (London, 1634); repr. with an Introduction by F. Wilson and bibliographical notes by S. Tyas (Stamford, 1996). For Powell, see the *DNB*, and Miles, *King Alfred in Literature*, p. 42.

beside a parallel 'Life' of King Charles, drawing parallels between the two rulers, allowing Charles to bathe in Alfred's reflected glory, yet suggesting by implication how Charles might bring himself into line. It should otherwise be noted that Alfred is hailed on the title-page not only as 'The First Institutor of Subordinate Government in this Kingdom', but also as 'Refounder of the University of Oxford', where 're-founder' was the operative word. For while Powell followed Camden in declaring that 'the institution of that famous Achademie was doubtless long before', he was determined to ensure that Alfred retained all the credit that was his due.[126]

The 'Life of King Alfred' written *c*. 1640 by Sir John Spelman (1594–1643), son of Henry, has a better claim to be regarded as the first 'modern' biography of the king; for it is Spelman's work, far more so than Powell's, which when first published in Latin translation in 1678, when published again in its original English form in 1709, and when used thereafter as the basis for more popular accounts of the king, effectively determined the parameters of Alfredian studies which have endured to the present day.[127] John Spelman was a close friend and adviser of King Charles I, and seems to have begun work on his 'Life of Alfred' in the late 1630s;[128] he completed it soon after the outbreak of the civil war, whilst serving in the royalist camp, at Oxford, in 1642. Whilst in Oxford, Spelman was based at Brasenose College, and died of camp disease on 25 July 1643.[129] The principal theme of Spelman's book is Alfred as the 'First Founder of the English Monarchy'; and to judge from the final section of the book (iii.122), and from the fact that it was dedicated to the twelve-year-old Charles, Prince of Wales, we may suppose that it was conceived by its author as a way of conveying to the reigning king, and to his heir, a picture of one of their most illustrious forebears, from whose experience they would be able to take comfort, and from whose example they might be able to draw inspiration. Charles I had inherited a united kingdom from James VI & I, in 1625; but whereas John Speed in his 'History' had presented James with a view of Britain as a whole, John Spelman was more concerned to apprise Charles I, and the Prince of Wales, of the political tradition inherited by a king of the English. The material is arranged in three books: book I, 'containing his wars and troublesome reign'; book II,

---

[126] Powell, *Life of Alfred*, pp. 37–47 (pp. 15–16 in the repr. ed.), citing Twyne as his authority.

[127] For the original English text, see T. Hearne, *The Life of Ælfred the Great, by Sir John Spelman Kt* (Oxford, 1709), hereafter Spelman, *Life of Alfred*. For the Latin translation, see [O. Walker], *Ælfredi Magni Anglorum regis invictissimi vita tribus libris comprehensa a clarissimo dno Johanne Spelman* (Oxford, 1678), hereafter Spelman, *Life of Alfred*, ed. Walker. See also Miles, *King Alfred in Literature*, pp. 43–4; Hagedorn, 'Received Wisdom: the Reception History of Alfred's Preface to the *Pastoral Care*', pp. 92–4; and Simmons, *Reversing the Conquest*, pp. 33–4.

[128] See further below, n. 132.

[129] For his father's account, see Gibson, *Reliquiæ Spelmannianæ*, sig. d; see also Obadiah Walker's preface to the edition of 1678 (below, n. 174).

'containing his laws and political government'; and book III, 'containing his magnificence, devotions, and private life'. Alfred is represented throughout as a mirror of princely behaviour; indeed, 'even the dust of his feet was not unworthy the collecting' (Author's Dedication). Yet this is no mere panegyric, or sustained exercise in sycophantic hyperbole, for Spelman's work was based on his own close examination of a wide range of material, in manuscript and print, and is suffused with displays of his own independence of judgement. It is true that he dwelt at some length on Alfred's foundation of the University of Oxford (ii.69–70, iii.20–67), explaining why the king chose to locate it there (ii.69),[130] and naming the members of the teaching staff (iii.65); yet although Spelman completed the work in Oxford, he did not take this indulgent line towards the story merely in order to gratify the University's self-esteem. The point is that Sir John Spelman was a Cambridge man: educated at Trinity College, like his father Sir Henry Spelman, and proud of it, like other Trinity men.[131] His concern, therefore, was to maintain the priority of Cambridge in the ratings; and to do this he naturally had to challenge the view that Oxford was already thriving in the fifth century, and to maintain instead that it had been not *re*founded but *founded* in the late ninth century by King Alfred. He took the trouble, therefore, to inspect the Cottonian manuscript of Asser, in order to establish whether or not the offending passage in Camden's edition was an authentic part of the text (iii.37).[132] It must be admitted that Spelman was somewhat less critical in his rather casual endorsement of the claim that Cambridge had been founded in the seventh century by Sigeberht, king of the East Angles (iii.60–3); but he felt sure that Oxford University would be proud 'henceforth to boast one Common Founder and Original with this our English Monarchy'.[133] Moving on to more weighty matters, Spelman regarded Alfred's surviving law-code as 'early', because Alfred was styled 'king of the West Saxons', and he presumed that there was a later code, now lost, in which the king had established shires and much else besides (ii.6). He made (or tried to make) good use of other manuscripts in the Cottonian library, including the 'Proverbs of Alfred' (ii.48–50),[134] and the

[130] Hearne countered Spelman's suggestion (that Oxford was a safe place) with a spirited assertion of the supposition that Alfred chose Oxford 'because Letters had flourished here so much before' (Spelman, *Life of Alfred*, ed. Hearne, pp. 144–5, n. 1; cf. pp. 225–6).
[131] He gave an honest reason for not wishing to impugn the antiquity of his own university: 'Besides having been of Trinity College in Cambridge, I would not be thought to have less affection to my Foster-Mother's Right, than the Author to the Apology [i.e. Twyne], Mr. Camden, Leland, and other Oxford Men have shewn for Oxford' (p. 191).
[132] Spelman, *Life of Alfred*, ed. Hearne, p. 182. A letter from John Spelman to Abraham Whelock, dated 6 April 1640 (in Cambridge, University Library, Dd. III. 12), reveals that for this purpose Spelman had sought Whelock's assistance in establishing the whereabouts of the manuscript used by Parker. [133] Spelman, *Life of Alfred*, ed. Hearne, p. 192.
[134] Spelman, *Life of Alfred*, ed. Hearne, pp. 125–31. See also Arngart, *Proverbs of Alfred* II, 20–5.

voyages of Ohthere and Wulfstan (ii.81).[135] There is little overt reference to King Charles's predicament at Oxford in the early 1640s, but plenty from which a king was clearly expected to learn. Although Alfred was 'sole sovereign of the whole island' (i.127), yet he was ruler of a free people (ii.3). Many of the kingdom's most cherished institutions had originated in his reign, including trial by jury and the Common Law (ii.15–19). He had been instrumental in the revival and promotion of learning (ii.51). He was not subservient to Rome (iii.114). There is also a striking emphasis on Alfred's willingness to 'hear the Opinion of his Counsel' (ii.89), whether his 'Great-Council' or his 'Privy-Council', and reference in the same connection (citing the *Mirror of Justices*, as cited by Coke) to the Assemblies convened twice a year at London (ii.92). In short, Spelman's 'Life of Alfred' has a serious claim on our attention, whether judged as a tract for its times, or as a forerunner of modern scholarship.[136] The autograph manuscript is, incidentally, preserved in the Bodleian Library;[137] and it is to be hoped that there may one day be a proper edition of the text, giving Spelman his due and revealing the processes of thought which lie behind the extensive authorial changes (all of which are concealed in the printed text). Other material relating to Spelman's 'Life' was formerly preserved at University College, Oxford, but sadly is now lost.[138]

The quality of Spelman's work on Alfred is thrown into relief when it is compared with the work of others writing more generally on the Anglo-Saxon period in the central decades of the seventeenth century. Sir Richard Baker (1568–1645), High Sheriff of Oxfordshire in 1620, fell on hard times in the 1630s and took up residence in the Fleet prison, where he wrote his *Chronicle of*

---

[135] It seems that Cotton Tiberius B. i was not available when Spelman visited the Cottonian library; see his *Life of Alfred*, ed. Hearne, pp. 152–6. See also D. S. Brewer, 'Sixteenth, Seventeenth and Eighteenth Century References to the Voyage of Ohthere', *Anglia* 71 (1952–3), 202–11, at 209.

[136] Spelman's portrayal of King Alfred deserves comparison with the line of argument pursued by him in some of his other more overtly polemical writings, on which see C. C. Weston and J. R. Greenberg, *Subjects and Sovereigns: the Grand Controversy over Legal Sovereignty in Stuart England* (Cambridge, 1981), pp. 108–13. The 'Life' is judged in another context by H. Carter, *A History of the Oxford University Press*, I: *To the Year 1780* (Oxford, 1975), pp. 112–13.

[137] Oxford, Bodleian Library, e Mus. 75 (S.C. 3696). Spelman's text was copied *c*. 1660 in Bodleian Library, Ballard 55 (S.C. 10841), and prepared by Hearne for the press in Bodleian Library, Rawlinson D. 324 (S.C. 15363).

[138] University College, MS. 131 ('Joan. Spelmanni notæ in vitam Ælfredi regis, 8vo') was perhaps a volume of Spelman's working notes. University College 136 ('Vita Ælfredi regis, primi monarchiæ Anglicanæ fundatoris, Anglicano sermone, folio'), if not an earlier manifestation of a local interest in King Alfred, was perhaps a copy of the finished work in its original English form. The descriptions are from E. Bernard, *Catalogi librorum manuscriptorum Angliae et Hiberniae in unum collecti* (Oxford, 1697), p. Univ 5, cited by H. O. Coxe, *Catalogus codicum MSS. qui in collegiis aulisque Oxoniensibus hodie adservantur*, 2 vols. (Oxford, 1852) I, 38 (by which time both were missing).

the *Kings of England* (1643), dedicated like Spelman's 'Alfred' to Charles, Prince of Wales.[139] Baker's *Chronicle* had reached its ninth edition by 1696, and enjoyed a revival in the early 1730s; and if only on that basis it is easy to appreciate how his view of events soon gained currency among the well-educated classes. He provides a cursory account of Anglo-Saxon England, on the standard model (Heptarchy/Egbert/Monarchy), from which Alfred emerges with all due credit for his various accomplishments, but the period is not represented as one from which great political principles are likely to have sprung. We turn with rather different expectations to John Milton (1608–74), who had little instinctive sympathy for the pretensions of monarchs. In *Eikonoklastes*, written in the aftermath of the execution of King Charles I (30 January 1649), and in response to *Eikon Basiliké*, Milton invoked Alfredian precedent on at least two occasions: he compared the provisions of the Triennial Act (1641) with King Alfred's provision for the holding of parliaments twice a year at London;[140] and in arguing that a coronation did not put the king above the law, he expressed the view that even Alfred, 'the most worthy king, and by som accounted first absolute Monarch of the Saxons heer', ordained that the king was subject to the law by his coronation oath.[141] Milton's *History of Britain, that Part Especially now call'd England*, although not in fact published until 1670, was written in the late 1640s and early 1650s, during the Commonwealth.[142] He adopted a healthily sceptical attitude towards the fanciful tales of King Arthur, yet was no more enthused or impressed than Baker had been with a period which struck him as scarcely more worthy of attention than 'the Warrs of Kites, or Crows, flocking and fighting in the Air'.[143] The tenor of the work is downbeat: the Danish invasions were a form of divine punishment for the sins of the English; Alfred is accorded his due ('Thus far, and much more might be said of his Noble Mind, which render'd him the Miror of Princes'), and had some worthy successors, but the rot set in after Edgar; and the Norman Conquest was a reason 'to fear from like Vices without amendment

---

[139] R. Baker, *Chronicle of the Kings of England* (London, 1643). For Baker, see the *DNB*, and M. W. Brownley, 'Sir Richard Baker's *Chronicle* and Later Seventeenth-Century English Historiography', *Huntington Lib. Quarterly* 52.4 (1989), 481–500.

[140] *Complete Prose Works* III, ed. Hughes, 398–400, with notes.

[141] *Ibid.* pp. 586–93. In both cases, Milton cites the *Mirror of Justices*.

[142] J. Milton, *The History of Britain, that Part Especially Now Call'd England, from the First Traditional Beginning Continu'd to the Norman Conquest* (London, 1670), repr. from the edition of 1677 in J. Milton, *The History of Britain*, with an Introduction by G. Parry (Stamford, 1991). For a modern edition, with full apparatus, see *Complete Prose Works of John Milton*, V.i: *1648?–1671*, ed. F. Fogle (New Haven, CT, 1971). See also T. A. Carnicelli, 'Milton's Knowledge of the Anglo-Saxon Period', *A Milton Encyclopedia*, ed. W. B. Hunter, *et al.*, 9 vols. (Lewisburg, 1978–83) I, 51–3, and G. D. Hamilton, 'The *History of Britain* and its Restoration Audience', *Politics, Poetics, and Hermeneutics in Milton's Prose*, ed. D. Loewenstein and J. G. Turner (Cambridge, 1990), pp. 241–55.

[143] *Complete Prose Works* V.i, ed. Fogle, 249; Milton, *History of Britain*, p. 216, with Parry's remarks, *ibid.* pp. 40–2.

the Revolution of like Calamities', whatever he might have had in mind.[144] At best, the period provided Milton with a number of subjects which in his opinion would provide suitable cases for treatment. He noted elsewhere, for example, that 'A Heroicall Poem may be founded somewhere in Alfreds reigne, especially at his issuing out of Edelingsey on the Danes, whose actions are wel like those of Ulysses'; but that is as far as it went.[145] We have to return, therefore, to those who started from a different standpoint. The herald and antiquary Sir William Dugdale (1605–86) had been at Oxford with the king, and Sir John Spelman, in 1642. In the first volume of his *Monasticon Anglicanum*, published in 1655, he produced a work which recognized the importance of ancient religious houses as repositories of historical records, and which (although of its nature apolitical) provided texts for the first time of a large number of royal charters, complementing the laws which had been in print for nearly one hundred years, providing instances of king and witan in action, and thereby giving credibility to the ancient polities of Anglo-Saxon England. On a completely different level, a closet drama by a certain 'R. Kirkham', entitled 'Alfred, or Right Re-Enthroned' (1659), presented the 'restoration' of King Alfred after his tribulations in 878 as an event which in spirit prefigured the prospective restoration of monarchy in the person of King Charles II.[146]

In the aftermath of the Restoration (1660), there was new enthusiasm for the institutions of monarchy. King Alfred was ready as always to take advantage of the change, and (as we shall see) did so most conspicuously in Oxford. Yet he still faced some serious competition from King Arthur,[147] and something more, like a change of dynasty, would be needed before the one would be favoured at the expense of the other. Moreover, Alfred had yet to gain widespread acceptance as the personification of the ancient English constitution, for a combination of several reasons. Circumstances had not been propitious during the Commonwealth and the Protectorate, and Sir John Spelman's 'Life' of Alfred was not yet in the public domain. There was also some strong competition from King Edgar.[148]

---

[144] *Complete Prose Works* V.i, ed. Fogle, 257–9 (Danish invasions), 276–92 (Alfred), 327–8 (decline after Edgar) and 403 (Norman Conquest); Milton, *History of Britain*, pp. 222–4, 238–51, 280 and 357.

[145] Cambridge, Trinity College, R. 3. 4, p. 38: Keynes, *Anglo-Saxon Manuscripts in the Library of Trinity College*, p. 52 (no. 38), with pl. XXXVIII; also in Milton, *History of Britain*, Appendix II (unpaginated), no. 24.

[146] Oxford, Bodleian Library, Rawlinson poet. 88, on which see A. H. Tricomi, 'R. Kirkham's Alfred, or Right Re-Enthroned', *OEN* 22.1 (1988), 30–1.

[147] See Brinkley, *Arthurian Legend*, pp. 80–7, and MacDougall, *Racial Myth in English History*, pp. 24–5.

[148] A verse play by Thomas Rymer (1641–1713), called *Edgar, or The English Monarch; an Heroick Tragedy* (London, 1678), 2nd ed. (London, 1693), was dedicated to King Charles II, and began with a poem comparing Charles and Edgar ('Thus . . . You alone, great Edgar's Person bear. / Unking'd, in Love, we represent him here'). Rymer became historiographer royal in 1692, and is better known for his *Foedera* (1704–17). For further comment, see J. M. Osborn, 'Thomas Rymer as Rhymer', *PQ* 54 (1975), 1–26.

Above all, however, it was still King Edward the Confessor who symbolized the pre-Conquest polity for most purposes. Edward had remained high in the affections of the Stuart kings,[149] and the new regalia, supplied in 1661 to replace what had recently been destroyed, included 'St Edward's Staff' and 'St Edward's Crown'.[150] There was still much interest in the symbolic importance of the so-called 'Laws of King Edward the Confessor',[151] and much debate about the circumstances and significance of the Norman Conquest.[152] In the view of Sir Matthew Hale (1609–76), for example, as expounded in his tract on 'The Prerogatives of the King' (*c.* 1660),[153] and in his 'History of the Common Law' (?1660s),[154] it was axiomatic that the laws of the English were the laws of Edward the Confessor, and that William was committed to uphold those laws as Edward's appointed successor.[155] Hale's view of the 'supposed Norman Conquest' was fundamentally at odds with the full-blooded doctrine of the 'Norman Yoke'; yet its currency helps to explain why those moved to propound the notion that William and his successors had *suppressed* the ancient liberties of the English people would be required, in effect, to look beyond Edward the Confessor and back to Alfred.[156] Alfred's advance in the later seventeenth century was also impeded by renewed emphasis, in certain quarters, on a more conservative or 'Normanist' interpretation of the Norman Conquest, and, in others, by competition from various alternative strategies. The stakes were raised in 1678, when Titus Oates aroused fears of a Popish plot against Charles II, and the pace of

---

[149] It is worth noting in this connection that the Wilton Diptych (above, n. 65) had passed into the possession of King Charles I; see Griffiths, *The Print in Stuart Britain*, pp. 92–3 (no. 48).

[150] S. Bury, 'St Edward's Crown', in *The Crown Jewels*, ed. Blair II, 3–25, and C. Blair, 'St Edward's Staff, 1661', *ibid.* II, 283–6.

[151] For the continued significance of the Laws of Edward the Confessor in seventeenth-century polemic, see J. Greenberg, 'The Confessor's Laws and the Radical Face of the Ancient Constitution', *EHR* 104 (1989), 611–37, and Weston, 'England: Ancient Constitution and Common Law', pp. 381–5.   [152] Above, n. 99.

[153] *Sir Matthew Hale's The Prerogatives of the King*, ed. D. E. C. Yale, Selden Soc. 92 (London, 1976).

[154] Hale's 'History of the Common Law' was first published in 1713, repr. in 1716 and 1739. It is repr. from the 3rd ed. in M. Hale, *The History of the Common Law of England*, ed. C. M. Gray (Chicago, 1971); but cf. D. E. C. Yale, *Hale as a Legal Historian*, Selden Soc. Lecture (London, 1976), pp. 5–6, on the transmission of the text. See also Cromartie, *Sir Matthew Hale*, pp. 104–9.

[155] *Prerogatives of the King*, ed. Yale, pp. 19–20; *History of the Common Law*, ed. Gray, pp. 5, 36–8, 42–3, 55–6, 62, 68–9 and 76 (and pp. 160–7, on trials by jury, without mention of Alfred). For Hale and the Norman Conquest, see also *ibid.* pp. xxvii–xxviii; *Prerogatives of the King*, ed. Yale, pp. xli–xlii; Cromartie, *Sir Matthew Hale*, pp. 33–6.

[156] In the early 1640s John Hare, in his tract *St Edwards Ghost, or Anti-Normanisme* (London, 1647), had developed a version of the 'Norman Yoke' which proposed the restoration of the laws of Edward the Confessor (Hill, 'The Norman Yoke', pp. 72–4), though it might have been realized subsequently that it was better to maintain differentials between the Norman and the English regimes.

political and historical debate quickened during the 'Exclusion Crisis' of 1679–81, when Whigs sought to exclude the catholic James, Duke of York, from succession to the throne. In 1680 William Petyt published a tract asserting that the freemen or commons of England had long been an essential and constituent part of parliament (significantly without reference to Alfred), thereby extending the notion of the 'Ancient Constitution' implicit in the writings of Selden, the elder Spelman, and others.[157] Petyt's argument was, however, promptly and quite effectively demolished by Dr Robert Brady (d. 1700), Master of Gonville and Caius College, Cambridge, and physician to Charles II and James II. Eager to reaffirm the royal prerogative, Brady gave articulate form to a 'Normanist' view of the Conquest itself, the impact of feudalism, the inwardness of Magna Carta, and the origins of Parliament.[158] Those moved, a few years later, to express their support for the Glorious Revolution of 1688–9, and for taking the oath of allegiance to William and Mary, justified their position in ways which were by no means exclusively dependent on the notion that the Revolution restored the ancient constitution.[159] Soon afterwards, Sir William Temple (1628–99), a friend of William III, produced his *Introduction to the History of England* (1695), which contained no more than a passing reference to Alfred, and otherwise focused attention on William I and the beneficial effects of the Norman Conquest.[160] The Normanist line was better history than some might have wished to imagine, whatever purpose it was made to serve; but clearly there was nothing in it for Alfred, who remained in the wings biding his time.

ALFRED THE GREAT IN THE UNIVERSITY OF OXFORD

Alfred's breakthrough in the eighteenth century may be attributed in one way or another to the support which he continued to enjoy, in the late seventeenth

---

[157] W. Petyt, *The Antient Right of the Commons of England Asserted; or, A Discourse Proving by Records and the Best Historians that the Commons of England were Ever an Essential Part of Parliament* (London, 1680), esp. Preface, pp. 1–75, at 6–16 (on 'Saxon government').

[158] Brady's response to Petyt's tract was first published in 1681, and revised in R. Brady, *An Introduction to the Old English History* (London, 1684); see also R. Brady, *A Complete History of England* (London, 1685), pp. 114–17. For Petyt and Brady, see Weston, 'England: Ancient Constitution and Common Law', pp. 404–10. See also D. C. Douglas, *English Scholars 1660–1730*, 2nd ed. (London, 1951), pp. 119–38; Butterfield, *The Englishman and his History*, pp. 75–8; Pocock, *Ancient Constitution*, pp. 182–228; R. J. Smith, *The Gothic Bequest: Medieval Institutions in British Thought, 1688–1863* (Cambridge, 1987), pp. 7–8; and P. Hicks, *Neoclassical History and English Culture: From Clarendon to Hume* (Basingstoke, 1996), pp. 82–109.

[159] For a conspectus of the arguments deployed c. 1690, see M. Goldie, 'The Revolution of 1689 and the Structure of Political Argument: an Essay and an Annotated Bibliography of Pamphlets on the Allegiance Controversy', *Bull. of Research in the Humanities* 83 (1980), 473–564, at 485–91 and 529.

[160] W. Temple, *An Introduction to the History of England* (London, 1695), 3rd ed. (London, 1708). For Temple, see the entry in *DNB*, and R. C. Steensma, '"So Ancient and Noble a Nation": Sir William Temple's History of England', *NM* 77 (1976), 95–107.

The cult of King Alfred the Great

century, in royalist Oxford. University College had long cherished its Alfredian associations, and there is every reason to believe that images of the king already adorned its windows and its walls.[161] In 1661–2, within a year or so of the Restoration (and, for that matter, of the restoration of Thomas Walker, Master of University College 1632–48), the college commissioned a portrait of its founder which was destined to fix an image of the king in the public mind. The college accounts for that year record a payment of 4s for 'the first draught of King Alfred's picture', and another payment of £3 10s for 'King Alfred's picture'. We may infer that a preliminary study was worked up after approval into a definitive portrait, though it seems that the final payment of £3 10s was made by the Master himself, as if the painting had been required by him for his own lodgings.[162] Further documentation from the eighteenth century clearly indicates the existence of a small portrait of Alfred which hung in the Master's Lodgings, as distinct from and considered older than a larger portrait which hung elsewhere in the college, probably in the Hall.[163] An engraving of a portrait of Alfred at University College, inscribed 'Alfredus Fundator', was published in 1678; an engraving of the same portrait, published in 1722, states specifically that it was taken 'ex antiquissima tabella in ædibus Magistri Coll. Univ. Oxon'.[164]

[161] Above, p. 236.

[162] The payments are recorded in the General Accounts for 1661/2 (UC:BU2/F1/1, 389r and 389v), cited by R. Lane Poole, *Catalogue of Portraits in the Possession of the University, Colleges, City, and County of Oxford*, 3 vols. (Oxford, 1912–26) II, 1, n. 1. A payment of £3 10s 'for King Alfreds picture', recorded in a private account book of Thomas Walker, Master of Univ 1632–48 and 1660–5, suggests, however, that the Master paid for the picture himself (UC:MA26/F4/1, 3v). I am most grateful to Dr Robin Darwall-Smith, Archivist of University College, for supplying and clarifying these references (letter, 4 Jan. 1999), and for determining that a further payment of £8 10s, 'to the painter', adduced in this connection by Lane Poole, probably had nothing to do with the picture of Alfred. A payment of 2s 6d was made in 1706 'for mending and varnishing King Alfred's picture' (UC:BU5/F2/1, p. 3).

[163] Cf. Hearne's remarks in his diary, 24 Feb. 1714: 'I saw this morning in the Master of University College's Dining Room a Picture of K. Alfred, painted a pretty many Years agoe. But tis nothing near as good as that I have printed from the Draught in Sr John Spelman's MS. The Beard is also wrong, & it makes him look too old. There is not that Briskness neither in the Face as should be.' (*Remarks and Collections of Thomas Hearne*, ed. C. E. Doble, *et al.*, 11 vols., Oxford Hist. Soc. 2, 7, 13, 34, 42–3, 48, 50, 65, 67, 72 (Oxford, 1885–1921) IV, 313–14.) In March 1721 Francis Wise addressed some queries on Alfredian matters to Arthur Charlett, including the age of the Cottonian manuscript of Asser and 'the Age of the Picture of King Alfred in the Master's Lodgings at University', which Charlett forwarded to Humfrey Wanley (BL, Add. 70477); Wanley dealt with the former, but avoided the latter (*Letters of Wanley*, ed. Heyworth, pp. 423–5 (no. 217) and 431–2 (no. 220)). In 1728 William Smith alluded to a 'very small' painting of King Alfred in the Lodgings which was considered to be older than another painting of Alfred which by implication was *not* in the Lodgings (*Annals of University-College* [below, n. 461], p. 251).

[164] See below, pp. 265 and 271. The engravings do not include the college's coat of arms, on which see above, n. 114.

It has long been assumed (by the scholarly world outside University College) that the original portrait behind this famous image of the king is lost.[165] It proves to be the case, however, that a small portrait of Alfred, painted on an oak panel (12 in. by 10 in.), which still hangs in the Master's Lodgings at University College, is none other than the portrait behind the engravings published in 1678 and 1722, and can thus be identified as the portrait commissioned in 1661–2 (pl. VIIIa). One should like to imagine that the image of the king – crowned, bearded, and clad in ermine robes – was a projection back into the distant past of the popular image of the late King Charles I, which might help to account for his somewhat downcast countenance; for certainly if the artist intended any reference to a Stuart king, it was not to the one who had been so recently restored to his throne.[166] Interestingly, Alfred is accompanied in the Master's Lodgings by a portrait supposed to be of his wife (Ealhswith), although the subject is clearly identified on the portrait itself as 'Elizabetha regina Angliæ', and looks not unlike Elizabeth of York (1465–1503), wife of King Henry VII; so one must suppose that at some (early) stage it was decided to provide Alfred with some female company.[167] The portrait of King Alfred in the Master's Lodgings at University College has considerable symbolic importance as a product of the seventeenth-century cult of Alfred in the University of Oxford, and as the origin of much of the eighteenth-century iconography of the king. Its identification implies, at the same time, that University College soon acquired a second portrait of Alfred, perhaps in the later seventeenth or early eighteenth century, which hung elsewhere in the college itself, and which is more certainly lost. The second portrait may or may not have been related in some way to what would then be a third portrait, proclaiming Alfred as Founder of University College in 872, which would appear to have originated in the late seventeenth

---

[165] The assumption derives from the fact that the portrait is not registered in Lane Poole, *Catalogue of Portraits* II [1926], even though the details of its origin in 1661–2 are given in a footnote (*ibid.* p. 1, n. 1).

[166] For some of the classic examples of Caroline portraiture, see R. Ollard, *The Image of the King: Charles I and Charles II* (London, 1979). For Charles I, see also D. Howarth, *Images of Rule: Art and Politics in the English Renaissance, 1485–1649* (London, 1997), pp. 132–52, and esp. J. Roberts, *The King's Head. Charles I: King and Martyr*, Exhibition Catalogue (London, 1999).

[167] The size and appearance of the portraits, the similar form of lettering on each, and the identical frames, suggest that they have long been hung as a pair; they were still regarded as a pair in 1902 (Carr, *University College*, pp. 7 and 225), and are recorded as a pair (though correctly identified) in the college inventory of 1943. The portrait of the queen conforms to the standard iconographic type for Elizabeth of York: see R. Strong, *Tudor and Jacobean Portraits*, 2 vols. (London, 1969) I, 97–8. I am grateful to Lord Butler (Master of University College), Ms Christine Ritchie (Librarian of University College), and Dr Jane Cunningham (Courtauld Institute) for their good offices in connection with these portraits; and to the occupants of the Blue Room, in the Master's Lodgings, for tolerating an intrusion when I came to see the portraits in March 1999.

century and which hung throughout the eighteenth century in the picture gallery at the Bodleian Library.[168] The portrait in the Bodleian Library showed the king with a sceptre in his right hand, and more ermine on his robe; sadly it too is now lost, but it is known well enough from reproductions published in the eighteenth and early nineteenth centuries.[169]

In 1676 Obadiah Walker (1616–99) became Master of University College, and soon found, as masters do, that he needed to raise funds for the completion of building works at what was then called 'the Mother of all Colleges'.[170] He devised a plan, and revealed it in a letter to the college's benefactors, dated 19 April 1677:

This is to returne the thanks of myselfe & the whole society unto you for youre bountifull & seasonable assistance of us. Seasonable I say, for it <*illeg.*> finisheth & maketh habitable our new buildings, discharging the glazier, ioyner, & such other work as are ornamentall as well as necessary. And I hope that by this your assistance as we shall fit up, so we shal also ere long fill all our new chambers, I wish I could say with good students. And now we cease building at least for a while, & are entring upon another worke, the success whereof we cannot so wel foresee as we did that of our building; this is the putting forth the life of our founder King Ælfred; the book is not made by any of us, but divers of the society have assisted with their paines & learning to fit it for the presse; & within a few daies by Gods blessing we hope it will be begun. For the society is willing that the world should know that theire benefactions are not bestowed upon <perfect *del.*> mere drones. We intend also to print it at the charge of the College, & hope to make some advantage by it towards finishing our chappel, & furnishing our Library, for no particular person desires anything for himself but onely to do a good work, which

---

[168] For the Bodleian picture gallery, see E. Waterhouse, 'Paintings and Painted Glass', *The History of the University of Oxford*, V: *the Eighteenth Century*, ed. L. S. Sutherland and L. G. Mitchell (Oxford, 1986), 857–64, at 857–9. I am grateful to Steven Tomlinson, Assistant Librarian, Bodleian Library, for his guidance in this connection.

[169] The Bodleian portrait appears to be a cross between the engraving of the portrait made in 1661–2 and the engraving of a medieval painting, said to represent King Alfred, in St Albans cathedral, published in Spelman, *Life of Alfred*, ed. Walker (1678), pl. II. It was presumably one of the portraits of founders commissioned for the picture gallery, *c.* 1670, by Willem Sonmans (William Sunman), who died in 1708. For the date '872', cf. Rous (above, pp. 236–7), who gives 873. A mezzotint of the Bodleian portrait was published in John Faber, *Founders of Colleges in Oxford and Cambridge* (London, 1712–14), inscribed: 'Alfredus Saxonum Rex Coll. Universitatis Oxon. Fundr. Circa Ao Chr. 872. Hujus summi Regis Effigiem a Tabula in Bibl. Bodleiana factam Reverendo Viro Arthuro Charlett S.T.P. et istius Collegii Magistro &c. Summa cum Humil. & Observantia D.D.D. J. Faber Ao 1712.' A particularly fine reproduction of the portrait, in colour, was published in R. Ackermann, *A History of the University of Oxford, its Colleges, Halls, and Public Buildings*, 2 vols. (London, 1814) I, opp. p. 25.

[170] For Obadiah Walker, see the account of his life in the *DNB*, and *VCH Oxon* III, 67–8. See also A. E. F[irth], 'Obadiah Walker', *University College Record* 1961, 95–106, and 1964, 261–73; R. Darwall-Smith, 'Obadiah Walker in his own Words', *University College Record* 1998, 56–68; L. Mitchell, 'Obadiah Walker: Addendum', *University College Record* 1998, 69–73; and Darwall-Smith, *University College: the First 750 Years*, pp. 16–18.

may express their gratitude to their freinds & benefactors; & advantage our posterity, as our Predecessors took care of us.[171]

Spelman's 'Life of King Alfred' had been left unpublished at his death in 1643, and was not, therefore, in the public domain; but by 'putting forth the life of our founder King Ælfred', Walker hoped to show the benefactors 'that their benefactions are not bestowed upon mere drones', and hoped at the same time to raise additional funds 'towards finishing our chappell and furnishing our library'. He prevailed upon Christopher Wase (1625–90), Superior Beadle of the Civil Law and printer to the University of Oxford, to translate Spelman's 'Life of Alfred' from English into Latin,[172] and sought assistance from Elias Ashmole in assembling material for the accompanying plates of Anglo-Saxon coins.[173] The book, published at Oxford in 1678,[174] was dedicated with all due pomp to His Majesty King Charles II (with a preface comparing the two rulers), and was clearly intended at one level as an affirmation of loyalty to the restored monarchy. It was also a work of some serious scholarship in its own right, represented by Walker's notes to the text,[175] and by an impressive set of

---

[171] Printed here from Walker's draft (UC:MA30/1/C/13). I am grateful to Dr Robin Darwall-Smith for supplying me with a photocopy. The letter is also cited by J. Newman, 'The Architectural Setting', *The History of the University of Oxford*, IV: *Seventeenth-Century Oxford*, ed. N. Tyacke (Oxford, 1997), pp. 135–77, at 145, and by R. A. Beddard, 'Tory Oxford', *Seventeenth-Century Oxford*, ed. Tyacke, pp. 863–905, at 864.

[172] Wase is named as the translator by Hearne, *Life of Alfred*, p. 225. He was educated at Eton and at King's College, Cambridge.

[173] The draft of Walker's letter to Ashmole (UC:MA30/3/C7/1) is printed by Darwall-Smith, 'Obadiah Walker in his own Words', p. 63. In the event, Walker published five engraved plates of coins, which are not in themselves unimportant in the history of Anglo-Saxon numismatics. The first (pl. III) shows the coins found at Harkirke, Lancs., in 1611 (M. Blackburn and H. Pagan, 'A Revised Check-List of Coin Hoards from the British Isles, c.500–1100', *Anglo-Saxon Monetary History*, ed. M. A. S. Blackburn (Leicester, 1986), pp. 291–313, at 295 and 303 (no. 92)), from a manuscript in Corpus Christi College, Oxford (MS. 255, 78v). The other four plates (pls. IV–VII) show a range of Anglo-Saxon coins from the collections of Sir John Cotton, Elias Ashmole, the Bodleian Library, and Dr Nicholas Jonston, but also including some said to be 'apud nos'. The device on the 'London Monogram' type was interpreted by Walker as evidence that the Alfred who issued it was king of Northumbria; cf. *Remarks and Collections*, ed. Doble, *et al.*, II, 189.

[174] [Walker], *Ælfredi Magni Anglorum regis invictissimi vita*. Walker's own copy, with extensive annotations, is preserved in the library of University College, Oxford. The original copperplates for all seven of the engraved plates are preserved in the college archives (UC:MA30/2/AR/1–7). I am grateful to Ms Christine Ritchie for enabling me to examine the book in November 1998.

[175] The notes include a text of the OE Coronation Oath, printed from a Junius transcript [Junius 60, 2r] of a (burnt) Cottonian manuscript [Cotton Vitellius A. vii] (p. 62); an interesting discussion of the Alfredian church at Athelney described by William of Malmesbury (pp. 130–1, with diagram), and some carefully chosen words on Alfred's foundation of Oxford University and of University College (p. 135).

The cult of King Alfred the Great

appendices.[176] There is no mistaking, however, that it was a book produced by the men of University College, in interests which were fundamentally their own. Prominence was given to a fine engraving of the portrait of King Alfred, and members of the college would be able to bathe in Alfred's reflected glory. It did not pass unnoticed, on the other hand, that in the notes to Spelman's text Walker displayed the tendencies which made him notorious as a closet Catholic.[177] Another symbol of Walker's campaign to proclaim and exploit the Alfredian credentials of University College was the life-size statue of the king which he caused to be placed in an empty niche over the outer arch of the gate-tower in January 1683.[178] For various reasons the statue was 'plucked down' from the gate-tower in October 1686, and placed over the doorway leading to the hall, where it was soon joined by a statue of St Cuthbert (patron saint of the college, in deference to William of Durham).[179] Walker's religious inclinations became increasingly apparent after the accession of James II, and generated much displeasure in Oxford, leading to his discomfiture at the time of the Glorious Revolution in 1688–9.[180] The statue of King Alfred still survived in the first half of the twentieth century, albeit rather the worse for the weather, and was last seen lurking in the rockery of the Master's Garden.[181]

Alfred made other appearances elsewhere in Oxford. According to Spelman, 'both the Story and the Glory of the Universitie's Foundation by Ælfred' was

---

[176] The appendices include the Latin version of King Alfred's will (from Parker), the prose and verse prefaces to Alfred's translation of Gregory's *Regula pastoralis* (from Parker), a text of the West Saxon regnal table (from Whelock), a chronology of Alfred's life, a text of the voyages of Ohthere and Wulfstan (presumably derived from a transcript of BL, Cotton Tiberius B. i), and an account of Alfred's descendants to King Charles II. See also Brewer, 'References to the Voyage of Ohthere', p. 209.

[177] A. Clark, *The Life and Times of Anthony Wood, Antiquary, of Oxford, 1632–1695, Described by Himself*, 5 vols., Oxford Hist. Soc. 19, 21, 26, 30, 40 (Oxford, 1891–1900) II, 421–2 and 449; see also Beddard, 'Tory Oxford', pp. 864–5, and Jones, *The English Nation*, pp. 107–14.

[178] The statue was given to the college by Dr Robert Plot, on his becoming a Fellow Commoner; see Smith, *Annals of University-College* [below, n. 461], pp. 251–2, and *VCH Oxon* III, 77. David Loggan's view of the rebuilt University College, published in his *Oxonia Illustrata* (1675), shows the outer face of the gate-tower with two niches for statues, both then empty; see *The Encyclopædia of Oxford*, ed. C. Hibbert (London, 1988), p. 475.

[179] Clark, *Life and Times of Wood* III, 35. Alfred was later replaced over the gate tower by Queen Anne, who remains *in situ*.

[180] See the account of his career in the *DNB*, and the references cited above, nn. 170 and 177. In 1687–8 Walker published a number of Catholic tracts from a printing-press at Univ (Clark, *Life and Times of Wood* III, 209, 218, 221), under an imprint with included King Alfred's head; see Carter, *History of the OUP*, pp. 118–19, and N. Tyacke, 'Religious Controversy', *Seventeenth-Century Oxford*, ed. Tyacke, pp. 569–619, at 610 and 614, with pl. 28.

[181] A photograph of the statue in the rockery, taken in 1915 (Oxfordshire Photographic Archive, Central Library, Oxford), is reproduced in J. Rhodes, *Oxford: the University in Old Photographs* (Stroud, 1988). See also *VCH Oxon* III, 77. The statue was still there in the 1940s, but is alas there no more.

Simon Keynes

beautifully set forth 'in a fair Window in St. Marie's Church' [the university church of St Mary the Virgin, on the High Street], both in picture and verses.[182] There was also a representation of King Alfred, as well as one of King Æthelstan (among others), in the windows of the Old Library at All Souls College, forming part of a larger scheme.[183] Some of the buildings bought for the University in the thirteenth century, with the money bequeathed by William of Durham, passed in course of time to Brasenose College; and since these buildings formed part of the supposedly 'Alfredian' foundation of the university, the fellows of Brasenose were, by extension, eager to assert an Alfredian identity of their own.[184] There was a seventeenth-century bust of King Alfred above the door of the Hall (or refectory), and a portrait of him within; the bust survives to this day on the outer north wall of the Hall (weathered and barely recognizable), but the portrait, which may not have been made before the mid-eighteenth century, is said to have been destroyed in the mid-twentieth century by fire.[185]

Obadiah Walker would have been gratified by the positive influence exerted by the cult of King Alfred in preparing the ground for the Oxford Anglo-Saxonists of the late seventeenth century, but of course it was as much the creative interaction between them, and the incomparable resources of the Bodleian Library, which gave them their edge.[186] The great Dutch scholar, Franciscus Junius (1589–1677), who was active in England in the second quarter of the seventeenth century and again at Oxford in the mid-1670s, had devoted much of his energy to the transcription and study of Anglo-Saxon texts. Among his papers were transcripts of the Alfredian translations of Boethius's 'Consolation of Philosophy', Gregory's 'Pastoral Care', and Augustine's 'Soliloquies';[187] and

---

[182] *Life of Alfred*, ed. Hearne, p. 190. The ancient stained glass in the west window has not survived; but for an account of it in the early seventeenth century, see T. G. Jackson, *The Church of St. Mary the Virgin Oxford* (Oxford, 1897), pp. 124 and 213–14.

[183] The representations of King Alfred and King Æthelstan were engraved for Spelman, *Life of Alfred*, ed. Walker, pl. II. The windows, which would appear to have originated *c.* 1600, were described by Hearne in 1724; see *Remarks and Collections*, ed. Doble, *et al.*, VIII, 225. For their later history, cf. *VCH Oxon* III, 186–7.   [184] Parker, *Early History of Oxford*, pp. 52–3.

[185] There are engravings of the bust in Spelman, *Life of Alfred*, ed. Walker, pl. I, and in Wise's edition of Asser (p. 1). The portrait (given to the college in 1769) showed Alfred in a 'red and ermine mantle over blue dress', holding a partly unrolled scroll in his left hand (Lane Poole, *Catalogue of Portraits* II, 243); cf. below, n. 312. I am grateful to Mrs Elizabeth Boardman, College Archivist, Brasenose College, and Ms Maria Chevska, curator of pictures, for apprising me of its unfortunate fate.

[186] For an excellent study of the wider context, see D. Fairer, 'Anglo-Saxon Studies', *History of the University of Oxford: the Eighteenth Century*, ed. Sutherland and Mitchell, pp. 807–29.

[187] Oxford, Bodleian Library, Junius 12 (S.C. 5124), 53 (S.C. 5165) and 70 (S.C. 5181). See also E. G. Stanley, 'The Sources of Junius's Learning as Revealed in the Junius Manuscripts in the Bodleian Library', *Franciscus Junius F.F. and his Circle*, ed. R. H. Bremmer Jr, Stud. in Lit. 21 (Amsterdam and Atlanta, GA, 1998), 159–76, at 166–7, 169 and 170.

The cult of King Alfred the Great

by leaving his manuscripts and collections to the Bodleian Library, and by thus making available a much greater variety of texts than was already accessible in print, he gave inspiration and direction to the development of Anglo-Saxon studies at Oxford in the closing decades of the century. George Hickes (1642–1715) was a fellow of Lincoln College in the 1670s, and remained for some time thereafter a major source of inspiration. The leader of the revival, however, was Edward Thwaites (1667–1711), of The Queen's College,[188] and its main hives of activity were at Queen's and across the High Street at University College. Edmund Gibson's edition of the 'E' text of the *Chronicle* (in the Bodleian Library) was published in 1692;[189] and Christopher Rawlinson's edition of the Alfredian Boethius was published (from a Junius transcript) in 1698.[190] On the other hand, William Elstob's projected edition of the Alfredian Orosius foundered in 1699,[191] and his edition of the corpus of Anglo-Saxon laws, undertaken with his sister Elizabeth Elstob, was not completed.[192] Thwaites himself produced an edition of the Old English Heptateuch in 1698, but his projected editions of the Orosius and of the 'Pastoral Care' failed to materialize.[193] Further stimulus and patronage was provided by Arthur Charlett, Master of University College (1692–1722). His view of the history of his own college is symbolized by its magnificent 'Benefactors' Book', which proclaims Alfred as the one who 'restored' the University of Oxford *c.* 870 [*sic*], and 'founded' the College of the Great Hall of the University, giving credit at the same time to William of Durham as the one who refounded the college *c.* 1200 [*sic*].[194] It was

---

[188] For an assessment of Thwaites's contribution, see Fairer, 'Anglo-Saxon Studies', pp. 812–20.

[189] E. Gibson, *Chronicon Saxonicum* (Oxford, 1692). Edmund Gibson (1669–1748) had entered The Queen's College in 1686. He also edited *Reliquiæ Spelmannianæ* (Oxford, 1698).

[190] *An. Manl. Sever. Boethi Consolationis Philosophiae Libri V, Anglo-Saxonice redditi ab Alfredo, inclyto Anglo-Saxonum rege*, ed. C. Rawlinson (Oxford, 1698). See Fairer, 'Anglo-Saxon Studies', pp. 813–14. Rawlinson (1677–1733) entered The Queen's College in 1695, and worked with assistance from Thwaites.

[191] For Elstob's Orosius, see Fairer, 'Anglo-Saxon Studies', pp. 822–3, and *Letters of Wanley*, ed. Heyworth, p. 46 n. 4. William Elstob (1673–1715) entered The Queen's College in 1691, and became a fellow of University College in 1696.

[192] One of three notebooks containing the material gathered by the Elstobs for their edition of the laws is now Oxford, Bodleian Library, MS. Eng. lang. c. 11 (S.C. 40391). For the Elstobs, see M. Gretsch, 'Elizabeth Elstob: a Scholar's Fight for Anglo-Saxon Studies', *Anglia* 117 (1999).

[193] For Thwaites and his Orosius, see Fairer, 'Anglo-Saxon Studies', p. 812. For the 'Pastoral Care', see Oxford, Bodleian Library, Rawl. D. 377, fols. 86–7. See also *A Chorus of Grammars*, ed. R. L. Harris, Pub. of the Dictionary of Old English 4 (Toronto, 1992), 108.

[194] For the 'Benefactors' Book', see Darwall-Smith, *University College: the First 750 Years*, pp. 5–6, with illustration showing the treatment of Alfred the Great and William of Durham on the opening page. I am informed by Dr Darwall-Smith that the last (? original) entry in the book is dated 1695, followed by two undated records which refer to Arthur Charlett, after which the book is blank.

267

Charlett who gave a room in the Master's Lodgings at University College to the indefatigable Humfrey Wanley (1672–1726), for a period of about five years from 1696 to 1700; and it was from this 'Alfredian' base that Wanley did so much to advance knowledge and understanding of Anglo-Saxon manuscripts.[195] Alfred, it seems, was never far from the collective mind. In 1698, Wanley told Hickes of various plans afoot in Oxford: 'we expect K. Ælfreds Boethius by Easter, after which Mr Thwaites will put P. Gregories Pastoral into the Press; for ought I know, when that comes out, an honest Gentleman of this College [i.e. Elstob], may publish Orosius, and so compleat our Royal Founders works'.[196] The two spectacular volumes of the (so-called) *Thesaurus*, published in 1703–5, are a monument to the industry of all these men,[197] but were indeed so impressive as almost to inhibit the further development of Anglo-Saxon studies for the duration of the eighteenth century.

The most important event for Alfred in the early eighteenth century was the publication in 1709 of Hearne's edition of the original English text of Spelman's 'Life', based on the manuscript in the Bodleian Library.[198] Thomas Hearne (1678–1735) was a deeply learned and highly opinionated character, who maintained an extensive correspondence with his friends and who for thirty years kept an extraordinarily detailed diary of his academic life in Oxford.[199] His contribution to scholarship is now measured by the numerous

---

[195] For Wanley, see *The Blackwell Encyclopaedia of Anglo-Saxon England*, ed. M. Lapidge, *et al.* (Oxford, 1999), pp. 466–7, and references; see also S. Gillam, 'Humfrey Wanley and Arthur Charlett', *Bodleian Lib. Record* 16.5 (1999), 411–29. One wonders whether Wanley might have had a hand in the production of the 'Benefactors' Book'.

[196] Wanley to Hickes, 18 Feb. 1698 (*Letters of Wanley*, ed. Heyworth, pp. 85–6); see also Fairer, 'Anglo-Saxon Studies', pp. 807–8.

[197] G. Hickes and H. Wanley, *Antiquæ literaturæ septentrionalis libri duo* (Oxford, 1703–5), comprising Hickes's *Linguarum vett. septentrionalium thesaurus grammatico-criticus et archæologicus* (in vol. I) and Wanley's *Librorum vett. septentrionalium, qui in Angliæ biblioth. extant, catalogus historico-criticus* (in vol. II).

[198] T. Hearne, *The Life of Ælfred the Great, by Sir John Spelman Kt* (Oxford, 1709). The sketch of Alfred which looms out of the page in Spelman's autograph manuscript (above, n. 137) was elaborated and engraved by Burghers for the frontispiece to Hearne's edition; but this portrait of the king made little impression on later Alfredian iconography. To judge from Hearne's own account (*Remarks and Collections*, ed. Doble, *et al.*, II, 179–83, 184–5 and 438), he prepared his edition *c.* 1705, and intended it as an expression of his gratitude to University College for kindnesses received; yet Dr Charlett, Master of Univ, was obstructive, in part because Hearne's edition was not dedicated to him, but also because he objected to the portrait (*ibid.* VIII, 39), evidently preferring the one in his own Lodgings, later engraved for Wise's edition of Asser (above, pp. 261–2, and below, p. 271). See also T. Harmsen, 'Bodleian Imbroglios, Politics and Personalities, 1701–16: Thomas Hearne, Arthur Charlett and John Hudson', *Neophilologus* 82 (1998), 149–68, at 153 and 155–6.

[199] For his diaries, and a digest of his correspondence, see *Remarks and Collections*, ed. Doble, *et al.*; described, with his other papers, in the Bodleian Library *Summary Catalogue*, under the Rawlinson collection. For Hearne's letters to James West, see *A Catalogue of the Lansdowne*

editions of texts which he put forth from his study in St Edmund Hall; yet all the while he paid a penalty for his commitment to the Jacobite cause, and for his refusal to take the oath of loyalty to the Hanoverian regime. None the less, Spelman might have hoped to find a more sympathetic editor, or least one who was less overtly hostile to his views. Hearne replaced Walker's notes with even more extensive notes of his own, and took the opportunity to mount a vehement defence of the disputed passage in Camden's edition of Asser,[200] giving vent in this process to the contempt of an Oxford antiquary for a Cambridge man whose only offence was to believe that his place was older than the other. For Alfred, however, all controversy was good publicity, and Hearne's edition of Spelman remains as interesting for the editorial comments as it remains essential for the original text. For their part, the university authorities soon had cause to be grateful. A small object found in a field in Somerset, in 1693, had been acquired soon afterwards by a local landowner, Colonel Nathaniel Palmer, and was first published five years later, in 1698. Palmer kept it during his lifetime, but intended that it should be given to the University of Oxford after his death, presumably in the fond belief that an inscription, applied to the object, applied no less appropriately to the university as a whole. Palmer's wish was duly fulfilled in 1718, and the Alfred Jewel took its place in the Ashmolean Museum.[201]

ALFRED THE GREAT IN THE EIGHTEENTH CENTURY

Alfred the Great entered the eighteenth century as the perfect image of a medieval king, resplendent in his ermine robes, radiating wisdom and justice, and honoured most especially in royalist Oxford. The Oxford Alfred was, however, fundamentally apolitical, and the reinvention of Alfred as a quintessentially 'British', popular, and constitutional monarch – the embodiment of the nation's political identity, the father of his people, and the defender of their liberties – was yet to be achieved. The political context for the further development of the cult of Alfred was the establishment of the Hanoverian dynasty in England; for while it was already axiomatic that kings ruled by parliamentary title, in the interests of their people, it remained necessary, after the Act of Union with Scotland in 1707, and the realization of the Hanoverian Succession in 1714, to impress upon the Hanoverians that they operated within a long tradition which they

---

Manuscripts in the British Museum II (London, 1819), 174–81. For a catalogue of his library, see *Antiquaries*, ed. S. Piggott, Sale Catalogues of Libraries of Eminent Persons 10 (London, 1974), 201–402. For his publications, see Carter, *History of the OUP*, pp. 263–9.

[200] Hearne, *Life of Ælfred the Great*, pp. 144, n. 1 and 177 [–80], n. 4.

[201] S. Keynes, 'The Discovery and First Publication of the Alfred Jewel', *Somerset Archaeol. and Nat. Hist.* 136 (1993 for 1992), 1–8; A. G. MacGregor and A. J. Turner, 'The Ashmolean Museum', *History of the University of Oxford: the Eighteenth Century*, ed. Sutherland and Mitchell, pp. 639–58, at 649; and S. Piggott, 'Antiquarian Studies', *ibid.* pp. 757–77, at 771. For the history of Alfred at Oxford in the later eighteenth century, see further below, pp. 322–4.

would be expected to uphold. The Act of Union did much to encourage the promotion of 'British' identity in the eighteenth century, fostering enthusiasm for any person or principle who or which could be represented as prototypically British.[202] Not, of course, that 'Britain' was anything new, or that a tendency prescriptive of Britain was ever proscriptive of England. The concept of *Britannia*, as a unity which encompassed other peoples as well as the English, was the rock upon which Bede had constructed his *Historia ecclesiastica gentis Anglorum*, and it had long held a special appeal for all those with serious political aspirations.[203] Such aspirations had been entertained on behalf of various Northumbrian, Mercian, and West Saxon rulers, in the eighth and ninth centuries; and there were even some Welshmen, like Asser, who could countenance an Englishman as 'ruler of all the Christians of the island of Britain'. The kingship of Britain became a political commonplace (if not exactly a reality) in the tenth century; and although Alfred was cast subsequently as the first monarch of all England, it came to be understood (by the English) that 'England' was what had formerly been called 'Britain', and it was thus by no more than the flight of a wishful thought that Alfred could be recast in the eighteenth century as the prototypical king of Britain. So just as Alfred had been held up to Charles I and Charles II as a model of English kingship, so too might he serve as a model of British kingship for the Hanoverians. At the same time, the foundations laid by Coke, the elder Spelman, and Selden, had been used by the younger Spelman in his portrayal of Alfred as a properly constitutional monarch, and the disembodied principles of the earlier generation had assumed a compellingly human form. Alfred was thus poised to embark upon his greatest role to date. For the new monarchs he was the personification of royal virtue, and an excellent source of reflected glory; but he was also the personification of the enlightened and democratic forms of government coveted by radical thinkers, and supposed by many to have been destroyed by the tyranny of the 'Norman Yoke'.[204] In other words Alfred would serve, during the reigns of George I (1714–27) and George II (1727–60), not only as a role-model for the kings but also as an emblem of the kind of monarchy favoured by disaffected Whigs, and also by those of 'Tory'

---

[202] On the emergence of 'British' identity in the eighteenth century, see L. Colley, *Britons: Forging the Nation 1707–1837* (New Haven, CT, 1992); see also F. O'Gorman, *The Long Eighteenth Century: British Political and Social History 1688–1832* (London, 1997), pp. 96–101, and A. Hastings, *The Construction of Nationhood: Ethnicity, Religion and Nationalism* (Cambridge, 1997), esp. pp. 35–65 ('England as Prototype'), at 61–5.

[203] S. Keynes, 'England, 700–900', *The New Cambridge Medieval History*, II: *c.700–c.900*, ed. R. McKitterick (Cambridge, 1995), 18–42, and *Encyclopaedia of ASE*, ed. Lapidge, *et al.*, p. 74.

[204] Above, pp. 247–8. For further discussion, see Hill, 'The Norman Yoke', pp. 95–9; R. Horsman, 'Origins of Racial Anglo-Saxonism in Great Britain before 1850', *Jnl of the Hist. of Ideas* 37 (1976), 387–410; G. Newman, *The Rise of English Nationalism: a Cultural History 1740–1830* (London, 1987), pp. 183–91 and 229–30; and Smith, *The Gothic Bequest*, esp. pp. 98–102.

The cult of King Alfred the Great

persuasion disappointed with the partisan tendencies of the reigning king. These were, however, rarefied tastes; and it was perhaps not until after the accession of George III (1760–1820) that Alfred was adopted more widely and affectionately by the people themselves, as the originator of their constitution and as a symbol of their national identity.

It was, of course, a heavy burden for Alfred to bear, and one does not cast him lightly in such a role. Three works published in the early 1720s helped to consolidate respect for King Alfred, and to strengthen the foundation on which his cult had come to depend. The first was David Wilkins's edition of the corpus of Anglo-Saxon legislation, published in 1721 and dedicated to King George I (1714–27).[205] The second was John Smith's edition of Bede's *Historia ecclesiastica*, and of the Old English translation of Bede credited to King Alfred, published in 1722.[206] The third was Francis Wise's edition of Asser, also published in 1722.[207] Of these, Wise's book is naturally of particular interest, if not so much for its text (more widely used in Camden's edition of 1602) as for its frontispiece, devised by the antiquary and engraver George Vertue (1684–1756).[208] The image of the king was derived from the portrait in the Master's Lodgings at University College, presumably via the engraving published by Walker in 1678, and pointedly shunning the portrait of Alfred which had appeared in Hearne's edition of Spelman in 1709;[209] but if the furrowed brow and distracted gaze of the earlier Oxford image made the king seem weighed down by the burden of his responsibilities, Vertue's Alfred looks up and ahead. The new image of the king is especially noteworthy for its introduction of a set of symbolic accessories: bow and arrows, harp, spear,

---

[205] D. Wilkins, *Leges Anglo-Saxonicæ ecclesiasticæ & civiles* (London, 1721). Wilkins was of Prussian origin (born Wilke), and is said to have been blessed with 'a width of erudition purchased with a certain want of accuracy' (*DNB*).

[206] J. Smith, *Historiae ecclesiasticae gentis Anglorum libri quinque, auctore Sancto & Venerabili Baeda* (Cambridge, 1722).

[207] F. Wise, *Annales rerum gestarum Ælfredi Magni, auctore Asserio Menevensi* (Oxford, 1722). Wise (1695–1767) was a fellow of Trinity College, Oxford. For his suggestion, made in 1738, that the White Horse of Uffington commemorated the English victory at Ashdown in 871, see Piggott, 'Antiquarian Studies', *History of the University of Oxford: the Eighteenth Century*, ed. Sutherland and Mitchell, pp. 757–77, at 765–70.

[208] For a portrait of Vertue as engraver, in the Society of Antiquaries of London, see E. Einberg, *Manners & Morals: Hogarth and British Painting 1700–1760*, Exhibition Catalogue (London, 1987), pp. 56–7 (no. 30); see also p. 93 (no. 71).

[209] There was no spirit of friendship between Wise and Hearne. In 1719 Wise (described by Hearne as 'a Pretender to Antiquities') had got the post of Second Librarian (Under-Keeper) in the Bodleian Library which had been denied to Hearne because of his refusal to take the oaths (*Remarks and Collections*, ed. Doble, *et al.*, VII, 81). This naturally affected Hearne's feelings towards Wise. Hearne was thus bound to have a low opinion of Wise's Asser, which he thought had been done 'purely out of opposition to me' (*ibid.* VIII, 30, 39–40 and 322, and IX, 121–2 and 123–4). Wise narrowly failed to become Bodley's Librarian in 1729, to Hearne's evident pleasure (*ibid.* X, 207).

scroll and books, the captured 'Raven' standard of the Danes, a ceremonial shield, and a shield bearing a version of King Alfred's coat of arms.[210] Vertue had presumably been prompted by his own imagination to incorporate the various accessories around his portrait of the king; and in this process he devised an image which, directly or indirectly, exerted a strong influence on the development of Alfredian iconography in the later eighteenth century.

It was, however, a fourth work, published towards the end of the 1720s, which proved to be of even greater importance in securing King Alfred's reputation: Rapin's *History of England*. Paul de Rapin-Thoyras (1661–1725) was a Huguenot who had fought for William of Orange in 1688.[211] After a spell in England, he had settled at Wesel in Germany. In 1707 he began work on his history, in a wish to explain English history for the benefit of French readers on the Continent; and ten years later he wrote a useful tract explaining the differences between Whigs (characterized as parliamentarians) and Tories (characterized as royalists). Rapin wanted above all to enlarge upon the origins of the English Constitution, and to this end he soon turned to the study of Anglo-Saxon history. In the words of his editor: 'He found this to be a very disagreeable and discouraging Task. But however, as he looked upon this Part of the English History as the Basis and Groundwork of all the rest, he waded through all Difficulties, and out of a confus'd Heap of Rubbish, without any Order or Connexion, he made a shift to carry on a Series of Facts, tho' often broken and interrupted.'[212] In its original form, in French, the *Histoire d'Angleterre* first appeared in eight volumes between 1724 and 1727, dedicated to King George I.[213] At once it was seen to represent an advance on anything which had yet appeared in English, and Nicholas Tindal (1687–1774), vicar of Great Waltham in Essex, set to work on an English translation (and continuation). The first two volumes of Rapin's *History of England* were published in monthly parts in 1726–8, completed in a further thirteen volumes by 1731.[214] A second (and

---

[210] The coat of arms (a cross potent fitched at foot) is a variation of the cross patonce or cross flory which represented the kingdom of all England, and was used for kings from Egbert to Eadwig, including Alfred (above, n. 114). The cross flory returns in a later version of Vertue's portrait (pl. II*b*)

[211] For Rapin, see H. R. Trevor-Roper, 'A Huguenot Historian: Paul Rapin', *Huguenots in Britain and their French Background, 1550–1800*, ed. I. Scouloudi (Basingstoke, 1987), pp. 3–19, and Hicks, *Neoclassical History and English Culture*, pp. 146–50.

[212] P. de Rapin Thoyras, *The History of England, as well Ecclesiastical as Civil* I (London, 1728), preface.   [213] P. de Rapin Thoyras, *Histoire d'Angleterre*, 8 vols. (The Hague, 1724–7).

[214] P. de Rapin Thoyras, *The History of England, as well Ecclesiastical as Civil* I–II (London, 1726–8). Vol. I [Julius Caesar – Edward the Martyr] is dated 1728, and was dedicated to Thomas, Lord Howard, Baron of Effingham. Vol. II.i [Æthelred II – Harold II, with the dissertation on the government of the Anglo-Saxons], dated 1726, and II.ii [William I – Stephen], dated 1728, was dedicated to Sir Charles Wager. For the manner and success of the publication, see R. M. Wiles, *Serial Publication in England before 1750* (Cambridge, 1957), pp. 96–7, 197 and 276–7.

The cult of King Alfred the Great

seemingly more widely distributed) edition of Rapin, in two folio volumes, was published in 1732–3,[215] followed by a third edition in 1743;[216] there was also an abridged edition, published in 1747.[217] Scarcely less important, perhaps, in the dissemination of Rapin's view of English history was John Lockman's *New History of England*, first published in 1729, based mainly on Rapin's book but revised 'for the entertainment of our youth of both sexes'.[218] In these various forms, Rapin's work rapidly established itself as the standard treatment of English history before and after the Norman Conquest.[219] Tindal seems to have respected Rapin's text, but he added greatly to its weight, and its appearance of authority, by his provision of an impressive apparatus of notes, enlarging upon details and citing published sources. Whether right or wrong, the *History* provided a suitably idealized view of the Anglo-Saxon constitution, and of early English society, in full accordance and sympathy with the 'Whig' conception of the origins of English liberties, and without undue glorification of kings. Egbert of Wessex was accorded his accustomed dignity as 'First King of England', though he was seen as little more than a conqueror of other peoples. Alfred was a different matter. At once we see how Spelman's view was injected into what would now become the mainstream of the historiographical tradition, for Rapin states at the outset that Spelman's 'Life' had served as his 'principal Guide'. The anecdotal element is relatively restrained, to the extent that the story of the cakes is represented only by an allusion to Alfred's enforced concealment in a neatherd's cottage, leaving Tindal to provide the story itself in a footnote (citing Camden's edition of Asser);[220] and although Rapin reported the monkish tale

---

[215] P. Rapin de Thoyras [*sic*], *The History of England*, 2nd ed., 2 vols. (London, 1732–3), originally published in weekly parts. For the folio edition, see Wiles, *Serial Publication in England*, pp. 106–8 and 285. Illustrations were added by subscription, from 1733 to 1736 (below, n. 293).

[216] P. Rapin de Thoyras, *The History of England*, 3rd ed., 2 vols. (London, 1743), originally published in weekly parts (Wiles, *Serial Publication in England*, p. 335).

[217] *An Abridgement of the History of England; being a Summary of Mr. Rapin's History and Mr. Tindal's Continuation, from the Landing of Julius Cæsar, to the Death of King George I*, 3 vols. (London, 1747), in which the narrative was reduced to single-sentence paragraphs, with marginal dates, though retaining some extended prose on 'The Character of Alfred the Great' (I, 39–45).

[218] J. Lockman, *A New History of England, by Question and Answer, extracted from the Most Celebrated English Histories, particularly M. Rapin de Thoyras* (London, 1729), which reached its 5th ed. in 1740, its 10th in 1758, its 15th in 1768, its 20th in 1784, and its 25th in 1811. For the illustrations which first appeared in the 6th ed. (1747), see below, p. 305. For Lockman (1698–1771), see the *DNB*. For a similar work by Richmal Mangnall (1769–1820), see below, n. 514.

[219] Butterfield, *The Englishman and his History*, pp. 90–6.

[220] Rapin, *History of England*, 2nd ed. I, 90–7 (on Alfred), at 92, n. 6: 'She having one Day set a Cake on the Coals, and being busied about something else, the Cake happen'd to be burnt; upon which she fell a scolding at the King for his Carelessness in not looking after the Cake, which she told him he could eat fast enough. Alfred was then sitting in the Chimney-corner, making Bows and Arrows, and other warlike Instruments. *Asser. Vit. Alfr.* p. 9.'). Cf. de Rapin Thoyras, *Histoire d'Angleterre* I, 307.

that Alfred was rescued from his wretched predicament by an appearance of St Cuthbert, he did so with evident disdain, and preferred to fasten instead on the news of the capture of the 'Raven' banner as the decisive turning-point in the king's fortunes. Rapin could not, however, resist the story of Alfred playing his harp in the Danish camp, leading to his great victory over the Danes. After completing the narrative, Rapin went on to consider Alfred in his capacity 'as a just, learned, and religious Prince, a Lover of his Subjects, and an indefatigable Promoter of Arts, Sciences, Justice and Religion', with all the usual elements. The lesson was never far from the author's mind. The king raised revenues, but only from his own hereditary estates, for 'It was not customary in those Days, for Princes to levy Taxes upon the People, in order to squander the Money in Luxury and Extravagancies'.

Alfred the Great and the establishment of the Hanoverian regime

So what of the Hanoverian connection? The most striking aspect of the development of the cult of Alfred in the first half of the eighteenth century is its particular association with Prince Frederick (1707–51), grandson of George I, son of George II and Caroline, and father of George III. Frederick had remained in Hanover during his grandfather's lifetime; but he came to England in 1728, in the year following his father's accession, and was created Prince of Wales in 1729. Sir Robert Walpole was at the height of his power, as George II's Prime Minister, and the Whigs were supreme. Prince Frederick's problem in modern historiography seems to be that his activities in the 1730s and 1740s are too easily judged from the vantage-point of someone aware that he died in 1751: a political irrelevance, a pawn in the hands of those who sought to profit from his friendship, at odds with his parents, and no more than a figurehead for those in opposition to Walpole.[221] Accordingly, he is generally given short shrift.[222] Yet his friends saw him differently, and in a more positive light. The more formal portraits of Prince Frederick display a sense of his promise for the future,[223] but he was most famously and charmingly depicted at Kew, playing the

---

[221] For a contemporary assessment of Prince Frederick, albeit from an interested party, see *Horace Walpole: Memoirs of George II*, ed. J. Brooke, 3 vols. (New Haven, CT, 1985) I, pp. 50–5.

[222] Extended modern studies are: G. Young, *Poor Fred: the People's Prince* (Oxford, 1937); A. Edwards, *Frederick Lewis, Prince of Wales* (London, 1947); and M. De-la-Noy, *The King Who Never Was: the Story of Frederick, Prince of Wales* (London, 1996). See also S. Jones, *Frederick, Prince of Wales, and his Circle*, Exhibition Catalogue [Gainsborough's House] (Sudbury, 1981); A. N. Newman, 'The Political Patronage of Frederick Lewis, Prince of Wales', *Hist. Jnl* 1 (1958), 68–75; P. Langford, *A Polite and Commercial People: England 1727–1783* (Oxford, 1989), pp. 36–7, 47–8 and 340; and Colley, *Britons*, p. 206.

[223] Among contemporary portraits of Prince Frederick, several in the Royal Collection are reproduced with discussion in C. Lloyd, *The Quest for Albion: Monarchy and the Patronage of British Painting*, Exhibition Catalogue (London, 1998).

cello.[224] There is no mistaking the hopes and expectations entertained by many of the heir to the throne of Great Britain, or the connection made between Prince Frederick and King Alfred the Great. In 1723 Sir Richard Blackmore (1654–1729), much ridiculed for his early attempts to harness the Arthurian legend in service of the Hanoverian cause,[225] though soon knighted for his services as physician to William III, blithely switched his frame of reference and dedicated an interminable epic poem about King Alfred to the 'Illustrious Prince Frederick of Hanover' (before Frederick had come over to join his father and grandfather in England).[226] Blackmore was sure that the young prince would learn the virtues of good kingship from his grandfather, George I, and from his father, George, Prince of Wales (later George II), but he felt at the same time that his poem would serve as an example of 'one of the greatest Monarchs that ever ruled this or any foreign Nation, a Prince sprung from the ancient Saxon Race of your own native Land' (Author's Dedication). His main source of historical information about Alfred was evidently Obadiah Walker's edition of Spelman's 'Life',[227] though it soon becomes apparent that the more important source would be his own imagination:

> I sing the Man, who left fair Albion's Shore,
> Mov'd by a generous Instinct to explore
> In various Realms the Customs, Arts, and Laws,
> Which Pow'r extend, and Peace and Plenty cause. (bk I, p. 2)

Books I to XI deal with Alfred's travels abroad, in effect on a Grand Tour of the approved kind. Ship-wrecked in Africa, the prince first wrestled with a panther, and then encountered a hermit, who asked him, not unreasonably, what he was up to in foreign parts. Alfred reflected for a moment on the sorry state of the Britain he had left, and explained that he had resolved to ascertain what systems of government were most likely to 'Make Subjects happy, and the Monarch Great', so that should he become king 'I might by wise and just and equal Laws / Advance the Realm, and aid Religion's Cause' (bk I, pp. 21–2). Alfred proceeded to enter into discussion with the hermit about prudent forms of civil government. Later he met Halla, king of Tunisia, and assured him of his intention, once king, to promote arts and sciences (bk III, pp. 74–5, 82–3). In book IV, Alfred's faithful companion Guithun told King Halla how they had passed

---

[224] Philippe Mercier (1689–1760), 'Frederick, Prince of Wales, and his Sisters making Music at Kew', reproduced with discussion in A. Laing, *In Trust for the Nation: Paintings from National Trust Houses*, Exhibition Catalogue (London, 1995), pp. 56–7.

[225] MacDougall, *Racial Myth in English History*, pp. 25–6.

[226] Sir Richard Blackmore, *Alfred: an Epick Poem in Twelve Books* (London, 1723). For Blackmore's life and works, see the *DNB*. See also Miles, *King Alfred in Literature*, pp. 52–7; and C. A. Simmons, 'The Historical Sources of Sir Richard Blackmore's *Alfred*', *ELN* 26 (1988), 18–23.

[227] Blackmore, *Alfred*, pp. xli–xliii.

through Germany and across the Alps to Rome, where Pope Leo had crowned Alfred king of Britain in succession to his father Atulpho (bk IV, pp. 124–5), and whence they had set off on their travels. After this, Alfred moved onwards via Parthenope and Ischia to Sicily (bk VI), where he avoided an eruption of Mount Etna, became embroiled with the fair Albana, and then set off for Spain. Alfred was shipwrecked again in Africa, had visions of heaven and hell, and was vouchsafed a vision of future political developments (bk VIII, pp. 286–93), culminating with Prince Frederick. As Alfred's guide remarked:

> By Thee, O Alfred, may he [Frederick] form his Mind
> To Science, Arts, and Arms, like Thee, inclin'd. (bk VIII, p. 292)

After further remarkable adventures in Africa (bk IX), Alfred reached Spain (bk X), where he heard of his father's death (p. 339), before sorting out some local difficulties in Navarre. He headed back through Burgundy and France, though briefly diverted his course in order to capture Toledo (bk XI). Finally, in book XII, Alfred returned to Britain, became king, beat the Danes, converted them to Christianity, married Elsitha, daughter of King Gunter, and made Augusta (London) his imperial seat (p. 448). Blackmore's poem must be judged as literature in connection with his detailed explanation of the nature and purpose of epic poetry, and, for our purposes, as evidence of Alfred's capacity to capture the imagination of those wishing to educate the incoming Hanoverians in the ways of English kingship; no less to the point, it is certainly an entertaining ride.

It was hard on Prince Frederick that he should have been subjected to this ordeal by poetry even before he set foot in England. It was, however, in much the same spirit that Nicholas Tindal dedicated the second edition of the English translation of Rapin's *History of England*, published in 1732–3, not to George II, but to Prince Frederick; and just in case the prince missed the point, Tindal explained precisely what lessons he might learn from English history, and how, in particular, he would see here 'the Origin and Nature of our Excellent Constitution, where the Prerogatives of the Crown, and Privileges of the Subject are so happily proportioned, that the King and the People are inseparably united in the same Interests and Views'. It was also in the same spirit that George Vertue devised, and dedicated to Prince Frederick, his set of engraved portraits and other plates made for the adornment of the *History*, published by subscription from 1733 and separately in 1736.[228] In this way Britannia and all she stood for made herself known to the incomers, and (one might add) made it easier for the British to accept Prince Frederick as one of their own. To their credit, the Hanoverians were not slow on the uptake. In 1735 Prince Frederick's mother,

---

[228] See further below, n. 293. For Vertue and Prince Frederick, see T. Clayton, *The English Print 1688–1802* (New Haven, CT, 1997), pp. 172–3.

The cult of King Alfred the Great

Queen Caroline, commissioned the sculptor Michael Rysbrack (1694–1770) to produce a series of portrait busts of kings and queens, beginning with Alfred the Great, apparently intended for the new Library at St James's Palace.[229] Frederick himself was renowned as a patron of the arts,[230] and was lavishing much attention on the furbishment of his home at Carlton House, in Pall Mall, and (with help from William Kent) on the layout of the gardens.[231] He is said to have regarded Edward the Black Prince as his pattern,[232] an unfortunate choice in as much as Edward had predeceased his father in 1376, yet he seems to have developed no less of a fixation on King Alfred the Great. In 1735 Prince Frederick ordered the construction of an Octagon Temple at Carlton House, from which there would have been a magnificent view westwards down the length of his garden, and filled it with paintings, sculpture and furniture;[233] at the same time he commissioned Rysbrack to produce marble busts of King Alfred and the Black Prince, placing them in niches on the steps leading up into the Temple, or in the Temple itself.[234] William Woollett's engraving of Carlton House Garden shows

---

[229] R. Gunnis, *Dictionary of British Sculptors 1660–1851* (London, 1953), rev. ed. (London, 1968), pp. 333–8; M. I. Webb, *Michael Rysbrack, Sculptor* (London, 1954), pp. 145–6; K. Eustace, *Michael Rysbrack Sculptor 1694–1770*, Exhibition Catalogue (Bristol, 1982), pp. 135–7 and 173; and K. Eustace, 'Stowe and the Development of the Historical Portrait Bust', *Apollo* 148 [no. 437] (July 1998), 31–40, at 37. For Queen Caroline and the arts, see O. Millar, *The Tudor, Stuart and Early Georgian Pictures in the Collection of Her Majesty The Queen* (London, 1963), pp. 27–8. The terracotta bust of Alfred (known from a photograph, reproduced in Eustace, *Rysbrack*, fig. 51), with others in the same series, fetched up on a shelf in the Orangery at Windsor Castle, and was destroyed when the shelf collapsed in 1906. There is an engraving, dated 1785, of a portrait of King Alfred as one of a series of royal portraits at Kensington Palace.

[230] Millar, *The Tudor, Stuart and Early Georgian Pictures in the Collection of Her Majesty The Queen*, pp. 28–30; K. Rorschach, 'Frederick, Prince of Wales (1707–51), as Collector and Patron', *Walpole Soc.* 55 (1989–90), 1–76; K. Rorschach, 'Frederick, Prince of Wales: Taste, Politics and Power', *Apollo* 134 [no. 356] (October 1991), 239–45.

[231] Rorschach, 'Frederick, Prince of Wales (1707–51), as Collector and Patron', esp. pp. 21–6; J. Harris, 'A Carlton House Miscellany: William Kent and Carlton House Garden', *Apollo* 134 [no. 356] (October 1991), 251–3.   [232] *Walpole: Memoirs of King George II*, ed. Brooke I, 50.

[233] The Octagon Temple drew architectural inspiration from Lord Burlington's Palladian villa at Chiswick, built in the 1720s, on which see *The Palladian Revival: Lord Burlington: his Villa and his Garden at Chiswick*, Exhibition Catalogue (New Haven, CT, 1994).

[234] According to a note in a contemporary publication, Rysbrack had finished 'the two fine Statues, which are to be erected on two marble Pedestals in the Octagon of the Garden of his R. H. the Prince of Wales in Pall-Mall' by July 1735 (*London Mag.* July 1735, 390). The inscription on the pedestal of the statue of Alfred read as follows: 'Alfredo Magno, / Anglorum Reipublicæ Libertatisque / Fundatori / Justo, Forti, Bono, / Legislatori, Duci, Regi, / Artium Musarumque / Fautori Eruditissimo, / Patriæ Patri / Posuit / F.W.P. / MDCCXXXV' (*ibid.*). In 1736 Prince Frederick paid Rysbrack £105 for the marble busts of Alfred and the Black Prince; see Webb, *Rysbrack*, pp. 156 and 210, and Eustace, 'Stowe and the Development of the Historical Portrait Bust', p. 38. Rorschach, 'Frederick, Prince of Wales (1707–51), as Collector and Patron', pp. 24–5, suggests that the statues were by the staircase of the Octagon Temple.

277

the view eastwards towards the Octagon Temple, in 1760;[235] sadly, this is the only known representation of the garden and its temple, for all was lost when the area was redeveloped in the 1820s.[236] It is interesting to note, however, that Prince Frederick's Octagon Temple, with its busts of King Alfred the Great and the Black Prince, would appear to have stood on precisely the spot where now stands No. 10 Carlton House Terrace, otherwise known as the British Academy.[237] Nor was Prince Frederick's interest in Alfred a passing infatuation. In 1738, Viscount Bolingbroke produced a tract for the intended benefit of Prince Frederick, on the role of the 'Patriot King', as one who rules in association with parliament and thereby saves a State from pervasive corruption;[238] and although Alfred is not mentioned, he cannot have been far from the author's or from the reader's mind. A year or two later Prince Frederick commissioned a drama on King Alfred, with words by James Thomson and David Mallet, and music by Thomas Arne. Thomson had previously hailed Alfred in contexts which established the king as one of the icons of the opposition to Walpole, by invoking him again in *Liberty, A Poem*, published in 1735 and dedicated to Prince Frederick, and he also added him to the roll-call of English patriots embedded in *The Seasons*;[239] so the prince would have known more or less what to expect.[240] The plot devised by Thomson

---

[235] For William Woollett (1735–85), appointed Engraver to King George III in 1775, see Clayton, *The English Print*, pp. 210–11; his engraving of the garden at Carlton House is reproduced *ibid*. p. 164.

[236] The battered and restored statue of a bearded king which stands in Trinity Church Square, Southwark, London S.E.1, is presumed by some to be Prince Frederick's Alfred, from Carlton House, but is supposed by others to be from the Palace of Westminster, *c*. 1400.

[237] The position of the Octagon Temple, at the eastern end of Carlton House gardens, can be seen in Rocque's map of London (1746), reproduced in Rorschach, 'Frederick, Prince of Wales (1707–51), as Collector and Patron', fig. 39, and in Jones, *Frederick, Prince of Wales, and his Circle*, p. 13. This map can be compared with maps in *Carlton House: the Past Glories of George IV's Palace*, Exhibition Catalogue (London, 1991), inside front and back covers, showing the house and gardens in 1799 and showing the house superimposed on a modern street plan of the same area.

[238] For Bolingbroke's text, which itself makes no reference to Alfred, see *Bolingbroke: Political Writings*, ed. D. Armitage (Cambridge, 1997), pp. 217–94; see also *Lord Bolingbroke: Contributions to the 'Craftsman'*, ed. S. Varey (Oxford, 1982). For pertinent comment, see Smith, *The Gothic Bequest*, pp. 57–70; Langford, *England 1727–1783*, p. 222; and esp. C. Gerrard, *The Patriot Opposition to Walpole: Politics, Poetry, and National Myth, 1725–1742* (Oxford, 1994), pp. 185–229.

[239] *The Complete Poetical Works of James Thomson*, ed. J. L. Robertson (Oxford, 1908), pp. 107 and 378; J. Thomson, *Liberty, The Castle of Indolence, and Other Poems*, ed. J. Sambrook (Oxford, 1986), p. 111; J. Thomson, *The Seasons and the Castle of Indolence*, ed. J. Sambrook (Oxford, 1972), pp. 77 and 225.

[240] For *Alfred: a Masque*, see Miles, *King Alfred in Literature*, pp. 58–62; D. Grant, *James Thomson: Poet of 'The Seasons'* (London, 1951), pp. 169–94; A. D. McKillop, 'The Early History of *Alfred*', *PQ* 41 (1962), 311–24; *Alfred: a Masque written by David Mallet and James Thomson, set to Music by Thomas Augustine Arne*, ed. A. Scott, Musica Britannica 47 (London, 1981), pp. xv–xx; M. Burden, 'A Mask for Politics: *The Masque of Alfred*', *Music Rev.* 48 (1988), 21–30, at 26–7; and Gerrard, *Patriot Opposition*, p. 117. See also *Cliveden*, National Trust Guide (London, 1994), pp. 16–19. A CD recording of extended excerpts from the masque was published by the *BBC Music Mag.* in June 1997. The masque was performed by Bampton Classical Opera, in the Deanery Garden, Bampton, in July 1998.

The cult of King Alfred the Great

and Mallet bears scarcely more resemblance to historical fact than Blackmore's poem, but the basic sequence of events is familiar enough: Alfred in hiding, Alfred restored, and Alfred triumphant. The drama was performed for the first time at Prince Frederick's house at Cliveden, in Buckinghamshire, on 1 August 1740, being the birthday of his daughter, the Princess Augusta, and the anniversary of King George I's accession in 1714, and symbolic, therefore, of the establishment of the Hanoverian regime. Nor would the original audience have missed the intended analogy between King Alfred and Prince Frederick: the one reduced to take refuge in a 'lowly cottage', and the other languishing at Cliveden, but both destined to save their country and people. The drama reaches its climax and comes to its end with a 'Grand Ode in Honour of Great Britain', sung in 1740 by Alfred and the assembled company, and sung to this day as the patriotic anthem 'Rule Britannia'. In addition to Carlton House, and Cliveden, Frederick also had a residence at Kew; and it was in about 1750 that he sought help from George Vertue in assembling likenesses of a number of ancient worthies for the statues that he wished to have made for his own recreation of Mount Parnassus. Busts of nine British worthies would be set beside their classical counterparts: Alfred would take his place alongside the others, and would be paired with the Spartan statesman and lawgiver, Lycurgus.[241] Sadly, Prince Frederick died in March 1751, before his grand scheme could be realized in stone.

The cult of King Alfred was associated in the second quarter of the eighteenth century not only with Frederick, Prince of Wales, but also with other peripheral or card-carrying members of the 'Patriot' opposition to Sir Robert Walpole.[242] It is not immediately obvious what to make of the gothic building known as 'Alfred's Hall', which stands in a secluded clearing in Oakley Wood on the estate of Lord Bathurst, at Cirencester Park, in Gloucestershire, except to say that it is an early manifestation of what would now be called medievalism. When first constructed, in the early 1720s, the building was known as 'The Wood House', or 'King Arthur's Castle', and seems to have been much used by Alexander Pope; some years later, a friend of Lord Bathurst's pointed out that 'Oakley Wood' itself had Alfredian associations, and the building in the clearing was renamed 'Alfred's Hall'.[243] A more elaborate feature in a landscape garden of far greater renown is

---

[241] Rorschach, 'Frederick, Prince of Wales (1707–51), as Collector and Patron', pp. 27–31, citing Vertue's notes in BL, Add. 19027, 80r.

[242] See Gerrard, *Patriot Opposition*; esp. pp. 102–7 and 116–21, and O'Gorman, *The Long Eighteenth Century*, pp. 71–86.

[243] J. Lees-Milne, *Earls of Creation: Five Great Patrons of Eighteenth-Century Art* (London, 1962, new ed. London, 1986), pp. 23–8; see also J. Burke, *English Art 1714–1800* (Oxford, 1976), p. 50, and M. McCarthy, *The Origins of the Gothic Revival* (New Haven, CT, 1987), p. 27 and pl. 21. The place where King Alfred stayed on the eve of the battle of Edington in 878, formerly identified as 'Oakley Wood' (among other places), is now identified as Iley Oak, near Warminster, Wilts. (*Asser's 'Life of King Alfred'*, ed. Stevenson, pp. 270–2; Keynes and Lapidge, *Alfred the Great*, p. 249).

more explicitly political. When Sir Richard Temple, 1st Viscount Cobham, began to develop the Elysian Fields in the grounds of his house at Stowe, Buckinghamshire, in the mid-1730s, he commissioned William Kent to devise a 'Temple of British Worthies', providing eight niches to the left of a central pyramid for busts of 'men of contemplation', and eight niches to the right for 'men of action'. The choice of worthies reflected Lord Cobham's own inclinations and sympathies, and above all his affiliation with the opposition to Walpole; and just in case any visitors to his gardens missed the point, inscriptions placed above the busts explained the significance of each. The busts of eight of the worthies had been made by Michael Rysbrack in the late 1720s, for an earlier Temple of Fame: Queen Elizabeth, Sir Francis Bacon, William Shakespeare, John Hampden, John Milton, John Locke, Sir Isaac Newton, and William III. Rysbrack's bust of Inigo Jones seems to have been freshly commissioned for the new Temple of British Worthies. These luminaries were then joined, in the later 1730s, by a series of busts made by Peter Scheemakers (1691–1781), to fill up the remaining niches:[244] Alfred the Great, the Black Prince, Sir Thomas Gresham, Sir Francis Drake, Sir Walter Ralegh, and Alexander Pope. A bust of Sir John Barnard, also by Scheemakers, was a later addition to the scheme. The accomplishments of King Alfred the Great were proclaimed in no uncertain terms: 'The mildest, justest, most beneficent of Kings; who drove out the Danes, secur'd the Seas, supported [*or* protected] Learning, establish'd Juries, crush'd Corruption, guarded Liberty, and was the Founder of the English Constitution.'[245] The figure itself was clearly modelled on Vertue's engraving for Rapin's *History of England*, but was provided with a different crown (more suited to stonework). There were others in the same circle who resorted to words, as opposed to stone, in order to vent their opposition. One was Samuel Johnson, whose poem 'London', first published in 1738, draws an explicit contrast between public order in 'Alfred's golden reign' and the situation which obtained in the present day;[246] and that it was more than a passing fancy on Dr Johnson's part is suggested by the fact that in 1746 he is said to have been contemplating writing a 'Life of Alfred'.[247] Another was

---

[244] Eustace, 'Stowe and the Development of the Historical Portrait Bust'; Webb, *Rysbrack*, pp. 135–6; G. Clarke, 'Grecian Taste and Gothic Virtue: Lord Cobham's Gardening Programme and its Iconography', *Apollo* 97 (June 1973), 566–71; M. Bevington, *Stowe: the Garden and the Park*, 2nd ed. (Stowe, 1995), pp. 37–8 and 94–6; and J. M. Robinson, *Temples of Delight: Stowe Landscape Gardens*, National Trust (London, 1990; new ed., 1994), pp. 90–3, with illustrations. See also *Stowe Landscape Gardens*, National Trust Guide (London, 1997), pp. 28–30.

[245] See *Descriptions of Lord Cobham's Gardens at Stowe (1700–1750)*, ed. G. B. Clarke, Buckinghamshire Record Soc. 26 (Aylesbury, 1990), 11, 75, 90, 107, 116 and 138.

[246] *Samuel Johnson: Poems*, ed. E. L. McAdam with G. Milne, Yale Edition of the Works of Samuel Johnson 6 (New Haven, CT, 1964), 45–61, at 60–1.

[247] *Boswell: Life of Johnson*, ed. R. W. Chapman, 3rd ed., rev. J. D. Fleeman (Oxford, 1970), p. 128. In 1781 Thomas Astle sent Johnson some notes on King Alfred's will: see *Liber Vitae*, ed. Keynes, p. 77.

The cult of King Alfred the Great

George, Lord Lyttelton (1709–73), who on his return from the grand tour in 1731 became equerry to (and chief favourite of) the Prince of Wales. It was to Lyttelton that Thomson had addressed *The Seasons*; and his own views on Alfred found expression some years later in his 'History of Henry II'.[248] Yet the most remarkable reflection of the cult of Alfred at this time, if only because it occurs in such an unexpected context, is William Hogarth's portrait of the heiress Mary Edwards (1705–43), made in 1742. The subject is represented as a princess in the Patriot cause: a copy of Elizabeth I's rousing speech to the troops at Tilbury, in 1588, is open on the table beside her, and busts of Queen Elizabeth and King Alfred are behind her on the wall.[249] One is left wondering whether the busts were provided from the artist's imagination, to enhance the symbolic effect, or whether they were sculptures commissioned by Mary herself, in order to bring the spirit of two patriots into her home.

King Alfred during the reign of King George III

The death of 'poor Fred', in 1751, dashed the hopes of those who had entertained such high expectations of him,[250] and denied the British people the pleasure of being ruled by one who seems to have taken King Alfred to heart. For his part, Alfred went on from strength to strength. The changing political and intellectual climate (reflected most obviously by the end of the Seven Years War in 1763, the American War of Independence in 1775–83, the outbreak of the French Revolution in 1789, and the French wars of 1793–1815) provided plenty of scope for Alfred to prosper both as a national icon, ever more closely identified with the Hanoverian cause, whenever the nation's security was threatened or when its sense of identity needed to be maintained, and as the originator and personification of what was fondly imagined to be a democratic constitution, whenever individual liberties were at stake. On the more personal level, the incapacity of George III, and the perception of his son George, Prince of Wales, as a dissolute wastrel, doubtless helped at the same time to keep Alfred to the fore as the very model of what a king should be. The perception of the king

---

[248] George, Lord Lyttelton, *The History of the Life of Henry the Second, and of the Age in which he Lived, in Five Books: to which is prefixed, A History of the Revolutions of England from the Death of Edward the Confessor to the Birth of Henry the Second*, 3 vols. (London, 1767–71), esp. II, 165 (navy), 175–6 (trade), 257 (slavery), 259 (view of Frankpledge) and 322 (learning).

[249] The painting is now in the Frick Collection, New York. See J. Uglow, *Hogarth: a Life and a World* (London, 1997), pp. 363–5, and Eustace, 'Stowe and the Development of the Historical Portrait Bust', p. 39.

[250] For the Jacobite jingle ('Here lies poor Fred, who was alive and is dead …'), see Young, *Poor Fred*, pp. 219–24. Prince Frederick's death was marked by the publication of numerous odes; and it is represented also by a pottery figure 'Britannia mourning for Frederick, Prince of Wales' (British Museum), reproduced in Jones, *Frederick, Prince of Wales, and his Circle*, p. 27. See also Langford, *England 1727–1783*, pp. 220–1.

which had developed in the seventeenth and early eighteenth centuries had by now become integral to the nation's perception of itself. Rapin's *History*, in the English form in which it had been first published in 1728, had been joined by some other substantial accounts of English history, such as William Guthrie's *General History of England* (1744),[251] complemented by accounts in the various forerunners of the *Dictionary of National Biography*,[252] but its position in the field had not been threatened. More serious threats began to take shape in the 1750s, initially in the form of a learned and somewhat austere *History of England* by David Hume (1711–76). Hume's work began to appear in 1754, and, moving steadily backwards, reached the Anglo-Saxon period in 1761.[253] Its success precipitated competition from Tobias Smollett (1721–71), who dashed out his own best-selling *Complete History of England*, first published in 1757–8;[254] but it was Hume, in effect, who set the view of English history which prevailed throughout the reign of George III. Hume's treatment of the reign of Alfred the Great is based squarely on the model provided by John Spelman, though shorn of obsession with the supposed antiquity of the University of Oxford and recast in the measured prose of the Enlightenment. On the anecdotal level, Hume fastened on the story of how Alfred took refuge in the house of a neatherd, and how he was berated by the neatherd's wife for allowing the cakes to burn, as a story of 'so much virtue and dignity reduced to such distress'. He also made good use of the story of Alfred entering the Danish camp, 'under the disguise of a harper', and of his display of magnanimity towards Hastings in 893. St Neot and St Cuthbert, on the other hand, do not make an appearance. The pitch is raised to a higher level when the time comes to project an image of the king as the perfect prince:

---

[251] W. Guthrie, *A General History of England, from the Invasion of the Romans under Julius Cæsar, to the Late Revolution in MDCLXXXVIII*, 4 vols. (London, 1744–51), originally published in weekly parts (Wiles, *Serial Publication in England*, pp. 148 and 339). The plates are in the form of engraved portraits, for rulers from William I onwards. For Guthrie (1707–70), see Smith, *The Gothic Bequest*, pp. 55–6, and Hicks, *Neoclassical History and English Culture*, pp. 155–8.

[252] J. P. Bernard, et al., *A General Dictionary, Historical and Critical: in which a New and Accurate Translation of that of the Celebrated Mr. Bayle is Included*, 10 vols. (London, 1734–41) I, 493–505 (on Alfred); *Biographia Britannica: or, The Lives of the Most Eminent Persons who have Flourished in Great Britain and Ireland, from the Earliest Ages, down to the Present Times*, 6 vols. in 7 (London, 1747–66) I, 45–57 (on Alfred). See also J. Ryland, *The Life and Character of Alfred the Great* (London, 1784), said to have been 'drawn from the more ample view of him in the first volume in folio of the Biographia Britannica, with other authors', which I have not seen.

[253] For the complex bibliography of this work, see T. E. Jessop, *A Bibliography of David Hume and of Scottish Philosophy* (London, 1938), pp. 27–33. For an exposition of Hume's historical writing, see Smith, *The Gothic Bequest*, pp. 74–84, and Hicks, *Neoclassical History and English Culture*, pp. 170–209.

[254] T. Smollett, *A Complete History of England*, 4 vols. (London, 1757–8), republished in weekly parts as 2nd ed. (London, 1758). On the popularity of this work, see Wiles, *Serial Publication in England*, pp. 5–6.

The cult of King Alfred the Great

The merit of this prince, both in private and public life, may with advantage be set in opposition to that of any monarch or citizen which the annals of any age or any nation can present to us. He seems indeed to be the model of that perfect character, which, under the denomination of a sage or wise man, philosophers have been fond of delineating, rather as a fiction of their imagination, than in hopes of ever seeing it really existing: so happily were all his virtues tempered together; so justly were they blended; and so powerfully did each prevent the other from exceeding its proper boundaries. He knew how to reconcile the most enterprising spirit with the coolest moderation; the most obstinate perseverance with the easiest flexibility; the most severe justice with the gentlest lenity; the greatest vigour in commanding with the most perfect affability of deportment; the highest capacity and inclination for science with the most shining talents for action.

Hume's Alfred was responsible, of course, for the division of all England into counties, and into hundreds, and into tithings; and if this arrangement might have seemed destructive of individual liberty, Hume assured his readers that 'it was well calculated to reduce that fierce and licentious people under the salutary restraint of law and government'. Yet nothing, Hume went on, 'could be more popular or liberal than [Alfred's] plan for the administration of justice'. In the monthly meetings of the hundreds lay the origin of juries, with the possibility of appeal to the biannual meetings of the shire and ultimately to the king in council. Alfred also 'framed a body of laws; which, though now lost, served long as the basis of English jurisprudence, and is generally deemed the origin of what is denominated the Common Law'. He encouraged learning, 'founded, or at least repaired, the university of Oxford', and led the way to his people 'in the pursuits of literature'. Alfred was, in short, 'one of the wisest and best that had ever adorned the annals of any nation'.[255] Hume's portrayal of Alfred is all the more remarkable because he was scathing in his treatment of the Anglo-Saxons in general, and eloquent on the beneficial effects of the Norman Conquest;[256] and the message was soon absorbed at the highest level. Sir William Blackstone (1723–80), appointed Vinerian professor of law at Oxford in 1758, and renowned as the author of *Commentaries on the Laws of England* (1765–9), subscribed (like Hume) to Spelman's notion of Alfred's 'lost' code of laws, and supposed that it contained 'the principal maxims of the common law, the penalties for misdemesnors, and the forms of judicial proceedings'; and although he seems to have been instinctively suspicious of the notion that it was necessarily

---

[255] D. Hume, *The History of England from the Invasion of Julius Caesar to the Revolution in 1688*, 6 vols. (London, 1759–62), new ed. in 8 vols. (London, 1778), reset in 6 vols., with a Foreword by W. B. Todd, Liberty Classics (Indianapolis, IN, 1983) I, 63–81. An abridged edition of Hume's *History* (Chicago, 1975), which does not include coverage of the Anglo-Saxon period, has an Introduction by R. W. Kilcup.

[256] E.g. Hume, *History of England* [1983] I, 168–9 and 185. See also Skinner, 'History and Ideology', pp. 155 and 177.

Alfred who invented trial by jury – noting the tendency to attribute so many things 'to the superior genius of Alfred the great; to whom, on account of his having done so much, it is usual to attribute everything' – he opined nonetheless that it was Alfred who reduced the whole kingdom 'under one regular and gradual subordination of government'.[257]

Manifestations of the cult of King Alfred proliferated in the second half of the eighteenth century, in ways which show that he remained a hero to those who operated at slightly less exalted levels of intellectual activity.[258] The time was ripe for the formation of organisations like the 'Laudable Society of Anti-Gallicans', and for an assault on the notion that English history began in 1066.[259] An anonymous play entitled 'Alfred the Great: Deliverer of his Country' was performed and published in 1753.[260] The action is set amidst the dramatic events of 878, but it has a stronger 'historical' plot than the masque of 1740 (though again with added love interest), moving rapidly from the Danish Camp on Salisbury Plain, via a Cottage in Athelney, to the Court at Winchester, culminating with Alfred's victory at Edington and a stirring speech on the need 'to guard against Future Invasions'. The play ends not so much with a rousing invocation of Britannia, as with King Alfred's unsubtle endorsement of the Hanoverian dynasty:

> *Alf.* Let all my subjects at their Homes with Chear,
> The first of August keep, in every Year:
> From Age to Age, may they continue free;
> And this be still the Day, mark'd out for Liberty.

In other words, all should respect the anniversary of the accession of King George I; at which point in comes Elfleda [= Æthelflæd, Alfred's daughter], 'in Man's Apparel', and delivers herself of an Epilogue apparently calculated to bring the house down. The view of the Anglo-Saxon past which lies behind the

---

[257] *The Sovereignty of the Law: Selections from Blackstone's 'Commentaries on the Laws of England'*, ed. G. Jones (London, 1973), pp. 46–8, 176 and 209–12. For Blackstone, see also Smith, *The Gothic Bequest*, pp. 91–4.

[258] See, in general, Miles, *King Alfred in Literature*; Stanley, 'The Glorification of Alfred'; R. Frank, 'The Search for the Anglo-Saxon Oral Poet', *Bull. of the John Rylands Univ. Lib. of Manchester* 75 (1993), 11–36; and L. Pratt, 'Anglo-Saxon Attitudes?: Alfred the Great and the Romantic National Epic', *Literary Appropriations of the Anglo-Saxons from the Thirteenth to the Twentieth Century*, ed. D. Scragg and C. Weinberg, CSASE 29 (Cambridge, 2000), 138–56. Miles (pp. 2–3) cites J. Loring Arnold, 'King Alfred in English Poetry', PhD Dissertation, Univ. of Leipzig (Meiningen, 1898), which I have not seen.

[259] See L. Colley, 'Radical Patriotism in Eighteenth-Century England', *Patriotism: the Making and Unmaking of British National Identity*, ed. R. Samuel, 3 vols. (London, 1989) I, 169–87, at 172–3, for an almanac issued by one of the Anti-Gallicans in 1750–1, featuring a print which listed the pre-Conquest rulers of England.

[260] *Alfred the Great, Deliverer of his Country: a Tragedy* (London, 1753). See also Miles, *King Alfred in Literature*, pp. 63–5, and Stanley, 'The Glorification of Alfred', pp. 432–3.

The cult of King Alfred the Great

poems written by the young Thomas Chatterton (1752–70), in 1768–9, and passed off by him as the works of a fictitious fifteenth-century poet called Thomas Rowley, is somewhat more difficult to fathom;[261] but just as Earl Leofwine invoked the name of Alfred in *Battle of Hastings II* ('Thinke of brave Ælfridus, yclept the grete'), so too did Chatterton, and the antiquary William Barrett, invoke Alfred in representing the Rowley papers as genuine.[262] On a different level, Obadiah Hulme pursued the radical line in his relentlessly polemical but beguilingly accessible *Historical Essay on the English Constitution* (1771), featuring Alfred the Great as the one who united the seven kingdoms of the Heptarchy and instituted the democratic systems of government which were then destroyed by Norman tyranny (and so on).[263] Alexander Bicknell conceived his *Life of Alfred*, published in 1777, as an attempt to render Spelman's earlier work 'more intelligible and entertaining to the generality of Readers',[264] and took his determination to popularize Alfred a stage further in 1788, with the play of his book, significantly entitled *The Patriot King*.[265] Two other works of Alfredian literature which originated in the 1770s exemplify Alfred's continued appeal to creative writers, whatever may have been on their agenda. John Home's drama on Alfred, performed in 1778, began with a defence of the dramatist's right to take liberties with historical truth in the interests of a romantic tale;[266] and in the same year Robert Holmes (1748–1805), Fellow of New College, Oxford, published a short but stirring ode on Alfred, ending 'Hail, British Alfred, patriot King, Great Father of thy people, Hail!'[267] One should add that Alfred seems to have made such an impression in the 1770s that he also earned a place for himself in some of the decorative schemes devised by Robert Adam (1728–92). At Kedleston Hall, in Derbyshire, two plaster roundels, one identified as Ethelred and the

---

[261] [T. Chatterton], *Poems, Supposed to have been Written at Bristol, by Thomas Rowley, and Others, in the Fifteenth Century* (London, 1777); see also T. Chatterton, *The Rowley Poems 1794* (Oxford and New York, 1990).

[262] *The Complete Works of Thomas Chatterton: a Bicentenary Edition*, ed. D. S. Taylor with B. B. Hoover, 2 vols. (Oxford, 1971) I, 72 (*Battle of Hastings* II, lines 135–8) and 273 (draft of a letter to Horace Walpole, April 1769).

[263] *An Historical Essay on the English Constitution: or, An Impartial Inquiry into the Elective Power of the People, from the First Establishment of the Saxons in this Kingdom, wherein the Right of Parliament, to Tax our Distant Provinces, is Explained, and Justified* (London, 1771), esp. pp. 22–33. For exposition of this work, see Newman, *The Rise of English Nationalism*, pp. 185–9, and Smith, *The Gothic Bequest*, pp. 100–2.

[264] A. Bicknell, *The Life of Alfred the Great, King of the Anglo-Saxons* (London, 1777). See Stanley, 'The Glorification of Alfred', p. 419.

[265] A. Bicknell, *The Patriot King: or Alfred and Elvida. An Historical Tragedy* (London, 1788), soon adapted for performance in Germany and provided with incidental music by Joseph Haydn (Stanley, 'The Glorification of Alfred', p. 423, n. 47). See also Miles, *King Alfred in Literature*, pp. 69–71.

[266] [J. Home], *Alfred. A Tragedy. As Performed at the Theatre-Royal, in Covent-Garden* (Dublin, 1777; London, 1778). For a synopsis of the plot, see Miles, *King Alfred in Literature*, pp. 66–9.

[267] R. Holmes, *Alfred. An Ode. With Six Sonnets* (Oxford, 1778).

Simon Keynes

other as Alfred, originally formed part of the decoration of the Tetrastyle Hall, and were later moved into Caesars' Hall;[268] while at Home House (20 Portman Square), in London, Alfred features with Queen Elizabeth in a painting forming part of the overmantel in the Library, or 'Asylum'.[269] Alfred even impressed himself on a prosperous and evidently enlightened merchant in the West Riding of Yorkshire. In 1769 one Jeremiah Dixon, of (Chapel) Allerton and Gledhow, near Leeds, erected a gothic structure in honour of King Alfred on Tunnel How Hill, overlooking the city, known locally as 'King Alfred's Castle' (but already ruinous when finally demolished in the mid-twentieth century).[270] No less remarkable is the case of the radical author, Catharine Macaulay (1731–91), who lived in the 1770s at Alfred House, 14 Alfred Street, Bath, with a bust of the king 'nodding o'er the patriotic portal' of her door. On the occasion of her birthday in 1777, she was presented with a set of six Odes, three of which invoked the name of King Alfred in her honour.[271]

---

[268] *Kedleston Hall, Derbyshire*, National Trust Guide (London, 1988, rev. 1998), p. 55; I am grateful to Ms Jill Banks, Archivist, Kedleston Hall, for her assistance in this connection. If only to judge from the portrait, 'Ethelred' was modelled on a *Helmet* penny of Æthelred II. Medallions of Alfred and Ethelred were among the items sold at the sale of the effects of a sculptor called Bridges in 1775 (Gunnis, *Dictionary of British Sculptors*, p. 61).

[269] The painting, made in 1776 by Antonio Zucchi (1726–95), shows Britannia, enthroned between Faith and Justice, being presented by Fame with portraits of Alfred the Great and Elizabeth I. Zucchi was working for Robert Adam, on behalf of Elizabeth, Dowager Countess of Home. See M. Whinney, *Home House: No. 20 Portman Square* (Feltham, 1969), pp. 39–40, with plate on p. 94, and Croft-Murray, *Decorative Painting in England* II, 298. The portrait of Alfred was based on the image devised by Vertue.

[270] An inscription on a tablet in the wall read as follows: 'To the Memory of / Alfred the Great / The Wise, the Pious and Magnanimous / The Friend of / Science, Virtue, Law, and Liberty / This Monument / Jeremiah Dixon of Allerton / Gledhow caused to be erected / A.D. MDC-CLXIX.' I am grateful to Chris Solomon for drawing my attention to 'Alfred's Castle'; to Vivien Cartwright (Local Studies Library, Central Library, Leeds) for providing me with press-cuttings (and a photograph of part of the structure taken shortly before it was demolished in May 1946); and to Brett Harrison (The Thoresby Society, Leeds) for providing me with a photograph of the inscription (from a lantern slide made in 1888). Jeremiah Dixon (1726–82) was High Sheriff of the county in 1758, and was made an FRS in 1773; he had bought the Gledhow estate in 1764. For the inscription on his tomb in the parish church of Leeds, see T. D. Whitaker, *Loidis and Elmete; or, An Attempt to Illustrate the Districts Described in those Words by Bede* (Leeds, 1816), p. 57, with pedigree of Dixon at pp. 130–1. See also R. V. Taylor, *The Biographia Leodiensis; or, Biographical Sketches of the Worthies of Leeds and Neighbourhood, from the Norman Conquest to the Present Time* (London, 1865), pp. 181–3.

[271] *Six Odes Presented to that Justly-Celebrated Historian, Mrs. Catharine Macaulay, on her Birth-Day, and Publicly Read to a Polite and Brilliant Audience, Assembled April the Second, at Alfred-House, Bath, to Congratulate that Lady on the Happy Occasion* (Bath, [1777]), esp. pp. 17–19, 35–8 and 39–45. For 'Alfred House', built *c*. 1772, see W. Ison, *Georgian Buildings of Bath from 1700 to 1830*, rev. ed. (Bath, 1980), pp. 7, 27, 97–9, 156–7 and 198 (showing the bust of Alfred, displaying all the features of its Vertue/Rysbrack model, over the Adamesque doorcase). For an account of her writings, see B. Hill, *The Republican Virago: the Life and Times of Catharine Macaulay, Historian* (Oxford, 1992), esp. pp. 31–2 and 79–80.

The cult of King Alfred the Great

It was at about this stage in the development of the Alfredian myth that a Frenchman contrived to complicate matters by injecting into the tale an element derived from a rather different context. M. Baculard d'Arnaud, described by an Englishman as 'the Richardson of France', included a short account of King Alfred at the beginning of his *Délassements* (1783), and told a fine story, in this connection, of how Alfred fell madly in love with a certain 'Ethelswitha', the most beautiful of the three daughters of the Lord d'Albanac, and how they married and lived happily ever after.[272] In fact (as it were), the story of Alfred and the daughters of the Lord d'Albanac relates to a different and wholly imaginary Alfred III, King of Mercia, who was the putative ancestor of the Dukes of Rutland;[273] and since this lesser-known Alfred had featured, in his own right, in a painting by Benjamin West, an engraving of which had been published in 1782, it would appear that M. Baculard d'Arnaud erred (deliberately or otherwise) in transferring the story to his better-known namesake. Whatever the case, the story of Alfred and 'Ethelwitha' [*sic*] soon found its way back to England, translated from Baculard d'Arnaud in the pages of *The Universal Magazine of Knowledge and Pleasure*, for 1784, with an engraved illustration by Thomas Stothard.[274] It was to enjoy some currency thereafter, in various manifestations of Alfredian poetry, drama, and prose.[275]

Alfred was still held up, in one way or another, as a model of behaviour for princes who had some prospect of becoming kings. In 1788 George III was afflicted by the malady which threatened to cost him his mind, and preparations were made for the dissolute George, Prince of Wales, to take over as regent; but in 1789 the king recovered his health, and plans for regency were for the time being set aside. Anne Fuller's novel *The Son of Ethelwolf*, published in 1789, was dedicated by permission to the Prince of Wales; and since the author makes a point in her preface of expressing her great relief that George III had just recovered from his illness,[276] it seems that she had decided, in the title of her novel, to represent Alfred as the son of his father, as a way of expressing her

---

[272] F. T. M. Baculard d'Arnaud, *Délassements de l'homme sensible, ou anecdotes diverses*, 6 vols. (Paris, 1783) I.i, 1–16 (with no indication of source). See R. L. Dawson, *Baculard d'Arnaud: Life and Prose Fiction*, 2 vols., Stud. on Voltaire and the Eighteenth Century 141–2 (Banbury, 1976) II, 474–518 (Baculard's medievalism) and 677–9 (*Délassements*); see also Miles, *King Alfred in Literature*, p. 111, and Stanley, 'The Glorification of Alfred', pp. 427–8.

[273] See further below, pp. 300–1.

[274] 'The Story of Alfred and Ethelwitha: with an Interesting Scene, Designed by Stothard', *Universal Mag. of Knowledge and Pleasure* (January, 1784), pp. 29–32.

[275] For example, in *Alfred: an Historical Tragedy* (London, 1789), on which see Miles, *King Alfred in Literature*, pp. 71–2, and in Fuller's novel (next note); also cited in *Observations on the Life and Character of Alfred the Great* (1794), on which see further below.

[276] A. Fuller, *The Son of Ethelwolf: an Historical Tale* (London, 1789), Preface: 'Heaven has restored to you a father, to England a sovereign, worthy of the tears that were recently shed for him, and of the happiness that his recovery now inspires.' For an effective discussion of the novel, see Stanley, 'The Glorification of Alfred', pp. 427–31.

loyalty to the reigning monarch and of impressing on the reader that Prince George remained his father's son. Fuller's tale is suffused with a strong romantic element, now involving 'Ethelswitha' (as opposed to the more historical 'Alswith'), and provides the hero with many opportunities for reflections of an Alfredian kind. Nor was Prince George expected to read only the novel. In an anonymous tract entitled *Lessons to a Young Prince*, published in 1790, dedicated and addressed directly to the Prince of Wales, the point is made that 'the jarring interests, claims, and principles produced by the union of the heptarchy, furnished the vigorous and comprehensive mind of Alfred with the first correct and rational idea of a political constitution which is recorded in history'.[277] The author goes on to assert that Alfred 'organised the free parts of the community into a political constitution, the best imagined and most effectual that has hitherto been exhibited in the world'; and then, to save the Prince the trouble of reading a verbal description of Alfred's 'Political Constitution of England', the author exhibits it in the form of a diagram, and proceeds to compare it with other diagrams representing English government in 1790, the constitution of the independent American states, and the constitution of revolutionary France.[278] The analogies were by no means inappropriate. The radical tradition reaching back past Obadiah Hulme's tract on the English constitution (1771), and Rapin's *History* (1726–31), to the lawyers of the early seventeenth century, had been absorbed by Thomas Jefferson, to the extent that he had 'Saxon' liberties at the back of his mind when he drafted the Declaration of Independence (1776) and later advocated the division of the West into what he fondly imagined would be the equivalent of Alfred's hundreds.[279] Soon after the outbreak of the War of Independence, in 1775, a 24-gun ship which had been built in Philadelphia in 1774, and named the *Black Prince*, was renamed *Alfred*, and proceeded to distinguish herself in battle against the British until captured in 1778.[280] Meanwhile, stirrings in Germany and France had prompted Albrecht von Haller to produce a rather curious 'Life of King Alfred', in 1773, dedicated

---

[277] *Lessons to a Young Prince, on the Present Disposition in Europe to a General Revolution* (London, 1790).
[278] The author of the tract was the Welsh radical David Williams (1738–1816). For his use of Alfred, see W. R. D. Jones, *David Williams: the Anvil and the Hammer* (Cardiff, 1986), esp. pp. 73 (in *A Plan of Association on Constitutional Principles* (1780)), 109–12 (in *Lesson to a Young Prince* (1790)), and 151 (in *Egeria, or Elementary Studies on the Progress of Nations in Political Oeconomy, Legislation, and Government* (London, 1803)).
[279] For further discussion, see R. Horsman, *Race and Manifest Destiny: the Origins of American Racial Anglo-Saxonism* (Cambridge, MA, 1981), pp. 9–24; S. R. Hauer, 'Thomas Jefferson and the Anglo-Saxon Language', *PMLA* 98 (1983), 879–98; and A. J. Frantzen, *Desire for Origins: New Language, Old English, and Teaching the Tradition* (New Brunswick, NJ, 1990), esp. pp. 204–7.
[280] *Dictionary of American Naval Fighting Ships*, 8 vols. (Washington, DC, 1959–81) I, 28. I owe my knowledge of the *Alfred*'s existence to the kindness of Professor Richard Abels, of the US Naval Academy, Annapolis, MD.

to King George III, in which the Alfredian regime was held up as the model of a moderate monarchy (*gemässigte Monarchie*), as opposed to absolute monarchy, moderate republic, or democracy.[281] A French edition of von Haller's 'Life of King Alfred' was published in 1775,[282] and was later said to have been among the works which hastened the French Revolution in 1789.

Alfred's light burned more brightly than ever in the 1790s, in ways which had more to do with contemporary politics, and with the impact of the Revolutionary and Napoleonic wars, than with any considerations of historical reality. In 1792 John Penn produced a play called 'The Battle of Eddington; or, British Liberty', which parades a contemporary political agenda in its dedication to the Prime Minister, William Pitt.[283] It contains some interesting discussion between Alfred and Ceolwulf about different political systems; and after lines like 'Long live great Alfred, patron of the Irish!', it ends as Alfred promises to make new laws for the united English, Scottish, Welsh and Irish people. In 1794 Daniel Isaac Eaton published an anonymous tract entitled 'Observations on the Life and Character of Alfred the Great', which proves to contain the text of two lectures on Alfred from a course on English history given by the unnamed author 'to a Society of Literary Gentlemen at Lyons' Inn', in the spring of 1793.[284] The author commended the excellent state of public order under Alfred, in contrast to the prevailing disorder under George III, and held up the witenagemot as a model of good government. A play by John O'Keeffe entitled 'Alfred, or the Magic Banner', which opened at the Haymarket in 1796, featured among many other dramatic moments a moving speech by Alfred about his invention of trial by jury.[285] The play was not, however, intended to serve a serious purpose, for as the theme became more familiar so too did it become fair game for satire, pantomime, and farce. Yet there was a limit to what even the British public could handle, and the play folded after three nights. There soon followed Lonsdale's 'Grand Historical Ballet of Action, with Airs, Chorusses, Etc.', entitled 'Alfred the Great; or The Danish Invasion', performed at Sadler's Wells theatre in 1798, which by all accounts was a stirring evocation of British

---

[281] A. von Haller, *Alfred König der Angel-Sachsen* (Göttingen and Bern, 1773). See also Miles, *King Alfred in Literature*, pp. 109–11, and Stanley, 'The Glorification of Alfred', pp. 417–18.

[282] A. von Haller, *Alfred, roi des Anglo-Saxons* (Lausanne, 1775).

[283] J. Penn, *The Battle of Eddington; or, British Liberty. A Tragedy* (London, 1792), 2nd ed. (London, 1796). See also Miles, *King Alfred in Literature*, pp. 73–4, and Stanley, 'The Glorification of Alfred', p. 424, n. 48.

[284] [Anon.], *Observations on the Life and Character of Alfred the Great* (London, 1794). The tale of Alfred and Ethelwitha was derived from Baculard d'Arnaud (above, n. 275). For the publisher, see the *DNB*, and M. T. Davis, '"That Odious Class of Men Called Democrats": Daniel Isaac Eaton and the Romantics 1794–1795', *History* 84 (1999), 74–92.

[285] J. O'Keeffe, *Dramatic Works*, 4 vols. (London, 1798) IV, 195–267. See also Miles, *King Alfred in Literature*, pp. 74–6, and Stanley, 'The Glorification of Alfred', pp. 424, n. 49, 426–7 and 437.

resistance to foreign oppression, at a time when Napoleon was active in Egypt.[286] Tales were also told at about this time of an English warship, called the 'Alfred', which had seen active service against the French.[287] Another fervent admirer of Alfred in the late eighteenth century was the political reformer Major John Cartwright (1740–1824), who in 1799 published his 'Appeal on the Subject of the English Constitution', in which he advocated the adoption of an Alfredian system of national defence which unlike other systems would not infringe civil liberties.[288]

ALFRED THE GREAT IN POPULAR HISTORY AND HISTORY PAINTING

The extensive exploitation of Alfredian themes for literary and polemical purposes in the second half of the eighteenth century raises some interesting questions. How was knowledge of English history conveyed to and absorbed by the people, and so by what means or stages did Alfred take his place in popular consciousness of the nation's historical identity? How did English history acquire its visual dimension? Which events, or persons, or subjects were deemed to suit an artistic purpose, and which were the first to catch the popular imagination? Some part must have been played by the educational process (though it is not clear how much detailed knowledge could have been acquired in this way), and some part by the popularity of the compendious histories written by Rapin, Hume, and others. It was, however, during the reign of King George III that the popularization of English history, and the fields of English painting, printmaking, and book illustration, began to interact upon each other in ways which add a further dimension to our understanding of King Alfred's place in the developing perception of the Anglo-Saxon past.[289]

Leaving aside the stylized woodcuts in Holinshed's 'Historie of England' (1577), and paying all due homage to the engravings of two events in Verstegan's *Restitution of Decayed Intelligence* (1605), it seems to have been some while before a

---

[286] For an account of this performance, see Miles, *King Alfred in Literature*, pp. 76–7.

[287] *Diary of Joseph Farington* [below, n. 443] III, 1055–6.

[288] J. Cartwright, *An Appeal, Civil and Military, on the Subject of the English Constitution* (London, 1799). For Cartwright, see the *DNB*, and J. W. Osborne, *John Cartwright* (Cambridge, 1972); see also Smith, *The Gothic Bequest*, pp. 137–9, and Simmons, *Reversing the Conquest*, pp. 36–9.

[289] On the popularity of history in the eighteenth century, see Langford, *England 1727–1783*, pp. 96–9, and Brewer, *Pleasures of the Imagination*, pp. 181–2. The *Universal History* mentioned by Langford had first appeared (part by part) in 7 folio volumes (1736–44), ranging widely across the ancient world (though including an account of the Anglo-Saxon invasion of Britain in VII.1, 438–55). An edition ranging across the modern world first appeared in 44 octavo volumes (1759–66), but did not cover Great Britain. A revised edition of the modern part, in 42 octavo volumes (1780–84), gave belated coverage to England, Scotland and Ireland (XXXIX–XLII); and Anglo-Saxon England is given relatively short shrift (XXXIX, 1–47, at 14–19 (Alfred)). See G. Abbattista, 'The Business of Paternoster Row: Towards a Publishing History of the *Universal History* (1736–65)', *Publishing Hist.* 17 (1985), 5–50.

The cult of King Alfred the Great

publisher deemed it desirable to attach a sequence of illustrations to a narrative of English history. The first edition of Rapin's *Histoire d'Angleterre* (1724) had been illustrated with some engraved portraits and decorative head-pieces, of no great artistic distinction, by F. M. La Cave.[290] In the first (octavo) edition of Tindal's translation (1726–8), the head-pieces were omitted, and La Cave's portraits were replaced by portraits devised for the purpose by George Vertue.[291] In the case of Alfred, Vertue developed the earlier engraving he had done for Wise's edition of Asser (1722), providing the same set of symbolic accessories (bow and arrows, harp, spear, scroll and books, Danish 'Raven' standard, and shield); interestingly, the other kings seem to have failed to catch his imagination in quite the same way. The second (folio) edition of the English translation (1732–3) revived the decorative head-pieces (rather badly redrawn for the purpose);[292] and from December 1733 the two-volume work could be embellished, by subscription, with a new and much more imposing set of symbolic portraits, again by George Vertue, which were themselves published as a complete collection (dedicated to Prince Frederick) in 1736.[293] Vertue's symbolic portraits naturally reflect Rapin's view of English history. Egbert, king of the West Saxons, is shown in his capacity as 'first Monarch of all England': the portrait is based on a coin (derived from Speed, or from Walker's edition of Spelman), and other symbols include some broken Roman statues, a runic inscription, and a map of the Heptarchy. Alfred (pl. VIII*b*), styled 'Ælfredus Magnus Rex Angl[orum]', is shown in the image devised by Vertue in the early 1720s (derived from Walker's edition of Spelman, and so from the portrait at University College, Oxford), with the same range of accessories (the captured

---

[290] Above, n. 213. The portraits include King Egbert (opp. p. 213), King Alfred (opp. p. 301), and King Cnut (opp. p. 406). The portraits were probably derived from the plates in Walker's edition of Spelman's 'Life' (1678), whether of the coins (for Egbert and Cnut) or of the painting at University College (Alfred). The headpieces include Vortigern and Rowena (p. 91), St Augustine preaching before King Æthelberht (p. 147), the three Anglian kings of Northumbria, Mercia, and East Anglia paying their respects to King Egbert (p. 277), the beheading of Swein's sister in the presence of King Æthelred (p. 383), and a meeting of the Witenagemot during the age of the Heptarchy (p. 475).

[291] Above, n. 214, vols. I, opp. pp. 293 (Egbert) and 323 (Alfred), and II.i, opp. title-page (Cnut).

[292] Above, n. 215, vol. I, 3 (a pastoral scene), 9 (Romans building), 30 (Rowena catching the eye of Vortigern), 45 (St Augustine before King Æthelberht), 82 (the three Anglian kings of Mercia, Northumbria and East Anglia acknowledging the sovereignty of King Egbert), 117 (execution of Gunnhild on the orders of King Æthelred in 1002), and 147 (government by heptarchy).

[293] G. Vertue, *The Heads of the Kings of England Proper for Mr Rapin's History, Translated by N. Tindal, M.A.* (London, 1736). Publication of the portraits began in December 1733, and was not completed until the summer of 1736; see Wiles, *Serial Publication in England*, pp. 285, 294 and 310, and Lippincott, *Selling Art in Georgian London*, pp. 149–50 and 190, n. 57. See also F. Haskell, *History and its Images: Art and the Interpretation of the Past* (New Haven, CT, 1993), p. 289, with fig. 168 (showing Vertue's portrait of Richard II).

Danish standard, bow and arrows, harp, several books, scroll, ruler and divider, and crown), over vignettes of a battle-field, the king playing his harp in the Danish camp, and a Viking fleet, and also the king's coat of arms.[294] The portrait of Cnut is developed from his coinage, surrounded by runes, a Raven (on a shield), and blazing torches, over a vignette of the king and his courtiers having a close encounter with the incoming tide. The portrait of William the Conqueror is again based on his coinage, though the vignette below (showing the enthroned conqueror holding Britannia in chains) is in strict accordance with the doctrine of the 'Norman Yoke'. Subsequent editions of Rapin's *History* were provided with some further illustrations, for the period after the Norman Conquest, but the illustrations did not extend to the full-page depiction of historical or pseudo-historical events.[295] Vertue's symbolic portraits were, moreover, scarcely adequate to convey much sense of the dignity and grandeur of the historical event, and can have made little impact on the popular imagination. Rapin's subject-matter, on the other hand, was more than enough to provide artists with a source of inspiration. As one distinguished critic has remarked: 'It [Rapin's *History of England*] promoted a widespread interest in national antiquity, inspired a school of English history painters from Kauffmann to Blake, and opened the era of English commercial engraving.'[296]

The illustration of Anglo-Saxon history

By the middle of the eighteenth century, knowledge of English history must have been reaching deeper and deeper into the collective consciousness of the reading public. Yet while there were many portraits of kings, imaginary or otherwise,[297] there was still little to help the public visualize the more significant or dramatic moments of the distant past. The term 'history painting', as opposed to portraiture, still life or landscape painting, is applied to a form of art in which subjects were drawn from classical and biblical sources in order to represent inspiring truths and noble themes.[298] The term is also used of paintings whose subjects

---

[294] For the image, see above, pp. 261–2 and 265; for the coat of arms, see above, nn. 65 and 114.

[295] The illustrations in the 3rd ed. of 1743, essentially the same as in the 2nd ed. of 1732–3, are said to be the best (*DNB*). They comprise the decorative headpieces, Vertue's symbolic portraits, drawings of particular monuments, and some additional portraits in vol. 2.

[296] D. V. Erdman, *Blake: Prophet Against Empire. A Poet's Interpretation of the History of his own Times*, 3rd ed. (Princeton, NJ, 1977), p. 66.

[297] For royal portraiture of the period, see James Granger, *Biographical History of England, from Egbert the Great to the Revolution* (1769); and for engraved portraits of Alfred, among others, see F. O'Donoghue and H. M. Hake, *Catalogue of Engraved British Portraits . . . in the British Museum*, 6 vols. (London, 1908–25) I, 34–5. For *Baziliologia* (1618), see above, n. 117.

[298] For the wider contexts of history painting, see E. Waterhouse, *Painting in Britain 1530–1790*, 5th ed. (New Haven, CT, 1994), pp. 271–84; Burke, *English Art 1714–1800*, esp. pp. 239–71; J. Brewer, *The Pleasures of the Imagination: English Culture in the Eighteenth Century* (London, 1997), esp. ch. 5 (pp. 206, 217, 245 and 246); and *The Dictionary of Art*, ed. J. Turner, 34 vols. (London, 1996) XIV, 581–9. Haskell, *History and its Images*, is concerned mainly with the use of art as

The cult of King Alfred the Great

were drawn from a nation's own history, for similar if not always exactly identical purposes. History painting in this more restricted sense flourished mightily in England during the period 1750–1850, and was long regarded as a high and indeed noble form of art, albeit one sustained more by the grandeur of its subject-matter than by the artistic quality of many of its products. It extended from paintings made in response to a particular commission, whether for display in a private home or a public place, to paintings or drawings made for public competitions and exhibitions; and it reached further out into print-making and print-selling,[299] and then downwards into the realms of contemporary book illustration.[300] It is true that connoisseurs returning to their grand houses from their Grand Tours would have treated much of this material with justifiable disdain, and that there are better pictures and more interesting prints to examine. It is also the case that in the estimation of discerning critics history paintings are now less well regarded than the portraits and landscapes produced by many of the same artists at the same time. For his part, an interloper in the field must acknowledge that just as the popular histories are no longer read as history, the pictures may scarcely rate as art. It is a matter, therefore, of indulging those who may have had more appetite than taste, limited resources, and some restrictions of space on their walls.

The development and progress of English history painting in the second half of the eighteenth century is (needless to say) inseparable from its political, social, and cultural contexts; and the increasing popularity of history painting, as artists began to draw upon what was seen to be a rich and for them a fresh source of inspiration, is thus but one aspect of a large and complex story. Many of the

---

historical evidence; but for the depiction of historical events in art, see esp. pp. 287–9. For 'English' history painting in particular, see J. Sunderland, 'Mortimer, Pine and Some Political Aspects of English History Painting', *Burlington Magazine* 116 (1974), 317–26; R. Strong, *And when did you last see your father? The Victorian Painter and British History* (London, 1978), focusing attention on the nineteenth century; J. Sunderland, 'John Hamilton Mortimer: His Life and Works', *Walpole Soc.* 52 (1986), esp. 12–22 and 70–5; *The Painted Word: British History Painting, 1750–1830*, ed. P. Cannon-Brookes (Woodbridge, 1991); and B. Allen, 'Rule Britannia? History Painting in 18th-Century Britain', *Hist. Today* 45 (June 1995), 12–18. See also M. Rochelle, *Historical Art Index, A.D. 400–1650: Peoples, Places, and Events Depicted* (Jefferson, NC, 1989). For other important aspects of the subject, see L. Lippincott, *Selling Art in Georgian London: the Rise of Arthur Pond* (New Haven, CT, 1983), and L. Lippincott, 'Expanding on Portraiture: the Market, the Public, and the Hierarchy of Genres in Eighteenth-Century Britain', *The Consumption of Culture: Word, Image, and Object in the Seventeenth and Eighteenth Centuries*, ed. A. Bermingham and J. Brewer (London, 1995), pp. 75–88.

[299] See D. Alexander, 'Print Makers and Print Sellers in England, 1770–1830', *The Painted Word*, ed. Cannon-Brookes, pp. 23–9, and Clayton, *The English Print*, esp. pp. 235–60.

[300] The British Museum's 'Catalogue of Prints and Drawings Illustrating English History, Unrevised and Unpublished' (1882), which reached page-proofs, but which was never published (BM, Dept of Prints and Drawings [hereafter P&D], O.3.5), lists material with 'Anglo-Saxon' subjects on pp. 19–110, including separate prints as well as plates removed from printed books. It contains much useful information, which has to be used with caution. The portfolios of English history prints in BM, P&D, of their nature contain no more than a small and random selection.

leading artists of the period feature in 'Anecdotes of Painters', written by Edward Edwards (1738–1806), himself one of their number, in the early years of the nineteenth century;[301] and it is striking how much can be understood in terms of the friendships and associations between them.[302] The work of Mason Chamberlin the Elder, Samuel Wale, and William Hamilton, to name but three of the artists who found inspiration in the Anglo-Saxon past, may pale into insignificance beside that of their contemporaries Sir Joshua Reynolds, George Stubbs, and Thomas Gainsborough, yet in their time they too formed part of the artistic élite.[303] The paintings themselves can be pursued at various levels, without any need to apologize for their lack of artistic distinction. The question arises, for example, whether the choice of subject was determined by the perceived or symbolic significance of particular events, or by the popularity of a subject for some other reason; whether the immediate source of the artist's inspiration was a work of historical scholarship, or of popular literature, or another painting; whether the artist's treatment of the chosen subject reveals anything about his attitude and intentions; whether there was a greater demand for one subject as opposed to another; and whether history painting of this kind affected later perceptions of English history, and thus entered the mainstream of English historical tradition, in ways from which the modern historian would do well to escape.

If we may ignore the isolated examples from earlier periods, the fashion for history painting began to gather momentum in the middle of the eighteenth century. In 1750 the publishers John and Paul Knapton (representing the firm which had published Blackmore's *Alfred* in 1728 and Rapin's *History* in 1732–3), acting in association with Robert Dodsley, decided to commission a series of engravings depicting great moments in the nation's history, beginning with a set of six engraved by Charles Grignion (1717–1810), and others, after designs by Francis Hayman (1708–76) and Nicholas Blakey (*fl.* 1750).[304] The engravings, known as 'English History Delineated', appeared in 1750–2, and were described by Edwards as 'the first attempt that was made in England to produce a regular

---

[301] E. Edwards, *Anecdotes of Painters who have Resided or been Born in England* (London, 1808), repr. with an Introduction by R. W. Lightbown (London, 1970). For Edwards, see further below, p. 310.

[302] W. T. Whitley, *Artists and their Friends in England 1700–1799*, 2 vols. (London, 1928), and Brewer, *Pleasures of the Imagination*, pp. 218–51.

[303] Edwards's treatment, in his *Anecdotes of Painters*, of Gainsborough (pp. 129–43) and Reynolds (pp. 184–212) should be compared with his treatment of, e.g., Blakey (pp. 3–4), Casali (pp. 22–4), Mortimer (pp. 60–5), Wale (pp. 116–18), Chamberlin (pp. 121–2), Pine (pp. 171–3), Wheatley (pp. 268–70), and Hamilton (pp. 272–5), all of whom are mentioned below among painters who depicted subjects drawn from Anglo-Saxon history.

[304] For details of this venture, see D. Alexander and R. T. Godfrey, *Painters and Engravers: the Reproductive Print from Hogarth to Wilkie* (New Haven, CT, 1980), pp. 23–4 (no. 35); Lippincott, *Selling Art in Georgian London*, pp. 156–8; B. Allen, *Francis Hayman* (New Haven, CT, 1987), pp. 146–8 (no. 78); Allen, 'History Painting', pp. 14–15 and 18; and Clayton, *The English Print*, pp. 92–3 and 258. For the Knaptons, see *Pope's Literary Legacy: the Book-Trade Correspondence of William Warburton and John Knapton*, ed. D. W. Nichol (Oxford, 1992), pp. li–lx.

suite of engravings from our national history'.[305] Only the first six of a projected fifty engravings were published, though fortunately for present purposes they came out in chronological order. The series begins appropriately enough with the landing of Julius Caesar (Blakey/Grignion).[306] We then move on past Caractacus's speech before the Emperor Claudius (Hayman/Grignion),[307] and the Druids (Hayman/Ravenet),[308] to the tale of Vortigern and Rowena (Blakey/Scotin).[309] The fifth engraving in the series is entitled 'Alfred in the Isle of Athelney, receiving news of a Victory over the Danes' (pl. IX*a*).[310] The central design, by Nicholas Blakey, shows the king in his fen-fastness receiving news of the capture of the Danish banner, set in dense woodland artfully provided by the French landscape expert Francis Vivares; the composition as a whole was engraved by Scotin. The imagined event had been adduced by Rapin as the turning-point of Alfred's fortunes in 878;[311] but in focusing attention on the Danish banner Blakey picked up one of the accessories used previously by Vertue, which would become a recurrent motif in later manifestations of Alfredian art.[312] The final engraving in the set shows the death of King Harold at the battle of Hastings (Hayman/Grignion).[313] The first four and the sixth of the six compositions in 'English History Delineated' gained wider currency from their inclusion (in redrawn and reduced versions) as engraved plates in the second edition of Smollett's *Complete History of England*, published in 1758;[314] the set as a whole was republished in 1778.[315]

---

[305] Edwards, *Anecdotes of Painters*, p. 4.
[306] Reproduced by Lippincott, *Selling Art in Georgian London*, p. 157.
[307] Reproduced by Allen, 'History Painting', p. 18.
[308] Reproduced by Allen, *Francis Hayman*, p. 147, and Allen, 'History Painting', p. 18.
[309] Reproduced by Clayton, *The English Print*, p. 97. See further below, n. 332.
[310] BM, P&D, 1877-6-9-1707; reproduced here from an impression in a private collection. Another impression in the BM (P&D, 1953-11-7-4) gives the title in English and French.
[311] *History of England* [2nd ed.], I, 92: 'The news of this Defeat [at Kinwith Castle in Devon], and the Death of the Danish General [Hubba], having reached Alfred in his retreat, he immediately considered how to turn this lucky Blow to his Advantage.'
[312] A portrait of Alfred engraved by B. Cole for the *New Universal Magazine* (1752) shows the king with a sceptre in his right hand, a partly unrolled scroll in his left hand, and the raven banner draped over the frame. The banner was used again by Samuel Wale in the 1760s (see further below).
[313] Reproduced by Allen, *Francis Hayman*, p. 148. It should be noted that (quite apart from the remarkable armour) the composition displays no influence from the Bayeux Tapestry (of which engravings were first published in 1729–30, though not published in England until 1750), and is to be compared in this respect with later representations of King Harold's death at the battle of Hastings, of which there are several.
[314] Smollett, *A Complete History of England* (above, n. 254), 2nd ed. I, opp. pp. 27 (Caesar), 54 (Caractacus), 111 (Druids), 125 (Vortigern), and 371 (Hastings). We also find engraved 'portraits' of Egbert (Miller), Alfred (Benoist) and Cnut (Benoist), evidently suggested by the images in Rapin's *History*.
[315] The engravings were reworked and republished by R. Sayer and J. Bennett, dated 12 Oct. 1778. 'Alfred in the Isle of Athelney' (BM, P&D, 1855-6-9-1829) was furnished with a six-line explanation of the historical background.

Simon Keynes

History painting in public exhibitions from 1760 onwards

In the second quarter of the eighteenth century it had been difficult for aspiring and established artists alike to exhibit their work to the public at large, while the lack of any corporate organisation among the artists hindered the development of a native school of art and at the same time denied them a much-needed sense of professional identity. The Society of Arts, also known as the Society for the Encouragement of Arts, Manufactures and Commerce (later the Royal Society of Arts), was established in 1754 with professional artists among its members, but disputes about aims and management soon prompted a majority of the artists to establish alternative arrangements.[316] The Society of Artists of Great Britain was formed in 1760 (known from 1765 as the Incorporated Society of Artists), while those who remained for the time being in loose association with the Society of Arts reformed themselves into the Free Society of Artists in 1761. The annual exhibitions sponsored by these organisations provided English artists with new and regular opportunities to exhibit their work, with the additional attraction for artists and the public alike of premiums, or prizes, for the best paintings in particular categories. The first exhibition took place under the aegis of the Society of Arts in 1760 (an exhibition which both the Society of Artists and the Free Society subsequently claimed as their own). There is a distinction thereafter between a series of exhibitions organized by the Society of Artists from 1761 to 1791, and a series organized by the Society of Arts from 1761 to 1764, by the artists themselves in 1765–6, and more formally by the Free Society of Artists from 1767 to 1783.[317] Among the premiums offered by the Society of Arts in the 1760s and early 1770s was one for 'Original Historical Pictures', to be chosen out of British or Irish history, 'containing not less than three Human Figures as large as Life'.[318]

Subjects drawn from early English history, although never threatening to overwhelm the profusion of portraits and landscapes, were well repre-

---

[316] H. Trueman Wood, *A History of the Royal Society of Arts* (London, 1913), esp. pp. 151–61 and 226–34; D. Hudson and K. W. Luckhurst, *The Royal Society of Arts 1754–1954* (London, 1954), esp. pp. 35–40.

[317] A complete (extra-illustrated and annotated) set of the catalogues of exhibitions at the Society of Artists, from 1760 to 1791, is in BM, P&D, presented by J. H. Anderdon in 1869. See also A. Graves, *The Society of Artists of Great Britain 1760–1791 / The Free Society of Artists 1761–1783. A Complete Dictionary of Contributors and their Work from the Foundation of the Societies to 1791* (London, 1907), with appendixes on the history of these organisations.

[318] For a list of the premiums bestowed for historical pictures from 1760 to 1773, see R. Dossie, *Memoirs of Agriculture, and Other Oeconomical Arts*, 3 vols. (London, 1768–82) III, 431–2. See also Sunderland, 'Political Aspects of English History Painting', pp. 321–2 and 325–6 (citing Minutes of the Society of Arts).

sented from the outset. In 1760 the Italian painter Andrea Casali (1705–84), who was active in England between 1741 and 1766,[319] won the second premium of fifty guineas for a historical painting, at the Society of Arts, with 'The story of Gunhilda' (daughter of King Cnut, who married the Emperor Henry III).[320] Two of the pictures exhibited by Casali at the Society of Arts/Free Society in 1761 had subjects drawn direct from Anglo-Saxon history. One is listed as 'An historical picture of K. Edgar, Elfrida, and Athelwold' (i.e. King Edgar's love for Ælfthryth, whose beauty had been concealed from him by Ealdorman Æthelwold),[321] and the other as 'An historical picture of Edward the Martyr' (i.e. the murder of King Edward the Martyr in 978).[322] At the Society of Arts/Free Society in 1763, Robert Edge Pine (1730–88) won the first premium of one hundred guineas for a history painting, with his representation of 'Canute reproving his courtiers for their

---

[319] For Casali, see Edwards, *Anecdotes of Painters*, pp. 22–4, and *Dictionary of Art*, ed. Turner.

[320] Society of Artists 1760 (2). The original painting was acquired by the Constable family, of Burton Constable Hall, nr Hull, East Yorkshire, where it remains; photograph in the file for the artist in the Paul Mellon Centre for Studies in British Art, 16 Bedford Square, London. The painting was engraved by Casali, c. 1760, entitled: 'The Champion; or Innocence Triumphant. The Empress Gunhilda being accused of Adultery, and her Innocence being to be tried by single Combat, the Champion for the Accusation (a Man of Gigantic Stature) is slain by her Page.' Casali's source was Guthrie, *General History of England*, pp. 292–3. An engraving by S. F. Ravenet was published by John Boydell in 1761, entitled: 'Gunhilda, Empress of Germany, daughter of Canute King of England, having been accused of adultery and treated as guilty by the Emperor, is defended by her Page, who in a public combat slays her accusers, after which she refuses to be reconciled to her Husband, & determines to retire into a Monastery.' There are impressions of both in BM, P&D.

[321] Free Society 1761 (15); he exhibited a sketch on the same subject at the Society of Artists in 1778 (32). The painting was at Fonthill House, and was sold in 1801 to Jeffrey (E. Croft-Murray, *Decorative Painting in England 1537–1837*, 2 vols. (London, 1962–70) II, 182), and is now untraced; it does not appear to have been engraved. The story of King Edgar and Ælfthryth (Elfrida) was derived ultimately from William of Malmesbury, *Gesta regum* ii.157 (ed. Mynors, *et al.*, pp. 256–8), and was given due attention by Rapin (*History of England* [2nd ed.] I, 109), Hume, and others. Its popularity may, however, reflect that of the various dramatic works on the same theme, e.g. Thomas Rymer's *Edgar* (1678, 1693; above, n. 148), but esp. William Mason's *Elfrida* (1752 onwards). The subject was depicted again by Wale c. 1770 (below, p. 308), by Kauffman in 1771 (below, p. 299), by Hamilton in 1774 (below, p. 299), and by Rigaud in 1796 (below, n. 334), among others.

[322] Free Society 1761 (20). A preliminary sketch for this composition was sold at Christie's, 15 Feb. 1974 (Lot 80); photograph in the Mellon Centre. The finished painting was acquired by the Constable family, of Burton Constable Hall, East Yorkshire, where it remains; photograph in the Mellon Centre. The painting was engraved by Casali c. 1761 (BM, P&D, 1867-12-14-387); cf. his drawing (BM, P&D, 1964-4-11-3). It was engraved again by S. F. Ravenet in 1767, and published by John Boydell in 1773 (BM, P&D, 1873-8-9-582); see below, p. 313. The subject had been depicted by Wale in 1747 (below, p. 305), and was depicted again by Wale in 1764 (below, p. 306), by Edwards in 1776 (below, p. 310), by Hamilton before 1786 (below, p. 313), and by Smirke in 1806 (below, p. 316), among others.

297

Simon Keynes

impious flattery'.[323] The second premium of fifty guineas went to Pine's pupil John Hamilton Mortimer (1740–79) for 'Edward the Confessor spoiling his mother at Winchester'.[324] King Alfred the Great made what would seem to have been his first appearance at the Society of Arts/Free Society in 1764, when Mason Chamberlin the Elder (?1727–87), a pupil of Francis Hayman, exhibited his 'King Alfred in a cottage; large as life'.[325] The original painting is untraced, and may or may not have been destroyed; but fortunately a large mezzotint of it was published in 1794, thirty years after it was first exhibited (pl. IX*b*).[326] Alfred himself cuts a particularly fine figure, transcending the wretched humiliation of his immediate predicament. The neatherd's wife points to a rather unappetizing 'cake' smouldering at his feet; her husband leers unknowingly at the king; and their dog looks at the husband. A curiously well-informed and even scholarly note is struck by the accessories cast down on the floor, among which we may identify not only the usual instruments of war but also a quire of the king's 'Handbook'.[327]

Further disputes within the Incorporated Society of Artists led a number of its élite to solicit the king's support for the foundation of the Royal Academy in December 1768,[328] creating a third series of exhibitions from 1769

---

[323] Free Society 1763 (159); also shown at the Society of Artists 1768 (89). The original painting is untraced; but the composition is known from an early copy (Sunderland, 'Political Aspects of English History Painting', fig. 48), and from an engraving made by F. G. Aliamet (BM, P&D, 1899-7-13-69), also published in 1772 by John Boydell. The subject had featured in the lower part of Vertue's portrait of Cnut, made in 1733 for the second (folio) edition of Rapin's *History* (above, p. 292), and had been depicted by Wale in 1747 (below, p. 305). The subject was depicted again by Edwards in 1777 (below, p. 310), by Hamilton (collection of His Grace the Duke of Devonshire; photograph in the Mellon Centre), and by Smirke in the 1790s (below, p. 316), among others. A mid-nineteenth-century view of Cnut and the waves, by John Martin (Laing Art Gallery, Newcastle-upon-Tyne), is illustrated in R. Humble, *The Saxon Kings* (London, 1980), pp. 164–5.

[324] Free Society 1763 (142). An oil sketch for the picture is in the Huntington Library and Art Gallery, San Marino, CA; see Sunderland, 'Mortimer: His Life and Works', pp. 16–19 and 122–3 (no. 8) and fig. 24. The original painting appeared at auction in 1878 (*ibid.* p. 122), but is now untraced. The picture seems not to have been engraved. The story is told by Rapin, *History of England* [2nd ed.] I, 131, among many others, and is ultimately from the *Anglo-Saxon Chronicle* for 1043.

[325] Free Society 1764 (30). Chamberlin, said to be of Stewart Street, Spittalfields, won a half-share of the second premium of 50 guineas for a history painting at the Society of Arts in 1764, for 'King Alfred at the Cottager's' (Dossie, *Memoirs of Agriculture* III, 432). The subject was depicted again by Edwards in 1776 (below, p. 310), by Wheatley in 1792 (below, pp. 315–16), and by Wilkie in 1806 (below, pp. 317–18), among others (below, pp. 339 and 340–1).

[326] See further below, p. 314. The mezzotint may have been first published some years earlier, and republished in 1794.

[327] The word 'handboc' is inscribed on the outer cover. The book was described as such in Savile's edition of William of Malmesbury's *Gesta regum* (*Rerum Anglicarum Scriptores Post Bedam praecipui*, p. 24); cf. *Gesta regum Anglorum*, ed. Mynors, *et al.*, p. 192, textual note *g*. For Alfred's 'Handbook', see Keynes and Lapidge, *Alfred the Great*, p. 268.

[328] S. C. Hutchison, *The History of the Royal Academy 1768–1986*, 2nd ed. (London, 1986), pp. 15–22 and 23–32; Brewer, *Pleasures of the Imagination*, pp. 228–36.

The cult of King Alfred the Great

onwards.[329] Again, subjects drawn from English history are well represented.[330] The Swiss artist Angelica Kauffmann (1741–1807), resident in London from 1766 to 1781,[331] produced a romantic pair comprising 'Vortigern, King of Britain, enamoured with Rowena, at the banquet of Hengist, the Saxon general', exhibited at the Royal Academy in 1770,[332] and 'The interview of King Edgar with Elfrida, after her marriage to Athelwold', exhibited in 1771.[333] In a similar vein, William Hamilton (1751–1801) exhibited 'King Edgar's first interview with Elfrida' at the Royal Academy in 1774.[334] The artist who dominated the field of history painting at this time was, however, Benjamin West (1738–1820), an American who had come to England in 1763, who had come to the attention of George III by 1768, and who was in a position to represent himself as 'Historical Painter' to the king by 1772.[335] West was principally renowned for his 'Death of General Wolfe', first painted in 1770, which attracted great attention

---

[329] A complete (extra-illustrated and annotated) set of the catalogues of exhibitions at the Royal Academy, from 1769 to 1849, is in BM, P&D, presented by J. H. Anderdon in 1867. See also A. Graves, *The Royal Academy of Arts: a Complete Dictionary of Contributors and their Work from its Foundation in 1769 to 1904*, 8 vols. (London, 1905–6).

[330] For the 'Anglo-Saxon' subjects represented in the Royal Academy exhibitions, in the wider context of all subjects drawn from British history, see Strong, *The Victorian Painter and British History*, pp. 155–68, at 155–7.

[331] W. Roworth, *Angelica Kauffmann: a Continental Artist in Georgian England* (London, 1993); *Dictionary of Art*, ed. Turner.

[332] Royal Academy 1770 (116). The original painting is at Saltram House, Devon (National Trust); photograph in the Mellon Centre. The subject had featured in one of the head-pieces in Rapin's *History* (above, nn. 290 and 292), and was depicted by Blakey in 1750 (above, p. 295) and by Fuseli in 1769; it was depicted again by Ryland (after Kauffmann) in 1772 (cf. photograph in the Mellon Centre), Mortimer in 1779 (Strong, *The Victorian Painter and British History*, pp. 19–20; Sunderland, 'Mortimer: His Life and Works', pp. 74–5 and 193), Rigaud in 1788 (photograph in the Mellon Centre), and Hamilton in 1795 (below, p. 315), among others.

[333] Royal Academy 1771 (113). The original painting is at Saltram (National Trust); photograph in the Mellon Centre. It was engraved by William Wynne Ryland and published in 1786 by Mary Ryland.

[334] Royal Academy 1774 (114). It seems that this composition should be distinguished from Hamilton's rendition of 'Edmund Ironside and Algitha', engraved by Bartolozzi and published in 1786 (below, p. 313), with which it is easily (and has been) confused. For John Francis Rigaud's painting, entitled 'The first interview of King Edgar and Elfrida' and exhibited at the Royal Academy in 1796, see 'Facts and Recollections of the XVIIIth Century in a Memoir of John Francis Rigaud Esq., R.A., by Stephen Francis Dutilh Rigaud', ed. W. L. Pressly, *Walpole Soc.* 50 (1984), 1–164, at 17–18, with pl. 66. For Hamilton's 'Edgar and Elfrida', first published in 1793, and again in 1802, see below, n. 447.

[335] For West and George III, see H. von Erffa and A. Staley, *The Paintings of Benjamin West* (New Haven, CT, 1986), p. 51; he became President of the Royal Academy in 1792. See also A. U. Abrams, *The Valiant Hero: Benjamin West and Grand-Style History Painting* (Washington DC, 1985); and D. H. Solkin, *Painting for Money: the Visual Arts and the Public Sphere in Eighteenth-Century England* (New Haven, CT, 1993), pp. 180–90 and 206–13. West is generally treated with studied contempt by art historians, not without reason: 'The monarch who could give lavish commissions to Benjamin West while neglecting Reynolds must have been sadly wanting in taste' (Whitley, *Artists and their Friends in England* I, 170).

when exhibited at the Royal Academy in 1771, and which enjoyed further success once engraved by Woollett and published by John Boydell, *et al.*, in 1776.[336] The choice for West's first experiment with an 'Anglo-Saxon' theme, exhibited at the Royal Academy in 1778,[337] was bizarre, to say the least: 'William de Albanac presents his three daughters to Alfred III, King of Mercia'. King Alfred III is one of the hitherto neglected figures of Anglo-Saxon England, and one suspects he would do best to remain so. His story was told in an 'old boke' which belonged in the sixteenth century to the Earls of Rutland, at Belvoir Castle in Leicestershire; but if the book still survives it is now inaccessible, and we are dependent for knowledge of its contents on a report provided by the antiquary John Leland, who had perused it in the 1540s. It turns out that Alfred III flourished in the 730s, and that he had been moved on one occasion to visit 'the stronge castell of Albanac nere Grantham' [Lincolnshire], where he encountered Guliam de A[l]banac and his three daughters (Adeline, Etheldrede, and Maude); in historical terms, therefore, he would have been a Middle Anglian ruler operating under the overlordship of Æthelbald, king of the Mercians. Alfred III was minded to take a fancy to one or other of the daughters, but Guliam threatened to kill with his sword whichever daughter he chose, rather than suffer the king to have her as his concubine; whereupon Alfred 'answerid that he meant to take one of them to wife, and chose Etheldrede that had fat bottoks, and of her he had Alurede that wan first [of] all the Saxons the monarchy of England'.[338] William de Albanac was one of the putative ancestors of the Earls, or later the Dukes, of Rutland, who were presumably brought up on this story at Belvoir Castle; and it was Charles Manners (1754–87), 4th Duke of Rutland, who commissioned the painting from West, presumably as part of a process of giving his family a sense of their historical identity.[339] The story was all too easily transferred from Alfred III of Mercia to Alfred the Great of

---

[336] Von Erffa and Staley, *Paintings of Benjamin West*, pp. 211–16 (nos. 93–100); A. McNairn, *Behold the Hero: General Wolfe and the Arts in the Eighteenth Century* (Liverpool, 1997), esp. pp. 109–64. General Wolfe was killed at Quebec in 1759.   [337] Royal Academy 1778 (331).

[338] *The Itineraries of John Leland the Antiquary*, ed. T. Hearne (Oxford, 1710–12) VIII, 58; 2nd ed. (Oxford, 1744–5) VIII, 25; 3rd ed. (Oxford, 1768–70) VIII, 26; *The Itinerary of John Leland in or about the Years 1535–1543*, ed. L. Toulmin Smith, 5 vols. (London, 1907–10) V, 148. It is possible that the book in question survives at Belvoir Castle, though it is not immediately identifiable in the reports made by the Historical Manuscripts Commission.

[339] For the family history, see J. Nichols, *The History and Antiquities of the County of Leicestershire*, 4 vols. in 8 (London, 1795–1811) II.i, 22–68, at 24. The original painting was recorded at Belvoir Castle in 1792 (*ibid.* pp. 69–73, at 73), but was destroyed there in the fire of 1816. It is known from an engraving by J. B. Michel, published by Boydell in 1782 (below, p. 313). See Von Erffa and Staley, *Paintings of Benjamin West*, pp. 186–7 (no. 47). A small outline drawing of the picture is in G. Hamilton, *The English School: a Series of the Most Approved Productions in Painting and Sculpture Executed by British Artists from the Days of Hogarth to the Present Time*, 4 vols. (London, 1831–2) IV, no. 56.

Wessex, but that was through no fault of either party.[340] West's other choice for an 'Anglo-Saxon' theme, also made in 1778, was rather more conventional: 'Alfred the Great dividing his Loaf with a Pilgrim', in other words the uplifting and familiar story of (the real) King Alfred's readiness, when in desperate straits at Athelney, to share his last morsel of food with a passing pilgrim, who turned out to be St Cuthbert. The supposed event took place in 878; and while one might suppose that West had been moved, therefore, by the muse of historical commemoration, it seems more likely that he had been reading Bicknell's 'Life of Alfred', which had been published the year before, in 1777.[341] West's composition shows a remarkably Christ-like king, who had been reading a book, retaining half of a loaf for his wife and small children, and offering the other half to the pilgrim, while a young boy (presumably Edward the Elder) stands calmly if disappointedly in the background. The preliminary version of the composition (50 × 64 cm), dated 1778,[342] was soon reworked on a much grander scale (228 × 279 cm, or over 7ft by 9ft), as befitted a mainline history painting, and exhibited at the Royal Academy in 1779.[343] It was then acquired by the publisher John Boydell, who presented the original to the Worshipful Company of Stationers and Newspaper Makers in 1780, and no doubt sought to recoup his expenses by publishing a large engraving of the picture in 1782.[344] It is striking, in this connection, that King George III's ninth son, born in 1780, was named Prince Alfred; sadly, the boy died two years later, and in 1783 West was inspired, or rather commissioned, to paint him in Heaven.[345]

The significance of Alfred in history-painting of the late eighteenth century is demonstrated most strikingly by the set of enormous murals made by James Barry (1741–1806), for the decoration of the Great Room in the new building occupied by the Society of Arts, in the Strand, from 1774.[346] The six paintings which make up the set were conceived in illustration of no less noble a theme than 'The Progress of Human Culture', and were accompanied by a book explaining the intended significance and symbolism of each.[347] The sixth picture

---

[340] See above, p. 287.
[341] Bicknell, *Alfred the Great*, pp. 149–51. For the subject, see above, n. 15. For the possibility that West's 'Alfredian' pictures were made in connection with a grander scheme, first formulated in 1778, see below, p. 313.   [342] Von Erffa and Staley, *Paintings of Benjamin West*, p. 188 (no. 49).
[343] Royal Academy 1779 (341). Von Erffa and Staley, *Paintings of Benjamin West*, pp. 187–8 (no. 48).
[344] For the engraving, see further below, p. 313; and for Hamilton's drawing of the same subject, see below, p. 310. Boydell became Alderman for Cheapside in 1785.
[345] Royal Academy 1784 (81). Von Erffa and Staley, *Paintings of Benjamin West*, pp. 480–1 (no. 575), in the Royal Collection. For a reproduction in colour, see C. Hibbert, *George III: a Personal History* (London, 1998), pl. 16.
[346] W. L. Pressly, *The Life and Art of James Barry* (New Haven, CT, 1981), pp. 86–122 (murals), at 113–19, and 233–4 (no. 27) and 294–8.
[347] J. Barry, *An Account of a Series of Pictures, in the Great Room of the Society of Arts, Manufactures, and Commerce, at the Adelphi* (London, 1783).

(roughly 12 feet high by 42 feet wide) is entitled 'Elizium, or the State of Final Retribution', and shows the gathering in Elysium of no fewer than 128 persons regarded by the artist as representative of the 'cultivators and benefactors of mankind'. The central group comprises legislators and wise rulers, and prominent among them is King Alfred the Great. As Barry explained, Alfred, 'the deliverer of his country, the founder of its navy, its laws, juries, arts, and letters, with his Dom book in one hand, is leaning with the other on the shoulder of that greatest and best of lawgivers, William Penn'.[348] An engraving of the whole composition was first published in 1792;[349] but for the purposes of an engraving showing just the central group of legislators, published in 1793, Barry decided to replace Penn with Cecilius Calvert, 2nd Lord Baltimore, whom he had come to regard as the true founder of political liberties in America.[350] Needless to say, King Alfred the Great retained his position giving inspirational support.

The first work exhibited at the Royal Academy by the young William Blake (1757–1827), in 1780, was 'The Death of Earl Goodwin', a watercolour which depicted Godwine, Earl of Wessex, receiving divine punishment for his complicity in the murder of the atheling Alfred.[351] It seems to have been one of an extensive series of drawings on the history of England made by Blake at this time, though never brought to completion; another was 'St Augustine converting King Ethelbert of Kent'.[352] Some years later, in 1793, Blake issued a prospectus offering a number of works for sale, including 'The History of England, a small book of Engravings';[353] and in a notebook written at the same time he made a list of what would appear to have been the projected contents of this book, including 'Alfred in the countryman's house'.[354] No copy of Blake's 'History of England' is known to exist, though several 'historical' drawings survive which may have been made *c.* 1793 in connection with it, some of which are worked up from the earlier series. Blake's watercolour representing 'The Ordeal of Queen Emma', as she cleared herself of various charges levelled against her, is presumed to be one of the drawings made in the early 1790s,[355] though the subject is not in fact among those listed in the projected contents of the 'History of England'. Another surviving drawing which shows an encounter

---

[348] *Ibid.* pp. 130–1, citing the Alfredian inscription on the statue of Fame at the Earl of Radnor's estate at Longford Castle. [349] Pressly, *Life and Art of James Barry*, pp. 263 and 274 (no. 22).
[350] *Ibid.* pp. 275–6 (no. 24); W. L. Pressly, *James Barry; the Artist as Hero* (London, 1983), no. 36.
[351] M. Butlin, *The Paintings and Drawings of William Blake*, 2 vols. (New Haven, CT, 1981) I, no. 60, and II, pl. 178.
[352] Butlin, *Paintings and Drawings of Blake* I, no. 57, and II, pl. 53, with pp. 16–25.
[353] G. Keynes, *Blake: Complete Writings* (Oxford, 1957), pp. 207–8. [354] *Ibid.* pp. 208–9.
[355] Butlin, *The Paintings and Drawings of William Blake*, I, no. 59, and II, pl. 177. For Wale's earlier drawing of the same subject, see below, p. 307. For discussion, see Erdman, *Blake: Prophet Against Empire*, pp. 45–7, and Sunderland, 'Political Aspects of English History Painting', pp. 321–2.

between a bearded man and a woman may well belong to the series made in the early 1780s; but the suggestion that it represents an earlier version of 'Alfred in the countryman's house', as known to have been projected in 1793, seems most unlikely, not least because the man is clearly in the position of advantage and control.[356] None the less, it is interesting that just as Milton should have contemplated writing an epic poem about Alfred at Athelney, so too should Blake have thought to include a drawing of Alfred and the cakes in his 'History of England'.

Illustrated history books

History painting as practised in the late eighteenth century, in the Grand Style and preferably on the grand scale, was supposed to be about elevated sentiments, noble gestures, and heroic deeds. The earliest subjects chosen from Anglo-Saxon history were doubtless suggested by a reading of the standard works of Rapin, Hume, and others, and fastened upon particular events in order to convey a salutary, improving or uplifting message: Vortigern captivated by the lovely Rowena, symbolizing a romantic truth behind the conquest of Britain by the Saxons; Alfred the Great reduced in adversity to the humblest and most humiliating of circumstances, from which he was able none the less to emerge triumphant; Alfred sharing his last morsel of food with a passing pilgrim; King Edgar deceived by one of his own nobles, and falling in love with the fair Elfrida; the young and innocent Edward the Martyr falling victim to his stepmother's treachery; Cnut demonstrating the impunity of earthly kings in relation to the superior power of God; and Edward the Confessor asserting his power over a woman who had plotted and schemed against him.[357] It was not long, however, before history painting was brought down to earth for the mundane purposes of narrative illustration. The weighty works of Rapin, Hume, Smollett, and others created new opportunities in the reign of George III for writers and publishers to exploit the popularity of English history. Some of those who took up the challenge, like Oliver Goldsmith (?1730–74), whose 'History of England' was published in 1764, followed by a more substantial 'History' in 1771,[358] were accomplished authors turning their literary skills to an

---

[356] Butlin, *Paintings and Drawings of Blake* I, no. 94 ('King Alfred and the swineherd's wife (?)'), and II, pl. 101. The drawing is obviously a study for no. 93, described more appropriately as 'A woodland encounter'.

[357] For a more 'political' (anti-monarchical) interpretation of the pictures of Cnut and Edward the Confessor, see Sunderland, 'Political Aspects of English History Painting', pp. 321–2, and 'Mortimer: His Life and Works', pp. 18–19. Cf. Strong, *The Victorian Painter and British History*, pp. 17–18.

[358] [O. Goldsmith], *An History of England, in a Series of Letters from a Nobleman to his Son*, 2 vols. (London, 1764), Letter VII, pp. 37–42 (on Alfred); O. Goldsmith, *The History of England, from the Earliest Times to the Death of George II*, 4 vols. (London, 1771) I, 71–84 (on Alfred), drawing on Hume; O. Goldsmith, *An Abridgement of the History of England, from the Invasion of Julius Cæsar, to the Year M.DCC.XC*, new ed. (Bath, 1795); etc.

Simon Keynes

historical purpose and the prospect of financial reward. Yet due consideration should also be given to a somewhat less familiar range of compendious histories of England, which must be presumed to have contributed much to the increased popularity and popular awareness of English history in the latter part of the eighteenth century.[359] They were written by men who may well deserve the neglect which posterity has thrust upon them. Thomas Mortimer (1730–1810), who seems to have the distinction of being the only one among their number to rate an entry in the *Dictionary of National Biography*, produced his three-volume 'History' in the mid-1760s, organizing his material reign by reign.[360] It was a work with serious academic pretensions (to the extent that it even took the author into the Cottonian library), and displays perfectly commendable command of Anglo-Saxon history. Rather less notable for whatever reason were those who followed him, and each other, in the field: William Henry Mountague;[361] Temple Sydney;[362] William Augustus Russel;[363] George Frederick Raymond;[364] Edward Barnard;[365] George William Spencer;[366] Charles Alfred Ashburton;[367] George Courtney Lyttleton;[368] Theophilus Camden;[369]

---

[359] Above, n. 289. For the success of serial publication of history in the first half of the eighteenth century, see Wiles, *Serial Publication in England*, esp. pp. 4–6, 96 and 108; and see also the pertinent remarks on lists of subscribers, *ibid.* pp. 229–31.

[360] T. Mortimer, *A New History of England*, 3 vols. (London, 1764–6), published in parts by J. Wilson and J. Fell, of Paternoster Row, London. The list of over 400 subscribers shows that it reached deep into the professional middle classes throughout the country.

[361] W. H. Mountague, *A New and Universal History of England*, 2 vols. (London, 1771–2), published by J. Cooke, of Paternoster Row, London.

[362] T. Sydney, *A New and Complete History of England* (London, 1773), published in 70 parts by J. Cooke, of Paternoster Row, London, with a list of over 400 subscribers. It would appear that one or two of the plates were issued with each part, in an order which bore no relation to the progress of the narrative. Instructions to the binder indicated where the plates were to be placed.

[363] W. A. Russel, *A New and Authentic History of England* (London, 1777–9), published in 80 parts by J. Cooke, of Paternoster Row, London.

[364] G. F. Raymond, *A New, Universal, and Impartial History of England* (London, 1777–90), published in 60 parts by J. Cooke [later C. Cooke], of Paternoster Row, London.

[365] E. Barnard, *A New, Comprehensive, and Complete History of England* (London, 1783), published in 70 weekly parts by Alexander Hogg, with a list of over 800 subscribers.

[366] G. W. Spencer, *A New, Authentic, and Complete History of England . . . to the Year 1795* (London, 1794), published in parts by Alexander Hogg.

[367] C. A. Ashburton, *A New and Complete History of England* (London, 1791–3), published in 80 weekly parts by W. and J. Stratford, with a list of over 1000 subscribers; reissued in 1795. It would appear that one engraved plate was issued with each part, in an order which bore no relation to the progress of the narrative. Instructions to the binder indicated where the plates were to be placed.

[368] G. C. Lyttleton, *The History of England, from the Earliest Dawn of Authentic Records, to the Ultimate Ratification of the General Peace at Amiens in 1802; and the Subsequent War in 1803*, 3 vols. (London, 1802–3), published in multiple parts by J. Stratford, with a list of nearly 2,500 subscribers.

[369] T. Camden, *The Imperial History of England*, 2 vols. (London, 1810–13), published by J. Stratford.

and doubtless several others.[370] It is not clear that any useful purpose would be served by reading the books produced by these men. It is more to the point that their histories were extensively illustrated, and that it was the range of illustrations in these works, as much as anyone's ringing prose, which helped to fix images of English history in the minds of the general public.

The most prolific of the illustrators was Samuel Wale (1721–86), a pupil of Francis Hayman (the principal artist involved in 'English History Delineated').[371] He exhibited work at the Society of Artists in the 1760s, became a Foundation Member of the Royal Academy in 1769, and was appointed the Academy's first Professor of Perspective; in 1778, after he was paralysed by a stroke, he became the Academy's librarian. The significance of Wale's work in the present context is that he was responsible for producing a series of drawings of a variety of historical scenes, which, however meagre in themselves, became widely known as engraved illustrations and thus exerted some influence on the development of history painting in the late eighteenth and early nineteenth centuries. A set of drawings made by Wale in 1746–7, covering the whole sweep of English history, would appear to represent the earliest artistic venture of its kind, devised perhaps significantly for a work at the very bottom end of the market. As we have seen, Lockman's *History of England*, based on Rapin, had first appeared in 1729.[372] The earliest editions were not illustrated, but for the sixth edition, which appeared in 1747, the publisher seems to have commissioned Wale to prepare a set of about thirty drawings suitable for the diminutive 12° format. The first two subjects chosen for illustration were 'Pope Adrian the IId crowns King Alfred at Rome' and 'Guy of Warwick overcomes Colbrand, the Danish champion', followed by 'Edward the Martyr stabb'd by order of his mother in law [*sic*]' and 'Canute commands the waves of the sea not to wet him'.[373] It was not an auspicious start, but the sequence as a whole retains a certain curiosity value. In 1753 Wale produced an elaborately allegorical

---

[370] E.g. R. Johnson [*alias* Cooper], *A New History of England* (London, 1780), published by F. Newbery; J. Baxter, *A New and Impartial History of England* (London, ?1796), published in parts by H. D. Symonds. One hardly dares think how many more there may have been.

[371] See entries on Wale in the *DNB*; E. Waterhouse, *The Dictionary of British 18th Century Painters in Oils and Crayons* (London, 1981); and *Dictionary of Art*, ed. Turner. See also Einberg, *Manners & Morals*, p. 182, and H. Hammelmann, *Book Illustrators in Eighteenth-Century England*, ed. T. S. R. Boase (New Haven, 1975), pp. 89–96.   [372] See above, p. 273.

[373] My understanding of the successive editions of Lockman's *History* from 1729 to 1800 is based on entries in the Eighteenth-Century Short Title Catalogue (ESTC), as available on the Internet (1998). The fifth edition (1740) was seemingly not illustrated. The sixth edition, published in weekly parts (1747), is the first said to be 'adorn'd with thirty-two copper-plates'; see also Wiles, *Serial Publication in England*, pp. 41, 46 and 352. There is a set of the engravings in the portfolio of prints after Wale, in BM, P&D, dated 1746 or 1747, removed from a copy of the sixth or later edition. The original engravings were subsequently replaced by some inferior (or even worse) engravings based on the same drawings, found already in the fifteenth edition (1768).

'Alfredian' design for the Oxford Almanack.[374] The set of illustrations for which Wale deserves most credit was, however, that devised for the compendious histories of England published in the 1760s and 1770s. The earliest selection of these drawings appeared in Mortimer's *New History of England* (1764–6), published by J. Wilson and J. Fell, of Paternoster Row, London. The drawings were engraved by Charles Grignion (1717–1810), as distinct from Reynolds Grignion (d. 1787), and set in elaborate borders; moreover, each plate was inscribed to a member of the nobility, with full heraldic apparatus, as if to lend the illustrations a grandeur commensurate with that of their subject matter. The first drawing depicts 'St Austin preaching to King Ethelbert & Queen Bertha, in the Isle of Thanet'.[375] The second represents King Alfred, who seems to have picked up some of the accessories from Vertue's portrait, and is shown doing what came most naturally to him: 'Alfred makes a Collection of Laws, and divides the Kingdom into Counties' (pl. X*a*).[376] It is the very image of the Georgian King Alfred, and the Roman garb seems especially well suited to an act of law-making. The other 'Anglo-Saxon' scenes suggest that the author, artist and publisher were not averse to exploiting some of the more sensational aspects of the subject: 'The Insolent Behaviour of Dunstan to King Edwy on the Day of his Coronation', dragging the king away from his women and back to the feast;[377] 'King Edward Stabb'd at the Gate of Corfe Castle by Order of his Mother', or rather his step-mother;[378] and 'The Massacre of the Danes', a particularly unpleasant scene representing the death of Gunnhild at the Massacre of St Brice's Day in November 1002.[379] Wale's imaginary views of historical events extend in Mortimer to the end of the seventeenth century, and for the eighteenth century the book was wisely provided only with portraits. Mountague's *New and Universal History of England* was published by J. Cooke [of Paternoster Row] in 1771. The publisher seems to have taken the opportunity in this case to publish a somewhat larger selection of Wale's drawings of some of the more dramatic moments in English history, perhaps including new drawings

---

[374] See below, n. 323.

[375] A sketch of this subject was exhibited by Wale at the exhibition of the Royal Academy in 1769. Grignion's engraving recurs in Mountague (1771) and Sydney (1773), but was re-engraved by Debroche for Russel (1777).

[376] A 'stained drawing' on the same theme (Alfred 'making a code of laws, dividing the kingdom into counties, and encouraging the arts and sciences') was exhibited by Wale at the Royal Academy in 1771 (208), now untraced. Grignion's engraving recurs in Mountague (1771), Sydney (1773), and Raymond (1777/90), but was re-engraved by White for Russel (1777).

[377] Grignion's engraving recurs in Mountague (1771) and Sydney (1773).

[378] Grignion's engraving recurs in Mountague (1771), Sydney (1773), and Raymond (1777/90), but was re-engraved by White for Russel (1777).

[379] The engraved version of the Massacre of St Brice's Day is not inscribed (or attributed), perhaps for obvious reasons; nor was it reused thereafter. The same theme was depicted in one of the head-pieces in Rapin's *History* (above, nn. 290 and 292).

The cult of King Alfred the Great

commissioned to illustrate a different narrative; as before, the drawings were engraved by Grignion. The 'Massacre of the Danes' was dropped; but the other illustrations in Mortimer's *History* were retained, though now without quite such grandiose packaging. Among the drawings by Wale which appear in Mountague for the first time, we find several relating to the Anglo-Saxon period: 'Berinus converting the Saxons to Christianity';[380] 'The Monks of Bangor put to the sword by Order of Ethelfrid';[381] 'The Abbess of Coldingham Monastery & her Nuns cutting off their Noses & upper Lips to prevent being Ravished by the Danes' (in 869);[382] 'Alfred taking the Danish Standard' (in 878);[383] 'Athelstan saves his Father's Life by taking Leofrid the Dane Prisoner';[384] 'Edmund stabbed by Leolf the Robber';[385] 'Combat between Edmund Ironside and Canute the Great';[386] and 'Queen Emma's Chastity Tried by Ordeal Fire'.[387] Wale's illustrations now continue into the eighteenth century, and include 'General Wolfe expiring in the Arms of a Grenadier & Volunteer at the Siege of Quebec' and 'The British Troops entering the Breach of the Moro Castle'.[388] Sydney's *New and Complete History of England* was published by Cooke in 1773. The illustrations used in Mortimer and Mountague were used again, with some differences: it was the Earl of Devon, not Alfred, who was given the credit for capturing the Danish standard; and a few of Grignion's engravings were replaced by new engravings of the same Wale drawings, made by other engravers. Among other drawings by Wale which appear in Sydney for the first time,

---

[380] The drawing was re-engraved by Walker for Sydney (1773).

[381] Grignion's engraving recurs in Sydney (1773).

[382] Grignion's engraving recurs in Sydney (1773). The story was part of the mainline 'St Albans' tradition, and had appeared in Rapin, *History of England* [2nd ed.] I, 89; see also *Parts Added to The Mirror for Magistrates*, ed. Campbell, pp. 463–8.

[383] Wale or Grignion erred in giving the credit to Alfred himself. Cf. *ASC*, s.a. 878, 'And there was captured the banner which they called "Raven"'. The drawing was re-engraved by Taylor for Sydney (1773), and the act reattributed to Odun, Earl of Devon; used again in Russel (1777). Taylor exhibited 'Alfred taking the Danish standard; engraved from Mr Wale' at the Society of Artists in 1770 (247).

[384] The drawing was re-engraved by Walker for Sydney (1773) and Raymond (1777/90). Cf. Rapin, *History of England* [2nd ed.] I, 99.

[385] Grignion's engraving recurs in Sydney (1773) and Raymond (1777/90); it was re-engraved by White for Russel (1777).

[386] Grignion's engraving recurs in Sydney (1773); it is also found in copies of Russel (1777), and Raymond (1777/90).

[387] The drawing was re-engraved by Walker for Sydney (1773). For Blake's drawing of the same subject, see above, p. 302. For the source, see Rapin, *History of England* [2nd ed.] I, 131.

[388] These events took place in 1759 and 1762 respectively. Wale's image of Wolfe was clearly based on an earlier painting by Penny (Von Erffa and Staley, *Paintings of Benjamin West*, p. 213). West's famous 'Death of Wolfe', painted in 1770 and first exhibited in 1771, was engraved by Woollett and published in 1776, re-engraved and reissued in 1791. See also Clayton, *The English Print*, pp. 238–40; McNairn, *Behold the Hero*, p. 230, apropos the reuse of Grignion's engraving of Wale's drawing in Sydney (1773), as reissued in 1775; and above, n. 336.

there are four which relate to the Anglo-Saxon period: 'Hengist and Horsa meeting King Vortigern, in the Isle of Thanet';[389] 'Paulinus baptizing Edwin, the first Christian King of Northumberland at York';[390] 'Alfred, disguised in the character of a harper, viewing the Danish camp';[391] and 'The first interview of Edgar and Elfrida'.[392] A selection of the familiar compositions by Wale was used yet again for the purposes of Russel's *New and Authentic History of England*, published by Cooke in 1777–9. For whatever reason, several more of Grignion's engravings were replaced by new engravings of the same drawings, made by other engravers, and several other illustrations were dropped. Two drawings by Wale which relate to the Anglo-Saxon period appear in Russel for the first time: 'Athelstan ordering the Bible to be translated into the Saxon Language';[393] and 'King Edgar rowed down the River Dee by Eight Tributary Kings attended by his principal Nobility'.[394] Raymond's *New, Universal, and Impartial History of England*, again published by Cooke, was issued in sixty parts between c. 1777 and 1790.[395] Raymond expunged Alfred burning the cakes, and Alfred dividing the loaf, from his history, as being 'nothing more than legendary tales'.[396] He gives us a slightly larger selection of Wale's drawings than in Russel, sometimes reverting to Grignion's engravings as used previously in Sydney; but, at least for the Anglo-Saxon period, there is none that appears here for the first time. The main innovation is that the figural scenes are interspersed in Raymond with pages of portraits, drawn by Metz, each depicting four leaders or kings, 'in the habits of the times in which they reigned'.[397]

A proper understanding of the relationship between the compendious histories published in the 1760s and 1770s, and their significance in popularizing particular events, perceptions, and images of English history, would require detailed comparison of the books themselves and examination of the whole range of

---

[389] Engraved by Walker; used again in Raymond (1777/90).

[390] Engraved by Walker; used again in Raymond (1777/90).

[391] Engraved by Grignion; used again in Raymond (1777/90). The subject had been incorporated in Vertue's symbolic portrait of Alfred (above, pp. 291–2) and was depicted again by Stothard c. 1793 (below, p. 317), Edwards (below, p. 310), Smirke (below, p. 311), and Claxton (below, p. 336), among others.

[392] Engraved by Rennoldson; used again in Raymond (1777/90).   [393] Engraved by Grignion.

[394] Engraved by Walker.

[395] One of the copies in the BL (L.23.b.3) is signed 'Wm Wright 1777' on the recto of the frontispiece, and continues to 1786 (p. 610); it was used as a register of births, marriages, and deaths in his family from the 1780s to the 1890s. The constituent parts are numbered, but not dated. A second copy in the BL (RB.31.c.153) differs from the first in so far as the text has been reset from p. 605 (1783) and continues to 1790.   [396] Raymond, *History of England*, p. 76 n. *.

[397] The leaders and kings are grouped as follows: (1) A Roman Commander, a Saxon Chief, a Danish General, and a Norman; (2) Egbert, Ethelwolf, Ethelbald, Ethelbert; (3) Ethelred, Alfred, Edward the Elder, Athelstan; (4) Edmund, Edred, Edwy, Edgar; (5) Ethelred II, Edward the Martyr, Edmund II, Canute the Great; (6) Harold I, Canute II, Edward the Confessor, Harold II. Cf. below, n. 408.

Wale's illustrations.[398] What was the role of the publisher of these works, and what were the methods and economics of publication? What do the lists of subscribers reveal about the intended market or readership? Who were the authors, and how did they compile their histories? To what extent were they independent of or dependent upon each other? When and under what circumstances were the drawings made by Samuel Wale, and to what extent was he responsible for the choice of subjects? Were all the drawings commissioned by the publisher in the early 1760s, and only a few of them engraved at that time for use in Mortimer's *History* (1764); and were more of them engraved later on, for use in Mountague's *History* (1771), Sydney's *History* (1773), and Russel's *History* (1777)? Or were they commissioned and executed in groups, in closer relationship to the particular requirements of the different narratives? Why were Grignion's engravings abandoned, and then used again? What influence did Wale's widely circulated illustrations exert on other manifestations of history painting and book illustration from the mid-1760s onwards? It is a subject with historiographical, bibliographical, and art-historical dimensions, and is probably best left to any one in need of displacement activity. For present purposes it must suffice to remark that in the context of the series as a whole Wale's three Alfredian scenes (the capture of the Danish banner; King Alfred making a law-code; and Alfred in the Danish camp disguised as a musician) reflect different aspects of Alfred's distinctive place in early English history: a brave and resourceful leader, who in his concern for the well-being of his people excelled all the other Anglo-Saxon kings.

In 1770, when Benjamin West so famously depicted the death of General Wolfe at Quebec with the protagonists in contemporary (as opposed to antique) clothing, his departure from artistic convention caused a minor sensation.[399] The sartorial anachronisms perpetrated by the painters of history paintings in the late eighteenth century, and the extent to which any of them paid any attention to the works published by Joseph Strutt in the mid-1770s,[400] would be another diverting

---

[398] To judge from the entries in ESTC, Mortimer was the most widely circulated of these works; but it may be that the works issued originally in parts did not have the same chance of preservation. For remarks on Mountague, Russel, and Raymond (without reference to Mortimer and Sydney), see T. S. R. Boase, 'Macklin and Bowyer', *Jnl of the Warburg and Courtauld Institutes* 26 (1963), 148–77, at 171–2. For the activities of the Paternoster Row publishers, and their ilk, in a different field, see B. Adams, *London Illustrated 1604–1851: a Survey and Index of Topographical Books and their Plates* (London, 1983). [399] McNairn, *Behold the Hero*, pp. 125–43.
[400] J. Strutt, *Horda Angel-cynnan; or, A Compleat View of the Manners, Customs, Arms, Habits, &c. of the Inhabitants of England, from the Arrival of the Saxons, till the Reign of Henry the Eighth*, 3 vols. (London, 1774–6), with numerous plates, in a rude and uncorrected state. Followed by J. Strutt, *The Chronicle of England; or, A Compleat History, Civil, Military and Ecclesiastical, of the Ancient Britons and Saxons, from the Landing of Julius Cæsar in Britain, to the Norman Conquest, with a Compleat View of the Manners, Customs, Arts, Habits, &c. of Those People*, 2 vols. (London, 1779), with numerous plates, with improvements. On the significance of Strutt, see Strong, *The Victorian Painter and British History*, pp. 50–2, and Haskell, *History and its Images*, pp. 292–5.

subject for further investigation; and one could start by comparing the output of Samuel Wale, in the 1760s, with that of Edward Edwards (1738–1806), in the later 1770s. Edwards, it has to be said, is a painter who is better known for his anecdotes of other painters than for his own paintings or drawings.[401] He did, however, make a number of drawings of historical scenes, engraved by John Hall and first published in *The Copper-Plate Magazine* in 1776–7,[402] at least three of which were derived from Anglo-Saxon history: 'Edward the Martyr stabbed by order of Elfrida' (published 1 April 1776); 'Alfred in the Neat-Herd's Cottage' (1 September 1776) (pl. X*b*); and 'Canute, commanding the sea to Retire' (1 April 1777).[403] Edwards seems also to have made a painting of 'Alfred in the Danish Camp', mentioned in the sale-catalogue of the contents of his house in 1807.[404] Edwards's drawings, engraved by Hall, were included in Barnard's *New, Comprehensive, and Complete History of England*, published in 1783 by Alexander Hogg, of 16 Paternoster Row, with more elaborate captions: 'King Alfred in disguise rebuked by the Neat Herd's Wife, for letting the Cakes burn which (she observed) he himself was so fond of'; 'Edward the Martyr stabbed by order of his Step Mother, Elfrida, at Corfe Castle in Dorsetshire'; 'Canute the Great, at the request of his Sycophants and Flatterers, ridiculously Commanding the Sea to retire'.[405] Edwards's drawings were accompanied in Barnard's *History* by a series of other drawings made by William Hamilton,[406] with equally laboured captions: 'Alfred the Great (during his Misfortunes occasioned by the Ravages of the Danes) Generously Dividing his Last Loaf with a Poor Pilgrim, who begged for something to satisfy his Hunger, at Athelney in Somersetshire'; 'The English (during the reign of Edward the Elder) Defeating the Danish Army near Watchet, in Somersetshire; a Few only Escaping, by Swimming to their Ships';

---

[401] For his *Anecdotes of Painters*, published posthumously in 1808, see above, n. 301. See also Hammelmann, *Book-Illustrators in Eighteenth-Century England*, pp. 30–1.

[402] *The Copper-Plate Magazine; or a Monthly Treasure for the Admirers of the Imitative Arts* was published by G. Kearsly, 46 Fleet Street, London. The title-page continues: 'In each Number of which will be given, A Portrait of some celebrated Personage, some interesting Historical Subject, and some curious Perspective View. Executed By the most capital Artists of Great Britain, and calculated to enrich the Cabinets of the Curious, or to ornament the Apartments of Persons of Real Taste.' The only set of the *Copper-Plate Magazine* in the British Library which dates from the 1770s contains portraits, with accompanying explanatory text.

[403] The portfolio of prints after Edwards in BM, P&D, contains loose impressions of these three compositions, with four others (also dated 1776–7) depicting later historical events, engraved by Hall or by Grignion.

[404] For further details, see Lightbown's Introduction to the reprint of Edwards, *Anecdotes of Painters* [above, n. 301], pp. xiii and xxiv.

[405] Barnard's *History* was presumably published in competition with the series of histories illustrated by Wale and published by the Cookes.

[406] For Hamilton, see above, p. 299, and Hammelmann, *Book-Illustrators in Eighteenth-Century England*, p. 48.

The cult of King Alfred the Great

and 'The renowned Battle of Hastings in Sussex, fought by Harold 2 and William, Duke of Normandy, wherein the former was killed, and the latter became Conqueror'.[407] The illustrative material for the early period otherwise includes some pages of portraits (drawn by Hamilton), each depicting four kings,[408] and a page showing a sequence of Anglo-Saxon coins.[409] Spencer's *New, Authentic, and Complete History of England* (1794), also published by Hogg, has the same four-up portraits by Hamilton, as well as the page of coins, and Hamilton's depiction of the battle of Hastings. The multiple-part compendious histories published by W. and J. Stratford, of 112 Holborn Hill, take the story onwards into the early nineteenth century, where perhaps it should be dropped. Five of the 'Anglo-Saxon' illustrations in Ashburton's *History of England* (1791–3), engraved in 'landscape' as opposed to 'portrait' format, were based (without acknowledgement) on previously published engravings of drawings by Samuel Wale,[410] with the addition of two engravings of drawings by other hands: one (by Chalmers) showed 'King Edgar laying aside his Crown on being reprimanded by Archbishop Dunstan for having seduced a nun', and the other (by Benezach) showed 'King Edward the Martyr expiring near a Blind Woman's House after having been Stabbed by order of his Step Mother Elfrida'. A similar range of illustrative material was used for Lyttleton's *History of England* (1802–3), although in this case compositions recognizably by Wale were attributed to Hamilton, and some new images were added.[411] Camden's *Imperial History of England*, published by Stratford in 1810–13, was provided with a fresh set of illustrations by Robert Smirke, including one of 'Alfred in the Danish camp'.[412]

---

[407] The drawing of Alfred dividing his loaf was evidently inspired or influenced by Benjamin West's earlier (1779) painting of the same subject (above, p. 301), an engraving of which had been published in 1782.

[408] The kings are grouped as follows: (1) Ethelbald, Ethelbert, Ethelred, Alfred; (2) Edward, Athelstan, Edmund, Edred; (3) Edwy, Edgar, Edward the Martyr, Ethelred; (4) Swein, Olaus, Edmund, Canute; (5) Harold, [Hartha]cnut, Edward, Harold. Cf. above, n. 397.

[409] The illustrations are derived from the plates of coins in Walker's edition of Spelman's 'Life of Alfred' (above, n. 173), with several erroneous identifications.

[410] The subjects chosen were St Augustine preaching to Æthelbert and Bertha, Alfred dividing England into counties, Athelstan ordering the Scriptures to be made public, Leolf stabbing King Edmund at Pucklechurch, and the landing of William the Conqueror at Pevensey.

[411] The Wale drawings now attributed to Hamilton include those mentioned in the previous note, as well as Alfred in the Danish camp, and Edgar on the river Dee. Among the new images we find Woodruff's 'Canute reproving the servile flattery of his courtiers', engraved by Tomlinson.

[412] Other subjects include 'The treachery of Elfrida' [murder of Edward the Martyr], 'The exposure of Prince Edwin' [with reference to the events of 933], and 'Canute reproving the flattery of his courtiers'. Smirke's drawings of Edward the Martyr and of Cnut differ in composition from his paintings engraved and published in 1806 as part of Bowyer's 'Historic Gallery'. Preliminary sketches for all of these compositions are to be found in the album of Smirke's drawings sold at Christie's, 11 July 1989, Lot 5. I am grateful to Dr Jane Cunningham for drawing this album to my attention.

Simon Keynes

Reproductive prints of history paintings

The rather low-grade drawings made by Samuel Wale, Edward Edwards, William Hamilton, and Robert Smirke (perhaps among others), not to mention an interestingly variant series published in Paris in 1784,[413] were engraved as illustrations for books intended for popular consumption. There was also a market at this time for larger reproductive engravings of existing, recently made, or specially commissioned paintings, of a size suitable for framing and hanging on walls (for which reason they came to be known as 'furniture prints').[414] An example had been set by 'English History Delineated', first published in 1751 (and republished in 1778), but the initial failure of that enterprise suggests that conditions were not conducive to the success of a purely 'historical' venture. The commercial potential of print publishing and printselling was soon realized, however, by John Boydell (1719–1804), an engraver turned publisher who became Alderman for Cheapside in 1785 and Lord Mayor of London in 1790–1.[415] The wide range of prints which became available from the 1760s onwards is best appreciated by perusing the catalogues issued by Boydell himself, and by other printsellers and publishers, in the late eighteenth and early nineteenth centuries.[416] Large numbers of impressions of a print could be made from each engraved plate; and while the prints were available separately for a few shillings or at most a guinea apiece, sets of prints were also gathered together in volumes, and sold by subscription as parts of series. It was, moreover, an international trade, so that the prints themselves might have their explanatory text in English and French, and sets of prints might soon find their way to France, Germany, and elsewhere. Boydell began to publish his *Sculptura Britannica: a Collection of Prints engraved after the Most Capital Paintings in England* in 1769, and by 1792 (as 'Boydell's Collection') it comprised a total of 571 prints available for purchase in nine large

---

[413] *Histoire d'Angleterre, représentée par figures, accompagnées de discours*, 3 vols. (Paris, 1784–1800), is a pictorial history of England constructed around a series of illustrations by various hands, engraved by François-Anne David, with explanatory text by P. P. F. Le Tourneur. The series includes 22 engravings of drawings of Anglo-Saxon subjects. One, engraved by David after Gois, is entitled 'Alfred abandonné de ses sujets, s'engage au service de son vacher en 875', showing Alfred in a farmyard at Athelney, without a burnt cake in sight.

[414] Brewer, *Pleasures of the Imagination*, pp. 456–8 and 461; Clayton, *The English Print, passim*. I am grateful to David Alexander (York), Norman Blackburn (printseller), Timothy Clayton (Worcester College, Oxford), Dafydd Davies (Grosvenor Prints, London), Craig Hartley (Fitzwilliam Museum, Cambridge), and Anthony Griffiths (BM, Dept of Prints & Drawings), for their guidance in connection with this material.

[415] *DNB*; S. H. A. Bruntjen, *John Boydell, 1719–1804: a Study of Art Patronage and Publishing in Georgian London* (New York, 1985); A. Griffiths and R. Williams, *The Department of Prints and Drawings in the British Museum: User's Guide* (London, 1987), p. 88; *Dictionary of Art*, ed. Turner.

[416] A. Griffiths, 'A Checklist of Catalogues of British Print Publishers *c*. 1650–1830', *Print Quarterly* 1 (1984), 4–22.

The cult of King Alfred the Great

volumes.[417] Among them we find engravings of history paintings by Andrea Casali ('Gunhilda, Empress of Germany, Daughter of Canute' [7s 6d], and 'Edward the Martyr, stabbed by order of Elfrida' [5s 0d]), Robert Edge Pine ('Canute the Great reproving his Courtiers' [10s 6d]), and Benjamin West ('Alfred, the Third King of Mercia' [£1 1s 0d] and 'Alfred the Great dividing his loaf with a pilgrim' [£1 1s 0d],[418] here taking their place beside 'The death of General Wolfe' [£1 1s 0d] and many others). Boydell was not, however, on his own. In 1778 Benjamin West, evidently conscious of his position as History Painter to the King, declared an intention to make pictures of 'some striking subjects of national importance', selected from 'British Story', which would then be engraved by William Woollett (Engraver to the King), and John Hall (engraver), 'to form a series, up to the reign of Alfred the Great'.[419] It is not exactly clear what West may have had in mind, since it would have been more natural to start rather than to end with Alfred. It may be significant, however, that West made his painting of 'Alfred III of Mercia', and first sketched the other Alfred dividing his loaf with a pilgrim, in 1778,[420] as if he had been thinking when he did so of his larger scheme; it is also the case that 'English History Delineated' was republished in the same year. In the event West was diverted by other tasks, Woollett died in 1785, and the project was abandoned. In 1786 Mary Ryland published an engraving of Angelica Kauffmann's 'Edgar and Elfrida', painted in 1771,[421] and the printseller James Birchall published an attractive pair of stipple engravings by Bartolozzi, after paintings by William Hamilton: one of 'Edward II the Martyr and Elfrida' (representing the murder of Edward the Martyr in 978),[422] and one of 'Prince Edmund, surnam'd Ironside and Algitha' (representing domestic politics in 1015).[423] Those with a particular taste for King

---

[417] *An Alphabetical Catalogue of Plates, Engraved by the Most Esteemed Artists, After the Finest Pictures and Drawings of the Italian, Flemish, German, French, English, and Other Schools, which Comprise the Stock of John and Josiah Boydell, Engravers and Printsellers, No. 90, Cheapside, and at the Shakespeare Gallery, Pall Mall* (London, 1803), pp. xv–xvii, followed by an alphabetical catalogue of Boydell's entire stock (pp. 1–60) from which the prints in his 'Collection' were selected. There are copies of this catalogue in the BL (787.k.13), and elsewhere. See also Bruntjen, *John Boydell*, pp. 40–4; Brewer, *Pleasures of the Imagination*, pp. 220 and 456; and Clayton, *The English Print*, esp. pp. 177, 196, 198 and 209–10.

[418] The painting (presented to the Worshipful Company of Stationers and Newspaper Makers) was copied by Josiah Boydell (now in the Fitzwilliam Museum, Cambridge). The copy was engraved by W. Sharp, and the engraving was published by John Boydell in 1782. The engraving is reproduced in *The Painted Word*, ed. Cannon-Brookes, p. 65 (no. 32), and in Clayton, *The English Print*, p. 237. I am grateful to Miss Jane Munro (Fitzwilliam Museum) for her help in this connection.

[419] From 'Proposals' issued by West, Woollett and Hall in 1778 and 1783, cited by Clayton, *The English Print*, pp. 240 and 306.   [420] Above, pp. 300–1.   [421] Above, p. 299.

[422] The original painting is untraced.

[423] The original painting is untraced. The subject (Rapin, *History of England* [2nd ed.] I, 122) is derived ultimately from the *Anglo-Saxon Chronicle*, s.a. 1015. When Birchall died, in 1795, 'Two half-sheet (squares), by Bartolozzi, of Edward the Martyr and Elfrida, and Prince Edmund and Algitha', with 2 coloured and 438 plain impressions, were sold for £73 (Clayton, *The English Print*, pp. 220, citing a catalogue of Birchall's effects, and 229).

Alfred would have been better satisfied in 1794, when the printsellers Darling and Thompson published a large mezzotint engraving of Mason Chamberlin's 'Alfred the Great in the neatherd's cottage' (pl. IX*b*).[424] It would be misleading, of course, to fasten on Anglo-Saxon history in particular, as opposed to English history in general; so the point is, simply, that by the end of the eighteenth century a cultivated Englishman not satisfied with history on his shelves could have had plenty more of it on his walls.

Bowyer's 'Historic Gallery'

The most ambitious venture giving visual form to the whole sweep of English history was itself a product of the 1790s. In 1791 the painter and publisher Robert Bowyer (*c.* 1758–1834) released a prospectus for his 'Complete History of England superbly embellished', a project which constitutes one of the most striking manifestations of the enthusiasm for history painting during the reign of King George III.[425] In effect, Bowyer commissioned a number of distinguished artists to produce paintings suggested by particular passages in David Hume's *History of England*, which were to be engraved and published in a sumptuous new edition of that work. In 1793 the paintings by then to hand were placed on permanent exhibition in Bowyer's so-called 'Historic Gallery', on Pall Mall;[426] and while the exhibition served to advertise the project, the work of engraving, printing, and publication could begin. The complete text of Hume's *History* was reset in magnificent form, and the separate parts were issued, with accompanying engravings, but for subscribers only, between 1793 and 1806. The work as a whole could be bound in five volumes, or in ten, according to

---

[424] BM, P&D, 1950-11-11-99, entitled 'Alfred the Great in the Neatherd's Cottage' [with an explanation in English and French], painted by Mason Chamberlin R.A., engraved by Charles Townley (styled Engraver to the King of Prussia), dedicated by permission to the Earl of Derby by John P. Thompson, and published on 1 Jan. 1794 by Darling & Thompson (Printsellers, &c., to their Royal Highnesses the Duke and Duchess of York), Great Newport St., & Mason Chamberlin [the Younger], 51 Great Russel St. A drawing of 'King Alfred and the burnt cakes', signed and dated 'H. S. 1794', appeared in a sale at Christie's, 11 February 1987, Lot 132.

[425] The BL copy of Bowyer's *Prospectus of the General Design and Conditions for a Complete History of England superbly embellished* (London, 1791) was destroyed by enemy action during World War II. Bowyer puts his case in *Elucidation of Mr Bowyer's Plan for a Magnificent Edition of Hume's History of England* (London, 1795), pp. 7–14, with a spirited statement of the desirability of delineating 'the most striking events of history', and a remark to the effect that 'till the present reign historical painting has been almost unknown in the British dominions'. For further discussion, see Boase, 'Macklin and Bowyer', pp. 169–76, and Strong, *The Victorian Painter and British History*, p. 21.

[426] *Exhibition of Pictures painted for Bowyer's Magnificent Edition of the History of England* (London, 1793), provides a list of paintings, with pertinent extracts from Hume. The *Catalogue of Pictures painted for Mr Bowyer's Magnificent Edition of Hume's History of England* (London, ?1800), registered in the BL catalogue, was destroyed during the war.

The cult of King Alfred the Great

taste and strength; and the engraved plates could be bound in where appropriate, or put together in a separate volume.[427] Bowyer's edition of Hume's *History* was hailed soon after its completion, albeit by Bowyer himself, as 'the most superb publication, without exception, in Europe'; but it had proved to be a financial disaster, and he was authorized by Act of Parliament to hold a public lottery in September 1806 (with 22,000 three-guinea tickets), against his total costs of over £100,000, and to dispose of all of the original paintings.[428] It is perhaps not surprising, under these circumstances, that only five of the ten paintings which dealt with Anglo-Saxon subjects are known to have survived,[429] making us dependent in the remaining cases on the published engravings. William Hamilton, who had exhibited a painting of 'Edgar and Elfrida' at the Royal Academy in 1774, who had made drawings of some 'Anglo-Saxon' subjects for Barnard's *History* in the early 1780s, and whose paintings of Edward the Martyr and Edmund Ironside had been engraved by Bartolozzi in 1786, was the natural choice for the inevitable 'Vortigern and Rovena'.[430] Henry Tresham produced 'St Augustine before Ethelbert'.[431] As usual, there is no sign of much interest in the great moments of Northumbrian, East Anglian, or Mercian history. There were, however, no fewer than three paintings of Alfred, and a portrait of him for good measure. Richard Westall (1765–1836) settled rather adventurously on 'Prince Alfred before Pope Leo III [*recte* IV]', showing the pope anointing the four-year-old Alfred at Rome in 853 (pl. XI*a*).[432] Francis

---

[427] D. Hume, *The History of England, from the Invasion of Julius Cæsar to the Revolution of 1688*, 5 vols. (London, 1806), printed by T. Bensley for Robert Bowyer, of which I have seen only the copy in the British Library (classmark 749.f.1), with its plates bound in a separate (sixth) volume. See Jessop, *Bibliography of Hume*, p. 31; and *David Hume and the Eighteenth Century British Thought: an Annotated Catalogue* (Tokyo, 1986), pp. 135–6. The fact that Bowyer's edition was published only by subscription means that copies may have found their way more easily into the private libraries of the well-to-do than into the public domain. A set sold at Sotheby's in July 1993 came from the library of the 1st Marquess of Buckingham, at Stowe, 'with Bowyer's autograph receipt in ink pasted to front endpaper of volume I (dated 1799)'. Another set, from Noseley Hall in Leicestershire, was sold at Sotheby's in September 1998.

[428] *Gentleman's Mag.* 86.1 (1806), 430–1; Burke, *English Art 1714–1800*, p. 256. The paintings were sold by Peter Coxe on 29–30 May 1807: see F. Lugt, *Répertoire des catalogues de ventes Publiques*, 3 vols. (The Hague, 1938–64) I [1600–1825], no. 7260, of which there are copies in the Courtauld Institute and in the Victoria and Albert Museum.

[429] For the scarcity of surviving paintings from Bowyer's 'Historic Gallery', see Boase, 'Macklin and Bowyer', pp. 176–7, though the records kept by the Mellon Centre make it much easier now (than it can have been *c.* 1960) to identify survivors from the series as a whole.

[430] The original painting was sold at Sotheby's, 12 July 1989 (Lot 98); photograph in the Mellon Centre. It was engraved for the Historic Gallery by Delatre, and published in 1795.

[431] The painting (untraced) was exhibited at the Royal Academy in 1795, engraved for the Historic Gallery by A. Smith, and published in 1794.

[432] The original painting was in the possession of Thos. Agnew and Sons in 1973; photograph in the Mellon Centre. It was engraved for the Historic Gallery by J. Stow, and published in 1794.

Wheatley (1747–1801) produced his own vision of 'Alfred in the House of the Neatherd' (1792), showing Alfred burning the cakes at Athelney in 878 (pl. XI*b*).[433] Henry Singleton (1766–1839) chose to illustrate 'Alfred liberating the family of Hastings', representing an event mentioned in the *Chronicle* for 893.[434] The portrait of Alfred is said to have been 'from the original picture in the University College, at Oxford', and is placed above a vignette showing the king in the act of building the University of Oxford.[435] The tone is lowered as we move into the tenth and eleventh centuries. William Hamilton further extended his repertoire with a dramatic rendition of 'Edwig and Elgiva', showing Abbot Dunstan, assisted by an elderly bishop, attempting to separate King Eadwig from the attentions of Ælfgifu.[436] Robert Smirke (1752–1845) had a go at 'The Treachery of Elfrida', depicting the murder of King Edward the Martyr,[437] and then moved on to 'Canute reproving his Courtiers'.[438] Finally, the events of the Norman Conquest were represented by P. J. de Loutherbourg (1740–1812), who produced an impressive 'Battle of Hastings',[439] and by Benjamin West, who fastened on 'William I, Receiving the Crown of England'.[440] The 'Anglo-Saxon' pictures in Bowyer's 'Historic Gallery' represent no more than the opening sequence in a series which contains well over 100 engraved plates in all, made up of about seventy historical scenes, over thirty portraits, and various head-pieces and vignettes; and in this wider context, the respect accorded to King Alfred the Great is a good reflection of the position he had come to occupy in public consciousness by the end of the eighteenth century.

---

[433] The original painting was sold at Christie's, New York, 4 October 1996 (Lot 57); photograph in the Mellon Centre. It was engraved for the Historic Gallery by W. Bromley, and published in 1795. See also M. Webster, *Francis Wheatley* (London, 1970), pp. 90–1 and 92 (fig. 129); and Strong, *The Victorian Painter and British History*, p. 21.

[434] The painting (untraced) was engraved for the Historic Gallery by W. Bromley, and published in 1798.

[435] Engraved by A. Skelton, and published in 1797. The portrait differs from the 'standard' image which originated in the engraving published in Spelman, *Life of Alfred*, ed. Walker, and may in fact have been based on an engraving of the portrait in the Bodleian Library.

[436] The painting was sold at Christie's, 3 May 1985 (Lot 83); it was acquired by Sarah Campbell Blaffer Foundation, Houston, Texas, and can be seen on the Foundation's website. It was engraved for the Historic Gallery by I. Taylor, and published in 1794; reproduced in Hammelmann, *Book Illustrators*, fig. 32. Cf. Wale's earlier drawing of the same subject (above, p. 306).

[437] The painting (untraced) was engraved for the Historic Gallery by W. Bromley, and published in 1806. Cf above, n. 412.

[438] The painting (untraced) was engraved for the Historic Gallery by G. Noble, and published in 1806. Cf above, n. 412.

[439] The painting (untraced) was engraved for the Historic Gallery by W. Bromley, and published in 1804.

[440] The painting, now in the Walker Art Gallery, Liverpool, was engraved for the Historic Gallery by G. Noble, and published in 1797. See von Erffa and Staley, *Paintings of Benjamin West*, pp. 188–9 (nos. 50–1).

Alfredian history painting in the early nineteenth century

The annual exhibitions at the Royal Academy continued to provide the best opportunities for artists to display their history paintings, complemented from 1806 by another series of exhibitions at the British Institution.[441] In 1799 Richard Westall, who had depicted the young Alfred and Pope Leo for Bowyer's 'Historic Gallery' in 1792, displayed an equally original choice of Alfredian subject-matter with his watercolour of 'Queen Judith reciting to Alfred the Great, when a child, the songs of the bards, describing the heroic deeds of his ancestors' (pl. XII*a*).[442] The picture was exhibited at the Royal Academy in 1800,[443] published as an aquatint *c.* 1801,[444] and exhibited again at the British Institution in 1806.[445] A vast picture of Alfred by a painter called Martin was also on show in 1800, at the Pantheon in Oxford Street.[446] Among other manifestations of pictorial Alfrediana in the early nineteenth century, we find several which reflect the conventional obsession with the events of 878. Thomas Stothard's representation of 'Alfred disguised as a harper in the Danish camp', of which an engraving was published in 1802 (pl. XII*b*) as part of an historical set of four, picked up a subject which focused attention on the king's cunning and resourcefulness in adversity.[447] The young David Wilkie (at the outset of his

---

[441] A. Graves, *The British Institution 1806–1867: a Complete Dictionary of Contributors and their Work from the Foundation of the Institution* (London, 1908).

[442] BM, P&D, Oo.3-12. See also L. Binyon, *Catalogue of Drawings by British Artists and Artists of Foreign Origin working in Great Britain, preserved in the Department of Prints and Drawings in the British Museum* IV (London, 1907), p. 321 (no. 16); and G. Smith, 'Watercolour: Purpose and Practice', in S. Fenwick and G. Smith, *The Business of Watercolour: a Guide to the Archives of the Royal Watercolour Society* (Aldershot, 1997), pp. 1–34, at 12, with fig. 11.

[443] Royal Academy 1800 (423). Cf. H. J. Pye, *Alfred; an Epic Poem, in Six Books* (London, 1801), p. 132: 'Alfred is said to have first caught the spirit both of poetry and heroism, from hearing his step-mother recite poems on the heroic actions of his ancestors. There is an excellent picture on the subject by Westall.' Joseph Farington reported in his diary that Westall's 'Alfred', and a companion drawing, were bought by West for Mr Udney for 100 guineas each, and that he would have given him double that sum: *The Diary of Joseph Farington*, ed. K. Garlick, *et al.*, 16 vols. (New Haven, CT, and London, 1978–84), with *Index*, ed. E. Newby (New Haven, CT, 1998) IV, 1395–6.

[444] At the Royal Academy in 1801 (569), Westall exhibited 'a print in imitation of a drawing', with the same title as the watercolour.   [445] British Institution 1806 (29).

[446] *Diary of Joseph Farington*, ed. Garlick, *et al.* IV, 1409 and 1410 (said to be about 14 feet by 10), identified in the index as the Swedish painter Elias Martin (1739–1818), but (as David Alexander points out to me) more likely to be the English historical painter William Martin (1752–*c.* 1831). Martin is known to have presented a picture of Alfred to the Bodleian Library in 1796: A à Wood, *The History and Antiquities of the University of Oxford* II, ed. J. Gutch (Oxford, 1796), 893.

[447] BM, P&D, 1849-7-21-1412, a stipple engraving published by Rudolph Ackermann in May 1802. For the publisher, see J. Ford, *Ackermann 1783–1983: the Business of Art* (London, 1983). The full set, first published by J. R. Smith, in 1793, and listed among 'Miscellaneous Prints' in R. Ackermann, *A Catalogue of Various Prints, Adapted for Furniture, Ornaments, etc.*

career, and working in response to a private commission) returned to Athelney with 'Alfred reprimanded by the neatherd's wife' (1806), rather more crowded than earlier paintings of the same subject but still retaining the basic features.[448] The painting itself remained in private hands, but an engraving of it was published in 1828 (pl. XIII*a*).[449] Richard Morton Paye exhibited his own vision of 'Alfred in the neat-herd's cottage' in 1807.[450] And in 1814–15 Henry Pierce Bone (1779–1855) exhibited 'The wife and sons of Hastings, the Danish chief, brought prisoners before Alfred the Great, etc.', at the Royal Academy and at the British Institution,[451] presumably having contracted the idea from the inclusion of the subject in Bowyer's edition of Hume.

The development of Alfredian iconography

It is now possible, should we be so inclined, to reflect upon the development of Alfredian iconography from *c.* 1660 to *c.* 1830. One cannot pretend that there is anything here to suggest that artists were possessed of a special ability to reach deep beneath the surface in order to capture the spirit of the historical King Alfred, but they caught his legendary namesake well enough. Although there are various 'medieval' representations of King Alfred, the familiar if no less stylized image of the king originated in the late seventeenth century, and is dominated by the portraiture emanating from Oxford. George Vertue picked up and developed the image in the 1720s and 1730s, introducing a range of accessories (including harp and spear), with a vignette of Alfred playing his harp in the Danish camp. For his part, Rysbrack immortalized the crowned, bearded, and benevolent king in stone. All that was needed was a kingdom for a stage,

---

(London, 1802)) comprised, Metz, 'Boadicea haranguing the Britons'; Hamilton, 'Vortigern and Rowena'; Stothard, 'Alfred disguised as a harper in the Danish camp'; and Hamilton, 'Edgar and Elfrida'. In iconographic terms, Stothard was following Wale (above, p. 308) and Edwards (above, p. 310). A drawing of 'King Alfred the Great', attributed to Stothard, appeared at Bonham's, London, in their sale on 12 December 1991, Lot 219.

[448] For this painting, now in a private collection, see H. A. D. Miles and D. B. Brown, *Sir David Wilkie of Scotland (1785–1841)* (Raleigh, NC, 1987), pp. 22–3, 26–7 and 123–7 (no. 6), with fig.; the reference to the existence of a related drawing in the Fitzwilliam Museum, Cambridge, seems to be erroneous. For a reproduction in colour, see B. Yorke, 'The Most Perfect Man in History?', *Hist. Today* 49.10 (1999), 8–14, at 12.

[449] The painting was engraved by James Mitchell, and published in 1828 by Boys & Graves (BM, P&D, 1836-11-24-3). It was engraved again by G. A. Periam, for the Wilkie Gallery (1848–50); and a small outline engraving by Normand *fils* was published in Hamilton, *The English School* I, no. 66. Versions of the same composition, based on one or other of the engravings, were made by the American artists J. Hall in 1840 and Thomas Sully in 1854. For the latter, see E. Biddle and M. Fielding, *The Life and Works of Thomas Sully (1783–1872)* (Charleston, SC, 1969), p. 335 (no. 2085). Sully's 'renowned' painting of Alfred appeared in a sale at Philadelphia in December 1914. I am grateful to Lance Humphries, of Baltimore, MD, for valuable guidance in connection with Sully. [450] British Institution 1807 (77).

[451] Royal Academy 1814 (352); British Institution 1815 (60).

some princes to act, and monarchs to behold the swelling scene. In 1751 Nicholas Blakey 'invented' an Alfredian event at Athelney, featuring one of Vertue's accessories; but the scene failed to capture the imagination, and spawned no imitators. Alfred the cake-burner was rather more successful. The basic formula, set in a dingy but not insubstantial 'cottage', with various accessories cast about on the floor, and other players in more or less threatening poses, would appear to have been devised by Mason Chamberlin in 1764. It was a theme to which other artists often returned: Edward Edwards in 1776, Francis Wheatley in 1792, and David Wilkie in 1806, to name but a few. Alfred the lawmaker, by Samuel Wale, had also appeared in 1764, and was the very model of the Georgian King Alfred. It may have lacked the human touch which gave other Alfredian subjects their special appeal, but it was picked up by Barry in the 1770s, and (as we shall see) would enjoy a revival in the 1840s. Alfred the harp-player, also by Wale, reappeared at about the same time, and became a favourite subject for popular illustration in the nineteenth century. The more worthy image of Alfred the loaf-giver was added to the canon, perhaps predictably by Benjamin West, in 1779, followed by William Hamilton in 1783. In 1792 Richard Westall, displaying somewhat greater imagination, focused his attention on Alfred's encounter with Pope Leo, and followed this in 1799 with his more homely vision of Alfred listening to a recital of English poetry at his stepmother's knee. Alfred the magnanimous in battle was immortalized by Henry Singleton in 1798, followed by Henry Pierce Bone in 1814. No doubt other Alfredian pictures were made in the later eighteenth and early nineteenth centuries which might enhance our understanding of how the king was perceived, and no doubt many other 'Anglo-Saxon' pictures were made which might help to put them in context among history paintings of the period. The basic truth is likely to remain, however, that Alfred attracted far more attention than any other Anglo-Saxon king. He was not so much the king who vanquished his enemies, although in that respect his time would come. He was, rather, the embodiment of good kingship, exuding all those qualities which set him apart as a national icon; for although reduced on one occasion to the humblest of circumstances, he was immediately identifiable as the father and protector of his people.

THE CULT OF THE LOCAL HERO

It seems clear that popular awareness of the broad sweep of English history, and consciousness of the nation's wider historical identity, would have increased dramatically in the second half of the eighteenth century. Rapin and Hume established the basic parameters of their subject, and the profusion of more popular histories suggests how the message was brought in more palatable form into the homes of an appreciative reading public. The range of history paintings made for the exhibitions of the Society of Artists and the Free Society of Artists in the 1760s, and for the exhibitions of the Royal Academy from 1769 onwards, reveals in a different but complementary way how particular subjects drawn from English history became particularly popular, and began to assume a visual form; while the fact that so many of the historical subjects were soon adapted for the trade in decorative prints suggests in another way how English history was received and absorbed by the public. It would appear, on the other hand, that the commemorative tendencies of the British people had not yet extended to figures of the dim and distant past, in the sense that there is no sign of any public commemoration of the potentially 'Alfredian' anniversaries in 1749 (birth), 1771 (accession), 1778 (salvation), or 1801 (death). The cult of Alfred was, however, driven forward at this stage by a widening range of local considerations: if not yet at Wantage (where he was born), then certainly at Athelney (where he earned renown), in Wiltshire (where he marshalled his forces), at Oxford (where he founded a university), and at Winchester (where he was buried).

Some particularly fine manifestations of the cult of King Alfred are to be found in the house and gardens at Stourhead, near Stourton, in Wiltshire, home of the wealthy banker Henry Hoare II (1705–85), known to his family as 'the Magnificent'. Hoare had lived through the reigns of George I and George II, but he regarded George III as the first truly British king. In 1762, inspired not only by George III's recent accession but also (as he admitted himself) by Voltaire's account of King Alfred,[452] Hoare resolved to erect a tower out of gratitude to Alfred on Kingsettle Hill, presumed to be the place (known as 'Egbert's stone') where the West Saxon forces had assembled in 878 for their counter-attack against the Danes; and in the tower there would be an inscription commemorating Alfred as the founder of the English Monarchy, founder of Oxford University, and much else besides. Hoare was aware that Rysbrack had once produced an imposing statue of 'Fame', holding a large medallion with a bust of Queen Anne; and he knew further that Queen Anne had been been replaced, after the victory at Culloden in 1746, with a bust of William Augustus, 1st Duke of Cumberland (younger brother of Prince Frederick), and that the statue had remained thereafter in Rysbrack's workshop. He now wanted the statue for himself, if only it would fit inside his projected tower on Kingsettle Hill, and intended to replace the Duke of Cumberland with King Alfred the Great.[453] Hoare may have realized that the plan would not work, for two years

---

[452] For eighteenth-century historical panegyrics on Alfred, including Voltaire's, see Stanley, 'The Glorification of Alfred', pp. 413–17.

[453] See K. Woodbridge, *Landscape and Antiquity: Aspects of English Culture at Stourhead 1718 to 1838* (Oxford, 1970), pp. 51–70, at 52–6, with the text of Hoare's letter to his son-in-law, dated 18 November 1762; see also K. Woodbridge, *The Stourhead Landscape, Wiltshire*, National Trust Guide (London, 1982), pp. 25–7 and 60.

The cult of King Alfred the Great

later, in 1764, he paid Rysbrack £100 for a fine marble bust of the king, modelled on the bust of Alfred which Rysbrack had made thirty years earlier for Queen Caroline, itself based on one or other of Vertue's engravings; the bust is now the property of the National Trust, and can be seen in the Library Ante-Room at Stourhead.[454] Rysbrack's statue of 'Fame' was purchased at a sale of his effects, in April 1767, by William Bouverie (1st Earl of Radnor), for £59, and was set up in the park at Longford Castle, near Salisbury, Wiltshire; two months later, in June 1767, Lord Radnor (perhaps following Hoare's original suggestion) replaced the Duke of Cumberland with a bust of Alfred, provided for £7 by Rysbrack's assistant, Gaspar Vanderhagen,[455] and, presumably at about the same time, caused to be added a long Latin inscription on the base celebrating the good name of 'Brittanic Alfred'.[456] Lord Radnor (who had received his education at University College in the 1740s) may have been moved in part by the new intensity of feeling for Alfred in the 1760s, but his wish to have Alfred ensconced in his park might also have been related to the fact that three of his sons were sent to his old college in the period 1767–72. In July 1767 Jacob Bouverie (1750–1828), 3rd Viscount Folkestone (later 2nd Earl of Radnor), was admitted to University College; interestingly, a drawing of Jacob, made on 29 December 1767, shows him holding a small medallion of King Alfred, as if to indicate that the son, like his father, drew inspiration from contemplation of so great a king.[457] Henry Hoare himself needed to resume work on 'Alfred's Tower'. Building began in 1769–70, and was completed in 1772. With help from

---

[454] For Rysbrack's bust of Alfred, see Webb, *Rysbrack*, p. 116, and fig. 46; Eustace, *Rysbrack*, pp. 171–3 (no. 79), with illustrations; and J. Kenworthy-Browne, 'Portrait Busts by Rysbrack', *National Trust Stud.* (1980), pp. 67–79, at 77–9. See also *Stourhead*, National Trust Guide (London, 1981, rev. 1997), p. 13.

[455] A number of small oval reliefs of King Alfred, in ivory (12 cm by 9 cm), presumed to date from the third quarter of the eighteenth century, are attributed to Vanderhagen after Rysbrack on the strength of the reference to Lord Radnor's commission; e.g. Sotheby's, 6 July 1995, Lot 151.

[456] See Webb, *Rysbrack*, p. 137; Eustace, *Rysbrack*, pp. 182–4; and Helen Matilda, Countess of Radnor, and W. B. Squire, *Catalogue of the Pictures in the Collection of the Earl of Radnor*, 2 pts (London, 1909) I, 43–6. One of the roundels on the base carries the inscription (in Latin): 'Whoever you may be, lover of liberty or letters, regard with reverent eyes the Portrait of this Man, who, when his Country was threatened by the Foe from abroad and struggling under Barbarian and shameful ignorance within, did raise it up by Arms, temper it by Laws, and embellish it by Learning. If you be a Briton, you may be proud, also, that the military prowess of Romulus, the politick Wisdom of Numa, and the philosophick Nobility of Aurelius, are uniquely comprehended in the name of BRITTANIC ALFRED.' The inscription subsequently found its way onto the engraved membership card of the University College Club, established by Jacob Bouverie, 2nd Earl of Radnor, in 1792, on which see further below, n. 468.

[457] I am grateful to Dr Jane Cunningham (Librarian, Photographic Survey, Courtauld Institute of Art) for bringing this drawing to my attention, and for her assistance in other connections. For Jacob Bouverie, see Countess of Radnor and Squire, *Catalogue of the Pictures* I, 76–9.

a cousin in Bath, Hoare secured the services of 'a young lad of 18' who came to Stourhead in early 1770 and in seven weeks 'finished a figure of Alfred the Great 10 feet high, from a model given him, to the Admiration of all the Spectators'; by the end of April the tower itself was 15 feet high, and Hoare remarked 'I hope it will be finished in as happy Times to this Isle as Alfred finished his Life of Glory in then shall I depart in peace.'[458] A suitably 'patriotic' inscription placed on a tablet underneath the statue proclaimed Alfred as (among other things) 'the founder of the English monarchy and liberty', and the tower rose upwards until it stood 160 feet high, commanding magnificent views over the surrounding countryside.[459]

The chief centre for the cultivation of Alfredophilia throughout the eighteenth century naturally remained the University of Oxford. The outcome of protracted hearings which followed the disputed election to the mastership of University College in 1722 (a dispute which could stand beside the most hotly contested royal successions of the tenth century) was the formal decision by a benchful of judges in 1727 that the college had been founded by King Alfred the Great, and that accordingly the Crown was the Visitor of the college and should determine the issue.[460] This reaffirmation of the traditional view was immediately challenged by William Smith (?1651–1735), himself a fellow of the college from 1675 to 1705 (and thus one who had served under Obadiah Walker), and from 1704 rector of Melsonby in Yorkshire, who restated in no uncertain terms the case for William of Durham (*c.* 1250).[461] Thomas Hearne was among those deeply committed to Alfredian Oxford, and in a defensive letter to the antiquary James West he dismissed Smith's book as 'a studied Rhapsody of Lyes', insisting none the less that his sole motive in editing Spelman's 'Life of Alfred' had been to serve the public interest.[462] More to the

---

[458] Letter from Henry Hoare to his daughter Susanna, 28 April 1770 (Woodbridge, *Landscape and Antiquity*, p. 61).

[459] *Ibid.* pp. 61 and 65; McCarthy, *The Origins of the Gothic Revival*, p. 31 and pl. 24. In its final (abbreviated) form, the inscription reads as follows: 'Alfred the Great AD 879 on this summit erected his standard against the Danish invaders. To him we owe the origin of juries, the establishment of a militia, the creation of a naval force. Alfred, the light of a benighted age, was a philosopher and a Christian; the father of his people, the founder of the English monarchy and liberty.' (Woodbridge, *The Stourhead Landscape*, p. 60.) On 'Alfred's Tower' as one of the proposed locations of 'Egbert's Stone', see J. Peddie, *Alfred the Good Soldier: His Life and Campaigns* (Bath, 1989), pp. 128–34.

[460] Carr, *University College*, pp. 172–6, and Darwall-Smith, *University College*, p. 18.

[461] W. Smith, *The Annals of University-College, Proving William of Durham the True Founder; and Answering all their Arguments who Ascribe it to King Alfred* (Newcastle upon Tyne, 1728). For Smith himself, see the entry on him in the *DNB*, and Carr, *University College*, pp. 176–9; see also Stanley, 'The Glorification of Alfred', p. 413, n. 19.

[462] TH to JW, 17 July 1728 (BL, Lansdowne 778, 95r). See also *Remarks and Collections*, ed. Doble, *et al.*, X, 27–9 and 33.

point, the views expressed so vehemently in Smith's *Annals of University-College* could scarcely compete with the traditions peddled in the far more widely-disseminated works of Rapin, Hume, and many others, and even or perhaps especially in Oxford his arguments made not the slightest difference to the pride which the University continued to take in its Alfredian identity. In 1735 the Oxford Almanack featured a general view of University College, designed by George Vertue, showing William of Durham and other benefactors paying their respects to an enthroned King Alfred.[463] In 1753 the Almanack featured an allegorical composition by Samuel Wale, showing King Alfred (identified by a celestial figure above him, and with Religion and Justice seated on either side of his throne) giving a charter to a group of figures representing the Arts and Sciences (Navigation, Architecture, Painting, Astronomy, Geography, Music), while at the same time gesturing to a view of University College, in the background, where they could all set to work.[464] No wonder, then, that a portrait of Sir Thomas Cookes, who had died in 1701 leaving money for the refoundation of Gloucester Hall, as Worcester College, showed Sir Thomas standing beside a bust of King Alfred, as one founder might acknowledge the inspiration of another.[465] Yet it was at University College, in particular, that Alfred continued to find his most enthusiastic supporters. A marble bas-relief of King Alfred was presented to the college in 1766 by Sir Roger Newdigate (1719–1806), as part of a major scheme undertaken in that year for the remodelling of the Hall;[466] a half-length portrait of Alfred, on glass, apparently based on the portrait then on display in the Bodleian picture gallery, was given to the college by the Hon. W. J. Skeffington in 1767;[467] and in 1771 Jacob Bouverie (3rd Viscount Folkestone), presumably on leaving the college, presented a marble bust of the king, and had

---

[463] H. M. Petter, *The Oxford Almanacks* (Oxford, 1974), pp. 59–60 (and fig.). A preliminary drawing for the composition is in the Ashmolean Museum: D. B. Brown, *Ashmolean Museum Oxford. Catalogue of the Collection of Drawings*, IV: *The Earlier British Drawings / British Artists and Foreigners working in Britain born before c. 1775* (Oxford, 1982), p. 641.

[464] Petter, *The Oxford Almanacks*, p. 67 (and fig.). For Wale's later work, see above, pp. 305–9.

[465] The portrait was painted presumably in the first half of the eighteenth century, and was given to the college by Dr Samuel Wanley (DD 1752). The college commissioned Robert Edge Pine to make a copy, executed in 1774 and described by a contemporary as 'a most shocking performance'. It seems not to be clear whether the portrait which now hangs in the library is the original, or Pine's copy. See Poole, *Catalogue of Portraits* III, 258–9. I owe my knowledge of the portrait at Worcester College to the kindness of Dr Timothy Clayton; and I am grateful to Dr J. H. Parker (Librarian, Worcester College) and to Dr Jane Cunningham (Courtauld Institute) for their help in the same connection.

[466] The Alfredian bas-relief was encased within an elaborate gothic chimneypiece; see *VCH Oxon* III, 80, and pl. opp. 76 (showing the Hall in 1814). Newdigate was an undergraduate at Univ in the late 1730s, and from 1750 to 1780 politically active as MP for the University. He was the founder of the Newdigate Prize for poetry, first awarded in 1806.

[467] For the picture in the Bodleian, see above, p. 263. There is a very similar painting, without the inscription naming Skeffington, in the Master's Dining Room.

it set up over the mantelpiece in the Senior Common Room.[468] It was also in the early 1770s that John Scott (1751–1838), of University College, presented himself for his MA degree at Oxford. He was examined in Hebrew and in History; and later recalled that the outcome of the examination had depended largely on his ability to answer correctly the question 'Who founded University College?'.[469] In 1775 the Chancellor's Prize for Latin Verse was awarded to John Warton, Scholar of Trinity College, for 'Alfredus Magnus'.[470] Yet perhaps the most important manifestation of the cult of Alfred at Oxford in the late eighteenth century was the publication, in 1788, of the original vernacular text of King Alfred's will, as preserved in the eleventh-century 'Liber Vitae' of the New Minster, Winchester. The 'Liber Vitae' had passed through a succession of private collections, and by 1770 had come into the hands of the distinguished antiquary and palaeographer Thomas Astle (1735–1803).[471] Astle prevailed upon the Revd Owen Manning to prepare a scholarly edition of the will, completed in 1776, and was subsequently instrumental in persuading the Delegates of the Oxford University Press to publish it, as 'a Monument which will reflect honour on the Memory of the Royal Founder of the University'.[472] Only in the nineteenth century does it appear that the tongue was moving into the cheek. In 1856 the Newdigate Prize for English Verse in the University of Oxford was

---

[468] The bust is by Joseph Wilton (1722–1803), and was evidently modelled on the statue by Rysbrack at Stourhead (above, p. 321). It was removed to the Library in 1938, where it remains (looking down the library towards the enormous statue of Lord Eldon, on whom see below); for a reproduction of it, see Lees, *Alfred the Great*, opp. p. 464. In 1791 Jacob Bouverie, who had succeeded his father as 2nd Earl of Radnor in 1776, proposed the foundation of a University College Dining Club, established in 1792, and gave it a strong sense of Alfredian identity; see L. Mitchell, 'The First Univ. Dining Club?', *University College Record* 1970, 351–8, with pl. I. I am most grateful to Christine Ritchie for her assistance in connection with the various items of Alfrediana at University College.

[469] John Scott is better known as George III's Lord Chancellor, created Baron Eldon in 1799 and 1st Earl of Eldon in 1821. For the story of his Oxford examination, see D. Petterson, 'Hebrew Studies', *History of the University of Oxford: the Eighteenth Century*, ed. Sutherland and Mitchell, pp. 535–50, at 546.

[470] *The Historical Register of the University of Oxford* (Oxford, 1888), p. 137. I owe this reference to the kindness of Dr John Pickles.

[471] The 'Liber Vitae' (BL Stowe 944) is first recorded in the possession of Walter Clavell (1676–1740), in 1710. It is next recorded in the hands of the Revd George North (1710–72), who remarked on its importance in a letter to the Revd William Cole, 25 Sept. 1748 (BL, Add. 5993, 78r), and later passed it on to Dr Michael Lort (1725–90), who gave it to Astle in 1769 or 1770. See *Liber Vitae*, ed. Keynes, pp. 73–7.

[472] *The Will of King Alfred* (Oxford, 1788), p. iii. It emerges from an earlier version of the preface that the publication had been superintended by Herbert Croft, of the Oxford Museum, 'out of Reverence for the Founder of University College, where I [*sc.* Croft] had the honour to be educated'. Astle suppressed this part of the preface, and elsewhere altered 'Royal Founder' to 'Royal Patron'; but the Press seems to have been determined to retain the reference to Alfred as 'Founder' of the University. For further details, see *Liber Vitae*, ed. Keynes, pp. 76–7.

The cult of King Alfred the Great

awarded to a certain William Powell James, of Oriel College, for a highly crafted poem on 'Alfred the Great contemplating Oxford University at the present day',[473] prompting Edwin Arnold, who had won the prize in 1852, to produce a light-hearted response from his rooms in University College.[474] And when the millennium of the foundation of University College was marked, in 1872, by a grand dinner attended by the college's most distinguished alumni, it is apparent that the occasion was not taken as seriously as might have been the case a hundred years before.[475]

Another natural centre for the cultivation of King Alfred's memory was at Winchester, where Alfred had seemingly established himself in the 890s, and where his son, Edward the Elder, was based in the early tenth century. After his death on 26 October 899 Alfred had been buried in the cathedral church of SS Peter and Paul, Winchester (later the Old Minster, or St Swithun's). Edward the Elder founded the New Minster, Winchester, adjacent to the cathedral, in 901, to cater (it seems) for the spiritual well-being of the 'kingdom of the Anglo-Saxons', and translated his father's mortal remains to a place of honour in the new church; so, when the community of the New Minster was relocated at Hyde Abbey, just north of the city walls, in 1110, Alfred's remains were translated again to a grave in front of the High Altar.[476] The putative resting-place of King Alfred at Hyde Abbey is known to have been disturbed in the immediate aftermath of the abbey's dissolution, in 1539, but the presumption naturally remained that the king's bones lay buried thereafter where the High Altar had once stood.[477] In the mid- or late 1780s the site was purchased from its owner by the county authorities, and cleared in readiness for the construction of a new gaol, or bridewell. On 23 December 1790, the Catholic divine John Milner (1752–1826), then resident at Winchester, wrote to a fellow antiquary, John Carter, giving an account of recent work on the site of Hyde Abbey.[478] The place which ought to be one of pilgrimage for all Englishmen, 'like disciples of Mahomet going to Mecca', had been desecrated: 'In the year 1785 this country,

---

[473] W. P. James, *King Alfred Surveying Oxford University at the Present Time: a Prize Poem, Recited in the Theatre, Oxford, June 4th, 1856* (Oxford, 1856). For the Newdigate Prize, see *The Historical Register of the University of Oxford* (Oxford, 1888), p. 147.

[474] (Sir) Edwin Arnold's poem is printed in *University College Record* 1961, 106–9.

[475] For the speeches made on this occasion, by the Master of University College, the Dean of Westminster, the Chancellor of the Exchequer, and others, see the report in the *Guardian*, 19 June 1872, pp. 808–9; see also Parker, *Early History of Oxford*, p. 62, and Carr, *University College*, pp. 7–8. The Regius Professor of Modern History is said to have presented the college with a parcel of burnt cakes; see *Encyclopædia of Oxford*, ed. Hibbert, p. 474.

[476] *Liber Vitae*, ed. Keynes, pp. 17, 43, 47 n. 308, and 81 (with references to the first reburial of Alfred's 'ashes' in the New Minster).   [477] *Liber Vitae*, ed. Keynes, pp. 47–8.

[478] For the wider context of Milner's particular interest in Alfred, see Smith, *The Gothic Bequest*, pp. 128–31.

being at a loss to fix on a proper place as a lay-stall for depositing the accumulated mass of moral filth and infection, could find none so proper for that purpose as the spot which covered the head of the divine Alfred and those of so many others of our great and good ancestors.' Milner went on to mention an inscribed stone 'which is in a garden adjoining to my house, and which, from certain tradition, I know to have been dug out of the ruins of Hyde Abbey some years ago'. The stone in question had been placed in a wall in St Peter's Street, and Milner enclosed a drawing of it, made in 1789, which was soon published by Carter,[479] and which was published more accurately by Milner himself in his 'Antiquities of Winchester' (1798).[480] The inscription reads 'ælfred rex dccclxxxi', in the kind of approximation of Insular letter-forms which one might find at any period from the twelfth century onwards. Milner added that the stone itself 'is now in the possession of Henry Howard, Esq., of Corby Castle', thus introducing a second Catholic into the tale. Henry Howard (1757–1842) was born at Corby Castle, near Carlisle, in Cumberland. His own Catholic upbringing had long denied him a place in the British army, but in 1795 he had been able to obtain a commission, and found himself stationed at Winchester in 1797–8. As a man with refined antiquarian tastes, and as one whose Whig sympathies found expression in the high veneration he felt 'for the character and principles of our renowned Alfred', Howard resolved while at Winchester 'to make the discovery of [Alfred's] tomb an object of research'.[481] He interviewed Mr Page, Keeper of the Bridewell, and was given details of the work on the site of Hyde Abbey when the gaol had been built there ten years before. The discoveries included 'a stone coffin cased with lead both within and without, and containing some bones and remains of garments', and two other coffins, found immediately to the west of some sculptural remains which seemed to have formed part of the High Altar. Howard suggested that the coffins might have contained the remains of Alfred, his wife Ealhswith, and Edward the Elder; he added that the bones were 'thrown about', and that the coffins were broken up and reburied where they lay. While based at Winchester Howard seems also to have acquired the inscribed stone from his fellow-Alfredophile, John Milner, and took it back home to Corby Castle, together with some fragments of sculpture and other monastic debris. The stone remained at Corby Castle throughout

---

[479] J. Carter, *Specimens of the Ancient Sculpture and Painting, now Remaining in this Kingdom* ... (London, 1780–94) II, 19–22, with plate.

[480] J. Milner, *The History, Civil and Ecclesiastical, and Survey of the Antiquities of Winchester*, 2 vols. (Winchester, 1798–1801), 2nd ed. (1809), opp. I, 374, and II, 239.

[481] H. Howard, 'Enquiries Concerning the Tomb of King Alfred, at Hyde Abbey, Near Winchester', *Archaeologia* 13 (1798), 2nd ed. (1807), 309–12, written in the form of a letter from Howard to George Nayler, dated 26 Feb. 1798, and communicated to the Society of Antiquaries on 29 March 1798.

the nineteenth century, but found its way back to Winchester in the 1930s, and is now preserved in the Winchester City Museum.[482] It is difficult to establish whether the inscription was made as early as the twelfth century, or as late as the eighteenth; and while we may assume that it was intended to commemorate an unspecified event itself presumed to have taken place in 881, we can but guess whether the event was the king's accession ('881' in error for 871)., or something else, such as the foundation of the burh at Winchester.[483] Whatever the case, one suspects that without Milner and Howard not even this curious piece of Alfrediana would have been preserved from the site of the king's last resting-place at Hyde Abbey.

The great enthusiasm for King Alfred in the late eighteenth century suggests that it would have been a good time to be the proprietor of the isle of Athelney, in the Somerset marshes, where the king had taken refuge in 878, where he had burnt the cakes, where he had had a vision of St Cuthbert, where he had built a fort, where he had heard the good news of the capture of the Raven banner, whence he had set off to the Danish camp disguised as a minstrel, and where he had later founded a monastery. In fact, plans to erect a monument on the presumed site of the monastery at Athelney were first hatched in 1798;[484] and although the monument was erected in a jubilee year (1801), the inscription suggests that it was as much a monument to the landowner as it had ever been intended to be a monument to the king.[485] The eighteenth century as a whole would seem also to have been a propitious time for the development of legends about places or objects with allegedly 'Alfredian' associations. 'King Alfred's blowing stone', which lies by the side of the road at Kingston Lisle, in the Vale of the White Horse, and which was used for summoning the English to battle

---

[482] Below, p. 351. For an illustration, see P. Bogan, 'Where is King Alfred Buried?', *Winchester Cathedral Record* 55 (1986), 27–34, at 28 (pl. 1); see also D. Tweddle, M. Biddle and B. Kjølbye-Biddle, *South-East England*, Corpus of AS Stone Sculpture 4 (Oxford, 1995), 341. A plaster cast of the stone was preserved in the Museum of the Society of Antiquaries in the early nineteenth century (A. Way, *Catalogue of Antiquities* ... (London, [1847]), p. 29). For further investigations into the burial-place of King Alfred, see below, pp. 345–6 and 352.

[483] The Winchester stone might be compared in this respect with the stone seen by William of Malmesbury, which commemorated Alfred's presumed foundation of the burh at Shaftesbury in 880; see Keynes, 'King Alfred the Great and Shaftesbury Abbey', p. 38.

[484] S. Keynes, 'George Harbin's Transcript of the Lost Cartulary of Athelney Abbey', *Somerset Archaeol. and Nat. Hist.* 136 (1993 for 1992), 149–59, at 151.

[485] The inscription on the monument is as follows: 'King Ælfred the Great, in the year of our Lord 879, having been defeated by the Danes, fled for refuge to the forest of Athelney, where he lay concealed from his enemies for the space of a whole year. He soon after regained possession of the throne; and in grateful remembrance of the protection he had received, under the favour of Heaven, he erected a monastery on this spot, and endowed it with all the lands contained in the Isle of Athelney. To perpetuate the memory of so remarkable an incident in the life of that illustrious prince, this edifice was founded by John Slade, Esq., of Maunsel, the proprietor of Athelney, and lord of the manor of North Petherton, A.D. 1801.'

against the Danes, is a case in point.[486] Another is the primitive tripod table from which King Alfred is alleged to have eaten the burnt cakes. The table was kept in the skittle alley of the King Alfred Hotel, at Burrowbridge, Somerset, in the 1930s, and was sold at auction in 1997.[487] If only to judge from a photograph, it would have been much at home in Mason Chamberlin's painting.

THE APOTHEOSIS OF KING ALFRED THE GREAT

The publication of Sharon Turner's *History of the Anglo-Saxons*, in 1799–1805, marked the beginning of a new age in the writing of Anglo-Saxon history.[488] Alfred's place in this story was naturally assured, but the cult had by now gathered enough momentum to rise way above the niceties of historical scholarship. The only question was how the Whig icon of the eighteenth century would come to be adopted as the embodiment of the nation's identity in the nineteenth century. Perhaps we should not expect to find any trace of the commemoration of the ninth centenary of the king's death, in 1801, in part because he was still too much the radical hero, and in part because it would take the jubilee of the accession of King George III, celebrated so enthusiastically in 1809, and the jubilee of the House of Hanover in 1814, to make people think in analogous terms of a ruler from the far more distant past.[489] It is other factors, therefore, which must be adduced to provide a background to Alfred's continued prosperity in the first half of the nineteenth century, though it is unlikely that the matter went so deep that the factors in question would have to be approached in anything other than the simplest of terms. The last stages of the Revolutionary and Napoleonic wars with France (1793–1815) would have strengthened Alfred's standing as one who had himself beaten off the threat of foreign conquest; and he continued to rise high with every increase in nationalistic fervour, whether prompted by the threat or actuality of war, or by pride in the extension and achievements of the British Empire, or by feelings of the innate superiority of

---

[486] *N&Q* 9th ser. 2 (1898), 373; Spinage, *King Alfred: Myths and Mysteries*, pp. 27–8. Francis Wise had suggested in 1738 that the White Horse at Uffington marked the site of the English victory at Ashdown in 871; see above, n. 207. For other 'Alfredian' sites in Berkshire and elsewhere, see P. Knott, 'Alfred's Wayte', *Berkshire Old and New* 7 (1990), 14–23, and Peddie, *Alfred the Good Soldier*.

[487] Finan, Watkins & Limm (The Square, Mere, Wiltshire), 5 April 1997, Lot 369.

[488] S. Turner, *A History of the Anglo-Saxons* (London, 1799–1805), 7th ed., 3 vols. (London, 1852), esp. I, 458–517, and II, 1–142. See also J. W. Burrow, *A Liberal Descent: Victorian Historians and the English Past* (Cambridge, 1981), pp. 116–19; MacDougall, *Racial Myth in English History*, pp. 92–5; Smith, *The Gothic Bequest*, p. 135; and Simmons, *Reversing the Conquest*, pp. 53–60.

[489] For such public celebrations during the reign of George III, see L. Colley, 'The Apotheosis of King George III: Loyalty, Royalty and the British Nation 1760–1820', *Past and Present* 102 (1984), 94–129. See also M. Chase, 'From Millennium to Anniversary: the Concept of Jubilee in Late Eighteenth- and Nineteenth-Century England', *ibid.* 129 (1990), 132–47; and R. Quinault, 'The Cult of the Centenary c. 1784–1914', *Hist. Research* 71 (1998), 303–23.

The cult of King Alfred the Great

one people over others.[490] The revival of the grandeur of monarchy during the reign of George IV, in the 1820s, would have encouraged all concerned to take up position under an Alfredian banner, while the feeling that George had succeeded only in bringing the monarchy into disrepute would have made others turn to Alfred as an example of what a king should be. At the same time, nothing (apart from scholarship) could deprive Alfred of his standing as the originator of all that was good in the British constitution, so the prospect of improvement following the accession of William IV, in 1830, and the return of the Whigs under Lord Grey, would have helped to promote Alfred as the founder and protector of political liberties, and as one who could be harnessed without much difficulty in the cause of social and educational reform. In even more general terms, the persistence of the Gothic Revival, and other aspects of nineteenth-century medievalism, would have done no harm to whosoever could climb on the bandwaggon as it lumbered past; while the sympathy, in a romantic age, for a person so interested in the poetry of his forebears, or for one seen to have experienced so much hardship and despair in looking after the interests of his people, would have endeared him to all those who cared.[491]

Given the intensity of indiscriminate Alfredophilia at the end of the eighteenth century, it is to be expected that manifestations of his cult should become more varied and widespread in the early nineteenth century, and more difficult to track down. Alfred soon fell prey to poets in search of subject-matter for exercises in epic poetry. In 1796 a certain Richard Poole had urged Coleridge to make Alfred the hero of an epic poem. Coleridge had other plans, and seems to have passed on the suggestion to his publisher, Joseph Cottle (1770–1853), of Bristol.[492] It was a bad move, for Cottle himself set to work, and in 1800 published a poem on Alfred in twenty-four books, focusing on the events of 878.[493] Although the work

---

[490] On the rise of 'racial Anglo-Saxonism', in England and in America, see Horsman, 'Origins of Racial Anglo-Saxonism in Great Britain before 1850'; Horsman, *Race and Manifest Destiny*; MacDougall, *Racial Myth in English History*, esp. pp. 89–124; and Frantzen, *Desire for Origins*.

[491] On the Anglo-Saxons in the nineteenth century, see O. Anderson, 'The Political Uses of History in Mid Nineteenth-Century England', *Past and Present* 36 (1967), 87–105, esp. 99–105. It would be interesting to know more of the incidence of 'Alfred' as a given name, in relation to other 'Anglo-Saxon' names and in relation to all personal names, during the eighteenth and nineteenth centuries. See further L. Dunkling, *The Guinness Book of Names*, 7th ed. (Enfield, 1995), pp. 47–8.

[492] D. Wu, 'Cottle's *Alfred*: Another Coleridge-Inspired Epic', *Charles Lamb Bull.* ns 73 (January 1991), 19–22. For an impression of Coleridge's views on Alfred, see S. T. Coleridge, *On the Constitution of the Church and State According to the Idea of Each* [1830], ed. J. Barrell (London, 1972), pp. 9, 41 and 82 n.; see also Smith, *The Gothic Bequest*, pp. 153–6.

[493] J. Cottle, *Alfred: an Epic Poem in Twenty-Four Books* (London, 1800), repr. in facsimile, with an introduction by D. H. Reiman (New York, 1979); see also J. Cottle, *Alfred: an Heroic Poem, in Twenty-Four Books*, 4th ed. (London, 1850), accompanied by Cottle's essay on 'The Heresiarch Church of Rome', pp. xix–cxvi. For discussion of the poem, see Miles, *King Alfred in Literature*, pp. 99–103; Stanley, 'The Glorification of Alfred', pp. 435–7; and Pratt, 'King Alfred in Mid-Late 18th Century Poetry'.

received some favourable notice,[494] it was derided by Coleridge, who is said to have remarked that 'it bore a lie on its title-page, for he called it *Alfred*, and it was never *halfread* by any human being'.[495] Henry James Pye (1745–1813), appointed Poet Laureate in 1790, had occasion to produce his own epic poem on Alfred, in six books, first published in 1801.[496] One might be disposed to assume that a poem on Alfred published in 1801 would commemorate the ninth centenary of the king's death, in 901, but a reading of the poem suggests that Pye was using Alfred as a means of promoting a rather different cause. The Poet Laureate clearly took the view that supernatural appearances were to be expected in Alfred's reign, but instead of Neot, or Cuthbert, we have a mysterious voice which first addressed the king from beneath a rock and then materialized in the form of a Druid bard. The bard reviewed the course of later English history, culminating with a stirring vision of King George III (bk III, lines 407–24). When we revert to the main theme, it is the combined forces of England, Wales, Scotland, and Ireland that gather together in order to repulse the Danes (bk IV, lines 717–35); and, after the triumph at Edington in 878, the bard returns with a prophetic vision of the unity of the British Isles (bk VI, lines 531–50), and of Alfred as first ruler of Britain (bk VI, lines 639–40). The point is, of course, that the poem marked not King Alfred's death but the Act of Union (1 January 1801), and the creation of the United Kingdom of Great Britain and Ireland. A third epic poem on Alfred, by John Fitchett, began to make its appearance in 1808. It is organized in 48 books, occupying a total of about 3000 pages or about 131,300 lines, making it approximately forty-one times longer than *Beowulf*. It must indeed be one of the longest poems in the English language, and might even qualify as the most unreadable. The incident of Alfred and the cakes can be located with some difficulty in book VII (lines 3148–70), and when the author died, in 1838, he was just approaching the battle of Edington, in book XLVII; at which point a friend took over, and brought the action swiftly to a close, in book XLVIII.[497] In 1813 Sir Walter Scott restrained himself with good reason from responding positively to the suggestion that he should write a poem about King Alfred.[498] Wordsworth

---

[494] *Gentleman's Mag.* 70 (1800), 975–6; but one suspects that the reviewer's tongue was firmly in his cheek.

[495] *Henry Crabb Robinson on Books and their Writers*, ed. E. J. Morley, 3 vols. (London, 1938) II, 663.

[496] H. J. Pye, *Alfred: an Epic Poem in Six Books* (London, 1801), republished in a different format (London, 1808). See also Miles, *King Alfred in Literature*, pp. 96–8.

[497] J. Fitchett, *King Alfred: a Poem*, ed. R. Roscoe, 6 vols. (London, 1841–2). It would appear from Roscoe's preface (I, viii) that a few copies of the first volume were privately printed, in 1808, only to be recalled afterwards by the author. See also Miles, *King Alfred in Literature*, pp. 104–6, and Stanley, 'The Glorification of King Alfred', p. 422.

[498] Letter from Sir Walter Scott to Richard Sainthill Jones, 12 March 1813, in *The Letters of Sir Walter Scott. III: 1811–1814*, ed. H. J. C. Grierson (London, 1932), pp. 234–5. I owe my knowledge of this letter to the kindness of Stewart Lyon.

was more effective with a short poem, composed in 1816 and first published in 1820, in which he juxtaposed 'A Fact' of Cnut failing to stem the tide and thereby demonstrating his powerlessness beside the power of God, with 'An Imagination' of Alfred consoling his men with the thought that while the tide was out they would have enough rest to allow their souls to press right on;[499] and his 'Ecclesiastical Sonnets', composed in 1821, include one on King Alfred, 'Lord of the harp and liberating spear'.[500] Richard Payne Knight's 'romance in rhyme' on Alfred, in twelve books (1823), bears little detectable relation to history, but the poet is not excluded by his flight of imagination from ending with sustained reflection on the late emperor Napoleon.[501] George Lewes Newnham Collingwood, FRS, on the other hand, was inspired by his reading of Sharon Turner's *History of the Anglo-Saxons* to produce an epic poem on Alfred in nine books (1836).[502] The poem deals, as usual, with the events of 878; and although the author was aware that the subject had been attempted by former writers, he justified his own contribution on the grounds that 'their success did not appear to be such as necessarily to preclude others from following the same track'.

The epic poems by Cottle, Pye, Fitchett, and others, represent a stage in Alfred's transition from the politicized legend of the eighteenth century into the more (but not exclusively) romanticized legend of the nineteenth, and perhaps we should not be surprised under these circumstances that he soon came to be regarded as a subject suitable for opera. The prose 'Lives' of King Alfred produced by von Haller and Bicknell in the 1770s were followed in 1815 by a 'Life' of Alfred by F. L. Graf zu Stolberg, based on Turner's *History of the Anglo-Saxons*;[503] so there would be no shortage of sources. Even so, it would be interesting to know, should anyone be minded to find out, precisely whence came the inspiration for the profusion of Alfredian libretti in the first half of the nineteenth century, and whether they possess any merit beyond a certain value as curiosities.[504] One of the earliest was that written by Theodore Körner in 1812, used many years later by Dvořák for the purposes of his first opera (1869–70).[505] Another was produced by Bartolomeo Merelli (1794–1879) in

---

[499] *The Poetical Works of William Wordsworth* IV, ed. E. de Selincourt and H. Darbishire (Oxford, 1947), 91–2.

[500] *Ibid.* III, ed. E. de Selincourt and H. Darbishire (Oxford, 1946), 354.   [501] R. P. Knight, *Alfred; a Romance in Rhyme* (London, 1823).

[502] G. L. Newnham Collingwood, *Alfred the Great: a Poem* (London, 1836).

[503] F. L. zu Stolberg, *Leben Alfred des Grossen, Königes in England* (Münster, 1815), 2nd ed. (Münster, 1836); with a portrait frontispiece derived from Vertue. See also Miles, *King Alfred in Literature*, pp. 118–19, and Stanley, 'The Glorification of Alfred', pp. 438–9.

[504] See also Stanley, 'The Glorification of King Alfred', p. 423, n. 47; Frank, *Search for the Anglo-Saxon Oral Poet*, p. 22, n. 63.

[505] J. Smaczny, '*Alfred*: Dvořák's First Operatic Endeavour Surveyed', *Jnl of the R. Musical Assoc.* 115 (1990), 80–106.

1820. A third, by Leone Tottola (d. 1831), enjoyed the distinction of being used by Donizetti, for an opera first performed in Naples on 2 July 1823. *Alfredo il Grande* is set in the Somerset marshes, and involves, besides Alfredo himself, Queen Amalia (soprano), General Edoardo (bass), a shepherd called Guglielmo (tenor), and a Viking general called Atkins (bass). Unfortunately, the opera appears to have been so utterly dreadful that the first performance proved also to be its last.[506] One might add that it is perhaps this general aspect of the cult of Alfred that should be invoked in order to account for the appearance in 1835 of a decidedly operatic vision of 'The Marriage of King Alfred the Great', by an Austrian painter called Sigmund Ferdinand von Perger (1778–1841).[507]

The rampant Alfredophilia of the early nineteenth century also encompasses the use of Alfred's name (and its associations) in the titles of several daily or weekly periodicals, both in London and in the west country,[508] and extends to the use of his name as a beacon of labour reform.[509] In 1800 (or thereabouts) the sculptor J. C. F. Rossi (1762–1839) was commissioned by the 11th Duke of Norfolk to produce a large stone relief showing 'King Alfred Instituting Trial by Jury on Salisbury Plain', installed at Arundel Castle.[510] Yet perhaps the most remarkable aspect of the cult of Alfred in this period is that in the 1820s he should have become part of the fabric of Buckingham Palace. Among designs made in 1826 by John Flaxman (1755–1826), for friezes to be placed on either side of the central bow on the Garden Front of the palace, were 'Alfred publishes his Laws', 'Alfred expelling the Danes', and 'King John signing Magna Carta'. George IV chose the two Alfredian themes; and although Flaxman died soon afterwards, his designs were developed by Richard Westmacott (1775–1856), and executed in 1827–8,[511] since when all garden parties at

---

[506] W. Ashbrook, *Donizetti and his Operas* (Cambridge, 1982), esp. pp. 292 ('There is little that mere music could do to introduce credibility into the unlikely meetings and furious confrontations that are liberally sprinkled through the tedious plot') and 537.

[507] The painting was sold at Sotheby's, 23 November 1988, Lot 481 (with illustration). I owe my knowledge of this item to Miss Jane Munro (Fitzwilliam Museum, Cambridge).

[508] E.g. *The Alfred and Westminster Evening Gazette*, continued as *The Alfred* (London, 1810–11); *The Alfred: West of England Jnl and General Advertiser* (Exeter, 1815–31); *The London Alfred, or The People's Recorder* (London, 1819); *The Alfred* (London, 1831–3). For further details, see Langenfelt, *Historic Origin of the Eight Hours Day*, pp. 119–22.

[509] On Alfred's contribution to labour legislation, see Langenfelt, *Historic Origin of the Eight Hours Day*, pp. 122–39, and Hill, 'The Norman Yoke', pp. 96–7 and 117.

[510] See J. M. Robinson, *Arundel Castle* (Chichester, 1995), pp. 28 and 35, with fig. 31. I am grateful to Dr Mark Goldie for drawing the sculpture to my attention.

[511] For the sculpture at Buckingham Palace, see J. M. Crook and M. H. Port, *The History of the King's Works*, VI: *1782–1851* (London, 1973), 263–302, at 298 and 301; and M. Busco, *Sir Richard Westmacott, Sculptor* (Cambridge, 1994), p. 58. Some of Flaxman's original designs were sold at Christie's, 24 March 1981, Lots 92–7, including 'King Alfred publishes his Laws' (Lot 96, with illustration). The friezes are just visible in J. Harris, *et al.*, *Buckingham Palace*, 2nd ed. (London, 1968), pp. 36–7.

The cult of King Alfred the Great

Buckingham Palace have been held in full view of King Alfred the Great. It so happens that the same Alfredian themes pervade James Sheridan Knowles's play, *Alfred the Great; or, The Patriot King*, written in the late 1820s, during the reign of George IV, but first performed and published in 1831, during the reign of his brother, William IV (1830–7).[512] The play was dedicated to the new king, described as 'a Patriot Monarch, destined, with the blessing of God, to restore the dilapidated fabric of his country's prosperity; and to rescue a devoted people from the ravages of the worst of invaders – CORRUPTION'. Alfred burns the cakes, and Christianity triumphs over paganism. The play ends dramatically as the king spares the central traitor from death at the hands of the mob, and institutes Trial by Jury in order to protect private rights from the exercise of arbitrary or corrupted power; at which point Guthrum remarks, quite decently under the circumstances, 'Blest are the heads that bow to sway like thine', whereupon Alfred, somewhat ungraciously, exhorts his countrymen to defend their country against all further invaders. The analogy between Alfred the Great and the Sailor King (or 'Silly Billy') was pursued in a different medium by the designer of a Sunderland mug, not in connection with their respective contributions to naval warfare, but in apparent connection with William's contribution to the passage of the Great Reform Act through Parliament in 1831–2. William was hailed on the mug as 'The only royal reformer since Alfred', perhaps causing many who drank from it to choke with surprise.[513]

King Alfred during the reign of Queen Victoria

It was during the long reign of Queen Victoria (1837–1901) that Alfred achieved his apotheosis. The presence of Prince Albert at Victoria's side, from 1840 until his death in 1861, and for some time in spirit thereafter, did Alfred's cause no harm. He was hailed as the founder of the Royal Navy, and even of the British Empire, as the father of English prose, and as the archetype of all heroic qualities. The view of Alfred inherited from the eighteenth-century histories, and now given a visual dimension, was soon absorbed into the kind of books which made the deepest impression at the most impressionable age. *Little Arthur's History of England*, by Maria Graham (later Lady Callcott), first appeared in 1835, and must have done as much as any other book, over the next hundred years or so, to familiarize households throughout the land with a picture of Alfred as every mother's dream and every boy's

---

[512] J. S. Knowles, *Alfred the Great; or, The Patriot King: An Historical Play* (London, 1831). For a synopsis of the plot, see Miles, *King Alfred in Literature*, pp. 80–5.
[513] For the mug, see L. Hallinan, *British Commemoratives: Royalty, Politics, War and Sport* (Woodbridge, 1995), p. 57, with pl. 97. Briggs (below, n. 576) alludes to a William IV plate bearing the king's head and the inscription 'The first radical monarch since Alfred'.

Simon Keynes

hero.[514] The multi-volume *Pictorial History of England*, which appeared in 1837–44, combined drawings of artifacts, and pages from decorated manuscripts, with a range of images derived from history-paintings of the late eighteenth century.[515] Whether intentionally or not, the association had the interesting effect of transferring authenticity from the genuine artifacts to the imaginary images. Works of this kind were soon mocked by Thackeray, in *Punch*, in a way which left Alfred exposed as one 'so good, and so wise, and so gentle, and so brave' that one could 'only love and honour his memory'.[516]

The Westminster competitions

Painters and sculptors of the early Victorian age continued to draw inspiration from the stories of Alfred's reign, even if the predictability of the subject-matter exposed a certain lack of imagination on their part.[517] The artist Richard Dadd (1817–86), like Blake before him, sought to establish his credentials at an early stage in his career by demonstrating his skill in history painting, still regarded as a higher form of art. In 1840 he exhibited a painting entitled 'Alfred the Great in disguise of a peasant, reflecting on the misfortunes of his country', at the Royal Academy; and in the same year he exhibited a painting entitled 'Elgiva the queen of Edwy in banishment', at Manchester.[518] The painting of Alfred, in particular, was well regarded, giving promise in the opinion of one reviewer 'that the artist will attain a high rank in his profession';[519] so it is not only the particular quality of Dadd's later work, produced under such tragic circumstances,[520] which makes one regret that his early 'Anglo-Saxon' history paintings are now untraced. The fact remained, however, that history painting needed sustained public patronage if it was ever to prosper.

---

[514] [M. Graham], *Little Arthur's History of England*, 2 vols. (London, 1835) I, 46–55, with a woodcut of the young Alfred at his mother's knee (p. 48); repr. many times, and reissued in a Century Edition in 1936. Richmal Mangnall's *Historical and Miscellaneous Questions for the Use of Young People* (1798) was also influential at the same level throughout the first half of the nineteenth century.

[515] G. L. Craik and C. Macfarlane, *The Pictorial History of England, being a History of the People, as well as a History of the Kingdom*, 6 vols. (London, 1841) I.i, 138–356, covering the period 449–1066.

[516] 'Miss Tickletoby's Lectures on English History', *Punch* 3 (1842), 29–30, repr. in W. M. Thackeray, *Miscellaneous Essays, Sketches and Reviews and Contributions to "Punch"* (London, 1886), pp. 367–416, at 379–81. The lectures continue with some pastiche in the form of poems on Æthelred and Cnut.

[517] For 'Anglo-Saxon', and specifically Alfredian, subjects in Victorian history painting, see Strong, *The Victorian Painter and British History*, pp. 114–18 and 155–7.

[518] P. Allderidge, *The Late Richard Dadd 1817–1886*, Exhibition Catalogue (London, 1974), pp. 16 and 54 (nos. 36 and 40).

[519] *The Art-Union* 2 (1840), 77; see also *ibid.* 5 (1843), 267–71.

[520] Dadd showed first signs of mental illness while travelling abroad in 1842, and killed his father soon after his return to England in 1843; whereupon he was certified insane, and passed the remainder of his life at Bethlem Hospital in London and at Broadmoor Hospital in Berkshire.

The cult of King Alfred the Great

On 16 October 1834 a fire which had started accidentally in the stoves of the House of Lords became the conflagration which led to the destruction of both Houses of Parliament at Westminster. In 1841, when the building of Sir Charles Barry's New Palace of Westminster was already under way, a select committee was appointed to consider matters of internal decoration.[521] The successive Reports of the Commissioners on Fine Arts, contained in the *Parliamentary Papers* from 1842 onwards, show in absorbing detail how they set about the task, and afford a view of the important place which 'historical' decoration of one kind and another was to have in their scheme. The first competition, announced in 1842, was for large 'cartoons' or drawings in chalk or charcoal, without colour, intended as preparatory designs for frescoes to be applied when the walls of the new building were ready to receive them.[522] Each artist was 'at liberty to select his subject from British history, or from the works of Spenser, Shakespeare, or Milton'; figures were to be not less than life-size; and there were to be nine prizes, of £300, £200, and £100. 140 cartoons were exhibited in Westminster Hall in the summer of 1843, of which 75 were 'historical', quite evenly distributed between the Roman (20), Anglo-Saxon (20) and medieval or early modern periods (35).[523] Of the 'Anglo-Saxon' subjects, no fewer than eleven concerned the conversion of the English to Christianity; of the rest, five were Alfredian,[524] two dealt with aspects of the burial of King Harold, and Edward the Martyr and Cnut could claim one apiece. Three of the eleven main prizes (increased from nine) went to cartoons on Anglo-Saxon subjects, which were thus among those published soon afterwards in the form of large lithographs:[525] one of three

---

[521] For the new building, see Crook and Port, *History of the King's Works* VI, 573–626, and T. S. R. Boase, 'The Decoration of the New Palace of Westminster, 1841–1863', *Jnl of the Warburg and Courtauld Institutes* 17 (1954), 319–58. See also *The Houses of Parliament*, ed. M. H. Port (New Haven, CT, 1976), pp. 238, 240 (sculptures of Saxon kings) and 268–81 (painting); and *Works of Art in the House of Lords*, ed. M. Bond (London, 1980).

[522] '[First] Report of the Commissioners on the Fine Arts', in *Parliamentary Papers* [hereafter *PP*] 1842 xxv, at 7.

[523] For the cartoons exhibited in 1843, see H. G. Clarke, *A Hand-Book Guide to the Cartoons now Exhibiting in Westminster Hall* (London, 1843), and *The Book of Art: Cartoons, Frescoes, Sculpture and Decorative Art, as Applied to the New Houses of Parliament*, ed. F. K. Hunt (London, 1846), pp. 79–112. For a review of the exhibition, see *The Art-Union* 5 (1843), 207–12; and for a depiction of the scene, see R. Strong, *The Spirit of Britain: a Narrative History of the Arts* (London, 1999), p. 555.

[524] Nos. 83 ([?], 'Alfred in the camp of the Danes'), 102 (James and George Foggo, 'Alfred the Great generously releases the wife and children of Hastings, the Danish invader', 103 (Marshall Claxton, 'Alfred in the camp of the Danes'), 104 (John Bridges, 'Alfred the Great submitting his code of laws for the approval of the witan'), and 105 (C. W. Cope, 'The first trial by jury').

[525] Reduced drawings of the original cartoons were made by John, James and William Linnell, engraved on stone, and published by Longman in *The Prize Cartoons; being the Eleven Designs to which the Premiums were Awarded by the Royal Commissioners on the Fine Arts in the Year 1843* (London, 1847), dedicated to the commissioners as 'the first fruits of their exertions to develop a high branch of art hitherto uncultivated in this country'.

Simon Keynes

prizes of £300 was awarded to Charles West Cope (1811–90) for 'The first trial by jury' (pl. XIII*b*);[526] one of three prizes of £200 was awarded to John Callcott Horsley (1817–1903) for 'St Augustine preaching to Ethelbert and Bertha'; and one of five prizes of £100 was awarded to John Bridges for 'Alfred submitting his code of laws for the approval of the witan' (pl. XIV*a*).[527] One of ten supplementary 'rewards' was given to Marshall Claxton (1813–68), for 'Alfred in the camp of the Danes' (pl. XIV*b*).[528] A second competition, for cartoons (on the same conditions as before) or for frescoes (on subjects of the artists' choice), and also for works in sculpture and other media, was announced in 1843.[529] The resulting exhibition took place at Westminster Hall in 1844.[530] Among the 84 pictures exhibited, we find four on Alfredian themes,[531] and otherwise, among the Anglo-Saxon subjects, only Queen Bertha, King Cnut, and Harold;[532] the sculptures included three of King Alfred, in suitably parliamentary mode.[533] A third competition, announced in 1844, was in respect of projected frescoes for six arched compartments in the House of Lords (with 'The Baptism of Ethelbert' among the specified subjects), and for statues of eminent legislators from Alfred onwards.[534] The various works of art were exhibited at Westminster Hall in 1845, and would appear to have included at least three statuettes of

---

[526] BM, P&D, 1854-12-11-135. Reproduced from the lithograph in A. G. Temple, *England's History as Pictured by Famous Painters* (London, 1896–7), p. 17; see also Boase, 'New Palace of Westminster', p. 328 and pl. 46c. A lithograph of the cartoon, engraved by H. S. Sadd, was published by Fishel, Adler & Schwartz, 373 Fifth Avenue, New York (BM, P&D, 1912-10-14-276).

[527] BM, P&D, 1854-12-11-142. Reproduced from the lithograph in Temple, *England's History as Pictured by Famous Painters*, p. 31. For a description of the composition, identifying the figures (including Grimbald, Asser, and others), see *The Book of Art*, ed. Hunt, p. 104.

[528] Claxton's 'Alfred in the Camp of the Danes, A.D. 880' (BM, P&D, 1852-6-12-421) was one of a set of smaller lithographs of the ten additional prize-winning cartoons, made by Frank Howard and published by T. McClean. It is described in this form as 'Prize Cartoon no. 103', being its number in the exhibition in 1843 (above, n. 524).

[529] 'Second Report of the Commissioners on the Fine Arts', in *PP* 1843 xxix, at 70.

[530] For the various items exhibited in 1844, see H. G. Clarke, *A Hand-Book Guide to the Cartoons, Frescoes, and Sculpture . . . now Exhibiting in Westminster Hall* (London, 1844), and *The Book of Art*, ed. Hunt, pp. 114–47. For a (scathing) review of the exhibition, see *The Art-Union* 6 (1844), 211–19; see also *ibid.* p. 293, for its popularity.

[531] Nos. 27 (Alexander Christie, 'Alfred the Great'), 35–6 (Harold John Stanley, 'Alfred compiling his laws, assisted by his friend Asser'), 50 (Henry C. Selous, 'Alfred submitting his code of laws to the wittena-gemot'), 59 (Marshall Claxton, 'The Building of Oxford University').

[532] John Martin's 'The Trial of Canute' was suggested by a passage in Turner, *History of the Anglo-Saxons* II, 293. For his painting of Cnut and the waves, see above, n. 323.

[533] Nos. 117 (Frederick S. Archer, 'Alfred the Great with the Book of Common Law'), 120 (James Sherwood Westmacott, 'Alfred the Great') and 173 (Edward B. Stephens, 'Alfred the Great propounding his Code of Laws'). Of these, Westmacott's was very highly praised (*The Art-Union* 6 (1844), 215), and Stephens's is illustrated in *The Book of Art*, ed. Hunt, p. 140; see also below, nn. 535 and 560.

[534] 'Third Report of the Commissioners on the Fine Arts', in *PP* 1844 xxxi, at 9 and 25.

The cult of King Alfred the Great

Alfred.[535] In 1845 the Commissioners published an interesting list of persons 'to whose memory statues might with propriety be erected in or adjoining the New Houses of Parliament', comprising an A-list (on which the commissioners were unanimous) and a B-list (on which they were not); the only Anglo-Saxons on the A-list were Bede and Alfred, and the only monarchs on the A-list were Alfred and Elizabeth.[536] A fourth competition, first announced in 1844 (for 1846), but then again in 1845 and in 1846 (for 1847), was for oil-paintings on any subject in religion, history, or poetry, with nine prizes of £500, £300, and £200; it was understood that paintings could be purchased by the nation for the decoration of unspecified rooms or apartments in the Palace at Westminster.[537] The exhibition, held at Westminster Hall in 1847, comprised 123 paintings, on a wide variety of different subjects.[538] Of seven 'Anglo-Saxon' pictures, three were Alfredian: Alexander Blaikley reverted to 'King Alfred the Great dividing his loaf with the beggar', dismissed by a critic as 'the most unfortunate version of this subject we have ever seen'; W. Philip Salter tried his hand at 'Queen Judith and the children of Ethelwulph' (i.e. the poetry competition), said to be 'faulty in treatment';[539] and G. F. Watts (1817–1904) won a £500 prize with his suitably jingoistic and highly acclaimed 'Alfred inciting the English to resist the Danes'.[540] In their Report for 1847, the commissioners announced elaborate plans for paintings on a range of specified 'historical' subjects considered suitable for the decoration of particular rooms throughout the palace of Westminster.[541]

---

[535] For the various items exhibited in 1845, see *The Book of Art*, ed. Hunt, pp. 169–89. For a review of the exhibition, see *The Art-Union* 7 (1845), 103–4 (sculpture) and 253–9 (cartoons). The statuettes of Alfred exhibited in 1845 were by James Sherwood Westmacott, Edward B. Stephens ('Alfred the Great as Legislator'), and John Henning; those by Westmacott and Stephens had been exhibited in 1844. See Gunnis, *Dictionary of British Sculptors*, pp. 198, 372 and 422.

[536] 'Fourth Report of the Commissioners on the Fine Arts', in *PP* 1845 xxvii, at 9. To judge from further sections of the same report, the commissioners had it in mind to accord Alfred a special place in the central Hall at Westminster.

[537] 'Third Report', p. 10; 'Fourth Report', pp. 16–17; also announced in the 'Fifth Report of the Commissioners on the Fine Arts', and in the 'Sixth Report of the Commissioners on the Fine Arts', in *PP* 1846 xxiv.

[538] For a review of the exhibition of paintings in 1847, incorporating a complete list of the 123 exhibited entrants, see *The Art-Union* 9 (1847), 265–72; and *ibid.* pp. 334 and 361, for the great success of the exhibition.

[539] For another Alfredian picture by Salter, see below, p. 338.

[540] For Watts's painting, which still hangs at Westminster, see T. Archer, *Pictures from Royal Portraits Illustrative of English and Scottish History* (London, 1878); Temple, *England's History as Pictured by Famous Painters*, p. 26; Boase, 'New Palace of Westminster', pp. 342–3 and 354; and esp. Strong, *The Victorian Painter and British History*, pp. 114–15 (fig. 131). For the prizes, see 'Seventh Report of the Commissioners on the Fine Arts', in *PP* 1847 xxxiii, at 19.

[541] 'Seventh Report of the Commissioners on the Fine Arts', in *PP* 1847 xxxiii, at 9–15. See also Boase, 'New Palace of Westminster', pp. 341–2. Cf. T. J. Gullick, *A Descriptive Handbook for the National Pictures in the Westminster Palace* (London, 1865).

'Anglo-Saxon' subjects feature in connection with St Stephen's Hall (a sitting of the witan, a trial by jury, and the conversion of the English to Christianity), the Central Corridor (English slave-boys on the market at Rome), the Royal Gallery (Alfred in the Danish camp, Edith finding Harold's body), the Lobby of the Guard Room (martyrdom of St Edmund), and the Norman Porch (Cnut reproving his courtiers, with the motto 'Nemo Dominus nisi Deus'). Daniel Maclise (1806–70) was moved to prepare a cartoon on the theme of Alfred in the Danish camp; and although nothing came of it at Westminster, he soon afterwards produced a vast painting of the same subject ('Alfred, the Saxon king, disguised as a minstrel, in the tent of Guthrum the Dane'), first exhibited at the Royal Academy in 1852.[542] John Callcott Horsley, who had been a prize-winner in 1843, seems to have tried his luck again with a pair of Alfredian paintings submitted for a decorative scheme at Westminster in 1851. One, entitled 'The boyhood of Alfred', shows a young Alfred listening attentively to a bard in full flow, and the other, entitled 'A model for Alfred's navy', shows him approving the model of a ship which he had designed in a seemingly anachronistic moment.[543]

It is not clear whether the nation's legislators would have felt inspired or overwhelmed by the presence of so much history painting in the Palace of Westminster, had all the schemes been implemented as first intended. Whatever the case, the competitions held in the 1840s created new opportunities for artists to display their pretensions and their talents in High Art, and at the same time generated much public interest in and awareness of the great moments in the nation's history. The Art-Union of London held its own competition in 1844 for 'an original picture illustrative of British History'. The main prize of £500 was won by H. C. Selous, for a later medieval subject; but among seven others deemed worthy of commendation to the public (out of a total of 28 entrants), we find G. Scharf's '"Non Angli sed Angeli"', W. B. Scott's 'Saxon alms-giving' (set in Alfred's time),[544] and W. P. Salter's 'Alfred, surrounded by his family, addresses Edward his son and successor', all of which are included in a set of lithographs published in 1847.[545] Anglo-Saxon, and particularly

---

[542] Royal Academy 1852 (122), now in the Laing Art Gallery, Newcastle-upon-Tyne. See R. Ormond, *Daniel Maclise (1806–1870)* (London, 1972), pp. 97–8 (no. 102), and Strong, *The Victorian Painter and British History*, p. 117 (fig. 135). The cartoon is at Stamford High School.
[543] Sotheby's sale, 6 Nov. 1991, Lot 219.   [544] British Institution 1848 (335), 5 ft 8 in by 7 ft 0 in.
[545] Art-Union of London, *Seven Designs in Outline, Reproduced from Cartoons Submitted in Competition for the Premium of Five Hundred Pounds Offered by the Society for an Historical Picture* (London, 1847), and *Gleanings from History, Illustrative of the Engravings Issued by the Art-Union of London, in 1847*, ed. J. Steward (London, 1847); cf. the strangely hostile remarks in *The Art-Union* 8 (1846), 92. The subject of Salter's cartoon was suggested by a passage in Turner, *History of the Anglo-Saxons* II, 105–6 (from the so-called 'Proverbs of Alfred'). For the wider context of this and other Art-Union competitions, see L. S. King, *The Industrialization of Taste: Victorian England and the Art Union of London* (Ann Arbor, MI, 1985), pp. 72–7.

Alfredian, subjects continued to make regular appearances in the public exhibitions, and doubtless in many other contexts as well. The saddest tale is that of the distinguished but more elderly historical painter, Benjamin Robert Haydon (1786–1846).[546] After a career dogged with penury and frustration, Haydon had been deeply disappointed in 1843 not to win one of the prizes at Westminster,[547] and resolved in November 1844 to produce a series of six huge paintings illustrating 'the best governments for mankind', based on a scheme which he had proposed many years before for the decoration of the House of Lords.[548] The first two canvases in the series were put on public exhibition in April 1846, but were unable to compete with the rival attraction of the famous dwarf, General Tom Thumb; and on 22 June 1846, while working on the third painting in the series ('Alfred and his First Trial by Jury'), Haydon took his own life.[549] The unfinished painting, splashed with Haydon's blood, fetched £8 18s 6d at the sale of Haydon's effects in March 1852.[550]

Most (though not all) of the other painters who turned to Alfred for inspiration in the central decades of the nineteenth century are barely more than names, and could not even begin to compete with Haydon as committed exponents of the High Art of history painting. The tradition of Alfred and the cakes was represented by J. Pain Davis, 'King Alfred in the Neatherd's Cottage' (1842),[551] and H. Warren, 'King Alfred in the Swineherd's Cottage' (1846).[552] The tradition of Alfred and the pilgrim was represented by Alexander Chisholm, 'King Alfred parting his remaining loaf with a poor pilgrim' (1841),[553] William Simson, 'Alfred the Great giving a portion of his last loaf to the pilgrim' (1842),[554] and William Cave Thomas, 'Alfred giving a portion of his

---

[546] E. George, *The Life and Death of Benjamin Robert Haydon, Historical Painter, 1786–1846*, 2nd ed. (Oxford, 1967); O. Clarke, *Benjamin Robert Haydon, Historical Painter* (Athens, GA, 1952); D. B. Brown, *et al.*, *Benjamin Robert Haydon, 1786–1846: Painter and Writer, Friend of Wordsworth and Keats*, Exhibition Catalogue (Grasmere, 1996). The major primary sources are *The Diary of Benjamin Robert Haydon*, ed. W. B. Pope, 5 vols. (Cambridge, MA, 1960–3), and F. W. Haydon, *Benjamin Robert Haydon: Correspondence and Table-Talk*, 2 vols. (London, 1876).

[547] George, *Haydon*, pp. 263–78; *Diary*, ed. Pope, V, 293–308; Haydon, *Correspondence* I, 218–24, and II, 57–8 (letter to Wordsworth).

[548] *Diary*, ed. Pope, III, 326–7 (the scheme in 1828, including 'Blessings of Law (Alfred establishing Trial by Jury)', and V, 399 and 405–6 (inception of the new series in 1844). See also George, *Haydon*, pp. 274–5, 280 and 282–3.

[549] *Diary*, ed. Pope, V, 516–51 (working on Alfred) and 553 (suicide); Haydon, *Correspondence and Table-Talk* I, 465 (advice on AS architecture), 467 (letter to his son, 4 May 1846, enclosing a sketch of 'Alfred'), and 230–7 (last days). Haydon's study for the head of Alfred, dated 1846, was sold at Sotheby's, 19 Nov. 1981, Lot 44. See also A. Hayter, *A Sultry Month: Scenes of London Literary Life in 1846* (London, 1965), pp. 80–1 and 108–10.   [550] George, *Haydon*, p. 392.

[551] British Institution 1842 (153), 6 ft 4 in by 6 ft 10 in.

[552] The picture was exhibited at the New Society of Watercolours and engraved in the *Illustrated London News*, 30 May 1846, p. 349.   [553] British Institution 1841 (158), 4 ft 6 in by 5 ft 5 in.

[554] Royal Academy 1842 (491); British Institution 1844 (60), 4 ft 6 in by 5 ft 4 in.

last loaf to the pilgrim' (1850).[555] The tradition of Alfred and his (step) mother was represented by Solomon Alexander Hart, 'Alfred the Great when a youth, encouraged by the Queen, listening to the heroic lay of a minstrel' (1836),[556] Alfred Stevens, 'King Alfred and his Mother' (*c.* 1848),[557] and Thomas Thorneycroft, 'Alfred the Great encouraged to the pursuit of learning by his mother' (1850).[558] And there was perhaps a new interest in Alfred as patron of learning, represented by John Gilbert, 'King Alfred the Great teaching the Anglo-Saxon youth' (1855).[559] Edward Bowring Stephens, who was among those who had produced statuettes of Alfred as legislator for the Westminster competitions in the mid-1840s, made another figure of the king in the early 1860s, showing the national icon in his more homely and approachable state.[560]

Although they proved popular with the public, the history paintings exhibited at the Royal Academy, at the British Institution, and in Westminster Hall attracted ridicule from the *cognoscenti*; and so it came about that the popularity of Alfredian art in the 1840s and 1850s helped only to accelerate the tendency for Alfred himself to be regarded (albeit affectionately) as a figure of fun. The competitions were mocked in the pages of *Punch*,[561] and their iconography soon entered into the standard imagery of political cartoonists.[562] In Thackeray's novel *The Newcomes* (published in 1853–5), Colonel Newcome and his son Clive encounter 'the eminent Mr Gandish, of Soho', an artist, whose exposition of the principles of "igh art' (in other words of history painting) extends to an explanation of his own painting of King Alfred burning the cakes:

You know the anecdote, Colonel? King Alfred, flying from the Danes, took refuge in a neat-'erd's 'ut. The rustic's wife told him to bake a cake, and the fugitive sovereign set

---

[555] Royal Academy 1850 (451). [556] British Institution 1836 (37), 5 ft by 4 ft 2 in.
[557] K. R. Towndrow, *The Works of Alfred Stevens in the Tate Gallery* (London, 1950), p. 67 (no. 72); Strong, *The Victorian Painter and British History*, p. 117 (fig. 134).
[558] Royal Academy 1850 (1299).
[559] The picture was engraved in the *Illustrated London News*, 30 June 1855, Supplement, p. 657, accompanied by a poem, by E. L. Hervey, in which Alfred exhorts the children to good deeds.
[560] 'Alfred the Great in the neatherd's cottage' was exhibited at the Royal Academy in 1863 (1060), and took its place in the Mansion House, London; see T. Beaumont James, *English Heritage Book of Winchester* (London, 1997), p. 43 (fig. 20). Other statuettes of Alfred were exhibited at the Academy in 1859 (by H. Armstead) and 1863 (by D. D. Ducker).
[561] E.g. *Punch* 5 (1843), 22, etc.; *ibid*. 13 (1847), 8–9 (W. M. Thackeray, *Travels in London . . . and other Contributions to Punch*, Harry Furniss Centenary Edition (London, 1911), pp. 280–5), with allusion to the prize-winning paintings by Pickersgill (burial of King Harold) and Watts (Alfred and the Danes), and with reference to a projected painting of Alfred and the cakes. For comment on the predictability of subjects exhibited at the Royal Academy, see *Punch* 34 (1858), 209. For the treatment of the art exhibitions in *Punch*, see also R. D. Altick, *Punch: The Lively Youth of a British Institution 1841–1851* (Columbus, OH, 1997), pp. 668–89, esp. 674–6.
[562] E.g. *Punch* 14 (1848), 201 (parody of Cnut and the waves); *ibid*. 15 (1848), 121 (parody of Alfred in the Danish camp); *ibid*. 43 (1862), 230–1 ('Ballad of King Alfred and the Grecian Cakes') and 239 ('Alfred the Little and Alfred the Great').

down to his ignoble task, and forgetting it in the cares of state, let the cake burn, on which the woman struck him. The moment chose is when she is lifting her 'and to deliver the blow. The King receives it with majesty mingled with meekness. In the background the door of the 'ut is open, letting in the royal officers to announce the Danes are defeated. The daylight breaks in at the aperture, signifying the dawning of 'Ope. That story, sir, which I found in my researches in 'ist'ry, has since become so popular, sir, that hundreds of artists have painted it, hundreds![563]

Mr Gandish asks rhetorically 'why is my "Alfred" 'anging up in this 'all?', and provides the answer himself: 'because there is no patronage for a man who devotes himself to 'igh art'. In one of Thackeray's shorter stories we meet 'George Rumbold, the historical painter', who like Mr Gandish inhabited the world which Haydon had left. Rumbold painted 'a picture of "Alfred in the Neatherd's Cottage", seventy-two feet by forty-eight', and in order to convey an idea of the size of the picture the narrator adds 'that the mere muffin, of which the outcast king is spoiling the baking, is two feet three in diameter'.[564] Noone in all seriousness would be able to depict the burning of the cakes again.

From one millennium to another (1849–1901)

Alfred continued to profit during Victoria's reign from his identification as the *fons et origo* of political stability in England, as distinct from the upheavals taking place elsewhere. In the opening months of 1848 (known on the Continent as the 'Year of Revolutions'), outbreaks of civil unrest had led to the establishment of the German National Assembly, which in the event lasted for barely a year.[565] Sympathy for the democratic principles which underlay the movement was, however, tempered in the minds of many contemporary observers with nervousness about what it might entail; and some looked to King Alfred as the personification of a typically English form of compromise. Reinhold Pauli's 'Life of King Alfred', published first in German (1851) and then in English translation (1852), might be regarded as the second 'modern' biography of the king (after Spelman, leaving aside von Haller and Bicknell).[566] It is certainly a work of serious scholarship, produced in 1848–50 while Pauli was based in Oxford and London; and it is distinguished not least for its assertion of faith in

---

[563] W. M. Thackeray, *The Newcomes: Memoirs of a Most Respectable Family*, ed. A. Pendennis, Harry Furniss Centenary Edition (London, 1911), pp. 181–90; ed. A. Sanders, World's Classics (Oxford, 1995), p. 221.

[564] 'Our Street' [1848], in *The Works of William Makepeace Thackeray*, XII: *The Christmas Books of Mr. M. A. Titmarsh* (London, 1872), at pp. 53–4; W. M. Thackeray, *Christmas Books*, Harry Furniss Centenary Edition (London, 1911), pp. 75–139, at 92.

[565] See J. Sperber, *The European Revolutions, 1848–1851* (Cambridge, 1994).

[566] R. Pauli, *König Aelfred und seine Stelle in der Geschichte Englands* (Berlin, 1851); R. Pauli, *The Life of King Alfred*, ed. T. Wright (London, 1852). See also [D.], 'Alfred and his Place in the History of England', *Gentleman's Mag.* ns 37 (1852), 115–20.

the authenticity of Asser's 'Life', in response to the doubts first raised in the early 1840s by Thomas Wright.[567] Yet as Pauli states in his preface, he had planned his work at Oxford 'in the November of the eventful year 1848, at a time when all German hearts trembled, as they had seldom done before, for the safety of their Fatherland; and, more especially, for the preservation of that particular state which Providence has chosen to be the defence and safeguard of Germany'; and he wrote his book 'principally for Germans'. In 1849 Francis Steinitz produced a translation of von Haller's 'Life of King Alfred' (originally published in 1773), stating in his preface that it had been written 'at a time when liberty and the wish for a constitutional form of government began to dawn in France and Germany' (and adding that it was one of many works which might have hastened the French revolution), so that Alfred could again take his place as a symbol of the most stable kind of political order ('moderate monarchy', as opposed to absolute monarchy, moderate republic, or democracy).[568] In England itself, John Mitchell Kemble was able to rise with the Anglo-Saxons above the gathering storm:

> On every side of us thrones totter, and the deep foundations of society are convulsed. Shot and shell sweep the capitals which have long been pointed out as the chosen abodes of order: cavalry and bayonets cannot control populations whose loyalty has become a proverb here, whose peace has been made a reproach to our own miscalled disquiet. Yet the exalted Lady who wields the sceptre of these realms, sits safe upon her throne, and fearless in the holy circle of her domestic happiness, secure in the affections of a people whose institutions have given to them all the blessings of an equal law.[569]

Kemble dedicated *The Saxons in England* to Queen Victoria, advertising it as a history 'of the principles which have given her empire its preeminence among the nations of Europe'.

There was, however, nothing like an anniversary to provide an excuse for further celebration of the king, and also an opportunity for self-aggrandizement on the part of any self-appointed organiser of the festivities. In July 1849 the renowned Victorian philosopher, Martin F. Tupper (1810–89), conceived the idea, in the dining-room of a friend's house in Soho Square, of commemorating King Alfred's one thousandth birthday.[570] The origin, inwardness, progress, and

---

[567] T. Wright, *Biographia Britannica Literaria: or Biography of Literary Characters of Great Britain and Ireland*, 2 vols. (London, 1842–6) I, 405–13. Cf. Pauli, *Life of Alfred*, pp. 6–18, and *Asser's 'Life of King Alfred'*, ed. Stevenson, pp. xcvi–cx.

[568] F. Steinitz, *The Moderate Monarchy, or Principles of the British Constitution, Described in a Narrative of the Life and Maxims of Alfred the Great and his Counsellors* (London, 1849). The double-page frontispiece juxtaposes a sub-Vertuesque portrait of Alfred, sporting sceptre, orb, and Alfred Jewel, with a portrait of Queen Victoria enthroned.

[569] J. M. Kemble, *The Saxons in England*, 2 vols. (London, 1849) I, v.

[570] See D. Hudson, *Martin Tupper: his Rise and Fall* (London, 1949), pp. 90–7; see also K. Philip, *Victorian Wantage* (Wantage, 1968), pp. 112–14.

aftermath of the celebrations at Wantage in October 1849 can be reconstructed in extraordinary detail from a scrapbook containing all correspondence and other documentation relating to the event, put together by Tupper himself and now preserved with the rest of his literary effects in the Research and Reference Center of the University Library of the University of Illinois at Urbana-Champaign.[571] It is a story which deserves to be told in full, as that of a man committed with all his heart to the Alfredian legend in all its glory, yet unable for whatever reason to secure much public support for a grandiose scheme; and it would need at the same time to be told in relation to the later and more successful festivities in 1878 and 1901.[572] In brief, however, it seems that Tupper circulated a printed prospectus to selected persons, encouraging them to participate; that he met with little support from the great and the good of the land, most of whom seem to have had more pressing engagements; that on 7 September 1849 he despatched a long, passionate and deeply patriotic letter on the subject of King Alfred to the Editor of *The Times*, which was not published ('Was this a letter to be rejected?', he scrawled across the top of his draft); and that he was forced to rely thereafter on a poster-campaign.[573] For their part, the

---

[571] Research and Reference Center, Library of the University of Illinois at Urbana-Champaign, x828/T8391, Album 14. I am grateful to Mrs Shirley Corke for drawing my attention in 1985 to the papers of Derek Hudson in the Guildford Muniment Room, Guildford, accumulated while writing his book on Martin Tupper, and for sending me a copy of the poster mentioned below; to Dr Nigel Ramsay for urging me to read Hudson's book; to the staff of the Guildford Muniment Room for steering me towards the Tupper archive in its present location; and to Derek Hudson himself (letter, 25 April 1998) for some further information.

[572] I am grateful to Dr Boyd Hilton for alerting me to the wider historical contexts which would make the subject more interesting, and which at the same time put it beyond my own reach.

[573] The wording of the poster will suffice to give a flavour of the event: 'To all good men & true, of Wantage and its neighbourhood. A great and unprecedented honour is thrust upon you: on Thursday, the 25th [October], will be commemorated, in his native town, KING ALFRED'S 1000th BIRTHDAY. From all parts of England your countrymen, together with some foreigners and American kinsmen, are expected to Flock to this Patriotic Celebration: and you need not be reminded how kindly, nor how warmly you will welcome the Guests who seek out WANTAGE on so happy an occasion. KING ALFRED is known to all the world as, perhaps, the Greatest Man, – Certainly the Best King, – that ever lived; and in his Institutions, Character, and Fame [he] is still and ever immortal amongst us. ... It is recommended to the Inhabitants of WANTAGE, that, in honour of their ILLUSTRIOUS TOWNSMAN, they decorate their streets and houses with flags, oak boughs, and such other tokens of patriotic feeling as they can muster; also, that they wear their holiday apparel, and the ALFRED MEDAL; – quantities of which, at a very cheap cost, will be in the town on Wednesday. ... Men of Berkshire, of all grades! you will not be wanting to yourselves on so glorious an occasion.' The poster is reproduced in Hudson, *Tupper*, front endpaper. In addition to reports published in newspapers, there is a revealing account of the proceedings in the Wantage Parish Diaries (Reading, Berkshire Record Office, D/P148/28), ed. A. J. Verdin, Berkshire Record Soc. (forthcoming); I am grateful to Lisa Spurrier (Archivist, Berks. R.O.) for her assistance in this connection.

townspeople of Wantage responded magnificently to Tupper's call, and paraded through the town on the appointed day singing the 'Alfred Jubilee Song' ('Alfred for ever! – to-day was He born, Day-star of England to herald her morn', etc.). It was Tupper who designed the commemorative medal;[574] his album contains a drawing of 'The Alfred Memorial' (designed by an architect called George Adam Burn), which never got any further; and it was he, ably assisted by the Revd Dr J. A. Giles, who masterminded the production of the 'Jubilee Edition' of *The Whole Works of King Alfred the Great* (1852), respectfully dedicated to Her Majesty the Queen.[575]

The sheer volume of Alfrediana produced in the second half of the nineteenth century, whether in the form of history, drama, literature, or book-illustration, is overwhelming, and testimony (as if any were needed) to the acceptance of Alfred as an integral part of the national myth. Some still preferred to write of Arthur, not Alfred, perhaps for the simple reason that the stories were much better, but there were many others who helped to maintain Alfred's profile with a relentless flow of words.[576] James E. Doyle's *Chronicle of England B.C. 55 – A.D. 1485* (1864) provided a conventional account of the king, and introduced some new images.[577] The public could otherwise rely on Edward Augustus Freeman (1823–92) to articulate the view of the professional historian.

'Alfred is the most perfect character in history . . . No other man on record has ever so thoroughly united all the virtues both of the ruler and of the private man. In no other man on record were so many virtues disfigured by so little alloy. A saint without superstition, a scholar without ostentation, a warrior all whose wars were fought in the defence of his country, a conqueror whose laurels were never stained by cruelty, a prince never

---

[574] L. Brown, *A Catalogue of British Historical Medals 1837–1901* (London, 1987), p. 141 (nos. 2344–5).

[575] J. A. Giles, ed., *The Whole Works of King Alfred the Great*, 2 vols. (Oxford and Cambridge, 1852). Those privileged to dine on 25 October 1849 at the Alfred's Head, in Wantage, under the chairmanship of Charles Eyston, Esq. ('a true English gentleman and both in heart and name a thorough Anglo-Saxon'), resolved on that occasion to bring forth the Jubilee Edition of Alfred's works, 'to be edited by the most competent Anglo-Saxon scholars who might be willing to combine for such a purpose' (Preface, pp. ix–x).

[576] The electronic or printed catalogues of the British Library give a good impression of the amount and variety of material on Alfred generated in the second half of the nineteenth century. The material in A. Hawkshaw, *Sonnets on Anglo-Saxon History* (London, 1854), pp. 96–105 and 117, gives expression to the usual sentiments. And for the lack of attention paid to the anniversary of the battle of Hastings, in 1866, which may have reflected a certain respect for the Anglo-Saxon past, see A. Briggs, 'Saxons, Normans and Victorians' [1966], repr. in *The Collected Essays of Asa Briggs*, 3 vols. (Brighton, 1985) II, 215–35.

[577] J. E. Doyle, *A Chronicle of England B.C. 55 – A.D. 1485* (London, 1864), pp. 46 (death of King Edmund), 50 (Alfred in the neatherd's cottage), 52 (baptism of Guthrum) and 57 (Alfred plans the capture of the Danish fleet). For the book's place in a wider context, see R. McLean, *Victorian Book Design and Colour Printing* (London, 1963), 2nd ed. (London, 1972), p. 184.

cast down by adversity, never lifted up to insolence in the hour of triumph – there is no other name in history to compare with his.'

Freeman proceeded to prove his point by comparing Alfred with St Louis of France, William the Silent, Charlemagne, Edward I, and George Washington, none of whom makes the grade. 'I repeat then', Freeman concludes, 'that Alfred is the most perfect character in history'.[578] It was, however, Thomas Hughes (1822–96), author of *Tom Brown's School Days* (1857) and a Member of Parliament from 1865 to 1874, who did more than any other person to determine the popular conception of King Alfred which prevailed in the last quarter of the nineteenth century. Hughes's 'Life' of Alfred was written in the late 1860s, expressly in order to assist 'ordinary English readers' in their search for 'deliverance from the dominion of arbitrary will'.[579] Hughes saw in Alfred the antithesis of the kind of imperial rule represented by Charlemagne; and he clearly felt, with regard to his own day, that Alfred helped by his example to expose what was wrong, in France, with the regime of the emperor Louis Napoleon, and why it was so necessary, in Britain, to assert the national will (as represented by the House of Commons) against the improper exercise of power by the House of Lords.[580]

Passing from the national to the parochial, we find Alfred pursued again at Winchester. The bridewell which had been built in the late 1780s on the site of Hyde Abbey, north of the city, was demolished in 1836, and the land sold in 1850.[581] Some years later, in 1866, an impoverished antiquary from Canterbury, called John Mellor, arrived in the town determined to rediscover the bones of King Alfred the Great where they had been left by Mr Page and his workmen eighty years before. Mellor started digging in earnest, and soon came up with the goods: 'a withered and much-dried severed and venerable head', obviously that of St Valentine given to the New Minster by Queen Emma in 1042; five skeletons, of which three were male (Alfred and his sons Edward and Æthelweard) and two female (Queen Ealhswith and Queen Ecgwynn); and an impressive quantity of other finds, including a silver sceptre, 'a plate of lead, with the king's name upon it', silver coins, gilt cloth, ermine,

---

[578] E. A. Freeman, *The History of the Norman Conquest of England*, 6 vols. (Oxford, 1867–79) I (2nd ed., 1870), 48–52. See also Skinner, 'History and Ideology', p. 177, and Burrow, *A Liberal Descent*, pp. 155–228.   [579] T. Hughes, *Alfred the Great* (London, 1871), p. 5.

[580] *Ibid*. pp. 3–6. The book was published in parts in 1869–71, and first issued in one volume in 1871. I am most grateful to Dr Boyd Hilton for elucidating the political context in 1869, when the preface would appear to have been written. The book's popularity is suggested by the fact that it had been reprinted nine times by 1904. It contains illustrations depicting a heroic Alfred at the battle of Ashdown, and a disgruntled ealdorman 'sedulously bent on acquiring learning'.

[581] Cf. *Punch* 18 (1850), 159 ('King Alfred going, going – gone!'). For the building of the bridewell in the 1780s, see above, pp. 325–6.

melted parts of the great cross given to the New Minster by Cnut and Emma, and embers of the fire in which the said cross had been destroyed in 1141.[582] To his surprise and consternation, Mellor was severely criticized in the pages of the *Hampshire Chronicle* (January 1867) and the *Gentleman's Magazine* (October 1868),[583] and beat a hasty retreat. The bones were placed by the local vicar in a vault lying outside the east end of the church of St Bartholomew, Hyde, under a plain stone slab, while Mellor himself tried to generate support in London for his proposal to have them placed in a more fitting resting-place (to be arranged at the expense, he suggested, of Brasenose College, or the University of Oxford). He met with no success, but he was not to be deterred. In 1867 Mellor moved westwards to Athelney, where he found more wonderful things, including 'a gold spur, a Saxon crook, silver coins, a Saxon knife, two keys of the abbey, a tile with a white horse's head, an incense chain, some stained glass and bronze spurs upon it, some lilies entwining', all of which he gave to the Taunton Museum. He reported a local tradition that underneath the monument at Athelney, which was said to cover 'the very hearthstone upon which the poor king let the cakes burn', lies a treasure placed there by the king himself, and added that he had also read of an underground passage running from the neatherd's cottage to the monument, and thence to the church of East Lyng.[584] If the two sets of discoveries are put together, the question arises whether Mellor was merely a lunatic, or whether he was pulling a West Saxon leg.

Two of the more public manifestations of the high Victorian cult of King Alfred were also the product of essentially local initiatives. The statue which stands to this day in the market-place at Wantage, designed and sculpted by H.S.H. Count Gleichen, presents an imposing image of the king. Alfred's mighty axe rests on the ground, its work done; he holds to his chest a parchment roll containing the laws which he has ordained for his people; and an inscription on the base rings out with all the cadences contrived by one determined to

---

[582] Letter from 'An Antiquarian' to the *Builder*, 12 Nov. 1870, printed in J. Mellor, *The Curious Particulars Relating to King Alfred's Death and Burial, Never Before Made Public* (Canterbury, 1871), pp. 21–2; letter from J. Mellor to the *Standard*, 9 Feb. 1871, not published but printed *ibid.* pp. 12–16. See also W. H. Draper, *Alfred the Great: a Sketch and Seven Studies*, 2nd ed. (1901), pp. 101–12; A. Bowker, *The King Alfred Millenary: a Record of the Proceedings of the National Commemoration* (London, 1902), pp. 62–8; and *Liber Vitae*, ed. Keynes, pp. 47–8.

[583] See extracts in Bogan, 'Where is King Alfred buried?' (above, n. 482), pp. 28–31.

[584] Letter to the *Morning Advertiser*, 23 Nov. 1870, in Mellor, *Curious Particulars*, p. 20; see also his letter to the *Standard*, 9 Feb. 1871, *ibid.* p. 13 (where the excavations are said to have taken place not in 1867 but in the autumn of 1870). A few years later, in August 1877, members of the Somersetshire Archaeological and Natural History Society convened for their twenty-ninth Annual Meeting at Bridgwater, and were taken to Athelney by the President, Bishop Clifford; but to judge from the account in *Proc. of the Somersetshire Archaeol. and Nat. Hist. Soc.* 23 (1877), 15–21 and 50–1, there was little left to show for the abbey, apart from some tiles.

match the language to the sentiment.[585] The statue was unveiled on 14 July 1877, by H.R.H. The Prince of Wales.[586] It owes its existence, however, not so much to a sudden, or belated, outburst of nationalistic fervour, as to the patronage of Col. Robert Loyd-Lindsay (1832–1901), of Lockinge, who had been awarded the Victoria Cross in 1857 for services in the Crimea, and who had entered Parliament in 1865 as Conservative member for Berkshire. The distinguished soldier, and aspiring politician, seems to have chosen to assume the mantle of King Alfred the Great; for the men of Wantage would have been able to recognize in Alfred the face of the colonel himself, and would have shared in his satisfaction when he was appointed financial secretary to the war office, in August 1877, under Lord Beaconsfield, and when he was created Baron Wantage of Lockinge in 1885.[587] The millennium in 1878 of the events which had taken place in 878 focused on the so-called 'Treaty of Wedmore' (all too easily confused with the extant treaty between Alfred and Guthrum). Proceedings on 7 August began with a sermon by the Bishop of Bath and Wells, in Wedmore Church, followed by a series of speeches in the Townhall. The speakers included the Catholic divine William Clifford (1823–93), Bishop of Clifton,[588] and the Revd. Professor Earle, Professor of Anglo-Saxon at Oxford, while the presence in the audience of Mr E. A. Freeman, unwell and prevented by his doctors from speaking himself, lent a certain air of historical dignity to the occasion. Luncheon in a spacious tent was followed by numerous patriotic and good-natured toasts. Finally, an assembled company of 800 persons settled down for tea, followed by 'a variety of out-door amusements'.[589]

---

[585] 'Alfred found learning dead, and he restored it. Education neglected, and he revived it. The laws powerless, and he gave them force. The Church debased, and he raised it. The land ravaged by a fearful enemy, from which he delivered it. Alfred's name will live as long as mankind shall respect the past.' Cf. Matt. V. 3–11 and XXV. 35–6.

[586] For an illustration of the scene, see *Illustrated Sporting and Dramatic News*, 21 July 1877, p. 425; and for the statue itself, see *White Horse Hill and its Surroundings, Issued in Commemoration of the Unveiling of the Statue of Alfred the Great, at Wantage, by H.R.H. The Prince of Wales, July 14th, 1877* (Wantage, [1877]), pp. 77–83. See also Philip, *Victorian Wantage*, pp. 114–16. A marble statuette of King Alfred, by Count Gleichen, based on the Wantage statue and dated 1878, is in the Royal Collection of Sculpture at Frogmore.

[587] For Loyd-Lindsay's military and political career, see Harriet Lady Wantage, *Lord Wantage, V.C., K.C.B.: a Memoir* (London, 1907), with frontispiece, and the *DNB*.

[588] Bishop Clifford was the President of the Somersetshire Archaeological and Natural History Society (above, n. 584), and had been vigorous in the defence of Asser, and Alfred, against the attacks launched by Henry Howorth in the *Athenaeum* in 1876–7 (below, n. 590). I am grateful to Thomás Kalmar for alerting me to the wider significance of Clifford's role in this context, and for much stimulating discussion of this and related matters.

[589] For the proceedings at Wedmore in 1878, see *An Account of the Celebration of the Thousandth Anniversary of the 'Peace of Wedmore', Signed by Alfred and Guthrum* (Wells, 1878), repr. from the *Wells Jnl*, 15 Aug. 1878. I am indebted to Tom Mayberry (Somerset Record Office) for providing me with a copy of this item.

It is not the case, however, that everything went Alfred's way in the nineteenth century. The authenticity of Asser's 'Life of King Alfred' had been challenged in the early 1840s, and was challenged again in the 1870s;[590] but for some time the momentum of the Alfredian myth was sufficient to carry it through. Besides, it was not the narrative or circumstantial detail which proved vulnerable to attack, but Alfred's accumulated credentials as the 'First Monarch' of England and as the originator of the nation's legal and administrative institutions. The more serious threat to Alfred's position came from the natural advance of historical scholarship: from a decline in the vitality or perceived relevance of the Whig tradition, coupled with the emergence of new preoccupations which shifted interest from one aspect of the period to another, and which put a different construction upon the course of events. There was a heightened awareness of Germanic roots, yet there was also a heightened appreciation of the way that medieval institutions had developed in response to changing circumstances and new influences. The 'Ancient Constitution' was buried under the massive weight and authority of Stubbs's *Constitutional History of England* (1873),[591] and few of those who noticed would have regretted its passing. There were some who may have been predisposed to maintain their faith in fundamental continuities, represented (for example) by Lord Selborne's tract on the history of tithes.[592] But Stubbs and his followers had their way. In 1895 J. H. Round (1854–1928) published his *Feudal England*, which, although it does not contain any discussion of Alfred, sounded the end not only for Freeman but also for the Whig interpretation of history, and placed the revival of the Norman supremacy on a new footing. In the same year, F. Pollock and F. W. Maitland presented a view of English legal history which, like Stubbs's, was in so many respects at odds with the notions inherited from the seventeenth and eighteenth centuries.[593] There was no longer any uncritical adulation of Alfred in these academic circles as the originator of anything. The shires, and other divisions, were now seen to be of far more complex origin, and trial by jury was

---

[590] The authenticity of Asser's 'Life of Alfred' was challenged by Thomas Wright in 1841, by Henry (later Sir Henry) Howorth in 1876–7, and by an anonymous author in *The Times* in 1898. For further details, see *Asser's Life of Alfred*, ed. Stevenson, pp. xcvi–cx (Wright), cx–cxxiv (Howorth, though without reference to Clifford's defence) and cxxiv–cxxv (*The Times*).

[591] W. Stubbs, *The Constitutional History of England in its Origin and Development*, 3 vols. (Oxford, 1873–8), 4th ed. (Oxford, 1883). See also Burrow, *A Liberal Descent*, pp. 126–51, and J. Campbell, 'William Stubbs (1825–1901)', *Medieval Scholarship: Biographical Studies on the Formation of a Discipline*, I: *History*, ed. H. Damico and J. B. Zavadil (New York, 1995), 77–87.

[592] R. Palmer [1st Earl of Selborne (1812–95)], *Ancient Facts and Fictions Concerning Churches and Tithes* (London, 1888).

[593] F. Pollock and F. W. Maitland, *The History of English Law before the Time of Edward I*, 2 vols. [1895], 2nd ed. (Cambridge, 1898), reissued with an introduction by S. F. C. Milsom (Cambridge, 1968).

credited to Norman administrative genius, as a prerogative derived by Duke William from Frankish practices.[594] Far from suppressing ancient liberties, the Normans had reduced an unruly mob to some semblance of order, and had brought the English out of their isolation and into the mainstream of European culture. It was a view (adumbrated by Daniel, Brady, Hume, and others) which had little popular appeal, yet it is one which has proved hard to dislodge.

In the late 1880s the nation began to gear itself up for the celebration of what was fervently believed to be the millennium of King Alfred's death, in October 1901. Alfred Austin, appointed Poet Laureate in 1896, brought forth the inevitable poem.[595] Plans for the 'National Commemoration' were announced, organizing committees were set up, and an appeal was launched for the £2000 needed for the projected statue of King Alfred to be raised on a vast granite block in the High Street of his capital at Winchester.[596] The many other manifestations of the millenary celebrations included a commemorative exhibition,[597] a replica of the Alfred Jewel,[598] and another commemorative medal.[599] Sadly, the Queen Empress died on 22 January 1901; but when the nation had recovered from her passing, it was able to recover its spirits by glorying in the millennium of King Alfred's death. The role of the impresario was assumed on this occasion by Mr Alfred Bowker, Mayor of Winchester, who produced soon afterwards a full account of the proceedings.[600] There was a pilgrimage to the

---

[594] Stubbs, *Constitutional History* I, 106–12 and 122–5 (shires, etc.), 269–70 (Norman genius), and 655–8 (trial by jury); Pollock and Maitland, *History of English Law* I, 140–3 (trial by jury) and 532–71 (shires, etc.). See also P. Wormald, 'Jury', *Encyclopaedia of ASE*, ed. Lapidge, *et al.*, p. 267.

[595] A. Austin, *England's Darling* (London, 1896); A. Austin, *Alfred the Great, England's Darling*, 5th ed. (London, 1901). See also Miles, *King Alfred in Literature*, pp. 92–5.

[596] A circular bound at the end of *Alfred the Great*, ed. A. Bowker (London, 1899), announced the 'National Commemoration' to be held in 1901, and invited contributions in respect of the statue by Hamo Thornycroft. Among the many other publications spawned by the millennium (registered in the electronic or printed catalogues of the British Library), J. C. Wall, *Alfred the Great: his Abbeys of Hyde, Athelney and Shaftesbury* (London, 1900) appears to have been conceived as an antidote to the air of militaristic triumphalism symbolized by the (then projected) statue at Winchester. Sir (William) Hamo Thornycroft (1850–1925) had previously crafted the statues of General Gordon in Trafalgar Square (1888) and of Oliver Cromwell in Old Palace Yard, Westminster (1899).

[597] *Alfred the Great Millenary Exhibition, 1901* (London, 1901), being the catalogue of an exhibition held at the British Museum; unfortunately, the BM (i.e. BL) copy was destroyed by enemy action in 1942.

[598] The publisher Elliot Stock, who published Wall's book, was also responsible for commissioning the production of fine commemorative replicas of the Alfred Jewel. See Keynes, 'The Discovery and First Publication of the Alfred Jewel', p. 8, n. 21.

[599] L. Brown, *A Catalogue of British Historical Medals 1760–1960*, III: *The Accession of Edward VII to 1960* (London, 1995), p. 11 (no. 3726).

[600] A. Bowker, *The King Alfred Millenary: a Record of the Proceedings of the National Commemoration* (London, 1902). The book's cover is decorated with a coat of arms for Alfred which differs from the norm (cf. above, n. 114). See also Simmons, *Reversing the Conquest*, pp. 185–91, and B. Yorke, *The King Alfred Millenerary in Winchester*, 1901, Hampshire Papers 17 (Winchester, 1999).

presumed site of Alfred's grave at Hyde Abbey, where the Mayor addressed the delegates at some length on matters of local history; the new and unashamedly militaristic statue of the king was unveiled; and the festivities culminated with the launching of HMS King Alfred, an armoured cruiser boasting a complement of 900 officers and men, and sporting a fine pair of 9.2 inch guns.

The big guns were also out in the groves of academe. In a sermon preached before the University of Oxford on the first Sunday after Queen Victoria's death, the Revd Charles Plummer, editor of Bede's *Ecclesiastical History* and of the *Anglo-Saxon Chronicle*, had drawn parallels between the late Queen and 'the greatest of her ancestors'. In October of the same year, Dr Plummer was in action again, delivering a series of Ford Lectures to his colleagues, on 'The Life and Times of Alfred the Great'.[601] 'We may not, here in Oxford', he said, 'claim Alfred as our founder; but surely our hearts may be uplifted at the thought, that in all that we do here in the cause of true learning and of genuine education, we are carrying on the work which Alfred left us to do'.[602]

ALFRED THE GREAT IN THE TWENTIETH CENTURY

A gap was by now opening up between the received myth and the perceived reality of early English history. The legendary Alfred had been cut back to size by a realization of what had been accomplished by his successors in the tenth century, by the adulation of Norman administrative genius, and by more dispassionate assessment of the differences between comparable institutions before and after the Conquest.[603] Yet he was remarkably adaptable. The sentiments which had raised Alfred to such great heights in the second half of the nineteenth century, culminating with the festivities of 1901, had much to do with pride in a nation's achievements during the age of Queen Victoria, and proved difficult to sustain for much longer in quite the same form. For while manifestations of the cult of Alfred in the twentieth century helped to perpetuate his fame as a national icon, and as a local hero, and while Alfred never lost his power to generate patriotic fervour in times of trouble, his true strength was now seen to lie in the service of more straightforwardly didactic ends. He remained one through whom parents might hope to inculcate their children with the principles of a virtuous life (a love of God, an interest in reading and writing, a respect for law and order, and a range of practical skills, coupled with courage and steadfastness in adversity, tempered with humility, generosity, and mercy); so the

---

[601] C. Plummer, *The Life and Times of Alfred the Great*, Ford Lectures 1901 (Oxford, 1902), with the text of Plummer's sermon at pp. 207–13. Cf. the remarks of F. M. Stenton, in *PBA* 15 (1929), 469. [602] Plummer, *Life and Times of Alfred the Great*, p. 193.
[603] See, e.g., W. S. Holdsworth, *A History of English Law* I–II (London, 1903), on the differences between the pre- and post-Conquest polities; see also C. Oman, *England before the Conquest* (London, 1910), on Alfred's laws.

The cult of King Alfred the Great

formula devised by Maria, Lady Callcott, in the early 1830s, and refined by Charles Dickens in his *Child's History of England*, in the early 1850s (with a picture of Alfred reading to his mother stamped on the cover), gave rise to specifically 'Alfredian' works such as *The Story of Alfred the Great* (c. 1880), the Colman's Mustard 'Life' of Alfred the Great (1900), and the Ladybird book of King Alfred the Great (1956).[604] It is fundamentally the same Alfred who lies behind the profusion of Alfredian novels published in the later nineteenth and throughout the twentieth centuries, and behind most other manifestations of modern Alfrediana. A few examples will suffice to illustrate the point. The impact of the millenary celebrations found reflection in an inscription on the stone wall of the 'King's Coffee House' (1906), at Knutsford (Cheshire), which gives King Alfred's 'last words', as reported in the *Proverbs of Alfred*.[605] In 1913 a statue of Alfred was raised at Pewsey, in Wiltshire, prompted in part by the knowledge that land there had been bequeathed by Alfred to his son Edward the Elder (later given by King Edmund to the New Minster, Winchester), and in part by the feeling that this was an appropriate way to commemorate the coronation of King George V (in 1911). The jingoistic spirit returned in 1927, when Colin Gill depicted 'Alfred's fleet defeating the Danes at sea' as part of a revived scheme for the decoration of St Stephen's Hall, Westminster.[606] A cartoon published in *Punch* on 28 June 1933 celebrated the king's attempted invention of the wristwatch, providing an instance of the continued exploitation of history for satirical or comic effect.[607] The inscribed stone which had been found on the site of Hyde Abbey in the late eighteenth century came back from Corby Castle to Winchester in 1934, and was put on display in the Winchester City Museum.[608] And so it went on. After the oratorio (1740) and the opera (1823), not to mention countless poems, plays, paintings, and novels, Alfred eventually received the ultimate accolade: the full-length feature film *Alfred the Great* (1969),

---

[604] For Callcott, see above, pp. 333–4. For Dickens on Alfred, see C. Dickens, *Master Humphrey's Clock* and *A Child's History of England*, New Oxford Illustrated Dickens 12 (London, 1958), 144–9. I owe my knowledge of the next two items to Dr Shaun Tyas, and of the Ladybird *King Alfred the Great* to my mother, who gave me a copy on my birthday in 1983.

[605] I am grateful to Mr Peter Hopton for drawing my attention to this inscription, and providing me with a photograph.

[606] For a reproduction in colour, see Yorke, 'The Most Perfect Man in History?', p. 14; see also *Houses of Parliament*, ed. Port, pp. 154 (showing the mural *in situ*) and 280.

[607] The cartoon was subsequently provided with a better caption (*Punch*, 19 July 1978, p. 114). Further study might reveal, however, that Cnut and the waves had greater political potential than Alfred and the cakes.

[608] Cf. above, n. 482. The stone was purchased by the City of Winchester from the estate of Philip Howard, of Corby Castle; report in the *Hampshire Observer*, 4 Aug. 1934. I am most grateful to Dr G. T. Denford (Museums Curator, Winchester Museums Service), for his assistance in this connection.

filmed in County Galway (Ireland), starring David Hemmings as Alfred and Michael York (himself a Univ man) as Guthrum.[609] Since then, the eleventh centenaries of selected events in Alfred's reign have been celebrated with all due solemnity. Alfred 'the truth-teller' may have given way to Alfred the propagandist; but the search is on, again, for Alfred's grave at Hyde Abbey,[610] and academics are gathering their thoughts for the conference commemorating his death.

THE CULT OF KING ALFRED

The main purpose of this exercise has been to show how the received tradition of King Alfred's 'greatness', from which we must try so hard to escape, is the product of a process of development which has extended well over a thousand years, and how Alfred's place in the mythology of English history was shaped during this period by an extraordinary range of factors, operating in competition or in combination with each other. We may be sure that the legend originated in Alfred's lifetime, and that it made some progress during the course of the tenth and eleventh centuries. It was not, however, until the twelfth and thirteenth centuries that Alfred began to emerge as a major political force: first, when William of Malmesbury chose for whatever reason to represent him as the originator of hundreds and tithings, and to credit him with the peace-keeping system familiar as 'frankpledge'; secondly, when the St Albans school of historians set him up as the 'First Monarch of all England'; and thirdly, when the author of the *Mirror of Justices* credited him with the invention of a constitution. Further developments in the fourteenth and fifteenth centuries cast him as the founder of the University of Oxford, and extended his inventive genius to include shires, as well as hundreds and tithings. Yet Alfred was still up against the cults of King Arthur and King Edward the Confessor, and up against those inclined to start English history with William the Conqueror. It helped, in the later sixteenth century, that a need arose to provide a distinctively English basis for the 'Ecclesia Anglicana', and, in the seventeenth century, that a line of Scottish kings developed pretensions which exceeded all reasonable expectations. Lawyers and antiquaries turned to Anglo-Saxon England in search of an ancient constitution, as a basis for their opposition to King James I; and in other respects the advance of scholarship gave greater credibility to the political orders and institutions of those days. It was then a Cambridge man, in the

---

[609] The film was directed by Clive Donner, and has a musical score by Raymond Leppard. For further details, see D. Elley, *The Epic Film: Myth and History* (London, 1984), pp. 154–5.

[610] Excavations co-ordinated by Winchester Museums, and directed by Kenneth Qualmann and Graham Scobie, have revealed the eastern end of the abbey, exposing the probable site of the High Altar, and thus the ground where lay the mortal remains of King Alfred the Great, and others, from *c.* 1110 to *c.* 1540. Further information is available from the Historic Resources Centre, 75 Hyde Street, Winchester SO23 7DW.

person of Sir John Spelman, who was first moved to draw the various threads together, and who, because he was at heart a royalist, arranged them in the form of a biography of King Alfred which he then presented to King Charles I and to the young Prince of Wales in the royalist camp at Oxford. After the Restoration, the good men of University College in Oxford soon seized the opportunity to reassert their dignity in respect of their own pretensions to antiquity; and, finding a 'Life' of King Alfred close at hand, which for reasons of its own gave particular emphasis to his role as their founder, they had it translated into Latin, and published it as part of a fund-raising exercise. What was good for University College was also good for the University of Oxford; and it was at Oxford, in the late seventeenth and early eighteenth centuries, that a group of scholars (at Univ, and across the road at Queen's) seized the initiative from Cambridge in the development of Anglo-Saxon studies, and gave them a pronounced Alfredian spin. The vital breakthrough for Alfred came after the Glorious Revolution of 1688–9 and the discomfiture of the catholic King James II; after the accession of William of Orange and Mary II in 1689; after the Act of Settlement (1701) had vested the succession in the line of Hanover; after the death of Queen Anne in 1714; and after the accession, therefore, of King George I (1714–27). In the meantime, Spelman's 'Life' had been published at Oxford in its original English form. It was now the changed political circumstances which gave Alfred the edge over Arthur, and which, with the further advance of the Whig interpretation of English history, soon gave him the edge over Edward the Confessor. Henceforth Alfred could serve as a paragon of enlightened and 'constitutional' kingship, as the originator and personification of the most cherished institutions of government, as the protector of liberty and order, as the defender of his people from foreign powers, as the guardian of their religious beliefs, and indeed as the very embodiment of British identity. He began to perform this multi-purpose role in the wings, as a symbol of opposition to a corrupt government, yet by the end of the eighteenth century his place was secure at the heart of the nation's perception of itself. The people had become familiar with Alfred in their history books, as well as in literature, in art, and on the stage; and, as in the late ninth century, there was nothing like the reality or threat of foreign invasion to unite the people with their monarchy and with their government in opposition to a common enemy, and so to concentrate the collective mind. One need not be surprised, therefore, that Alfred was accorded a place in the decorative sculpture on the Garden Front of Buckingham Palace, ten years before the accession of Queen Victoria in 1837. The deep and well-entangled roots sustained the further development of the cult of King Alfred in the later nineteenth century; and while it is arguable that more damage than good was done to his cause by the excesses of Victorian adulation, it is the high Victorian myth which remains the basis of his popular identity. It should be noted that the development of the Alfredian myth was not in itself dependent upon the development of knowledge of Anglo-Saxon language and literature, that it did not depend upon the authenticity (or otherwise) of a particular primary source, and that at no point, except perhaps in the late ninth century, did it depend for its promotion upon anything approximating to an 'Establishment'. The monarchy, and parliament, were always free, and welcome, to wrap themselves in his mantle, but Alfred (dare one say it) remained essentially the people's king.

The cult of King Alfred delivered to posterity a creature of whom, perhaps, the less said the better; and it only remains to consider, albeit briefly, how the modern conception of the historical King Alfred accords with his legendary namesake.[611] As we have seen, many of the basic continuities which lay at the heart of the Whig interpretation of English history, in the seventeenth and eighteenth centuries, had been set aside by the end of the nineteenth, and the tendency instead was to emphasize Norman and Angevin innovations: while the Anglo-Saxons were content to lumber about in pot-bellied equanimity, the Normans took off, and the Angevins leapt forward. More recently, it has been the turn of the Anglo-Saxonists to strike back. In historical terms, the steady reassessment of Anglo-Saxon England was led by and is still primarily associated with the names of Sir Frank Stenton and Dorothy Whitelock; and of course their lead has since been followed by many others. The cumulative achievement has been, not surprisingly, a much higher and more sophisticated estimation of the Anglo-Saxon achievement, albeit in ways which might not have impressed those who had espoused Alfred's cause in the past. Those who wrote about Anglo-Saxon England in the seventeenth and eighteenth centuries tended to be on the side of the people, and their inclination was to resent any hint of the infringement of liberties. Modern writers about Anglo-Saxon England tend for whatever reason to be on the side of the kings: their inclination is to extol strong government and a unified kingdom, and to reward with their praise those kings who seek by whatever means to maintain the rule of law and order. When King Alfred is given credit for his role in setting up the kingdom of the English, it seems at first sight to be a pleasant reassertion of the Whig interpretation of history, in accordance with which our liberties, and our most cherished institutions, are held to have originated long before the Norman Conquest. In fact it is quite the reverse. The doctrine of the 'Norman Yoke', representing the imposition of an alien regime at the expense of ancient English liberties, is now giving way to a doctrine of the 'Anglo-Saxon Yoke', if by that we

---

[611] The primary material is assembled in Keynes and Lapidge, *Alfred the Great*. See also A. Smyth, *Alfred the Great* (Oxford, 1995); S. Keynes, 'On the Authenticity of Asser's *Life of King Alfred*', *JEH* 47 (1996), 529–51; and R. Abels, *Alfred the Great: War, Kingship and Culture in Anglo-Saxon England* (London, 1998).

may signify a unified English people kept under firm or at least notional control by the far-reaching aspirations and centralized institutions of a strong royal government. It is debateable, within this context, how much (if anything) should be credited to the overlords and other megastars of the seventh and eighth centuries; and it is arguable that we should not allow the aspirations to obscure the practicalities. We might do well, in other words, to look closely at Ine, Ecgberht, and Æthelwulf, for their respective contributions to the development, in Wessex and in its south-eastern extension, of a polity very different from the earlier 'Mercian' overlordship; yet not to overlook the further developments in the tenth and eleventh centuries which put Alfred's achievements in their appropriate perspective.[612] Alfred takes his place at the end of a line of West Saxon kings, and at the beginning of a line of those who aspired to be kings of the English. He drew strength from all that had gone before, and he rose well to the challenge, yet he also had the vision which gave him, and his successors, an extraordinary sense of purpose and direction.[613] It was Alfred who fastened on the importance of London, even if he was stuck for the time being in Winchester; it was Alfred who invented the 'kingdom of the Anglo-Saxons' in the 880s, and who was known to his admirers as 'king of the Anglo-Saxons', even if in some contexts he persisted in calling himself 'king of the West Saxons'; and it was Alfred who paved the way for the extension and transformation of the 'kingdom of the Anglo-Saxons' into the 'kingdom of the English', during the course of the tenth century. He saw and he seized the opportunity to assert the power and the dignity of his royal office, and did so in ways which could be construed as necessary for the defence of his realm and for the protection of his people. We may respect him for his military achievements, if more for his construction of a defensive network of fortresses in the 880s than for whatever abilities he displayed in the field in the 870s or in the 890s. We may also respect him for the arrangements which lie behind his coinage, his will, and his law-code, which illuminate his rule in ways now much better understood than ever before; though it remains a matter of great importance in our perception of late Anglo-Saxon state-formation whether it was Alfred who instituted everything, or whether some space should be left for his successors, most notably Edward the Elder, Æthelstan, and Edgar, to introduce some further

---

[612] Keynes, 'England, 700–900', pp. 39–42; S. Keynes, 'England, 900–1016', *The New Cambridge Medieval History*, III: *c. 900–1024*, ed. T. Reuter (Cambridge, 1999), 456–84.

[613] The vision can be understood in different ways: see, e.g., P. Wormald, '*Engla Lond*: the Making of an Allegiance', *Jnl of Hist. Sociology* 7 (1994), 1–24; J. Campbell, 'The United Kingdom of England: the Anglo-Saxon Achievement', *Uniting the Kingdom? The Making of British History*, ed. A. Grant and K. J. Stringer (London, 1995), pp. 31–47; S. Foot, 'The Making of *Angelcynn*: English Identity before the Norman Conquest', *TRHS* 6th ser. 6 (1996), 25–49; and Keynes, 'King Alfred and the Mercians', esp. pp. 34–9, and entry on the 'kingdom of the Anglo-Saxons' in *Encyclopaedia of ASE*, ed. Lapidge, *et al.*, pp. 37–8.

refinements. Above all, perhaps, we may respect him for the promotion during his reign of an extraordinary scheme for the revival of religion and learning among his people, not for its own sake (far from it) but because, like David and Solomon, he saw it as a means to an end. It is now recognized, better than ever before, that all of this was driven by the circle of learned men assembled at King Alfred's court, of Frankish, Welsh, Mercian, and West Saxon extraction. Yet above it all was the presiding genius of the king himself, known to us from the sympathetic narrative of the *Anglo-Saxon Chronicle*, from Asser's extraordinarily perceptive 'Life', and from the corpus of the king's own writings. We may recognize in the legendary Alfred the product of many hundreds of years of English history, and indeed it is this that gives the legend its particular and abiding interest. If, on the other hand, we choose to restrict ourselves to contemporary material bearing on Alfred's life and reign, we find that the genuine Alfred of the late ninth century was a very different but no less extraordinary man.

Bibliography for 1998

DEBBY BANHAM, CARL T. BERKHOUT, CAROLE P. BIGGAM, MARK BLACKBURN, CAROLE HOUGH, SIMON KEYNES and TERESA WEBBER

This bibliography is meant to include all books, articles and significant reviews published in any branch of Anglo-Saxon studies during 1998. It excludes reprints unless they contain new material. It will be continued annually. The year of publication of a book or article is 1998 unless otherwise stated. The arrangement and the pages on which the sections begin are as follows:

1. GENERAL AND MISCELLANEOUS — page 359
2. OLD ENGLISH LANGUAGE — 365
   Lexicon and glosses, 365; *Syntax, phonology and other aspects*, 368
3. OLD ENGLISH LITERATURE — 374
   General, 374; *Poetry*, 375 (*General*, 375; '*Beowulf*', 376; *Other poems*, 379); *Prose*, 383
4. ANGLO-LATIN, LITURGY AND OTHER LATIN ECCLESIASTICAL TEXTS — 384
5. PALAEOGRAPHY, DIPLOMATIC AND ILLUMINATION — 388
6. HISTORY — 392
7. NUMISMATICS — 398
8. ONOMASTICS — 399
9. ARCHAEOLOGY — 401
   General, 401; *Towns and other major settlements*, 405; *Rural settlements, agriculture and the countryside*, 408; *Pagan cemeteries and Sutton Hoo*, 411; *Churches, monastic sites and Christian cemeteries*, 413; *Ships and seafaring*, 415; *Miscellaneous artifacts*, 416; *Bone, stone and wood*, 416; *Metal-work*, 417; *Pottery and glass*, 419; *Textiles*, 419; *Inscriptions*, 419
10. REVIEWS — 420

Carl Berkhout has been mainly responsible for sections 2, 3 and 4, Teresa Webber for section 5, Debby Banham for section 6, Mark Blackburn for section 7, Carole Hough for section 8 and Carole Biggam for section 9. References to publications in Japan have been supplied by Professor Yoshio Terasawa. Simon Keynes has been responsible for co-ordination.

The following abbreviations occur where relevant (not only in the bibliography but also throughout the volume):

AAe   *Archaeologia Aeliana*
AB   *Analecta Bollandiana*
AC   *Archæologia Cantiana*

Bibliography for 1998

AHR	American Historical Review
AIUON	Annali, Istituto Universitario Orientale di Napoli: sezione germanica
ANQ	American Notes and Queries
AntJ	Antiquaries Journal
ANS	Anglo-Norman Studies
ArchJ	Archaeological Journal
ASE	Anglo-Saxon England
ASNSL	Archiv für das Studium der neueren Sprachen und Literaturen
ASPR	Anglo-Saxon Poetic Records
ASSAH	Anglo-Saxon Studies in Archaeology and History
BAR	British Archaeological Reports
BBCS	Bulletin of the Board of Celtic Studies
BGDSL	Beiträge zur Geschichte der deutschen Sprache und Literatur
BIAL	Bulletin of the Institute of Archaeology (London)
BN	Beiträge zur Namenforschung
BNJ	British Numismatic Journal
CA	Current Archaeology
CBA	Council for British Archaeology
CCM	Cahiers de civilisation médiévale
CCSL	Corpus Christianorum, Series Latina
CMCS	Cambrian Medieval Celtic Studies
CSASE	Cambridge Studies in Anglo-Saxon England
CSEL	Corpus Scriptorum Ecclesiasticorum Latinorum
DAEM	Deutsches Archiv für Erforschung des Mittelalters
EA	Études anglaises
EconHR	Economic History Review
EEMF	Early English Manuscripts in Facsimile
EETS	Early English Text Society
EHR	English Historical Review
ELN	English Language Notes
EME	Early Medieval Europe
EPNS	English Place-Name Society
ES	English Studies
FS	Frühmittelalterliche Studien
HBS	Henry Bradshaw Society Publications
HS	Historische Sprachforschung
HZ	Historische Zeitschrift
IF	Indogermanische Forschungen
JBAA	Journal of the British Archaeological Association
JEGP	Journal of English and Germanic Philology
JEH	Journal of Ecclesiastical History
JEPNS	Journal of the English Place-Name Society
JMH	Journal of Medieval History
JTS	Journal of Theological Studies

LH	*The Local Historian*
MA	*Medieval Archaeology*
MÆ	*Medium Ævum*
MGH	Monumenta Germaniae Historica
MLR	*Modern Language Review*
MP	*Modern Philology*
MS	*Mediaeval Studies*
MScand	*Mediaeval Scandinavia*
N&Q	*Notes and Queries*
NChron	*Numismatic Chronicle*
NCirc	*Numismatic Circular*
NH	*Northern History*
NM	*Neuphilologische Mitteilungen*
OEN	*Old English Newsletter*
PA	*Popular Archaeology*
PBA	*Proceedings of the British Academy*
PL	Patrologia Latina
PMLA	*Publications of the Modern Language Association of America*
PQ	*Philological Quarterly*
RB	*Revue bénédictine*
RES	*Review of English Studies*
RS	Rolls Series
SBVS	*Saga-Book of the Viking Society for Northern Research*
SCBI	Sylloge of Coins of the British Isles
SCMB	*Seaby's Coin and Medal Bulletin*
SettSpol	*Settimane di studio del Centro italiano di studi sull'alto medioevo* (Spoleto)
SM	*Studi Medievali*
SN	*Studia Neophilologica*
SP	*Studies in Philology*
TLS	*Times Literary Supplement*
TPS	*Transactions of the Philological Society*
TRHS	*Transactions of the Royal Historical Society*
YES	*Yearbook of English Studies*
ZAA	*Zeitschrift für Anglistik und Amerikanistik*
ZDA	*Zeitschrift für deutsches Altertum und deutsche Literatur*
ZVS	*Zeitschrift für vergleichende Sprachforschung*

1. GENERAL AND MISCELLANEOUS

Andersson, Theodore M., Fred C. Robinson, Marie Borroff and Constance B. Hieatt, 'John Collins Pope', *Speculum* 73, 956–8

Baker, Peter S., and Nicholas Howe, ed., *Words and Works: Studies in Medieval English Language and Literature in Honour of Fred C. Robinson*, Toronto OE Ser. 10 (Toronto)

Banham, Debby, Carl T. Berkhout, Carole P. Biggam, Mark Blackburn, Simon Keynes and Alexander Rumble, 'Bibliography for 1997', *ASE* 27, 295–344

Barker, Katherine, and Timothy Darvill, ed., *Making English Landscapes, Changing Perspectives: Papers presented to Christopher Taylor at a Symposium Held at Bournemouth University on 25th March 1995*, Bournemouth Univ. School of Conservation Sciences Occasional Paper 3, Oxbow Monograph 93 (Oxford, 1997)

Barnwell, P. S., 'Late Antiquity and the Early Middle Ages (300–900)', *Ann. Bull. of Hist. Lit.* 81 (1997), 12–21

'Late Antiquity and the Early Middle Ages (300–900)', *Ann. Bull. of Hist. Lit.* 82, 10–18

Beck, Heinrich, 'Andreas Heusler (1865–1940)', *Medieval Scholarship*, ed. Damico, pp. 283–96

Berkhout, Carl T., 'Laurence Nowell (1530–ca. 1570)', *Medieval Scholarship*, ed. Damico, pp. 3–17

'Old English Bibliography 1997', *OEN* 31.4, 3–28

Bernstein, Melissa, 'New and Updated Anglo-Saxon Resources on the Internet for 1998', *OEN* 32.1, 14–15

Blackburn, Mark A. S., and David Dumville, ed., *Kings, Currency and Alliances: History and Coinage of Southern England in the Ninth Century*, Stud. in AS Hist. 9 (Woodbridge)

Bøye, Merete, 'Hallen og havet som eskatologiske modsætninger – i den angelsaksiske poesie og hos Grundtvig', *Grundtvig Studier*, pp. 120–41

Brewer, Charlotte, 'Walter William Skeat (1835–1912)', *Medieval Scholarship*, ed. Damico, pp. 139–49

Carr, Gerald F., Wayne Harbert and Lihua Zhang, ed., *Interdigitations: Essays for Irmengard Rauch* (New York)

Clarke, Howard B., Máire Ní Mhaonaigh, and Raghnall Ó Floinn, ed., *Ireland and Scandinavia in the Early Viking Age* (Dublin)

Clement, Richard W., 'Richard Verstegan's Reinvention of Anglo-Saxon England: a Contribution from the Continent', *Reinventing the Middle Ages and the Renaissance*, ed. William F. Gentrup, Arizona Stud. in the Middle Ages and the Renaissance 1 (Turnhout), 19–36

Clunies Ross, Margaret, 'Revaluing the Work of Edward Lye, an Eighteenth-Century Septentrional Scholar', *Stud. in Medievalism* 9 (1997), 66–79

Colish, Martha L., *Medieval Foundations of the Western Intellectual Tradition 400–1400* (New Haven, CT, 1997) [including Anglo-Latin and Old English]

Collinson, Patrick, 'One of Us? William Camden and the Making of History', *TRHS* 6th ser. 8, 139–63

Crawford, Barbara E., ed., *Conversion and Christianity in the North Sea World*, St John's House Papers 8 (St Andrews)

Damico, Helen, ed., with Donald Fennema and Karmen Lenz, *Medieval Scholarship. Biographical Studies on the Formation of a Discipline*, II: *Literature and Philology* (New York)

De Bièvre, Elisabeth, ed., *Utrecht: Britain and the Continent: Archaeology, Art and Architecture*, Brit. Archaeol. Assoc. Conference Trans. 18 (London, 1996)

Dekker, Kees, 'The Old Frisian Studies of Jan van Vliet (1622–1666) and Thomas Marshall (1621–1685)', *Amsterdamer Beiträge zur älteren Germanistik* 49, 113–38

Doerr, Joe Frances, 'Conjuring Æþelflæd', *OEN* 32.1, 11 [poem]

Downing, Jack, 'Meeting the Vikings', *Yorkshire Jnl* 21, 30–5 [Danelaw Village, Murton Park]

Dronke, Peter, and Ursula Dronke, *Growth of Literature: the Sea and the God of the Sea*, H. M. Chadwick Memorial Lecture 8 (Cambridge)

Düwel, Klaus, ed., with Sean Nowak, *Runeninschriften als Quellen interdisziplinärer Forschung. Abhandlungen des Vierten Internationalen Symposiums über Runen und Runeninschriften in Göttingen vom 4.–9. August 1995*, Ergänzungsbände zum Reallexikon der Germanischen Altertumskunde 15 (Berlin)

Ferrari, Michele Camillo, *Sancti Willibrordi venerantes memoriam: Echternacher Schreiber und Schriftsteller von den Angelsachsen bis Johann Bertels: ein Überblick* (Luxembourg, 1994)

Fisiak, Jacek, and Akio Oizumi, ed., *English Historical Linguistics and Philology in Japan*, Trends in Ling., Stud. and Monographs 109 (Berlin)

Frank, Roberta, 'When Lexicography Met the Exeter Book', *Words and Works*, ed. Baker and Howe, pp. 207–21

Frankis, John, 'Views of Anglo-Saxon England in Post-Conquest Vernacular Writing', *Orality and Literacy in Early Middle English*, ed. Herbert Pilch, ScriptOralia 83 (Tübingen, 1996), 227–47

Frantzen, Allen J., *Before the Closet: Same-Sex Love from 'Beowulf' to 'Angels in America'* (Chicago, IL)

'Prior to the Normans: the Anglo-Saxons in *Angels in America*', *Approaching the Millennium: Essays on 'Angels in America'*, ed. Deborah R. Geis and Steven F. Kruger (Ann Arbor, MI, 1997), pp. 134–50

'Straightforward', *Parergon* 16.1, 93–104 [interview by David Matthews]

Gatch, Milton McC., 'Humfrey Wanley (1672–1726)', *Medieval Scholarship*, ed. Damico, pp. 45–57

Gneuss, Helmut, 'Old English Texts and Modern Readers: Notes on Editing and Textual Criticism', *Words and Works*, ed. Baker and Howe, pp. 127–41

Graham, Timothy, and Andrew G. Watson, *The Recovery of the Past in Early Elizabethan England: Documents by John Bale and John Joscelyn from the Circle of Matthew Parker*, Cambridge Bibliographical Soc. Monograph 13 (Cambridge)

Gransden, Antonia, ed., *Bury St Edmunds: Medieval Art, Architecture, Archaeology and Economy*, Brit. Archaeol. Assoc. Conference Trans. 20 (Leeds)

Harmsen, Theodor, 'Bodleian Imbroglios, Politics and Personalities, 1701–1716: Thomas Hearne, Arthur Charlett and John Hudson', *Neophilologus* 82, 149–68

Harris, Richard L., 'George Hickes (1642–1715)', *Medieval Scholarship*, ed. Damico, pp. 19–32

Hill, Joyce, 'Medieval English Studies at the University of Leeds', *Med. Eng. Stud. Newsletter* 39, 29–31

Hill, Joyce, and Mary Swan, ed., *The Community, the Family and the Saint: Patterns of Power in Early Medieval Europe* (Turnhout)

Hill, Thomas D., Susan E. Deskis and Charles D. Wright, 'James E. Cross', *Speculum* 73, 958–9

Hines, John, ed., *The Anglo-Saxons from the Migration Period to the Eighth Century: an Ethnographic Perspective*, Stud. in Hist. Archaeoethnology (Woodbridge, 1997)

Hogg, James, 'Spare Us *Beowulf* and the *Regula Pastoralis*: Alternatives for Old-English at a Foreign University', *Text and Context: Essays in English and American Studies in Honour of Holger M. Klein*, ed. Sabine Coelsch-Foisner and Wolfgang Görtschacher (Rheinfelden), pp. 17–29

Hooper, Jennie, 'The "Rows of the Battle-Swan": the Aftermath of Battle in Anglo-Saxon Art', *Armies, Chivalry and Warfare in Medieval Britain and France*, ed. Matthew Strickland, Harlaxton Med. Stud. ns 7 (Stamford), 82–99

Howe, Nicholas, 'Praise and Lament: the Afterlife of Old English Poetry in Auden, Hill and Gunn', *Words and Works*, ed. Baker and Howe, pp. 293–310

Jackson, Peter, 'Fontes Anglo-Saxonici: a Register of Written Sources Used by Authors in Anglo-Saxon England. Thirteenth Progress Report', *OEN* 31.3, 12–15

Jesch, Judith, 'Professor Christine E. Fell, OBE', *Nottingham Med. Stud.* 42, iv–vi

Kay, Christian, 'David Donald Murison, 1913–1997, and Adam John Aitken, 1921–1998', *Med. Eng. Stud. Newsletter* 38, 1–4

Kiernan, Kevin S., 'N. R. Ker (1908–1982)', *Medieval Scholarship*. ed. Damico, pp. 425–37

Kristensson, Gillis, 'Olof Arngart 1905–1997', *JEPNS* 30 (1997–8), 155–7

Lasko, Peter, 'The Bayeux Tapestry and the Representation of Space', *Medieval Art: Recent Perspectives*, ed. Owen-Crocker and Graham, pp. 26–39

Lewis, C. P., 'The Central Middle Ages (900–1200) (i) British History', *Ann. Bull. of Hist. Lit.* 81 (1997), 22–3

'The Central Middle Ages (900–1200) (i) British History', *Ann. Bull. of Hist. Lit.* 82, 19–31

Lowe, Kathryn A., 'In Memoriam: Christine Elizabeth Fell (1938–1998)', *OEN* 32.1, 10–11

MacKay, Angus, with David Ditchburn, ed., *Atlas of Medieval Europe* (London, 1997)

MacMahon, Michael K. C., 'Henry Sweet (1845–1912)', *Medieval Scholarship*, ed. Damico, pp. 167–75

Mason, Emma, 'The Works of Frank Barlow', *Med. Hist.* (Bangor) 2.1 (1992), 134–9

Milroy, James, 'Linguistic Ideology and the Anglo-Saxon Lineage of English', *Speech Past and Present: Studies in English Dialectology in Memory of Ossi Ihalainen*, ed. Juhani Klemola, Merja Kytö and Matti Rissanen, Bamberger Beiträge zur englischen Sprachwissenschaft 38 (Frankfurt am Main, 1996), 169–86

Mora, María José, and María José Gómez-Calderón, 'The Study of Old English in America (1776–1850): National Uses of the Saxon Past', *JEGP* 97, 322–36

Morris, John, *Arthurian Sources*, 6 vols. (Chichester, 1995)

Nativel, Colette, 'Junius (Franciscus F. F.) (1591–1677)', *Centuriæ Latinæ*, ed. C. Nativel, Travaux d'Humanisme et Renaissance 314 (Geneva, 1997), 439–48

Niles, John D., 'The Wasteland of Loegria: Geoffrey of Monmouth's Reinvention of the Anglo-Saxon Past', *Reinventing the Middle Ages and the Renaissance*, ed. William F. Gentrup, Arizona Stud. in the Middle Ages and the Renaissance 1 (Turnhout), 1–18

Oergel, Maike, 'The Redeeming Teuton: Nineteenth-Century Notions of the "Germanic" in England and Germany', *Imagining Nations*, ed. Geoffrey Cubitt (Manchester), pp. 75–91

Oizumi, Akio, 'English Historical Linguistics and Philology in Japan 1950–1994. A Survey with a List of Publications Arranged in Chronological Order', *Language History and Linguistic Modelling*, ed. Hickey and Puppel, pp. 771–89

'English Historical Linguistics and Philology in Japan 1950–1995: a Bibliographical Survey', *English Historical Linguistics and Philology in Japan*, ed. Fisiak and Oizumi, pp. 1–19

O'Keeffe, Katherine O'Brien, 'Edward Burroughs Irving, Jr. 1923–1998', *Med. Eng. Stud. Newsletter* 39, 1–2

'In Memoriam: Edward B. Irving Jr. (1923–98)', *OEN* 31.3, 10

O'Sullivan, Deirdre, 'Changing Views of the Viking Age', *Med. Hist.* (Bangor) 2.1 (1992), 3–13

Owen-Crocker, Gale R., 'Introduction', *Bull. of the John Rylands Univ. Lib. of Manchester* 79.3 (1997), 11–13 [special issue on 'Anglo-Saxon Texts and Contexts']

Page, R. I., 'Christine Elizabeth Fell 1938–1998', *Med. Eng. Stud. Newsletter* 39, 3–5

'Professor James E. Cross (1920–96)', *SBVS* 25.1, 83–4

'Two Runic Notes', *ASE* 27, 289–94

Palmer, Richard, 'Reginald Dodwell, Lambeth Librarian 1953–1958', *Medieval Art: Recent Perspectives*, ed. Owen-Crocker and Graham, pp. 224–30

Parry, Graham, 'An Incipient Medievalist in the Seventeenth Century: William Somner of Canterbury', *Stud. in Medievalism* 9 (1997), 58–65

Pope, John C., 'Eduard Sievers (1850–1932)', *Medieval Scholarship*, ed. Damico, pp. 177–99

Prescott, Andrew, 'The Published Writings of Janet Backhouse', *Illuminating the Book: Makers and Interpreters. Essays in Honour of Janet Backhouse*, ed. Michelle P. Brown and Scot McKendrick (London), pp. 299–305

Pulsiano, Phillip, 'Benjamin Thorpe (1782–1870)', *Medieval Scholarship*, ed. Damico, pp. 75–92

'Record of the Eighth Conference of the International Society of Anglo-Saxonists, at Università di Palermo, 7–12 July 1997', *ASE* 27, 1–4

'Research in Progress', *OEN* 31.4, 29–35

Rendall, Jane, 'Tacitus Engendered: "Gothic Feminism" and British Histories, *c.* 1750–1800', *Imagining Nations*, ed. Geoffrey Cubitt (Manchester), pp. 57–74

Robins, Robert Henry, 'Against the Establishment: Sidelines on Henry Sweet', *Productivity and Creativity: Studies in General and Descriptive Linguistics in Honor of E. M. Uhlenbeck*, ed. Mark Janse with An Verlinden, Trends in Ling., Stud. and Monographs 116 (Berlin), 167–78

Robinson, Benedict Scott, '"Darke speech": Matthew Parker and the Reforming of History', *Sixteenth Century Jnl* 29, 1061–83

Robinson, Fred C., 'Philological Criticism', *Poetica* (Tokyo) 50, 3–15

Robinson, Fred C., R. I. Page and Derek Pearsall, 'Tauno F. Mustanoja', *Speculum* 73, 962–3

Sandred, Karl Inge, 'Olof Arngart 15/4 1905–4/4 1997', *Namn och Bygd* 86, 119–20
'Rune Forsberg 1908–1997', *JEPNS* 30 (1997–8), 158–9
'Rune Forsberg 1908–1997', *Ortnamnssällskapets i Uppsala årsskrift*, pp. 79–81
Sauer, Hans, 'Knowledge of Old English in the Middle English Period?', *Language History and Linguistic Modelling*, ed. Hickey and Puppel, pp. 791–814
'Max Förster (1869–1954)', *Medieval Scholarship*, ed. Damico, pp. 339–49
Savage, Anne, 'Pagans and Christians, Anglo-Saxons and Anglo-Saxonists: the Changing Face of Our Mythical Landscape', *Reinventing the Middle Ages and the Renaissance*, ed. William F. Gentrup, Arizona Stud. in the Middle Ages and the Renaissance 1 (Turnhout), 37–49
Schichler, Robert L., ed., 'Abstracts of Papers in Anglo-Saxon Studies', *OEN* 31.3, A1–A47
Scott, Anne, 'The Legend of Saint Mildred in the *Nova legenda Anglie*', *Allegorica* 19, 63–81
Short, Harold, and Jane Roberts, 'Lynne Grundy 1957–1997', *Lit. and Ling. Computing* 13, 55
Skemer, Don C., see sect. 2a (*Expositio Vocabulorum*)
Smith, Arden R., 'Old English Influence on the Danian Language of J. R. R. Tolkien', *Interdigitations*, ed. Carr *et al.*, pp. 231–7
Smol, Anna, 'Pleasure, Progress and the Profession: Elizabeth Elstob and Contemporary Anglo-Saxon Studies', *Stud. in Medievalism* 9 (1997), 80–97
Spevack-Husmann, Helga, 'Rosemary Woolf (1925–1978)', *Medieval Scholarship*, ed. Damico, pp. 439–52
Stephens, Alan D., 'The Germanic Heroic Tradition and the Cultural Context of the Bayeux Tapestry', *Med. Hist.* (Bangor) 3 (1993), 51–8
Sutherland, Kathryn, 'Elizabeth Elstob (1683–1756)', *Medieval Scholarship*, ed. Damico, pp. 59–73
Szarmach, Paul E., M. Teresa Tavormina and Joel T. Rosenthal, ed., *Medieval England: an Encyclopedia* (New York)
[Szarmach, Paul E., *et al.*], *A Tribute to Ted Irving* (Kalamazoo, MI)
Thomas, Charles, 'C. A. Ralegh Radford', *MA* 42, 104–6
Trahern, Joseph B., Jr, ed., 'The Year's Work in Old English Studies 1995', *OEN* 30.2 (1998 for 1997), 3–148
Turner, Jane, ed., *The Dictionary of Art*, 34 vols. (London, 1996) [numerous articles under 'Anglo-Saxon']
Warner, Peter, *The Origins of Suffolk* (Manchester, 1996)
Wilcox, Jonathan, ed., *Old English Newsletter* 31.1–4 (Kalamazoo, MI, 1997–8) [issue 31.2 forthcoming]

2. OLD ENGLISH LANGUAGE

a. Lexicon and glosses

Anderson, Earl R., 'Interpretatio Romana: an Influence on Old English Vocabulary', *Foreign Lang. Education* [Xi'an Foreign Lang. Univ.] 4 (1997), 11–27

Baker, Peter S., 'The Inflection of Latin Nouns in Old English Texts', *Words and Works*, ed. Baker and Howe, pp. 187–206

Bammesberger, Alfred, 'Das altenglische Glossenwort *afigaen/afigen*', *Anglia* 116, 492–7

'An Old English Word for "butter"', *N&Q* 45, 41–6

see also sect. 2*b* and 3*bii*

Berger, Christiane, *Altenglische Paarformeln und ihre Varianten*, Münsteraner Monographien zur englischen Literatur 13 (Frankfurt am Main, 1993)

Biggam, C. P., *Grey in Old English: an Interdisciplinary Semantic Study* (London)

Biggs, Frederick M., 'The Exeter *Exeter Book*? Some Linguistic Evidence', *The Dictionary of Old English*, ed. Toswell, pp. 63–71

Blockley, Mary, 'The Irresistible Force, the Immovable Object and the *Dictionary of Old English*', *The Dictionary of Old English*, ed. Toswell, pp. 9–21

Boutkan, D. F. H., 'On the Form of North European Substratum Words in Germanic', *Historische Sprachforschung* 111, 102–33

Bredehoft, Thomas A., see sect. 9*l*

Breeze, Andrew, 'A Brittonic Etymology for Old English *stor* "incense"', *Anglia* 116, 227–30

Cassidy, Frederic G., 'The Anglo-Saxon Interjection', *Bright is the Ring of Words: Festschrift für Horst Weinstock*, ed. Clausdirk Pollner, Helmut Rohlfing and Frank-Rutger Hausmann (Bonn, 1996), pp. 45–8

'English – a Germanic Language?', *Interdigitations*, ed. Carr *et al.*, pp. 75–9

Cathey, James E., '*Interpretatio Christiana Saxonica*: Redefinition for Reeducation', *Interdigitations*, ed. Carr *et al.*, pp. 163–72

Cederlöf, Mikael, *The Element -stōw in the History of English*, Acta Universitatis Upsaliensis/Studia Anglistica Upsaliensia 103 (Uppsala)

Coates, Richard, 'The Scriptorium of the Mercian Rushworth Gloss: a Bilingual Perspective', *N&Q* 44 (1997), 453–8

see also sect. 5

Dalton-Puffer, Christiane, 'From *unasecgendlic* to *unspeakable*: the Role of Domain Structure in Morphological Change', *Advances in English Historical Linguistics*, ed. Fisiak and Krygier, pp. 33–51

Dekeyser, Xavier, 'Loss of Prototypical Meanings in the History of English Semantics or Semantic Redeployment', *Historical Linguistics 1995, Volume II: Germanic Linguistics*, ed. Richard M. Hogg and Linda van Bergen, Current Issues in Ling. Theory 162 (Amsterdam), 63–71

Fischer, Andreas, '"With this ring I thee wed": the Verbs *to wed* and *to marry* in the History of English', *Language History and Linguistic Modelling*, ed. Hickey and Puppel, pp. 467–81

Foot, Sarah, see sect. 6

Fujiwara, Yasuaki, 'On Identifying Old English Adverbs', *English Historical Linguistics and Philology in Japan*, ed. Fisiak and Oizumi, pp. 21–41

Goossens, Louis, 'Meaning Extension and Text Type', *ES* 79, 120–43

Gwara, Scott, 'New Old English Words from Dry-Point Aldhelm Glosses: *mennischær* and *ellenmod*', *ANQ* 11.1, 5–7

see also sect. 4 and 5

Healey, Antonette diPaolo, 'Wood-Gatherers and Cottage-Builders: Old Words and New Ways at the *Dictionary of Old English*', *Tracing the Trail of Time: Proceedings from the Second Diachronic Corpora Workshop*, ed. Raymond Hickey *et al.* (Amsterdam, 1997), pp. 33–46

Holland, Joan, 'Dictionary of Old English: 1998 Progress Report', *OEN* 32.1, 12–13

Hough, Carole, 'OE *brūn* in Place-Names', *ES* 79, 512–21

'Place-Name Evidence for Old English Bird-Names', *JEPNS* 30 (1997–8), 60–76 [OE *bemere*, OE *horn-blāwere*, OE *pīpere*, OE *hearpe*]

'Place-Name Evidence relating to the Interpretation of Old English Legal Terminology', *Leeds Stud. in Eng.* 27 (1996), 19–48

Howlett, David, 'Old English *ondgierwan, ongierwan, ungierwan*', *Anglia* 116, 223–6

Ishiguro, Taro, 'Verbs of Negative Import: a Syntactic Study that Benefited from the *Dictionary of Old English*', *The Dictionary of Old English*, ed. Toswell, pp. 23–32

Jucker, Andreas H., 'The Discourse Marker *well* in the History of English', *Eng. Lang. and Ling.* 1 (1997), 91–110

Kahlas-Tarkka, Leena, '– THING in English: a Case of Grammaticalization?', *Language History and Linguistic Modelling*, ed. Hickey and Puppel, pp. 281–91

Keefer, Sarah Larratt, see sect. 4

Kitson, P. R., 'Old English Bird Names (II)', *ES* 79, 2–22

'The Root of the Matter: OE *wyrt, wyrtwale, -a, wyrt(t)rum(a)* and Cognates', *Language History and Linguistic Modelling*, ed. Hickey and Puppel, pp. 127–41

Kittlick, Wolfgang, see sect. 2*b*

Kornexl, Lucia, 'Ahd. *gifatero* / ae. *gefædera* und ihr "paradoxes Femininum"', *Historische Sprachforschung* 111, 305–46

Liberman, Anatoly, 'The English F-Word and its Kin', *Interdigitations*, ed. Carr *et al.*, pp. 107–20

Lloyd, Albert L., 'The "Shaping" of German *Farbe*: Cathedral Renovations and the Rebuilding of an Etymology', *Interdigitations*, ed. Carr *et al.*, pp. 121–8

Lucas, Peter J., 'From *Jabberwocky* Back to Old English: Nonsense, Anglo-Saxon and Oxford', *Language History and Linguistic Modelling*, ed. Hickey and Puppel, pp. 503–20

Markey, Tom, 'Studies in Runic Origins 1: Germanic *maþl-/*mahl-* and Etruscan meΘlum', *Amer. Jnl of Germanic Ling. and Literatures* 10, 153–200

Markey, Thomas L., 'English *dung* "manure": Early Animal Husbandry and Etymology', *North-Western European Lang. Evolution* 34, 3–13

McGowan, Joseph, 'More Glosses in Early Medieval English Manuscripts', *N&Q* 45, 166–8

Mottausch, Karl-Heinz, '"Gehen" und "stehen" im Germanischen: Versuch einer Synthese', *Historische Sprachforschung* 111, 134–62

Nevanlinna, Saara, '"To Make Merry", its Variants in Middle English and the Helsinki Corpus', *Language History and Linguistic Modelling*, ed. Hickey and Puppel, pp. 521–42

Oguy, A., 'Some Notes about Semantic Regularity of Some Polysemantic Words', *Jnl of Quantitative Ling.* 5, 62–6

Ono, Shigeru, 'Old English Verbs of Possessing', *English Historical Linguistics and Philology in Japan*, ed. Fisiak and Oizumi, pp. 297–311

Österman, Aune, '*There* Compounds in the History of English', *Grammaticalization at Work*, ed. Matti Rissanen, Merja Kytö and Kirsi Heikkonen, Topics in Eng. Ling. 24 (Berlin, 1997), 191–276

Park, Soon-Ham, 'A Study of the Diglossic Situations in the Old English and Middle English Period: With Reference to the Celtic Substratum and the French Superstratum', *Hist. of Eng.* (Seoul, 1997) 4, 31–48

Peeters, Christian, 'On Germanic Etymology', *General Ling.* 36, 117–18

Pintzuk, Susan, and Ann Taylor, 'Annotating the Helsinki Corpus: the *Brooklyn-Geneva-Amsterdam-Helsinki Parsed Corpus of Old English* and the *Penn-Helsinki Parsed Corpus of Middle English*', *Tracing the Trail of Time: Proceedings from the Second Diachronic Corpora Workshop*, ed. Raymond Hickey *et al.* (Amsterdam, 1997), pp. 91–104

Polomé, Edgar C., 'Some Comments on the Vocabulary of Emotion in Germanic', *Interdigitations*, ed. Carr *et al.*, pp. 129–40

Porter, David W., 'Dogs That Won't Hunt and Old English Ghost Words', *N&Q* 45, 168–9

Ramisch, Heinrich, 'Re-Examining the Influence of Scandinavian on English: the Case of *ditch/dike*', *Language History and Linguistic Modelling*, ed. Hickey and Puppel, pp. 561–9

Raumolin-Brunberg, Helena, and Leena Kahlas-Tarkka, 'Indefinite Pronouns with Singular Human Reference', *Grammaticalization at Work*, ed. Matti Rissanen, Merja Kytö and Kirsi Heikkonen, Topics in Eng. Ling. 24 (Berlin, 1997), 17–85

Richards, Mary P., 'The *Dictionary of Old English* and Old English Legal Terminology', *The Dictionary of Old English*, ed. Toswell, pp. 57–61

Rissanen, Matti, '*Maþelian* in Old English Poetry', *Words and Works*, ed. Baker and Howe, pp. 159–72

'The Pronominalization of *one*', *Grammaticalization at Work*, ed. Matti Rissanen, Merja Kytö and Kirsi Heikkonen, Topics in Eng. Ling. 24 (Berlin, 1997), 87–143

'Towards an Integrated View of the Development of English: Notes on Causal Linking', *Advances in English Historical Linguistics*, ed. Fisiak and Krygier, pp. 389–406

Roberts, Jane, 'On the *Thesaurus of Old English*', *Med. Eng. Stud. Newsletter* 39, 8–21

'*A Thesaurus of Old English*: One Snapshot of a Vanished World', *North-Western European Lang. Evolution* 33, 133–53

Rusche, Philip G., 'What Type of Treasure is Kept in a *goldhordhus*?', *N&Q* 45, 14–16

Sauer, Hans, 'On the Analysis and Structure of Old and Middle English Plant Names', *Hist of Eng.* (Seoul, 1997) 3, 133–62

Schaffner, Stefan, 'Zu Wortbildung und Etymologie von altenglisch *nihol, niowol* und lateinisch *procul*', *Münchener Studien zur Sprachwissenschaft* 56 (1996), 131–71

Skemer, Don C., '*Expositio Vocabulorum*: a Medieval English Glossary as Archival Aid', *Jnl of the Soc. of Archivists* 19, 63–75

Speirs, Nancy, 'Lexicography and Corpus-Tagging: Enhancing the *Dictionary of Old English Corpus in Electronic Form*', *Tracing the Trail of Time: Proceedings from the Second Diachronic Corpora Workshop*, ed. Raymond Hickey *et al.* (Amsterdam, 1997), pp. 137–49

Stanley, E. G., 'Words for the *Dictionary of Old English*', *The Dictionary of Old English*, ed. Toswell, pp. 33–56

Takeuchi, Schin'ichi, see sect. 3*c*

Tanabe, Harumi, 'In Search of Synonyms in the *Historical Thesaurus of English* and the Second Edition of the *OED* on *CD*', *Stud. in Eng. Lang. and Lit.* [Seikei Univ.] 1, 57–71

Terasawa, Yoshio, *The Kenkyusha Dictionary of English Etymology* (Tokyo, 1997)

'Some Etymological and Semasiological Notes on *girl*', *English Historical Linguistics and Philology in Japan*, ed. Fisiak and Oizumi, pp. 401–16

Toswell, M. J., ed., *The Dictionary of Old English: Retrospects and Prospects*, with a preface by Antonette diPaolo Healey, *OEN* Subsidia 26 (Kalamazoo, MI)

Wright, Michael J., 'Anglo-Saxon Midwives', *ANQ* 11.1, 3–5

Zbierska-Sawala, Anna, 'Word-Formation and the Text in Early English: the Axiological Functions of Old English Prefixes', *Language History and Linguistic Modelling*, ed. Hickey and Puppel, pp. 593–602

b. Syntax, phonology and other aspects

Abraham, Werner, '"Jespersen's Cycle": the Evidence from Germanic', *Interdigitations*, ed. Carr *et al.*, pp. 63–70

Allen, Cynthia L., 'The Development of an "Impersonal" Verb in Middle English: the Case of *behoove*', *Studies in Middle English Linguistics*, ed. Fisiak and Winter, pp. 1–21

'Genitives and the Creolization Question', *Eng. Lang. and Ling.* 2, 129–35

'Middle English Case Loss and the "Creolization" Hypothesis', *Eng. Lang. and Ling.* 1 (1997), 63–89

Anderson, John, 'A Core Morphology for Old English Verbs', *Eng. Lang. and Ling.* 2, 199–222

'Subjecthood and the English Impersonal', *Language History and Linguistic Modelling*, ed. Hickey and Puppel, pp. 251–63

Bammesberger, Alfred, 'The Germanic Preterite-Present **ann/unn-*', *North-Western European Lang. Evolution* 34, 15–21

'Runic Frisian *weladu* and Further West Germanic Nominal Forms in *-u*', *North-Western European Lang. Evolution* 33, 121–32

Barrack, Charles M., 'Mother Reveals Why Intervocalic Coronals Misbehave', *Interdigitations*, ed. Carr *et al.*, pp. 71–4

Sievers' Law in Germanic, Berkeley Insights in Ling. and Semiotics 22 (New York)
Bech, Kristin, 'Pragmatic Factors in Language Change: XVS and XSV Clauses in Old and Middle English', *Folia Linguistica Historica* 19, 79–102
Bermúdez-Otero, Ricardo, 'Prosodic Optimization: the Middle English Length Adjustment', *Eng. Lang. and Ling.* 2, 169–97
Blockley, Mary E., 'Apposition and the Subjects of Verb-Initial Clauses', *Words and Works*, ed. Baker and Howe, pp. 173–86
Denton, Jeanette Marshall, 'Phonetic Perspectives on West Germanic Consonant Gemination', *Amer. Jnl of Germanic Ling. and Literatures* 10, 201–35
Derolez, René, 'On the "Otherness" of the Anglo-Saxon Runes and the "Perfect Fit" of the Fuþark', *Runeninschriften*, ed. Düwel, pp. 103–16
Ehala, Martin, 'How a Man Changed a Parameter Value: the Loss of SOV in Estonian Subclauses', *Historical Linguistics 1995, Volume II: Germanic Linguistics*, ed. Richard M. Hogg and Linda van Bergen, Current Issues in Ling. Theory 162 (Amsterdam), 73–88
Fischer, Olga, 'The Grammaticalisation of Infinitival *to* in English Compared with German and Dutch', *Language History and Linguistic Modelling*, ed. Hickey and Puppel, pp. 265–80
Fisiak, Jacek, and Marcin Krygier, ed., *Advances in English Historical Linguistics (1996)*, Trends in Ling., Stud. and Monographs 112 (Berlin)
Fisiak, Jacek, and Werner Winter, ed., *Studies in Middle English Linguistics*, Trends in Ling., Stud. and Monographs 103 (Berlin, 1997)
Fitzmaurice, Susan, 'Grammaticalisation, Textuality and Subjectivity: the Progressive and the *Anglo-Saxon Chronicle*', *The Virtues of Language: History in Language, Linguistics and Texts*, ed. Dieter Stein and Rosanna Sornicola, Stud. in the Hist. of Lang. Sciences 87 (Amsterdam), 21–49
Freeborn, Dennis, *From Old English to Standard English: a Course Book in Language Variation across Time*, 2nd ed. (London)
Fulk, Robert D., 'Ambisyllabicity in Old English: a Contrary View', *Insights in Germanic Linguistics II: Classic and Contemporary*, ed. Irmengard Rauch and Gerald F. Carr, Trends in Ling., Stud. and Monographs 94 (Berlin, 1997), 29–45
'The Chronology of Anglo-Frisian Sound Changes', *Amsterdamer Beiträge zur älteren Germanistik* 49, 139–54
'Evaluating the Evidence for Lengthening before Homorganic Consonant Clusters in the *Ormulum*', *Interdigitations*, ed. Carr *et al.*, pp. 201–9
'The Role of Syllable Structure in Old English Quantitative Sound Changes', *North-Western European Lang. Evolution* 33, 3–35
Garrett, Andrew, 'On the Origin of Auxiliary *do*', *Eng. Lang. and Ling.* 2, 283–330
Gąsiorowski, Piotr, *The Phonology of Old English Stress and Metrical Structure*, Bamberger Beiträge zur englischen Sprachwissenschaft 39 (Frankfurt am Main, 1997)
'Words in *-ate* and the History of English Stress', *Studies in Middle English Linguistics*, ed. Fisiak and Winter, pp. 157–80
Goh, Gwang-Yoon, 'Relative Obliqueness and Subcategorization Inheritance in Old English Preposition-Verb Compound Verbs', *Ohio State Univ. Working Papers in Ling.* 51, 59–93

Green, D. H., *Language and History in the Early Germanic World* (Cambridge)
Ham, William H., 'A New Approach to an Old Problem: Gemination and Constraint Reranking in West Germanic', *Jnl of Comparative Germanic Ling.* 1 (1997–8), 225–62
Han, Sang-Woo, 'A Study of Verb Movement in Old English', *Hist. of Eng.* (Seoul) 5, 93–104 [in Korean]
Hewson, John, 'The Evolution of Definite and Indefinite Articles in English', *Language History and Linguistic Modelling*, ed. Hickey and Puppel, pp. 101–11
Hickey, Raymond, and Stanisław Puppel, ed., *Language History and Linguistic Modelling: a Festschrift for Jacek Fisiak on his 60th Birthday*, Trends in Ling., Stud. and Monographs 101 (Berlin, 1997)
Hogg, Richard M., 'On the Ideological Boundaries of Old English Dialects', *Advances in English Historical Linguistics*, ed. Fisiak and Krygier, pp. 107–18
'The Morphology and Dialect of Old English Disyllabic Nouns', *Language History and Linguistic Modelling*, ed. Hickey and Puppel, pp. 113–26
Hulk, Aafke, and Ans van Kemenade, 'Negation as a Reflex of Clause Structure', *Negation and Polarity: Syntax and Semantics*, ed. Danielle Forget *et al.*, Current Issues in Ling. Theory 155 (Amsterdam, 1997), 183–207
Hutton, John, 'The Development of Secondary Stress in Old English', *Historical Linguistics 1995, Volume II: Germanic Linguistics*, ed. Richard M. Hogg and Linda van Bergen, Current Issues in Ling. Theory 162 (Amsterdam), 115–30
'Stress in Old English, *giet ongean*', *Linguistics* 36, 847–85
Hwang, Intae, 'Stylistics and an Interpretation of *The Wanderer*, an Old English Lyric', *Hist. of Eng.* (Seoul) 6, 47–67
Jin, Koichi, *Aspects of English Syntax and Style: a Comparative Study* (Tokyo, 1997)
'(Pro-)Nominal Reference in Old English and the Origin of the *that*-Clause', *English Historical Linguistics and Philology in Japan*, ed. Fisiak and Oizumi, pp. 111–36
Kastovsky, Dieter, 'Morphological Restructuring: the Case of Old English and Middle English Verbs', *Historical Linguistics 1995, Volume II: Germanic Linguistics*, ed. Richard M. Hogg and Linda van Bergen, Current Issues in Ling. Theory 162 (Amsterdam), 131–47
Killie, Kristin, 'The Spread of *-ly* to Present Participles', *Advances in English Historical Linguistics*, ed. Fisiak and Krygier, pp. 119–34
Kilpiö, Matti, 'On the Forms and Functions of the Verb *be* from Old to Modern English', *English in Transition: Corpus-Based Studies in Linguistic Variation and Genre Styles*, ed. Matti Rissanen, Merja Kytö and Kirsi Heikkonen, Topics in Eng. Ling. 23 (Berlin, 1997), 87–120
Kishida, Takayuki, 'On the Accusative–Dative Syncretism in *The Parker Chronicle* (1070–1154)', *Ann. Collection of Essays and Stud.* (Gakushuin Univ.), 45, 59–96 [in Japanese]
Kitson, Peter, 'When Did Middle English Begin? Later Than You Think!', *Studies in Middle English Linguistics*, ed. Fisiak and Winter, pp. 221–69
Kittlick, Wolfgang, *Die Glossen der Hs. British Library, Cotton Cleopatra A.III: Phonologie, Morphologie, Wortgeographie*, Europäische Hochschulschriften XIV, 347 (Frankfurt am Main)

Kleiner, Yuri, '*Fernassimilation*: Germanic Palatal Umlaut and Breaking', *Interdigitations*, ed. Carr *et al.*, pp. 93–106

Koopman, Willem F., 'Inversion after Single and Multiple Topics in Old English', *Advances in English Historical Linguistics*, ed. Fisiak and Krygier, pp. 135–50

'Topicalization in Old English and its Effects. Some Remarks', *Language History and Linguistic Modelling*, ed. Hickey and Puppel, pp. 307–21

Kroch, Anthony, and Ann Taylor, 'Verb Movement in Old and Middle English: Dialect Variation and Language Contact', *Parameters of Morphosyntactic Change*, ed. Ans van Kemenade and Nigel Vincent (Cambridge, 1997), pp. 297–325

Krygier, Marcin, 'Epenthesis and *Mouillierung* in the Explanation of *i*-umlaut: the Rise and Fall of a Theory', *Advances in English Historical Linguistics*, ed. Fisiak and Krygier, pp. 151–9

From Regularity to Anomaly: Inflectional 'i'-umlaut in Middle English, Univ. of Bamberg Stud. in Eng. Ling. 40 (Frankfurt am Main, 1997)

'Nominal Markedness Changes in Three Old and Middle English Psalters – Using the Past to Predict the Past', *Language History and Linguistic Modelling*, ed. Hickey and Puppel, pp. 143–52

'On a Synchronic Approach to Old English Morphology', *Folia Linguistica Historica* 19, 119–28

Lee, Phil-Hwan, 'Cliticization of Old English Personal Pronouns', *Hist. of Eng.* (Seoul) 5, 73–92 [in Korean]

López-Couso, María José, and Belén Méndez-Naya, 'On Minor Declarative Complementizers in the History of English: the Case of *but*', *Advances in English Historical Linguistics*, ed. Fisiak and Krygier, pp. 161–71

Los, Bettelou, 'Bare and *to*-Infinitives in Old English: Callaway Revisited', *Advances in English Historical Linguistics*, ed. Fisiak and Krygier, pp. 173–88

'The Rise of the *to*-Infinitive as Verb Complement', *Eng. Lang. and Ling.* 2, 1–36

Manabe, Kazumi, 'Finite and Non-Finite Clauses in the English of Alfred's Reign: a Study of Syntax and Style in Old English', *English Historical Linguistics and Philology in Japan*, ed. Fisiak and Oizumi, pp. 189–207

McCully, Christopher B., 'Stress, Survival and Change: Old to Middle English', *Studies in Middle English Linguistics*, ed. Fisiak and Winter, pp. 283–300

Minkova, Donka, 'Constraint Ranking in Middle English Stress-Shifting', *Eng. Lang. and Ling.* 1 (1997), 135–75

Minkova, Donka, and Robert P. Stockwell, 'The Origins of Long-Short Allomorphy in English', *Advances in English Historical Linguistics*, ed. Fisiak and Krygier, pp. 211–39

Moessner, Lilo, 'Economy as a Principle of Syntactic Change', *Language History and Linguistic Modelling*, ed. Hickey and Puppel, pp. 357–72

Molencki, Rafał, 'Modals in Past Counterfactual Conditional Protases', *Advances in English Historical Linguistics*, ed. Fisiak and Krygier, pp. 241–51

Moon, An-Nah, 'A Blocking Effect of a Prosodic Word Boundary in Old English Fricative Voicing', *Hist. of Eng.* (Seoul) 6, 89–112

Mottausch, Karl-Heinz, 'Die reduplizierenden Verben im Nord- und Westgermanischen: Versuch eines Raum-Zeitmodells', *North-Western European Lang. Evolution* 33, 43–91

Nagle, Stephen J., and Sara L. Sanders, 'Downsizing the Preterite-Presents in Middle English', *Advances in English Historical Linguistics*, ed. Fisiak and Krygier, pp. 253–61

Nagucka, Ruta, 'The Instrumental in Old English', *Language History and Linguistic Modelling*, ed. Hickey and Puppel, pp. 153–66

Nakao, Toshio, 'The Hiatus in English Historical Phonology', *Language History and Linguistic Modelling*, ed. Hickey and Puppel, pp. 59–64

Nielsen, Hans Frede, *The Continental Backgrounds of English and its Insular Development until 1154*, North-Western European Lang. Evolution Suppl. 19 (Odense)

Niwa, Yoshinobu, 'Cumulative Phenomena between Prefixes and Verbs in Old English', *Language History and Linguistic Modelling*, ed. Hickey and Puppel, pp. 167–78

Nuñez Pertejo, Paloma, 'On the Origin and History of the English Prepositional Type *a-hunting*: a Corpus-Based Study', *Revista Alicantina de Estudios Ingleses* 9 (1996), 105–17

Oaks, Dallin D., 'Historical Roots of Structural Ambiguity in English: a Survey of Some Selected Grammatical Features', *General Ling.* 36, 59–70

Ogawa, Hiroshi, '*þa* Temporal Clauses in Two Old English *Lives of St Martin*: a Study of Prose Styles in the Blickling and Ælfrician Versions', *Stud. in Med. Eng. Lang. and Lit.* (Tokyo) 13, 45–60

Ogura, Michiko, 'Ælfric Believed *on* God', *N&Q* 45, 273–5

'The Grammaticalization in Medieval English', *Advances in English Historical Linguistics*, ed. Fisiak and Krygier, pp. 293–314

'On Double Auxiliary Constructions in Medieval English', *English Historical Linguistics and Philology in Japan*, ed. Fisiak and Oizumi, pp. 229–36

Ohkada, Masayuki, 'On Nominative Case Assignment in Old English', *Advances in English Historical Linguistics*, ed. Fisiak and Krygier, pp. 345–59

Okazaki, Masao, 'A Constraint on the Well-Formedness of Old English Alliterative Verse', *Eng. Ling.* (Tokyo) 15, 243–80

Oliver, Lisi, 'Irish Influence on Orthographic Practice in Early Kent', *North-Western European Lang. Evolution* 33, 93–113

Paddock, Harold, 'Effects of Mood Loss and Aspect Gain on English Tenses', *Language History and Linguistic Modelling*, ed. Hickey and Puppel, pp. 1527–36

Penzl, Herbert, 'The Germanic *i*-umlaut Revisited', *Insights in Germanic Linguistics II: Classic and Contemporary*, ed. Irmengard Rauch and Gerald F. Carr, Trends in Ling., Stud. and Monographs 94 (Berlin, 1997), 189–95

Phillips, Betty S., 'The Peterborough Chronicle Diphthongs', *Studies in Middle English Linguistics*, ed. Fisiak and Winter, pp. 429–38

Pintzuk, Susan, 'Old English Verb-Complement Word Order and the Change from OV to VO', *York Papers in Ling.* 17 (1996), 241–64

'Post-Verbal Complements in Old English', *Historical Linguistics 1995, Volume II: Germanic Linguistics*, ed. Richard M. Hogg and Linda van Bergen, Current Issues in Ling. Theory 162 (Amsterdam), 233–46

Plotkin, Vulf Y., 'A Case of Divergent Phonological Evolution in West Germanic', *Language History and Linguistic Modelling*, ed. Hickey and Puppel, pp. 873–7

Pocheptsov, George G., 'Quasi-Impersonal Verbs in Old and Middle English', *Studies in Middle English Linguistics*, ed. Fisiak and Winter, pp. 469–88

Poussa, Patricia, 'Derivation of *it* from *þat* in Eastern Dialects of British English', *Language History and Linguistic Modelling*, ed. Hickey and Puppel, pp. 691–9

Rissanen, Matti, 'Optional *THAT* with Subordinates in Middle English', *Language History and Linguistic Modelling*, ed. Hickey and Puppel, pp. 373–83

Ruiz Moneva, M. Angeles, 'A Relevance Theory Approach to the Scandinavian Influence upon the Development of the English Language', *Revista Alicantina de Estudios Ingleses* 10 (1997), 183–91

Seppänen, Aimo, 'The Genitive and the Category of Case in the History of English', *Language History and Linguistic Modelling*, ed. Hickey and Puppel, pp. 193–214

Sonoda, Katsuhide, 'On the Inseparable Nature of Verb-Auxiliary Combinations in Old English', *English Historical Linguistics and Philology in Japan*, ed. Fisiak and Oizumi, pp. 313–21

Steins, Carsten, 'Against Arbitrary Features in Inflection: Old English Declension Classes', *Phonology and Morphology of the Germanic Languages*, ed. Wolfgang Kehrein and Richard Wiese, Linguistische Arbeiten 386 (Tübingen), 241–65

Stepanovicius, Albertas, 'Middle (and Old) English Prerequisites for the Great Vowel Shift', *Studies in Middle English Linguistics*, ed. Fisiak and Winter, pp. 561–72

Swan, Toril, 'Adverbialization and Subject-Modification in Old English', *Advances in English Historical Linguistics*, ed. Fisiak and Krygier, pp. 443–56

Taillé, Michel, *Histoire de la langue anglaise* (Paris, 1995)

Terajima, Michiko, 'The Syllable Structure and Phonological Processes in the History of English', *English Historical Linguistics and Philology in Japan*, ed. Fisiak and Oizumi, pp. 361–85

Terasawa, Jun, 'The Passive as a Perfect in Old English', *The Locus of Meaning: Papers in Honor of Yoshihiko Ikegami*, ed. K. Yamanaka and T. Ohori (Tokyo), 306–24

Teresi, Loredana, 'Computer-Assisted Linguistic Analysis in Anglo-Saxon Manuscripts: an Experimental Study', *Bull. of the John Rylands Univ. Lib. of Manchester* 79.3 (1997), 133–48

Valentin, Paul, '*Wirdhu* and the Germanic Passive', *Interdigitations*, ed. Carr *et al.*, pp. 141–6

Van den Eynden, Nadine, 'Aspects of Preposition Placement in English', *Speech Past and Present: Studies in English Dialectology in Memory of Ossi Ihalainen*, ed. Juhani Klemola, Merja Kytö and Matti Rissanen, Bamberger Beiträge zur englischen Sprachwissenschaft 38 (Frankfurt am Main, 1996), 426–46

van Gelderen, Elly, 'The Future of *for to*', *Amer. Jnl of Germanic Ling. and Literatures* 10, 45–71

van Kemenade, Ans, 'Topics in Old and Middle English Negative Sentences', *Language History and Linguistic Modelling*, ed. Hickey and Puppel, pp. 293–306

Venneman, Theo, 'The Development of Reduplicating Verbs in Germanic', *Insights in Germanic Linguistics II: Classic and Contemporary*, ed. Irmengard Rauch and Gerald F. Carr, Trends in Ling., Stud. and Monographs 94 (Berlin, 1997), 297–336

Vezzosi, Letizia, 'Passive Constructions: the Case of Old English', *Folia Linguistica Historica* 19, 53–64

La sintassi della subordinazione in anglosassone, Pubblicazioni dell'Istituto di linguistica 3 (Naples)

Waltz, Heidi, 'Causative Psych-Verbs in the History of English', *Insights in Germanic Linguistics II: Classic and Contemporary*, ed. Irmengard Rauch and Gerald F. Carr, Trends in Ling., Stud. and Monographs 94 (Berlin, 1997), 337–43

Wełna, Jerzy, 'The Functional Relationship between Rules (Old English Voicing of Fricatives and Lengthening of Vowels before Homorganic Clusters)', *Advances in English Historical Linguistics*, ed. Fisiak and Krygier, pp. 471–84

'Weak-to-Strong: a Shift in English Verbs?', *Language History and Linguistic Modelling*, ed. Hickey and Puppel, pp. 215–28

Yamada, Norio, 'On the Functional Motivation of Phonological Changes in English', *English Historical Linguistics and Philology in Japan*, ed. Fisiak and Oizumi, pp. 417–37

3. OLD ENGLISH LITERATURE

a. General

Alamichel, Marie-Françoise, and Josseline Bidard, trans., *Des animaux et des hommes*, Cultures et civilisation médiévales 17 (Paris)

Åström, Berit, 'The Creation of the Anglo-Saxon Woman', *SN* 70, 25–34

Brown, Marjorie A., 'The Feast Hall in Anglo-Saxon Society', *Food and Eating in Medieval Europe*, ed. Martha Carlin and Joel T. Rosenthal (London), pp. 1–13

Carruthers, Leo, comp., *La Ronde des saisons: saisons dans la littérature et la société anglaises du Moyen Age*, Cultures et civilisations médiévales 16 (Paris)

Coatsworth, Elizabeth, 'Cloth-Making and the Virgin Mary in Anglo-Saxon Literature and Art', *Medieval Art: Recent Perspectives*, ed. Owen-Crocker and Graham, pp. 8–25

Crépin, André, 'Notes sur l'enfance dans l'Angleterre du haut moyen âge', *PRIS-MA* (Poitiers) 12 (1996), 157–65

Elliott, Ralph W. V., 'Runes in English Literature: from Cynewulf to Tolkien', *Runeninschriften*, ed. Düwel, pp. 660–6

Knappe, Gabriele, 'Classical Rhetoric in Anglo-Saxon England', *ASE* 27, 5–29

Lendinara, Patrizia, see sect. 6

Locherbie-Cameron, M. A. L., 'Friend or Foe? The Portrayal of Enemies in Anglo-Saxon Literature', *Med. Hist.* (Bangor) 2.1 (1992), 34–44

Luiselli Fadda, Anna Maria, see sect. 9*l*

Magennis, Hugh, '*Godes þeow* and Related Expressions in Old English: Contexts and Uses of a Traditional Literary Figure', *Anglia* 116, 139–70

Potkay, Monica Brzezinski, and Regula Meyer Evitt, *Minding the Body: Women and Literature in the Middle Ages, 800–1500* (London, 1997) ['Redeeming Ornament: Women in Old English Literature', pp. 31–46 and 204–6]

Raffel, Burton, ed. and trans., and Alexandra H. Olsen, ed., *Poems and Prose from the Old English* (New Haven, CT)

Rat, Jean-Michel, 'Les Activités maritimes du Haut Moyen Age en relation avec les saisons', *La Ronde des saisons*, ed. Carruthers, pp. 23–35

Schaefer, Ursula, 'Twin Collocations in the Early Middle English Lives of the *Katherine*

Group', *Orality and Literacy in Early Middle English*, ed. Herbert Pilch, ScriptOralia 83 (Tübingen, 1996), 179–98

Shirai, Naoko, 'Traditions of Beheading: a Comparative Study of Classical Irish and Anglo-Saxon Cultures', *Medieval Heritage: Essays in Honour of Tadahiro Ikegami*, ed. Masahiko Kanno *et al.* (Tokyo, 1997), pp. 315–28

Stanley, Eric Gerald, 'Personification without the Distinction of Capitalization, Mainly in Early Middle English', *Orality and Literacy in Early Middle English*, ed. Herbert Pilch, ScriptOralia 83 (Tübingen, 1996), 199–226

Thundy, Zacharias P., *Millennium: Apocalypse and Antichrist and Old English Monsters c. 1000 A.D.* (Notre Dame, IN)

Tkacz, Catherine Brown, 'Heaven and Fallen Angels in Old English', *The Devil, Heresy and Witchcraft in the Middle Ages: Essays in Honor of Jeffrey B. Russell*, ed. Alberto Ferreiro (Leiden), pp. 327–44

Treharne, E. M., 'Old English Literature [1995]', *Year's Work in Eng. Stud.* 76, 110–30

b. Poetry

i. General

Acker, Paul, *Revising Oral Theory: Formulaic Composition in Old English and Old Icelandic Verse* (New York)

Alamichel, Marie-Françoise, '"Sumer is icumen in": chants et saisons dans la Grande-Bretagne médiévale', *La Ronde des saisons*, ed. Carruthers, pp. 51–60

Anderson, Earl R., *A Grammar of Iconism* (Madison)

Conner, Patrick W., 'Beyond the ASPR: Electronic Editions of Old English Poetry', *New Approaches to Editing Old English Verse*, ed. Keefer and O'Keeffe, pp. 109–26

Dance, Richard, 'The Lycanthropic Language of Old English Poetry; or, a Light in the Dark Ages', *University College [Oxford] Record* 12.1 (1997), 64–76

Dubois, Marguerite-Marie, 'Le Rondeau du coucou', *La Ronde des saisons*, ed. Carruthers, pp. 15–21

Erzgräber, Willi, *Mittelalter und Renaissance in England. Von den altenglischen Elegien bis Shakespeares Tragödien* (Freiburg im Breisgau, 1997) [collected papers]

Highfield, John, '*Mod* in the Old English "Secular" Poetry: an Indicator of Aristocratic Class', *Bull. of the John Rylands Univ. Lib. of Manchester* 79.3 (1997), 79–92

Hill, Thomas D., 'Two Notes on the Old Frisian *Fia-eth*', *Amsterdamer Beiträge zur älteren Germanistik* 49, 169–78

Honegger, Thomas, 'Form and Function: the Beasts of Battle Revisited', *ES* 79, 289–98

Huisman, Rosemary, *The Written Poem: Semiotic Conventions from Old to Modern English* (London)

Irving, Edward B., Jr, 'Editing Old English Verse: the Ideal', *New Approaches to Editing Old English Verse*, ed. Keefer and O'Keeffe, pp. 11–20

Jackson, Elizabeth, '"Not Simply Lists": an Eddic Perspective on Short-Item Lists in Old English Poems', *Speculum* 73, 338–71

Keefer, Sarah Larratt, and Katherine O'Brien O'Keeffe, ed., *New Approaches to Editing Old English Verse* (Cambridge)

Macrae-Gibson, O. D., and J. R. Lishman, 'Variety of Old English Metrical Usage', *NM* 99, 139–71

Minkova, Donka, 'Velars and Palatals in Old English Alliteration', *Historical Linguistics 1997*, ed. Monika S. Schmid, Jennifer R. Austin and Dieter Stein, Current Issues in Ling. Theory 164 (Amsterdam), 269–89

Neville, Jennifer, 'The Seasons in Old English Poetry', *La Ronde des saisons*, ed. Carruthers, pp. 37–49

O'Keeffe, Katherine O'Brien, 'Introduction', *New Approaches to Editing Old English Verse*, ed. Keefer and O'Keeffe, pp. 1–9

'The Performing Body on the Oral-Literate Continuum: Old English Poetry', *Teaching Oral Traditions*, ed. John Miles Foley (New York), pp. 46–58

Poole, Russell, *Old English Wisdom Poetry*, Annotated Bibliographies of Old and Middle Eng. Lit. 5 (Cambridge)

Rissanen, Matti, see sect. 2*a*

Scragg, D. G., 'Towards a New Anglo-Saxon Poetic Records', *New Approaches to Editing Old English Verse*, ed. Keefer and O'Keeffe, pp. 67–77

Stévanovitch, Colette, 'Le Menu des banquets dans la poésie vieil-anglaise', *Banquets et manières de table au moyen âge*, Sénéfiance 38 (Aix-en-Provence, 1996), 375–89

Stodnick, Jacqueline A., 'Cynewulf as Author: Medieval Reality or Modern Myth?', *Bull. of the John Rylands Univ. Lib. of Manchester* 79.3 (1997), 25–39

Terasawa, Jun, 'The *helle* Sequence in Old English Poetry', *English Historical Linguistics and Philology in Japan*, ed. Fisiak and Oizumi, pp. 387–99

Tranter, Stephen N., 'Significant Choices: the Interplay of Rhyme and Alliteration in Medieval English Poetry', *Literaturwissenschaftliches Jahrbuch* 39, 75–94

Wendler, Antje, *Die Figuren der Diskurspartner und ihre Verwendung in der altenglischen Dichtung*, Internationale Hochschulschriften 263 (Münster)

ii. *'Beowulf'*

Baker, Peter S., 'The Reader, the Editor and the Electronic Critical Edition', *A Guide to Editing Middle English*, ed. Vincent P. McCarren and Douglas Moffat (Ann Arbor, MI), pp. 263–83 [*Brunanburh* and *Beowulf*]

Bammesberger, Alfred, 'The Half-Line *freond on frætewum* (*Beowulf* 962a)', *NM* 99, 237–9

'The Half-Line *Grendeles mægum* (*Beowulf* 2353b)', *N&Q* 45, 2–4

'The Reading of *Beowulf*, 1. 31b', *NM* 99, 125–9

Barringer, Bob, 'Adding Insult to the Inquiry: a Study of Rhetorical Jousting in *Beowulf*', *In Geardagum* 19, 19–26

Blockley, Mary E., see sect. 2*b*

Booth, Paul Anthony, 'King Alfred versus Beowulf: the Re-Education of the Anglo-Saxon Aristocracy', *Bull. of the John Rylands Univ. Lib. of Manchester* 79.3 (1997), 41–66

Breizmann, Natalia, '*Beowulf* as Romance: Literary Interpretation as Quest', *MLN* 113, 1022–35

Carruthers, Leo, *Beowulf* (Paris)

Čermák, Jan, '*Hie dygel lond warigeað*: Spatial Imagery in Five *Beowulf* Compounds', *Linguistica Pragensia* 1996, no. 1, pp. 24–34

Crépin, André, 'Beowulf: monstre ou modèle?' *EA* 51, 387–98

Dockray-Miller, Mary, 'Beowulf's Tears of Fatherhood', *Exemplaria* 10, 1–28

Dumville, David N., 'The *Beowulf*-Manuscript and How Not to Date It', *Med. Eng. Stud. Newsletter* 39, 21–7

Earl, James W., '*Beowulf*: the Raw and the Cooked – an Experimental Translation', *OEN* 31.3, 16–27

'Freud on Epic: the Poet as Hero', *New Methods in the Research of Epic / Neue Methoden der Epenforschung*, ed. Hildegard L. C. Tristram, ScriptOralia 107 (Tübingen), 161–71

Eaton, Trevor, *'Beowulf', Read in Anglo-Saxon* (Wadhurst, 1997) [2 CDs and 12-page booklet]

Enright, Michael J., 'The Warband Context of the Unferth Episode', *Speculum* 73, 297–337

Faraci, Dora, 'La caccia al cervo nel *Beowulf*', *Romanobarbarica* 14 (1998 for 1996–7), 375–420

Fjalldal, Magnús, *The Long Arm of Coincidence: the Frustrated Connection between 'Beowulf' and 'Grettis saga'* (Toronto)

Fortson, Benjamin W., IV, 'Some Work on Old Problems: the Meter of *Beowulf*', *Diachronica* 15, 325–37

Fulk, Robert D., 'Secondary Stress Phenomena in the Meter of *Beowulf*', *Interdisciplinary Jnl for Germanic Ling. and Semiotic Analysis* 3, 279–304

Garde, Judith N., 'Christian and Folkloric Tradition in *Beowulf*: Death and the Dragon Episode', *Lit. & Theol.* 11 (1997), 325–46

Gerritsen, Johan, '*Beowulf* Revisited', *ES* 79, 82–6

Goetsch, Paul, 'Der koloniale Diskurs in *Beowulf*', *New Methods in the Research of Epic / Neue Methoden der Epenforschung*, ed. Hildegard L. C. Tristram, ScriptOralia 107 (Tübingen), 185–200

Hala, James, 'The Parturition of Poetry and the Birthing of Culture: the *ides aglæcwif* and Beowulf', *Exemplaria* 10, 29–50

Hall, J. R., 'F. J. Furnivall's Letter to the Royal Library, Copenhagen, Asking That the Thorkelin Transcripts of *Beowulf* Be Sent to London for the Use of Julius Zupitza', *N&Q* 45, 267–72

Hall, Simon, see sect. 6

Herschend, Frands, 'Beowulf and St. Sabas: the Tension between the Individual and the Collective in Germanic Society around 500 A.D.', *Tor: tidskrift för arkeologi* 24 (1992), 145–64

Hubert, Susan J., 'The Case for Emendation of *Beowulf* 250b', *In Geardagum* 19, 51–4

Jensen, S. R., trans., *Beowulf and the Monsters, Adapted and Abridged from the Old English Poem, 'Beowulf'* (Sydney, 1997)

Karasawa, Kazutomo, 'On the Connotation of "*þa metod nolde*" in *Beowulf*', *Soundings* (Tokyo) 24, 105–21

Kiernan, Kevin S., 'The Conybeare-Madden Collation of Thorkelin's *Beowulf*', *Anglo-Saxon Manuscripts and Their Heritage*, ed. Pulsiano and Treharne, pp. 117–36

Lee, Alvin A., *Gold-Hall and Earth-Dragon: 'Beowulf' as Metaphor* (Toronto)

Liberman, Anatoly, 'The "Icy" Ship of Scyld Scefing: *Beowulf* 33', *Bright Is the Ring of*

Words: Festschrift für Horst Weinstock, ed. Clausdirk Pollner, Helmut Rohlfing and Frank-Rutger Hausmann (Bonn, 1996), pp. 183–94

Lionarons, Joyce Tally, *The Medieval Dragon: the Nature of the Beast in Germanic Literature* (Enfield Lock)

McGowan, Joseph, 'Readings from the *Beowulf* Manuscript, ff. 94r–98r (the *St. Christopher* Folios)', *Manuscripta* 39 (1995), 26–9

Mitchell, Bruce and Fred C. Robinson, ed., *'Beowulf': an Edition with Relevant Shorter Texts* (Oxford) [includes 'Archaeology and *Beowulf*' by Leslie Webster]

Müller-Zimmermann, Gunhild, 'Beowulf: zur Datierungs- und Interpretationsproblematik', *Medieval Insular Literature between the Oral and the Written II: Continuity of Transmission*, ed. Hildegard L. C. Tristram, ScriptOralia 97 (Tübingen, 1997), 29–64

Niles, John D. 'Reconceiving *Beowulf*: Poetry as Social Praxis', *College Eng.* 61, 143–66

Ogura, Michiko, 'An Ogre's Arm: Japanese Analogues of *Beowulf*', *Words and Works*, ed. Baker and Howe, pp. 59–66

Olsen, Alexandra H., '*Beowulf*', *Teaching Oral Traditions*, ed. John Miles Foley (New York), pp. 351–8

Osborn, Marijane, 'The Real Fulk Fitzwarine's Mythical Monster Fights', *Words and Works*, ed. Baker and Howe, pp. 271–92

Oshifari, Kinshiro, 'A Swimming Bird or a Flying Bird? – "*Fugle gelicost*" (*Beowulf* 218b)', *Fleur-de-lis Rev.* (Shirayuri College) 34, 89–99 [in Japanese]

Owen-Crocker, Gale R., 'Telling a Tale: Narrative Techniques in the Bayeux Tapestry and the Old English Epic *Beowulf*', *Medieval Art: Recent Perspectives*, ed. Owen-Crocker and Graham, pp. 40–59

Peter, Steve, 'Healfdene's Honey: a Bear Bearn in *Beowulf*', *Mír Curad: Studies in Honor of Calvert Watkins*, ed. Jay Jasanoff, H. Craig Melchert and Lisi Oliver (Innsbruck), pp. 573–84

Prescott, Andrew, 'Constructing Electronic *Beowulf*', *Towards the Digital Library: the British Library's 'Initiatives for Access' Programme*, ed. Leona Carpenter, Simon Shaw and Andrew Prescott (London), pp. 30–49

Puhvel, Martin, 'The Aquatic Contest in *Hálfdanar saga Brönufóstra* and Beowulf's Adventure with Breca. Any Connection?', *NM* 99, 131–8

Reichert, Hermann, 'Runeninschriften als Quellen der Heldensagenforschung', *Runeninschriften*, ed. Düwel, pp. 66–102

Risden, E. L., '*Beowulf*, Tolkien and Epic Epiphanies', *Jnl of the Fantastic in the Arts* 9, 192–9

Robinson, Fred C., 'Some Reflections on Mitchell and Robinson's Edition of *Beowulf*', *Med. Eng. Stud. Newsletter* 39, 27–9

Rosensfit, Gail Rae, *Beowulf*, Maxnotes (Piscataway, NJ, 1995)

Russom, Geoffrey, *'Beowulf' and Old Germanic Metre*, CSASE 23 (Cambridge)

Schaefer, Ursula, 'Epik und Stil: Überlegungen zu einer analytischen Kategorie', *New Methods in the Research of Epic / Neue Methoden der Epenforschung*, ed. Hildegard L. C. Tristram, ScriptOralia 107 (Tübingen), 173–83

Scherb, Victor I., 'Setting and Cultural Memory in Part II of *Beowulf*', *ES* 79, 109–19

Schneider, Karl, 'On Some Onomatopoetic Elements in the Textual Formulation of the *Beowulf* Epic', *Poetica* (Tokyo) 49, 97–102

Schwetman, John W., 'Beowulf's Return: the Hero's Account of his Adventures among the Danes', *Med. Perspectives* 13, 136–48

Senra Silva, Immaculada, 'The Rune "Eþel" and Scribal Writing Habits in the *Beowulf* MS', *NM* 99, 241–7

Shilton, Howard, 'The Nature of Beowulf's Dragon', *Bull. of the John Rylands Univ. Lib. of Manchester* 79.3 (1997), 67–77

Shippey, T. A., and Andreas Haarder, ed., *'Beowulf': the Critical Heritage* (London)

Sohn, Chang Yong, 'Reclassification of Light Verses in *Beowulf*', *The Hist. of Eng.* (Seoul) 6, 69–87

Stanley, Eric Gerald, 'Courtliness and Courtesy in *Beowulf* and Elsewhere in English Medieval Literature', *Words and Works*, ed. Baker and Howe, pp. 67–103

Stévanovitch, Colette, *'Beowulf': de la forme au sens* (Paris)

Stockwell, Robert P., and Donka Minkova, 'Against the Notion "Metrical Grammar"', *Insights in Germanic Linguistics II: Classic and Contemporary*, ed. Irmengard Rauch and Gerald F. Carr, Trends in Ling., Stud. and Monographs 94 (Berlin, 1997), 243–55

Suzuki, Seiichi, 'Anacrusis in the Meter of *Heliand*', *Interdigitations*, ed. Carr *et al.*, pp. 189–99

'The Metrical Prominence Hierarchy in Old English Verse', *Language History and Linguistic Modelling*, ed. Hickey and Puppel, pp. 73–84

Taylor, Paul Beekman, *Sharing Story: Medieval Norse–English Literary Relationships* (New York)

Thieme, Adelheid L. J., 'The Gift in *Beowulf*: Forging the Continuity of Past and Present', *Michigan Germanic Stud.* 22 (1996), 126–43

Thompson, Stephen P., comp., *Readings on 'Beowulf'* (San Diego, CA)

Tripp, Raymond R., Jr, '*Beowulf* 301–308: the Mock-Heroic Arrival of the Hero', *ELN* 36.1, 1–8

Tristram, Hildegard L. C., 'What's the Point of Dating "Beowulf"?' *Medieval Insular Literature between the Oral and the Written II: Continuity of Transmission*, ed. Hildegard L. C. Tristram, ScriptOralia 97 (Tübingen, 1997), 65–80

Wang, Ji-hui, *The Concept of Kingship in Anglo-Saxon and Medieval Chinese Literature: a Comparative Study of Beowulf and Xuanhe Yishi* (Beijing, 1996)

Waterhouse, Ruth, '*Beowulf* as Palimpsest', *Monster Theory: Reading Culture*, ed. Jeffrey Jerome Cohen (Minneapolis, MN, 1996), pp. 26–39

Webster, Leslie, see Bruce Mitchell and Fred C. Robinson, ed.

Wehlau, Ruth, '"Seeds of Sorrow": Landscapes of Despair in *The Wanderer*, *Beowulf*'s Story of Hrethel and *Sonatorrek*', *Parergon* 15.2, 1–17

Wilkinson, Paul, and Griselda Cann Mussett, *Beowulf in Kent*, Faversham Papers 64 (Faversham)

Wodzak, Victoria, 'Of Weavers and Warriors: Peace and Destruction in the Epic Tradition', *Midwest Quarterly* 39, 253–64

iii. Other poems

Baker, Peter S., see sect. 3*bii* [*Brunanburh*]

Blockley, Mary, 'Cædmon's Conjunction: *Cædmon's Hymn* 7a Revisited', *Speculum* 73, 1–31

Bragg, Lois, 'The Modes of the Old English Metrical Charms – the Texts of Magic', *New Approaches to Medieval Textuality*, ed. Mikle David Ledgerwood (New York), pp. 117–40

Bredehoft, Thomas A., 'A Note on Robinson's *Rewards of Piety*', *N&Q* 45, 5–8 [*Exhortation to Christian Living* and *Summons to Prayer*]

Buzzoni, Marina, *Il 'genere' incantesimo nella tradizione anglosassone: aspetti semantico-pragmatici e sviluppo diacronico*, Pubblicazioni della Facoltà di lettere e filosofia dell'Università di Pavia 83 (Florence, 1996)

Cain, Christopher M., 'The "Fearful Symmetry" of *Maldon*: the Apocalypse, the Poet, and the Millennium', *Comitatus* 28 (1997), 1–16

Cavill, Paul, 'Maxims in *The Battle of Maldon*', *Neophilologus* 82, 631–44

Coates, Richard, see sect. 8 [*Brunanburh*]

Coppola, Maria Augusta, 'Ags. *synrust*', *Helikon* 33–4 (1996 for 1993–4), 309–33 [*Christ III*]

'... *swa þæt scire glæs*: sui segni della beatitudine e della dannazione nel *Cristo III*', *Helikon* 33–4 (1996 for 1993–4), 121–58

Crane, David, trans., *De situ Dunelmi = On Durham: the Last Poem in Old English* (Bath, 1996)

de Lacy, Paul, 'Thematic and Structural Affinities: *The Wanderer* and Ecclesiastes', *Neophilologus* 82, 125–37

Deskis, Susan E., 'Jonah and Genre in *Resignation B*', *MÆ* 67, 189–200

DiNapoli, Robert, 'The Heart of the Visionary Experience: *The Order of the World* and its Place in the Old English Canon', *ES* 79, 97–108

'Poesis and Authority: Traces of an Anglo-Saxon *agon* in Cynewulf's *Elene*', *Neophilologus* 82, 619–30

Doane, A. N., 'Spacing, Placing and Effacing: Scribal Textuality and Exeter Riddle 30a/b', *New Approaches to Editing Old English Verse*, ed. Keefer and O'Keeffe, pp. 45–65

Dockray-Miller, Mary, 'Female Community in the Old English *Judith*', *SN* 70, 165–72

Donoghue, Daniel, 'An *anser* for Exeter Book Riddle 74', *Words and Works*, ed. Baker and Howe, pp. 45–58

Drout, Michael D. C., '*The Fortunes of Men* 4a: Reasons for Adopting a Very Old Emendation', *MP* 96, 184–7

Ericksen, Janet Schrunk, 'Runesticks and Reading *The Husband's Message*', *NM* 99, 31–7

Forester, Lee, 'On the Semiotics of Germanic Alliterative Verse', *Interdigitations*, ed. Carr et al., pp. 81–91 [*Brunanburh* and *Maldon*]

Francovich Onesti, Nicoletta, 'Roman Themes in the Franks Casket', *L'Antichità nella cultura europea del Medioevo / L'Antiquité dans la culture européenne du Moyen Age, Ergebnisse der internationalen Tagung in Padua 27.09–01.10.1997* (Greifswald), pp. 295–313

Glanz, Elaine, '*Standan steame bedrifenne* in *The Dream of the Rood*', *Mediaevalia* 21 (1997), 189–208

Griffiths, Bill, trans., *The Phoenix* (Market Drayton)

Griffiths, Mark, 'Dialect and Literary Dialect in *The Battle of Maldon*', *N&Q* 45, 272–3

Harbus, Antonina, 'Exeter Book Riddle 39 Reconsidered', *SN* 70, 139–48

Hillary, David, trans., '*The Dream of the Rood*', *Epworth Rev.* 24 (1997), 46–9
Hiltunen, Risto, 'Functions of Speech in *The Battle of Maldon*', *Stud. in Med. Eng. Lang. and Lit.* (Tokyo) 13, 29–43
Hoek, Michelle, 'Violence and Ideological Inversion in the Old English *Soul's Address to the Body*', *Exemplaria* 10, 271–85
Holderness, Graham, trans., 'The Wanderer', *English* 47, 99–102
Hough, Carole, '*The Battle of Maldon* Line 33', *RES* 49, 322–6
  'Odda in *The Battle of Maldon*', *N&Q* 45, 169–72
  'Place-Names and the Provenance of Riddle 49', *Neophilologus* 82, 617–18
  '*The Wife's Lament* Line 15b and *Daniel* Line 499b: Two Notes on Place-Name Evidence', *ELN* 35.4, 1–4
Ivanov, Vyacheslav V., 'Traces of Indo-European Medical Magic in an Old English Charm', *Interdigitations*, ed. Carr *et al.*, pp. 1–24
Johnson, David F., 'The Fall of Lucifer in *Genesis A* and Two Anglo-Latin Royal Charters', *JEGP* 97, 500–21
Keefer, Sarah Larratt, 'Respect for the Book: a Reconsideration of "Form", "Content" and "Context" in Two Vernacular Poems', *New Approaches to Editing Old English Verse*, ed. Keefer and O'Keeffe, pp. 21–44 [*Psalm 50* and *Prayer*]
Laszlo, Renate, *Köcherfliege und Seidenraupe in den altenglischen Rätseln* (Marburg, 1997)
  Die Sonne bringt es an den Tag: ein altenglisches Rätsel des siebten Jahrhunderts und seine Lösung (Marburg) [Riddle 40]
Lionarons, Joyce Tally, 'Cultural Syncretism and the Construction of Gender in Cynewulf's *Elene*', *Exemplaria* 10, 51–68
Marsden, Richard, see sect. 5 [Riddle 26]
Mitchell, Bruce, '*The Dream of the Rood* Repunctuated', *Words and Works*, ed. Baker and Howe, p. 143–57
Molinari, Maria Vittoria, 'Overcoming Pagan Suffering in *Deor*', trans. Richard Davies, *Linguistica e filologia* (Bergamo) 8, 7–28
Niles, John D., 'Exeter Book Riddle 74 and the Play of the Text', *ASE* 27, 169–207
Obst, Wolfgang, and Florian Schleburg, ed. and trans., *Lieder aus König Alfreds Trostbuch: die Stabreimverse der altenglischen Boethius-Übertragung*, Anglistische Forschungen 259 (Heidelberg)
Olsen, Karin, 'The Dichotomy of Land and Sea in the Old English *Andreas*', *ES* 79, 385–94
Orton, Peter, 'The Transmission of the West Saxon Versions of Cædmon's Hymn: a Reappraisal', *SN* 70, 153–64
Page, R. I., 'The Icelandic Rune-Poem', *Nottingham Med. Stud.* 42, 1–37 [*Rune Poem*]
Petrescu, Ioana I., '*Wulf and Eadwacer* and the 19th Century Romantic Poems', *Orality and Literacy in Early Middle English*, ed. Herbert Pilch, ScriptOralia 83 (Tübingen, 1996), 167–77
Powell, Stephen D., 'The Journey Forth: Elegiac Consolation in *Guthlac B*', *ES* 79, 489–500
Salvador Bello, Mercedes, 'Direct and Indirect Clues: Exeter Riddle No. 74 Reconsidered', *NM* 99, 17–29

Stévanovitch, Colette, 'Envelope Patterns in Translation: the Old English *Metres of Boethius*', *Med. Translator* 6, 101–13

'The Translator and the Text of the Old English *Genesis B*', *Med. Translator* 5 (1996), 130–45

Sub-Deacon Bede [Tripp, Raymond P., Jr], trans., 'The Riddle of the Soul', *In Geardagum* 19, 55–6 [*Wife's Lament*]

Szarmach, Paul E., '*Anthem*: Auden's *Cædmon's Hymn*', *Medievalism in the Modern World: Essays in Honour of Leslie Workman*, ed. Richard Utz and Tom Shippey, Making the Middle Ages 1 (Turnhout), 329–40

Thieme, Adelheid L. J., 'Gift Giving as a Vital Element of Salvation in *The Dream of the Rood*', *South Atlantic Rev.* 63.2, 108–23

Toswell, M. J., 'How Pedantry Meets Intertextuality: Editing the Old English Metrical Psalter', *New Approaches to Editing Old English Verse*, ed. Keefer and O'Keeffe, pp. 79–93

Vickrey, John, '*Genesis* 549–51 and 623–25: Narrative Frame and Devilish Cunning', *PQ* 76 (1997), 347–68

Wehlau, Ruth, 'The Power of Knowledge and the Location of the Reader in *Christ and Satan*', *JEGP* 97, 1–12

see also sect. 3*bii* [*Wanderer*]

Williams, Ann, 'The Battle of Maldon and "The Battle of Maldon": History, Poetry and Propaganda', *Med. Hist.* (Bangor) 2.2 (1992), 35–44

Znojemská, Helena, '"The Ruin": a Reading of the Old English Poem', *Litteraria Pragensia* 15, 15–33

c. Prose

Atherton, Mark, see sect. 5

Benison, Líam, 'Translation during King Alfred's Reign: the Politics of Conversion and Truth', *Med. Translator* 6, 82–100

Bhattacharya, Prodosh, 'An Analogue, and Probable Source, for a Metaphor in Alfred's Preface to the Old English Translation of Augustine's *Soliloquies*', *N&Q* 45, 161–3

Butcher, Maria, 'A Homily for the Nativity of the Virgin Mary', *Bull. of the John Rylands Univ. Lib. of Manchester* 79.3 (1997), 93–118

Caie, Graham D., 'Infanticide in an Eleventh-Century Old English Homily', *N&Q* 45, 275–6

Carruthers, Leo, 'Apocalypse Now: Preaching and Prophecy in Anglo-Saxon England', *EA* 51, 399–410

Chapman, Don, 'Motivation for Producing and Analyzing Compounds in Wulfstan's Sermons', *Advances in English Historical Linguistics*, ed. Fisiak and Krygier, pp. 15–21

Clayton, Mary, *The Apocryphal Gospels of Mary in Anglo-Saxon England*, CSASE 26 (Cambridge)

Davis, Graeme, *The Word-Order of Ælfric* (Lewiston, NY, 1997)

Discenza, Nicole Guenther, '"Wise wealhstodas": the Prologue to Sirach as a Model for Alfred's Preface to the *Pastoral Care*', *JEGP* 97, 488–99

Fitzmaurice, Susan, see sect. 2*b*

Gilles, Sealy, 'Territorial Interpolations in the Old English Orosius', *Text and Territory: Geographical Imagination in the European Middle Ages*, ed. Sylvia Tomasch and Sealy Gilles (Philadelphia, PA), pp. 79–96

Gneuss, Helmut, see sect. 5

Green, Eugene, 'Speech Acts and the Question of Self in Alfred's *Soliloquies*', *Interdigitations*, ed. Carr *et al.*, pp. 211–18

Hill, Joyce, 'Translating the Tradition: Manuscripts, Models and Methodologies in the Composition of Ælfric's *Catholic Homilies*', *Bull. of the John Rylands Univ. Lib. of Manchester* 79.1 (1997), 43–65

    'Ælfric, Gregory and the Carolingians', *Roma, magistra mundi: itineraria culturae medievalis. Mélanges offerts à père L. E. Boyle*, ed. Jacqueline Hamesse (Louvain-la-Neuve), pp. 409–23

    see also sect. 4

Hollis, Stephanie, 'The Old English "Ritual of the Admission of Mildrith" (London, Lambeth Palace 427, fol. 210)', *JEGP* 97, 311–21

Horner, Shari, 'The Violence of Exegesis: Reading the Bodies of Ælfric's Female Saints', *Violence against Women in Medieval Texts*, ed. Anna Roberts (Gainesville, FL), pp. 22–43

Ishikawa, Yuli, 'Paris Psalter: King Alfred's Old English Translation of the Psalms', *Research Bull. of Obihiro Zootechnical Univ.: the Humanities and Social Sciences*, 9.4 (1997), 1–23 [in Japanese]

Johnson, Richard F., 'Archangel in the Margins: St. Michael in the Homilies of Cambridge, Corpus Christi College 41', *Traditio* 53, 63–91

Lionarons, Joyce Tally, 'Another Old English Text of the *Passio Petri et Pauli*', *N&Q* 45, 12–14

Liuzza, Roy Michael, see sect. 5

Marx, C. W., 'The Gospel of Nicodemus in Old and Middle English', *The Medieval Gospel of Nicodemus*, ed. Zbigniew S. Izydorczyk, Med. & Renaissance Texts & Stud. 158 (Tempe, AZ, 1997), 207–59

Moye, Ray, '"Pleasing Passages": Style in the Old English *Pastoral Care*', *Jnl of the Rocky Mountain Med. and Renaissance Assoc.* 16–17 (1995–6), 25–51

Nakamura, Koichi, 'Rhetorical Analysis of *Historia Apollonii Regis Tyri* and OE *Apollonius of Tyre*', *Jnl of Humanities* (Meiji Univ.) 3 (1997), 1–32

Ogawa, Hiroshi, 'Syntactical Revision in Wulfstan's Rewritings of Ælfric', *English Historical Linguistics and Philology in Japan*, ed. Fisiak and Oizumi, pp. 215–28

Ogura, Michiko, see sect. 2*b*

O'Keeffe, Katherine O'Brien, 'Body and Law in Late Anglo-Saxon England', *ASE* 27, 209–32

    see also sect. 5

Oliver, Lisi, '*Cyninges fedesl*: the King's Feeding in Æthelberht, ch. 12', *ASE* 27, 31–40

Proud, Joana, 'The Old English *Life of Saint Pantaleon* and its Manuscript Context', *Bull. of the John Rylands Univ. Lib. of Manchester* 79.3 (1997), 119–32

Pulsiano, Phillip, see sect. 5
Ranum, Ingrid, '*Blickling Homily X* and the Millennial Apocalyptic Vision', *In Geardagum* 19, 41–9
Stanton, Robert, 'The (M)other Tongue: Translation Theory and Old English', *Translation Theory and Practice in the Middle Ages*, ed. Jeanette Beer, Stud. in Med. Culture 38 (Kalamazoo, MI, 1997), 33–46
Swan, Mary, 'The *Apocalypse of Thomas* in Old English', *Leeds Stud. in Eng.* 29, 333–46
see also sect. 5
Szarmach, Paul E., 'Abbot Ælfric's Rhythmical Prose and the Computer Age', *New Approaches to Editing Old English Verse*, ed. Keefer and O'Keeffe, pp. 95–108
see also sect. 5
Takeuchi, Schin'ichi, 'Archaism in the Vocabulary of Ælfric', *English Historical Linguistics and Philology in Japan*, ed. Fisiak and Oizumi, pp. 341–59

4. ANGLO-LATIN, LITURGY AND OTHER LATIN ECCLESIASTICAL TEXTS

Alberi, Mary, 'The Evolution of Alcuin's Concept of the *Imperium Christianum*', *The Community, the Family and the Saint*, ed. Hill and Swan, pp. 3–18
'The "Mystery of the Incarnation" and Wisdom's House (Prov. 9:1) in Alcuin's *Disputatio de vera philosophia*', *JTS* 48 (1997), 505–16
Armstrong, Dorsey, 'Holy Queens as Agents of Christianization in Bede's *Ecclesiastical History*: a Reconsideration', *Med. Encounters* 4, 228–41
Baker, Peter S., see sect. 2a
Bayless, Martha, 'The *Collectanea* and Medieval Dialogues and Riddles', *Collectanea pseudo-Bedae*, ed. Bayless and Lapidge, pp. 13–24
Bayless, Martha, and Michael Lapidge, ed., *Collectanea pseudo-Bedae*, Scriptores Latini Hiberniae 14 (Dublin)
Bayless, Martha, 'The *Collectanea* and Medieval Dialogues and Riddles', *Collectanea pseudo-Bedae*, ed. Bayless and Lapidge, pp. 13–24
Beare, Rhona, 'Swallows and Barnacle Geese', *N&Q* 45, 5
Berry, Mary, *Liturgical Music in Anglo-Saxon Times: Deerhurst Leacture 1988* (Deerhurst, 1988)
Biggs, Frederick M., 'Bede's Use of Augustine: Echoes from Some Sermons?', *RB* 108, 201–13
Bragg, Lois, 'Visual-Kinetic Communication in Europe before 1600: a Survey of Sign Lexicons and Finger Alphabets Prior to the Rise of Deaf Education', *Jnl of Deaf Stud. and Deaf Education* 2 (1997), 1–25 [Bede]
Bullough, D. A., 'Alcuin's Cultural Influence: the Evidence of the Manuscripts', *Alcuin of York*, ed. Houwen and MacDonald, pp. 1–26
see also sect. 5
Coates, Simon, 'The Construction of Episcopal Sanctity in Early Anglo-Saxon England: the Impact of Venantius Fortunatus', *Hist. Research* 71, 1–13

Bibliography for 1998

Consolino, Franca Ela, 'L'invenzione di una biografia: Almanno di Hautvillers e la vita di sant'Elena', *Hagiographica* 1 (1994), 81–100

Cünnen, Janina, '*Amicitia* in Old English Letters: Augustine's Ideas of "Friendship" and their Reception in Eangyth's Letter to Boniface', *Revista Alicantina de Estudios Ingleses* 10 (1997), 35–46

Dales, Douglas, *Called To Be Angels: an Introduction to Anglo-Saxon Spirituality* (Norwich)

de Jong, Mayke, 'From Scolastici to Scioli: Alcuin and the Formation of an Intellectual Élite', *Alcuin of York*, ed. Houwen and MacDonald, pp. 45–57

Diem, Albrecht, 'The Emergence of Monastic Schools: the Role of Alcuin', *Alcuin of York*, ed. Houwen and MacDonald, pp. 27–44

Di Pilla, Alessandra, 'La presenza del *De Genesi contra Manichaeos* di Agostino nell'*In principium Genesis* di Beda', '*De Genesi contra Manichaeos,*' '*De Genesi a litteram liber imperfectus*' *di Agostino d'Ippona*, ed. Luigi Franco Pizzolato and Giovanni Scanavino, Lectio Augustini, Settimana agostiniana pavese 8 (Palermo, 1992), 99–113

Driscoll, Michael S., '*Ad pueros sancti Martini*: a Critical Edition, English Translation and Study of the Manuscript Transmission', *Traditio* 53, 37–61

Elfassi, Jacques, 'Germain d'Auxerre, figure d'Augustin de Cantorbéry. La réécriture par Bède de la "Vie de saint Germain d'Auxerre"', *Hagiographica* 5, 37–47

Engels, L. J., 'Priscian in Alcuin's *De orthographia*', *Alcuin of York*, ed. Houwen and MacDonald, pp. 113–42

Englisch, Brigitte, *Die Artes Liberales im frühen Mittelalter (5.–9. Jh): das Quadrivium und der Komputus als Indikatoren für Kontinuität und Erneuerung der exakten Wissenschaften zwischen Antike und Mittelalter*, Sudhoffs Archiv, Beihefte 33 (Stuttgart, 1994) [includes Bede etc.]

Garrison, Mary, 'The *Collectanea* and Medieval Florilegia', *Collectanea pseudo-Bedae,* ed. Bayless and Lapidge, pp. 42–83

'Letters to a King and Biblical Exempla: the Examples of Cathuulf and Clemens Peregrinus', *EME* 7.3, 305–28 [possible English connections]

'The Social World of Alcuin: Nicknames at York and at the Carolingian Court', *Alcuin of York*, ed. Houwen and MacDonald, pp. 59–79

Gorman, Michael, 'The *Argumenta* and *Explanationes* on the Psalms Attributed to Bede', *RB* 108, 214–39

Gwara, Scott, 'Second Language Acquisition and Anglo-Saxon Bilingualism: Negative Transfer and Avoidance in Ælfric Bata's Latin *Colloquia*, ca. A.D. 1000', *Viator* 29, 1–24

see also sect. 5 [Aldhelm]

Haggenmüller, Reinhold, *Die Überlieferung der Beda und Egbert zugeschriebenen Bußbücher*, Europäische Hochschulschriften III, 461 (Frankfurt am Main, 1991)

Herren, Michael W., 'The Transmission and Reception of Graeco-Roman Mythology in Anglo-Saxon England, 670–800', *ASE* 27, 87–103

Hill, Joyce, 'Winchester Pedagogy and the *Colloquy* of Ælfric', *Leeds Stud. in Eng.* 29, 137–52

Houwen, L. A. J. R., and A. A. MacDonald, ed., *Alcuin of York, Scholar at the Carolingian Court. Proceedings of the Third Germania Latina Conference, Held at the University of*

Groningen, May 1995, Germania Latina 3, Mediaevalia Groningana 22 (Groningen)

Howlett, D. R., *British Books in Biblical Style* (Dublin, 1997)

Cambro-Latin Compositions: Their Competence and Craftsmanship (Dublin)

'Miscouplings in Couplets', *Bulletin Du Cange / Archivum Latinitatis Medii Aevi* 55 (1997), 271–6

'Insular Acrostics, Celtic Latin Colophons', *CMCS* 35, 27–44

Jackson, Gordon, trans., *Alcuin: Selected Poems* (Lincoln)

Jackson, Peter, 'Herwagen's Lost Manuscript of the *Collectanea*', *Collectanea pseudo-Bedae*, ed. Bayless and Lapidge, pp. 101–20

Johnson-South, Ted, see sect. 6

Jones, Christopher A., *Ælfric's Letter to the Monks of Eynsham*, CSASE 24 (Cambridge)

'Ælfric of Eynsham as a Medieval Latin Author', *Jnl of Med. Latin* 8, 1–57

'Two Composite Texts from Archbishop Wulfstan's "Commonplace Book": the *De ecclesiastica consuetudine* and the *Institutio beati Amalarii de ecclesiasticis officiis*', *ASE* 27, 233–71

'The Book of the Liturgy in Anglo-Saxon England', *Speculum* 73, 659–702

Jordan, Victoria B., 'Chronology and Discourse in the *Vita Ædwardi Regis*', *Jnl of Med. Latin* 8, 122–55

Jullien, Marie-Hélène, 'Les Hymnes dans le milieu alcuinien', *De Tertullien aux Mozarabes: Mélanges offerts à Jacques Fontaine*, ed. Louis Holtz and Jean-Claude Fredouille (Paris, 1992) II, 171–82

Kaczynski, Bernice M., 'The Seventh-Century School of Canterbury: England and the Continent in Perspective', *Jnl of Med. Latin* 8, 206–15

Keefer, Sarah Larratt, 'Looking at the Glosses in London, BL Additional 57337 (the Anderson Pontifical)', *Anglia* 116, 215–22

Knappe, Gabriele, see sect. 3*a*

Kneepkens, C. H., 'Some Notes on Alcuin's *De perihermeniis* with an Edition of the Text', *Alcuin of York*, ed. Houwen and MacDonald, pp. 81–112

Körntgen, Ludger, *Studien zu den Quellen der frühmittelalterlichen Bußbücher*, Quellen und Forschungen zum Recht im Mittelalter 7 (Sigmaringen, 1993)

Lapidge, Michael, 'The Origin of the *Collectanea*', *Collectanea pseudo-Bedae*, ed. Bayless and Lapidge, pp. 1–12

see also sect. 5

Lebecq, Stéphane, 'Les saints anglais et le milieu marin. Contribution de quelques textes hagiographiques à la connaissance du milieu littoral dans l'Angleterre du début du moyen âge', *Comptes rendus des séances de l'Académie des Inscriptions et Belle-Lettres* 1995, no. 1, pp. 43–56

Lendinara, Patrizia, 'Mixed Attitudes to Ovid: the Carolingian Poets and the Glossographers', *Alcuin of York*, ed. Houwen and MacDonald, pp. 171–213

Leonardi, Claudio, 'Alcuino e la retorica', *Dialektik und Rhetorik im früheren und hohen Mittelalter*, ed. Johannes Fried (Munich, 1997), pp. 171–4

Luiselli, Bruno, 'Dal latino della Britannia romana ai più antichi latinismi del celtico insulare e dell'anglosassone', *La transizione dal latino alle lingue romanze. Atti della Tavola* rotonda di linguistica storica, Università Ca' Foscari di Venezia, 14–15 giugno 1996, ed. József Herman with Luca Mondin (Tübingen), pp. 213–27

Lutterbach, Hubertus, 'Die Speisegesetzgebung in den mittelalterlichen Bußbüchern (600–1200). Religionsgeschichtliche Perspektiven', *Archiv für Kulturgeschicte* 80, 1–37

Lynch, Joseph H., see sect. 6

Marsden, Richard, 'The Biblical Text of the *Collectanea*', *Collectanea pseudo-Bedae*, ed. Bayless and Lapidge, pp. 35–41

'*Manus Bedae*: Bede's Contribution to Ceolfrith's Bibles', *ASE* 27, 65–85

Martin, Lawrence T., 'Augustine's Influence on Bede's *Homeliae euangelii*', *Collectanea Augustiniana. Augustine: 'Second Founder of the Faith'*, ed. Joseph C. Schnaubelt and Frederick Van Fleteren (New York, 1990), pp. 357–69

McBride, Oswald, 'Of Cathedras and Kings: a Study of the Place of the King in Tenth–Eleventh Century Monastic Liturgies in England', *Ecclesia Orans* 15, 91–114

McCulloh, John M., 'The "Pseudo-Bede of Cologne": a Martyrology of the "Gorzean" Reform', *Forschungen zur Reichs-, Papst- und Landesgeschichte, Peter Herde zum 65. Geburtstag*, ed. Karl Borchardt and Enno Bünz (Stuttgart) I, 81–99

Meens, Rob, *Het tripartite boeteboek: overlevering en betekenis van vroegmiddeleeuwse biechtvoorschriften (met editie en vertaling van vier 'tripartita')*, Middeleeuwse studies en bronnen 41 (Hilversum, 1994)

Montgomery, George, and Arthur F. Dimmock, *Venerable Legacy: Saint Bede and the Anglo-Celtic Contribution to Literary, Numerical and Manual Language* (Edinburgh)

Morton, Jennifer, 'Doubts about the Calendar: Bede and the Eclipse of 664', *Isis* 89, 50–65

O'Briain, Helen Conrad, 'Bede's Use of Classical Poetry *In Genesim, De temporum ratione* and *Epistola ad Wicthedum*', *Hermathena* 161 (1996), 43–51

O'Keeffe, Katherine O'Brien, see sect. 3*c*

Orchard, Andy, 'The Verse-Extracts in the *Collectanea*', *Collectanea pseudo-Bedae*, ed. Bayless and Lapidge, pp. 84–100

Parsons, David, see sect. 9*e*

Petroff, Valery V., 'The *De templo* of Bede as the Source of an Ideal Temple Description in Eriugena's *Aulae sidereae*', *Recherches de théologie et philosophie médiévales* 65, 97–106

Pfaff, Richard W., *Liturgical Calendars, Saints and Services in Medieval England*, Variorum Collected Stud. Ser. 610 (Aldershot)

'The Study of Medieval Liturgy', in his *Liturgical Calendars*, no. I

'The Hagiographical Peculiarity of Martha's Companion(s)', in his *Liturgical Calendars*, no. IV

'Why do Medieval Psalters have Calendars?', in his *Liturgical Calendars*, no. VI

Pons, Christian-Marie, 'L'*Illittérature* en images', *Etudes Littéraires* 30.1 (1997), 97–104, [Alcuin]

Prescott, Andrew, see sect. 5

Romero-Pose, Eugenio, 'La Biblia de Alcuino y el perdido comentario al Apocalipsis de Ticonio', *Revista Española de Teología* 55 (1995), 391–7

Rosser, Susan, 'Æthelthryth: a Conventional Saint?', *Bull. of the John Rylands Univ. Lib. of Manchester* 79.3 (1997), 15–24

Ruff, Carin, 'Misunderstood Rhetorico-Syntactical Glosses in Two Anglo-Saxon Manuscripts', N&Q 45, 163–6
Sauer, Hans, 'Die Exkommunikationsriten aus Wulfstans Handbuch und Liebermanns Gesetze', *Bright Is the Ring of Words: Festschrift für Horst Weinstock*, ed. Clausdirk Pollner, Helmut Rohlfing and Frank-Rutger Hausmann (Bonn, 1996), pp. 283–307
Spitzbart, Günter, ed. and trans., *Venerabilis Bedae Historia Ecclesiastica Gentis Anglorum*, rev. ed. (Darmstadt, 1997)
Stanley, E. G., 'St Cædmon', N&Q 45, 4–5
Stanton, Robert, 'National Martyrs and Willing Heroes: Piety and Patriotism in Two English Saints' Lives', *The Propagation of Power in the Medieval West: Selected Proceedings of the International Conference, Groningen, 20–23 November 1996*, ed. Martin Gosman, Arjo Vanderjagt and Jan Veenstra (Groningen, 1997), pp. 191–204 [Abbo on Edmund of East Anglia, and Osbern on Alfheah]
Thacker, Alan, 'Memorializing Gregory the Great: the Origin and Transmission of a Papal Cult in the Seventh and Early Eighth Centuries', *EME* 7, 59–84
Thorley, John, *Documents in Medieval Latin* (London)
Trebbin, Heinrich, 'Die Visionen der Heiligen Antonius und Guthlac', *Antoniter-Forum* 5 (1997), 47–55
Verey, Christopher, see sect. 5
Viarre, Simone, 'Un portrait d'Angilbert dans la correspondance d'Alcuin?', *De Tertullien aux Mozarabes: Mélanges offerts à Jacques Fontaine*, ed. Louis Holtz and Jean-Claude Fredouille (Paris, 1992) II, 267–74
Ward, Benedicta, *The Venerable Bede*, rev. ed. (London)
Wieland, Gernot R, see sect. 5
Wright, Charles D., 'Alcuin's Ambrose: Polemics, Patrology and Textual Criticism', *Alcuin of York*, ed. Houwen and MacDonald, pp. 143–69
Wright, Neil, 'The Sources of the *Collectanea*', *Collectanea pseudo-Bedae*, ed. Bayless and Lapidge, pp. 25–34

5. PALAEOGRAPHY, DIPLOMATIC AND ILLUMINATION

Atherton, Mark, 'The Image of the Temple in the *Psychomachia* and Late Anglo-Saxon Literature', *Bull. of the John Rylands Univ. Lib. of Manchester* 79.3 (1997), 263–85 [iconography]
Bischoff, Bernhard, *Katalog der festländischen Handschriften des neunten Jahrhunderts (mit Ausnahme der wisigotischen) I: Aachen-Lambach* (Wiesbaden)
Bistřický, Jan, ed., *Typologie der Königsurkunden*, Acta Colloquii Olomucensis 1992 (Olmütz)
Brown, Michelle P., 'Sir Robert Cotton: Collector and Connoisseur?', *Illuminating the Book: Makers and Interpreters: Essays in Honour of Janet Backhouse*, ed. Michelle P. Brown and Scot McKendrick (London), pp. 281–98
Budny, Mildred, *Insular, Anglo-Saxon, and Early Anglo-Norman Manuscript Art at Corpus Christi College, Cambridge: an Illustrated Catalogue*, 2 vols. (Kalamazoo, MI, 1997)

Bullough, Donald A., 'A Neglected Early-Ninth-Century Manuscript of the Lindisfarne *Vita S. Cuthberti*', *ASE* 27, 105–37

Campos Vilanova, Xavier, 'The Busy Ups and Downs of an Anglo-Saxon *Codex Aureus* in the Spain of the Habsburgs', *SELIM 1996: Proceedings of the Ninth International Conference of the Spanish Society for Medieval English Language and Literature*, ed. Margarita Bon Giménez and Vickie Olsen (Zaragoza, 1997), pp. 42–8

Coates, Richard, 'The Scriptorium of the Mercian Rushworth Gloss: a Bilingual Perspective', *N&Q* 44 (1997), 453–8

Coatsworth, Elizabeth, 'Clothmaking and the Virgin Mary in Anglo-Saxon Literature and Art', *Medieval Art*, ed. Owen-Crocker and Graham, pp. 8–25

Collier, Wendy E. J., 'A Thirteenth-Century User of Anglo-Saxon Manuscripts', *Bull. of the John Rylands Univ. Lib. of Manchester* 79.3 (1997), 149–65

Cooke, Jessica, 'Worcester Books and Scholars, and the Making of the Harley Glossary (British Library MS. Harley 3376)', *Anglia* 115 (1997), 441–68

Crowley, J., 'Greek Interlinear Glosses from the Beginnings of the Monastic Reform in Worcester: B.L. Royal 2.A.xx', *Sacris Erudiri* 37 (1997), 133–9

D'Aronco, Maria Amalia, 'Il MS. Londra, British Library, Cotton Vitellius C.III dell'erbario anglosassone e la tradizione medica di Montecassino', *Incontri di popoli e culture tra V e IX secolo*, ed. Marcello Rotili (Naples), pp. 117–27

D'Aronco, M.A., and M. L. Cameron, ed., *The Old English Illustrated Pharmacopoeia: British Library Cotton Vitellius C.III*, EEMF 27 (Copenhagen)

Deshman, Robert, 'Another Look at the Disappearing Christ: Corporeal and Spiritual Vision in Early Medieval Images', *Art Bull.* 79 (1997), 518–46

Dumville, David N., see sect. 3*bii* [*Beowulf* manuscript]

Ferrari, Michele Camillo, see sect. 1

Gneuss, Helmut, 'A Newly-Found Fragment of an Anglo-Saxon Psalter', *ASE* 27, 273–87

Graham, Timothy, 'Abraham Wheelock's Use of CCCC MS 41 (Old English Bede) and the Borrowing of Manuscripts from the Library of Corpus Christi College', *Cambridge Bibliographical Soc. Newsletter* (1997), 10–16

  'Cambridge, Corpus Christi College 57 and its Anglo-Saxon Users', *Anglo-Saxon Manuscripts*, ed. Pulsiano and Treharne, pp. 21–69

Gransden, Antonia, 'Some Manuscripts in Cambridge from Bury St Edmunds Abbey: Exhibition Catalogue', *Bury St Edmunds*, ed. Gransden, pp. 228–85

Gullick, Michael, 'Professional Scribes in Eleventh- and Twelfth-Century England', *English Manuscript Studies 1100–1700* 7, 1–24

Gwara, Scott, 'Further Old English Scratched Glosses and Merographs from Corpus Christi College, Cambridge MS 326 (Aldhelm's *Prosa de Virginitate*)', *ES* 78 (1997), 201–36

  'The Transmission of the "Digby" Corpus of Bilingual Glosses to Aldhelm's *Prosa de Virginitate*', *ASE* 27, 139–68

Hawkes, Jane, see sect. 9*a*

Henderson, Isabel, see sect. 9*h*

Hill, Joyce, see sect. 3*c*

Insley, Charles, 'Charters and Episcopal Scriptoria in the Anglo-Saxon South-West', *EME* 7, 173–97

Kelly, S. E., ed., *Charters of Selsey*, AS Charters 6 (Oxford)

Kiernan, Kevin, S., see sect. 3*bii*

Kubouchi, Tadao, 'What is the Point? Manuscript Punctuation as Evidence for Linguistic Change', *The Locus of Meaning: Papers in Honor of Yoshihiko Ikegami*, ed. K. Yamanaka and T. Ohori (Tokyo), 17–32

Lapidge, Michael, 'Byrhtferth at Work', *Words and Works*, ed. Baker and Howe, pp. 25–43

Lasko, Peter, 'The Bayeux Tapestry and the Representation of Space', *Medieval Art*, ed. Owen-Crocker and Graham, pp. 26–39

Liuzza, Roy Michael, 'Who Read the Gospels in Old English?', *Words and Works*, ed. Baker and Howe, pp. 3–24

Lowe, Kathryn A., 'Lay Literacy in Anglo-Saxon England and the Development of the Chirograph', *Anglo-Saxon Manuscripts*, ed. Pulsiano and Treharne, pp. 161–204

'The Nature and Effect of the Anglo-Saxon Vernacular Will', *Jnl of Legal Hist.* 19.1, 23–61

'The Development of the Anglo-Saxon Boundary Clause', *Nomina* 21, 63–100

MacLean, Douglas, see sect. 9*h*

Marchesin, Isabelle, 'Le Corps musical dans les miniatures psalmiques carolingiennes et romanes', *Le Geste et les gestes au moyen âge*, Sénéfiance 41 (Aix-en-Provence), 401–27 [Vespasian Psalter]

Marsden, Richard, '"Ask what I am called": the Anglo-Saxons and their Bibles', *The Bible as Book*, ed. Sharpe and Van Kampen, pp. 145–76

see also sect. 4

Meehan, Bernard, *The Book of Durrow* (Dublin, 1996)

Mews, Constant J., 'Two Unnoticed Manuscripts in Poland Copied before 900: Gregory's *Regula pastoralis* in Anglo-Saxon Minuscule in Warsaw and an Uncial New Testament in Cracow', *Scriptorium* 51 (1997), 303–13

Muñoz de Miguel, María, 'The Iconography of Christ *Victor* in Anglo-Saxon Art: a New Approach to the Study of the "Harrowing of Hell" Relief in Bristol Cathedral', *'Almost the Richest City': Bristol in the Middle Ages*, ed. Lawrence Keen ([London], 1997), pp. 75–80

Murray, Peter, and Linda Murray, see sect. 9*a*

Noel, William, 'The Lost Canterbury Prototype of the 11th-Century Bury St Edmunds Psalter', *Bury St Edmunds*, ed. Gransden, pp. 161–71

O'Keeffe, Katherine O'Brien, 'Reading the C-Text: the After-Lives of London, British Library, Cotton Tiberius B. I', *Anglo-Saxon Manuscripts*, ed. Pulsiano and Treharne, pp. 137–60

Owen-Crocker, Gale R., see sect. 3*bii*

Owen-Crocker, Gale R., and Timothy Graham, ed., *Medieval Art: Recent Perspectives. A Memorial Tribute to C. R. Dodwell* (Manchester)

Page, R. I., see sect. 9*l*

Parsons, David, 'Byrhtferth and the Runes of Oxford, St. John's College, Manuscript 17', *Runeninschriften*, ed. Düwel, pp. 439–47

Pfaff, Richard W., see sect. 4

Prescott, Andrew, 'The Ghost of Asser', *Anglo-Saxon Manuscripts*, ed. Pulsiano and Treharne, pp. 255–91

Proud, Joana, see sect. 3*c*

Pulsiano, Phillip, 'A Middle English Gloss in the Lambeth Psalter', *ANQ* 10 (1997), 2–9

'The Prefatory Matter of London, British Library, Cotton Vitellius E. xviii', *Anglo-Saxon Manuscripts*, ed. Pulsiano and Treharne, pp. 85–116

Pulsiano, Phillip, and Elaine M. Treharne, ed., *Anglo-Saxon Manuscripts and their Heritage* (Aldershot)

Schipper, William, 'The Worcester Tremulous Scribe and the Ælfric Manuscripts', *Jnl of Eng. Ling.* 25 (1997), 183–201

Scragg, D. G., 'Cambridge, Corpus Christi College 162', *Anglo-Saxon Manuscripts*, ed. Pulsiano and Treharne, pp. 71–83

Sharpe, John L., and Kimberly Van Kampen, ed., *The Bible as Book: the Manuscript Tradition* (London)

Swan, Mary, 'Memorialized Readings: Manuscript Evidence for Old English Homily Composition', *Anglo-Saxon Manuscripts*, ed. Pulsiano and Treharne, pp. 205–17

Szarmach, Paul E., 'Æðelflæd of Mercia: *mise en page*', *Words and Works*, ed. Baker and Howe, pp. 105–26

Teviotdale, E. C., 'An Episode in the Medieval Afterlife of the Caligula Troper', *Anglo-Saxon Manuscripts*, ed. Pulsiano and Treharne, pp. 219–26

Toswell, M. J., 'The Late Anglo-Saxon Psalter: Ancestor of the Book of Hours?', *Florilegium* 14 (1995–6), 1–24

Treharne, Elaine M., 'The Dates and Origins of Three Twelfth-Century Old English Manuscripts', *Anglo-Saxon Manuscripts*, ed. Pulsiano and Treharne, pp. 227–53

Verey, Christopher, 'A Northumbrian Text Family', *The Bibly as Book*, ed. Sharpe and Van Kampen, pp. 105–122

Webber, Teresa, 'The Provision of Books for Bury St Edmunds Abbey in the 11th and 12th Centuries', *Bury St Edmunds*, ed. Gransden, pp. 186–93

Werner, Martin, 'Three Works on the Book of Kells', *Peritia* 11 (1997), 250–326

Wieland, Gernot R., 'Gloss and Illustration: Two Means to the Same End?', *Anglo-Saxon Manuscripts*, ed. Pulsiano and Treharne, pp. 1–20

Williams, C. L. Sinclair, 'The *Cwylla* of King Edmund's West Malling Charter', *AC* 89 (1975 for 1974), 135–9

Withers, Benjamin, 'Interaction of Word and Image in Anglo-Saxon Art II: Scrolls and Codex in the Frontispiece to the *Regularis Concordia*', *OEN* 31.1 (1997), 36–40

Wüstefeld, W. C. M., 'Missionaries, Masters and Manuscripts: a Survey of the Oldest Books and their Patrons in the Diocese of Utrecht (until c. 1200)', *Utrecht*, ed. De Bièvre, pp. 145–62

6. HISTORY

Abels, Richard, *Alfred the Great: War, Kingship and Culture in Anglo-Saxon England* (London)
Abrams, Lesley, 'History and Archaeology: the Conversion of Scandinavia', *Conversion and Christianity*, ed. Crawford, pp. 109–28
  'The Conversion of the Scandinavians of Dublin', *ANS* 20, 1–29
Angenendt, Arnold, 'Willibrord tussen bisschopszetel en klooster', *Millennium* 10 (1996), 100–10
Arrand, Donald, *Britain Under and After the Romans*, Northfield Society Occasional Papers 23 (Birmingham, 1997)
Bailey, Keith, 'Aspects of Anglo-Saxon Middlesex: Harrow and Hayes', *ASSAH* 9 (1998 for 1996), 63–74
Bailey, Maggie, see sect. 9*b*
Baillie, M. G. L., see Section 9*a* [eclipses in *ASC*]
Baker, Nigel, and Richard Holt, 'The Origins of Urban Parish Boundaries', *The Church in the Medieval Town*, ed. T. R. Slater and Gervase Rosser (Aldershot), pp. 209–35
Banham, Debby, 'Herbs in Anglo-Saxon Medicine', *Herbs* 23.4, 8–9
Barnwell, Paul, '*Hlafaeta, Ceorl, Hid* and *Scir*: Celtic, Roman or Germanic?', *ASSAH* 9 (1998 for 1996), 53–61
Barrett, Derek, see sect. 9*a*
Bassett, Steven, *The Origins of the Parishes of the Deerhurst Area*, Deerhurst Lecture 1997 (Deerhurst)
Bates, David, ed., *Regesta regum Anglo-Normannorum: the Acta of William I (1066–1087)* (Oxford)
Bauer, Nancy, 'Abbess Hilda of Whitby: All Britain was Lit by her Splendor', *Medieval Women Monastics: Wisdom's Wellsprings*, ed. Miriam Schmitt and Linda Kulzer (Collegeville, MN, 1996), pp. 13–31
Beale, Philip, *A History of the Post in England from the Romans to the Stuarts* (Aldershot) ['From the Romans to the Norman Conquest', pp. 1–18]
Berry, Roger, 'The Funding of the Norman Conquest and Some Financial Indicators', *Rev. of the Guernsey Soc.* 51.1 (1995), 6–12
Bliese, John R. E., 'Saint Cuthbert and War', *JMH* 24, 215–41
Booth, Paul Anthony, see sect. 3*bii*
Bradbury, Jim, *The Battle of Hastings* (Stroud)
Bremmer, Rolf J., 'Widows in Anglo-Saxon England', *Between Poverty and the Pyre: Moments in the History of Widowhood*, ed. Jan Bremmer and Lourens van den Bosch (London, 1995), pp. 58–88
Brett, Martin, 'The Church at Rochester, 604–1185', *Faith and Fabric: a History of Rochester Cathedral, 604–1994*, ed. Nigel Yates and Paul W. Wesley (Rochester, 1996), pp. 1–27
Brooke, Daphne, *Wild Men and Holy Places: St Ninian, Whithorn, and the Medieval Realm of Galloway* (Edinburgh)
Brown, Majorie A., 'The Feast Hall in Anglo-Saxon Society', *Food and Eating in Medieval Europe*, ed. Martha Carlin and Joel T. Rosenthal (London), pp. 1–13

Cathers, Kerry, 'Hierarchy or Anarchy: an Examination of the Leadership Structures within the Anglo-Saxon Military', *The Propagation of Power in the Medieval West: Selected Proceedings of the International Conference, Groningen, 20–23 November 1996*, ed. Martin Gosman, Arjo Vanderjagt and Jan Veenstra (Groningen, 1997), pp. 97–111

Charles-Edwards, Thomas, 'Alliances, Godfathers, Treaties and Boundaries', *Kings, Currency and Alliances*, ed. Blackburn and Dumville, pp. 47–62

  'Anglo-Saxon Kinship Revisited', *The Anglo-Saxons*, ed. Hines, pp. 171–210

Chibnall, Marjorie, '"Clio's Legal Cosmetics": Law and Custom in the Work of Medieval Historians,' *ANS* 20, 31–43

Clarke, Howard B., 'Proto-Towns and Towns in Ireland and Britain in the Ninth and Tenth Centuries', *Ireland and Scandinavia in the Early Viking Age*, ed. Clarke *et al*., pp. 331–80

Coates, S., 'Perceptions of the Anglo-Saxon Past in the Tenth-Century Monastic Reform Movement', *The Church Retrospective*, ed. R. N. Swanson, Stud. in Church Hist. 33 (Woodbridge, 1997), 61–74

Cole, Dick, 'The Cornish Identity and Genetics: an Alternative View', *Cornish Stud.* 2nd ser. 5 (1997), 21–9

Coleman, Julie, 'Rape in Anglo-Saxon England', *Violence and Society in the Early Medieval West*, ed. Guy Halsall (Woodbridge), pp. 193–204

Conn, Marie A., 'Rites of King-Making in Tenth-Century England', *The Propagation of Power in the Medieval West: Selected Proceedings of the International Conference, Groningen, 20–23 November 1996*, ed. Martin Gosman, Arjo Vanderjagt and Jan Veenstra (Groningen, 1997), pp. 111–27

Cownie, Emma, *Religious Patronage in Anglo-Norman England 1066–1135*, R. Hist. Soc. Stud. in Hist. ns (Woodbridge)

  'The Cult of St Edmund in the Eleventh and Twelfth Centuries: The Language and Communication of a Medieval Saint's Cult', *NM* 99, 177–97

Davis, R. H. C., and Marjorie Chibnall, ed. and trans., *The Gesta Gullielmi of William of Poitiers*, Oxford Medieval Texts (Oxford)

Dumville, David N., 'Anglo-Saxon and Celtic Overkingships: a Discussion of Some Shared Historical Problems', *Bull. of the Inst. of Oriental and Occidental Stud., Kansai Univ.* 31, 81–100

  'Ireland and Britain in *Táin bó Fraích*', *Études celtiques* 32 (1997 for 1996), 175–87 [names of peoples and territories, including Old English, and political implications]

  'The Terminology of Overkingship in Early Anglo-Saxon England', *The Anglo-Saxons*, ed. Hines, pp. 345–73

Edgington, Susan B., *et al*., trans., *Ramsey Abbey's Book of Benefactors, Part One: the Abbey's Foundation* (Huntingdon)

Faith, Rosamund, 'The Topography and Social Structure of a Small Soke in the Middle Ages: the Sokens, Essex', *Essex Archaeol. and Hist.* 27 (1996), 202–13

Farrant, John H., 'John Collingwood Bruce and the Bayeux Tapestry', *AAe* 5th ser. 25 (1997), 109–13

Fleming, Robin, *Domesday Book and the Law: Social and Legal Custom in Early Medieval England* (Cambridge)

Foot, Sarah, 'Language and Method: the Dictionary of Old English and the Historian', *The Dictionary of Old English*, ed. Toswell, pp. 73–87

Gardiner, Mark, 'The Colonisation of the Weald of South-East England', *Med. Settlement Research Group Ann. Report* 12 (for 1997), 6–8

see also sect. 9*a*

Garner, H. W., 'The Danes on the Rame Peninsula', *Devon and Cornwall Notes and Queries* 38, 76–83

Getz, Faye, *Medicine in the English Middle Ages* (Princeton, NJ)

Hall, Richard, see sect. 9*e*

Hall, Simon, 'Beowulf: New Light on the Dark Ages', *Hist. Today* 48.12, 4–5 [Paul Wilkinson's proposal that action takes place in Kent]

Härke, Heinrich, see sect. 9*a*

Harmeling, Deborah, 'Tetta, "Noble in Conduct", and Thecla, "Shining like a Light in a Dark Place"', *Medieval Women Monastics: Wisdom's Wellsprings*, ed. Miriam Schmitt and Linda Kulzer (Collegeville, MN, 1996), pp. 99–114

Hayashi, Hiroshi, *Essays in Anglo-Saxon Law*, 4 vols. (Tokyo, 1990–4)

A Study of the Charter-Criticism of the Anglo-Saxon Period, its Theory and Practice: a Preliminary Handbook, 2nd ed., 2 pts (Tokyo)

Heighway, Carolyn, *Deerhurst St Mary & Gloucester St Oswald: Two Saxon Minsters*, 6th Deerhurst Lecture ([Deerhurst], [1989?])

Henson, Donald, *A Guide to Late Anglo-Saxon England from Ælfred to Eadgar II* (Hockwold-cum-Wilton)

Hill, David, 'Anglo-Saxon Technology: 1. The Oxcart; 2. *Win geard seax*: the Anglo-Saxon Vine Dresser's Knife', *Med. Life* 10, 13–20

Hines, John, 'Religion: the Limits of Knowledge', *The Anglo-Saxons*, ed. Hines, pp. 375–410

Hollis, Stephanie, 'The Minister-in-Thanet Foundation Story', *ASE* 27, 41–64

Hooke, Della, *The Anglo-Saxon Landscape of North Gloucestershire*, 7th Deerhurst Lecture ([Deerhurst], 1990)

The Landscape of Anglo-Saxon England (London)

'The Anglo-Saxons in England in the Seventh and Eighth Centuries: Aspects of Location in Space', *The Anglo-Saxons*, ed. Hines, pp. 65–99

Huff, Chris, 'The Introduction of Falconry to the Anglo-Saxon Kingdoms: a Consideration of the Evidence from Anglo-Saxon and Continental Sources', *Med. Life* 10, 5–12

Horsfall, Anne, 'Domesday Woodland in Dorset', *Proc. of the Dorset Nat. Hist. and Archaeol. Soc.* 118 (1997), 1–6

Insley, Charles, 'Charters and Episcopal Scriptoria in the Anglo-Saxon South-West', *EME* 7, 173–97

Janes, Dominic, 'God, Gold, Corruption and Poverty', *Hist. Today* 48.12, 8–12 [treasure and saints' cults, including St Cuthbert]

Jewell, Helen M., *Women in Medieval England* (Manchester, 1996)

Johnson-South, Ted, 'Changing Images of Sainthood: St Cuthbert in the *Historia de Sancto Cuthberto*', *Saints: Studies in Hagiography*, ed. Sandro Sticca, Med. & Renaissance Texts & Stud. 141 (Binghamton, NY, 1996), 81–94

Jones, Timothy S., 'The Outlawry of Earl Godwin from the *Vita Ædwardi Regis*', *Medieval Outlaws: Ten Tales in Modern English*, ed. Thomas H. Ohlgren (Stroud), pp. 1–11

Keefer, Sarah Larratt, '*Ut in omnibus honorificetur Deus*: the *corsnæd* Ordeal in Anglo-Saxon England', *The Community, the Family and the Saint*, ed. Hill and Swan, pp. 237–64

Keene, Derek, 'Metalworking in Medieval London: an Historical Survey', *Jnl of the Hist. Metallurgy Soc.* 30.2 (1996), 95–102 [from A.D. 1000]

Kelly, S. E., see sect. 5

Keynes, Simon, *Anglo-Saxon History: a Select Bibliography*, 3rd ed., OEN Subsidia 13 (Kalamazoo, MI)

    'Queen Emma and the *Encomium Emmae Reginae*', *Encomium Emmae Reginae*, ed. A. Campbell, Camden Classic Reprints 4 (Cambridge), [xii]–[lxxxvii]

    'King Alfred and the Mercians', *Kings, Currency and Alliances*, ed. Blackburn and Dumville, pp. 1–45

Kleinschmidt, Harald, 'The Geuissae and Bede: On the Innovativeness of Bede's Concept of the *Gens*', *The Community, the Family and the Saint*, ed. Hill and Swan, pp. 77–102

    'Überlegungen zur Entstehung von Siedlungsraumgrenzen am Beispiel des frühmittelalterlichen Sussex', *Migration und Grenze*, ed. Andreas Gestrich and Marita Krauss, Stuttgarter Beiträge zur Historischen Migrationsforschung 4 (Stuttgart), 84–102

Kobayashi, Ayako, 'Queen Emma and the Last Kings of the Anglo-Saxon Dynasty', *Stud. in Eng. Lang. and Lit.* 4, 43–55 [in Japanese]

Kurasawa, Ichitaro, 'Problems Concerning the Succession to the Throne of England in 1066', *Bummei* 76 (1997), 35–52 [in Japanese]

Lamb, Raymond, 'Pictland, Northumbria and the Carolingian Empire', *Conversion and Christianity*, ed. Crawford, pp. 41–56

Lazzari, Loredana, 'Regine, badesse, sante: il contributo della donna anglosassone all'evangelizzazione (secc. VII e VIII)', *SM* 3rd ser. 39, 601–32

Lendinara, Patrizia, 'The Kentish Laws', *The Anglo-Saxons*, ed. Hines, pp. 211–43

Lewis, Suzanne, *The Rhetoric of Power in the Bayeux Tapestry* (Cambridge)

Lynch, Joseph H., *Christianizing Kinship: Ritual Sponsorship in Anglo-Saxon England* (Ithaca, NY)

MacQuarrie, Alan, *The Saints of Scotland: Essays in Scottish Church History, A.D. 450–1093* (Edinburgh, 1997) [includes St Margaret]

Magilton, John, see sect. 9*b*

Mason, Emma, 'Monastic Habits in Medieval Worcester', *Hist. Today* 48.5, 37–43

Maxwell, I. S., 'The Identification and Location of *Caellincg*', *Jnl of the R. Inst. of Cornwall* 3.1, 39–41

McLynn, Frank, *1066: the Year of the Three Battles* (London)

Metcalf, D. M., see sect. 7

Miyama, Tasuku, 'Bede's World', *Jnl of the Dept. of Liberal Arts* (Asia University, Tokyo) 57, 115–26 [in Japanese]

Morris, John, see sect. 1

Mynors, R. A. B., ed. and trans., completed by R. M. Thomson and M. Winterbottom, *William of Malmesbury, Gesta regum Anglorum: the History of the English Kings* I, Oxford Medieval Texts (Oxford)

Bibliography for 1998

Nagai, Ichiro, 'The Celtic Fringe and England: the Case of Wales', *Iwanami's World History*, ns 7, ed. S. Sato (Tokyo), pp. 81–107 [in Japanese]

Nelson, Janet L., 'Early Medieval Rites of Queen-Making and the Shaping of Medieval Queenship', *Queens and Queenship in Medieval Europe*, ed. Anne J. Duggan (Woodbridge, 1997), pp. 301–15

Nicholas, David, *The Growth of the Medieval City: from Late Antiquity to the early Fourteenth Century* (London, 1997)

Nilsson, Bertil, 'Vikings Deceased in England – Commemorated by Whom? Runic Memorials in Sweden', *The Community, the Family and the Saint*, ed. Hill and Swan, pp. 379–90

O'Keeffe, Katherine O'Brien, see sect. 3*c*

Oliver, Lisi, '*Cyninges fedesl*: the King's Feeding in Æthelberht, ch. 12', *ASE* 27, 31–40

'Towards Freeing a Slave in Germanic Law', *Mír Curad: Studies in Honor of Calvert Watkins*, ed. Jay Jasanoff, H. Craig Melchert and Lisi Oliver (Innsbruck), pp. 549–60

Palmer, J. J. N., 'The Conqueror's Footprints in Domesday Book', *The Medieval Military Revolution: State, Society and Military Change in Medieval and Early Modern Europe*, ed. Andrew Ayton and J. L. Price (London, 1995), pp. 23–44

Parsons, David, see sect. 9*e*

Pelteret, David A. E., 'Bede's Women', *Women, Marriage and Family in Medieval Christendom: Essays in Memory of Michael M. Sheehan, C.S.B.*, ed. Constance M. Rousseau and Joel T. Rosenthal, Stud. in Med. Culture 37 (Kalamazoo, MI), 19–46

'Saint Wilfrid: Tribal Bishop, Civic Bishop or Germanic Lord?', *The Community, the Family and the Saint*, ed. Hill and Swan, pp. 159–80

Pewsey, Stephen, 'Two More Lost Essex Saints: the Mysterious Martyrs of Wakering', *Essex Archaeol. and Hist. News* 127, 9–10 [SS Æthelbert and Æthelred]

Pohl, Walter, 'Ethnic Names and Identities in the British Isles: a Comparative Perspective', *The Anglo-Saxons*, ed. Hines, pp. 7–40

Potts, W. T. W., 'Brettaroum, Bolton-le-Sands, and the Late Survival of Welsh in Lancashire', *Contrebis* 19 (1994), 61–76

Rader, Rosemary, 'St Frideswide: Monastic Founder of Oxford', *Medieval Women Monastics: Wisdom's Wellsprings*, ed. Miriam Schmitt and Linda Kulzer (Collegeville, MN, 1996), pp. 33–47

Reid, Bill, 'The Anglo-Saxon Chronicle: Fact or Fiction?', *Glevensis* 31, 25–6

Reuter, Timothy, 'The Making of England and Germany, 850–1050: Points of Comparison and Difference', *Medieval Europeans*, ed. Smyth, pp. 53–70

Richards, Mary P., 'Anglo-Saxonism in the Old English Laws', *Anglo-Saxonism*, ed. Frantzen and Niles, pp. 40–59

Rodger, N. A. M., *The Safeguard of the Sea: a Naval History of Britain*, I, *660–1649* (London, 1997)

Rollason, D. W., with D. Gore and G. Fellows-Jensen, *Sources for York History to A.D. 1100*, The Archaeology of York 1 (York)

Rollason, David, ed., *Symeon of Durham: Historian of Durham and the North*, Studies in North-Eastern Hist. 1 (Stamford)

Russo, Daniel G., *Town Origins and Development in Early England, c. 400–950 A.D.* (Westport, CT)

Sawyer, P. H., *Anglo-Saxon Lincolnshire*, History of Lincolnshire 3 (Lincoln)
  From Roman Britain to Norman England, 2nd ed. (London) [with Postscript]
Scull, Christopher, see sect. 9*b*
Semple, Sarah, 'A Fear of the Past: the Place of the Prehistoric Burial Mound in the Ideology of Middle and Later Anglo-Saxon England', *World Archaeol.* 30.1, 109–26
Sharp, Sheila M., 'England, Europe and the Celtic World: King Athelstan's Foreign Policy', *Bull. of the John Rylands Univ. Lib. of Manchester* 79.3 (1997), 197–220
Slater, T. R., 'Benedictine Town Planning in Medieval England: the Evidence from St Alban's', *The Church in the Medieval Town*, ed. T. R. Slater and Gervase Rosser (Aldershot), pp. 155–76
Smith, Malcolm, 'Genetic Variation and Celtic Population History', *Cornish Stud.* 6, 7–22
Smyth, Alfred P., 'The Emergence of English Identity, 700–1000', *Medieval Europeans*, ed. Smyth, pp. 24–52
Smyth, Alfred P., ed., *Medieval Europeans: Studies in Ethnic Identity and National Perspectives in Medieval Europe* (Basingstoke)
Snyder, Christopher A., *An Age of Tyrants: Britain and the Britons, A.D. 400–600* (Stroud)
Stafford, Pauline, 'Emma: the Powers of the Queen in the Eleventh Century', *Queens and Queenship in Medieval Europe*, ed. Anne J. Duggan (Woodbridge, 1997), pp. 3–26
Stewartby, Lord, see sect. 7
Story, J. E., 'Carolingian Northumbria and the Legatine Mission of 786', *Conversion and Christianity*, ed. Crawford, pp. 93–107
Swanton, Michael, '*The Deeds of Hereward*', *Medieval Outlaws: Ten Tales in Modern English*, ed. Thomas H. Ohlgren (Stroud), pp. 12–60
  'The Bayeux Tapestry: Epic Narrative, not Stichic but Stitched', *The Formation of Culture in Medieval Britain: Celtic, Latin and Norman Influences on English Music, Literature, History and Art*, ed. Françoise H. M. Le Saux (Lampeter, 1995), pp. 149–69
Thormann, Janet, 'The *Anglo-Saxon Chronicle* Poems and the Making of the English Nation', *Anglo-Saxonism and the Construction of Social Identity*, ed. Allen J. Frantzen and John D. Niles (Gainesville, FL, 1997), pp. 60–85
Tomizawa, Reigan, 'Church and State in Early Medieval England', *Shisen* 85 (1997), 1–18 [in Japanese]
Tsurushima, Hirokazu, 'England: its Place and Structure in the Making of Europe', *Iwanami's World History*, ns 8, ed. O. Egawa, pp. 221–49 [in Japanese]
Tyler, Damian J., 'Bede, the Anglo-Saxon Chronicle, and Early West Saxon Kingship', *Southern Hist.* 19 (1997), 1–23
Venarde, Bruce L., *Women's Monasticism and Medieval Society: Nunneries in France and England, 890–1215* (Ithaca, NY, 1997)
Vogtherr, Thomas, 'Zwischen Benediktinerabtei und bischöflicher Cathedra. Zu Auswahl und Amtsantritt englischer Bischöfe im 9.–11. Jahrhundert', *Die Früh- und Hochmittelalterliche Bischofserhebung im europäischen Vergleich*, ed. Franz-Reiner Erkens (Vienna), pp. 287–320
Wamers, Egon, see sect. 9*g*
Warner, Peter, *The Origins of Suffolk*, The Origins of the Shire (Manchester, 1996)

Wood, Ian, 'Before and After the Migration to Britain', *The Anglo-Saxons*, ed. Hines, pp. 41–64 [includes discussion]
Wormald, Patrick, 'Frederic William Maitland and the Earliest English Law', *Law and Hist. Rev.* 16.1, 1–25
Wybourne, Catherine, 'Leoba: a Study in Humanity and Holiness', *Medieval Women Monastics: Wisdom's Wellsprings*, ed. Miriam Schmitt and Linda Kulzer (Collegeville, MN, 1996), pp. 81–96
Yorke, Barbara, 'The Bonifacian Mission and Female Religious in Wessex', *EME* 7.2, 145–72

7. NUMISMATICS

Bateson, J. D., and I. G. Campbell, *Byzantine and Early Medieval Western European Coins in the Hunter Coin Cabinet, University of Glasgow* (Glasgow) [includes two rare sixth-century Anglo-Saxon coins]
B[esly], E. M., and N. McQ. H[olmes], ed., 'Coin Register 1997', *BNJ* 67 (1997), 125–47
Bibire, Paul, 'Moneyers' Names on Ninth-Century Southumbrian Coins: Philological Approaches to Some Historical Questions', *Kings, Currency and Alliances*, ed. Blackburn and Dumville, pp. 155–66
Blackburn, Mark, 'The London Mint in the Reign of Alfred', *Kings, Currency and Alliances*, ed. Blackburn and Dumville, pp. 105–23
Blackburn, Mark, and Richard Ashton, ed., 'Coin Hoards 1998', *NChron* 158, 287–331 [includes 5 Anglo-Saxon hoards, at 294–5 and 298–300]
Blackburn, Mark, and Andy Gillis, 'A Second Coin of King Eardwulf of Northumbria and the Attribution of the Moneyer Coins of King Ælfwald', *BNJ* 67 (1997), 97–9
Blackburn, Mark, and Simon Keynes, 'A Corpus of the *Cross-and-Lozenge* and Related Coinages of Alfred, Ceolwulf II and Archbishop Æthelred', *Kings, Currency and Alliances*, ed. Blackburn and Dumville, pp. 125–50
Bonser, Michael, 'Single Finds of Ninth-Century Coins from Southern England: a Listing', *Kings, Currency and Alliances*, ed. Blackburn and Dumville, pp. 199–240
Booth, James, "Monetary Alliance or Technical Co-Operation? The Coinage of Berhtwulf of Mercia (840–852)', *Kings, Currency and Alliances*, ed. Blackburn and Dumville, pp. 63–103
Clarke, Stephen, 'The Monmouth Hoard of Æthelred II Coins', *Archaeol. in Wales* 34 (1994), 16
Edwards, B. J. N., see sect. 9*i*
Elliott, L., 'A "Porcupine" Sceat from Adbolton Deserted Medieval Village, Nottinghamshire', *Trans. of the Thoroton Soc. of Notinghamshire* 100 (1996), 169–70
Lyon, C. S. S., 'The "Expanding Cross" Type of Edward the Confessor and the Appledore (1997) Hoard', *NCirc* 106, 426–8
Metcalf, D. M., *An Atlas of Anglo-Saxon and Norman Coin Finds, c. 973–1086* (London)
'The Monetary Economy of Ninth-Century England South of the Humber: a

Topographical Analysis', *Kings, Currency and Alliances*, ed. Blackburn and Dumville, pp. 167–97

'Runes and Literacy: Pondering the Evidence of Anglo-Saxon Coins of the Eighth and Ninth Centuries', *Runeninschriften*, ed. Düwel, pp. 434–8

Pagan, H. E., 'The Oxford Alpinist's Uncle's Hoard', *NCirc* 106, 206 [hoard of uncertain Anglo-Saxon pennies discovered 1893–4]

Smart, Veronica, see sect. 8

Staecker, Jörn, see sect. 9*i*

Stewartby, Lord, 'Moneyers in the Written Records', *Kings, Currency and Alliances*, ed. Blackburn and Dumville, pp. 151–3

Wiechmann, Ralf, 'Souvenirs aus England? Zwei northumbrische "Stycas" gefunden in Schleswig-Holstein', *Studien zur Archäologie des Ostseeraumes von der Eisenzeit zum Mittelalter: Festschrift für Michael Müller-Wille*, ed. Anke Wesse (Neumünster), pp. 453–60 [Æthelred II, moneyers Leofthegn and Monne]

Williams, Gareth, 'A Hoard of "Expanding Cross" Pennies from Appledore: Preliminary Report', *NCirc* 106, 152–3

8. ONOMASTICS

Atkin, M. A., 'Places Named "Anstey"', *Proceedings of the XIXth Congress of Onomastic Sciences*, ed. Nicolaisen II, 15–23

'Places Named "Anstey" : a Gazetteer', *JEPNS* 30 (1997–8), 83–98

Baines, Arnold H. J., 'Hambleden: the Bent Valley', *Records of Buckinghamshire* 37 (1997 for 1995), 138–40

Breeze, Andrew, 'The *Anglo-Saxon Chronicle* for 949 and Olaf Cuaran', *N&Q* 44 (1997), 160–1

'A Celtic Etymology for *Ouse Burn*, Newcastle', *AAe* 5th ser. 26, 57–8

'The Celtic Place-Name Loders', *Proc. of the Dorset Nat. Hist. and Archaeol. Soc.* 119 (1997), 183

'Four Devon Place-Names', *Nomina* 21, 157–68 [Clyst, Countisbury, Creedy, Croyde]

'The Kent Place-Name Brenchley', *Nomina* 21, 154–6

'The Lancashire Place-Names Alkincoats and Heskin', *Nomina* 21, 149–53

'The Name of Sock Dennis and Old Sock, near Yeovil', *Somerset and Dorset Notes and Queries* 34, 248–50

'The Name of Trusham', *Devon and Cornwall Notes and Queries* 38, 74–6

'The Name of Trysull, Near Wolverhampton', *Staffordshire Studies* 10, 77–8

'The Place-Name *Onn* at High Onn and Little Onn', *Trans. of the Staffordshire Archaeol. & Hist. Soc.* 37, 139

Cameron, Kenneth, *A Dictionary of Lincolnshire Place-Names*, EPNS popular ser. 1 (Nottingham)

Cederlöf, Mikael, see sect. 2*a*

Coates, Richard, 'Æthelflæd's Fortification of *Weardburh*', *N&Q* 45, 8–12

'Dumpford Hundred', *Sussex Past and Present* 86, 5 and 7

'A Further Snippet of Evidence for Brunanburh = *Bromborough*', *N&Q* 45, 288–9
'Liscard and Irish Names in Northern Wirral', *JEPNS* 30 (1997–8), 23–6
'Merrow and Some Related Brittonic Matters in Surrey', *JEPNS* 30 (1997–8), 16–22
'A New Explanation of the Name of London', *TPS* 96, 203–29
'A Surviving Latin Place-Name in Sussex: Firle', *JEPNS* 30 (1997–8), 5–15
see also sect. 2*a*

Cox, Barrie, *The Place-Names of Leicestershire*, I. *The Borough of Leicester*, EPNS 75 (Nottingham)
'Baumber in Lindsey', *JEPNS* 30 (1997–8), 27–32

Ellerington, Enoch, 'The Origin of the Place-Name, Bradon', *Somerset and Dorset Notes and Queries* 34 (1997), 115–17

Faith, Rosamund, see sect. 6

Fellows-Jensen, Gillian, 'Little Thwaite, Who Made Thee?', *Proceedings of the XIXth Congress of Onomastic Sciences*, ed. Nicolaisen II, 101–6

Forsberg, Rune, *The Place-Name 'Lewes': a Study of its Early Spellings and Etymology*, Acta Universitatis Upsaliensis/Studia Anglistica Upsaliensia 100 (Uppsala, 1997)

Gelling, Margaret, 'Essex Place Names Project', *Essex Archaeol. and Hist. News* 126 (1997), 2–5
'The Etymology of Rouncil', *JEPNS* 30 (1997–8), 105–6
'Place-Names and Landscape', *The Uses of Place-Names*, ed. Simon Taylor (Edinburgh), pp. 75–100

Hesse, Mary, 'The Field Called "Augey" in Ickleton: an Anglo-Saxon Enclosure?', *Proc. of the Cambridge Ant. Soc.* 85 (1997 for 1996), 159–60

Hilton, G., 'The Origin of the Name Rouncil, Kenilworth, Warwickshire', *JEPNS* 30 (1997–8), 99–104

Hooke, Della, '*Lamberde Leie, Dillameres Dic*: a Lost or a Living Landscape?', *Making English Landscapes*, ed. Barker and Darvill, pp. 26–45

Hough, Carole, 'Bonhunt: an Essex Place-Name', *Anglia* 113 (1995), 207–12
'The Place-Name Felderland', *N&Q* 42 (1995), 420–1
'The Place-Name Cotterstock', *ES* 77 (1996), 375–8
'Old English *rōt* in Place-Names', *N&Q* 43 (1996), 128–9
'The Place-Name Thursley', *N&Q* 43 (1996), 387–9
'The Hill-Name Haldon', *Devon and Cornwall Notes and Queries* 38 (1997), 23–8
'Old English **Ducemann*', *Neophilologus* 81 (1997), 605–8
'The Earliest Old English Place-Names in Scotland', *N&Q* 44 (1997), 148–50
'The Place-Name Hardy', *N&Q* 44 (1997), 168–9
'OE *lāf* in Place-Names', *N&Q* 44 (1997), 304–6
'The Place-Name Kingston and the Laws of Æthelberht', *SN* 69 (1997), 55–7
'Farmlands and Farming Woods: Two Place-Names Reconsidered', *Proceedings of the XIXth Congress of Onomastic Sciences*, ed. Nicolaisen II, 192–8
'Old English **Coppa*', *JEPNS* 30 (1997–8), 53–9
'Stallingborough in Lincolnshire', *N&Q* 45, 286–8
'The Place-Name Satterleigh', *NM* 99, 173–5
'The Place-Name Ousden', *SN* 70, 149–52

see also sect. 2*a* (three items) and 3*biii* (four items)

Insley, John, 'Harby – a Place-Name Complex in the Danelaw', *SN* 70, 9–23

Jones, Graham, 'Penda's Footprint? Place-Names Containing Personal Names Associated with those of Early Mercian Kings', *Nomina* 21, 29–62

Keene, Barbara, and Michael Sampson, 'Identifying the Domesday Manors of Nochecote and Loteland', *Devon and Cornwall Notes and Queries* 38 (1997), 15–16

Kemble, James, 'The Essex Place-Names Project', *Essex Archaeol. and Hist.* 28 (1997), 311–13

'Essex Place-Names Project', *Essex Archaeol. and Hist. News* 128, 3–4

Mills, A. D., *A Dictionary of English Place-Names*, 2nd ed. (Oxford)

Morris, John, see sect. 1

Morris, Richard, 'Journey Through History to Penda's Fen', *Brit. Archaeol.* 39, 15

Nicolaisen, W. F. H., ed., *Proceedings of the XIXth Congress of Onomastic Sciences, Aberdeen, August 4–11, 1996: 'Scope, Perspectives and Methods of Onomastics'*, 3 vols. (Dept of Eng., Univ. of Aberdeen)

Parsons, David, 'British *Caratīcos*, Old English *Cerdic*', *CMCS* 33 (1997), 1–8

Proudfoot, Edwina, and Christopher Aliaga-Kelly, see sect. 9*g*

Robertson, Barbara, 'Evercy: a Lost Place-Name in Wellow', *Somerset and Dorset Notes and Queries* 34, 222–4 [identified by A.D. 861 charter bounds]

Russell, Pamela B., 'Everton – Not a *tūn*?', *JEPNS* 30 (1997–8), 77–81

Smart, Veronica, 'Onomasticon Anglo-Saxonicum Numismaticum: Indexing and Database', *Proceedings of the XIXth Congress of Onomastic Sciences*, ed. Nicolaisen I, 319–24

Styles, Tania, 'Whitby Revisited: Bede's Explanation of *Streanaeshalch*', *Nomina* 21, 133–48

Townend, Matthew, '*Ella*: an Old English Name in Old Norse Poetry', *Nomina* 20 (1997), 23–35

English Place-Names in Skaldic Verse, EPNS es 1 (Nottingham)

Turner, Dennis, 'Thunderfield, Surrey – Central Place or Shieling', *Med. Settlement Research Group Ann. Report* 12 (1998 for 1997), 8–10

Watts, V. E., 'Some Northumbrian Fishery Names IV: the River Tweed', *Durham Archaeol. Jnl* 13 (1997), 89–98

Wilkinson, Paul, 'Finding Beowulf in Kent's Landscape', *Brit. Archaeol.* 39, 8–9

9. ARCHAEOLOGY

a. General

Ambers, J., and S. Bowman, 'Radiocarbon Measurements from the British Museum: Datelist XXIV', *Archaeometry* 40.2, 413–35 [includes Anglo-Saxon]

Anderson, Trevor, 'Human Bone Studies', *Canterbury's Archaeol.* (1993 for 1992–3), 59–64 [includes Anglo-Saxon dental drilling]

[Anon.], 'Archäologischer Teil: Ausgrabungen, archäologische Denkmäler, Museen', *Die Römer in Nordrhein-Westfalen*, ed. Horn, pp. 319–656 [useful for pre-Migration evidence]

'Recent Work of the County Archaeological Section', *Essex Archaeol. and Hist. News* 128, 11–16 [includes Anglo-Saxon]
'Work of the County Archaeological Section', *Essex Archaeol. and Hist. News* 119 (1994), 11–16 [includes Anglo-Saxon]
'Work of the County Archaeological Section', *Essex Archaeol. and Hist. News* 120 (1994), 6–11 [includes Anglo-Saxon]
'Work of the County Archaeological Section', *Essex Archaeol. and Hist. News* 121 (1994), 6–15 [includes Anglo-Saxon]
'Work of the County Archaeological Section', *Essex Archaeol. and Hist. News* 125 (1997), 10–16 [includes Anglo-Saxon]
'Work of the County Archaeological Section', *Essex Archaeol. and Hist. News* 127, 11–16 [includes Anglo-Saxon]
'Work of the County Council Archaeology Section', *Essex Archaeol. and Hist. News* 118 (1993), 9–16 [includes Anglo-Saxon]
'Work of the County Council Archaeology Section', *Essex Archaeol. and Hist. News* 122 (1995), 9–16 [includes Anglo-Saxon]
Arnold, C. J., *An Archaeology of the Early Anglo-Saxon Kingdoms*, 2nd ed. (London, 1997)
Baillie, M. G. L., *A Slice Through Time: Dendrochronology and Precision Dating* (London, 1995)
Barnatt, John, and Ken Smith, *English Heritage Book of the Peak District: Landscapes Through Time* (London, 1997) [includes Anglo-Saxon]
Barrett, Derek, 'The Marston St. Lawrence Area, Northamptonshire: Archaeology and Early History', *Cake and Cockhorse* 14.4, 97–105 [includes Anglo-Saxon]
Bennett, Alison, ed., 'Archaeology in Essex 1996', *Essex Archaeol. and Hist.* 28 (1997), 205–27 [includes Anglo-Saxon]
Bennett, Alison, ed., 'Work of the Essex County Council Archaeology Section, 1996', *Essex Archaeol. and Hist.* 28 (1997), 181–204 [includes Anglo-Saxon]
Bennett, Alison, and P. J. Gilman, ed., 'Archaeology in Essex 1995', *Essex Archaeol. and Hist.* 27 (1996), 261–76 [includes Anglo-Saxon]
Blair, John, and Nigel Ramsay, ed., *English Medieval Industries: Craftsmen, Techniques, Products* (London, 1991)
Brown, Nigel, 'The Archaeology of South East Essex, Sixty Years On', *Essex Jnl* 33.1, 12–16 [includes a section on the Anglo-Saxon period]
Brown, Tony, and Glenn Foard, 'The Saxon Landscape: a Regional Perspective', *The Archaeology of Landscape: Studies presented to Christopher Taylor*, ed. Paul Everson and Tom Williamson (Manchester), pp. 67–94
Capelle, Torsten, *Die Sachsen des frühen Mittelalters* (Stuttgart)
Carrington, Peter, comp., *From Flints to Flower Pots: Current Research in the Dee-Mersey Region: Papers from a Seminar Held at Chester, February 1994*, [Chester City Council] Archaeol. Service Occasional Paper 2 (Chester, 1994)
Chapman, John, and Helena Hamerow, ed., *Migrations and Invasions in Archaeological Explanation*, BAR International Ser. 664 (Oxford, 1997)
Clark, Anthony, *Seeing Beneath the Soil: Prospecting Methods in Archaeology* (London, 1990) [includes brief accounts of surveys at Pewsey Anglo-Saxon cemetery, and a settlement at Wraysbury]

Clough, T. H. McK., ed., 'Rutland History in 1995–96', *Rutland Record* 17 (1997), 314–15 [includes Anglo-Saxon archaeology]
'Rutland History in 1996–97', *Rutland Record* 18, 361–8 [includes Anglo-Saxon archaeology]
Davison, Brian, *Picturing the Past Through the Eyes of Reconstruction Artists* (London, 1997) [includes Anglo-Saxon]
Dent, John, and Rory McDonald, *Early Settlers in the Borders* (Melrose, 1997) [includes brief information on the Angles in the Scottish borderland]
Dyer, James, *Discovering Archaeology in England and Wales*, 6th ed. (Princes Risborough, 1997) [includes a small section on Anglo-Saxon England]
Ellis, C., and A. G. Brown, 'Archaeomagnetic Dating and Palaeochannels Sediments: Data from the Mediaeval Channel Fills at Hemington, Leicestershire', *Jnl of Archaeol. Science* 25.2, 149–63 [includes early medieval evidence]
English, Barbara, 'Towns, Mottes and Ringworks of the Conquest', *The Medieval Military Revolution: State, Society and Military Change in Medieval and Early Modern Europe*, ed. Andrew Ayton and J. L. Price (London, 1995), pp. 45–61
Fagan, Brian M., ed., *The Oxford Companion to Archaeology* (Oxford, 1996) [includes articles of Anglo-Saxon interest]
Fokkens, Harry, *Drowned Landscape: the Occupation of the Western Part of the Frisian-Drentian Plateau, 4400 BC–AD 500* (Assen)
Fulford, Michael, Timothy Champion, and Antony Long, ed., *England's Coastal Heritage: a Survey for English Heritage and the RCHME*, Eng. Heritage Archaeol. Report 15 (London, 1997) [includes a section on Anglo-Saxon England]
Gardiner, Mark, 'The Exploitation of Sea-Mammals in Medieval England: Bones and their Social Context', *ArchJ* 154 (1998 for 1997), 173–95 [includes a catalogue of cetacean bone finds from medieval contexts]
Gechter, Michael, 'Das römische Heer in der Provinz Niedergermanien', *Die Römer in Nordrhein-Westfalen*, ed. Horn, pp. 110–38
Gerrard, Sandy, *English Heritage Book of Dartmoor: Landscapes Through Time* (London, 1997) [includes a small section of Anglo-Saxon interest]
Graham-Campbell, James, 'The Early Viking Age in the Irish Sea Area', *Ireland and Scandinavia in the Early Viking Age*, ed. Clarke, Ní Mhaonaigh and Ó Floinn, pp. 104–30 [includes north-west England]
Hamerow, H., 'Migration Theory and the Anglo-Saxon "Identity Crisis"', *Migrations and Invasions in Archaeological Explanation*, ed. Chapman and Hamerow, pp. 33–44
Härke, Heinrich, 'Early Anglo-Saxon Military Organisation: an Archaeological Perspective', *Military Aspects of Scandinavian Society in a European Perspective, A.D. 1–1300 (2nd May, 1996; National Museum, Copenhagen)*, ed Anne Nørgård Jörgensen and Birthe L. Clausen, Stud. in Archaeol. and Hist. 2 (Copenhagen, 1997), 93–101
'Early Anglo-Saxon Social Structure', *The Anglo-Saxons*, ed. Hines, pp. 125–70
Harrison, Lesley, 'Palaeoenvironmental Work in West Cheshire', *From Flints to Flower Pots*, comp. Carrington, pp. 4–12 [includes Anglo-Saxon]
Hässler, Hans-Jürgen, 'Völkerwanderungs- und Merowingerzeit', *Ur- und Frühgeschichte in Niedersachsen*, ed. Hässler, pp. 285–320

Hässler, Hans-Jürgen, ed., *Ur- und Frühgeschichte in Niedersachsen* (Stuttgart, 1991)
Hawkes, Jane, 'Symbolic Lives: the Visual Evidence', *The Anglo-Saxons*, ed. Hines, pp. 311–44 [includes discussion]
Hayes, Andrew, *Archaeology of the British Isles wth a Gazetteer of Sites in England, Wales, Scotland and Ireland* (London, 1993) [includes Anglo-Saxon]
Higgins, Tony, Peter Main, and Janet Lang, ed., *Imaging the Past: Electronic Imaging and Computer Graphics in Museums and Archaeology*, Brit. Museum Occasional Paper 114 (London, 1996)
Hines, John, 'Britain After Rome: Between Multiculturalism and Monoculturalism', *Cultural Identity and Archaeology: the Construction of European Communities*, ed. Paul Graves-Brown, Siân Jones, and Clive Gamble (London, 1996), pp. 256–70 see also sect. 6
Hinton, David, *Saxons and Vikings* (Wimborne) [about Dorset]
Hodges, Richard, 'The Not-So-Dark Ages', *Archaeology* 51.5, 61–3 and 65
Holroyd, Isabel, and Jeremy Oetgen, ed., *Brit. and Irish Archaeol. Bibliography* 2.1 and 2.2
Horn, Heinz Günter, 'Das Leben im römischen Rheinland', *Die Römer in Nordrhein-Westfalen*, ed. Horn, pp. 139–317
Horn, Heinz Günter, ed., *Die Römer in Nordrhein-Westfalen* (Stuttgart, 1987) [including pre-Migration Saxons]
Howard, Bruce, ed., *Archaeology in Hampshire: Annual Report for 1997* (Winchester) [see 'Index to Sites by Period', pp. 55–6]
Hunter-Mann, Kurt, 'Understanding the Archaeology of Post-Roman Britain', *Med. Life* 1 (1995), 5–7
Jackson, Gary, Cath Maloney, and Dinah Saich, 'Archaeology in Surrey 1994–5', *Surrey Archaeol. Collections* 84 (1997), 195–243 [includes Anglo-Saxon]
Jackson, Phyllis, 'Footloose in Archaeology 1997', *CA* 156 (1998), 456–7 [Anglo-Saxon feet]
Jordan, David, David Haddon-Reece and Alex Bayliss, *Radiocarbon Dates from Samples Funded by English Heritage and Dated Before 1981* (London, 1994) [includes Anglo-Saxon samples]
Klæsøe, Iben Skibsted, 'Plant Ornament: a Key to a New Chronology of the Viking Age', *Lund Archaeol. Rev.* 1997, 73–87
Kunow, Jügen, 'Die Militärgeschichte Niedergermaniens', *Die Römer in Nordrhein-Westfalen*, ed. Horn, pp. 27–109
McAdam, Ellen, 'Rural Post-Excavation and the *IDEA* Database from Aarhus', *Imaging the Past*, ed. Higgins, Main and Lang, pp. 73–84 [cases include Saxon sites: an early cemetery at Lechlade, a settlement near Abingdon, and Yarnton-Cassington, Oxon.]
Maloney, Cath, 'Fieldwork Round-Up 1997', *London Archaeologist* 8, supplement 3, 75–109 [includes Anglo-Saxon]
Matthews, Keith, 'Archaeology Without Artefacts: the Iron Age and Sub-Roman Periods in Cheshire', *From Flints to Flower Pots*, ed. Carrington, pp. 51–62
Morris, John, see sect. 1
Murray, Peter, and Linda Murray, *The Oxford Companion to Christian Art and Architecture* (Oxford, 1996) [includes section a Anglo-Saxon art]

Park, David, 'Simony and Sanctity: Herbert Losinga, St Wulfstan of Worcester and Wall-Paintings in Norwich Cathedral', *Studies in Medieval Art and Architecture presented to Peter Lasko*, ed. David Buckton and T. A. Heslop (Stroud, 1994), pp. 157–70

Ritchie, Anna, and David J. Breeze, *Invaders of Scotland: an Introduction to the Archaeology of the Romans, Scots, Angles and Vikings, Highlighting the Monuments in the Care of the Secretary of State for Scotland* (Edinburgh, 1991)

Ritchie, Graham, and Anna Ritchie, *Scotland: Archaeology and Early History* (Edinburgh, 1991) [contains a section on the Angles in Scotland]

Rüger, Christoph B., 'Zur Erforschung der römischen Zeit im Rheinland und in Westfalen', *Die Römer in Nordrhein-Westfalen*, ed. Horn, pp. 13–26

Saunders, Tom, 'Economy and Society: Technological Change in Early Medieval England', *Jnl of Theoretical Archaeol.* 5–6 (1998 for 1995–6), 125–54

Schwarz, Wolfgang, 'Römische Kaiserzeit', *Ur- und Frühgeschichte in Niedersachsen*, ed. Hässler, pp. 238–84

Strachan, David, *Essex from the Air: Archaeology and History from Aerial Photographs* (Chelmsford) [includes Anglo-Saxon material]

Todd, Malcolm, 'Barbarian Europe, A.D. 300–700', *The Oxford Illustrated Prehistory of Europe*, ed. Barry Cunliffe (Oxford, 1994), pp. 447–82

[Various authors], 'Bedfordshire', *South Midlands Archaeol.* 28, 1–19 [includes Anglo-Saxon]

'Buckinghamshire', *South Midlands Archaeol.* 28, 20–31 [includes Anglo-Saxon]

'Fieldwork', *Canterbury's Archaeol.* (1993 for 1992–3), 1–45 [reports on sites throughout Kent]

'Northamptonshire', *South Midlands Archaeol.* 28, 31–46 [includes Anglo-Saxon]

'Oxfordshire', *South Midlands Archaeol.* 28, 46–92 [includes Anglo-Saxon]

'Scarborough and its Area: Proceedings of the 143rd Summer Meeting of the Royal Archaeological Institute, 1997', *ArchJ* 154 (1998 for 1997), 228–96 [includes Anglo-Saxon]

Watson, Bruce, 'The Archaeology and Ecology of the Tidal Thames: a Conference Review', *Bull. of the Surrey Archaeol. Soc.* 325, 2–6 [includes Anglo-Saxon fish-traps and timber revetments]

Wulf, Friedrich-Wilhelm, 'Ausblick: Archäologie des Mittelalters und der Neuzeit in Niedersachsen', *Ur- und Frühgeschichte in Niedersachsen*, ed. Hässler, pp. 369–553

'Karolingische und ottonische Zeit', *Ur- and Frühgeschichte in Niedersachsen*, ed. Hässler, pp. 321–68

b. Towns and other major settlements

Andrews, P., ed., *Excavations at Hamwic, II: Excavations at Six Dials*, CBA Research Reports 109 (York, 1997)

Aston, Michael, and James Bond, *The Landscape of Towns* (London, 1976) [includes a chapter on Anglo-Saxon and Scandinavian towns]

Ayre, Julian, and Robin Wroe-Brown, with Richard Malt, 'Æthelred's Hythe to Queenhithe: the Origin of a London Dock', *Med. Life* 5 (1996), 14–25

Bailey, Maggie, 'Towns and Markets in a Regional Administrative Landscape: the

Development of the Late Saxon Urban Network in East Anglia', *Bull. of the John Rylands Univ. Lib. of Manchester* 79.3 (1997), 221–49

Blackmore, Lyn, *et al.*, 'Royal Opera House', *CA* 158, 60–3 [Saxon London]

Carrington, Peter, ed., *'Where Deva Spreads her Wizard Stream': Trade and the Port of Chester: Papers from a Seminar Held at Chester, November 1995*, Chester Archaeol. Occasional Paper 3 (Chester, 1996)

Chester City Council, *Discovering Chester: City Walls Walk* (Chester, 1991)

Clark, Kate M., 'An Anglo-Saxon Dog from Salter Street, Stafford', *International Jnl of Osteoarchaeology*, 8.1, 61–5

Coy, Jennie, 'Comparing Bird Bones from Saxon Sites: Problems of Interpretation', *International Jnl of Osteoarchaeology* 7.4 (1997), 415–21 [the evidence is predominantly from Southampton]

Dixon, Philip, *et al.*, *Newark Castle Studies: Excavations 1992–1993* (Newark, 1994) [includes early and late Anglo-Saxon occupation, and Christian burials]

Evans, D. T., 'Excavations at the Former Davygate Centre', *Interim: Archaeology in York* 22.4 (1997), 5–9 [includes evidence for Anglo-Saxon occupation]

Gardiner, Mark, and Christopher Greatorex, 'Archaeological Excavations in Steyning, 1992–95: Further Evidence for the Evolution of a Late Saxon Small Town', *Sussex Archaeol. Collections* 135 (1997), 143–71

Griffiths, David, 'The Maritime Economy of the Chester Region in the Anglo-Saxon Period', *'Where Deva Spreads her Wizard Stream'*, ed. Carrington, pp. 49–60

Hall, Allan R., and Philippa Tomlinson, 'Archaeological Records of Dye Plants – an Update – With a Note on Fullers' Teasels', *Dyes in Hist. and Archaeol.* 8 (1989), 19–21 [includes evidence from Anglo-Scandinavian York]

Hall, Richard, 'Ports of the East and South Coasts in the Anglo-Saxon Era: an Overview', *'Where Deva Spreads her Wizard Stream'*, ed. Carrington, pp. 40–8

Hinton, Peter, and Roger Thomas, 'The Greater London Publication Programme', *ArchJ* 154 (1998 for 1997), 196–213 [the background to forthcoming publications, including a list of Saxon projects]

Hodges, Richard, 'Dark Age York Discovered: New Excavations Throw Light on Missing 8th and 9th Centuries', *Minerva* 9.2, 42–3

Huggins, Rhona, 'London and the River Lea', *London Archaeologist* 8.9, 241–7 [includes Anglo-Saxon]

James, Tom Beaumont, *English Heritage Book of Winchester* (London, 1997) [includes a chapter on Anglo-Saxon Winchester]

Keen, Laurence, ed., *'Almost the Richest City': Bristol in the Middle Ages*, Brit. Archaeol. Assoc. Conference Trans. 19 (London, 1997)

Kenyon, John R., *Castles, Town Defences and Artillery Fortifications in Britain: a Bibliography, 1945–74*, CBA Research Report 25 (London, 1978) [contains publications on Anglo-Saxon town defences]

Castles, Town Defences and Artillery Fortifications in Britain and Ireland: a Bibliography, Volume 2, CBA Research Report 53 (London, 1983) [contains publications on Anglo-Saxon town defences]

Castles, Town Defences and Artillery Fortifications in Britain and Ireland: a Bibliography,

Volume 3, CBA Research Report 72 (London, 1990) [contains publications on Anglo-Saxon town defences]

Leech, Roger H., 'The Medieval Defences of Bristol Revisited', *'Almost the Richest City'*, ed. Keen, pp. 18–30 [includes the Late Saxon town walls]

Magilton, John, 'Chichester, the Burghal Hidage and the Diversion of the River Lavant', *The Archaeology of Chichester and District 1996: a Review of Fieldwork and Research by Southern Archaeology and Others in Chichester District*, comp. Sue Woodward (Chichester, [1996?]), pp. 37–41

Maltby, Mark, *Faunal Studies on Urban Sites: the Animal Bones from Exeter 1971–1975*, Exeter Archaeol. Reports 2 (Sheffield, 1979) [includes a small amount of eleventh-century evidence]

Marshall, Pamela, and John Samuels, *Guardian of the Trent: the Story of Newark Castle* (Newark, 1997) [includes early and late Saxon occupation, and a Christian Saxon cemetery]

McCarthy, M. R., *A Roman, Anglian and Medieval Site at Blackfriars Street, Carlisle: Excavations 1977–9*, Cumberland and Westmorland Ant. and Archaeol. Soc. Research Ser. 4 (Kendal, 1990)

Mulkeen, S., and T. P. O'Connor, 'Raptors in Towns: Towards an Ecological Model', *International Jnl of Osteoarchaeology* 7.4 (1997), 440–9 [includes early medieval evidence]

Museum of London Archaeological Service, 'No 1, Poultry', *CA* 158, 50–6 [includes a summary of the post-Roman evidence]

'Saxon London', *Rescue News* 71 (1997), 5

Musty, John, 'John Musty's Science Diary', *CA* 158, 64–6 [includes Late Saxon pollution of the Thames]

Samuels, John, 'Newark Castle', *CA* 156, 458–61 [includes Anglo-Saxon occupation and a Late Saxon cemetery]

Scull, Christopher, 'Urban Centres in Pre-Viking England?', *The Anglo-Saxons*, ed. Hines, pp. 269–310

Shimmin, D., and G. Carter, 'Excavations at Angel Yard, High Street, Colchester, 1986 and 1989', *Essex Archaeol. and Hist.* 27 (1996), 35–83 [includes possible Late Saxon pits, and some pottery]

Swain, Hedley, and Alex Werner, 'London Bodies: How the Museum of London is Putting Our Ancestors on Display', *Minerva* 9.6, 16–18 [includes Anglo-Saxon]

Wacher, John, *The Towns of Roman Britain*, 2nd ed. (London, 1995) [last chapter discusses Anglo-Saxon settlement]

Ward, Simon, 'The Course of the River Dee at Chester', *'Where Deva Spreads her Wizard Stream'*, ed. Carrington, pp. 4–11 [includes Anglo-Saxon period]

Ward, Simon, et al., *Chester City Ditches, a Slice of History: Excavations at 5–7 Foregate Street 1991*, Chester Archaeol. Service Guidebook 1 (Chester, 1992)

Watson, Bruce, 'The Future of London's Past Revisited and Expanded – a Conference Review', *London Archaeologist* 8.8, 213–20 [includes Anglo-Saxon]

Webber, Mike, 'Time and Tide: the Thames Archaeological Survey Two Years On', *Rescue News* 73 (1997), 1–2 [includes Anglo-Saxon]

Wroe-Brown, Robin, 'Bull Wharf: Queenhithe', *CA* 158, 75–7 [Saxon London]

c. Rural settlements, agriculture and the countryside

Allen, Tim, with Nicholas Barton and Andrew Brown, *Lithics and Landscape: Archaeological Discoveries on the Thames Water Pipeline at Gatehampton Farm, Goring, Oxfordshire 1985–92*, Oxford Archaeol. Unit Thames Valley Landscapes Monograph 7 (Oxford, 1995) [includes a Saxon *Grubenhaus*]

[Anon.], 'Fieldwork and Excavation in 1997', *Med. Settlement Research Group Ann. Report* 12 (1998 for 1997), 29–43

'Thames Valley Archaeological Services', *CBA Wessex Newsletter* October, 14–15 [includes a *Grubenhaus* and two pits at Wraysbury]

Astill, Grenville, 'An Archaeological Approach to the Development of Agricultural Technologies in Medieval England', *Medieval Farming and Technology: the Impact of Agricultural Change in Northwest Europe*, ed. Grenville Astill and John Langdon (Leiden, 1997), pp. 193–223

Barnes, Ian, Keith M. Dobney and J. Peter W. Young, 'The Molecular Palaeoecology of Geese: Identification of Archaeological Goose Remains Using Ancient DNA Analysis', *International Jnl of Osteoarchaeology* 8.4, 280–7

Bassett, Steven, 'Continuity and Fission in the Anglo-Saxon Landscape: the Origins of the Rodings (Essex)', *Landscape Hist.* 19 (1997), 25–42

Beresford, Maurice, and John Hurst, *English Heritage Book of Wharram Percy: Deserted Medieval Village* (London, 1990)

Berryman, R. D., *Use of the Woodlands in the Late Anglo-Saxon Period*, BAR Brit. Ser. 271 (Oxford)

Butler, Chris, 'Rescue Archaeology in Mid-Sussex', *CA* 156, 464–7 [includes a *Grubenhaus* and a possible Anglo-Saxon pagan shrine]

Chapelot, Jean, and Robert Fossier, *The Village and House in the Middle Ages* (London, 1985)

Coles, John, and David Hall, 'The Fenland Project: from Survey to Management and Beyond', *Antiquity* 71 (1997), 831–44

Cook, Martin, *Medieval Bridges* (Princes Risborough)

Drewett, Peter, and Sue Hamilton, 'The Saxons on Caburn?', *Sussex Past and Present* 86, 6–7

Elsdon, Sheila M., *Old Sleaford Revealed: a Lincolnshire Settlement in Iron Age, Roman, Saxon and Medieval Times: Excavations 1882–1995* (Oxford, 1997)

Fasham, P. J., D. E. Farwell and R. J. B. Whinney, *The Archaeological Site at Easton Lane, Winchester*, Hampshire Field Club and Archaeol. Soc. Monograph 6 (Andover, 1989)

Fasham, P. J. and R. J. B. Whinney, *Archaeology and the M3: the Watching Brief, the Anglo-Saxon Settlement at Abbots Worthy and Retrospective Sections*, Hampshire Field Club and Archaeol. Soc. Monograph 7 (Andover, 1991)

Finn, Neil, 'Secrets of the Wreake Valley: Excavations at Eye Kettleby, Leicestershire', *Rescue News* 72 (1997), 4–5

Ford, Steve, 'The Excavation of Late Saxon and Medieval Features at Kintbury Square, Kintbury, Berkshire, 1995', *Berkshire Archaeol. Jnl* 75 (1997 for 1994–7), 75–92

Foreman, Stuart, 'Medieval Boreham: Excavations at the Former Buxted Chicken

Factory, Boreham, 1992–93', *Essex Archaeol. and Hist.* 28 (1997), 103–12 [includes traces of early medieval tofts]

Fowler, Peter J., 'Farming in Early Medieval England: Some Fields for Thought', *The Anglo-Saxons*, ed. Hines, pp. 245–68

――'"A Trifle Historical": Making Landscapes in Northumbria', *Making English Landscapes*, ed. Barker and Darvill, pp. 55–69 [includes the 'new' early medieval farm at Bede's World, Jarrow]

Gilbert, Pippa, 'The Pre-Conquest Landscape at Kingston Seymour on the North Somerset Levels: Report on Survey 1996', *Archaeology in the Severn Estuary 1996*, ed. Rippon, pp. 53–7

'Hester', 'Around the County', *Bedfordshire Mag.* 26, 292–9 [Harrold]

Holbrook, Neil, *et al.*, 'The Roman and Early Anglo-Saxon Settlement at Wantage, Oxfordshire: Excavations at Mill Street, 1993–4', *Oxoniensia* 61 (1997 for 1996), 109–79

Hurst, J. D., ed., *A Multi-Period Salt Production Site at Droitwich: Excavations at Upwich*, CBA Research Report 107 (York, 1997)

Insole, Peter, 'An Investigation of a Medieval and Post Medieval Field Boundary Complex at British Gas Seabank, on the North Avon Levels', *Archaeology in the Severn Estuary 1996*, ed. Rippon, pp. 95–105 [includes an eleventh-century ditch]

Ivens, R. J., *et al.*, *Tatenhoe & Westbury: Two Deserted Medieval Settlements in Milton Keynes*, Buckinghamshire Archaeol. Soc. Monograph Ser. 8 (Aylesbury, 1995)

Jackson, R. P. J., and T. W. Potter, *Excavations at Stonea, Cambridgeshire 1980–85* (London, 1996)

Kidd, Sandy, 'Back from the Brink: Two Recent Planning Cases from Northamptonshire', *Rescue News* 71 (1997), 1–2 [includes an Anglo-Saxon settlement at Higham Ferrers]

Kristiansen, Mette Svart, and Ditlev L. D. Mahler, 'Some Perspectives in Danish Medieval Archaeology: Taarnby Village', *Med. Settlement Research Group Ann. Report* 12 (1998 for 1997), 21–6

Lobb, S. J., and P. G. Rose, *Archaeological Survey of the Lower Kennet Valley, Berkshire*, Wessex Archaeol. Report 9 (Salisbury, 1996)

Loveluck, C. P., 'The Development of the Anglo-Saxon Landscape, Economy and Society "On Driffield", East Yorkshire, 400–750 A.D.', *ASSAH* 9 (1998 for 1996), 25–48

Magilton, John, and Spencer Thomas, 'The Origin and Growth of Midhurst', *The Archaeology of Chichester and District 1997: a Review of Fieldwork and Research by Southern Archaeology and Others in Chichester District*, comp. Sue Woodward (Chichester), pp. 29–33

May, Jeffrey, *Dragonby: Report on Excavations at an Iron Age and Romano-British Settlement in North Lincolnshire*, 2 vols., Oxbow Monograph 61 (Oxford, 1996)

Meates, G. W., 'A Standing Stone at Eynsford', *AC* 94 (1979 for 1978), 260–2

Medlycott, Maria, 'Excavations at Othona', *Essex Archaeol. and Hist. News* 117 (1993), 14–15

Miles, David, ed., *Archaeology at Barton Court Farm, Abingdon, Oxon.*, CBA Research Report 50, Oxford Archaeol. Unit Report 3 (Oxford, 1986)

Millett, Martin, and David Graham, *Excavations on the Romano-British Small Town at Neatham, Hampshire, 1969–1979*, Hampshire Field Club and Archaeol. Soc. Monograph 3 (Andover, 1986) [includes two *Grubenhäuser*]

Moloney, Colm, *Catterick Past and Present* (Wakefield) [Anglo-Saxon cemetery and buildings]

Morley, Beric, and David Gurney, *Castle Rising Castle, Norfolk*, East Anglian Archaeol. Report 81 (Gressenhall, 1997)

Muir, Richard, *The Yorkshire Countryside: a Landscape History* (Edinburgh, 1997)

Mynard, Dennis C., *Excavations on Medieval and Later Sites in Milton Keynes 1972–1980*, Buckinghamshire Archaeol. Soc. Monograph Series 6 (Aylesbury, 1994)

Oosthuizen, Susan, 'Medieval Settlement Relocation in West Cambridgeshire: Three Case-Studies', *Landscape Hist.* 19 (1997), 43–55

— 'The Origins of Cambridgeshire', *AntJ* 78, 85–109

— 'Prehistoric Fields into Medieval Furlongs? Evidence from Caxton, Cambridgeshire', *Proc. of the Cambridge Ant. Soc.* 86, 145–52

Ortner, Donald J., and Simon Mays, 'Dry-Bone Manifestations of Rickets in Infancy and Early Childhood', *International Jnl of Osteoarchaeology*, 8.1, 45–55

Philp, Brian, *The Roman Villa Site at Orpington, Kent*, Kent Monograph Series 7 (Dover, 1996)

Powlesland, Dominic, 'Early Anglo-Saxon Settlements, Structures, Form and Layout', *The Anglo-Saxons*, ed. Hines, pp. 101–24

Reeves, Anne, 'Earthworks Survey, Romney Marsh', *AC* 116 (1997 for 1996), 61–92

Rippon, Stephen, 'Puxton (North Somerset) and Early Medieval "Infield" Enclosures', *Med. Settlement Research Group Ann. Report* 12 (1998 for 1997), 18–20

— 'Roman and Medieval Settlement on the North Somerset Levels: Survey and Excavation at Banwell and Puxton, 1996', *Archaeology in the Severn Estuary 1996*, ed. Rippon, pp. 39–52

— *The Severn Estuary: Landscape Evolution and Wetland Reclamation* (London, 1997)

Rippon, Stephen, ed., *Archaeology in the Severn Estuary 1996 (Volume 7): Annual Report of the Severn Estuary Levels Research Committee* (Exeter, 1997)

Rowley, Trevor, and Mélanie Steiner, ed., *Cogges Manor Farm, Witney, Oxfordshire: the Excavations from 1986–1994 and the Historic Building Analysis* (Oxford, 1996)

Silvester, Bob, 'Historic Settlement Surveys in Eastern Clwyd', *From Flints to Flower Pots*, comp. Carrington, pp. 63–8

Taylor, Christopher, 'Dorset and Beyond', *Making English Landscapes*, ed. Barker and Darvill, pp. 9–25

Tyler, S., and N. P. Wickenden, 'A Late Roman and Saxon Settlement at Great Waltham', *Essex Archaeol. and Hist.* 27 (1996), 84–91

Vyner, Blaise, 'Air Photographic Evidence for Medieval Settlement and Land-Use in the Lower Tees Valley', *Medieval Rural Settlement in North-East England*, ed. B. E. Vyner, Archit. and Archaeol. Soc. of Durham and Northumberland Research Report 2 (Durham, 1990), 9–18

Wager, Sarah J., *Woods, Wolds and Groves: the Woodland of Medieval Warwickshire*, BAR Brit. Ser. 269 (Oxford)

White, Robert, *English Heritage Book of the Yorkshire Dales: Landscapes Through Time* (London, 1997) [includes Anglian and Norse settlement]

Wilkinson, Keith N., 'Of Sheep and Men: GIS and the Development of Medieval Settlement in the Cotswolds', *Imaging the Past*, ed. Higgins, Main and Lang, pp. 271–81

Williams, R. J., P. J. Hart and A. T. L. Williams, *Wavendon Gate: a Late Iron Age and Roman Settlement in Milton Keynes*, Buckinghamshire Archaeol. Soc. Monograph Ser. 10 (Aylesbury, 1995)

Woodward, Sue, ed., *The Archaeology of Chichester and District 1993: a Review of Fieldwork and Research Carried Out by Chichester District Archaeological Unit and Others During the Year in Chichester District* (Chichester, [1993?])

Worthington, Margaret, 'Wat's Dyke: an Archaeological and Historical Enigma', *Bull. of the John Rylands Univ. Lib. of Manchester* 79.3 (1997), 177–96

d. Pagan cemeteries and Sutton Hoo

Allen, Roland, 'A Stag Stands on Ceremony: Evaluating some of the Sutton Hoo Finds', *Bull. of the John Rylands Univ. Lib. of Manchester* 79.3 (1997), 167–75

Aston, Mick, and Tim Taylor, *Atlas of Archaeology* (London) [includes Anglo-Saxon burials at Winterbourne Gunner, Wiltshire]

Atkinson, Mark, 'Archaeological Evaluation of the Proposed M11 Widening Scheme', *Essex Archaeol. and Hist. News* 117 (1993), 13–14 [includes an Anglo-Saxon cemetery]

Barnatt, John, and John Collis, *Barrows in the Peak District: Recent Research* (Sheffield, 1996) [includes Anglian primary and intrusive burials, with a catalogue]

Bowden, Mark, *Pitt Rivers: the Life and Archaeological Work of Lieutenant-General Augustus Henry Lane Fox Pitt Rivers, DCL, FRS, FSA* (Cambridge, 1991) [includes an account of Anglo-Saxon intrusive barrow burials at Winkelbury Hill]

Boyle, A., et al., *Two Oxfordshire Anglo-Saxon Cemeteries: Berinsfield and Didcot* (Oxford, 1996)

Boyle, A., et al., ed., *The Anglo-Saxon Cemetery at Butler's Field, Lechlade, Gloucestershire, I: Prehistoric and Roman Activity and Anglo-Saxon Grave Catalogue* (Oxford)

Canterbury Archaeological Trust and the Trust for Thanet Archaeology, 'Interim Report on Excavations in Advance of the Dualling of the A253 Between Monkton and Mount Pleasant, Thanet', *AC* 116 (1997 for 1996), 305–10 [includes a small Anglo-Saxon cemetery]

Caruth, Jo, 'Behind the Headlines: RAF Lakenheath Anglo-Saxon Cemetery', *Rescue News* 74, 1–2

Carver, Martin, *Sutton Hoo: Burial Ground of Kings* (London)

'Conversion and Politics on the Eastern Seaboard of Britain: Some Archaeological Indicators', *Conversion and Christianity*, ed. Crawford, pp. 11–40

'Immemorial Mounds', *National Trust Mag.* 83, 54–7 [Sutton Hoo]

Crawford, Sally, 'Britons, Anglo-Saxons and the Germanic Burial Ritual', *Migrations and Invasions in Archaeological Explanation*, ed. Chapman and Hamerow, pp. 45–72

Bibliography for 1998

Drinkall, Gail, Martin Foreman and Martin G. Welch, *The Anglo-Saxon Cemetery at Castledyke South, Barton-on-Humber*, Sheffield Excavation Report 6 (Sheffield)

Fitzpatrick, A. P., with Andrew B. Powell *et al.*, *Archaeological Excavations on the Route of the A27 Westhampnett Bypass, West Sussex, 1992, II: the Late Iron Age, Romano-British, and Anglo-Saxon Cemeteries*, Wessex Archaeol. Report 12 (Salisbury, 1997)

Hawkes, Sonia Chadwick, and A. C. Hogarth, 'The Anglo-Saxon Cemetery at Monkton, Thanet: Report on the Rescue Excavations of May / June 1971', *AC* 89 (1975 for 1974), 49–89

Jones, Julie, 'What's in the Box?', *Interim: Archaeol. in York* 22.1 (1997), 20–5

Lloyd-Jones, Jeff, 'Calculating Bio-Distance Using Dental Morphology', *Computing and Statistics in Osteoarchaeology: Proceedings of the Second Meeting of the Osteoarchaeological Research Group Held in London on 8th April 1995*, ed. Sue Anderson and Katherine Boyle (Oxford, 1997), 23–30 [comparison of Romano-British and Anglo-Saxon material suggests relatively small numbers of Saxon immigrants]

Lucy, Sam, *The Early Anglo-Saxon Cemeteries of East Yorkshire: an Analysis and Reinterpretation*, BAR Brit. Ser. 272 (Oxford)

Malim, Tim, and John Hines, with Corinne Duhig, *The Anglo-Saxon Cemetery at Edix Hill (Barrington A), Cambridgeshire: Excavations 1989–1991 and a Summary Catalogue of Material from 19th Century Interventions*, CBA Research Report 112 (York)

Mayes, P., and M. J. Dean, *An Anglo-Saxon Cemetery at Baston, Lincolnshire*, Occasional Papers in Lincolnshire Hist. and Archaeol. 3 (Sleaford, 1976)

[National Trust, East Anglia Regional Office], *The National Trust Sutton-Hoo – Statement of Significance* (Blickling)

Meadows, Ian, 'The Pioneer Helmet: a Dark-Age Princely Burial from Northamptonshire', *Med. Life* 8 (1997), 2–4

Newman, John, 'New Light on Old Finds – Bloodmoor Hill, Gisleham, Suffolk', *ASSAH* 9 (1998 for 1996), 75–9

O'Sullivan, Deirdre, 'A Group of Pagan Burials from Cumbria?', *ASSAH* 9 (1998 for 1996), 15–23

Parfitt, Keith, 'An Unrecorded? Anglo-Saxon Cemetery at Water's End, Near Dover', *Kent Archaeol. Rev.* 134, 89–90

Pearson, Michael Parker, 'Tombs and Territories: Material Culture and Multiple Interpretation', in Ian Hodder *et al.*, *Interpreting Archaeology: Finding Meaning in the Past* (London, 1995), pp. 205–9 [Sutton Hoo]

Phillips, Charles W., *My Life in Archaeology* (Gloucester, 1987) [includes the Sutton Hoo excavation, and other Anglo-Saxon burials]

Richards, M. P., *et al.*, 'Stable Isotope Analysis Reveals Variations in Human Diet at the Poundbury Camp Cemetery Site', *Jnl of Archaeol. Science* 25.12, 1247–52

Semple, Sarah, see sect. 6

Smith, Andy, 'Trauma Most Foul: the Human Remains from Kintbury, Berkshire', *Current and Recent Research in Osteoarchaeology: Proceedings of the Third Meeting of the Osteoarchaeological Research Group Held in Leicester on 18th November 1995*, ed. Sue Anderson and Katherine Boyle (Oxford), pp. 27–30

Taylor, Alison, *et al.*, 'An Anglo-Saxon Cemetery at Oakington, Cambridgeshire', *Proc. of the Cambridge Ant. Soc.* 86, 57–90

Timby, Jane R., *The Anglo-Saxon Cemetery at Empingham II, Rutland: Excavations Carried Out Between 1974 and 1975*, Oxbow Monograph 70 (Oxford, 1996)

Welch, Martin G., *Highdown and its Saxon Cemetery*, Worthing Museum and Art Gallery Publication 11 (Worthing, 1976)

Williams, Howard, 'Monuments and the Past in Early Anglo-Saxon England', *World Archaeol.* 30.1, 90–108 [Anglo-Saxon burials in Roman and prehistoric structures]

e. Churches, monastic sites and Christian cemeteries

Ahrens, Claus, 'An English Origin for Norwegian Stave Churches?', *Med. Life* 4 (1996), 3–7

Bagshaw, Steve, 'Early Medieval Church to Tractor Shed: Building Survey at Leonard Stanley Priory', *Glevensis* 31, 3–12

Bailey, Richard N., 'Seventh-Century Work at Ripon and Hexham', *The Archaeology of Cathedrals*, ed. Tatton-Brown and Munby, pp. 9–18

Blair, John, 'Bampton: an Anglo-Saxon Minster', *CA* 160, 124–30

'St. Frideswide's Monastery: Problems and Possibilities', *Saint Frideswide's Monastery at Oxford*, ed. Blair, pp. 221–58

'Thornbury, Binsey: a Probable Defensive Enclosure Associated with Saint Frideswide', *Saint Frideswide's Monastery at Oxford*, ed. Blair, pp. 3–20

Blair, John, ed., *Saint Frideswide's Monastery at Oxford: Archaeological and Architectural Studies* (Gloucester, 1990)

Blockley, Kevin, Margaret Sparks and Tim Tatton-Brown, *Canterbury Cathedral Nave: Archaeology, History and Architecture*, Archaeol. of Canterbury, ns 1 (Canterbury, 1997)

Boyle, Angela, 'The Bones of the Anglo-Saxon Bishop and Saint, Chad: a Scientific Analysis', *Church Archaeol.* 2, 35–8

Cessford, Craig, 'Exogamous Marriages Between Anglo-Saxons and Britons in Seventh-Century Northern Britain', *ASSAH* 9 (1998 for 1996), 49–52

Chapman, Andy, 'Brackmills, Northampton: an Early Iron Age Torc', *CA* 159, 92–5 [includes an early Christian cemetery]

Chester Archaeology, *A Church for All Ages: Chester Cathedral Excavations in 1996 and 1997* (Chester, 1997)

[Clarke, Amanda], 'Seeking St Ninian and his Legacy: Excavations at Whithorn', *Interim: Archaeology in York* 22.2 (1997), 17–27

Cramp, Rosemary, *et al.*, 'St Mary's, Deerhurst – a Retrospective', *Church Archaeol.* 2, 19–28

Dean, Stephen, 'Southampton, St Mary's', *Church Archaeol.* 2, 58

Detsicas, A. P., 'Excavations at Eccles, 1973: Twelfth Interim Report', *AC* 89 (1975 for 1974), 119–34 and 216–17 [includes an Anglo-Saxon cemetery]

Dixon, Philip, *et al.*, see sect. 9*b*

Everson, Paul, and David Parsons, 'Brixworth Church – Are the Bricks Really Roman?', *Roman Brick and Tile: Studies in Manufacture, Distribution and Use in the Western Empire*, ed. Alan McWhirr, BAR International Ser. 68 (Oxford, 1979), 405–11

Fasham, P. J., and G. Keevill, with D. Coe, *Brighton Hill South (Hatch Warren): an Iron Age Farmstead and Deserted Medieval Village in Hampshire*, Wessex Archaeol. Report 7 (Salisbury, 1995)

Bibliography for 1998

Foster, Charlotte, 'Round-Up: England', *Church Archaeol.* 1 (1997), 52–62

Gem, Richard, *English Heritage Book of St Augustine's Abbey, Canterbury* (London, 1997)

Gilchrist, Roberta, *Gender and Material Culture: the Archaeology of Religious Women* (London, 1994)

Hall, Richard, 'Revelation (over Ripon Cathedral's Crypt) Chapter 2', *Interim: Archaeology in York* 22.3 (1997), 26–35

  'Ripon: Early Days', *Interim: Archaeology in York* 22.1 (1997), 26–32

Heighway, Carolyn, see sect. 6

Hicks, Carola, *Cambridgeshire Churches* (Stamford, 1997)

Higgitt, John, see Potter, T. W. and R. D. Andrews

Jones, Julie, see sect. 9*d*

Kelly, Jean, and Michael Ferrar, 'Wood Hall: the Mystery of an Anglo-Saxon Cathedral', *Ancient* 6.61, 15–18

King, Cyril, 'A Look at Old Byland Church', *Ryedale Historian* 17 (1994–5), 10–12

Loveluck, C. P., 'A High-Status Anglo-Saxon Settlement at Flixborough, Lincolnshire', *Antiquity* 72, 146–61

Lyne, Malcolm, *Lewes Priory: Excavations by Richard Lewis, 1969–82* (Lewes, 1997)

Marshall, Pamela, and John Samuels, see sect. 9*b*

McCarthy, M. R., 'The Origins and Development of the Twelfth-Century Cathedral Church at Carlisle', *The Archaeology of Cathedrals*, ed. Tatton-Brown and Munby, pp. 31–45

Milne, Gustav, *St Bride's Church, London: Archaeological Research 1952–60 and 1992–5*, Eng. Heritage Archaeol. Reports 11 (London, 1997)

Parsons, David, *Liturgy and Architecture in the Middle Ages*, Deerhurst Lecture 1986 (Deerhurst, 1989)

  'England and the Low Countries at the Time of St Willibrord', *Utrecht*, ed. De Bièvre, pp. 30–48

Parsons, David, and Christopher J. Brooke, 'Recording Churches and Cathedrals', *Buildings Archaeology: Applications in Practice*, ed. Jason Wood, Oxbow Monograph 43 (Oxford, 1994), 129–54

Pickles, C. J. R., 'The Anglo-Saxon Cathedral of Canterbury', *Med. Life* 1 (1995), 13–19

Potter, T. W., and R. D. Andrews, 'Excavation and Survey at St Patrick's Chapel and St Peter's Church, Heysham, Lancashire, 1977–8', *Contrebis* 21 (1996), 29–73 [includes 'The Sculpture' by R. J. Cramp, 'The Wall Plaster: Decoration and Lettering' by John Higgitt, and 'The Bone Comb' by Alison Cook and Colleen Batey]

Rahtz, Philip and Lorna Watts, *Kirkdale Archaeology 1996–1997*, Supplement to the *Ryedale Historian* 19 (1998–9)

  'Kirkdale, St Gregory's Minster', *Church Archaeol.* 2, 63

Reilly, Lisa A., *An Architectural History of Peterborough Cathedral*, Clarendon Stud. in the Hist. of Art 17 (Oxford, 1997)

Rijntjes, Raphaël, '*Porticus* or *Pastophorion*?: Eighth-Century St Martin, Utrecht, Between Anglo-Saxon and Frankish Traditions', *Utrecht*, ed. De Bièvre, pp. 49–57

Rodwell, Warwick, 'Above and Below Ground: Archaeology at Wells Cathedral', *The Archaeology of Cathedrals*, ed. Tatton-Brown and Munby, pp. 115–33 [includes Anglo-Saxon]

'Landmarks in Church Archaeology: a Review of the Last Thirty Years', *Church Archaeol.* 1 (1997), 5–16

Ryder, Peter F., 'Durham Churches: a Programme of Archaeological Assessment', *Church Archaeol.* 1 (1997), 35–41

'Durham Churches 1996 / 1997: an Archaeological Assessment', *Church Archaeol.* 2, 57–8

Medieval Churches of West Yorkshire (Wakefield, 1993)

Samuels, John, see sect. 9*b*

Scott, Ian R., *Romsey Abbey: Report on the Excavations 1973–1991*, Hampshire Field Club and Archaeol. Soc. Monograph 8 (Andover, 1996)

Scull, Christopher, 'Excavations in the Cloister of St Frideswide's Priory, 1985', *Saint Frideswide's Monastery at Oxford*, ed. Blair, pp. 21–73

Smith, Ian, 'The Archaeology of the Early Christian Church in Scotland and Man, A.D. 400–1200', *Church Archaeology: Research Directions for the Future*, ed. John Blair and Carol Pyrah, CBA Research Report 104 (York, 1996), 19–48

Stöver, Jos, 'Willibrord's Cathedral: an Investigation of the First Phases of the Construction of the Salvatorkerk in Utrecht', *Utrecht*, ed. De Bièvre, pp. 69–81

Tatton-Brown, Tim, 'New Survey of Kent Churches', *Church Archaeol.* 1 (1997), 47–8

Tatton-Brown, Tim, and Julian Munby, ed., *The Archaeology of Cathedrals*, Oxford Univ. Committee for Archaeol., Monograph 42 (Oxford, 1996)

Taylor, Martin, 'Two Relics of English Christianity Before the Arrival of St Augustine', *Kent Archaeol. Rev.* 132, 32–8 [St Martin's Church and hoard]

Van Welie, Eeko, 'St Salvator's, St Martin's and Pepin the Younger', *Utrecht*, ed. De Bièvre, pp. 58–68

Vigar, John E., *Kent Churches* (Stroud, 1995)

Ward, Simon, 'Archaeology in Chester Cathedral 1995–97', *Church Archaeol.* 2, 39–44

Watts, Lorna, Jane Grenville and Philip Rahtz, *Archaeology at Kirkdale*, Supplement to the *Ryedale Historian* 18 (1996 for 1996–7)

Wilkinson, David J., and Alan D. McWhirr, *Cirencester: Anglo-Saxon Church and Medieval Abbey*, Cirencester Excavations 4 (Cirencester)

Woodward, Sue, ed., *The Archaeology of Chichester and District 1992: a Review of Fieldwork and Research Carried Out by Chichester District Archaeological Unit and Others During the Year in Chichester District* (Chichester, [1992?]) [includes an investigation of the part pre-Conquest church at Stoughton]

Woodward, Sue, ed., *The Archaeology of Chichester and District 1994: a Review of Fieldwork and Research by Chichester District Archaeological Unit, Southern Archaeology and Others in Chichester District* (Chichester, [1994?]) [includes a newly revealed Anglo-Saxon doorway in Woolbeding church]

f. Ships and seafaring

Bjornstad, Tom, 'Sinking Viking Ship?', *Archaeology* 51.1, 25 [ship burial at Stein in Hole, Ringerike, Norway]

Bonde, Niels, 'Found in Denmark, but Where Do They Come From?', *Archaeol. Ireland* 12.3, 24–9 [concerns one of the Skuldelev ships, built in Ireland]

Crumlin-Pedersen, Ole, 'Large and Small Warships of the North', *Military Aspects of Scandinavian Society*, ed. Jørgensen and Clausen, pp. 184–94

Delgado, James P., ed., *Encyclopaedia of Underwater and Maritime Archaeology* (London, 1997) [includes accounts of several Anglo-Saxon and Viking ships]

Hutchinson, Gillian, *Medieval Ships and Shipping* (London, 1994)

Kelly, Eamonn P., and Edmond O'Donovan, 'A Viking *Longphort* Near Athlunkard, Co. Clare', *Archaeol. Ireland* 12.4, 13–16 [includes evidence from Anglo-Saxon England]

McGrail, Seán, *Ancient Boats in North-West Europe: the Archaeology of Water Transport to A.D. 1500*, reissued with corrections and additions (London)

Marsden, Peter, *English Heritage Book of Ships and Shipwrecks* (London, 1997) [includes the Sutton Hoo, Graveney and Clapton boats]

Wooding, Jonathan M., *Communication and Commerce Along the Western Sealanes, A.D. 400–800*, BAR International Ser. 654 (Oxford, 1996)

g. Miscellaneous artifacts

Biddle, Martin, and Birthe Kjølbye-Biddle, 'An Early Medieval Floor-Tile from St Frideswide's Minster', *Saint Frideswide's Monastery at Oxford*, ed. Blair, pp. 259–63

MacGregor, Arthur, and Flora Holly, *Ashmolean Museum Oxford: a Summary Catalogue of the Continental Archaeological Collections (Roman Iron Age, Migration Period, Early Medieval)*, BAR International Ser. 674 (Oxford, 1997)

Proudfoot, Edwina, and Christopher Aliaga-Kelly, 'Towards an Interpretation of Anomalous Finds and Place-Names of Anglo-Saxon Origin in Scotland', *ASSAH* 9 (1998 for 1996), 1–13

Ryan, Pat, *Brick in Essex from the Roman Conquest to the Reformation* (Chelmsford, 1996)

Wamers, Egon, 'Insular Finds in Viking Age Scandinavia and the State Formation of Norway', *Ireland and Scandinavia in the Early Viking Age*, ed. Clarke, Ní Mhaonaigh and Ó Floinn, pp. 37–72

h. Bone, stone and wood

Baker, Nigel, 'Underground Shrewsbury', *CA* 159, 108–14 [includes reused interlace-decorated stones]

Cook, Alison, and Colleen Batey, see sect. 9*e* [under Potter, T. W., and R. D. Andrews]

Cramp, R. J., see sect. 9*e* [under Potter, T. W., and R. D. Andrews]

Earwood, Caroline, *Domestic Wooden Artefacts in Britain and Ireland from Neolithic to Viking Times* (Exeter, 1993)

Edwards, Ben, 'A Cross at Lancaster in the Late Sixteenth Century', *Contrebis* 23, 36–9 [drawing of 1562 which may depict a lost pre-Conquest cross]

Flynn, P., 'Excavations at St Michael, Workington', *Church Archaeol.* 1 (1997), 43–5

Foster, Sally M., ed., *The St Andrews Sarcophagus: a Pictish Masterpiece and its International Connections* (Dublin)

Francovich Onesti, Nicoletta, see sect. 3*biii* [Franks Casket]

Gibson, Margaret, *The Liverpool Ivories: Late Antique and Medieval Ivory and Bone Carving in Liverpool Museum and the Walker Art Gallery* (London, 1994) [includes an English carving of the Nativity of the late tenth century]

Henderson, Isabel, '*Primus inter pares*: the St Andrews Sarcophagus and Pictish Sculpture', *The St Andrews Sarcophagus*, ed. Foster, pp. 97–167 [includes references to Anglo-Saxon sculpture, manuscript art, and seaxes]

Lang, J. T., and S. Wrathmell, 'A Fragment of Anglian Sculpture from Dewsbury, West Yorkshire', *AntJ* 77 (1997), 375–80

Le Pard, Gordon, 'Medieval Sundials in Dorset', *Proc. of the Dorset Nat. Hist. and Archaeol. Soc.* 119 (1998 for 1997), 65–86

Lonie, W., 'Newstead (Melrose Parish)', *Discovery and Excavation in Scotland* (1998 for 1997), 67

MacGregor, Arthur, 'Antler, Bone and Horn', *English Medieval Industries: Craftsmen, Techniques, Products*, ed. Blair and Ramsay, pp. 355–78

MacLean, Douglas, 'The Northumbrian Perspective', *The St Andrews Sarcophagus*, ed. Foster, pp. 179–201

Muñoz de Miguel, María, 'Anglo-Saxon Figure Sculpture at St Mary's Priory Church, Deerhurst', *Trans. of the Bristol and Gloucestershire Archaeol. Soc.* 115 (1997), 29–40

'The Iconography of Christ *Victor* in Anglo-Saxon Art: a New Approach to the Study of the "Harrowing of Hell" Relief in Bristol Cathedral', *'Almost the Richest City'*, ed. Keen, pp. 75–80

Pàroli, Teresa, 'The Carrand Panel of the Auzon Casket: Stories and History', *Germanic Studies in Honor of Anatoly Liberman*, ed. Karl Gustav Goblirsch, Martha Berryman Mayou and Marvin Taylor (Odense, 1997) [*North-Western European Lang. Evolution* 31/32], 277–304

Parsons, David, 'Stone', *English Medieval Industries: Craftsmen, Techniques, Products*, ed. Blair and Ramsay, pp. 1–27

Plunkett, Steven J., 'The Mercian Perspective', *The St Andrews Sarcophagus*, ed. Foster, pp. 202–26

Potts, W. T. W., 'Two Romanesque Capitals in Halton Church', *Contrebis* 21 (1996), 12–13

Rawes, Julian, 'The Historical Importance of Churchyard Memorials', *Glevensis* 31, 33–41

Ryder, Peter F., *The Medieval Cross Slab Grave Cover in County Durham*, Archit. and Archaeol. Soc. of Durham and Northumberland Research Report 1 (Durham, 1985)

Sermon, Richard, see sect. 9*l*

Sidebottom, Philip C., 'The Ecclesfield Cross and "Celtic" Survival', *Trans. of the Hunter Archaeol. Soc.* 19 (1997), 43–55

Stocker, David, '*Fons et Origo*: the Symbolic Death, Burial and Resurrection of English Font Stones', *Church Archaeol.* 1 (1997), 17–25

Thomas, Charles, 'Form and Function', *The St Andrews Sarcophagus*, ed. Foster, pp. 84–96 [discussion of Anglo-Saxon shrines and sarcophagi]

i. Metal-work

Ager, Barry, 'A Quoit Brooch Style Belt-Plate from Meonstoke, Hampshire', *ASSAH* 9 (1998 for 1996), 111–14

Bayley, Justine, *Anglo-Scandinavian Non-Ferrous Metalworking from 16–22 Coppergate*, Archaeol. of York 17.7 (London, 1992)

Charge, B. B., 'A Field Survey of Castle Camps, Cambridgeshire', *Jnl of the Haverhill and District Archaeol. Group* 6.3 (1997), 132–237 [spearhead and girdle-hanger fragment]

Clogg, Phil, and Chris Caple, 'Conservation Image Enchancement at Durham

University', *Imaging the Past*, ed. Higgins, Main and Lang, pp. 13–22 [cases include a pattern-welded sword-blade and an Anglo-Saxon gold pendant]

Cuddeford, Michael J., 'Some Recent Finds of Late Anglo-Saxon Metalwork from Essex', *Essex Archaeol. and Hist.* 27 (1996), 319–22

Daniels, R., L. Brewster and J. Jones, 'An Eighth-Century Pin from Hartlepool', *ArchJ* 154 (1998 for 1997), 214–20

Edwards, B. J. N., 'A Gold Foil Rediscovered', *Contrebis* 22 (1997), 11–12

Egan, Geoff, 'Some Archaeological Evidence for Metalworking in London c. 1050 AD–c. 1700 AD', *Jnl of the Hist. Metallurgy Soc.* 30.2 (1996), 83–94

Gaimster, Märit, *Vendel Period Bracteates on Gotland: on the Significance of Germanic Art*, Acta Archaeologica Lundensia, Ser. in 8°, 27 (Stockholm)

Geddes, Jane, 'Iron', *English Medieval Industries: Craftsmen, Techniques, Products*, ed. Blair and Ramsay, pp. 167–88

Gifford, Chris, 'The View from a Bridge – a Perspective on Metal Detecting', *CBA Wessex Newsletter* October, 30–1 [photograph of a stirrup-mount]

Graham-Campbell, J. A., 'The Gold Finger-Ring from a Burial in St Aldate's Street, Oxford', *Saint Frideswide's Monastery at Oxford*, ed. Blair, pp. 263–6

Green, Miranda J., 'Vessels of Death: Sacred Cauldrons in Archaeology and Myth', *AntJ* 78, 63–84

Hårdh, Birgitta, *Silver in the Viking Age: a Regional-Economic Study*, Acta Archaeologica Lundensia, Ser. in 8°, 25 (Stockholm, 1996) [Scandinavian material for comparative studies]

Henderson, Isabel, see sect. 9*h*

Ladle, Lilian, 'Spotlight on the Bestwall Quarry Project, Wareham, Dorset', *CBA Wessex Newsletter* October (1997), 22–5 [includes a copper alloy mount in Ringerike style]

Margeson, S., 'Ball-Headed Pins: A Typological Puzzle', *East Anglian Studies: Essays presented to J. C. Barringer on his Retirement, August 30 1995, University of East Anglia, Norwich*, ed. Adam Longcroft and Richard Joby (Norwich, 1995), 161–5

Penman, Alastair, 'Botel Bailey', *CA* 156, 473–5 [includes an Anglian bow-brooch from this site in Galloway]

Rogers, Nicky, 'Strapped for an Answer?', *Interim: Archaeology in York* 22.2 (1997), 38–40 [a probable strap-distributor]

Staecker, Jörn, 'Brutal Vikings and Gentle Traders', *Lund Archaeol. Rev.* 1997, 89–103 [concerning the reasons for hoard deposition, including British evidence]

Taylor, Martin, see sect. 9*e*

Thomas, Gabor, 'Silver Wire Strap-Ends from East Anglia', *ASSAH* 9 (1998 for 1996), 81–100

Truc, Marie-Cécile, 'Les fibules ansées symétriques en Normandie', *Archéologie médiévale* 27 (1997), 1–58 [equal-arm brooches in Normandy]

Walsh, Aidan, 'A Summary Classification of Viking Age Swords in Ireland', *Ireland and Scandinavia in the Early Viking Age*, ed. Clarke, Ní Mhaonaigh and Ó Floinn, pp. 222–35

Watson, P. J., *et al.*, 'Antiquities from Berkshire in West Midlands Museums', *Berkshire*

Archaeol. Jnl 75 (1997 for 1994–7), 121–4 [includes an Anglo-Saxon axehead from Maidenhead]

Williams, David, *Late Saxon Stirrup-Strap Mounts, a Classification and Catalogue: a Contribution to the Study of Late Saxon Ornamental Metalwork*, CBA Research Report 111 (York, 1997)

'Two Anglo-Scandinavian Harness Cheek-Pieces from Tandridge and Nutfield', *Surrey Archaeol. Collections* 84 (1997), 192–3

j. Pottery and glass

Adams, Lauren, *Medieval Pottery from Broadgate East, Lincoln 1973*, Lincoln Archaeol. Trust Monograph Ser. 17.1 (Lincoln, 1977)

Davison, Jim, and Geoff Porter, 'Excavations at 14 Whitgift Street, Croydon, 1987–88 and 1995', *London Archaeologist* 8.9, 227–32 [includes a sherd of fifth-century pottery]

Edwards, Julie, 'Post-Roman Pottery from Chester', *From Flints to Flower Pots*, ed. Carrington, pp. 69–75

Ford, Steve, 'Loddon Valley (Berkshire) Fieldwalking Survey', *Berkshire Archaeol. Jnl* 75 (1997 for 1994–7), 11–33 [includes probable Anglo-Saxon sherds]

Marks, Richard, *The Medieval Stained Glass of the County of Northamptonshire* (Oxford, 1997)

Mellor, Maureen, *Pots and People That Have Shaped the Heritage of Medieval and Later England* (Oxford, 1997)

Osborne, June, *Stained Glass in England*, rev. ed. (Stroud, 1993)

k. Textiles

FitzGerald, Maria, 'Insular Dress in Early Medieval Ireland', *Bull. of the John Rylands Univ. Lib. of Manchester* 79.3 (1997), 251–61

Jørgensen, Lise Bender, 'A Coptic Tapestry and Other Textile Remains from the Royal Frankish Graves of Cologne Cathedral', *Acta Archaeologica* 56 (1985), 85–100 [includes a summary of North European textiles in the Merovingian period, including Anglo-Saxon]

Staniland, Kay, *Embroiderers* (London, 1991)

l. Inscriptions

Bredehoft, Thomas A., 'First-Person Inscriptions and Literacy in Anglo-Saxon England', *ASSAH* 9 (1998 for 1996), 103–10

Derolez, R., *The Origin of the Runes: an Alternative Approach*, Koninklijke Academie voor Wetenschappen, Letteren en Schone Kunsten van België, Academiae Analecta – Klasse der Letteren 60.1 (Brussels)

Hines, John, 'Grave Finds with Runic Inscriptions from Great Britain', *Runeninschriften*, ed. Düwel, pp. 186–96

Holman, Katherine, 'Scandinavian Runic Inscriptions as a Source for the History of the British Isles: the St Paul's Rune-Stone', *Runeninschriften*, ed. Düwel, pp. 629–38

Luiselli Fadda, Anna Maria, 'Aspetti e significati della compresenza delle scritture romana e runica nelle iscrizioni anglosassoni', *Incontri di popoli e culture tra V e IX secolo*, ed. Marcello Rotili (Naples), pp. 89–101

Page, R. I., 'Two Runic Notes', *ASE* 27, 289–94
Sermon, Richard, 'A Reassessment of the Franks Casket Cryptic Inscription', *Glevensis* 31, 17–21

10. REVIEWS

Abrams, Lesley, *Anglo-Saxon Glastonbury* (Woodbridge, 1996): S. Coates, *History* 83, 298–9; D. Hooke, *Jnl of Hist. Geography* 24, 224–5; C. Insley, *EHR* 113, 405–6

Abramson, A. I. J., ed., *Yorkshire Numismatist* 3: M. Archibald, *NChron* 158, 341–3

Allen, Cynthia L., *Case Marking and Reanalysis* (Oxford, 1995): A. van Kemenade, *Jnl of Ling.* 34, 227–32

Bailey, Richard N., *England's Earliest Sculptors* (Toronto, 1996): D. A. Hinton, *MA* 41, 332–4; D. Kahn, *Speculum* 73, 150–2; S. J. Plunkett, *ArchJ* 154, 322–3

Baker, Peter S., and Michael Lapidge, ed., *Byrhtferth's 'Enchiridion'* (Oxford, 1995): R. M. Liuzza, *Speculum* 73, 153–4; D. G. Scragg, *RES* 49, 72–3

Berga, Tatjana, *Latvian Collections: Anglo-Saxon and Later British Coins*, (Oxford, 1996): S. Keynes, *EME* 7, 126–7; J. Steen Jensen, *Nordisk Numismatisk Unions Medlemsblad*, p. 26; T. Talvio, *BNJ* 67, 153–4

Biggam, C. P., *Blue in Old English* (Amsterdam, 1997): R. Dance, *MÆ* 67, 178; S. van Romburgh, *ES* 79, 469–70

Bjork, Robert E., ed., *Cynewulf: Basic Readings* (New York, 1996): N. Howe, *Speculum* 73, 152–3

Bjork, Robert E., and John D. Niles, ed., *A Beowulf Handbook* (Lincoln, NE, 1997): S. Irvine, *N&Q* 45, 483–4

Blockley, K., et al., *Excavations in the Marlowe Car Park and Surrounding Areas* (Canterbury, 1995): M. Millett, *AC* 116, 341–6

Boddington, A., *Raunds Furnells: the Anglo-Saxon Church and Churchyard* (London, 1996): P. Rahtz, *Church Archaeol.* 1, 64

Booth, James, *Northern Museums: Ancient British, Anglo-Saxon, Norman and Plantagenet Coins to 1279*, SCBI 48 (Oxford, 1997): C. Barclay, *BNJ* 67, 153; J. C. Moesgaard, *Nordisk Numismatisk Unions Medlemsblad*, p. 25

Bradbury, Jim, *The Battle of Hastings* (Stroud, 1998): R. Jones, *Sussex Past and Present* 86, 12

Brooks, Nicholas P., and Catherine Cubitt, ed., *St Oswald of Worcester* (London, 1996): E. G. Whatley, *JEH* 49, 160–1

Brown, Michelle P., *The Book of Cerne* (London, 1996): R. Gameson, *N&Q* 45 (1998), 100–1; M. Henig, *AntJ* 78, 494–5

Bruni, Sandra, ed., *Alcuino: De Orthographia* (Florence, 1997): P. Riché, *Revue d'histoire ecclésiastique* 93, 654

Cameron, Kenneth, *English Place Names*, rev. ed. (London, 1996): C. Hough, *Nomina* 20 (1997), 99–102; V. Watts, *Names* 46, 63–5

Cameron, M. L., *Anglo-Saxon Medicine* (Cambridge, 1993): R. Zaffuto, *SchM* 28–9 (1995), 127–30

Carver, Martin, *Sutton Hoo: Burial Ground of Kings?* (Philadelphia, 1998): [Anon.], *CA* 160, 147

Clark, Cecily, *Words, Names and History*, ed. P. Jackson (Cambridge, 1995): B. R. Hutcheson, *Jnl of Eng. Ling.* 26, 266–9

Clark, Francelia Mason, *Theme in Oral Epic and in 'Beowulf'* (New York, 1995): M. D. Cherniss, *Speculum* 73, 489–91

Clarke, Peter A., *The English Nobility under Edward the Confessor* (Oxford, 1994): K. Schnith, *Deutsches Archiv für Erforschung des Mittelalters* 54, 397–8

Clemoes, Peter, *Interactions of Thought and Language in Old English Poetry* (Cambridge, 1995): R. E. Bjork, *Speculum* 73, 491–3; A. Crépin, *ASNSL* 235, 154–6; J. M. Hill, *MP* 96, 61–5

Clemoes, Peter, ed., *Ælfric's Catholic Homilies. The First Series: Text* (Oxford, 1997): J. Wilcox, *Envoi* 7, 23–9

Conner, Patrick W., ed., *The Abingdon Chronicle* (Cambridge, 1996): C. Insley, *EHR* 113, 136; H. O'Donoghue, *RES* 49, 71–2; A. R. Rumble, *History* 83, 124–5

Coppens, Christian, Albert Derolez and Hubert Heymans, *Codex Eyckensis: an Insular Gospel Book from the Abbey of Aldeneik, a Facsimile with an Introduction* (Antwerp, 1994): R. McKitterick, *EME* 7, 233–4

Cramp, Rosemary, *Grammar of Anglo-Saxon Ornament* (Oxford, 1991): D. A. Hinton, *MA* 41 (1997), 332–4

Crépin, André, and Hélène Taurinya Dauby, *Histoire de la littérature du Moyen Âge* (Paris, 1993): J. Dor, *CCM* 41, 187–9

Cross, J. E., et al., ed., *Two Old English Apocrypha and their Manuscript Source* (Cambridge, 1996): J.-C. Haelewyck, *Revue d'histoire ecclésiastique* 93, 641–2

Cross, J. E., and Jennifer Morrish Tunberg, ed., *The Copenhagen Wulfstan Collection* (Copenhagen, 1993): H. Gneuss, *Anglia* 116, 88–9

Cubbin, G. P., ed., *MS D* (Cambridge, 1996): E. M. Treharne, *RES* 49, 200–1; B. Yorke, *History* 83, 524

Cubitt, Catherine, *Anglo-Saxon Church Councils c. 650–c. 850* (Leicester, 1995): R. Meens, *Tijdschrift voor Geschiedenis* 110 (1997), 63–4

Dales, Douglas, *Light to the Isles: a Study of Missionary Theology in Celtic and Anglo-Saxon Britain* (Cambridge, 1997): D. N. Dumville, *Expository Times* 109 (1997–8), 348; D. P. Kirby, *JEH* 49, 715–16; B. Mitchell, *Hist. Today* 48.3, 56–7; L. Olson, *Jnl of Religious Hist.* 23, 131–3

Dark, K. R., ed., *External Contacts and the Economy of Late Roman and Post-Roman Britain* (Woodbridge, 1996): M. Henig, *EHR* 113, 961; R. Reece, *Britannia* 29, 471–2

Darlington, R. R., and P. McGurk, ed., *The Chronicle of John of Worcester, II* (Oxford, 1995): D. Rollason, *EHR* 113, 967–8

Davis, Craig R., *'Beowulf' and the Demise of Germanic Legend in England* (New York, 1996): S. E. Deskis, *JEGP* 97, 232–5; R. Gleißner, *Mediaevistik* 10 (1998 for 1997), 378–9; S. Irvine, *RES* 49, 201–2; J. D. Niles, *Speculum* 73, 497–9; J. S. Ryan, *Parergon* 16.1, 142–4

Davril, Anselme, ed., *The Winchcombe Sacramentary* (Woodbridge, 1995): M. Metzger, *CCM* 41.164 bis, 21*–22*; V. Ortenberg, *History* 83, 703

Deshman, Robert, *The Benedictional of Æthelwold* (Princeton, NJ, 1995): J. Alexander, *Speculum* 73, 168–70

Deskis, Susan E., *'Beowulf' and the Medieval Proverb Tradition* (Tempe, AZ, 1996): J.

Čermák, *MÆ* 67, 324–6; N. Howe, *Speculum* 73, 836–8; C. Larrington, *RES* 49, 336–7

DiNapoli, Robert, *An Index of Theme and Image to the Homilies of the Anglo-Saxon Church: Comprising the Homilies of Ælfric, Wulfstan, and the Blickling and Vercelli Codices* (Hockwold-cum-Wilton, 1995): E. M. Tyler, *EME* 7, 131–2

Doane, A. N., *Anglo-Saxon Manuscripts in Microfiche Facsimile*, 1 (Binghamton, NY, 1994): H. Gneuss, *Anglia* 116, 248–50

Düwel, Klaus, ed., *Runische Schriftkultur in kontinental-skandinavischer und -angelsächsischer Wechselbeziehung* (Berlin, 1994): J. E. Knirk, *Mediaevistik* 10 (1998 for 1997), 379–81

Dumville, David N., *English Caroline Script and Monastic History* (Woodbridge, 1993): U. Lenker, *Anglia* 116, 90–3

Dumville, David N., ed., *Facsimile of MS F: the Domitian Bilingual* (Cambridge, 1995): H. Gneuss, *Anglia* 116, 88–9

Eales, Richard, and Richard Sharpe, ed., *Canterbury and the Norman Conquest* (London, 1995): N. Brooks, *History* 83, 704–5

Earl, James W., *Thinking about 'Beowulf'* (Stanford, CA, 1994): J. Tally Lionarons, *Jnl of the Rocky Mountain Med. and Renaissance Assoc.* 16–17 (1995–6), 219–21; K. Reichl, *Anglia* 116, 526–33; J. S. Ryan, *Parergon* 16.1, 150–2

Eaton, Trevor, *Beowulf* [recording] (Wadhurst, 1997): R. Dance, *MÆ* 67, 128–9

Enright, Michael, *Lady with a Mead Cup: Ritual, Prophecy and Lordship in the European Warband from La Tène to the Viking Age* (Blackrock, 1996): P. Stafford, *EME* 7, 133–5

Evans, Stephen S., *The Lords of Battle: Image and Reality of the Comitatus in Dark-Age Britain* (Woodbridge, 1997): S. Fanning, *EME* 7, 136–7; D. P. Kirby, *Welsh Hist. Rev.* 19 (1998–9) 146–8; S. Morillo, *AHR* 103, 1232–3; B. Yorke, *Albion* 30, 253–4

Evison, Vera I., and Prue Hill, *Two Anglo-Saxon Cemeteries at Beckford, Hereford and Worcester* (York, 1996): S. Bassett, *MA* 41 (1997), 330–1; C. Scull, *ArchJ* 154 (1998 for 1997), 322

Faith, Rosamond, *The English Peasantry and the Growth of Lordship* (Leicester, 1997): R. Fossier, *Revue historique* 602, 691–2; P. Stafford, *History* 83, 701–2

Fletcher, Richard, *The Conversion of Europe: from Paganism to Christianity, 371–1386* (London, 1997): R. I. Moore, *TLS* 6 February 1998, 24

Foley, John Miles, *Immanent Art* (Bloomington, IN, 1991): R. Alexander, *Jnl of Amer. Folklore* 111, 442–4

The Singer of Tales in Performance (Bloomington, IN, 1995): R. Alexander, *Jnl of Amer. Folklore* 111, 442–4

Fox, Peter, ed., *The Book of Kells: MS 58, Trinity College Library Dublin* (Luzern, 1990): M. Werner, *Peritia* 11, 250–326

Frantzen, Allen J., and John D. Niles, ed., *Anglo-Saxonism and the Construction of Social Identity* (Gainesville, FL, 1997): J. Čermák, *MÆ* 67, 366–7; M. Pettinger, *Envoi* 7, 35–8

Gameson, Richard, *The Role of Art in the Late Anglo-Saxon Church* (Oxford, 1995): S. A. Brown, *AHR* 102 (1997), 433

Gameson, Richard, ed., *The Early Medieval Bible: its Production, Decoration and Use* (Cambridge, 1994): T. O'Loughlin, *Peritia* 11, 413–15

Gameson, Richard, ed., *The Study of the Bayeux Tapestry* (Woodbridge, 1997): D. J. Bernstein, *Albion* 30, 258–60; C. Cannon, *MÆ* 67, 356–7

Geake, Helen, *The Use of Grave-Goods in Conversion-Period England, c. 600–c. 850* (Oxford, 1997): A. Dodd, *JBAA* 151, 230–1

Gneuss, Helmut, *Books and Libraries in Early England* (Aldershot, 1996): H. Sauer, *Anglia* 116, 381–6

Language and History in Early England (Aldershot, 1996): H. Sauer, *Anglia* 116, 381–6

Griffith, Mark, ed., *Judith* (Exeter, 1997): B. O'Donoghue, *TLS* 25 September, p. 27 [replies by V. Cunningham, 16 October, p. 17, and H. Wilson, 11 December, p. 17]

Griffiths, Bill, *An Introduction to Early English Law* (Hockwold-cum-Wilton, 1995): W. Pencack, *Law and Hist. Rev.* 16 (1998), 174–5

Gunstone, A. J. H., *South Eastern Museums: Ancient British, Anglo-Saxon, and Later Coins to 1279* (Oxford, 1992): J. C. Moesgaard, *Nordisk Numismatisk Unions Medlemsblad*, p. 25

Hagen, Ann, *A Second Handbook of Anglo-Saxon Food & Drink* (Hockwold-cum-Wilton, 1995): J. Musty, *CA* 158, 66

Hall, Richard, *English Heritage Book of Viking Age York* (London, 1994): J. D. Richards, *Yorkshire Archaeol. Jnl* 70, 162

Head, Pauline, *Representation and Design* (Albany, NY, 1997): B. O'Donoghue, *RES* 49, 488–9; M. Swan, *MÆ* 67, 323–4

Healey, Antonette diPaolo, *et al.*, ed., *Dictionary of Old English: A* (Toronto, 1996): M. Griffith, *MÆ* 67, 127–8; G. Owen-Crocker, *RES* 49, 70–1

Dictionary of Old English: E (Toronto, 1996): J. Bately, *N&Q* 45, 88–9

Higham, N. J., *The Convert Kings: Power and Religious Affiliation in Early Anglo-Saxon England* (Manchester, 1997): D. P. Kirby, *JEH* 49, 716–17; B. Mitchell, *Hist. Today* 48.3, 56–7; B. Yorke, *Southern Hist.* 19, 149–50

The English Conquest (Manchester, 1994): M. E. Jones, *AHR* 103, 1568–9

An English Empire (Manchester, 1995): M. E. Jones, *AHR* 103, 1568–9; D. Rollason, *History* 83, 119–20

Hill, David, and Alexander R. Rumble, ed., *The Defence of Wessex* (Manchester, 1996): J. Blair, *EHR* 113, 1263–4

Hill, John M., *The Cultural World in 'Beowulf'* (Toronto, 1995): K. Reichl, *Anglia* 116, 526–33; T. A. Shippey, *MLR* 93, 169–70

Hines, John, ed., *The Anglo-Saxons from the Migration Period to the Eighth Century* (Woodbridge, 1997): J. M. McCulloh, *Albion* 30, 659–60

Hooke, Della, *Pre-Conquest Charter-Bounds of Devon and Cornwall* (Woodbridge, 1994): M. J. Swanton, *Agricultural Hist. Rev.* 46, 223–5

Houwen, L. A. J. R., and A. A. MacDonald, ed., *Beda Venerabilis* (Groningen, 1996): R. Meens, *Millennium* 11 (1997), 62–5

Howlett, D. R., *British Books in Biblical Style* (Dublin, 1997): K. Foster, *Envoi* 7, 44–54

Hutcheson, B. R., *Old English Poetic Metre* (Cambridge, 1995): D. Donoghue, *MP* 95, 506–9; G. Russom, *Anglia* 116, 404–6; E. G. Stanley, *N&Q* 45, 94–6

Insley, John, *Scandinavian Personal Names in Norfolk* (Uppsala, 1994): K. I. Sandred, *Nomina* 20 (1997), 106–9; V. Watts, *Anglia* 116, 86–7

Irvine, Martin, *The Making of Textual Culture* (Cambridge, 1994): H.-J. Diller, *ASNSL* 235, 147–9; G. Silagi, *Deutsches Archiv für Erforschung des Mittelalters* 54, 265; G. L. Bursill-Hall, *Manuscripta* 39, 70–3

Jack, George, ed., *'Beowulf': a Student Edition* (Oxford, 1994): K. Reichl, *ASNSL* 235, 455–6

Jackson, R. P. J., and T. W. Potter, *Excavations at Stonea, Cambridgeshire, 1980–85* (London, 1996): H. Hamerow, *MA* 41 (1997), 365–6

Jacobsson, Mattias, *Wells, Meres, and Pools* (Uppsala, 1997): D. Waugh, *SN* 70 (1998), 247

John, Eric, *Reassessing Anglo-Saxon England* (Manchester, 1996): P. Bange, *Tijdschrift voor Geschiedenis* 111, 109–10; D. Hooke, *Jnl of Hist. Geography* 24, 224–5; D. B. McCulloch, *Revue d'histoire ecclésiastique* 93, 635–6; J. S. Myerov, *European Legacy* 3.2 (1998), 146–7

Jolly, Karen Louise, *Popular Religion in Late Saxon England* (Chapel Hill, NC, 1996): J. Blair, *Albion* 29, 271–2; L. L. Coon, *Speculum* 73, 196–8; P. Dendle, *Medievalia et Humanistica* 24 (1997), 193–4; R. I. Page, *JEH* 49, 161–2; R. W. Pfaff, *AHR* 102 (1997), 797–8; P. Stafford, *EHR* 113, 404–5

Jones, Michael E., *The End of Roman Britain* (Ithaca, NY, 1996): N. J. Higham, *AHR* 102 (1997), 1461–2; N. W. Nolte, *Albion* 29.2, 269–71 R. Reece, *Britannia* 29, 471–2; P. Salway, *Welsh Hist. Rev.* 19 (1998–9), 143–6

Jørgensen, Lise Bender, *North European Textiles Until A.D. 1000* (Aarhus, 1992): K. Tidow, *Bonner Jahrbücher* 195, 649–51

Keats-Rohan, K. S. B., and David E. Thornton, *Domesday Names* (Woodbridge, 1997): P. Cavill, *MÆ* 67, 368

Kelly, S., ed., *Charters of St Augustine's Abbey*: (Oxford, 1995): F. Neininger, *DAEM* 54, 679

Kelly, S. E., ed., *Charters of Shaftesbury Abbey* (Oxford, 1996): J. C. Crick, *EHR* 113, 965–6; A. Williams, *JEH* 49, 159–60

Keynes, Simon, ed., *The Liber Vitae of the New Minster and Hyde Abbey Winchester* (Copenhagen, 1996): J. Backhouse, *AntJ* 78, 495–7; S. Coates, *History* 83, 522–3; J. R. Maddicott, *EHR* 113, 1265–6; R. McKitterick, *TLS* 31 July, p. 28; A. Mentzel-Reuters, *Deutsches Archiv für Erforschung des Mittelalters* 54, 251–2; D. Rollason, *EME* 7, 366

Kiernan, Kevin S., *'Beowulf' and the 'Beowulf' Manuscript*, rev. ed. (Ann Arbor, 1996): J. Gerritsen, see sect. 3*bii*

Knappe, Gabriele, *Traditionen der klassischen Rhetorik im angelsächsischen England* (Heidelberg, 1996): M. Camargo, *Rhetorica* 16, 233–5; E. G. Stanley, *N&Q* 45, 89–91

Laing, Lloyd, and Jennifer Laing, *Early English Art and Architecture* (Stroud, 1996): R. Gameson, *JEH* 49, 344–6; M. Henig, *EHR* 113, 695–6

Lapidge, Michael, ed., *Archbishop Theodore* (Cambridge, 1995): D. B. McCulloch, *Revue d'histoire ecclésiastique* 93, 638–9

Lapidge, Michael, Malcolm Godden, and Simon Keynes, ed., *Anglo-Saxon England* 25 (Cambridge, 1996): A. J. Kabir, *N&Q* 45, 93–4

Lass, Roger, *Old English: a Historical Linguistic Companion* (Cambridge, 1994): R. Zaffuto, *SchM* 28–9 (1995), 176

Bibliography for 1998

Laszlo, Renate, *Das mystische Weinfaß* (Marburg, 1996): A. Hindorf and D. Schneider, *ZAA* 46, 76–7

Lester, G. A., *The Language of Old and Middle English Poetry* (London, 1996): C. Larrington, *RES* 49, 73–4; H. Magennis, *ES* 79, 87–8; E. G. Stanley, *N&Q* 45, 1; M. Tajiri, *Stud. in Med. Eng. Lang. and Lit.* 13, 61–74

Lewis, Carenza, Patrick Mitchell-Fox and Christopher Dyer, *Village, Hamlet and Field: Changing Medieval Settlements in Central England* (Manchester, 1997): M. G. Thompson, *Rural Hist.* 9, 239–40

Lindsay, W. M., *Studies in Early Medieval Latin Glossaries*, ed. Michael Lapidge (Aldershot, 1996): H. D. Jocelyn, *Classical Rev.* 48, 519

Lord, Albert Bates, *The Singer Resumes the Tale* (Ithaca NY, 1995): J. D. Niles, *Speculum* 73, 560–2

Love, Rosalind C., ed. and trans., *Three Eleventh-Century Anglo-Latin Saints' Lives* (Oxford, 1996): J. Blair, *JEH* 49, 533–5; M. Philpott, *EHR* 113, 136–7; D. Rollason, *History* 83, 125–6

MacNamara, Jo Ann Kay, *Sisters in Arms: Catholic Nuns Through Two Millennia* (Cambridge, MA, 1996): C. Walker, *Jnl of Religious Hist.* 23, 130–1

Magennis, Hugh, *Images of Community in Old English Poetry* (Cambridge, 1996): N. Howe, *JEGP* 97, 581–3

Malmer, Brita, *The Anglo-Scandinavian Coinage c. 995–1020* (Stockholm, 1997): S. H. Gullbekk, *BNJ* 67, 154–5

Margeson, Sue, *The Vikings in Norfolk* (Norwich, 1997): R. Hodges, *Hist. Today* 48.1, 58–9

Markus, R. A., *Gregory the Great and his World* (Cambridge, 1997): H. Chadwick, *TLS* 6 March, p. 32

Marsden, Richard, *The Text of the Old Testament in Anglo-Saxon England* (Cambridge, 1995): J. R. Hall, *Speculum* 73, 229–31; U. Lenker, *Anglia* 116, 519–22

Mason, Emma, *Westminster Abbey and its People, c. 1050–1216* (Woodbridge, 1996): M. Altschul, *Albion* 30, 260–1

McCready, William D., *Miracles and the Venerable Bede*, (Toronto, 1994): G. H. Brown, *Peritia* 11, 406–9

McCully, C. B., and J. J. Anderson, ed., *English Historical Metrics* (Cambridge, 1996): R. D. Fulk, *Language* 74, 844–7

McKitterick, Rosamond, ed., *The New Cambridge Medieval History*, 2, *c. 700–c. 900* (Cambridge, 1995): J. Campbell, *EHR* 113, 680–4

Meehan, Bernard, *The Book of Kells: an Illustrated Introduction to the Manuscript in Trinity College Dublin* (London, 1994): M. Werner, *Peritia* 11, 250–326

Metcalf, D. M., *Thrymsas and Sceattas in the Ashmolean Museum, Oxford*, 3 vols. (London, 1993–4): M. Archibald, *BNJ* 67, 150–3

Milfull, Inge B., *The Hymns of the Anglo-Saxon Church* (Cambridge, 1996): P.-A. Deproost, *Revue d'histoire ecclésiastique* 93, 642–3; R. W. Pfaff, *EME* 7, 246–7; E. G. Stanley, *N&Q* 45, 101–3; J. Stevenson, *Heythrop Jnl* 39, 200–1

Mills, A. D., *The Place-Names of the Isle of Wight* (Stamford, 1996): W. F. H. Nicolaisen, *Names* 46, 151–3

Mitchell, Bruce, *An Invitation to Old English and Anglo-Saxon England* (Oxford, 1995): J. Bately, *Reading Med. Stud.* 22 (1996), 110–11

Momma, H., *The Composition of Old English Poetry* (Cambridge, 1997): R. D. Fulk, *PQ* 77, 239–42; M. Griffith, *N&Q* 45, 238–9; M. Swan, *MÆ* 67, 323–4

Morillo, Stephen, ed., *The Battle of Hastings* (Woodbridge, 1996): J. Bradbury, *Albion* 30, 78–9; D. J. A. Matthew, *EHR* 113, 407–8

Noel, William, *The Harley Psalter* (Cambridge, 1995): C. M. Kauffmann, *AHR* 103, 495

North, Richard, *Heathen Gods in Old English Literature* (Cambridge, 1997): O. Falk, *Envoi* 7, 54–64

O'Keeffe, Katherine O'Brien, ed., *Reading Old English Texts* (Cambridge, 1997): S. Horner, *Envoi* 7 (1997), 175–82

O'Mahony, Felicity, ed., *The Book of Kells: Proceedings of a Conference at Trinity College Dublin, 6–9 September 1992* (Aldershot, 1994): M. Werner, *Peritia* 11, 250–326

Orchard, Andy, *The Poetic Art of Aldhelm* (Cambridge, 1994): S. Gwara, *Speculum* 73, 877–9; M. W. Herren, *Peritia* 11, 403–6

Pride and Prodigies (Cambridge, 1995): J. B. Friedman, *MLR* 93, 455–6; J. Hill, *Anglia* 116, 406–9; J. M. Hill, *MP* 96, 58–61; K. S. Kiernan, *Speculum* 73, 879–81; P. Sorrell, *Parergon* 15.2, 246–50; E. M. Tyler, *ASNSL* 235, 156–9

Orme, Nicholas, *English Church Dedications: with a Survey of Devon and Cornwall* (Exeter, 1996): K. Jankulak, *JEH* 49, 531–2; J. R. Maddicott, *EHR* 113, 695

Page, R. I., *Runes and Runic Inscriptions* (Woodbridge, 1995): E. H. Antonsen, *JEGP* 97, 402–4; P. Orton, *SBVS* 25, 99–108

Pasternack, Carol Braun, *The Textuality of Old English Poetry* (Cambridge, 1995): J. Köberl, *ASNSL* 235, 150–4; M. J. Toswell, *EME* 7, 249–50

Pelteret, David A. E., *Slavery in Early Mediaeval England* (Woodbridge, 1995): S. Fanning, *JEGP* 97, 235–6; P. Freedman, *AHR* 102 (1997), 435–6

Phythian-Adams, Charles, *Land of the Cumbrians: a Study in British Provincial Origins, A.D. 400–1120* (Aldershot, 1996): E. Klingelhofer, *Albion* 30, 255–7; N. J. Higham, *Northern Hist.* 34, 228–9

Pulsiano, Phillip, *Anglo-Saxon Manuscripts in Microfiche Facsimile* 2 (Binghamton, NY, 1994): H. Gneuss, *Anglia* 116, 248–50

Rahtz, Philip, and Lorna Watts, *St Mary's Church, Deerhurst, Gloucestershire: Fieldwork, Excavations and Structural Analysis, 1971–1984* (Woodbridge, 1997): J. Blair, *EME* 7, 370–1; A. E. Brown, *History* 83, 300–1

Raw, Barbara C., *Trinity and Incarnation in Anglo-Saxon Art and Thought* (Cambridge, 1997): R. Gameson, *Albion* 30, 463–4; H. Magennis, *N&Q* 45, 91–2

Remley, Paul G., *Old English Biblical Verse* (Cambridge, 1996): A. N. Doane, *JEGP* 97, 407–10; S. M. Kim, *Jnl of Religion* 78, 609–10; C. L. Patton, *Old Testament Abstracts* 20 (1997), 560; P. J. Semper, *N&Q* 45, 92–3

Richards, Mary P., ed., *Anglo-Saxon Manuscripts: Basic Readings* (New York, 1994): P. Acker, *Manuscripta* 39, 73–4

Richter, Martin, ed., *Die altenglischen Glossen zu Aldhelms 'De laudibus virginitatis'* (Munich, 1996): J. D. Pheifer, *N&Q* 45, 482–3

Röber, Ralph, *Die Keramik der frühmittelalterlichen Siedlung von Warendorf* (Bonn, 1990): M. Kühlborn, *Bonner Jahrbücher* 196, 896–9

Roberts, Jane, and Christian Kay, with Lynne Grundy, *A Thesaurus of Old English*

(London, 1995): P. W. Conner, *Speculum* 73, 887–9; M. Görlach, *Anglia* 116, 398–401

Roberts, Jane, and Janet L. Nelson, with Malcolm Godden, ed., *Alfred the Wise*: H. Steiner, *DAEM* 54, 861–3

Robinson, Fred C., *The Editing of Old English* (Oxford, 1994): R. P. Tripp, Jr, *Reading Med. Stud.* 22 (1996), 129–31

The Tomb of Beowulf and Other Essays on Old English (Oxford, 1993): D. J. Williams, *Reading Med. Stud.* 21 (1995), 112–14

Robinson, Fred C., and E. G. Stanley, ed., *Old English Verse Extracts from Many Sources: a Comprehensive Collection*, EEMF 23 (Copenhagen, 1991): P. E. Szarmach, *Peritia* 11, 409–11

Rumble, Alexander R., ed., *The Reign of Cnut* (London, 1994): T. Reuter, *DAEM* 54, 303–4

Rumble, Alexander R., and A. D. Mills, ed., *Names, Places and People: an Onomastic Miscellany in Memory of John McNeal Dodgson* (Stamford, 1997): P. Cavill, *Nottingham Med. Stud.* 42, 242–5

Russell, James C., *The Germanization of Early Medieval Christianity: a Sociohistorical Approach to Religious Transformation* (Oxford, 1994): A. Angenendt, *JEH* 49, 156–7; R. Simek, *Mitteilungen des Instituts für österreichische Geschichtsforschung* 104 (1996), 143–5

Russom, Geoffrey, *'Beowulf' and Old Germanic Metre* (Cambridge, 1998): D. Minkova, *Folia Linguistica Historica* 19, 173–82

Sandred, Karl Inge and Bengt Lindström, *The Place-Names of Norfolk*, I. *The Place-Names of the City of Norwich* (Nottingham, 1989); and Sandred, Karl Inge, *et al.*, *The Place-Names of Norfolk*, II. *The Hundreds of East and West Flegg, Happing and Tunstead*, (Nottingham, 1996): J. Insley, *Namn och Bygd* 86, 103–17

Sato, Shuji, ed., *Back to the Manuscripts* (Tokyo, 1997): M. Griffith, *N&Q* 45, 412–13; R. Hanna III, *MÆ* 67, 368

Schipperges, Stefan, *Bonifatius ac socii eius* (Mainz, 1996):R. Schieffer, *DAEM* 54, 298

Schneider, Karl, *Runstafas* (Münster, 1994): J. Hines, *Anglia* 116, 246–7

Schwyter, J. R., *Old English Legal Language* (Odense, 1996): J. Holland, *Speculum* 73, 593–5; H. Peters, *Language* 74, 223–4

Smyth, Alfred P., *King Alfred the Great* (Oxford, 1995): M. Altschul, *AHR* 102 (1997), 1463–4; K. Davis, *Medievalia et Humanistica* 24 (1997), 211–15; J. L. Nelson, *EME* 7, 115–24; D. A. E. Pelteret, *Speculum* 73, 263–5; H. Vollrath, *DAEM* 54, 243–4

Snyder, Christopher A., *Sub-Roman Britain (AD 400–600)* (Oxford, 1996): J. duQ. Adams, *Arthuriana* 8.2, 142–3

Spitzbart, Günter, ed. and trans., *Venerabilis Bedae Historia Ecclesiastica Gentis Anglorum*, rev. ed. (Darmstadt, 1997): A. Classen, *Mediaevistik* 10 (1998 for 1997), 372–3

Stafford, Pauline, *Queen Emma and Queen Edith: Queenship and Women's Power in Eleventh-Century England* (Oxford, 1997): I. Baumgärtner, *Historische Zeitschrift* 267, 171–2; L. Carruthers, *EA* 51, 342–3; M. Chibnall, *THES* 13 February, 29; E. Mason, *Med. Prosopography* 19, 240–2; M. A. Meyer, *Albion* 30, 464–6; J. C. Parsons, *Canadian Jnl of Hist.* 33, 87–8; P. Skinner, *Gender and Hist.* 10, 144–5; J. A. Smith, *Parergon* 15.2, 279–81; A. Wareham, *EME* 7, 258–9; B. Yorke, *History* 83, 702

Stanley, E. G., *In the Foreground: 'Beowulf'* (Woodbridge, 1994): J. Harris, *JEGP* 97, 404–6; P. J. Lucas, *RES* 49, 337–8; K. Reichl, *Anglia* 116, 526–33

Stevenson, Jane, *The 'Laterculus Malalianus' and the School of Archbishop Theodore* (Cambridge, 1995): R. W. Pfaff, *Speculum* 73, 601

Sturdy, David, *Alfred the Great* (London, 1995): M. Henig, *JBAA* 151, 232

Suzuki, Seiichi, *The Metrical Organization of 'Beowulf'* (Berlin, 1996): B. W. Fortson IV, see sect. 3*bii*; R. D. Fulk, see sect. 3*bii*; M. Griffith, *MÆ* 67, 179; G. Russom, *Speculum* 73, 269–71; E. G. Stanley, *N&Q* 45, 96–9

Swanton, M. J., trans. and ed., *The Anglo-Saxon Chronicle* (London, 1996): N. P. Brooks, *EHR* 113, 401–2; K. O'Brien O'Keeffe, *Speculum* 73, 905–7; A. R. Rumble, *History* 83, 523–4; J. C. Weale, *Med. Life* 9, 35–6

Szarmach, Paul, E., ed., *Holy Men and Holy Women* (Albany, NY, 1996): K. L. Jolly, *Biography* 21, 74–9; M. Swan, *Med. Sermon Stud.* 42, 62–4

Thomas, Charles, *And Shall These Mute Stones Speak?* (Cardiff, 1994): E. Okasha, *ArchJ* 154 (1998 for 1997), 321

Timby, Jane R., *The Anglo-Saxon Cemetery at Empingham II, Rutland* (Oxford, 1996): C. Hills, *MA* 41 (1997), 366

Toswell, M. J., ed., *Prosody and Poetics in the Early Middle Ages* (Toronto, 1995): H. Magennis, *ES* 79, 89–90

Tweddle, Dominic, *et al.*, *Corpus of Anglo-Saxon Stone Sculpture*, 4: *South-East England* (Oxford, 1995): I. Henderson, *JEH* 49, 158–9; D. A. Hinton, *MA* 41 (1997), 332–4; J. West, *ArchJ* 154 (1998 for 1997), 323–4

van der Horst, Koert, William Noel and Wilhelmina C. M. Wüstefeld, ed., *The Utrecht Psalter in Medieval Art: Picturing the Psalms of David* (London, 1996): P. Bange, *Tijdschrift voor Geschiedenis* 111, 109–10; D. Marner, *JEH*, 49, 524–6

Venarde, Bruce L., *Women's Monasticism and Medieval Society: Nunneries in France and England 890–1215* (Ithaca, NY, 1997): M. Aurell, *Annales: histoire, sciences sociales* 53, 1290–2; R. Gilchrist, *JEH* 49, 714–15; J. H. Lynch, *Catholic Hist. Rev.* 84, 530–1; P. Stafford, *EHR* 113, 969

von Padberg, Lutz E., *Mission und Christianisierung* (Stuttgart, 1995): W. H. C. Frend, *EHR* 113, 964–5; W. Hartmann, *Deutsches Archiv für Erforschung des Mittelalters* 54, 297

Walker, Ian W., *Harold, the Last Anglo-Saxon King* (Stroud, 1997): E. Cavell, *Parergon* 16.1, 205–7; P. Tudor-Craig, *Hist. Today* 48.9, 56–7

Warner, Peter, *The Origins of Suffolk* (Manchester, 1996): M. E. Hall, *Speculum* 73, 917–18; M. Todd, *Albion* 29, 459–60

Wehlau, Ruth, *The Riddle of Creation* (New York, 1997): J. Toswell, *Univ. of Toronto Quarterly* 68 (1998–9), 425–6

Williams, Ann, *The English and the Norman Conquest* (Woodbridge, 1995): S. Mooers Christelow, *Speculum* 73, 627–9; K.-U. Jäschke, *HZ* 267, 462–4; K. Schnith, *DAEM* 54, 771–2; R. V. Turner, *AHR* 102 (1997), 798

Williams, David, *Late Saxon Stirrup Mounts* (York, 1997): A. Dodd, *JBAA* 151, 231

York Archaeological Trust and The National Museum of Denmark, *The World of the Vikings*, CD-ROM for Windows (York, 1996): K. Holman, *SBVS* 25, 113–18

Zimmermann, Gunhild, *The Four Old English Poetic Manuscripts* (Heidelberg, 1995): G. Knappe, *Anglia* 116, 523–5